Decoding China

Decoding China

Hard Perspectives from India

EDITED BY
ASHOK K. KANTHA

BLOOMSBURY
NEW DELHI • LONDON • OXFORD • NEW YORK • SYDNEY

BLOOMSBURY INDIA
Bloomsbury Publishing India Pvt. Ltd
Second Floor, LSC Building No. 4, DDA Complex, Pocket C – 6 & 7,
Vasant Kunj, New Delhi, 110070

BLOOMSBURY, BLOOMSBURY INDIA and the Diana logo
are trademarks of Bloomsbury Publishing Plc

First published in India 2025

Copyright © The Vivekananda International Foundation, 2025

All rights reserved. No part of this publication may be: i) reproduced or transmitted in any form, electronic or mechanical, including photocopying, recording or by means of any information storage or retrieval system without prior permission in writing from the publishers; or ii) used or reproduced in any way for the training, development or operation of artificial intelligence (AI) technologies, including generative AI technologies. The rights holders expressly reserve this publication from the text and data mining exception as per Article 4(3) of the Digital Single Market Directive (EU) 2019/790

Bloomsbury Publishing Plc does not have any control over, or responsibility for, any third-party websites referred to or in this book. All internets addresses given in this book were correct at the time of going to press. The author and publisher regret any inconvenience caused if addresses have changed or sites have ceased to exist, but can accept no responsibility for any such changes

ISBN: HB: 978-93-61313-60-8; eBook: 978-93-61316-73-9
2 4 6 8 10 9 7 5 3 1

Typeset in Adobe Garamond Pro by Manipal Technologies Limited
Printed and bound in India in India by Thomson Press India Ltd

To find out more about our authors and books visit www.bloomsbury.com and sign up for our newsletters

For sale in the Indian subcontinent only

Contents

Part One Decoding China: The Big Picture
1. India's China Challenge — 3
   Ashok K. Kantha
2. Emerging Trends in China — 75
   Arvind Gupta

Part Two Decoding China's Strategic Ambitions
3. Russia and China in the Post-Cold-War World — 99
   P.S. Raghavan
4. Biden Administration's Responses to the China Challenge — 119
   Arun K. Singh
5. China's Foreign Policy Under Xi Jinping: Transformations and Problems — 135
   Srikanth Kondapalli
6. Strategic Competition in Southeast Asia and the Indo-Pacific — 150
   Biren Nanda
7. An Assessment of Chinese Inroads in South Asia — 168
   Sreeradha Datta
8. Pakistan–China Relations — 184
   Tilak Devasher
9. China and West Asia: A Solid Trajectory — 197
   Anil Trigunayat
10. A Decade of the Belt and Road Initiative — 216
    Commodore Gopal Suri

Part Three Decoding China's Domestic Preoccupations
11. China After the 20th Party Congress: Political, Economic and Technological Developments — 243
    Ananth Krishnan
12. China's Economic Trajectory: Politics in Command — 253
    Manoj Kewalramani
13. Science and Technology Innovation in China — 275
    Group Captain Chandan Sharda
14. Impact of Zero-COVID Policy on China — 288
    Santosh Pai

15. COVID-19 and Public Health Crisis in China: Central and
    Local Responses   303
    Madhurima Nundy
16. Further Decline of Human Rights Scenario in Xinjiang Under
    COVID-19 Restrictions   313
    Debasish Chaudhuri
17. The Tibet Question   332
    Jayadeva Ranade

Part Four   Decoding China's Military Universe

18. Instrument of the Chinese Dream: A Military Appreciation of
    the 'New Era' People's Liberation Army   347
    Lieutenant General Gautam Banerjee
19. India–China Border: Crystal-Gazing into the Foreseeable Future   367
    Lieutenant General Rakesh Sharma
20. Contest for the Heavens: China's Space Programme   378
    Air Marshal Diptendu Choudhury
21. The Strategy of Military–Civil Fusion in China   395
    Prerna Gandhi

Index   409
About the Editor   423
About the Contributors   424

Part One

Decoding China: The Big Picture

1

India's China Challenge
Ashok K. Kantha

I.

Where We Are: Eastern Ladakh Crisis and Beyond

As of March 2025, India and China are poised at an ambiguous and transitional juncture in their relations. There is a tactical thaw and a rebuilding phase in the relationship after an extended period of sharp decline following transgressions by Chinese forces across the Line of Actual Control (LAC) at multiple locations in Eastern Ladakh in the summer of 2020, the amassing of troops by China, counter-deployment by India and the brutal clash in Galwan Valley in mid-June 2020.

'Complete disengagement' of Indian and Chinese troops, deployed in close proximity, has reportedly been achieved, but many questions remain about what has been agreed upon after protracted negotiations. There is continuing military deployment in abnormally high numbers on both sides in forbidding terrain for the fifth successive winter, and the process of de-escalation and de-induction of troops has not yet commenced. Relations have thus stabilised but are still far from normal. We are witnessing a re-engagement rather than a reset in ties, which will require addressing numerous structural challenges accumulated in the relationship.

On 21 October 2024, Foreign Secretary Vikram Misri stated at a media briefing that an 'agreement has been arrived at on patrolling arrangements along the Line of Actual Control in the India–China border areas, leading to disengagement and a resolution of the issues that had arisen in these areas in 2020'.[1] The next day, the Chinese Foreign Office spokesperson also remarked that 'China and India have reached resolutions on issues concerning the border area'.

Prime Minister Narendra Modi and President Xi Jinping met on 23 October 2024 on the margins of the BRICS (Brazil, Russia, India, China, and South Africa) Summit in Kazan, where re-engagement was agreed upon. This was the first structured bilateral meeting between the two leaders in nearly five years. PM Modi and President Xi agreed that the special representatives (SRs) on the India–China boundary question would meet to oversee the management of peace and tranquillity in the border areas and to explore a fair, reasonable and mutually acceptable solution to the boundary question. The relevant dialogue mechanisms at the level of foreign ministers and other officials would also be utilised to stabilise and rebuild bilateral relations.

The Indian readout of the meeting referred to the two leaders welcoming 'the recent agreement for complete disengagement and resolution of issues that arose in 2020 in the India–China border areas'.[2] The Chinese readout was more circumspect and mentioned that Modi and Xi 'commended the important progress the two sides had recently made through intensive communication on resolving the relevant issues in the border areas'.[3]

After the summit-level meeting at Kazan, there have been high-level interactions, including between the External Affairs Minister (EAM) and the member of the Politburo of the Central Committee of the Communist Party of China (CPC) and Foreign Minister Wang Yi at Rio de Janeiro on 18 November 2024 on the margins of the G20 Summit (and again on 21 February 2025 in Johannesburg on the sidelines of the G20 foreign ministers' meeting), the resumption of the dialogue between the SRs after five years with National Security Adviser (NSA) Ajit Doval meeting his Chinese counterpart, Wang Yi, in Beijing on 18 December 2024; and Foreign Secretary Vikram Misri visiting Beijing on 26–27 January 2025.

The Chinese side has maintained that the normalisation of relations should not be linked to the boundary question and the situation along the borders, which should be handled in a compartmentalised manner. Even before the understanding of October 2024 on disengagement, they were pressing for overall relations to be brought back to the normal track. In Track 1.5 and Track 2 conversations with us, Chinese scholars and officials did not deny that the status quo had been changed but expected India to accept the altered facts and move on to normalcy in relations. They had reiterated four specific demands: a level playing field for Chinese companies; facilitation of visas; resumption of direct flights and permitting Chinese journalists to be stationed in India. In response, we pointed out that those issues were merely symptoms of a more fundamental problem they had created and that they must redress it first.

Post-disengagement, the Chinese interlocutors gave an expanded wish list for moving India–China ties to the 'pre-2020 normal' to visiting Indian journalists in November 2024. Additional demands included the withdrawal of restrictions on Chinese apps in India and the free flow of scholars and tourists.[4]

During the meeting of the EAM with Wang Yi on the sidelines of the G20 Summit on 19 November 2024, the next steps in India–China relations, including the resumption of the Kailash–Mansarovar pilgrimage, data sharing on trans-border rivers, direct flights and media exchanges were discussed.[5]

According to the Ministry of External Affairs (MEA) readout of the 23rd meeting of the SRs on 18 December, they 'provided positive directions for cross-border cooperation and exchanges including resumption of the Kailash–Mansarovar Yatra, data sharing on trans-border rivers and border trade'; 'discussed various measures to maintain peace and tranquillity on the border and advance effective border management', drawing on the 'learnings from the events of 2020'; and 'resolved to inject more vitality into [the] process' of the search for a 'fair, reasonable and mutually acceptable framework for settlement of the boundary question'.[6] The statement released by the Chinese Ministry of Foreign Affairs referred to a 'six-point consensus' reached between the SRs[7], which was broadly in line with the Indian statement but with different priorities. The Chinese side continued to downplay the salience of the border issue, asserting that it should be 'properly handled from the overall situation of bilateral relations so as not to affect the development of bilateral relations'.

During his visit to Beijing just before the Chinese New Year, Foreign Secretary Misri had substantive discussions not only with his counterpart Vice Foreign Minister Sun Weidong but also with Wang Yi and Minister of the International Department of the Communist Party of China Liu Jianchao.

The statements issued by the two foreign offices confirmed that both sides have taken 'certain people-centric steps to rebuild and stabilise ties', including direct air links, the Kailash–Manasarovar pilgrimage and interactions between the media and think tanks.[8] The Chinese foreign office statement also referred to the 'mutual dispatch of journalists'.[9] Both sides also agreed to mark the 75th anniversary of the establishment of diplomatic relations in 2025. These are building blocks for the normalisation of relations, but that objective will be difficult to achieve without more progress on the management of the borders and the redressal of the outstanding issues in the relationship.

The statement made by the EAM in Lok Sabha on 3 December 2024 (and in Rajya Sabha on 4 December 2024) was his first substantive statement in Parliament on developments in India–China relations since the Chinese intrusions in Eastern Ladakh in the summer of 2020 and placed the relationship in perspective.[10]

The EAM recalled the amassing of troops by China, India's forceful counter-deployment and protracted negotiations, resulting in a disengagement of forces, but his statement was economical in giving details of the arrangements for disengagement from 'friction points' (a recent and inapt coinage in India–China border negotiations to describe areas of Chinese transgressions across the LAC). Without using the term 'buffer zones', the minister alluded to the construct when he remarked that in a few places where 'friction' occurred in 2020, 'steps of a temporary and limited nature' had been taken. He said, 'This … applies to both sides and can be revisited as the situation demands.' He flagged the disengagement of troops as 'an immediate priority' but no such urgency has been attached to the termination of 'steps of a temporary and limited nature'.

Even while stating that the immediate priority of disengagement had been achieved, the EAM made it clear that more work remained to be done on 'de-escalation as well as effective management of our activities in the border areas'. He reiterated India's consistent position that 'the maintenance of peace and tranquillity in border areas is a pre-requisite for the development of our ties', a critical linkage China has sought to disavow in recent years. Dr Jaishankar did not suggest that the border areas had returned to a state of normalcy.

While the EAM did not say so, credit must be given to the government for showing strategic patience in protracted negotiations and for being able to persuade China to agree to the resumption of patrolling by Indian troops to their 'traditional patrolling points' in Depsang and Demchok, an issue that the Chinese side was not even prepared to discuss earlier.

The EAM was also accurate in not suggesting a major forward movement in overall relations, indicating instead that recent developments have set our ties in the direction of 'some improvement' and adding that the conclusion of the disengagement phase 'allows us to consider other aspects of our bilateral engagement in a calibrated manner, keeping our national security interests first and foremost'. He was right to pour cold water on the suggestion coming from certain quarters about a 'reset' in India–China relations.

Looking ahead, the Indian side will do well to bear in mind four key propositions spelt out by the EAM, including in his statements in Parliament on 3 and 4 December 2024.

First, the state of India–China relations will reflect the state of borders, and the maintenance of peace and tranquillity, respecting the LAC and not altering the status quo unilaterally are essential prerequisites for the normal development of relations.

Second, 'steps of a temporary and limited nature' were adopted to 'obviate the possibility of further friction' in other 'friction points', which can be revisited.

Third, after the completion of disengagement, 'the next priority will be to consider de-escalation, that would address the massing of troops along the LAC with associated accompaniments'.

Finally, bilateral engagement in other domains will be taken forward 'in a calibrated manner, keeping our national security interests first and foremost'.

What are the implications of these propositions?

Let us begin with the situation along the borders, which is still far from normal, as articulated publicly by the Chief of the Army Staff (COAS) General Upendra Dwivedi. General Dwivedi has acknowledged that a 'degree of standoff' persists along the LAC, ruled out any reduction in troop deployments during the winter months, and emphasised that 'we want to go back to status quo of April 2020'[11]. Disengagement has included 'steps of a temporary and limited nature', involving denial of access to some patrolling points and pastures on our side of the LAC to our troops and graziers respectively. If these arrangements become permanent, the Chinese side would have achieved its objective of making incremental changes in the ground situation while staying under the threshold of an outright armed conflict. We cannot let the present situation freeze and become the 'new normal'. The COAS continues to call for 'go[ing] back to status quo of April 2020'[12], though the MEA no longer refers to the restoration of the status quo ante.

There is also an absence of clarity on the nature of understandings reached on disengagement. For instance, reports in *The Hindu* newspaper and other credible media outlets suggest that India agreed to formalise patrolling by China in Yangtse and possibly in the Subansiri Valley in Arunachal Pradesh.[13] We had seen occasional attempted intrusions by the People's Liberation Army (PLA) of China in Yangtse, which were foiled as India was well-entrenched militarily in that area; the last such reported intrusion by a large group of Chinese troops was in December 2022 when Indian troops were credited with taking effective preventive measures. Likewise, there have been occasional Chinese intrusions in the Subansiri Valley, but earlier media reports had quoted 'government sources' as saying that the Chinese demands for patrolling rights in Yangtse and the Subansiri Valley were 'unreasonable' and 'devoid of logic'.[14]

Post-disengagement, the two sides were expected to discuss de-escalation of troops, but these negotiations have not yet commenced. The Agreement on Confidence Building Measures in the Military Field along the LAC of November 1996 provides that any ceilings on military forces and armaments must take into account 'parameters such as the nature of the terrain, road communication and other infrastructure and time taken to induct/de-induct troops and armaments'. We have a disadvantage vis-à-vis China in these domains, which must be taken on board in the de-escalation talks.

We must see how the process of disengagement, de-escalation and de-induction works out along the LAC. It is undoubtedly in the interest of both countries to bring down tensions along the borders, but we should not forget what happened in April–May 2020 when what was seen to be a routine military exercise was used by China for multiple transgressions across the LAC under the shadow of the COVID-19 pandemic.

The most important challenge will be careful calibration of further development of bilateral relations and not falling into the trap of reverting to 'business as usual', as China would prefer. If we do so, there will be little incentive for China to address the outstanding issues, including the altered status quo along the borders.

While China has done well in making progress on its wish list conveyed to us in Track 2 interactions, it is particularly keen to see movement on its demand that Chinese companies be given a 'level playing field' in India. The Indian government has been cautious in this regard as we will discuss later.

Faced with economic difficulties, geopolitical pushback and challenges linked to the second Trump administration, China is a little more inclined to reach out to us, but there is not much evidence to suggest that this outreach is more than tactical. Nevertheless, we must utilise this opening and test how far China is interested in accommodating our concerns and interests. This calls for a closer but cautious re-engagement, but not a reset in ties. We are unlikely to see any diminution of the strategic challenge that China poses to the rise of India.

At the same time, it must be acknowledged that we are at a reordering point in the geopolitical landscape which will influence how we deal with China as our primary strategic challenge. We are witnessing a complex and head-spinning churn in the international situation, partly in continuance of trends in evidence for some time and partly as a result of the forces unleashed by the second Trump administration in the US.

Possibly the most important development is the US breaking ranks with its transatlantic European allies and re-engaging with Russia, in effect abandoning the policy of dual containment targeting Russia and China. On balance, the US moving away from the position of treating Russia as a permanent enemy will be a positive development for us, though it is doubtful that China and Russia can be driven apart by the US in what is being called a 'reverse Nixon', a reference to President Richard Nixon's rapprochement with Beijing in 1972 exploiting the worsening relations between China and the Soviet Union. Russia's relations with China are much stronger today, anchored in shared interests as also a close personal relationship between Vladimir Putin and Xi Jinping.

Donald Trump is keen on the quick termination of the Ukraine war but it is far from certain that the relative disengagement of the US in the European theatre will necessarily result in greater targeting of China in the Indo-Pacific, as senior Trump officials have indicated. Trump is himself sending out mixed signals on China. The strategic rivalry between the US and China is likely to continue, though Trump is interested in a 'deal' with China, which the Chinese are quite keen to explore. Even a limited understanding between the two countries will have significant implications for India and we will be watching that space very closely.

Besides, Trump's surreal meeting with President Volodymyr Zelenskyy of Ukraine in the Oval Office on 28 February, his cavalier and almost cruel treatment of the European allies as also Canada and Mexico, the US withdrawal from organisations like the WHO, its undermining of global trade architecture with the introduction of the concept of reciprocal tariffs, questioning climate change, and gutting of instruments like United States Agency for International Development (USAID) are creating space for China, in Europe, the Global South and multilateral platforms.

Moreover, the transactional and somewhat whimsical Trumpian approach should make us carefully ponder over the efficacy of external balancing in our China strategy.

II.

India–China Relations: A Broken Paradigm

Now that India has reached an understanding on the resumption of patrolling in Eastern Ladakh and the process of rebuilding ties has commenced, are we moving towards a reset in relations? The answer is: not so soon.

Indeed, the EAM also stated on 16 November 2024 that the latest disengagement of Indian and Chinese troops on the LAC is only part of a process that must lead to de-escalation and resolution of other issues linked to the bilateral relationship and does not signify a reset in ties at this stage.[15]

The understanding reached in October last year was limited in nature; a step towards the diminution of tensions, it represented more a nudge than a major shift, a tactical adjustment rather than any fundamental realignment. The process of normalisation of India–China borders has indeed commenced and made some headway; there is greater stability now but restoration of normalcy will take time. As long as the borders remain abnormal and highly militarised, India cannot rush towards a complete normalisation of overall relations. Our expectations in this regard must be carefully managed.[16]

However, while considering any reset of ties, we should not lose sight of the fact that apart from the unfinished agenda of the redressal of disruption caused to the status quo by Chinese transgressions in Eastern Ladakh, there are major structural problems in the relationship which need to be addressed. Indeed, the basic paradigm that had buttressed the relationship for over three decades has irrevocably broken down and the search for a new equilibrium will be a protracted process.

The old paradigm can be traced back to the visit of Prime Minister Rajiv Gandhi to China in December 1988. Until then, India had insisted that, before any normalisation could take place, the boundary issue had to be settled. The decision to develop relations and seek normalisation of overall relations was a major break from our past policy.[17]

However, the linkage between an early settlement of the boundary question and further development of bilateral relations was not altogether dropped. Thus, the 'India–China Joint Press Communiqué' issued on 23 December 1988 notes that the leaders 'agreed to settle this [boundary] question through peaceful and friendly consultations. They also agreed to develop their relations actively in other fields and work hard to create a favourable climate and conditions for a fair and reasonable settlement of the boundary question while seeking a mutually acceptable solution to this question. In this context, concrete steps will be taken, such as establishing a joint working group on the boundary question.'[18]

There was another aspect of the basic compact that the Chinese have ignored in recent years – pending a boundary settlement, both sides would respect the status quo along the borders and not seek to change it unilaterally and that the maintenance of peace and tranquillity in the border areas was an essential prerequisite for the continued development of bilateral relations. This understanding was reflected in subsequent joint statements. Thus, the joint statement issued on 15 May 2015 during PM Modi's visit to China recalled, 'The two sides will resolve outstanding differences, including the boundary question, in a proactive manner. Those differences should not be allowed to come in the way of continued development of bilateral relations. Peace and tranquillity on the India–China border was recognized as an important guarantor for the development and continued growth of bilateral relations.'[19]

It is relevant to recall that Rajiv Gandhi's visit to China took place against the backdrop of the Wangdung crisis of 1986–87, which had also led to a surge in tensions, heavy military deployments by both sides and the threat from China of teaching India a lesson. Counterintuitively, the Wangdung incident set the stage for PM Gandhi's visit to China, which culminated in a new framework for the management of the relationship that lasted until 2020. Can we utilise the latest border crisis to move towards a new compact for the relationship through patient negotiations?

Though the boundary question has defied a solution, the two sides had managed to put in place a relationship that had the basic attributes of normal state-to-state and people-to-people engagement, including an extensive architecture of confidence-building measures along the borders, dialogue mechanisms concerning various bilateral, regional and multilateral issues, vibrant though lopsided trade, two-way investment flows, the presence of nearly 25,000 Indian students in China and a much smaller number of Chinese students in India (before the COVID-19 pandemic), a modest flow of tourists, partnership on global issues like climate change and so on.

All this came crashing down in the wake of Chinese border transgressions in the Western Sector and the deadly clash in the Galwan Valley on the night of 15–16 June 2020, resulting in 20 fatalities on our side and an unknown number of casualties on the Chinese side. This was the first clash along the borders involving the loss of life since 1975, and it undermined a basic pillar sustaining a difficult but critical relationship – that the continued development of relations was predicated on the maintenance of peace and tranquillity in the border areas. The EAM put it succinctly: the state of the borders will determine the state of the relationship and, as long as the borders are abnormal, the overall relations cannot return to the normal track.

III.

Modi Years and the Persistence of Structural Problems in India–China Relations

India's policy towards China during the past decade has been marked by a large measure of continuity along with significant initiatives. This process was disrupted in the summer of 2020.

The Narendra Modi government inherited a complex relationship with China in May 2014 that was simultaneously stable and fraught. The stability stemmed from the fact that the two countries had broadly subscribed to a basic template since 1988, as discussed above.

One major change after the NDA government assumed office was that the leaders of the two countries, Narendra Modi and Xi Jinping, took charge of India–China relations. Until then, it was the Chinese Premier who was the primary interlocutor for the prime minister of India. When I met President Xi during the presentation of credentials as the new Indian ambassador to China in March 2014, he told me that he saw improving relations with India as his 'historic mission'.[20] Likewise, Modi took a personal interest in the relationship with China, a country he had visited earlier as the chief minister of Gujarat.

In fact, immediately after the Modi government was sworn in, Xi sent Foreign Minister Wang Yi to New Delhi as his special emissary in early June 2014 to initiate preparations for his own state visit to India, which took place in September 2014. In an unusual move, it was conveyed by the Chinese side that Xi would like to commence his visit in Modi's home state of Gujarat and, if possible, meet him there. In a departure from protocol, Modi travelled to Ahmedabad to receive Xi in a 'hometown diplomacy' gesture. Xi reciprocated in May 2015 by receiving Modi in his own hometown of Xi'an. As the Indian ambassador in Beijing, I was closely involved with these two visits.

Prior to the COVID-19 pandemic and the developments in Eastern Ladakh, we had sought a constructive engagement with China. Our leaders met frequently; PM Modi and President Xi had as many as eighteen meetings between 2014 and 2019, including two informal summits at Wuhan (April 2018)[21] and Chennai (October 2019).[22] These interactions resulted in some key understandings of 'Closer Developmental Partnership' (September 2014)[23] and managing 'the simultaneous re-emergence of India and China as two major powers in the region and the world' in a mutually supportive manner with 'both sides showing mutual respect and sensitivity to each other's concerns, interests and aspirations' (May 2015)[24]. During the 2014–19 period, there was significant momentum in trade and investment linkages, people-to-people contacts and the deepening and widening of dialogue mechanisms at various levels.

At the same time, India's concerns and interests were being projected forcefully. Thus, while receiving Xi in Ahmedabad on 17 September 2014, Modi, during a walk along the Sabarmati riverbank, conveyed privately to the Chinese leader his strong concerns regarding the Chinese intrusions in Chumar and Demchok, which had escalated the previous evening. The message registered with Xi, and talks commenced the same evening on the de-escalation and withdrawal of Chinese troops; the status quo ante was restored through a written understanding reached in Beijing later in the month.

In the summit talks in Xi'an in May 2015, Modi pressed Xi on the imperative of an early boundary settlement. The joint statement issued in Beijing the following day 'affirmed that an early settlement of the boundary question serves the basic interests of the two countries and should be pursued as a strategic objective by the two governments.'[25]

Likewise, subsequent summit meetings were utilised to convey strong messages on a range of issues, including the boundary question, the need to move towards a more balanced economic relationship, India's membership of the Nuclear Suppliers Group (NSG) and the blocking by China of the listing of Pakistan-based terrorists under the UN Security Council's 1267 Committee.[26]

Yet the government was acutely aware of the challenges in the relationship. There was no illusion about the fact that we were dealing with a country that was undergoing unprecedented transformation and was aggressive in its pursuit of unilateral territorial claims and self-defined core interests. India assessed that after the 2008–09 global financial crisis, China had come to the conclusion that the West was in terminal decline and that time and momentum were on its side. Xi Jinping's 'China Dream' of the 'great rejuvenation of the Chinese nation', articulated soon after he became the general secretary of the CPC in October 2012, involved the 'restoration' of China's 'rightful role' as the leading power in the region and beyond.[27]

There were also serious doubts about whether informal summits were resulting in progress on these structural challenges in the relationship. The Chinese are traditionally averse to using summit-level meetings as platforms for negotiations on contentious issues. It has also been our experience that meetings at the highest level with China have been fruitful only when preceded by extensive preparatory negotiations, including through the deployment of special emissaries.

In its bilateral dealings with India, China was not showing much interest in resolving the boundary question and clarifying the LAC. Likewise, it was not responsive to India's concerns, interests and aspirations on a range of issues, such as trade imbalance, India's permanent membership of the UN Security Council (UNSC), its inclusion in the NSG and the listing of known terrorists under the aegis of the UNSC.

Therefore, even while the relations appeared to be on an even keel, ominous clouds were building up due to the accumulation of unresolved issues and irritants. There were structural challenges in the relationship that predated Galwan. This pattern appears to be continuing as there is little evidence of any keenness on the part of China to address those outstanding issues. Let us illustrate with an emerging challenge involving trans-border rivers.

A Xinhua report of 25 December 2024[28] on the 'approval' given by the Chinese government to build the world's largest hydropower project in the lower reaches of the Yarlung Tsangpo River in Tibet is a reminder of how stubborn issues in the relationship will continue to surface and create fresh complications. According to the Hong Kong-based *South China Morning Post*, the project is expected to generate nearly 300 billion kilowatt-hours (kWh) of electricity annually, more than thrice the installed capacity of the Three Gorges Dam (88.2 billion kWh), which is presently the world's largest hydropower plant. 'Total investment in the dam could exceed 1 trillion yuan (US$137 billion), which would dwarf any other single infrastructure project on the planet.'[29]

This decision, apparently taken without any prior consultations with the lower riparian countries, India and Bangladesh, has huge implications for them. Though the exact location of the project has not been officially announced, it is likely to be developed at the 'Big Bend' in the Yarlung Tsangpo, very close to the place where the river enters Arunachal Pradesh. This venture will have major downstream impacts on water flows in the Brahmaputra River system in India and further below in Bangladesh. Ominously, the construction of a colossal hydropower plant with a massive impounding of water in an ecologically unstable and earthquake-prone region involves the risk of disaster on an unprecedented scale[30], as geospatial studies by Dr Y. Nithiyanandam and others have shown.[31]

Uniquely placed as an upper riparian vis-à-vis its neighbours, China has an unfortunate track record of ignoring their interests and concerns with disastrous consequences in the Mekong River basin and elsewhere. As China proceeds with its massive project in Tibet, it is likely to emerge as another major irritant in the relationship.

We must also acknowledge that the worldviews of India and China have become highly divergent. As China's strategic contestation with the US intensified with the Trump administration beginning to take a more hardline position vis-à-vis China in 2016 and the revival of the Quad in 2017, Beijing was increasingly looking at its relations with New Delhi through the prism of its rivalry with Washington. In 2018, Wang famously dismissed the Quad as nothing more than 'sea foam' that would dissipate, but soon the Chinese were voicing their strong concerns regarding the mechanism and India's participation in the 'small clique' diplomacy of the US aimed at countering and containing China.[32]

The bottom line is that in the midst of the geopolitical reordering taking place today, China is possibly the only major country which is not supportive of the rise of India. It is promoting a hierarchical order with China as the pre-eminent power while we favour a multipolar Asia and multipolar world. It actively hinders India's interests in South Asia and the Indian Ocean Region (IOR). It is aggressively seeking to project its influence in a manner that is detrimental to our interests. It opposes our permanent membership of the UN Security Council. On its part, China is suspicious of our strategic linkages with the US and initiatives like the Quad which it believes are aimed at containing China.

On the Indian side, there is a realisation that China is not inclined to deliver on the understanding reached in May 2015 that the simultaneous rise of the two countries should progress in a mutually supportive manner. Given the asymmetries in the economic and military power of the two countries, China is not prepared to work towards a relationship between equals.

The challenge of dealing with China has been seriously affected by the growing gap in the comprehensive national strength of India and China. Thus, in 2023, the GDP of China was US$17.79 trillion, which was five times as large as the GDP of India at US$3.55 trillion (World Bank data).[33] The chart in Figure 1.1 shows how a yawning gap has opened between the GDPs of the two countries, which were broadly comparable until the year 2000:

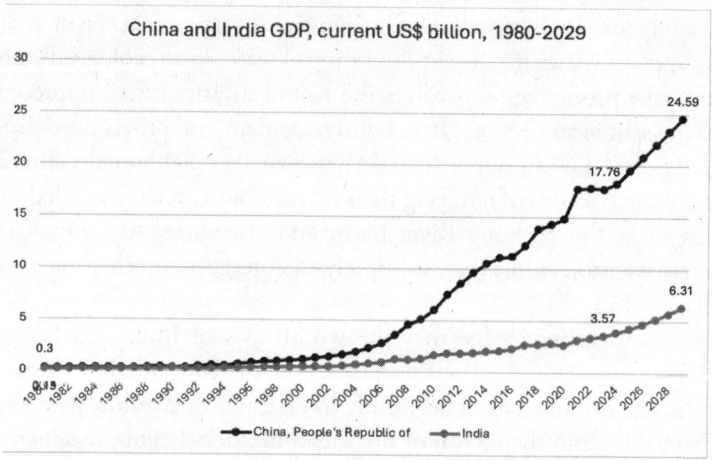

Figure 1.1 China and India's GDP (in US$ billion), 1980–2029
Note: 2024–29 are projections of growth
Source: IMF World Economic Outlook, October 2024

Likewise, the defence budgets and capabilities of India and China have become increasingly asymmetrical. According to the Stockholm International

Peace Research Institute (SIPRI) data for 2023, China's defence budget was approximately US$296 billion, as compared to US$84 billion for India.[34] China's real defence spending is assessed to be significantly higher than its officially acknowledged budget.

Let us look at the growing gap between the capabilities of the Indian Navy and the PLA Navy (PLAN) even though it is an area where we have relatively strong domestic manufacturing capabilities, unlike our ground and air forces, which depend heavily on imported defence hardware. According to data available from SIPRI and other public sources[35], the PLAN surpasses the Indian Navy in both quantity and quality across major platforms. China's larger fleet – 3 aircraft carriers (2 operational), 41 destroyers, 44 frigates, 71 corvettes and over 70 submarines – dwarfs India's 2 carriers, 10 destroyers, 13 frigates, 28 corvettes, and 18 submarines. China now has the largest navy in the world with 370 warships, though the US Navy still has a significant edge in terms of technological sophistication and displacement. India has about 150 warships (including auxiliary vessels), though with much lower sophistication and total displacement value compared to the PLAN. What is more worrisome is the expanding asymmetry in both numbers and quality. Chinese naval shipyards are adding about 20 warships every year while the corresponding number for India is 3–4 ships on average. This gap is progressively eroding the advantage India has in the IOR due to its strategic location and peninsular geography.

The situation along the land borders had become more challenging even prior to 2020. Apart from Chinese intrusions into the Depsang Plains in 2013, and into Demchok and Chumar in 2014, there was a prolonged standoff in the Doklam (Dolam) area of Bhutan in 2017, which was resolved but it proved to be a short-lived respite as the Chinese soon reinforced their deployments and infrastructure within the Bhutanese territory.

One major consequence of what has happened in Eastern Ladakh since the summer of 2020 is that the border issue is back at the centre of India–China relations. The relative calm that had prevailed along the India–China borders for over four decades is unlikely to be restored anytime soon. The borders have become active, with high levels of deployments on both sides. It is the new reality now. The challenge is compounded by the fact that the Chinese have not been ready to clarify the LAC, let alone resolve the boundary question, as they have used the unsettled border as a pressure point in the relationship.

China is not interested in an early resolution of the boundary question for a variety of reasons. The Chinese seem to believe that time is on their side. There has not been any breakthrough in talks on the boundary question between the SRs since April 2005 when an agreement was signed on the political parameters and guiding principles for a boundary settlement. They are demanding 'meaningful adjustments' by India in the Eastern Sector, that is, in Arunachal Pradesh (referred to by them as 'Zangnan' or 'South Tibet'), including Tawang, before they will consider making 'corresponding concessions' in the Western Sector (so-called 'dong tiao xi rang' or 东调西让, translated as 'adjustments in the east and concessions in the west'). No government in India can consider making such major 'adjustments' in Arunachal Pradesh. The Chinese stance is at variance with the position earlier conveyed by Zhou Enlai and Deng Xiaoping, which seemed to suggest a package solution largely based on the recognition of the status quo in the border areas.

The Chinese have likewise gone back on the clear-cut understanding of the clarification and confirmation of the LAC contained in the bilateral agreements of 1993 and 1996. In the agreement of 7 September 1993, the two sides agreed to 'jointly check and determine the segments of the line of actual control where they have different views as to its alignment'. This understanding was further amplified in the agreement on military confidence-building measures (CBMs) of 29 November 1996, which called for the two sides to arrive at a 'common understanding' of the alignment of the LAC and agree to exchange maps indicating their respective perceptions of the entire alignment of the LAC as early as possible. The maps were exchanged for the Middle Sector but the process was unilaterally halted by the Chinese side in June 2002 when maps of the Western Sector were shown to each other. The Chinese claimed that we had expanded our claims and refused to exchange maps. There has been no progress in the LAC clarification exercise over the past 22 years.

Differences even on the LAC are now being defined by China in terms of sovereignty. This is a departure from the elaborate architecture of CBMs we have put in place since the Border Peace and Tranquillity Agreement of September 1993, based on the two sides respecting and observing the LAC without prejudice to their respective positions on the boundary question.

There are growing concerns in India about a host of other issues, including the denial of market access to Indian products and services and growing dependencies on imports from China in critical areas. Disruptions in supply chains have exacerbated import dependency on China during the COVID-19 pandemic and underscored the need for resilience in India's supply sources.

The Chinese are not inclined to address India's long-standing problem of a huge bilateral trade deficit and the impediments faced by Indian companies in accessing the Chinese market. According to International Trade Centre data[36], China's trade surplus with India exceeded US$102 billion in 2024 (up from US$46 billion in 2024); while its exports to India increased from US$67 billion in 2020 to US$121 billion in 2024, its imports from India declined from US$21 billion in 2020 to US$18 billion in 2024 (see Figure 1.2). There has been no improvement in India's import dependencies vis-à-vis China in critical sectors like active pharmaceutical ingredients, electronics, chemicals, machinery and green energy products, which is a source of great vulnerability, as China has an established track record of weaponising such dependencies.

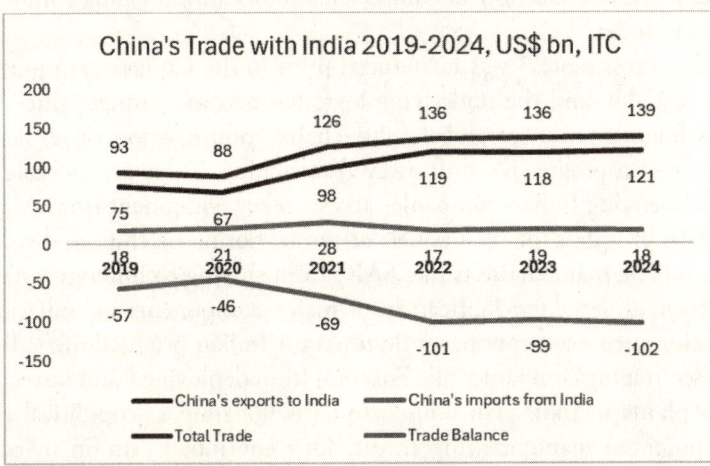

Figure 1.2 China's Trade with India (in US$ billion), 2019–24
Source: International Trade Centre

Even before the Chinese intrusions in May 2020, the policy on welcoming investment from China was being revisited. Thus, Press Note 3 issued by India's Department for Promotion of Industry and Internal Trade on 17 April 2020 put all foreign direct investment (FDI) from China (and other countries sharing a land border with India) in the prior approval category.[37] It was a significant shift in policy.

The government has also taken measures to reduce dependencies on China-dominated supply chains by attempting to build domestic capabilities through production-linked incentives in 14 sectors, tapping alternative supply sources and banning over 350 Chinese apps. This policy of derisking vis-à-vis China will be a difficult and protracted but necessary process. In May 2021, the Government of India decided to leave out Chinese telecom entities Huawei and ZTE from its 5G trials (and the subsequent rollout).

Earlier, in November 2019, India had decided not to join the Regional Comprehensive Economic Partnership (RCEP) even though it had participated in the negotiations on the agreement. India decided to opt out of RCEP as several of its key demands were not addressed in the agreement,[38] but concerns about China were possibly the most significant factor in India's decision. The apprehension was that the Indian market could be overwhelmed by cheaper Chinese goods, adversely affecting India's manufacturing and agricultural sectors.[39] This was compounded by broader geopolitical tensions and trade imbalances between India and China.

Economic security vis-à-vis China has its compelling logic. It would be naïve to expect that China will help build up our manufacturing capabilities, unless it essentially involves assembly of components sourced from China with low-value addition in India.

Indeed, Press Note 3 was introduced prior to the Chinese transgressions in Eastern Ladakh, and the underlying logic has become stronger since then, as there is fragmentation of global value chains, prioritisation of resilience and security, and a progressive shift away from China. There are credible reports of China denying Indian companies access to key equipment (for instance, for fabrication of wafers for solar panels or tunnel boring machines), discouraging electric vehicle manufacturers like SAIC from sharing technology with Indian partners or undertaking fabrication of major components in India, delaying export clearance for components destined for Indian production facilities and even discouraging companies like Foxconn from deploying Chinese technicians at their plants in India. For China, India is not only a geopolitical rival but also a potential manufacturing threat. Our continued caution in economic engagement with China is warranted.[40]

However, the Chinese transgressions in Eastern Ladakh in May 2020 created a qualitatively different situation and a turning point in the relationship. Unlike previous standoff incidents, the Chinese have not restored the status quo as of April 2020, even though progress has been made towards the disengagement of troops, as discussed above.

Despite the understandings reached on the disengagement of troops, the LAC remains live and militarised. The Chinese have stepped up infrastructure building in border areas and India has reciprocated. The infrastructure gap in favour of China remains sizeable and is still increasing. China continues to significantly enhance long-term deployment capabilities along the entire LAC. Three major railway projects coming close to the India–China borders – Nyingchi, Yadong and Gyrong in Tibet – are under development, as are several highways, including G695 in Aksai Chin. The Chinese are prepared for an entrenched military presence close to the LAC.

China's aggressive behaviour in the shared periphery, land and maritime, has also been a major source of anxiety for India. Some key aspects of China's approach towards South Asia should be flagged.

One, China has regarded South Asia as a region of interest right since the 1950s but in recent years it has started looking at the region as its immediate strategic periphery. We have seen the evolution of China's strategic outlook towards South Asia, especially since the convening of the 'Work Forum on Chinese Diplomacy Towards the Periphery' by the CPC Central Committee in October 2013. Frankly, we are struggling to unpack China's strategic behaviour towards our region. We are not clear whether China seeks expanded influence or whether its objective verges on strategic dominance. China is increasingly entangled in the domestic affairs of our neighbours and is seeking to shape political outcomes.

Two, there is also greater willingness to invest sizeable resources in South Asia under the Belt and Road Initiative (BRI) and its subset, the China–Pakistan Economic Corridor (CPEC). South Asia has emerged as a key component in China's Maritime Silk Road and Indian Ocean strategies. However, there are questions about the viability of many of these projects and the ability of the recipients to handle the large debt that these projects involve. Sri Lanka's debt distress resulted in Chinese entities acquiring the Hambantota Port on a 99-year lease. While handing over the port to China in November 1921, the Sri Lankan government justified the decision to lease the Hambantota Port to Chinese entities as a necessary measure to manage the country's debt.[41] Many of these unsustainable projects have roots in elite capture by China.

Three, China's trade with South Asia has also expanded but has become increasingly imbalanced in its favour. Thus, according to International Trade Centre data for 2023, China exported US$166 billion to the SAARC (South Asian Association for Regional Cooperation) region and imported only US$23 billion. It had a trade surplus of US$143 billion, of which India accounted for over US$100 billion. Such a skewed trade structure is not sustainable.

Another defining element of China's engagement with South Asia is defence cooperation. According to SIPRI data, Pakistan and Bangladesh are the top two defence export destinations of China. A combined 63.4 per cent of China's conventional weapons sales between 2010 and 2020 have found their way to Pakistan, Bangladesh and Myanmar.[42] With Pakistan, there is a long history of overt and covert cooperation in strategic sectors like nuclear weapons and missile development.

Finally, as China is the second largest economy and the leading trading nation in the world with a growing presence in different parts of the world, it is not surprising that its engagement with South Asia has also expanded. However, how China expands its presence in our neighbourhood, both land and maritime, matters to India. There are natural anxieties when projects are undertaken in violation of India's sovereignty and territorial integrity (for instance, projects in Pakistan-occupied Kashmir). More so as there is a deliberate pattern of India's vital interests being undermined and the positioning of China as a countervailing force vis-à-vis India comes in the way of the realisation of the potential for intra-regional cooperation.

In the maritime domain, China is progressively deploying a 'two-ocean' strategy in the Pacific and the IOR. The Western Pacific, particularly the Taiwan Strait and the first island chain, remains the area of primary interest for China. However, beginning with anti-piracy operations in the IOR in 2008, the PLAN has gradually 'normalised' its operations in our maritime neighbourhood. The Chief of Naval Staff Admiral R. Hari Kumar stated on 1 December 2023 that China now has 'a sustained presence' in the IOR with six to eight warships deployed at any given time, apart from research or spy vessels and its fishing fleet.[43]

China now considers its emergence as a maritime power and its protection of overseas interests as strategic priorities. In the Chinese white paper on military strategy released in May 2015, there was a major change in the focus of the PLAN with the addition of 'open seas protection' to its existing role of 'offshore waters defence'.[44] The white paper stated that the 'traditional mentality that land outweighs the sea must be abandoned'. This doctrinal shift, the rolling out of the Maritime Silk Road initiative, rapid buildup of PLAN and its assets, major reforms and modernisation underway in the Chinese military, militarisation of reclaimed/augmented features in the South China Sea, near-continuous naval presence and regular submarine deployments in the IOR, development of its first overseas facility and deployment of the PLA Marines at Djibouti in 2017 and other actions taken by China are progressively resulting in a much bigger footprint of the PLAN in the Indian Ocean beyond the Western Pacific, in consonance with China's stated policy of becoming a maritime power. China's long-term strategy in the IOR is to move from one of selective sea denial to a strategy of deflective sea control.

However, the Chinese presence in South Asia and the IOR is not necessarily meant as a countervailing force to India; it is increasingly a part of the larger Chinese strategy to expand its regional and global footprint in consonance with its great power ambitions.

In recent months, China has made a tactical outreach not only to the US but also to the European Union, Japan, South Korea, Vietnam and Australia to restore greater stability in those relationships. This tactical flexibility has now been extended to India, though earlier we were an outlier in China's charm offensive, as was evident from Xi's absence at the G20 Summit in New Delhi in September 2023 and the fact that the post of the Chinese ambassador in New Delhi had remained vacant for 16 months.

We have discussed earlier the geopolitical reordering that is currently unfolding with unpredictable outcomes. As India prepares to recalibrate relations with China after the understanding on the disengagement of troops in the Depsang Plains and Demchok, and bilateral re-engagement at the highest level, the nature of the challenge posed by China not only to India but also to other major countries, as well as the evolving response of those countries, must be assessed carefully.

IV.
Sources of China as a Global Challenge and Pushback

The rise of China over the past 45 years has been the most important geopolitical development of this period. The country has been transformed and has emerged as the second-largest economy in the world, the largest manufacturer (with 30 per cent of global manufacturing exports), the largest trading nation, a formidable military power and second only to the US in its comprehensive national power. China has not only pulled over 750 million of its citizens out of poverty[45] but has also contributed immensely to the global economy as the leading beneficiary of globalisation. However, there are aspects of China's rise and its pursuit of parochial 'core interests' that have been deeply disturbing. While for India, China is the primary strategic challenge for the reasons discussed earlier, its behaviour poses a significant global challenge. Some of the sources of this challenge are examined below.

A. China's Worldview and Grand Strategy

We are at a time when China's worldview and its leadership ambitions have crystallised but at the same time it is facing growing pushback.

What is China's grand strategy? It is a complex subject but a good place to start is Xi Jinping's 'Chinese Dream' of 'great rejuvenation of the Chinese nation', which was articulated soon after he took over as the Chinese leader in October 2012 at the 17th Party Congress.

The Chinese Dream essentially involves achieving two centenary goals that China has set for itself. The first of these goals has been achieved, that is, by 2021 (the 100th anniversary of the founding of the CPC), China, by its reckoning, emerged as a moderately affluent society, doubling its 2010 GDP and income per capita. The second centenary goal is to be reached by 2049 (the 100th anniversary of the People's Republic of China [PRC]) when it should have become a strong, prosperous and harmonious country. This will also involve fostering China's role as a leading nation in the world, a leader which helps shape and guide the global governance system, is a rule-setter, promotes Chinese values and safeguards its core interests.

Under Xi, China has been more explicit about its regional and global ambitions and more aggressive in pursuit of its unilaterally defined 'core interests'. This, when seen along with his domineering role as the supreme leader of China and his radical departures from the policy prescriptions of Deng Xiaoping and his cohort in both domestic and external domains, has given rise to a perception that these changes are being uniquely driven by Xi Jinping and his ideological worldview. Thus, in his new book, *On Xi Jinping: How Xi's Marxist Nationalism Is Shaping China and the World*, Kevin Rudd has argued that 'these changes, together with those in foreign policy and national security policy, have been driven from the top. Or as Xi himself has often proclaimed, through the agency of "top-level design". For these reasons, the central argument ... remains that we need to understand the nature of Xi's ideational worldview as a means of unlocking where he has taken China so far, as well as where he may take it next.'[46]

There is little doubt about the 'agency' of Xi Jinping as a unique leader, the most influential since the establishment of the PRC in 1949, along with Mao Zedong and Deng Xiaoping, in shaping and driving changes within China and in its external aspirations and behaviour since 2012. Yet, it would be a mistake to underestimate the structural factors behind these developments, which predate Xi and will continue to mould the Chinese Dream even after his departure. The fact that Xi Jinping is part of a continuum in the evolution of China's worldview, rather than a sui generis phenomenon, has significant implications when we seek to anticipate China's future behaviour. There will no doubt be course corrections from time to time depending on circumstances and some of his policies may be abandoned, as has happened during Xi's stewardship of the party-state, but a common thread running through China's contemporary history should not be lost sight of.

There are two keywords which have strongly resonated in Chinese narratives. The first word is 'fuqiang' (富强), which means economically prosperous and militarily strong. It has been a constant theme in the Chinese narrative since the early 20th century. The second term is 'fuxing' (复兴) or rejuvenation, which is the restoration of China's perceived rightful leadership role, first in the Asia-Pacific and eventually globally. China is, after all, 'Zhongguo', the 'Middle Kingdom', with its sense of centrality, destiny and entitlement. In the Chinese narrative that is the historical norm, the 'century of humiliation' being an aberration which must be set right.

The century of humiliation came to an end with the establishment of the PRC under the leadership of Mao Zedong, and the rejuvenation of the Chinese nation commenced. In the essential narrative of the party-state, under Mao Zedong (1949–76), China 'stood up' ('zhanqilaile', 站起来了); under Deng Xiaoping (1978–92), China 'became rich' ('fuqilaile', 富起来了) and under Xi Jinping (2012–present), China has 'become strong' ('qiangqilaile', 强起来了). It is still a mission incomplete as the Chinese Dream will be realised by the middle of the century when the country regains its 'rightful' role as the 'leading nation'.

We will not dwell on the Mao period, which was one of great upheavals, but Xi Jinping refers to those revolutionary years of ideological focus with great pride. Unlike Mao, he puts stability above everything else but that has not prevented him from reviving the language of 'struggle' and 'rectification'.

He does not believe in a 'permanent revolution' but has his own variant of a never-ending anti-corruption campaign. He is not in the business of 'exporting revolution' but does believe that the Chinese model of development and his 'community of shared destiny' offer a viable alternative to the US-led order.

The legacy of Deng Xiaoping is the policy of 'reform and opening-up' which resulted in the unprecedented transformation of China. He recognised China's weaknesses after the ravages of the Cultural Revolution and focused on modernisation and economic development rather than pursuing unrealistic foreign policy expectations and attracting the ire of the US, with whom he sought strategic alignment to counter the threat from the Soviet Union. Deng sought to integrate China into the global economy, fostering trade relations and attracting foreign technology and investment. He prioritised normalising relations with the United States and other Western countries. His pragmatic strategic line is contained in the principle 'taoguang yanghui', meaning to hide one's capabilities and bide one's time. Indeed, the scope of this strategy can be better understood from Deng's 24-character dictum: Observe calmly (冷静观察), secure our position (站稳脚跟), cope with affairs calmly (沉着应付), hide our capacities and bide our time (韬光养晦), be good at maintaining a low profile (善于守拙) and never claim leadership (绝不当头).

This strategy emphasises a cautious and measured approach to international relations, focusing on internal development and avoiding unnecessary provocations. This shift significantly transformed China's international standing and economic trajectory. However, this was meant to be a temporary and preparatory phase rather than a permanent worldview or strategic stance of the PRC.

As China's economy grew, so did its ambitions. In 2004, China's leaders briefly talked of a 'peaceful rise' (heping jueqi) of China to reflect the reality of China's resurgence. It generated anxieties within and outside China and was quickly replaced with the anodyne mantra of 'peaceful development' (heping fazhan).[47] But China started ramping up its economic presence worldwide, including in Africa and Latin America.

It was only after the Global Financial Crisis of 2008–09 that we saw the first major wave of assertiveness by China in claiming a leadership role. As previously mentioned, it was China's assessment that the US-led West, which was the epicentre of the crisis, was in terminal decline and that China's time had come. China played a critical role in dealing with the financial crisis, including through a massive stimulus package, which reinforced its position as a major engine of the world economy, contributing about one-third of global growth.

At an ambassadorial conference in 2009, Hu Jintao subtly suggested a significant revision in China's grand strategy. He noted that there had been 'a major change in the balance of international forces' in reference to the financial crisis and that the 'prospects for multipolarity were now more obvious'.⁴⁸ Concepts like 'international balance of power' (国际力量对比) and 'multipolarity' (多极化) are euphemisms for the decline of American power. As Rush Doshi has observed, China's leaders have made clear that their adherence to 'hiding capabilities and biding time' was never permanent but instead contingent on the 'international balance of power'.⁴⁹ Thus, Hu explained to China's foreign policy apparatus: 'Adhering to hide and bide (韬光养晦) is a strategic decision made by the centre based on comprehensively analysing the entire international balance of power.'⁵⁰ If China's strategy was dependent on the 'international balance of power', and if the 'international balance of power' had changed', then it meant China's grand strategy needed revision.⁵¹

Hu proposed the change at the conference. He declared that China needed to modify Deng's 'hiding capabilities and biding time' by more 'actively accomplishing something' (积极有所作为). This seemingly semantic shift – the addition of the word 'actively' to one part of Deng's doctrine – heralded a more proactive and assertive approach to China's foreign policy.

Two years after Hu's speech, China outlined the concept of a 'Community of Common Destiny' in a white paper, which suggested China's preferences for an Asia where others were dependent on China economically and divorced from US alliances militarily. On the economic and institutional side, China said the 'Community of Common Destiny' was a state of being 'interconnected' and 'intertwined'; on the security side, it defined it as being against the 'Cold War mentality', which is an implicit critique of the US and its alliance system. The phrase then reappeared in Hu's 18th Party Congress Political Report and later became the cornerstone of Xi's order-building project.⁵²

Under Hu's leadership, China started adopting a more muscular policy to 'reclaim' its 'lost territory' in the Senkaku (Diaoyu) Islands in the East China Sea and took a firmer stance on its territorial claims in the South China Sea. This included increased patrolling and the establishment of administrative units to govern disputed areas. The successful hosting of the 2008 Olympics was a demonstration of China's growing confidence and desire to showcase its achievements on the global stage. On 23 July 2010, Foreign Minister Yang Jiechi delivered a famous line at a meeting of the Association of Southeast Asian Nations (ASEAN) Regional Forum in Hanoi (after Secretary of State Hillary Clinton had criticised China's South China Sea claims) that seemed to capture China's new diplomacy: 'China is a big country and other countries are small countries, and that's just a fact.'⁵³

Another key shift with roots in the Asian Financial Crisis of the late 1990s related to adjusting the ends of the country's strategy away from a narrow focus on blunting American power towards a broader focus on building regional order. This effort was subsumed under concepts like 'peripheral diplomacy'

(周边外交). In the past, China saw its periphery as a source of threat, fearing that the US would organise a balancing coalition within it to challenge China. Now, after the Global Financial Crisis, China saw the periphery not only as a place to push back on the 'China threat theory' but as an arena for a more affirmative and less defensive Chinese strategy.[54]

In the military domain, the Global Financial Crisis accelerated China's shift away from a singular focus on blunting American power through sea denial, which had prioritised mines, missiles and submarines. China would instead shift its focus to building regional order through sea control and amphibious capabilities, which emphasised aircraft carriers, more capable surface vessels, amphibious units, overseas facilities and a variety of capabilities it had deliberately neglected.[55]

These actions marked a move towards a more confident and engaged stance in international affairs, reflecting China's growing economic and military power. Hu's approach aimed to balance maintaining a low profile with taking more initiative in global governance and regional issues, reflecting a shift towards a more proactive and confident foreign policy and setting the stage for China's rapid rise on the global stage. However, under Hu Jintao, China formally stuck to Deng Xiaoping's 24-character dictum.

A more explicitly assertive and ambitious phase started with Xi Jinping's accession to power in late 2012. It was possible for Xi to conceive an ambitious Chinese Dream because of the massive makeover that China had achieved over the past four decades.

Externally, Xi no longer refers to Deng's dictum. Instead, there is talk of 'Fenfa Youwei', which means 'striving for achievement' or a more proactive foreign policy. He is pursuing the policy of shaping the periphery of China, through initiatives like 'One Belt One Road', by launching new institutions like the Asian Infrastructure Investment Bank (AIIB), forcefully asserting China's core interests and unabashedly pursuing 'great power diplomacy'. In November 2014, Xi convened a rare Central Foreign Affairs Work Conference, which made it clear that China is going global. The main theme of the conference was an appeal to build 'great power diplomacy with Chinese characteristics'. It laid down the goal of building a 'global network of partnerships', leveraging China's enhanced global role and utilising the 'strategic opportunity' available today.

As China's leading international relations (IR) scholar Yan Xuetong put it in 2013, 'In the past we had to keep a low profile because we were weak while other states were strong ... Now, with "Striving for Achievement", we are indicating to neighbouring countries that we are strong and you are weak. This is a change at a very fundamental level.'[56]

In his work report to the 19th Party Congress (October 2017), Xi Jinping remarked, 'Both China and the world are in the midst of profound and complex changes. China is still in an important period of strategic opportunity for development; the prospects are bright but the challenges are severe.' This theme has been further developed by Xi through the characterisation of the current period as one of 'unprecedented changes not seen in a century'. An implicit message is that China is the primary beneficiary of these changes, which will result in a restructured international order.

Xi Jinping's 19th Party Congress report put 'rejuvenation' at the centre of his 'China Dream' and his 'new era' for China. He referred to the tragedy of the Opium Wars and declared rejuvenation as 'the original aspiration and mission of the Chinese Communists' – one that only the CPC could achieve.[57]

At the 19th Party Congress, we witnessed a clear articulation by Xi Jinping of China's great power ambitions. Xi talked about China becoming 'a global leader of composite national strength and international influence' and moving 'closer to the centre stage' by mid-century. A Xinhua commentary put it more explicitly: 'By 2050 … China is set to regain its might and re-ascend to the top of the world'. Xi referred to China as a 'strong country' or 'great power' as many as 30 times in his report.

Earlier, on 17 February 2018, speaking at a top-level national security seminar in Beijing, Xi Jinping stated that China should take the lead in shaping the 'new world order' and safeguarding international security. This new approach was quickly dubbed in the official Chinese media as the 'Two Guides' (Liangge Yindao) policy. However, China is still reluctant to expand its international responsibility too rapidly. It selectively seeks leadership on global issues like climate change and globalisation. It also selectively engages in handling regional trouble spots – South Sudan, Ukraine, Iran–Saudi re-engagement and so on. It is not yet prepared to invest substantial resources towards playing a mediatory role.

In his work report at the 20th Party Congress (October 2022), Xi Jinping clearly defined China's overarching goal: 'After basically realizing modernization, we will continue to work hard and build China into a great modern socialist country that leads the world in terms of composite national strength and international influence by the middle of the century.'[58]

A key thrust area of Xi Jinping's foreign policy has been regional order-building through 'peripheral diplomacy'. In July 2013, President Xi held an unprecedented work forum on peripheral diplomacy, which signified a strategic focus on the neighbourhood. As a *People's Daily* online article noted shortly after Xi's landmark 2013 meeting, 'the conference raised peripheral diplomacy to the level of national rejuvenation in its importance'.[59] Here again, Xi is building on concepts that originated in the Hu Jintao period.

Second, China is now prepared to deploy its considerable political, economic, military and diplomatic influence in pursuit of its strategic objectives. Xi has asserted that under no circumstances will China sacrifice its core national interests, including contested territorial claims. Its core national interests are being projected in progressively expansive terms: first Taiwan and Tibet, then islands in the East China Sea and still ambiguous claims in the South China Sea. Its preferred strategy involves what is described in the Western strategic literature as 'grey-zone operations'. China is ready to use its economic power as an instrument of coercion, the way it did against South Korea after it deployed the Terminal High Altitude Area Defence (THAAD) missile defence system in 2016, or impose sanctions against Australia, which had the temerity to call for investigations into the origins of the COVID-19 pandemic in 2020.

Third, China seeks to expand its role in the Asia-Pacific at the expense of the US. It is working towards strategic decoupling between the US and countries of Southeast Asia, in particular. The current trend line in terms of the changing balance of forces is towards China.

It has been observed that Xi's proactive foreign policy in Asia offers a deal: China will deliver trade, investment and other economic goods, and progressively act as a net security provider to those partners who accommodate, or at least do not challenge, its core interests.

The rapid accumulation of power by China has led to balancing and hedging by the countries of the region but this has not deterred it. China has assessed that the long-term benefits of its assertive stance outweigh the attendant risks. For instance, it is prepared to pay the price of some diplomatic damage as it entrenches its physical and military presence in the South China Sea. It is counting on its economic pull, the US ambivalence and the reluctance of ASEAN to take sides between the US and China.

This growing discontent among Southeast Asians with the US was reflected, most notably, in the annual survey conducted in early 2024 by the ISEAS–Yusof Ishak Institute, a think tank based in Singapore. This survey, for the first time, reveals that 'China continues to be seen as the most influential economic (59.5 per cent) and political–strategic (43.9 per cent) power in the region, outpacing the United States by significant margins in both domains'. It also revealed, most notably, that 'China has edged past the United States to become the prevailing choice (50.5 per cent) if the region were forced to align itself in the ongoing US–China rivalry'.[60]

Fourth, as noted earlier, China is assiduously shaping the international environment in its periphery with initiatives like the BRI and the AIIB.

The BRI is the signature initiative of President Xi Jinping, which has been backed by huge resources. The BRI has several pragmatic considerations linked to China's connectivity agenda: the quest for new growth engines for its slowing economy, utilisation of its surplus capacity, development of new markets as it moves up the value chain, more gainful deployment of its foreign exchange reserves, internationalisation of the renminbi and the desire to develop and stabilise its western regions.

However, the BRI is also a geostrategic initiative by China aimed at shaping its periphery and carving out a continental-cum-maritime realm with China as the anchor and central player. It is a 'grand strategy' for promoting economic integration (first regionally, then globally) through physical connectivity and gradually extending China's economic and political influence. It helps China achieve its geopolitical objectives by binding other countries more closely to its own growth story.

There are growing concerns about the BRI's modalities, lack of transparency and China-centric orientation; the loans given for BRI projects have progressively come down since 2018. A Centre for Strategic and International Studies (CSIS) report brings out that most of the BRI projects are cornered by Chinese companies through opaque processes.[61] The absence of due diligence and proper viability studies results in recipient countries taking on projects that are not sustainable and well beyond their repayment capabilities. Sri Lanka, where the government has been forced to hand over the Hambantota Port to Chinese entities on a 99-year lease under a debt–equity swap, is a cautionary tale. A 2021 study by the Center for Global Development, a US think tank, analysed sixty-eight countries hosting BRI projects and found twenty-three at risk of debt distress, including eight at high risk: Pakistan, Djibouti, the Maldives, Laos, Mongolia, Montenegro, Tajikistan and Kyrgyzstan.[62]

BRI investments peaked between 2016 and 2018, then sharply retracted in 2020 due to the economic impact of the COVID-19 pandemic. Overall investment remains well below the 2016–18 peak. In 2023, the relative composition of the BRI investment across financial investment and construction continued the trends that started in 2022 with financial investment at 52 per cent of overall BRI investments and the remaining 48 per cent dedicated to construction.[63]

At the same time, the BRI holds considerable attraction and over 130 countries have jumped on its bandwagon, as per the official BRI website (https://eng.yidaiyilu.gov.cn/).

Fifth, with the rapid accumulation of its power, China is no longer keen on multipolarity even though it continues to pay lip service to it. Instead, it talks of a 'new model of major power relations'.

In his work report to the 19th Party Congress, Xi Jinping remarked, 'Both China and the world are in the midst of profound and complex changes. China is still in an important period of strategic opportunity for development; the prospects are bright but the challenges are severe.'

Given the self-doubt in the West and its perceived decline, Trump's 'America First' policy and his ambivalence over the US's global leadership role and its alliances during his first term, the Biden administration's preoccupation with the conflicts in Ukraine and the Middle East and the expectation that the second Trump administration will be transactional in its approach, China continues to discern a strategic opening to further expand its regional and global profile, particularly in the Global South.

At the same time, the geopolitical contestation with the US-led West has intensified. China is today a country in a hurry as it is keen to lock in its advantage during the current window of strategic opportunity. This window may not be available for long given the slowdown of the Chinese economy, internal fault lines in the country, its ageing population and growing pushback against its assertive behaviour.

China is taking ambitious steps to accrue national power by increasing its investments in assets that established American authority in the previous century: overseas interests, overseas bases, foreign assistance, maritime power, global rule-setting and new technologies.

B. Navigating the Past: Chinese Narratives

It is important to understand the narratives developed by the party-state in China about the inevitable rise of China, which serves both domestic legitimacy and international positioning, portraying China's rise as a natural, inevitable 'restoration' of its historical prominence while adapting its Marxist foundations to incorporate Confucian traditions.

The CPC asserts that China's current trajectory of rapid development is a return to its rightful place at the centre of the world stage, a position it claims to have held for much of recorded history. The party emphasises the grandeur of imperial China, particularly during dynasties like the Han, Tang, and Ming, when China was a dominant economic and cultural force. It portrays the period from the Opium Wars (mid-19th century) to the mid-20th century – often dubbed the 'century of humiliation' – as an aberration, a temporary disruption caused by foreign aggression and internal weakness. Xi Jinping frequently invokes this framing, suggesting that China's rise today is a correction of that historical anomaly.

While emphasising China's presumed historical role as the world's largest economy for centuries, the Chinese completely ignore the fact that during extended periods in history, India was the largest economy. In his seminal work, *The World Economy: A Millennial Perspective*, Angus Maddison argues that India and China were the largest economies from the early centuries CE up until the 18th century; India was mostly the largest economy from 1 CE until 1000 CE and again from 1500 CE until 1700 CE, when the Chinese economy surpassed India's.[64]

The narrative positions China as the cradle of an enduring, sophisticated civilisation, contrasting it with the relatively 'young' West. This is tied to the concept of 'tianxia' (all under heaven), a traditional Confucian worldview in which China sits at the centre of a hierarchical, harmonious global order. The CPC adapts this to suggest that China's rise restores a more stable, moral and multipolar world, as opposed to Western hegemony. Xi has spoken of China as the only great uninterrupted civilisation, again ignoring India being a similarly placed civilisation.

Under Xi Jinping, the 'China Dream' and the 'great rejuvenation of the Chinese nation' posit China's resurgence as a historical inevitability, aligning with the Marxist idea of historical materialism but infused with nationalist fervour. The CPC argues that China's unique system – 'socialism with Chinese characteristics' – is the vehicle for this restoration, proving its superiority over Western liberal democracy. The party has had a complex relationship with past traditions but now it is blending Marxist socialism with Confucian heritage. This selective appropriation of Confucianism requires an ideological tightrope walk.

By leveraging China's rich cultural heritage and philosophical traditions, Xi Jinping aims to reinforce the legitimacy of CPC rule, presenting it as an essential part of China's historical continuity and future progress. Indeed, Xi calls Confucianism 'the cultural soil that nourishes the Chinese people'. This is in strong contrast to how Mao assessed Confucius. In Qufu, Confucius's tomb was blown up. *When Marx Met Confucius* is a recent party-state-sponsored cultural product. In the story, Marx meets Confucius, and they end up agreeing that communism is compatible with Confucianism. In a *Foreign Affairs* essay on the 'Real Roots of Xi Jinping Thought: Chinese Political Philosophers' Long Struggle with Modernity', Rana Mitter observes that 'Xi's effort to synthesize Confucius and Marx is not invalid, as an exercise'.[65]

Whether or not valid, this Xi-led enterprise to redefine China's ideological underpinnings feels increasingly urgent as an economic slowdown and deficit in the well-being quotient have fostered public distrust at home and underlined the need for a revised social contract between the party-state and various stakeholders in China.

There are four other aspects of this narrative that are problematic and can be challenged. One, there is nothing inevitable about the 're emergence' of China (and India, for that matter) as a pre-eminent power, even though the rise of China has been a reality rooted in the country's remarkable economic achievements over the past four decades.

Two, the construct of the centrality of China and the Sinosphere is deployed to legitimise the contemporary Chinese project of seeking the country's primacy in the region, disregarding the historical fact that most of the Indo-Pacific, including India, was never a part of this presumed China-centric universe.

Three, China claims its 'historical rights' as the basis for its contested territorial claims in the South China Sea, along the India–China borders and elsewhere. Such claims are often based on a contrived history. For instance, the categorical award of the International Court of Arbitration in The Hague on 12 July 2016, which ruled unanimously in favour of the Philippines on the issue of the South China Sea, concluded that there was no legal basis for China to claim so-called 'historical rights' to resources within the sea areas encompassed by the 'nine-dash line' and that there was no evidence that China had exercised exclusive control over the waters or their resources. Nevertheless, China has gone ahead and augmented its ability to control disputed features and nearby maritime space as well as its force projection capability in the South China Sea.

There are also implications for India with China claiming sovereignty over part or all of its territory 'from time immemorial', as we can see in tensions along the borders.

Finally, Xi Jinping's BRI has effectively co-opted the notion of the 'Silk Road'. The idea of a Silk Road was completely unknown in ancient or medieval times: not a single ancient record, either Chinese or Western, refers to its existence. Instead, it was invented as late as 1877 by a Prussian geographer, Baron von Richthofen. China was far from being the central node of ancient trade routes, in which India figured more prominently. As William Dalrymple has argued in his recent book, *The Golden Road: How Ancient India Transformed the World*, silk was never the main commodity imported to the West from the East; it was always far exceeded in value by imports of Indian pepper, spices, ivory, cotton, gems, teak and sandalwood. The Sinocentric reframing and rebranding of history portraying the trading world of the Silk Road as a network of peaceful global exchange centred on China is deployed to serve a contemporary objective.

C. Challenges to the Realisation of China's Grand Strategy

China faces a challenging road towards the realisation of its dream of 'great rejuvenation' by the middle of the century.

The first point to note is that China today is at multiple inflection points in its economy, diplomacy and polity with uncertain outcomes. China is adjusting to a 'new normal' not only in its economy but also in its polity and diplomacy. The new normal in politics and diplomacy involves the emergence of the 'core' leader Xi Jinping who is systematically pursuing the 'Chinese Dream'. At the same time, the Chinese economy is slowing down with a host of structural challenges, even while the country deals with an ageing population, internal security risks and other domestic issues. If the Chinese economy stagnates, many of its ambitious plans will be difficult to realise. We have the cautionary tale of Japan, which was going to sweep everything before it but has been stuck in fitful stagnation for over three decades.

Second, there is the aspect of pushback by the US and its allies and friends. The US is unlikely to yield its pre-eminent position easily. The country is still ahead in economic, military and technological strength. While Europe is declining, the same is not true of the US, which has a tremendous capacity for self-renewal. The geopolitical contestation between the US and China came out in the open during the first Trump administration, which questioned the policy of engagement with China and unleashed a tariff war against China in 2018. There was a sharp decline in US–China relations after the outbreak of the COVID-19 pandemic, which Trump publicly called the 'China virus'.

Contrary to Chinese expectations, the Biden administration continued the enhanced tariffs on imports from China imposed by Trump. Biden pivoted to an industrial policy with the Creating Helpful Incentives to Produce Semiconductors (CHIPS) and Science Act and the Inflation Reduction Act, which had a clear focus on rebuilding capabilities to counter China. Additionally, the Biden administration introduced export controls in high-tech areas like advanced semiconductors under NSA Jake Sullivan's 'small yard, high fence' approach, working closely with allies like Japan and the Netherlands. Sullivan articulated this approach in an important speech at the Brookings Institution in April 2023, which described the Biden administration's policy of allowing most trade and economic relations with China to continue while heavily restricting a core area of products, technologies and business activities that are deemed critical to national security.[66]

China and the US are both pursuing a de-risking strategy, reducing their dependencies on each other. However, given the extensive interlinkages between the two economies, any decoupling is not viable.

China's 'strategic enabling' of the Russian invasion of Ukraine, as the US and its NATO allies perceived it, has further complicated its relations with Western countries. However, while the European countries are upset with the 'partnership without limits' between China and Russia, they were not keen to follow the US lead in pursuing a de-risking strategy towards China. Now, of course, the discourse has been altered with the return of Donald Trump to the White House.

In the first 60 days of his second term, Trump initially adopted a relatively measured approach compared to the aggressive rhetoric of his 2024 campaign. Trump invited Xi Jinping to his inaugural function, which was attended by Vice President Han Zheng on Xi's behalf. Trump has spoken positively about his personal relationship with Xi Jinping, while also highlighting his intent to secure favourable deals for the US. On 23 January 2025, after speaking with

Xi, Trump told CNBC, 'I've always had a great relationship with President Xi Jinping', and expressed optimism about 'getting along with China'. Trump portrays his relationship with Xi as a unique asset, rooted in mutual respect and past camaraderie, which he believes can facilitate deals benefiting the US.

Notably, Trump refrained from immediately imposing the 60 per cent tariffs on Chinese imports he had promised, instead starting with a more modest 10 per cent tariff on Chinese goods, alongside a delay in enforcing a TikTok ban for 75 days. At the same time, the Trump administration continues to characterise China as a strategic adversary and has initiated several economic measures directed against China, including the following:

> On 1 February 2025, Trump issued an executive order imposing a 10 per cent tariff on all imports from China, effective 4 February 2025. This was followed by an additional 10 per cent tariff on Chinese imports starting 4 March 2025. On 10 February 2025, Trump signed proclamations setting a 25 per cent tariff on all steel imports and raising aluminium tariffs from 10 per cent to 25 per cent, effective 12 March 2025. These apply globally but significantly impact China, a major producer, despite its relatively small direct exports to the US. The measures close loopholes exploited by China via third countries like Mexico, aiming to curb its influence on global metal markets. More reciprocal tariffs are expected to be announced on 2 April 2025.

On 20 January, the US Department of the Treasury introduced regulations restricting US investments in China's critical sectors, including semiconductors, quantum information technologies and AI, to prevent China from leveraging US capital for technological advancement. A 25 February 2025 executive memorandum further directed limits on US investments to China in these industries. The 20 January 2025 'America First Trade Policy' memorandum instructed agencies to assess inbound Chinese investments, signalling tighter controls.

Reports indicate the Trump administration intends to maintain and likely expand the Biden administration's restrictions on exporting advanced semiconductors and related high-tech items to China. The 20 January 2025 executive order on trade builds on Biden's export controls, ordering a review of technology export policies with a 1 April 2025 deadline.

Indeed, the 'America First Trade Policy' memorandum of 20 January 2025 launched several China-focused investigations, with reports due by 1 April 2025.

Overall, the Trump administration's approach blends economic nationalism with strategic containment. A 'grand deal' could soften this trajectory, but it is difficult to make any firm prediction at present. The second Trump administration's China policy is still evolving, though the relationship remains underpinned by deep structural tensions. Trump's appointments of China hawks like Senator Marco Rubio as secretary of state and Representative Michael Waltz as NSA signal a hardline stance, reinforcing the perception in Beijing that the US views China as its primary adversary.

Initially, China responded with relatively conciliatory rhetoric and modest retaliatory tariffs on US goods, such as a 10 per cent tariff on crude oil and agricultural machinery, and export controls on rare earth metals. However, in response to the new round of US tariffs introduced on 4 March, China retaliated with tariffs of up to 15 per cent on US agricultural goods and banned shipments to some US defence companies. The spokesperson of the Chinese Ministry of Foreign Affairs deployed much harsher language on 4 March: 'If war is what the U.S. wants, be it a tariff war, a trade war or any other type of war, we're ready to fight till the end.'[67]

China sees Trump's tariff threats as well as restrictions on investment and technology flows as a direct challenge to its export-driven economy, already under pressure. The prospect of even a limited economic decoupling, with the US pushing to reduce reliance on Chinese supply chains, further complicates China's recovery strategy. The Biden-era restrictions on semiconductors and advanced technologies have been retained and are likely to expand under Trump. China perceives this as an attempt to stifle its technological rise, particularly in areas like AI, biotech and renewable energy, which are critical to its long-term ambitions.

While Chinese scholars recognise that there is a bipartisan consensus in the US on countering the strategic challenge posed by China, they also regard Trump's transactional nature as a potential opening. Unlike Biden's multilateral containment strategy, Trump's focus on bilateral deals could allow China to negotiate trade-offs.

China anticipates that Trump's 'America First' policies may strain US alliances, providing Beijing with leverage to deepen ties with Europe, Japan, India and those in the Global South. By routing exports through third countries and enhancing economic partnerships, China aims to mitigate the impact of US tariffs and reduce reliance on the American market, a strategy already in motion since Trump's first term.

China is better prepared to deal with any 'Trump shock' and at the same time, more vulnerable as its economy is in a difficult spot. Seven years of navigating tariffs, tech restrictions and trade tensions have given Xi Jinping and his advisers a deeper understanding of the US President's playbook. China has developed its own toolkit of retaliatory measures, including the weaponisation of control over critical materials, its sanctions and counter-sanctions regimes, and greater co-option of its private sector companies to subserve the interests of the party-state, apart from retaliatory tariffs, where China has less headroom given its huge trade surplus with the US.

However, the most important preparatory steps have involved developing its domestic technological capabilities over the past decade (discussed later) and reducing dependence on the US market since the first round of tariffs imposed by the first Trump administration on imports from China. Since the 2017–18 Trump tariffs, China has reduced its dependence on the US market by 6–7 percentage points (19 per cent to 12–13 per cent), redirecting exports to the EU (+1–2 points), ASEAN (+3–4 points) and the Global South (+7–8 points). This diversification, accelerated by tariffs and geopolitical tensions, showcases China's adaptability, though it remains vulnerable to retaliatory measures and supply chain scrutiny.

The Chinese preference seems to be to seek a 'deal' and avoid escalation without showing weakness. This stance is broadly reflected in the vigorous debate taking place within the Chinese strategic community, which suggests both nervousness about the US tariffs and Trump's unpredictability, accompanied by a tentative hope that he would undermine the US alliance system and show isolationist tendencies and retrenchment from regional and global commitments (and thus create strategic space for China), or might be prepared to deal with China, given his transactional approach and self-image as the master of the 'art of the deal'.

Most discussions of a 'grand deal' between the US and China focus on economic issues of trade imbalances, tariffs and investment – for example, perhaps China fulfilling the Phase One trade deal's US$200 billion purchase commitment or offering (albeit reluctantly) financial concessions like a stronger renminbi. While the Trump administration has taken steps to tighten inward and outward investment flows linked to China, many Chinese companies like CATL have shown interest in investing in the US.

This economic focus makes geopolitical concessions like Taiwan or spheres of influence much less likely, since the strategic contestation between the US and China is unlikely to abate. There is a basic contradiction in the worldviews and strategic aspirations of the US and China. Shorn of the rhetoric on both sides, the bottom line is that the US is determined to maintain its primacy while China seeks pre-eminence in the Asia-Pacific region first and eventually globally. In strategic terms, it will be difficult to reconcile Trump's 'Make America Great Again' and Xi's 'China Dream'.

Under the first Trump administration, the US shifted its strategic stance towards China from a decades-long policy of 'engagement' to one of 'strategic competition'. This transformation marked a significant departure from the post-Cold War approach, which had emphasised economic integration and cooperation with China to encourage its liberalisation and integration into the global order. The Trump administration reframed China as a primary geopolitical and economic rival, a stance crystallised in the National Security Strategy (NSS) released on 18 December 2017.[68]

The US NSS of October 2022 under the Biden administration was categorical in its assessment that the PRC is the only competitor with both the intent to reshape the international order and increasingly the economic, diplomatic, military and technological power to do so and that China has ambitions to create an enhanced sphere of influence in the Indo-Pacific and to become the world's leading power.[69]

This author's Chinese interlocutors are acutely aware of the fact that there is bipartisan consensus in the US that China is the rival determined to displace it from its global perch and that the confrontation between the US (the established hegemon) and China (the aspirant hegemon) will be the determining feature of the strategic landscape of the Indo-Pacific in the foreseeable future. They are convinced that the US is seeking to not only maintain its competitive edge over China in military, economic and technological domains but also to work proactively to slow down the growth of Chinese capacities in these areas. Their assessment is not without basis.

However, in this geopolitical contest, Russia has moved closer to China, which has also gained ground in the Global South. China is possibly watching recent developments in US–Russia relations with a degree of anxiety. If Trump manages to normalise relations with Russia after an extended period of the US-led West treating Moscow as a perennial adversary, that will amount to a huge geopolitical shift. It will open up more strategic and economic space for Russia and reduce its dependence on China in a relationship which has become progressively unequal in favour of China since the Russian annexation of Crimea in 2014 and subsequent Western sanctions, which were scaled up after the Russian invasion of Ukraine in February 2022.

However, as noted earlier, a 'reverse Nixon' gambit involving the US weaning Russia away from China is unlikely. From Moscow's perspective, there is no certainty that the current trajectory of American policies will be sustained. Just like American allies and partners have worried about US unpredictability, so will Russia. Both China and Russia will look beyond the Trump administration.

However, both Xi and Putin felt it necessary to reassure each other in a lengthy virtual meeting on 24 February 2025. According to the *People's Daily*, Xi conveyed to Putin, 'Our bilateral relationship has a strong internal driving force and unique strategic value. It is neither targeted at any third party nor affected by any third party… No matter how the international landscape changes, our relationship shall move forward at its own pace.'[70]

According to the Chinese readout, Putin assured Xi, 'Developing relations with China is a strategic choice made by Russia with a view to the long term; it is not an act of expediency, not affected by any temporary incidents, and not subject to interference by external factors.'

Yet even a limited rapprochement between the US and Russia will give the latter more options and influence the nature of Sino-Russian relations. It will also create more strategic space for India.

However, it is not yet clear how US–China relations will evolve under the second Trump administration. Freed of the burden of dual containment targeting China and Russia, will the US deal with the China challenge in a more forthright manner with greater focus on the Indo-Pacific? We will have to monitor the evolving developments closely and not rush to premature conclusions.

The Biden administration spent four years building a united front with Europe to counter China. That united front is becoming collateral damage as the new Trump administration dramatically upends Joe Biden's approach, befriending Russia and alienating Europe. China is stepping up its efforts to probe opportunities to build its own united front with Europe and drive a wedge between it and the US.[71]

Europe's relations with China are poised to evolve in a delicately balanced manner, shaped by the pressures of a strained transatlantic alliance with the US and the perceived existential threat posed by Russia, the pull of China as an economic behemoth and growing concerns about its mercantilist policies and the risk of 'China shock 2.0' faced by hi-tech manufacturing in Europe.

Sino-European relations were already under pressure in the post-COVID period, and more so after the Russian invasion of Ukraine, for which China was seen as a strategic enabler. There are also growing apprehensions about China's dominance of green energy manufacturing (electric vehicles, lithium-ion batteries and solar power equipment) as well as other 'future' industries, leading to retarded industrialisation in Europe, if not hollowing out of manufacturing on the continent. These concerns have led to the European Union imposing countervailing tariffs, ranging from 7.8 per cent to 35.3 per cent, on imports of electric vehicles from China on 30 October 2024. Earlier, in May 2021, the European Parliament had effectively shelved the ratification of the Comprehensive Agreement on Investment negotiated with China over human rights concerns and the exchange of sanctions. On the other hand, the EU countries are loath to weaken their trade and investment links with China (bilateral trade in goods of €585 billion in 2024 and China's significant role in two-way investment flows and in supplying materials for Europe's green transition).

Against this complex, changing and unpredictable backdrop, Europe may tilt towards cautious accommodation with China. China, meanwhile, will keep probing transatlantic weak spots. Economic necessity and the lack of immediate alternatives encourage Germany and France, economic heavyweights, to prioritise trade stability; Germany's reliance on Chinese markets for its auto industry is a case in point. At the same time, the EU's de-risking rhetoric, backed by actions like screening Chinese investments, trade measures on EV imports from China and boosting domestic technology, suggests a middle path: engagement with guardrails.

China is rapidly expanding its strategic and business presence in the developing countries of the Global South. According to a report in the *Economist* (1 August 2024), for instance, greenfield direct investments by Chinese firms tripled in 2023, to US$160 billion, expanding their globalised supply chains. Much of that was in setting up manufacturing facilities in countries from Malaysia to Morocco, partly to circumvent barriers being raised by developed countries on direct Chinese exports and partly to take advantage of free trade agreements that those countries have. Since 2016, listed Chinese firms have quadrupled their sales in the Global South to US$800 billion and now sell more there than in rich countries.[72] A Rhodium Group report (16 September 2024)[73] confirms that, after years of slow growth, China's outward FDI has picked up post-pandemic and is shifting away from advanced economies towards Asia and emerging economies, focusing on diversification of markets, circumventing trade restrictions in the US and boosting China's position in global supply chains. This trend of enhanced Chinese presence and engagement with the Global South is likely to be reinforced not only in the economic and commercial fields but also in political, diplomatic, military and people-to-people linkages, more so if the US under the Trump administration abdicates space for China.

We have discussed earlier how China is showing greater tactical flexibility in its relations with Japan, Australia and even India and had made some headway, without changing its stance on outstanding issues or lowering its strategic ambitions.

At the same time, China is rising in a crowded geopolitical field, with the rise of India and others. There is a lot of hedging and balancing going on. China is nowhere close to matching the US advantage in having a vast and effective network of alliances, though this strength is being questioned by the new administration in Washington DC. China is also a 'partial power' as Sinologist David Shambaugh puts it, given its deficiencies in great power attributes like soft power. One can argue that it has suffered from premature hubris and excessive aggression, leading to the undermining of some of its key relationships, including with India.

Additionally, there is a set of domestic challenges to the realisation of China's grand strategy, which are discussed in a later section on the party-state and its anxieties.

D. China's Unfinished Territorial Project and Grey-Zone Warfare

However, before we turn to the domestic preoccupations and challenges of China, let us explore a key aspect of China's external behaviour, that is, its 'grey-zone operations'.

Xi Jinping has consistently emphasised China's unwavering stance on not compromising on its territorial integrity and sovereignty. Thus, in a speech before the National People's Congress on 20 March 2018, Xi declared, 'Every inch of our great motherland absolutely cannot and absolutely will not be separated from China. All acts and tricks to split the motherland are doomed to failure and will be condemned by the people and punished by history!'[74] The problem is that China's unfinished territorial project includes unilaterally defined claims based on contrived history in the South China Sea, East China Sea, the India–China borders, Bhutan and of course the 'reunification' of Taiwan. With the rising tide of nationalism in China, the room for finding a negotiated settlement based on give-and-take, as was the case in earlier land boundary agreements, has shrunk.

China's preferred playbook for achieving its objectives in these theatres is what is called 'grey-zone operations', which fall below the threshold of an outright armed conflict. Such 'warfare' involves China deploying a variety of tactics to advance its interests, including incremental gains in territory ('salami slicing'), creation of a 'new normal', which becomes the basis for further creeping encroachments, military and economic coercion, cyber operations, 'law enforcement' through the China Coast Guard (CCG) and maritime militia activities and influence operations.[75] These operations are designed to achieve strategic objectives without triggering a full-scale military response. China has avoided a full-fledged conflict or intervention by the US yet advanced its territorial claims in various theatres, including the South China Sea, East China Sea, Taiwan, the India–China borders and Bhutan.

In the South China Sea, China has been forcefully pursuing its territorial claims despite the award of the International Arbitral Tribunal at The Hague which ruled unanimously in favour of the Philippines in July 2016 and 'concluded that there was no legal basis for China to claim historic rights to resources within the sea areas falling within the "nine-dash line"'. The Tribunal also 'found that China had violated the Philippines' sovereign rights in its exclusive economic zone by (a) interfering with Philippine fishing and petroleum exploration, (b) constructing artificial islands and (c) failing to prevent Chinese fishermen from fishing in the zone'. The Tribunal also held that fishermen from the Philippines (like those from China) had traditional fishing rights at Scarborough Shoal and that China had interfered with these rights by restricting access.[76]

It is remarkable how successfully China has overcome this major legal setback and progressively changed the facts on the ground in its favour and to the disadvantage of other claimant nations of ASEAN. Over the last decade, China has undertaken reclamation around disputed land features in the South China Sea on an unprecedented scale (3,200 acres across seven features it occupies in the Spratlys) and built civil and military facilities, including four 3,000-metre-long airfields, which can support the largest military aircraft in the Chinese inventory. This has augmented China's ability to control disputed features and nearby maritime space as well as its force projection capability in the South China Sea and beyond in the IOR.

In the Senkaku Islands (called Diaoyu Islands by China), Japan has firm control and does not recognise the existence of any international dispute over the territorial sovereignty of those islands. Yet, China has made incremental gains through 'lawfare', aggressive actions by the CCG and orchestrated public campaigns against Japan. Thus, in 2014, China persuaded Japan to agree to a 'four-point consensus', which, inter alia, included both countries recognising that they had different views regarding the tensions in the East China Sea. Since then, China has stepped up coercive activities by CCG vessels around Senkaku/Diaoyu. In 2023, a total of 1,287 Chinese government vessels were spotted in the contiguous zone around the Senkaku Islands on 352 out of 365 days, setting a record for the highest number of days since record-keeping began in 2008.[77]

Likewise, in the Taiwan Straits, China has deployed an array of tools for economic, military and diplomatic coercion of the Democratic People's Party (DPP) government and utilises contingency situations to normalise an escalating ladder of coercive measures, as it did after the US Speaker Nancy Pelosi's visit to Taiwan in August 2022 and, more recently, after inaugural remarks by President Lai Ching-te on 20 May 2024. These involve routine incursions by PLA aircraft across the median line in the Taiwan Straits (which China had respected earlier), large-scale simulation of quarantine measures and 'law enforcement' by the Coast Guard vessels in 'prohibited waters' around Taiwan's Jinmen and Mazu islands, which the Chinese government vessels were not entering earlier.

We have discussed China's creeping encroachments across the India–China LAC in violation of agreements to respect the LAC. Likewise, in Bhutan, China has been systematically encroaching on Bhutanese territory notwithstanding an agreement it had signed with Bhutan in 1998 in which both parties proclaimed 'mutual respect for each other's sovereignty and territorial integrity' and agreed 'not to resort to unilateral action to alter the status quo of the border'. A report released in October 2024 suggests that China has built as many as 22 villages and settlements within Bhutan's customary borders.[78]

These tactics have allowed China to advance its strategic interests while avoiding direct military confrontation. They have been carefully kept under a threshold which could trigger a military response by the US and others; yet this bar has been raised continuously, creating a 'new normal' that others are expected to get used to.

V.
The Party-State and Its Anxieties

Xi Jinping is a leader in his own mould. China under Xi Jinping has progressively moved away from Deng Xiaoping's legacy in key areas: domestically, economically and in its external behaviour. Yet, we have discussed earlier that the changes in the foreign policy domain, though striking, are broadly in sync with the trendline of the pre-Xi period. One can argue that the course change is more pronounced in domestic and economic policies.

Personalised Polity: Politically, China has shifted towards a personalised polity dominated by a supreme leader and has abandoned collective leadership and periodic, institutionalised succession. It has reverted to the era of the 'Great Helmsman', harking back to the Mao period, with Xi variously hailed within the CPC as 'lingxiu' (the supreme leader), 'tongshuai' (commander-in-chief) and 'linghang zhangduo' (the pilot at the helm), with 'Xi Jinping Thought' enshrined in the party charter and the state constitution, Xi's opponents weeded out, term limits removed and a personality cult put in place. With the removal of the two-term limit for the presidency in the state constitution in March 2018, Xi Jinping can hold all three key positions – general secretary of the party, chairman of the Central Military Commission and state president – indefinitely.

This shift has its attendant risks. Deng Xiaoping had institutionalised collective leadership in China to correct the problems of the 'excessive concentration of power' witnessed under Mao. The erosion of checks and balances that the supreme leader syndrome entails has serious risks not only for China but also for the rest of the world as China is now a major actor regionally and globally.

The risks were on full display during the COVID-19 pandemic. After the initial suppression of information about the deadly virus, which allowed it to spread, the party-state intervened forcefully with its Zero-COVID policy, which seemed to bring the pandemic under control while the rest of the world, including the advanced countries, struggled with escalating fatalities. This was claimed as evidence of the Chinese model over Western capitalism. However, the Zero-COVID policy, driven personally by Xi, was allowed to continue for too long, leading to protests in Shanghai and elsewhere and a huge impact on the economy and society. It was lifted in a precipitous manner in early December 2022 without adequate preparation, leading to a large number of deaths that were not reported. A Centers for Disease Control and Prevention report estimated that SARS-CoV-2 infections caused 1.41 million deaths in China during December 2022–February 2023, substantially higher than those reported through official channels.[79] Was the mismanagement of the pandemic a glaring example of a broken feedback mechanism under the scenario of an over-concentration of authority in one person?

But there is also a bargain on offer: the supreme leader will deliver on the Chinese Dream of the great rejuvenation of the Chinese nation. What is his economic roadmap for delivering on this social contract?

Statist Tilt in Economy: Xi has shown a distinct preference for interventions and control of the party-state in the economy and has moved away from the larger autonomy given to the private sector under the policies of Deng Xiaoping and his cohort. China's crackdown on the private sector has been a significant development in recent years, impacting various industries and high-profile figures, including Jack Ma. In 2020, Chinese regulators halted the initial public offering of Ant Group, a financial technology company founded by Jack Ma shortly after he delivered a speech criticising Chinese financial regulators.[80] The Chinese government has implemented stringent regulations across multiple sectors, including technology, education and real estate. This has led to a significant drop in the market value of many private companies.

The third Plenum of the eleventh Central Committee of the CPC (July 2024) made it clear that China would continue to employ industrial policies to further enhance its manufacturing capacities and trade dominance, in particular in strategic industries. This is even though, as Vice Premier Liu He noted in September 2021, the private sector contributes more than 50 per cent of the tax revenue, more than 60 per cent of GDP and over 70 per cent of technological innovations; it also provides more than 80 per cent of urban employment and accounts for more than 90 per cent of market entities in China.[81]

In Xi Jinping's vision, innovation and high-tech manufacturing have emerged as key drivers for the future growth of China and considerable headway has been made towards that objective, as we will discuss later. The Chinese leadership is also hoping that innovation will be the key to boosting total factor productivity (TFP). The adoption of AI and robotics,[82] investments in R&D, technical standardisation, the digital economy and advanced manufacturing protocols have given China an advantage in the high-tech manufacturing and services sector.[83]

Outreach to the Private Sector: As several reports by the Mercator Institute for China Studies (MERICS) have highlighted, the CPC under Xi Jinping has fundamentally reshaped China's political economy to align with national strategic priorities.[84] Xi does not want to suppress the private sector, which is the primary driver of growth. The objective instead is to tame and co-opt private capital in subserving the strategic interests laid down by the CPC.[85] The party-state's controls and guidance over economic actors have been expanded drastically. Xi Jinping's policies focus less on the profitability of companies; instead, economic resources should be geared towards strategic sectors in the real economy – mainly high-tech manufacturing and emerging technologies such as AI and green energy, rather than sectors such as real estate or the consumer internet, which were seen as non-strategic and/or destabilising.

However, as the economic slowdown persists, there has been some course correction, as signified in a high-profile symposium with top business leaders attended by Xi himself on 17 February 2025. The party is keen to revive the spirits of entrepreneurs and remove some bureaucratic obstacles to their progress, more so after it has already established firm control over the private sector. China has tightened rules for overseas listings, bolstered the influence of party committees within private companies and imposed new laws on data collection and transfer. The US hostility to Chinese companies has driven them closer to their home market and government. As America denies China access to vital inputs such as high-end computer chips, private firms are joining the party's mission to achieve self-reliance. Xi's vision for the private sector is about promoting 'Chinese-style modernisation', with private capital aligning with the party's goals.

Economic Slowdown: The overall picture, however, is that China's economic growth has slowed down significantly compared to its rapid expansion in previous decades. Factors such as high debt levels, the real estate crisis, a preference for the less productive state sector compared to the private sector, diminishing returns on investment, relative stagnation in TFP, sluggish domestic demand, an ageing population, a shrinking workforce and geopolitical tensions with the US and other advanced economies are cited as reasons behind the economic slowdown. The lower growth trajectory is structural rather than cyclical, and no ready answers are available for its reversal. While China's growth has moderated, its global economic influence endures, with overtaking the US remaining a distant and uncertain prospect.

The Chinese leadership is inclined to accept a lower growth rate but cannot afford to have a downward spiral in the economy, which is now close to deflation. Krishna Srinivasan, director of the International Monetary Fund's (IMF's) Asia-Pacific department, said in an interview with *Nikkei Asia* in early November 2024 that 'deflation risks are rising', calling that 'a worry' considering the country's recent low inflation rate and weak domestic demand. Core inflation, which excludes food and fuel prices, measured 0.1 per cent in September, down from 0.3 per cent in August; the 'GDP deflator has been negative for some time'.[86] Given such concerns, Srinivasan said consumer 'confidence has been coming down', followed by the stagnant property sector, which has continued to underperform in sales, new construction and investment. Indeed, the Producer Price Index has been falling for 29 consecutive months and the Consumer Price Index is barely in positive territory. The heightened risk of deflation has fuelled talk of the 'Japanification' of the Chinese economy, with the country falling into structural economic deceleration, which does not respond to stimulus measures.[87]

In a policy correction, the Chinese leadership has taken some significant steps since September 2024 to stimulate the economy, help local authorities with their unsustainable debt burden and revive the property sector, which contributed over 25 per cent to GDP but has been declining in recent years. It is far from clear that these measures will kickstart the economy. A large fiscal stimulus package is expected if Trump were to impose even higher tariffs on imports from China.[88]

Foreign companies face unprecedented challenges as China has prioritised national security over economic growth, tightened its grip on the business hub of Hong Kong and unleashed tight control over the private sector. As a result, a growing number of companies have reached 'a tipping point', where the challenges of doing business in China are starting to outweigh returns, said Jens Eskelund, head of the EU Chamber of Commerce, in China in September 2024.[89]

China's economy is navigating a complex transition, marked by slower growth, demographic challenges, a weak pivot towards consumption and strong emphasis on self-reliance. Weak domestic demand, overcapacity and trade tensions pose significant downside risks, but opportunities in the continued expansion of exports, green energy, technology and the growing global footprint of Chinese companies offer growth prospects. Chinese companies are building factories around the world and forging new global supply chains, driven by a desire to circumvent tariffs and secure access to markets. They are setting up manufacturing plants in large target markets, such as the EU and Brazil, as well as in 'connector countries' like Mexico and Vietnam that provide access to developed markets through trade agreements. At the same time, China has sought to ensure its own centrality in these new China-friendly global supply chains by limiting the export of key technology, including for batteries, EVs, rare earth processing and lithium extraction. This is a reversal of China's standard practice of leveraging access to its market to acquire technology from other countries. China's reluctance to share certain technologies can cause problems with partner countries and has already emerged as a concern with Chinese EV investments in the EU.[90] There are also growing concerns that despite the talk of the 'Dual Circulation' strategy, which aims to balance internal and external economic drivers, domestic consumer spending has refused to pick up, and there is excessive dependence on exports as a driver of growth.

A recent Bruegel study by Alicia García-Herrero and Xu Jianwei points out that Japan's experience does not answer definitively the question of whether a focus on technological progress alone can reverse the decline in growth, especially if increases in industrial capacity are not accompanied by greater domestic consumption. The external market ultimately served as only a temporary solution for Japan, because rising protectionist measures in the West limited its ability to export its way out of economic stagnation. China faces a similar challenge of an oversupply relative to demand.[91]

China as a Mercantilist Economic Power: Exports are one sector of the economy doing well. There are concerns that China is trying to export its way out of its current economic predicament, which is not a viable proposition for a US$18 trillion economy and will be highly disruptive for other economies. Post-COVID-19, China has again built up large overcapacities in several sectors, including green energy products and equipment. Given China's industrial policy, its determination to dominate future industries (including the 'Three New' of solar power equipment, lithium-ion batteries and electric vehicles), opaque subsidies, massive economies of scale and unrivalled supply chains, there are concerns among both developed and emerging economies about imports from China flooding their markets and leading to their own delayed industrialisation. The US has imposed additional tariffs on imports from China, including a 100 per cent duty on electric vehicles, even before the second Trump administration launched new tariffs and other measures targeting China (discussed earlier). The EU too introduced countervailing import duty on EVs from China, which has retaliated with countermeasures. Emerging economies like India have similar concerns. This is setting the stage for greater frictions in China's external economic engagement.

Legitimacy of the CPC: The social contract devised by Deng and his cohort involved delivering economic growth and higher standards of living for the people and in return the CPC retaining the monopoly on political power. That performance legitimacy is getting eroded with slower growth and growing social malaise (high youth unemployment, the 'lying flat' phenomenon with young people opting out of the rat race, the narrative of the 'garbage time of history' reflecting despondency and so on). Under these circumstances, there is greater invocation of ideology, nationalism and an imagined narrative of the past as sources of legitimacy for the dominance of political, economic and societal space by the CPC.

Politics in Command, Stability above All Else: Under Xi, we have politics in command; in his work report at the 20th Party Congress, he prioritised control of the party, ideology, national security, political stability and 'waging struggles' against both domestic and foreign rivals ahead of economic development or opening up the country. There were 91 references to 'security' as compared to 60 to 'economy'. For the CPC, regime perpetuation is the overriding priority and stability triumphs over other considerations. China comes across as a country with great ambitions but also imbued with an odd combination of triumphalism and profound anxieties.

'Top Design' vs 'Crossing the River Feeling Stones': The debate between 'top design' and 'crossing the river while feeling stones' reflects two distinct approaches to governance and economic reform in China, each associated with different eras of leadership and ideological priorities under Xi Jinping and Deng Xiaoping respectively.

Under the leadership of Deng Xiaoping and his cohort, China pursued a pragmatic, experimental strategy, which involved a cautious, step-by-step approach to reform, emphasising trial and error over rigid planning. After the chaos of the Mao era, Chinese leaders sought to modernise China's economy without a preconceived blueprint, prioritising practical results over ideological purity. This philosophy underpinned the economic reforms of the late 20th century, such as the introduction of the 'household responsibility system' or contract farming in the countryside in the late 1970s–early 1980s, the rapid growth of township and village enterprises (TVEs) in the 1980s and the establishment of Special Economic Zones (SEZs) like Shenzhen, where policies were tested locally before being scaled up nationally. It allowed China to transition from a centrally planned economy to a socialist market economy, fostering rapid growth while avoiding large-scale disruption. It gave space to local initiatives and improvisation. Deng famously remarked on the unexpected success of TVEs, saying something to the effect of: 'The rapid development of township and village enterprises was not something we foresaw. It wasn't a product of the central government's design – our rural policies opened the door, but the peasants themselves took the initiative.'[92]

In contrast, 'top design' has been a hallmark of Xi Jinping's governance since he assumed power in 2012. This approach emphasises centralised, strategic planning and a comprehensive, systemic vision crafted at the highest levels of the CPC. Xi has argued that China's challenges, ranging from economic inequality to environmental crises and technological competition, require coordinated, long-term policies rather than piecemeal experimentation. 'Top design' reflects Xi's push for stronger party control, as seen in projects like the BRI, the Made in China 2025 plan and sweeping anti-corruption campaigns. It's about setting a clear direction from above and ensuring all parts of the system align with that vision, with less tolerance for local deviation or improvisation.

Critics of Xi's method argue that it stifles creativity and local initiative, risking rigidity in a fast-changing world. Supporters say Deng's gradualism is outdated for a superpower that needs bold, unified action. However, Xi's preferred approach also results in situations like the pursuit of the 'Zero-COVID' policy for far too long and its abrupt jettisoning in December 2022, as we have discussed earlier.

China's Long COVID: While initially effective, the prolonged duration of Xi's 'Zero-COVID' policy inflicted economic damage – disrupting supply chains, stifling consumption and straining businesses – and provoked social unrest, evident in protests and declining trust. It left China with a bruised economy, a society subjected to vastly enhanced technology-driven surveillance, and a country that was more inward-looking. The China that exited 'zero COVID' was indeed different – economically scarred, socially transformed and systemically more controlled – than the one that entered it, underscoring the policy's lasting legacy. Although the 'Zero-COVID' measures are gone, the party-state has clung to a strategy of accelerating government intervention in Chinese life. In his article entitled 'Xi's Age of Stagnation: The Great Walling-off of China' published in *Foreign Affairs* (September–October 2023), Ian Johnson has argued that China's 'economic problems are part of a broader process of political ossification and ideological hardening'.[93] 'For anyone who has observed the country closely over the past few decades, it is difficult to miss the signs of a new national stasis, or what the Chinese call neijuan. Often translated as "involution", it refers to life twisting inward without real progress.' There is some merit in this argument.

Never-ending Anti-Corruption Campaign: Xi Jinping's anti-corruption campaign, launched in 2012 and continuing relentlessly since then, is another example of 'top design' that has caused considerable disruption. Beyond addressing corruption, the campaign is widely seen as a strategic tool for Xi to consolidate his political power, removing rivals and ensuring loyalty within the party and its affiliated institutions. As of 2023, the campaign had punished approximately 2.3 million party and government officials.

The Chinese military has been a favourite target of the campaign. According to a recent tabulation in the respected Chinese journal *Caixin*[94], more than 80 generals have been ensnared in China's anti-corruption campaign since it kicked off in the wake of the 18th National Party Congress held in October 2012. A total of 13 full generals, 18 lieutenant generals and more than 50 major generals have fallen from grace in graft probes in the past dozen years, a *Caixin* compilation has found. Notable officials include two vice chairmen of the Central Military Commission (Xu Caihou and Guo Boxiang), two defence ministers (Li Shangfu and his predecessor, Wei Fenghe), as well as virtually the entire leadership of the PLA Rocket Force. In recent years, many of the top officials targeted have been proteges of Xi, including Miao Hua, director of the Political Work Department of the CMC, who was suspended in November 2024. These purges have raised questions about the level of corruption in the Chinese military and its morale, operational readiness and the selection of top cadres, apart from the efficacy of the anti-corruption campaign itself.

Authoritarian but Not Totalitarian: Under Xi, China is firmly in a 'neo-authoritarian' period. It is a country rolling out a nationwide social credit system which, according to a State Council document, will 'allow the trustworthy to roam everywhere under heaven while making it hard for the discredited to take a single step'.[95] The 'surveillance state' was turbocharged during the Zero-COVID period with an infusion of technological solutions to the gigantic task of monitoring individuals and communities. In China, the internal security budget rivals, if not exceeds, the national defence spending.

However, China is far from being a totalitarian state. Personal choices available to an average Chinese citizen are much greater today, compared to the early 1980s when I had my first diplomatic assignment in Beijing. Though this space has shrunk to some extent under Xi and his technology-assisted surveillance state, the state interventions in personal affairs are not so intrusive and social media is still vibrant as long as the red lines are observed. The intrusions by the party-state increased during the Zero-COVID regime though some of it has been scaled back.

VI.

Random Thoughts on the Future of China

What is the future of China? Is it a juggernaut inexorably poised to emerge as the leading economy and military power of the world, as the Chinese narrative would suggest? Alternatively, will it meet the fate of Japan, which was once seen as displacing the US as the largest economy in the world but then became caught up in an endless loop of stagnation, albeit at a high level of per capita income and technological excellence?

A. Peak China?

There is an argument doing the rounds that China has 'peaked', that is, it has reached or is nearing the zenith of its economic, political and military power, and it may face a decline or stagnation in the near future.[96] Familiar arguments are advanced in favour of this proposition: economic slowdown, middle-income economy trap, debt burden, ageing population ('old before rich' syndrome), 'imperial' overreach, geopolitical tensions, domestic crises and so on. As Hal Brands and Michael Beckley have argued in *Foreign Affairs*, 'China is tracing an arc that often ends in tragedy: a dizzying rise followed by the spectre of a hard fall.'[97] In their view, it is now or never if China wants to redraw the world map.

All these arguments have some merit, but they ignore the fact that there is still considerable appetite and potential for growth left in the Chinese economy. Prognostications of an impending collapse of China have proved wrong time and again since the turn of the century.

While the slowdown of the Chinese economy is structural rather than cyclical, as we have discussed earlier, there are persuasive arguments for concluding that China has not yet peaked.

Innovation Power: China has emerged as a major innovation nation and continues to lead in various high-tech sectors, including green technology, high-speed rail and electric vehicles. The country also files more patents than any other nation. As the Chinese economy continues to decelerate, the central government is investing heavily in innovation, doubling down on R&D spending and STEM-oriented human capital.[98] There are bottlenecks, no doubt, including a flagging reform process; over-reliance on government funding and the state sector; the technology-denial regime of the US and its allies in key areas like advanced semiconductors, AI and quantum computing; fragmentation in global technology networks and retarded globalisation, which benefited China immensely; bias towards applied research as opposed to basic research, which is usually associated with breakthrough and general-purpose technologies and so on.

Under Xi Jinping, we have seen increasing emphasis on 'new quality productive forces' (新质生产力) since late 2023. *Xinhua News* explains this concept as 'advanced productivity that plays a leading role in innovation and breaks away from the traditional economic growth mode and productivity development path'. Increasingly, Xi is emphasising an innovation- and technology-led development model for China, as traditional drivers of growth like real estate continue to drag down the Chinese economy.

A recent Bloomberg Intelligence and Bloomberg Economics report[99] points out that China is forging ahead in many of the 13 key technologies Xi Jinping outlined in 2015 as part of Made in China 2025, a priority for his country's development. Though this flagship initiative is no longer highlighted in official Chinese pronouncements because of the backlash it generated in the West, the industrial policy blueprint intended to make the nation a leader in emerging tech has largely been successful. Electric vehicles, high-speed rail and solar panels are among the five areas in which China has achieved global leadership positions, while it is catching up fast in another seven sectors.

Likewise, an August 2024 update of the 'Critical Technology Tracker' of the Australian Strategic Policy Institute (ASPI)[100] reveals a stunning shift in research leadership towards China. The US led in sixty of sixty-four technologies in the five years from 2003 to 2007, but in the most recent five years (2019–23), has led in only seven. China led in just three of sixty-four technologies in 2003–07 but is now the lead country in fifty-seven of sixty-four technologies in 2019–23. However, this report perhaps exaggerates Chinese dominance as it doesn't take into account much of the cutting-edge research being undertaken outside the public gaze.

The US continues to have a significant edge in critical areas like AI, though the recent unveiling of 'DeepSeek' by a Chinese company showed that its lead over China may not be as pronounced as previously thought.

Economic Resilience: Despite challenges, China's economy remains robust in many areas, such as manufacturing and infrastructure development. The Chinese government has shown a capacity for economic adaptation and innovation. Under Xi Jinping, the spirit of 'crossing the river by feeling the stones' might have been replaced by 'top-down design' but the Chinese people still retain their resilience and the capacity to course-correct and find solutions.

Domestic Consumption/Dual Circulation: Domestic consumption remains a vastly untapped resource as part of China's 'Dual Circulation' strategy. Economic policies announced in November 2024 were aimed at fostering consumption and, with a structurally high savings rate, there is scope for enhanced demand to emerge as a future growth driver.

China's Export Dominance: China's global trade in goods surplus exceeded US$988 billion in 2024 after a 19 per cent rise over the previous year (ITC Trade Map).[101] Not only does it enjoy surpluses with most countries, but it also dominates certain critical products where it has strategically built manufacturing strengths. China's exports are 70 per cent higher than the second-largest exporter, the US, and double that of Germany.[102] It is the largest exporter of the top traded items, other than fuels, of electronics (where Hong Kong is the second-largest exporter) and machinery and occupies strategic space in EVs, solar equipment, shipping containers and critical minerals among other products, apart from more mundane items like plastics, furniture and bedding, apparel and others. Its footprint is strong enough to make it difficult for other countries to diversify trade sources even if they wanted to. For developing countries, China's cost competitiveness represents a compelling advantage that is unlikely to recede any time soon. Thus, the world's dependence on Chinese products will continue for the foreseeable future despite attempts to restructure global value chains and impose tariffs.

Military Strength: Likewise, China's military strength continues to expand and is nowhere near peaking. China continues to invest heavily in its military capabilities, both conventional and strategic, which enhances its power projection.

Therefore, one would argue that the notion of China peaking is premature. In all likelihood, it will get over the middle-income economy trap. Alicia Garcia-Herrero of Bruegel has projected that while China's structural deceleration is unavoidable, its GDP per capita should still reach US$25,000 by 2035.[103]

At the same time, the fact remains that earlier projections that China will emerge as the largest economy in the world towards the end of this decade, overtaking the US in GDP is no longer likely. A fundamental misassessment about the decline of the US-led West has been rife in China. A post-Brexit Europe, grappling with its domestic political, social and economic malaise, dealing with a protracted conflict in Ukraine, uncertainties in the transatlantic alliance and a perceived existential threat from Russia, and not being able to develop a coherent policy towards China, is possibly going through an extended period of angst and decline; but despite its numerous problems and divisions, the United States cannot yet be dismissed as a declining power, inexorably sliding towards decay. According to IMF data, the GDP of China as a percentage of the

GDP of the US declined from 76 per cent in 2021 to 70 per cent in 2022 and 66 per cent in 2023. In other words, instead of catching up with the US, China is falling further behind now. This decline is largely due to the appreciation of the US dollar and the differing growth rates between the two economies.

As theories of 'Peak China' are premature, likewise, the Chinese assessment that the US is in terminal decline is flawed.

The most likely scenario is the continued growth of the Chinese economy, though at a progressively slower rate. China has not yet reached the peak of its power,[104] but it may not be able to emerge as the pre-eminent power of the world. For India, a multipolar world and a multipolar Asia without a hegemon is the preferred international order.

B. Personality Traits of China as a Great Power

It has been noted that China is growing in a crowded neighbourhood where its dominance is being challenged not only by the established hegemon, the US, but also by other rising powers like India. China talks of a transition towards a multipolar world, but its preference is for a hierarchical Asia where it is the pre-eminent power. Even globally, a multipolar order will be a halfway house for it as a means to end the US pre-eminence, which China would like to displace as the leading power by the middle of the 21st century, as Xi Jinping articulated at the 19th and 20th Congresses of the CPC in October 2017 and October 2022 respectively. Whether China will achieve that objective remains doubtful.

However, there is no doubt about the fact that China is a great power which practises 'major power diplomacy'. What are the traits of China as a newly emergent great power?

China appears to be a great power in a hurry that recognises that its window of strategic opportunity might be closing, as its economy slows down, its population ages rapidly and the geopolitical pushback from the US and its allies and partners intensifies. It has shed any pretence of hiding its capabilities and biding its time. It is pursuing its unilaterally defined 'core interests' aggressively and is willing to take some reputational damage, convinced that the gains outweigh the diplomatic cost.

However, China is unlikely to emulate the US as a great power in many important areas. It is not seeking to put in place a vast network of allies, as the US has. Instead, it is building up partnerships and a universe of institutions and initiatives, which are China-led, China-centric and often initiated by it, rather than being multilateral in character. This includes the BRI (involving funding, mostly commercial loans, supposedly adding up to around US$1 trillion, though it is difficult to give an accurate number), a nebulous and ill-defined 'Community of Shared Destiny' and more frugal projects like the Global Development Initiative (GDI), Global Security Initiative (GSI) and

Global Civilisational Initiative (GCI), apart from an extensive bilateral outreach covering all continents and umbrella regional platforms like the Forum on China–Africa Cooperation (FOCAC).

While the BRI has enabled it to expand its presence globally and also advance its geopolitical agenda, the project is being recalibrated and scaled down, as it has faced closer scrutiny and the inability of many of the partner countries to pay back loans. The impact of other initiatives like the GSI, GDI and GCI is still rather limited, even though they have been embraced by a large number of countries. China's greatest strength is its economic heft, the fact that it is the leading trading partner of over 120 countries, the largest manufacturer which is increasingly dominating advanced industries, possibly the most important node in the global value chains, the third-largest source of FDI and the leading source of outward tourism. However, as the Chinese economy decelerates, China's capacity for external engagement will be constrained to some extent.

Even while China sets up new institutions centred around it, it is seeking to expand its influence through the existing organisations, including the UN and its organs and the Bretton Woods institutions through more proactive participation, greater voluntary funding, systematic deployment of Chinese nationals and so on. In that respect, it is a status quoist power which is blocking the reform of the UNSC as it would like to preserve its status as the only developing nation among its five permanent members. Thus, China combines status quoist tendencies with its endeavours to upstage the US-led Western order as a revisionist power.

As China's naval presence expands globally, the requirements of the PLAN for logistics and other support facilities will also grow. At present, China has one modest base at Djibouti and access facilities at several other locations. While the number of Chinese bases where the PLAN can station its troops and specialised facilities for repair and maintenance of its naval assets will increase, it does not seem likely that China will have an extensive network of bases matching that of the US. It is more likely to utilise dual-use facilities, in addition to a smaller number of bases. According to a database maintained by the Council on Foreign Relations (August 2024), there are 129 port projects in which Chinese entities have acquired varied equity ownership or operational stakes.[105] China operates or has ownership in at least one port on every continent except Antarctica. Of the 129 projects, 115 are active, while the remaining 14 port projects have become inactive due to cancellation or suspension by the end of July 2024. The report claims that of these, there are 14 port projects with a majority of Chinese ownership where there is physical potential for naval use.

Going by present trends, China as a great power is unlikely to be as interventionist as the US, both by choice and due to resource constraints. It is not inclined to be involved in faraway wars as the US has done and against which there is strong domestic pushback within America. There is a much lower appetite in China to shed blood and invest resources for 'peacekeeping' or 'nation-building'. Contrary to arguments advanced by scholars like Kevin Rudd, China is not eager to export its ideology or development model, as it recognises that its growth model or 'socialism with Chinese characteristics' is deeply anchored in Chinese soil and is not amenable to being transplanted elsewhere. Xi Jinping has talked about an ideological contestation with the West but that is more to secure China's position on issues like universal human rights or to counter the Western narrative of a rules-based international order. China is more likely to focus on advancing its national interests rather than pursue a proselytising internationalist agenda. All nations pursue national interests, but China will be a particularly selfish major power.

C. China after Xi Jinping

As things stand, health permitting, Xi Jinping is expected to get at least another term as the general secretary of the CPC at the 21st Party Congress in late 2029. So far, he has not groomed any successor. While factionalism is a time-tested characteristic of the CPC, Xi has managed to ensure that there is no alternative leadership that can become a rallying point against him. To the extent we can understand the highly secretive and opaque party machinery in China, Xi's authority is not being challenged at present, despite policy missteps like the Zero-COVID policy, economic slowdown, a growing sense of malaise in society, a confrontational foreign policy which has generated geopolitical pushback and a near-continuous anti-corruption campaign that has hurt a very large number of party cadres, government functionaries and the armed forces at different levels. At the 20th Party Congress in 2022, Xi was able to pack the leadership with his supporters on an unprecedented scale. With Xi Jinping Thought enshrined in the state and party constitutions, he is the chief ideologue and interpreter of the party line, which places him in a unique position, without precedent except in the case of Mao Zedong Thought.

Yet, Xi Jinping (born 15 June 1953) is already 71 years old and will either demit office or be eased out at some point. Do we expect major changes post-Xi, as happened after the demise of Mao in 1976, or will there be policy continuity as we saw after Deng passed away in 1997? One may expect course correction as China is faced with major domestic and external challenges. We may not see the emergence of another supreme leader and a possible return to collective leadership may occur. The decision to move towards greater centralisation of authority in the party-state was a conscious choice made after the Jiang–Hu years which had witnessed policy drift and a high level of corruption. The pendulum may swing in the opposite direction post-Xi after a period of unprecedented concentration of power in his persona. If the Chinese economy is unable to shake off its slow and imbalanced growth trajectory and as the feeling grows that the next generation might be worse off compared to the current generation, there might be significant changes in economic policies.

However, it is unlikely that the Chinese Dream pursued across generations will be jettisoned. We have discussed earlier that Xi Jinping is a unique leader and yet he is part of a continuum as far as China's quest for its perceived destiny is concerned. Therefore, the nature of the China challenge might be fine-tuned depending on altered circumstances, but it is unlikely to change fundamentally.

VII.

Search for a New Equilibrium in India–China Relations

Keeping in view the above assessment of the China challenge, some suggestions on the management of India–China relations in the near to medium term are offered.

Border Management: Looking ahead, India must work on the basis of a clear-eyed assessment of the situation, deny China any gains of its 'salami-slicing' tactics along the border, look at the latest disengagement in the Depsang Plains and Demchok as a step towards the normalisation of the LAC rather than the completion of a process, continue discussions on the restoration of the status quo as of early 2020 in terms of patrolling activities and grazing rights, and move with caution on the subsequent steps of de-escalation and de-induction of troops. It should be made clear to the Chinese interlocutors, through Track 1 and Track 2 channels, that while India favoured bringing down tensions in the border areas, the status quo had been disturbed and there is an unfinished agenda of normal management of borders that must be addressed before overall relations can return to full normalcy. It is premature to talk of any reset in ties at this stage. Any reset will not be a realistic proposition without meaningful progress on structural challenges in the relationship. This will require a frank strategic dialogue and readiness to resolve the accumulated problems steadily, rather than wishing them away.

During the meeting between Prime Minister Narendra Modi and President Xi Jinping at Kazan on 23 October, the two leaders 'agreed that the Special Representatives on the India–China boundary question will meet at an early date to oversee the management of peace and tranquillity in border areas and to explore a fair, reasonable and mutually acceptable solution to the boundary question'.[106] The agenda of this dialogue, as also conversations between the foreign ministers as well as through other diplomatic channels should, inter alia, include an early dismantling of the so-called buffer zones and the resumption of patrolling by Indian troops (and traditional grazing by Indian graziers) to patrolling points and pastures they were visiting in the Galwan Valley, Gogra, Hot Springs and the Pangong Lake area in Eastern Ladakh, without giving the Chinese concessions in other sectors.

In parallel, there should be greater visibility on what has been agreed upon in different phases of disengagement, without compromising our negotiating position. It may be recalled that after Chinese intrusions in the Sumdorong Chu and Namkha Chu valleys in 1986–87, there were frank discussions in Parliament. In fact, greater transparency on the part of the government helped buttress our position in the negotiations and we could resist intense pressure from China (including the threat of 'teaching India a lesson' conveyed by Deng Xiaoping through the then US Defence Secretary Casper Weinberger) to vacate the Hathongla–Lungrola–Sulula ridgeline that Indian troops had occupied in Brigade strength after the Chinese set up a post at Wangdung in June 1986. The matter was de-escalated through quiet diplomacy and the stage was set for Prime Minister Rajiv Gandhi's visit to China in December 1988. The disengagement at Wangdung was eventually reached in 1995 without in any way affecting the deployment of Indian troops along the Hathongla–Lungrola–Sulula ridgeline and its northern slopes and their patrolling activities in the two valleys. There is a need to show similar perseverance and strategic patience, which might in fact encourage China to consider a more durable modus vivendi with India.

Any de-escalation of troops will have to be done very carefully, keeping in mind our disadvantages vis-à-vis the nature of the terrain and infrastructure, and consequently the longer reinduction time required by us.

In this context, we should bear in mind Article III(3) of the Agreement on Confidence Building Measures in the Military Field Along the LAC in the India–China Border Areas of November 1996 which reads as follows:

> The two sides shall exchange data on the military forces and armaments to be reduced or limited and decide on ceilings on military forces and armaments to be kept by each side within mutually agreed geographical zones along the line of actual control in the India-China border areas. The ceilings shall be determined in conformity with the requirement of the principle of mutual and equal security, with due consideration being given to parameters such as the nature of terrain, road communication and other infrastructure and time taken to induct/de-induct troops and armaments.[107]

As the army chief has repeatedly emphasised, the subsequent steps will also require rebuilding trust, which was seriously undermined when Chinese troops pivoted after what was misread as a routine military exercise and crossed the LAC at multiple locations, taking advantage of the distraction caused by the COVID-19 pandemic. If adequate and verifiable safeguards are not put in place before any de-escalation of troops, there is a distinct risk of the past behaviour being repeated by the Chinese (as they did on the Doklam Plateau in Bhutan where the Chinese moved in and entrenched their position on the ground soon after the disengagement in 2017).

We cannot be in any hurry to deinduct additional troops as we are at a disadvantage when it comes to the reinduction of troops. However, a situation of enhanced deployment of troops of the two countries in close proximity over the long run is also not desirable as it can lead to accidents. India must therefore keep exploring ways and means of achieving de-escalation of troops through patient negotiations.

As discussed earlier, Article X(1) of the Agreement on Military CBMs of November 1996 contained a categorical agreement on the two sides 'arriving at a common understanding of the alignment of the line of actual control in the India–China border areas', 'agree[ing] to speed up the process of clarification and confirmation of the line of actual control' and also 'agree[ing] to exchange maps indicating their respective perceptions of the entire alignment of the line of actual control as soon as possible'.

The process of clarification of the LAC must be resumed. Even if a common understanding of the entire alignment of the LAC is not arrived at, ways and means can be found for handling those pockets where the two sides have different perceptions. Indeed, that will make it possible to implement understandings like notification of military exercises and even move towards force limitation in mutually identified geographical zones as provided for in the agreement of 1996.

Boundary Settlement: As for the task given to the SRs by the two leaders at Kazan to resume their work on a boundary settlement, there is little evidence to suggest any breakthrough in the talks that has eluded the SRs since they concluded the Agreement on Political Parameters and Guiding Principles for Boundary Settlement in April 2005. However, a clear message must be conveyed to the Chinese SR that, as a result of Chinese transgressions in Eastern Ladakh and elsewhere, their resurrection of the narrative of 'Zangnan' and repeated protests about our routine and normal activities in Arunachal Pradesh, the border issue has returned to the centre of India–China discourse and it is increasingly difficult not to let it come in the way of normal development of relations. The two sides should therefore ponder over the letter and spirit of the breakthrough agreement of 2005 and seek a political settlement which will safeguard the vital interests of the two countries rather than return to the futile exercise of repeating their respective narratives which can never be reconciled.

Strategic Dialogue: An important task performed by the SRs (as well as foreign ministers) in the past has been to engage in strategic consultations on regional and global trends as well as future directions of India–China relations. It is particularly important to have such a dialogue at a time of churn in the international environment.

The geopolitical milieu in which China is pursuing its ambitious agenda has been complicated by its strategic contestation with the US. China's predicament might become more complicated in the second Trump administration. Faced with geopolitical pushback and economic headwinds, will China show greater tactical flexibility vis-à-vis India, even though it is unlikely to dilute its strategic objectives? India too could do with more elbow room to pursue its multi-alignment strategy amidst more pronounced pressures from the US and its allies and uncertainty stemming from an unpredictable incumbent in the White House.

This strategic dialogue can explore whether the simultaneous rise of India and China can be managed in a less confrontational manner. However, we must show staying power and strategic perseverance and should not lower the bar to seek an elusive détente with China.

Asymmetric Deterrence: The key to discouraging China from again deploying its favourite playbook of grey-zone operations against us is continued investment in our deterrence capabilities and preparedness for multi-domain warfare. The deterrence will be primarily defensive in character but not without quid pro quo options. Given the large gap between the capability endowments of India and China, we will have to pursue asymmetric deterrence, rather than seeking parity with China in terms of military hardware. For China, it is the US which is its primary strategic challenge. In fact, China tends to deliberately downplay India as a challenge or threat, though its deployments vis-à-vis us remain robust.

In our assessment, the risk of a full-fledged armed conflict with China is relatively low in the near term but clearly there is no scope for complacency.

The more likely scenario is probing by China along the LAC where there are differing interpretations on the two sides. In a recent Track 1.5 conversation, a Chinese scholar with a PLA background ominously suggested that China has not yet reached its claim line in the Western Sector. Likewise, the so-called 'LAC of 7th November 1959' is raised from time to time. The Chinese had pushed for our acceptance of this construct in discussions on border-related understandings. In response, we have consistently rejected this notional alignment, which is not based on the facts on the ground and keeps changing as per Chinese predilections.

In the Eastern Sector, both sides agree that the LAC is along the McMahon Line of 1914, but we favour the interpretation of the alignment based on the watershed principle (as explained by Henry McMahon in his final memorandum), while the Chinese would like a literal transposition of the McMahon Line as shown in small-scale maps (appended to the Shimla Convention of 1914) onto modern maps (which is neither logical nor in keeping with cartographic principles). We are aware of the pockets with differing interpretations, some formally acknowledged and some tacitly recognised, but opportunistic probing by China elsewhere cannot be ruled out. Our response has to be reading Chinese intentions correctly with improved intelligence, surveillance and reconnaissance (ISR) capabilities (where there was apparently a shortfall in not anticipating large-scale Chinese transgressions in May 2020), foiling attempts by China to alter the LAC and if that happens remaining prepared to embarrass it with countermeasures elsewhere ('quid pro quo' options).

In this regard, continued improvement in border infrastructure is essential. It is important to recall that the Indian Army reviewed its reservations regarding developing roads close to the LAC (due to apprehensions that such roads could become ingress routes for the PLA) way back in the mid-1990s when a list of roads was developed in the China Study Group (called 'the CSG roads') but progress was relatively tardy until a few years ago.

While the Chinese military conventional and strategic capabilities are much larger compared to ours, they have major commitments elsewhere, particularly in the Western Pacific. Besides, effective deterrence involves not matching China's overall military might (which we cannot do in the foreseeable future) but having a comparable capability to bring to bear forces along the LAC (which is doable) and retaining an edge in the deployment of our air power (where the terrain favours us) and naval assets (where we have the 'home field' advantage due to our peninsular geography and strategic location in the IOR). This capability can be asymmetric in character. However, there are four policy choices we must make at the earliest.

One, India's defence budget is inadequate to cope with a two-front situation that exists vis-à-vis China and Pakistan, which have a track record of strategic collusion. Studies by PRS Legislative Research bring out the inconvenient fact that in recent years, the central government's expenditure on defence has decreased as a share of its total expenditure – from 17.1 per cent in 2014–15 to 13 per cent in 2025–26 (BE). Can we afford this downward trend?

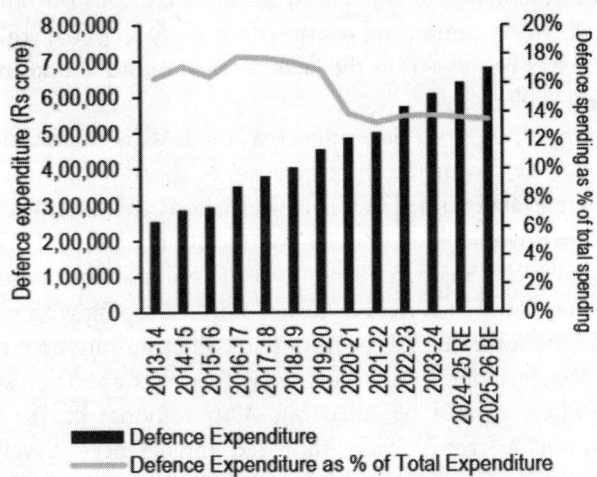

Figure 1.3 Defence Expenditure as Share of Central Government's Total Expenditure
Source: Union budget documents (various years); PRS Legislative Research

Two, a lasting consequence of the Chinese transgressions in Eastern Ladakh will be a further preoccupation of the Indian armed forces with its land borders. Our northern frontiers with China will require enhanced deterrence and continuous vigilance. This will have an impact on inter-service prioritisation, even though the maritime domain offers greater opportunities to our defence planners to take advantage of the IOR chokepoints and China's other vulnerabilities. This happens at a time when, in a reversal of the trends spanning several centuries, China does not have a serious continental threat and can focus more on building up its maritime capabilities as it is doing. The imperative of not ignoring any of the three services (as well as the strategic forces) reinforces the case for a progressive enhancement of our defence budget.

Three, we must grapple with a conundrum relating to the 'Agniveer' scheme which has caused deep misgivings among our armed forces and within the strategic community. This initiative, though well-meaning, needs an urgent review with an open mind and an appropriate course correction.

Finally, can we keep delaying effective measures towards jointness of our three services and the theatreisation of command? Xi Jinping forced the PLA to bite the bullet, and the restructuring of the Chinese military has made considerable headway in the past decade.

Strategic Capabilities: In our discourse, we tend to overlook recent changes in China's strategic capabilities and its nuclear posture, and the implications of these developments for India. Traditionally, even though India–China relations have been fraught, nuclear deterrence has not been a major feature of the relationship. Strategic communities of the two countries seldom talk about the possibility of escalation of potential conventional conflict along borders into the nuclear dimension. Nuclear weapons have mostly remained in the shadows, including in the border standoff in Eastern Ladakh.

However, the basic stability of India–China nuclear deterrence is now under some stress due to several developments, namely: the rapid expansion of China's nuclear warheads (assessed by the US Department of Defence to be in the 'low 200s' in 2020 but over 600 operational nuclear warheads as of early 2024; over 1,000 operational nuclear warheads by 2030, much of which will be deployed at higher readiness levels; and 1,500 warheads by 2035);[108] increasing diversification and sophistication of its nuclear arsenal (including more accurate delivery systems like CSS-5 and CSS-10 missiles, reportedly allocated for missions against India); acquisition of counterforce and ballistic missile defence (BMD) capabilities which are not yet mature enough to be effective against the US but could potentially erode India's limited second-strike capability; and problematic changes in China's nuclear doctrines, including relatively rapid retaliation and an 'early warning counterstrike' posture.

India has maintained a conservative nuclear posture, reflected in the modest size of its nuclear inventory and its consistent nuclear doctrines. However, as the gap between the nuclear arsenals of India and China increases, and as Pakistan continues to enlarge its nuclear arsenal, we will have to carefully assess the implications of these developments. India's nuclear doctrine, including 'No First Use', has been clearly articulated and is consistent; previous reviews have not indicated any need for modification. However, what is a 'credible minimum deterrent' under the scenario of the nuclear threat from China and Pakistan, which have an extensive history of collusion and both of whom are expanding their nuclear weapon capabilities and delivery systems?

China refuses to have meaningful dialogue with India on nuclear and strategic issues. It is essential that nuclear matters be discussed at the least between the strategic communities of India and China, if not at an intergovernmental level.

External Balancing: Much of our answer to the challenge posed by China will have to be found in enhancing our own deterrence and capabilities, and reducing the capability gap with China, but a policy of external balancing, working with the US, Japan, Australia and other like-minded countries, will be an essential part of our response. We will have to help build up each other's competencies, work together to innovate and develop advanced technologies, promote more diversified and resilient regional and global value chains not excessively dependent on one country, enhance our combined deterrence to discourage China from opting for disruptive behaviour and seek a more equitable order reflecting contemporary realities. The objective is not to contain China but to nudge it to be a more responsible stakeholder in the global commons where it is not pursuing its narrowly defined 'core interests' to the detriment of other countries.

In this process, it will be important to manage our expectations from the US and its allies, and their expectations of us in conflict situations, whether along the India–China borders or in the Indo-Pacific and the IOR.

Given the transactional approach being adopted by the second Trump administration towards the US allies and partners, we will have to continuously monitor the efficacy of external balancing against China, prioritising essentially our own deterrence capabilities.

While it is unlikely that India would consider direct military involvement in a crisis in the Taiwan Strait or the South China Sea, there is a menu of options available to India, ranging from diplomatic signalling to logistic support, depending on the scenario that develops and our assessment of the country's interests in those theatres, the preference being deterrence and prevention of any armed conflict.

Economic Security: There is a seductive logic in the arguments being advanced in many quarters that closer economic engagement with China, delinked from the broader relationship, greater integration with Chinese supply chains and the wooing of inflows of investment from that country, will address many of our economic challenges. Most of these arguments fail to factor in the complex dynamics of both India–China relations as well as the China factor in India's economic security which has been analysed by V.S. Seshadri in a recent study (September 2024).[109]

We have already discussed the issue of an unsustainable trade deficit with China and growing dependencies on imports from China in critical sectors that create vulnerabilities. It cannot be business as usual with China (which is the Chinese preference) when overall relations and the situation along the borders remain fraught. Some other considerations should be kept in mind while deciding the level of economic security we seek vis-à-vis China.[110]

One, both the US-led West and China are increasingly securitising their economies and de-risking and diversifying vis-à-vis each other. According to a Rhodium Group report, India has the highest score (2.86) of all emerging and developing countries as a potential alternative investment destination to China.[111] If India seeks closer integration with Chinese supply chains, global companies might be discouraged from considering India as their alternative node for global value chains. In the unlikely event of Chinese companies developing India as a major manufacturing hub to circumvent tariffs and other entry restrictions in the US and European markets, there will be a high risk of India being targeted by those countries to plug the loophole in their regimes vis-à-vis China. It is already happening in the case of exports of solar panels through ASEAN countries, and Canada and Mexico being pressurised to follow enhanced US tariffs on Chinese products so that there could be a 'fortress North America from the flood of Chinese imports that's coming out of the most unbalanced economy in the history of modern times,' as the US Treasury Secretary Scott Bessent put it.[112]

Two, China is still not a market economy. China's objective of dominating future industries and its preference for exporting its way out of its economic difficulties, rather than prioritising domestic consumption, will aggravate existing tensions in economic relations with both advanced economies and emerging economies such as India.

Three, China's rigorous scrutiny of outward flows of investment and technology by its companies aims to maximise domestic value chains and make the country indispensable to global technology production, as a recent Mercator Institute for China Studies (MERICS) study brings out.[113] A Bloomberg report suggests that China has strongly advised its carmakers to ensure that advanced electric vehicle technology stays in the country and that they produce key parts domestically and export so-called knock-down kits to their foreign plants.[114] India has been specifically mentioned in this regard.

Going by past experience, it would be naive to expect that China will help build India's manufacturing capacities. Instead, Chinese companies have preferred to invest in sensitive sectors in India, including through acquisitions, which led to Press Note 3 in April 2020. Giving free access to Chinese companies will attract low-value-addition investments, potential investments in sensitive sectors where data security can be an issue, and suspicious investments, and be a recipe for stunted industrialisation in a large number of sectors in which China seeks to dominate the world or act globally.

Four, the expectation that imports from China can be reduced by boosting FDI from China is not borne out by the experience of other geographies which have received substantial Chinese investments. For instance, the ASEAN imports from China increased from US$386 billion in 2021 to US$438 billion in 2023, as sourcing of intermediates from China soared.

Thus, proceeding from strategic, security and economic perspectives, India would do well to take a differentiated policy towards economic relations with China. India cannot decouple itself from the economy of China, the world's largest manufacturer and exporter. But India must decide which sectors of its economy it can selectively allow Chinese FDI into based on its manufacturing strengths and strategies, and keep in mind the interests of its national security and industrial development.[115]

Anticipating Crises: In a relationship that is complex and accident-prone, preparing for turbulence on sensitive issues is advisable. Just to give an example, Tibet has traditionally been a difficult issue in the relationship. The joint statement issued on 24 June 2003 during Prime Minister Atal Bihari Vajpayee's visit to China had the following formulation on Tibet: 'The Indian side recognizes that the Tibet Autonomous Region is part of the territory of the People's Republic of China and reiterates that it does not allow Tibetans to engage in anti-China political activities in India.'[116] The problem with the formulation is that soon the Chinese resurrected the term 'Zangnan' (or 'South Tibet'), which includes most of Arunachal Pradesh. Besides, the 'Tibet Autonomous Region' as shown in the PRC maps claims most of Arunachal Pradesh. Therefore, it was not tenable to use the language of the TAR being 'part of the territory' of the PRC.

Looking ahead, the passing away of the 14th Dalai Lama, who will soon reach the age of 90 years, will generate a problematic situation. The question of who selects the reincarnation of the Dalai Lama is debatable as Vijay Gokhale brings out in his recent Carnegie India monograph.[117] The PRC claims that the imperial ordinance of 1793 (known as the Imperially Approved Ordinance for Better Governance of Tibet or the 29-Article Ordinance) stipulates the procedure for the reincarnation of the Living Buddhas (including the Dalai Lama) and subjects the selected candidate to approval by Beijing. In 2007, the State Religious Affairs Bureau issued Order No. 5 titled 'Measures on the Management of the Reincarnation of Living Buddhas of Tibetan Buddhism', which made it clear that the central government intended to control the entire process of selection and appointment of the Living Buddhas. Tibetans reject the idea that China has the authority to exercise legal jurisdiction over the process of selecting the Dalai Lama (and other Living Buddhas of Tibet).[118] In fact, the Chinese claim was rejected by the 14th Dalai Lama himself and he observed in a statement issued on 24 September 2011: '[The] person who reincarnates has sole legitimate authority over where and how he or she takes rebirth and how that reincarnation is to be recognized.'[119] The Dalai Lama added: 'When I am about ninety I will consult the high Lamas of the Tibetan Buddhist traditions, the Tibetan public, and other concerned people who follow Tibetan Buddhism, and re-evaluate whether the institution of the Dalai Lama should continue or not. On that basis we will take a decision.'

However, the Chinese authorities will undoubtedly seek to control the reincarnation of the 14th Dalai Lama, which will generate considerable controversy. We need to prepare for that contingency.

Working with China in SCO, BRICS and G20: During the past four-plus years, even while bilateral relations between India and China were at a low ebb, the two countries continued to work together in minilateral platforms like the Shanghai Cooperation Organisation (SCO), BRICS and G20. During the EAM's meeting with Foreign Minister Wang Yi on the margins of the G20 Summit on 19 November 2024, both ministers made a positive evaluation of the cooperation in the three groupings. According to the MEA readout: 'EAM noted that India and China have both differences and convergences. We have worked constructively in the BRICS and the SCO framework. Our cooperation in the G20 has also been evident.'[120] Xinhua quoted Wang Yi as making a similar assessment.[121] India's continued proactive involvement in these forums will be in keeping with its stance of strategic autonomy and will advance its agenda. Its participation will also help ensure that these groupings do not become instruments for geopolitical contestation and instead seek concrete and positive outcomes.

New Paradigm: As discussed earlier, the old paradigm governing the relationship has broken down, but a new paradigm is yet to be forged. While we may initiate dialogue in this regard, it is premature to fashion such an overarching framework for the resumption of constructive engagement with China. There is still unfinished business in sorting out the disruption caused by Chinese behaviour along the borders and making some progress on accumulated grievances on both sides before it can be declared that the relationship is back on the normal track and a reset can be attempted. However, channels of communication and dialogue must be kept open at different levels between the two governments and the strategic communities of India and China.

Given Xi Jinping's primacy in the Chinese party-state, our PM's continued engagement with him is desirable but without any undue expectations that these summit-level meetings will provide a negotiating platform to resolve outstanding issues. With China, productive summit-level meetings require extensive preparatory work and even then, they can be deployed to seek breakthroughs in the relationship only when the circumstances are favourable and there is readiness on both sides. Such a juncture eludes the two countries at present.

In conclusion, our working hypothesis should be that the Chinese economy will continue on its growth path, albeit at a progressively slower rate. The geopolitical pushback it is facing, including its strategic contestation with the US for pre-eminence, is unlikely to abate until a new equilibrium is reached, though there might be tactical adjustments from time to time. There is still considerable uncertainty about the trajectory of China's relations with the US under the Trump administration. Donald Trump poses a special challenge because the Chinese leadership is not comfortable when it cannot predict and game out its rivals and competitors (as has happened with India as well), but China will play the long game and ride out the Trump years, if needed. It will seek to protect its privileged relationship with Russia, drive a wedge between Europe and the US, stabilise relations with Japan, Australia and other US allies, continue to grow its footprint in the Global South, and utilise openings created by the retrenchment of the US from multilateral platforms like the WHO. India too must show strategic patience in its dealings with China, make a clear-eyed assessment of the China challenge without demonising its largest neighbour, build its own capabilities, reinforce its deterrence, not shy away from external balancing without any exaggerated hopes, keeping in mind the larger geopolitical picture (where a degree of stability in relations with China gives it more elbow room) and seek cooperation wherever possible and desirable, bilaterally and on multilateral and global issues, without yielding on its own interests, concerns and aspirations, and without harbouring any unrealistic expectations.

Notes

1. Ministry of External Affairs, 'Transcript of Special Briefing by Foreign Secretary on Prime Minister's Visit to Russia', 21 October 2024, https://www.mea.gov.in/media-briefings.htm?dtl/38441/Transcript+of+Special+Briefing+by+Foreign+Secretary+on+Prime+Ministers+Visit+to+Russia+October+21+2024
2. Ministry of External Affairs, 'Meeting of Prime Minister with Mr. Xi Jinping, President of the People's Republic of China on the margins of the 16th BRICS Summit', 23 October 2024, https://www.mea.gov.in/press-releases.htm?dtl/38457/

Meeting+of+Prime+Minister+with+Mr+Xi+Jinping+President+of+the+Peoples+Republic+of+China+on+the+margins+of+the+ 16th+BRICS+Summit

3. Chinese Ministry of Foreign Affairs, 'President Xi Jinping Meets with Indian Prime Minister Narendra Modi', 24 October 2024, https://www.mfa.gov.cn/eng/xw/zyxw/202410/t20241023_11514914.html

4. Roy, S., 'Beijing Bid to Move Ties to Pre-2020 Normal: China officials', *Indian Express*, available at: https://indianexpress.com/article/india/delhi-beijing-bid-to-move-ties-to-pre-2020-normal-china-officials-9665097/

5. Ministry of External Affairs, 'EAM's meeting with Foreign Minister Wang Yi on the margins of G20 Summit', 19 November 2024, https://www.mea.gov.in/press-releases.htm?dtl/38543/External_Affairs_Ministers_meeting_with_Member_of_the_Communist_Party_of_China_CPC_Political_Bureau_and_Foreign_Minister_HE_Mr_Wang_Yi_on_the_sideline

6. Ministry of External Affairs, '23rd Meeting of the Special Representatives of India and China', 18 December 2024, https://www.mea.gov.in/press-releases.htm?dtl/38805/23rd+Meeting+of+the+Special+Representatives+of+India+and+China

7. Ministry of Foreign Affairs, 'People's Republic of China, China-India special representatives reach 6 consensus points at meeting on border issue', 18 December 2024, https://www.fmprc.gov.cn/wjbzhd/202412/t20241218_11501563.shtml

8. Ministry of External Affairs, 'Visit of Foreign Secretary to China', 27 January 2025, https://www.mea.gov.in/press-releases.htm?dtl/38946/Visit_of_Foreign_Secretary_to_China

9. Chinese Ministry of Foreign Affairs, 'China–India Vice Foreign Ministers/Secretaries Dialogue Held in Beijing', 28 January 2025, https://www.fmprc.gov.cn/wjbxw_new/202501/t20250128_11547219.shtml

10. Kantha, A.K., 'A Good Beginning but China Negotiations Must Continue', *The Hindu*, 9 December 2024, https://www.thehindu.com/opinion/lead/a-good-beginning-but-china-negotiations-must-continue/article68962353.ece.

11. *The Hindustan Times*, 'Degree of standoff exists along LAC, need to restore trust: Indian Army Chief', 14 January 2025, https://www.hindustantimes.com/india-news/degree-of-standoff-exists-along-lac-need-to-restore-trust-indian-army-chief-101736826667532.html

12. *The Hindu*, 'We are trying to restore trust, reassure each other, other stages will follow through: Army Chief', 22 October 2024, https://www.thehindu.com/news/national/army-chief-gen-upendra-dwivedi-speaks-about-india-china-talks-breakthrough/article68782428.ece

13. *The Hindu*, 'India, China to undertake "coordinated patrolling"', 25 October 2024, https://www.thehindu.com/news/national/india-china-disengagement-process-to-be-completed-by-october-29/article68796102.ece

14. *The Tribune*, 'Chinese Seek "Unreasonable" Patrolling Rights at Two LAC Spots along Arunachal Pradesh', 22 September 2024, https://www.tribuneindia.com/news/india/the-tribune-exclusive-chinese-seek-unreasonable-patrolling-rights-at-two-lac-spots-along-arunachal-pradesh/

15 *Hindustan Times*, 'Disengagement on LAC is Not a Reset, says Jaishankar at HTLS', 16 November 2024, https://www.hindustantimes.com/india-news/htls-2024-jaishankar-says-lac-disengagement-must-lead-to-deescalation-101731745452500.html
16 Kantha, A.K., 'Weighing in on Business as Usual with China', *The Hindu*, 24 September 2024, https://www.thehindu.com/opinion/lead/weighing-in-on-business-as-usual-with-china/article68674839.ece
17 Kalha, R.S., 2014, 'India-China Boundary Issues: Quest for Settlement', ICWA.
18 Ranganathan, C.V. and V.C. Khanna, 2000, *India and China: The Way ahead after 'Mao's India War'*, Har-Anand Publications.
19 Ministry of External Affairs, 'Joint Statement between India and China during Prime Minister's visit to China', 15 May 2015, https://www.mea.gov.in/bilateral-documents.htm?dtl/25240/Joint_Statement_between_the_India_and_China_during_Prime_Ministers_visit_to_China
20 *The Hindu*, 'My Mission is to better India ties: Xi', 16 November 2021, https://www.thehindu.com/news/international/world/my-mission-is-to-better-india-ties-xi/article5810706.ece
21 Ministry of External Affairs, 'India–China Informal Summit at Wuhan', 28 April 2018, https://www.mea.gov.in/press-releases.htm?dtl/29853/IndiaChina_Informal_Summit_at_Wuhan
22 Ministry of External Affairs, '2nd India–China Informal Summit', 12 October 2019, https://www.mea.gov.in/press-releases.htm?dtl/31938/2nd_IndiaChina_Informal_Summit
23 Ministry of External Affairs, 'Joint Statement between the Republic of India and the People's Republic of China on Building a Closer Developmental Partnership', 19 September 2014, https://www.mea.gov.in/bilateral-documents.htm?dtl/24022/Joint+Statement+between+the+Republic+of+India+and+the+Peoples+ Republic+of+China+on+Building+a+Closer+ Developmental+Partnership
24 Ministry of External Affairs, 'Joint Statement between India and China during Prime Minister's visit to China', 15 May 2015, https://www.mea.gov.in/bilateral-documents.htm?dtl/25240/Joint_Statement_between_the_India_and_China_during_Prime_Ministers_visit_to_China
25 Ministry of External Affairs, 'Joint Statement between India and China during Prime Minister's visit to China', 15 May 2015, https://www.mea.gov.in/bilateral-documents.htm?dtl/25240/Joint_Statement_between_the_India_and_China_during_Prime_Ministers_visit_to_China
26 Haidar, S., 2022, 'Explained: Held up by the Chinese', *The Hindu*, 19 October, https://www.thehindu.com/news/international/explained-held-up-by-the-chinese/article66032861.ece
27 Xi Jinping, 'Achieving Rejuvenation Is the Dream of the Chinese People', 29 November 2012, https://china.usc.edu/xi-jinping-achieving-rejuvenation-dream-chinese-people-november-29-2012
28 *Xinhua*, 'China Approves Construction of Hydropower Project in Lower Reaches of Yarlung Zangbo River', 25 December 2018, https://english.news.cn/20241225/3b1298a2f02d4428bd76e65929571cd3/c.html

29. *South China Morning Post*, 'China Approves Tibet Mega Dam that Could Generate 3 Times More Power Than Three Gorges', 25 December 2024, https://sc.mp/oqkmg?utm_source=twitter&utm_campaign=3292267&utm_medium=share_widget… via @scmpnews
30. Thread of posts on 'X', Ashok K. Kantha, 26 December 2024, https://x.com/ashokkkantha/status/1872152759698600364
31. Nithiyanandam, Dr Y., 2003, 'Raising the Stakes: China's Mega Dam Project Heightens Tensions at the Roof of the World', Takshashila Geospatial Bulletin No. 2, 7 July, https://geospatialbulletin.takshashila.org.in/p/2-raising-the-stakes-chinas-mega
32. Tyler, M.C., 2024, 'The future of the Quad in the Indo-Pacific', ORF, 22 February, https://www.orfonline.org/expert-speak/the-future-of-the-quad-in-the-indo-pacific
33. https://data.worldbank.org/?locations=CN-IN
34. https://www.sipri.org/databases/milex
35. https://www.sipri.org/publications/2011/european-union-and-modernisation-peoples-liberation-army-navy-limits-europes-strategic-irrelevance
    US Department of Defence, China Military Power Report 2024, issued on 18 December 2024, https://www.defense.gov/News/Publications/?Page=2
    Naval Technology, India vs China: A comparison of the Indian and Chinese (PLA) Navies, https://www.naval-technology.com/features/india-vs-china-indian-and-chinese-pla-navies-compared/
    Center for Strategic & International Studies, Unpacking China's Naval Buildup, 5 June 2024, https://www.csis.org/analysis/unpacking-chinas-naval-buildup
36. International Trade Center Trade Map, bilateral trade between China and India, – China's trade balance with India: https://www.trademap.org/Bilateral_TS.aspx?nvpm=1%7c156%7c%7c699%7c%7cTOTAL%7c%7c%7c2%7c1%7c1%7c3%7c2%7c1%7c1%7c1%7c1%7cl
    China's exports to India: https://www.trademap.org/Bilateral_TS.aspx? nvpm=1%7c156%7c%7c699%7c%7cTOTAL%7c%7c%7c2%7c1%7c1%7c2%7c2%7c1% 7c1%7c1%7c1%7cl
    China's imports from India: https://www.trademap.org/Bilateral_TS.aspx?nvpm= 1%7c156%7c%7c699%7c%7cTOTAL% 7c%7c%7c2%7c1%7c1%7c1%7c2%7c 1%7c1%7c1%7c1%7cl
37. Press Information Bureau, 'Restricting FDI Inflows from China in The Strategic Sector', 10 December 2021, https://pib.gov.in/PressReleaseIframePage.aspx?PRID=1780251
38. Press Information Bureau, 'India's on-Going Trade Negotiations', 13 March 2020, https://pib.gov.in/pressreleasepage.aspx?prid=1606300
39. Hussain, Z. and A.K. Gupta, 2024, 'Opinion', *The Hindu Business Line*, 18 January, https://www.thehindubusinessline.com/opinion/india-did-well-in-not-joining-rcep/article67753310.ece; SAIS Review of International Affairs, Simi Mehta, 19 February 2020, https://saisreview.sais.jhu.edu/the-rcep-minus-india-reasons-and-implications/

40 *The Economic Times*, 'How China wants to press pause on India's Apple success story', 14 January 2025, https://economictimes.indiatimes.com/industry/cons-products/electronics/how-china-wants-to-press-pause-on-indias-apple-success-story/articleshow/117232349.cms?from=mdr
TheQuint, China Has Silently Put 'Industrial Sanctions' on India: Will New Delhi Respond?, Sanjay Kapoor, 19 January 2025, https://www.thequint.com/news/world/india-china-sanctions-iphone-narendra-modi-galwan-xi-jinping High Capacity, China is trying to reshape global supply chains, Kyle Chan, 28 February 2025, https://www.high-capacity.com/p/china-is-trying-to-reshape-global

41 *The Hindu*, 'Sri Lanka formally hands over the Hambantota Port on 99-year lease to China', 1 December 2021, https://www.thehindu.com/news/international/sri-lanka-formally-hands-over-hambantota-port-on-99-year-lease-to-china/article61847422.ece

42 China Power Team, CSIS, 'How Dominant Is China in the Global Arms Trade?', 26 April 2018, updated 27 May 2021, https://chinapower.csis.org/china-global-arms-trade

43 *The Times of India*, 'India keeping close tabs on China–Pak collusion in the IOR, revising plans: Navy Chief', 1 December 2023, https://timesofindia.indiatimes.com/india/india-keeping-close-tabs-on-china-pak-collusion-in-the-ior-revising-plans-navy-chief/articleshow/105664264.cms

44 Information Office of the State Council, People's Republic of China, China's Military Strategy, May 2015, https://english.www.gov.cn/archive/white_paper/2015/05/27/content_281475115610833.htm

45 UNDP assessment, 2019, https://www.undp.org/china/blog/what-changes-after-china-defeats-poverty

46 Rudd, K., 2024, *On Xi Jinping: How Xi's Marxist Nationalism Is Shaping China and the World*, Oxford University Press.

47 Information Office of the State Council, People's Republic of China, 'China's Peaceful Development', September 2011, http://english.gov.cn/archive/white_paper/2014/09/09/content_281474986284646.htm

48 Jintao, H., 2016, *Hu Jintao Selected Works*, Vol. 3, Beijing: People's Press.

49 Doshi, R., 2021, *The Long Game: China's Grand Strategy to Displace American Order (Bridging the Gap)*, Oxford University Press.

50 Jintao, H., 2016, *Hu Jintao Selected Works*, Vol. 3, Beijing: People's Press.

51 Doshi, R., 2021, *The Long Game: China's Grand Strategy to Displace American Order (Bridging the Gap)*, Oxford University Press.

52 Report of Hu Jintao to the 18th CPC National Congress, 'Firmly March on the Path of Socialism with Chinese Characteristics and Strive to Complete the Building of a Moderately Prosperous Society in All Respects', 8 November 2012, http://www.china.org.cn/china/18th_cpc_congress/node_7167318.htm

53 Doshi, R., 2021, *The Long Game: China's Grand Strategy to Displace American Order (Bridging the Gap)*, Oxford University Press.

54 Ibid.
55 Ibid.
56 Ibid.

57 Jinping, X., 'Secure a Decisive Victory in Building a Moderately Prosperous Society in All Respects and Strive for the Great Success of Socialism with Chinese Characteristics for a New Era' [决胜全面建成小康社会 夺取新时代中国特色社会主义伟大胜利], 19th Party Congress Political Report, 18 October 2017, https://www.andrewerickson.com/2017/10/full-text-of-xi-jinpings-19th-national-party-congress-work-report-related-documents/

58 Jinping, X., Full text of the report to the 20th National Congress of the Communist Party of China, 25 October 2022, https://english.news.cn/20221025/8eb6f5239f984f01a2bc45b5b5db0c51/c.html

59 Renmin Wang [人民网], 'China's Peripheral Diplomacy: Advancing Grand Strategy [中国周边外交：推进大战略]', 28 October 2013, http://theory.people.com.cn/n/2013/1028/c136457-23344720.html

60 State of Southeast Asia Survey 2024, https://www.iseas.edu.sg/category/centres/asean-studies-centre/state-of-southeast-asia-survey/#:~:text=The per cent20State per cent20of per cent20Southeast per cent20Asia,economic per cent20tensions per cent20between per cent20major per cent20powers.

61 Hillman, J.E., 2019, 'Corruption Flows Along China's Belt and Road', Center for Strategic & International Studies (CSIS), 18 January, https://www.csis.org/analysis/corruption-flows-along-chinas-belt-and-road

62 Hurley, J., Morris, S. and G. Portelance, 'Examining the Debt Implications of the Belt and Road Initiative from a Policy Perspective', Center for Global Development, https://www.cgdev.org/sites/default/files/examining-debt-implications-belt-and-road-initiative-policy-perspective.pdf

63 US Department of Defence, 'China Military Power report 2024', 18 December 2024, https://www.defense.gov/News/Publications/?Page=2

64 Maddison, A., *The World Economy: A Millennial Perspective* (OECD, 2001); *Chinese Economic Performance in the Long Run, 960–2030 AD* (OECD, 2007); and *Contours of the World Economy, 1–2030 AD* (Oxford University Press, 2007).

65 Mitter, R., 'The Real Roots of Xi Jinping Thought: Chinese Political Philosophers' Long Struggle with Modernity', *Foreign Affairs*, March–April 2024, https://www.foreignaffairs.com/reviews/china-real-roots-xi-jinping-thought

66 White House, 'Remarks by NSA Jake Sullivan on Renewing American Economic Leadership at the Brookings Institution', 23 April 2023, https://www.whitehouse.gov/briefing-room/speeches-remarks/2023/04/27/remarks-by-national-security-advisor-jake-sullivan-on-renewing-american-economic-leadership-at-the-brookings-institution/

67 Chinese Ministry of Foreign Affairs, 'Regular Press Conference of Foreign Ministry Spokesperson Lin Jian', 4 March 2025, https://www.fmprc.gov.cn/eng/xw/fyrbt/lxjzh/202503/t20250304_11568271.html

68 The US National Security Strategy, 18 December 2017, https://trumpwhitehouse.archives.gov/wp-content/uploads/2017/12/NSS-Final-12-18-2017-0905.pdf

69 The US National Security Strategy, White House, 12 October 2022, available on https://www.whitehouse.gov/wp-content/uploads/2022/10/Biden-Harris-Administrations-National-Security-Strategy-10.2022.pdf

70 https://trackingpeoplesdaily.substack.com/p/xi-talks-to-putin-is-a-reverse-kissinger?utm_source=substack&publication_id=264786&post_id=157862731&utm_medium=email&utm_content=share&utm_campaign=email-share&triggerShare=true&isFreemail=true&r=tc8&triedRedirect=true

71 Pike, L., 2025, 'Trump's Europe Shock Creates an Opening for China', Foreign Policy, 20 February, https://foreignpolicy.com/2025/02/20/trump-europe-china-tariffs-defense-spending/?tpcc=editors_picks&utm_source=Sailthru&utm_medium=email&utm_campaign=Editors per cent27 per cent20Picks per cent20- per cent 2002212025&utm_term=editors_picks

72 *The Economist*, 'Chinese companies are winning the global south', 1 August 2024, https://www.economist.com/leaders/2024/08/01/chinese-companies-are-winning-the-global-south

73 Rhodium Group, 'The Next Generation of China's Outbound Investment', 16 September 2024, https://cbm.rhg.com/research-note/next-generation-chinas-outbound-investment

74 Associated Press, 'Emboldened Xi to protect "every inch" of China territory', 20 March 2018, https://apnews.com/article/ddcb059166e84c78bff013c67736b937

75 Lin, B., Garafola, C.L., McClintock, B., Denton, S.W., et al., 2022, 'A New Framework for Understanding and Countering China's Gray Zone Tactics', Rand Corporation, 30 March, https://www.rand.org/pubs/research_briefs/RBA594-1.html

76 Permanent Court of Arbitration, 'The South China Sea Arbitration (The Republic of Philippines vs The People's Republic of China)', https://pca-cpa.org/en/cases/7/

77 *The Diplomat*, 'China Sets Record for Activity Near Senkaku/Diaoyu Islands in 2023', 4 January 2024, https://thediplomat.com/2024/01/china-sets-record-for-activity-near-senkaku-diaoyu-islands-in-2023/

78 Barnett, R., 2024, 'The Politics of China's Land Appropriation in Bhutan', *The Diplomat*, 15 October, https://thediplomat.com/2024/10/the-politics-of-chinas-land-appropriation-in-bhutan/

79 Du, Z., Wang, Y., Bai, Y., Wang, L., Cowling, B.J. and L.A. Meyers, 'Estimate of COVID-19 Deaths', Centers for Disease Control and Prevention, December 2022–February 2023, https://wwwnc.cdc.gov/eid/article/29/10/23-0585_article

80 Zhai, K., Zhu J. and Ch. Leng, 2020, 'How billionaire Jack Ma Fell to Earth and Took Ant's Mega IPO with Him', Reuters, 5 November, https://www.reuters.com/article/world/asia-pacific/how-billionaire-jack-ma-fell-to-earth-and-took-ants-mega-ipo-with-him-idUSKBN27L2GW/

81 *Xinhua*, The State Council of PRC, 'Vice-premier stresses promoting digital economy for high-quality development', 6 September 2021, https://english.www.gov.cn/statecouncil/liuhe/202109/06/content_WS6135af9fc6d0df57f98dfc4a.html

82 Wang, K.L., Sun T.T. and R.Y. Xu, 2023, 'The Impact of Artificial Intelligence on Total Factor Productivity: Empirical Evidence from China's Manufacturing Enterprises', https://doi.org/10.1007/s10644-022-09467-4

83 Wang, Sh., Zheng, Y. and Q. Wang, 2023, 'Technical standardization and total factor productivity in innovation-driven development: Evidence from China', PLOS, 5 October, https://doi.org/10.1371/journal.pone.0287109
84 MERICS, 'The Party Knows Best: Aligning Economic Actors with China's Strategic Goals', October 2023, https://merics.org/en/report/party-knows-best-aligning-economic-actors-chinas-strategic-goals
85 Ibid.
86 *Nikkei Asia*, 'China's Rising Deflation Risk Worrisome: IMF Regional Director – Nikkei Asia', 8 November 2024, https://asia.nikkei.com/Economy/China-s-rising-deflation-risk-worrisome-IMF-regional-director?dicbo=v2-zCX7xmD
87 Kessler, A., 2024, 'China Is Turning Japanese: The Mainland Expects a Sharp Decline in Its Economic Growth, Sound Familiar?' *The Wall Street Journal*, 13 October, https://www.wsj.com/opinion/china-is-turning-japanese-asia-economy-downturn-history-1990s-real-estate-stimulus-2054e267
88 *Nikkei Asia*, 'China Unveils $1.4tn Debt Swap Programme to Ease Local Government Pain', 8 November 2024, https://asia.nikkei.com/Economy/China-unveils-1.4tn-debt-swap-program-to-ease-local-government-pain?utm
89 *The Wire China*, 'The Tipping Point', 10 November 2024, https://www.thewirechina.com/2024/11/10/the-tipping-point-foreign-companies-china/
90 Chan, K., 'China is trying to reshape global supply chains', High Capacity, https://www.high-capacity.com/p/china-is-trying-to-reshape-global
91 García-Herrero, A. and X. Jianwei, 2025, 'Will China's economy follow the same path as Japan's?', Bruegel policy brief, 27 February, https://www.bruegel.org/policy-brief/will-chinas-economy-follow-same-path-japans
92 Xiaoping, D., 1992, Excerpts from Talks Given in Wuchang, Shenzhen, Zhuhai and Shanghai, https://www.marxists.org/reference/archive/deng-xiaoping/1992/10.htm
93 Johnson, I., 'Xi's Age of Stagnation: The Great Walling-Off of China', *Foreign Affairs*, September–October 2023, https://www.foreignaffairs.com/china/xi-jinping-age-stagnation
94 *Caixin Global*, 'Chart of the Day: The Military Brass Ensnared in China's Anti-Corruption Campaign', 27 December 2024, https://www.caixinglobal.com/2024-12-27/chart-of-the-day-the-military-brass-ensnared-in-chinas-anti-corruption-campaign-102272883.html?utm_source=Subscription+Pool&utm_campaign=341673c856-EMAIL_CAMPAIGN_5_13_2020_3_37_COPY_02&utm_medium=email&utm_term=0_4f3ff79ef1-341673c856-71822435
95 State Council Notice concerning Issuance of the Planning Outline for the Construction of a Social Credit System (2014–20), translation: https://digichina.stanford.edu/work/planning-outline-for-the-construction-of-a-social-credit-system-2014-2020/
96 Beckley, M. and H. Brands, 2022, *Danger Zone: The Coming Conflict with China*, W.W. Norton and Co.; Khanna, P., 2020, 'Has China Peaked Already?', Noēma, 13 October, https://www.paragkhanna.com/has-china-peaked-already/

97 Beckley, M. and H. Brands, 2021, 'The End of China's Rise: Beijing Is Running Out of Time to Remake the World', *Foreign Affairs*, 1 October, https://www.foreignaffairs.com/articles/china/2021-10-01/end-chinas-rise

98 García-Herrero, A. and R., 'China's quest for innovation: Progress and bottlenecks', Bruegel Working Paper, No. 08/2023, https://hdl.handle.net/10419/274214

99 Wilkins, R.C., 2024, 'The US Drive to Stem China's Tech Rise Is Stalling', Bloomberg', 30 October, https://www.bloomberg.com/news/newsletters/2024-10-30/the-us-drive-to-stem-china-s-tech-rise-is stalling?cmpid=BBD110624_CN&utm_medium=email&utm_source=newsletter&utm_term=241106&utm_campaign=china

100 Leung, Dr J.W., Robin, S. and D. Cave, 'Critical Technology Tracker', ASPI, August 2024, https://www.aspi.org.au/report/aspis-two-decade-critical-technology-tracker

101 ITC Trade Map, 'Bilateral Trade between China and the World', accessed on https://www.trademap.org/Bilateral_TS.aspx?nvpm=1%7c156%7c%7c000%7c%7cTOTAL%7c%7c%7c2%7c1%7c1%7c3%7c2%7c1%7c1%7c1%7c1%7c1

102 International Data Centre data accessed on 22 November 2024.

103 Presentation by Alicia Garcia-Herrero at a seminar with the Institute of Chinese Studies and India International Centre on 'China's Growth Prospects: Zooming into Trade, Supply Chains and Industrial Policy', New Delhi, 26 October 2024.

104 Mastro, O.S., and D., 'China Hasn't Reached the Peak of Its Power', *Foreign Affairs*, 22 August 2022, https://www.foreignaffairs.com/china/china-hasnt-reached-peak-its-power

105 Council on Foreign Relations, 'Tracking China's Control of Overseas Ports', August 2024, https://www.cfr.org/tracker/china-overseas-ports#chapter-title-0-2

106 Ministry of External Affairs, 'Meeting of Prime Minister with Mr Xi Jinping, President of the People's Republic of China on the margins of the 16th BRICS Summit', 23 October 2024, https://www.mea.gov.in/press-releases.htm?dtl/38457/Meeting+of+Prime+Minister+with+Mr+Xi+Jinping+President+of+the+Peoples+Republic+of+China+on+the+margins+of+the+16th+ BRICS+Summit

107 Ministry of External Affairs, 'Agreement between the Government of the Republic of India and the Government of the People's Republic of China on Confidence-Building Measures in the Military Field along the Line of Actual Control in the India–China Border Areas', CH96B1124PDF (www.mea.gov.in)

108 The US Department of Defence annual report on 'Military and Security Developments Involving the People's Republic of China', 18 December 2024, https://www.defense.gov/News/Publications/?Page=2
The US Department of Defence annual report on 'Military and Security Developments Involving the People's Republic of China', 19 October 2023, https://www.defense.gov/News/Releases/Release/Article/3561549/dod-releases-2023-report-on-military-and-security-developments-involving-the-pe/; The US Department of Defence 2022 Report on 'Military and Security Developments Involving the People's Republic of China', 29 November 2022, https://www.defense.gov/News/Releases/Release/Article/3230516/2022-report-on-military-and-security-developments-involving-the-peoples-republi/

109 Seshadri, V.S., 2024, 'The China Factor in India's Economic Security', Delhi Policy Group, 26 September, https://www.delhipolicygroup.org/publication/policy-briefs/the-china-factor-in-indias-economic-security.html
110 Kantha, A.K., 'Weighing in on business as usual with China', *The Hindu*, 24 September 2024, https://www.thehindu.com/opinion/lead/weighing-in-on-business-as-usual-with-china/article68674839.ece
111 Rhodium Group, China Diversification Framework Report, June 2024, https://www.businessroundtable.org/china-diversification-framework-report
112 Reuters, 'Treasury chief urges Canada, Mexico to match US tariffs on China as deadline looms', 28 February 2025, https://www.ctvnews.ca/world/trumps-tariffs/article/treasury-chief-urges-canada-mexico-to-match-us-tariffs-on-china-as-deadline-looms/
113 MERICS, 'Keeping Value Chains at Home: How China Controls Foreign Access to Technology and What It Means for Europe', 8 August 2024, https://merics.org/en/report/keeping-value-chains-home
114 Bloomberg.com, 'China Asks Its Carmakers to Keep Key EV Technology at Home', 11 September 2024, https://www.bloomberg.com/news/articles/2024-09-12/china-asks-its-carmakers-to-keep-key-ev-technology-at-home
115 Pant, H.V. and K.A. Mankikar, 2024, 'The Fatal Flaw in India's China Strategy: Economic Dependence Will Make New Delhi Forever Vulnerable to Beijing', *Foreign Affairs*, 14 November, https://www.foreignaffairs.com/india/fatal-flaw-indias-china-strategy
116 Press Information Bureau, 'Declaration on Principles for Relations and Comprehensive Cooperation Between the Republic of India and the People's Republic of China', 24 June 2003, https://archive.pib.gov.in/release02/lyr2003/rjun2003/24062003/r2406200318.html
117 Gokhale, V., 'The Next Dalai Lama: Preparing for Reincarnation and Why It Matters to India', *Carnegie India*, November 2024, https://carnegieendowment.org/research/2024/11/the-next-dalai-lama-preparing-for-reincarnation-and-why-it-matters-to-india?lang= en&center=india
118 State Religious Affairs Bureau, 'Management Measures for the Reincarnation of Living Buddhas in Tibetan Buddhism', Order No. Five, Issued on 18 July 2007, https://www.cecc.gov/resources/legal-provisions/measures-on-the-management-of-the-reincarnation-of-living-buddhas-in-0.
119 'Statement of His Holiness the Fourteenth Dalai Lama, Tenzin Gyatso, on the Issue of His Reincarnation', 24 September 2011, https://tibetoffice.org/media-press/featured-news/statement-of-his-holiness-the-fourteenth-dalai-lama-tenzin-gyatso-on-the-issue-of-his-reincarnation
120 Ministry of External Affairs, 'External Affairs Minister's meeting with Member of the Communist Party of China (CPC) Political Bureau and Foreign Minister, H.E. Mr. Wang Yi on the sidelines of G20 Summit', 19 November 2024, available on https://www.mea.gov.in/press-releases.htm?dtl/38543/External_Affairs_Ministers_meeting_with_Member_of_the_Communist_Party_of_China_CPC_Political_Bureau_and_Foreign_Minister_HE_Mr_Wang_Yi_on_the_sideline

121 *Xinhua*, 'Indian FMs Meet on Bilateral Ties', 19 November 2024, available on https://english.news.cn/20241119/69a51054f6a146ab80bd29fc02903c1b/c.html

2

Emerging Trends in China

Arvind Gupta

At the 20th Party Congress of the Communist Party of China (CPC) held in October 2022, Xi Jinping was reaffirmed as the General Secretary of the CPC for the third time. This was in a major departure from the CPC custom of two-term limit on the top posts. In March 2023, the National People Congress elected him as President of People's Republic of China for the third time. This was a mere formality as the decision had been taken much earlier. Xi Jinping is now the president for the foreseeable future. He is also the Chairman of Central Military Commission (CMC). Xi Jinping's 'Thoughts on Socialism with Chinese Characteristic for a New Era' have been incorporated in the constitution of the CPC along with Mao's thoughts, making them part of the reigning CPC ideology which every Party member is obliged to follow. The fourteen-point list outlining Xi's thought seeks to ensure CPC's absolute dominance in all forms of work in China, and ensure CPC's 'absolute leadership' over the People's Liberation Army (PLA). Xi Jinping has been given the status of the 'core leader' of the Central Committee. These developments indicate that he has succeeded in strengthening his position politically, legally and constitutionally. He has emerged as the strongest leader since Mao, enjoying unfettered power over the Party, the military and the state institutions.

Since the 18th Party Congress, Xi Jinping has proceeded in a systematic way to establish his supremacy in the Party and the military. By using anti-corruption campaigns in the Party, military, government organs and State Owned Enterprises (SOEs), he has ruthlessly nullified all possible opposition to him. However, being at the top with untrammelled power is risky. Supremacy can never be taken for granted. He will have to remain ever vigilant in ensuring that no challenger emerges in the future. He now has the onerous task of delivering on the promises he has made. Their non-fulfilment will make him vulnerable.

In the last decade, Xi Jinping has given a definite direction to the Party, military and the country. He has reversed or mitigated the laxity that emerged during the tenures of his predecessor when China opened up to the rest of the world. Xi's key focus has been to strengthen the ideological foundation of the Party and establish its supremacy over all aspects of the country's political, economic, social and cultural life. Since the 18th Party Congress in 2012,

Xi has underlined the goal of turning China into a 'prosperous, democratic, culturally advanced, and harmonious modern socialist country by 2049', which coincides with the centenary of the establishment of People's Republic of China. He has resolutely underlined the guiding principle of 'Socialism with Chinese Characteristic', in which the Party and its 'core' leadership would play the leading role. He has warned against entertaining the 'erroneous views at abandoning socialism'. There has been relentless stress on ideological purity amongst the cadres of the Party. The cadre's loyalty to the Party's ideology and to Xi himself is the main criterion for their survival and advancement. One of the key insights Xi provides to the Party is that the USSR collapsed due to the weakening of the influence of the Communist Party of Soviet Union (CPSU) over the country. CPC cannot afford to go the CPSU way. It must remain in the leadership role in all aspects. It must ensure that socialist principles are followed at all levels. That is the core of Xi's thoughts on socialism for 'new era'. While China still remains open to the rest of the world, Xi Jinping has ensured that such opening up is strictly watched and regulated. In the name of the opening up, ideological purity cannot be compromised. Socialism should not be swept aside due to the influx of foreign ideas. Deviations from Party line and ideology are strictly disallowed and severely dealt with. Modern technology has been extensively used for heightened surveillance and monitoring of Chinese citizens.

Since the 18th Party Congress, Xi Jinping has given several slogans and a broad framework to guide reforms and work of the Party. The notable ones are 'Socialism for a New Era', 'China Dream', 'Beautiful China', 'Peaceful Development', 'Belt and Road Initiative', 'Co-Prosperity', 'Dual Circulation', 'Global Development Initiative', 'Global Security Initiative', 'Global Civilisational Initiative', 'Community of Shared Interests', 'Major country relations', etc. Every day, new slogans emerge. Party functionaries and Politburo members downwards are urged to muster and imbibe these slogans. Xi himself conducts regular 'study sessions' for Politburo members on ideological issues. The Party, the state institutions and their powerful propaganda machines amplify Xi's messages to create awareness about his thinking.

Under Xi, China has jettisoned the Deng's dictum of 'hide your strength, bide your time'. The 18th Party Congress set about the task of achieving a 'moderately prosperous society' by 2020 and realising 'China Dream' of national rejuvenation. Xi declared, 'We will not let any country force China to betray its core interests or undermine our country's sovereignty, security and developmental interests.... China does not covet other countries' rights and interests, nor do we give up our legitimate rights and interests.'[1] China has become far more assertive and aggressive in its behaviour while professing its peaceful intentions. This is evident in the case of South China Sea, East China Sea, Taiwan Straits and India–China border. The South China Sea islands and reefs have been captured and unilaterally made into China's sovereign territories in complete disregard of the international law. China has consciously adopted a vigorous strategy of enhancing its influence across the world. Xi is the author of Belt and Road Initiative, which has been used as a principal instrument for extending China's influence. Chinese diplomats routinely pressurise and intimidate their counterparts. The aggressive style of Chinese diplomacy has been dubbed by observers as 'wolf warrior' diplomacy. To enhance its influence in multilateral institutions, China used money, power and other means to capture positions there.

On the economic front, China's record under Xi has been mixed. Its GDP in 2012 was $8.45 trillion and, in 2022, $17.94 trillion,[2] but the annual growth rate has come down from about 8.8 per cent to about 3 per cent. Nevertheless, China has emerged as the second largest economy in the world, the largest trading nation, a major technological power and it now has the largest military in the world in terms of number of troops, etc. Xi can be credited with some of these achievements. However, the task before Xi would be to sustain reasonably high economic growth in the foreseeable future. This may not be easy. Despite notable achievements, the Chinese economy continues to face structural shortcomings and global uncertainties. During the COVID-19 years, the economic growth dropped sharply. China bears the responsibility of mishandling the COVID-19 outbreak in Wuhan, which resulted in it becoming a global pandemic. China's misplaced Zero-COVID policy also disrupted the global supply chains. While the Chinese economy has begun to recover, the future remains cloudy.

China's future is closely tied with the prospects of the US–China relations. Together, the two countries account for nearly 42 per cent of global GDP (in 2022) in nominal terms. China owes its rise to benign US policies. The US went out of its way to get China into the global mainstream by facilitating its entry into the World Trade Organisation (WTO) in 2001, even though China was not a market economy at the time. Attracted by China's market and its open economic policies, Western companies were encouraged to shift their production lines to China. In the process, China grew at the expense of the US. Within a few years of joining the WTO, China overtook the US as the largest manufacturer of goods and the largest trader. The US industrial ecosystem was hollowed out by its manufacturing shift to China. A similar trend was observed in respect of Europe and Japan. China became the factory of the world.

China's rise has triggered a new power balance, particularly in the Indo-Pacific. The global order is experiencing contradictory tendencies. There is rise in multipolarity but, at the same time, China and the US are the two most powerful countries. They treat each other as strategic rivals. While the US has a well-defined sphere of influence, which has emerged after the Second World

War, China is trying to create its own area of influence. Given their economic interdependence, the strategic rivalry between the US and China is playing out in complex and unpredictable ways.

It is in this backdrop that we discuss the emerging political, economic and security trends in China, particularly after the 20th Party Congress.

The 20th Party Congress

The most important outcome of the 20th Congress (October 2022) was to cement Xi Jinping's status as the unrivalled, unchallenged leader of the Party. The CPC had been following the limit on Party leadership to avoid the formation of a personality cult. On 11 March 2018, the National People Congress amended its Constitution, allowing the president to have unlimited number of terms. The 20th Party Congress has ensured that Xi emerges as a cult figure. In a press conference held by the senior officials of the Central Committee of the CPC, senior officials of the Party gave a briefing on the main outcomes of the 20th CPC National Congress. According to them, the Congress provided a 'political manifesto and a guideline for action to achieve new victories on socialism with Chinese characteristic for a New Era'.[3] The report of the Central Committee to the 20th CPC National Congress provided 'new theoretical innovation', namely, integrating the basic tenets of Marxism with China's reality and traditional culture. China would oppose any country imposing its own development model on China. Utmost focus will be on the 'quality of development, rule of law and self-reform'. Despite the remarkable achievements of the anti-corruption fight over the past decades, the situation still remained 'grave and intricate, and the battle against the corruption is fierce and must be won' and 'anti-corruption momentum' would be sustained.[4] Since the 20th Party Congress, National People Congress (NPC) and the National Committee of Chinese People's Political Consultative Conference (NCCPPCC) held their sessions in March 2023.

In the short period that has elapsed since the 20th Party Congress, one can see a considerable continuity since 2012 as also renewed stress on achieving the 'Centenary goal' by 2049. Speaking at his first session, the 14th National People's Congress on 13 March 2023, Xi Jinping defined the task of the Party to build China into 'a great modern socialist country in all respects and advance national rejuvenation on all fronts'. The focus remains on 'rejuvenation', an all-encompassing term aimed at conveying the tasks ahead. In 2022, the Party officially announced that its goal to overcome poverty, one of its two centenary goals, had been achieved. Now the emphasis was shifting to achieving higher prosperity levels by 2049. In this context, Xi underlined the urgency to 'speed up Chinese modernisation, strive in unity and continue breaking new ground ... on the new journey'.[5] One should expect Xi and the Party to redouble its efforts to implement ideas, plans and projects that have originated since the 18th Party Congress.

All organs of state and parties have kept busy holding meetings and discussions to advance the goal set by the 20th Party Congress. At the 3rd Plenum of the 20th Central Committee (held on 7 November 2023) chaired by Xi Jinping, the focus was on realising 'beautiful China' by 2035, enhancing ecological diversity and sustainability and strengthening control over its monopoly sector. The Standing Committee of Chinese People's Political Consultative Conference (CPPCC) deliberated from 31 October to 2 November 2023 over the 'beautiful China' theme, strategy for promotion of culture through the use of digital technology, in museums, exhibitions and displays, for instance, and establishment of a green energy industry. At the sixth session of the Standing Committee of the 14th National People's Conference on 24 October 2023, Defence Minister Lee Shangfu and Foreign Affairs Minister King Gan were removed from their posts. The Central Financial Work Conference (30–31 October 2023) took up the theme of management of local and central government debts. At the State Councils' fourth study session held on 31 October 2023, the focus was on the creation of an advanced intellectual property section and high-quality industrial intellectual property.

The Party

Absolute control over Party machinery is central to Xi Jinping's strategy. Even in 2012, Xi had highlighted the shortcomings in the Party's work. In the last ten years, Xi has sought to return the Party to its purist ideological moorings and establish its unchallenged supremacy in all spheres, including political, economic, military and social. Xi Jinping has iterated in no uncertain terms that the Party will continue to lead the country in every sphere. That principle will not be compromised. That is the crux of Xi's 'Thoughts', which are now the fundamental doctrine of the Party. No deviation from this doctrine will be tolerated. Xi has the last word on doctrinal issues. Party discipline is to be strictly enforced. The fight against corruption and deviation from socialist principles will continue. The Party will continue to control the military 'absolutely', and the latter would have to work under its guidance at all times.

The goal of Xi's policies remains China's 'rejuvenation' and 'complete reunification'. The independence of Taiwan will not be tolerated. While no date for reunification has been set, the One-China principle is sacrosanct—that is the crux of China's foreign policy.

The Chinese Communist Party and other institutions have got busy in implementing the decision of the 20th Party Congress. The first task is to communicate the philosophy, doctrine, strategy and plans of the Party, internally and externally. The second plenary session of the 20th Central Committee of CPC was held on 28 February 2023. It emphasised that institutional reform must be guided by 'Xi Jinping Thought'. It highlighted the need for 'high-quality development' and 'coordination' amongst the Party's Central Committee, NPC, the State Council and the NCCPPCC. The socialist modernisation would incorporate science and technology, optimisation of resources, creation of appropriate institutional mechanisms and more efficient operation and management. It was emphasised that Party and state institutions should 'deeply understand' the significance of the 'two establishments', 'four consciousness', 'four self-confidences' and 'two safeguards'. These code words basically stand for unflinching loyalty to Xi Jinping Thought and Xi Jinping himself as the 'core leader' of the Party.[6] Emphasis was also placed on study, publicity and implementation of the legislation of the 20th Party congress in all government agencies, enterprises, institutions, urban and rural communities, campuses, military camps and various new economic and social organisations.[7] The Party propaganda machinery has got busy with this job. In the coming months and years, we can expect several new slogans, goals and strategies to be put forward by the Party as the task of national 'rejuvenation' advances.

Military

In the rise of China, military strength has arguably been assigned the most important priority. The logic is that without a strong military, China will be vulnerable to external pressure. Xi has vowed to make PLA into a 'world-class' military and a 'steel wall'.

Recognising the importance of the military in China's growth strategy, Xi, as the Chairman of the CMC, has presided over fundamental restructuring of the military since 2012. The Party's control over the military has been strengthened. The CMC has been reorganised. Defence budget has been enhanced significantly. Resources have been provided for military modernisation, including induction of new technologies. A policy of military–civil fusion have been followed. New theatre commands (TCs) have been established. A PLA rocket force has been created out of the former Second Artillery. The People Armed Police (PAP) looking after internal security has been brought under the CMC. The 18th Party Congress had identified modernisation of the military as a priority task for the 'new era'. Continuing in that direction, the 20th Party Congress talked about 'further modernising national defence and the military'. The aim is to elevate armed forces to a world-class level by 2049 through professionalisation of the armed forces and developing high-quality talent by training and education.[8]

Party–military relationship is a critical area of focus for Chinese leadership. One constant theme running through the modernisation process is upholding the 'absolute leadership of the Party over the military to 'ensure that guns are always grasped by those who are loyal and reliable to the Party'.[9]

An economically strong China has ample resources to devote to military modernisation. China's defence expenditure, at $224.79 billion (as of 2022) is second only to that of the US. New equipment and platforms have been provided to the armed forces. A vast, self-reliant defence industrial infrastructure has been created. Military–Civil Fusion (MCF), an old concept, has been given fresh impetus by Xi Jinping. MCF strategy implies development of dual-use technologies like artificial intelligence, big data analytic, 5G, quantum computing, etc. for civil as well as military purposes. Considerable effort has been made in the last two years to 'informationalise' the PLA.

Since he became the General Secretary of the CPC in 2012, Xi has insisted upon civil-military integration on a number of occasions. In 2017, Xi Jinping set up a Central Commission for Military–Civil Fusion (MCF). In June 2017, he declared, 'we must accelerate the formation of a full-element, multi-domain, and high-return military-civil fusion deep development pattern, and gradually build up China's unified military-civil system of strategies and strategic capability.'[10] The 13th Five Year Plan (2015–2020) contained several references to MCF. The idea is to achieve 'comprehensive, multi-domain, and high-efficiency military-civil technology fusion' to promote the sharing of military and civilian S&T resources.[11] However, the references to MCF have since been dropped for some reason.

There is renewed stress on the borders and maritime security. The military is being given the capability to fight and win wars. China is modernising its strategic arsenal and delivery systems. It has built hypersonic glide vehicles, quantum satellites, a space station, deep sea exploration vehicles, nuclear submarines, warships and fighter aircrafts. Cyber and space have also been integrated into its military war machinery.[12]

China's 2019 defence white paper gives considerable details about the ongoing military reforms and transformation in China.[13] In a fundamental reorganisation of the older PLA structure reform, the command system of the PLA has been reorganised with the aim of 'winning war in the information age'. The CMC exercises overall leadership over the newly established TCs. PLA has established a joint operation command system comprising permanent as well as specialised command establishments for both peacetime and wartime operations. Presently, the Eastern, Southern, Western, Northern and Central TCs are supervised by the CMC under Xi's leadership. In addition, CMC has also established a Discipline Inspection Commission and a Supervision Commission to tighten ideological doctrinal control and the military units. Approximately 300,000 personnel have been reduced to bring the PLA's strength to 2 million troops. The earlier eighteen-group armies have been reorganised into thirteen new ones. The People Armed Police (PAP) has been strengthened and restructured. Given the importance of technology, a CMC Steering Committee has been formed to promote and imbibe military scientific research. The Academy of Military Sciences and various research institutes have also been reorganised. With a view to professionalise the military, several new laws have been enacted to introduce a 'career officers' system. Military welfare and support mechanism have been strengthened. In a notable shift from earlier times, the armed forces have also withdrawn from business activities.[14] The sweeping restructuring measures have covered the PLA Army, Navy, Air Force and the Second Artillery. A new Rocket Force, PLA Strategic Support Force and PLA Joint Logistic Support Force have also been created.[15]

Establishing the Party's political control over the military has been Xi's top priority since 2012. He has been relentless in purging the armed forces to ensure that officers and cadres are loyal to him. Purges within the armed forces have continued even after the 20th Party Congress, which cemented his dominance in the Party and the state. In 2023, well after the Party Congress, China's defence minister, the chief and the deputy chief of the rocket force were sacked without any reason being stated. The foreign minister was also summarily removed. This shows that the system has not settled down even after the 20th Party Congress.[16]

Economy

Chinese leaders are acutely conscious of the challenges and headwinds that the Chinese economy is facing in the aftermath of COVID-19, the Russia–Ukraine war and the US trade and technology restrictions. Economic growth has come down sharply in the last few years. Local administrations have run up huge debts. China's debt-to-GDP ratio (around 300 per cent) is among the highest in the world. Xi's policies have put tremendous pressure on the private sector, and investment in the sector is slowing down.

In a speech delivered on 15 December 2022[17] at the Central Economic Work Conference, Xi Jinping identified the 'major issues in economic work'. The top priority for the country, according to him, is to 'expand domestic demand'. He emphasised that economic development will be led by the public sector while the 'non-public sector' would be provided guidance. He also emphasised the need to upgrade China's industrial system. The 'low return' and lack of 'innovative capability' in the State-Owned Enterprises (SOEs) would be addressed. The SOEs would need to 'balance' their economic and social responsibilities and adopt modern 'corporate governance with distinctive Chinese features' to become 'world class enterprises'. The private sector would not be neglected as it plays an important role in economic and social developments. Property rights of private enterprises would be protected. Fair competition would be created. The government would maintain a 'cordial relationship' with business. Acknowledging that private investment is low, the government plans to increase public investment, while also encouraging private investment by providing wider market access.

For the last four decades, Foreign Direct Investment (FDI) has played a crucial role in the emergence of China as an economic powerhouse. China leveraged its vast market and made itself an attractive destination for FDI. In the process, it also made sure that relatively backward domestic enterprises entered into joint ventures with foreign companies to learn modern methods and imbibe new technologies. Giant Special Economic Zone (SEZs) were set up to attract foreign investors and encourage exports. However, Xi's policies have created doubts in the minds of foreign investors. During the COVID-19 years, foreign companies contemplated 'decoupling' from China. China, however, remains important for foreign investors as its economy begins to recover. The talk of decoupling has now been replaced by 'de-risking'. Xi Jinping has emphasised the need 'not only to retain existing high quality foreign investments but also attract more' by expanding market access and improving business environment.

High local government debt, weak financial system and a speculative real estate sector pose major risk to Chinese economy. In 2021, China's second largest real estate company Evergrande had accumulated a debt of $305 billion. It came under financial stress due to the 2020 policies to control the debt level of major property developers. It needed limited financial support to survive. Several other real estate companies are in deep financial stress as well.[18] Xi has warned against speculation and rising debts, and has spoken about transitioning to a 'new model of development for the real estate sector'. He emphasised the need to guard against 'systemic risks and moral hazards', calling for reform in the financial system. In this regard, he has also called for 'resolute supervision' of local government debt and steps to curb the increase of new debt. He also underlined the need to improve the local taxation system and provide local governments with basic financial resources.

Regional disparities in China are glaring. Xi has consistently pointed out that the growing rich–poor divide has deepened, threatening social stability. The Party has emphasised 'co-prosperity', which implies regulation of high wealth generators and crackdown on illegal earning and redistribution of income through taxation measures. The government has broken up several private sector companies to promote co-prosperity and enhanced Party control over the private sector. This has led to fear in and weakening of the private sector. Breaking up the major companies has less to do with economic principles and more to do with ensuring that they do not acquire autonomy over the Party-state system.

Amidst the prospect of economic slowdown, China has started the preparations for its 15th Five Year Plan (2026–2030). The National Development Reform Commission of China, the body responsible for economic planning, held its meeting on 19 December 2023, where it considered the main themes for the next five-year plan. Steady growth of the private economy, stability of foreign trade and foreign investment, growth of digital economy, achieving carbon neutrality, clean energy and promoting a circular economy are high on the agenda of the economic planners.[19]

Culture

Traditionally, Communists look down upon culture as backward and anti-socialist. Civilisation, traditions and religion have been considered as taboo. The central revolution of the 1960s and 1970s was aimed at demolishing the vestiges of Chinese culture and establishing Communism firmly in the country. However, Xi is changing that narrative. China is rediscovering its culture, albeit in a selective manner. In the building of a prosperous socialist society in China, culture will play an important role. Xi Jinping has time and again emphasised the need for inculcating pride in China's culture and its civilisational achievements. He is using culture in his discourse to promote Chinese nationalism and patriotism, and for projecting a benign image of the country. He regularly visits archaeological sites, museums, art galleries and other cultural centres and interacts with artists, academics, experts and professionals in the sphere. His refrain has been that China's long history and culture must be studied carefully. Studying the past will help China build its future. The government has launched an all-encompassing 'China's Civilisational Project' to give a boost to research into China's history, culture and civilisation. The effort is to project China as a continuous civilisation where different ethnicities have always lived in harmony and peace. This is to blunt the criticism about China's treatment of its minorities, like the Uyghurs and Tibetans. Chinese civilisation's contribution to global well-being is regularly highlighted.

Xi has identified five prominent features of Chinese civilisation: 'consistency', 'originality', 'uniformity', 'inclusivity' and 'peaceful nature'. Consistency implies that Chinese people would follow their 'own path' and originality refers to the 'enterprising' spirit of the Chinese people. Uniformity means that the various ethnicities of China are integrated and have lived together even during times of crisis. 'Inclusivity' shows 'harmonious co-existence of diverse religious belief in China and open mindedness towards other civilisations'. Overall, the narrative is that Chinese civilisation has been peaceful in the internal as well as external domains. The emphasis on culture and soft power has a political purpose to portray China's rise as peaceful, benign and helpful towards the rest of the world. The idea is to develop a new theory of culture in accordance with Marxist principles. Xi calls it a 'New Cultural Mission'.[20]

In all this, Xi has been careful to emphasise that 'Socialism with Chinese Characteristics in the New Era' will remain the guiding principle for Party work and policies. There would be no compromise on socialist principles. The Party's thought is that China's civilisation and culture do not contradict Marxism in any way. It is necessary to 'Sinicise' Marxism by integrating it into China's history and culture. The strong emphasis on culture is one of the most important initiatives of Xi Jinping.

Technology

Chinese leaders have well understood that self-reliance in technology is indispensable to China's rise and managing competition with the West. Under President Xi, a great deal of importance has been placed on increasing expenditure on research and development (R&D), STEM education, intellectual property rights, building strengths in critical emerging technology, creating a digital economy and embedding it into the real economy. Huge resources are being spent on basic and applied research and training and capacity building. China is trying its best to reduce its dependence on the Western companies in so far as high technologies is concerned. In 2022, China spent about $443 billion – 2.55 per cent of its GDP – on R&D. This brought China to the twelfth place globally, ahead of France.[21] On fundamental research, China spent about 195.1 billion Yuan (about $27 billion).[22] It is also building global Chinese companies in the high-tech areas. It has achieved some notable successes in this regard, particularly in 5G communication, deep sea exploration, quantum computing and artificial intelligence.

China is giving special impetus to the development of digital economy, embedding it into the real economy, developing digital industry in key areas and building world-class industry infrastructure. Addressing the thirty-fourth group study session of the Politburo of the 19th CPC Central Committee on 18 October 2021, Xi underlined the importance of developing appropriate mechanisms for ensuring security and control of key infrastructure, strategic resources, major science and tech project and leading enterprises. He emphasised the need for strengthening theoretical research in the digital economy as well.[23] New technologies are to be developed while keeping in mind 'the larger strategic picture of national rejuvenation and the once-in-a-century changes occurring in the world'. China would upgrade the traditional industry, foster new industry, new business forms and new business models to build up the strength, quality and size of China's digital economy,[24] he said.

China's Worldview and Its Foreign Policy

China's rise as a global power is unmistakable. The Chinese do not hide their ambition for the same, thereby challenging the US hegemony. China's foreign policy is geared to support the strategic goal of realising its dream. Its efforts are directed at ensuring that its rise is not contained by any power.

After the 18th Party Congress, Xi Jinping devoted considerable attention to developing new concepts for China's foreign policy and diplomacy. The assessment at that time was that the world was becoming multipolar, economic globalisation was deepening and the opportunities for collaboration were increasing. While China would safeguard its core interests, its development would be peaceful and its rise would be beneficial for the whole world. At the 19th Party Congress, Xi made the assessment that although China's future was 'bright', the challenges were also 'serious'. 'All comrades must aim high and look far, be alert to the danger even in the times of calm, have the courage to pursue reform and break new ground,' he said.[25] Speaking at the 20th Party Congress, Xi described China as changing 'like never before' and having reached 'a crossroads in history'. While he envisaged the long-term trend as that of 'peace, development, cooperation and mutual benefits', at the same time, he came down heavily against 'all forms of hegemonies and power politics, the Cold War mentality, interference in other country and double standards'. But China will 'never seek hegemony or engage in expansionism'.[26] In the last decade, China's confidence in its future has grown but so has the perception that the challenges are also becoming complex.

There is greater focus on shaping the global environment through a variety of initiatives and instruments. At the 20th Party Congress, Xi outlined the key trends of China's foreign policy. He spoke of China building 'major countries relations featuring peaceful coexistence, overall stability' and promised to pursue the policy of 'opening to the outside world', and 'building an open global economy'. China would promote trade and investment liberalisation, and create 'new drivers for global growth'. It would also safeguard the 'international system with the United Nation at its core', and strengthen the WTO, Asia Pacific Economic Cooperation (APEC), BRICS and Shanghai Cooperation Organization (SCO). It would pursue the cause of common good. Xi's ideas are captured in his latest initiatives, 'Global Development Initiative' (GDI), 'Global Security Initiative' (GSI) and 'Global Civilisation Initiative' (GCI).[27]

Between 2012 and 2022, Xi unveiled several proposals with far-reaching implications. Outlining the main principle of China's foreign policy at the Central Conference on Foreign Affairs on 28 November 2014, Xi said China should explain to the international community the 'global implication and impact of Chinese Dream'.[28] He declared that China had broken 'new ground' in 'diplomatic theory and practice' and developed 'a distinctive diplomatic approach befitting its role as a major country'.[29] He said that China had advocated 'a new model of international relations' based on 'shared interests' and 'common, comprehensive, cooperative and sustainable security'.[30] He outlined the contours of a 'new model of major country relations' and the neighbourhood policy, based on 'amity, good faith, mutual benefit and inclusiveness'.³¹ He warned his colleagues that they should be aware of the 'protracted nature of contest over the international order'. While China's neighbourhood environment was uncertain, he also assessed that 'the general trend of prosperity and stability in the Asia Pacific region will not change'.³² He had developed these ideas during his numerous visits, meeting and interactions to the other nations in the region.³³

The 'Belt and Road Initiative' (BRI), formerly known as 'One Belt One Road', is Xi Jinping's flagship project which has now extended to most parts of the world. He proposed building the Silk Road Economic Belt in Kazakhstan in the fall of 2013 and the 21st-century Maritime Silk Road in Indonesia. The two proposals are collectively known as the Belt and Road Initiative. Conceived as a $1 trillion mega connectivity project, the BRI has served in the recent years as a major platform for extending China's influence. In 2016, Xi Jinping declared that more than 100 countries and international organisations had joined the initiative.³⁴ China also took the lead in setting up the Asian Infrastructure Investment Bank (AIIB), a Silk Road Fund to promote the BRI. With time, the scope of the BRI was expanded beyond infrastructure and hard connectivity to include trade and investment, innovation and cultural connectivity.

Undaunted by the fact that several countries have fallen into debt traps due to the debt-driven financing model of BRI, China is expanding its scope. The third Belt and Road Forum for international cooperation was held in Beijing on 17 October 2023, in which Xi recounted ten years of BRI's achievements and outlined its future direction. According to the data given by him, more than 150 countries and thirty international organisations have signed onto the BRI. It has gone beyond physical connectivity to include institutional connectivity. Twenty multilateral cooperation platforms are functioning under it. Announcing eight major steps in support of cooperation under the BRI, Xi promised that China Development Bank and Export-Import Bank of China will each establish a RMB 350 billion financing window. An additional RMB 80 billion will be provided to Silk Road Fund. Multilateral cooperation platforms covering energy, taxation, finance, green development, disaster reduction, think tank cooperation, media, culture and several other fields will be set up.³⁵

In the last one year, the BRI has also been supplemented with the GDI, GSI and GCI, as mentioned before. The GDI was launched in 2021, with fifty cooperation projects in its ambit. According to an official statement, more than ten of these projects have been completed. These projects are focused on the needs of developing countries and help them in realising the 2030 sustainable development goal.³⁶

The Global Security Initiative, unveiled in February 2023, has been designed to establish China's stakes in global security challenges. This is in keeping with China's rising ambition to become a global power. A concept paper issued in this regard talked about 'multiple risks' and 'deficits' in peace, development, security and governance the world was facing.[37] Much of the concept note was a rehash of what Xi Jinping has been stating all along concerning respect for values of non-interference, multilateral system with UN at its core, respect for sovereignty and territorial integrity, etc. It talked about resolution of conflicts through consultations and dialogues, and warns against unilateral sanctions. It urges a holistic approach to traditional and non-traditional security issues involving 'extensive consultations, joint contributions and shared benefits in global governance'. There are specific references to regional situations in different parts of the world and also to global issues like climate change, information security, space security, nuclear disarmament, food security, etc. Chinese leaders have begun to promote GSI at all fora. China put forward a twelve-point programme for the resolution of Russia–Ukraine conflict and also brokered the Saudi Arabia–Iran reconciliation. At a high-profile international conference organised by President Macron of France in Paris in June 2023, China made certain proposals aimed at stabilising the international financial system and meeting the financial needs of developing countries. It has also made proposals on digital governance, health, climate change, the environment, etc. All this has given China considerable profile and publicity. Essentially, China is positioning itself as a stakeholder in global governance, multilateralism and global and regional security issues.[38]

China's rise and its assertiveness, however, has attracted strong backlash. Realising the harm done to the US, President Trump launched major trade and technological war against China to protect its industrial and technological competitiveness. President Biden continued with restrictive policies and tightened measures to prevent China's access to the US high-end semiconductor and chips. Trade and tech competition between the US and China will be a determining factor for the future of global trade. The US National Security Strategy has described China as a strategic rival. China on its part has condemned the US for trying to 'contain' it. The relations between the two are fraught and dangerously poised.

To China's discomfort, the Quad of the US, India, Japan and Australia has been revived. Initially, China dismissed it as being of no consequence. However, the Quad has evolved over the years into a formidable grouping. China now sees it as an instrument designed by the US to contain and curb it. A new military grouping (AUKUS) was formed in September 2021 by Australia, the UK and the US to build nuclear submarines. Several European countries have formulated individual Indo-Pacific strategies. China is alarmed at the growing engagement of North Atlantic Treaty Organization (NATO) in the Indo-Pacific. Japan and South Korea have attended NATO meetings, and it is even opening an office in Japan. These developments have led to heightened tensions in the Taiwan Straits.

China is acutely aware that its emergence can be thwarted. It has reacted sharply to what it sees as the US's containment efforts. Following the US Speaker Nancy Pelosi's visit to Taiwan in 2022, China has intensified its military manoeuvres in the Taiwan Straits manifold to pressurise Taiwan. China's relations with Japan and Australia have deteriorated sharply as well. Japan has increased its defence budget. China has also acted by strengthening its grip over Association of Southeast Asian Nations (ASEAN), developing strategic partnerships with Russia, challenging India on the borders and increasing its influence in South Asia, the Middle East and the Pacific. It played a role in bringing together Iran and Saudi Arabia. It has increased its influence in Europe by forming a seventeen-plus grouping. China also took steps to build and strengthen its high technology base within the country. Xi Jinping has devoted huge attention to the strengthening of the military, and China has directed its efforts to position itself as a global power capable of challenging the Western hegemony.

In Chinese assessment, the US is bent upon containing its and preventing its rise. China is preparing itself to meet the long-term challenges posed by the US by building up its economy, technology, military and influence. The Indo-Pacific is emerging as a battleground for US–China competition. The Chinese are also studying the progress of Russia–Ukraine war and its global impact. The war has pushed Russia into China's corner, to its advantage, and China is sure to take advantage of the new power equations. It is concerned that the coming together of the US, Japan, India and Australia could prove to be a big obstacle in China's rise. China is deeply concerned about the developments in Taiwan and the growing US presence there as well as in the South China Sea and other areas. China is adopting a variety of strategies, including increasing its diplomatic heft in Eurasia, the Middle East, Pacific Islands, Africa and Latin America. It is also working proactively in international organisations to negate the West's influence and win new friends.

Although Chinese leaders claim that they are not interested in exporting the Chinese system or model of development to any country, the fact remains that China is building its own sphere of influence. Despite its pious declaration, China's hegemonic tendencies are all too visible. The Russia–Ukraine war has provided China with an opportunity for it as well. Having fallen out with the West, Russia is pivoting towards the East and has developed a strategic dependence on China. The Russia–Ukraine war has aggravated China's differences with Europe as well. At the same time, despite the talk of China-plus-one and other strategies, Europe and the US have not been able to significantly dilute their economic connections with it. Faced with the US sanctions, China is positioning itself as a champion of free trade.

China's rise cannot be taken for granted. It will have to contend with its strategic rivalry with the US. Although the US itself is beset with lots of problems internally and externally, its political, military, economic, scientific and technological heft remains considerable. The Chinese and the US economy are still intertwined and likely to remain so in the future, despite the deepening of their strategic rivalry. Both sides realise that they will have to manage the tense relationship while ensuring that they do not get involved in a major military conflict. The President Joe Biden–Premier Xi Jinping meeting in San Francisco on 15 November 2023 was aimed at chalking out a framework to manage their relations in view of this. The Chinese readout of the meeting was interesting. According to the Chinese foreign office statement, President Xi told President Biden that 'turning their back on each other is not an option … conflict and confrontation has unbearable consequences for both sides … The world is big enough to accommodate both countries, and one country's success is an opportunity for the other.'[39] According to the US readout of the meeting, President Biden said that while the US would always stand up for its interests, its values and its allies and partners, there was a need for both the US and China to 'manage competition responsibly to prevent it from veering into conflict, confrontation, or a new Cold War'.[40]

Conclusion

Following the 20th Party Congress, leaders' attention will be on achieving the centenary goal of making China a developed country. The following trends need to be highlighted:

- **Authoritarianism is on the rise in China:** Xi has emerged as the strongest Chinese leader since Mao. His authority is unchallenged at the moment. This trend will continue and strengthen under Xi; however, he will have to remain alert and vigilant. Anti-corruption campaigns are likely to continue under Xi to weed out any dissent and future challengers. Mindful of the complexities of governance, he is taking personal interest in ensuring that the Party cadre at all levels remain loyal to him and his thinking. He is putting in a lot of emphasis on socialist ideology and 'Xi Jinping's Thought'.
- **Difficulties lie ahead for the Chinese economy:** The Chinese economic miracle of the last forty years is losing steam. Export-led growth dependent upon foreign investment may not work anymore due to the hyper-globalisation trends in the global economy; China will have to find new triggers of growth. Sustaining high economic growth for longer periods will be a challenge. Regional disparity and income inequalities have also become acute. There are signs of social discontent caused by lack of equity and skewed development. The per capita income in China is still low by developed-country standards. Addressing socio-economic problems in

an authoritarian setting will be a major issue for the Party. Initiatives like 'co-prosperity' are bound to scare the private sector, which accounts for over half of China's GDP.
- **Worsening international environment:** The international environment has changed dramatically, and long-term rivalries are re-emerging. China recognises the risks of this, but still sees this as a period of opportunities for itself and a 'bright' future ahead. While economic interdependence mitigates strategic competition to some extent, China will have to prepare itself for a long-term, multipronged confrontation with the US. A military conflict would not be in China's interest, but it is readying a world-class military, equipped and capable of fighting and winning wars. Whether it can do so is still a question that remains to be answered at this stage.
- **As trade and technology wars intensify, China would not hesitate to use its dominance in critical material supply chains:** Most countries are dependent upon China for importing solar panels and other vital material needed for transition to clean energy. China is paying a great deal of attention to building its scientific and technological capabilities. It is trying to catch up with the US in high-tech areas with some success. It is building a large number of scientific and technological (S&T) institutions and training skilled manpower to sustain its S&T growth. It has had some success in building civil-military technologies. Military cadres are being encouraged to become familiar with modern science and technology.
- **Leveraging culture and civilisation to project itself as a benign power:** 'Wolf warrior' diplomacy, the treatment of Uyghur and Tibetan minorities, occupation of South China Sea islands, the use of BRI created to trap unsuspecting countries into unviable projects, etc. have tarnished the global image of China. A great deal of effort is being made by China to improve and project a benign image. Yet, its assertiveness and aggression is there for all to see. China's diplomacy is geared towards increasing its global and regional influence. These trends are likely to intensify in the future under Xi. In India's neighbourhood, China has followed a systematic policy of enhancing its influence through the BRI and specific initiatives. Much of China's South Asia policy has a consequence for India. China is approaching India's neighbours in the framework of common and shared future through 'thick and thin'.
- **The Chinese system is brittle:** Having concentrated most powers in his own hands, Xi Jinping is in an unassailable position. But that is also his weakness. Under his watch, China has taken a turn towards greater authoritarians. This will make the society brittle. A black swan event or a misstep, a costly involvement in an unproductive conflict or further worsening of the international environment can deliver a huge shock to the country.

Xi is putting in place the policies and strategies aimed at ensuring China's rise as a major economic, military and technological power rivalling the US. China's rise and Russia's weaknesses have fundamentally altered the balance of power in the world. The next ten years are critical to China's trajectory. The world will be closely watching Xi's policies and how they are implemented.

Notes

1. Xi Jinping, *The Governance of China*, Vol. II (Beijing: Foreign Language Press, 2017), 43.
2. 'China's Provincial GDP Figures in 2012', China Briefing, 16 May 2013, available at: https://www.china-briefing.com/news/chinas-provincial-gdp-figures-in-2012/; 'China's GDP Sinks To 3% In 2022, Second Lowest In 50 Years', *Outlook*, 17 January 2023, https://www.outlookindia.com/business/china-s-gdp-sinks-to-3-in-2022-second-lowest-in-50-years-news-254289#:~:text=here%20on%20Tuesday.-,The%20annual%20GDP%20of%20China%20totalled%202-1.02%20trillion%20yuan%20(%24,of%20Statistics%20(NBS)%20said.
3. 'China Focus: Senior Officials Explain Key Report at Party Congress', Xinhua, 25 October 2022, https://english.news.cn/20221025/bf8734c11d01456c9c884925a4aab204/c.html
4. Ibid.
5. 'Full Text of Xi Jinping's Speech at the First Session of 14th NPC', Xinhua, 15 March 2023, http://english.scio.gov.cn/m/topnews/2023-03/15/content_85168965.htm.
6. 'Resolution on the Major Achievements and Historical Experience of the Party over the Past Century', Wikiwand, https://www.wikiwand.com/en/Resolution_of_the_CPC_Central_Committee_on_the_Major_Achievements_and_Historical_Experience_of_the_Party_over_the_Past_Century.
   According to the CPC historical resolution (8–11 November 2021), the Two Establishes are:
   (i) 'To establish the status of Comrade Xi Jinping as the core of the Party's Central Committee and of the whole Party'
   (ii) 'To establish the guiding role of Xi Jinping Thought on Socialism with Chinese Characteristics for the New Era'
   This document was the third of its kind after 'historical resolutions' adopted by Mao Zedong and Deng Xiaoping, with the document declaring that CPC General Secretary Xi Jinping's leadership was 'the key to the great rejuvenation of the Chinese nation'.
   Four consciousness imply staunch loyalty to 'the Communist Party of China (CPC) Central Committee, [its] General Secretary Xi Jinping as well as to Party theories, guidelines, principles and policies,' according to a recent commentary published by *Qiushi Journal*, the flagship magazine of the CPC Central Committee. 'China champions "four consciousnesses," conforming with Xi', en.people.cn, 3 March 2016. Available at: https://en.people.cn/n3/2016/0303/c90000-9024163.html.

According to the Sixth Plenum of the 19th Central Committee of the CPC, the Two Safeguards are: [1] 'Safeguard the "core" status of General Secretary Xi Jinping within the CPC' [2] 'To safeguard the centralized authority of the Party'. During the 20th National Congress of the CPC, the Two Safeguards were added to the CPC Constitution. See: 'Two Establishes and Two Upholds', Wikipedia. https://en.wikipedia.org/wiki/Two_Establishes_and_Two_Safeguards.

In 2017, the 19th CPC National Congress added the Four Confidences to the Party's Constitution, inserting 'firm confidence in its path, theory, system, and culture', along with other doctrines proposed by Xi Jinping. The doctrine was first discussed at the 18th Party Congress held in November 2012 in a speech by then Party General Secretary Hu Jintao. Four Confidences, Wikipedia. https://en.wikipedia.org/wiki/Confidence_doctrine.

7 'Communique of Second Plenary Session of 20th Central Committee of the Communist Party of China', Xinhua, 1 March 2023., https://english.news.cn/20230301/049a55576b884e5687f9f127da078ae5/c.html.

8 Ibid.

9 Speaking at a study session of Politburo of the CPC central committee on 30 July 2022, Xi stressed that cultivating a new type of 'high quality and professional military personnel' is critical for building a world class military. Xi has repeatedly underlined the importance of study of high-end military technologies by the military personnel. In this context, the Chinese military's training and teaching institutions have been reformed. 'Xi: Build world class military', http://eng.chinamil.com.cn/SpecialReport/2023/T/244583/16207073.html.

10 Quoted in Maj Gen P.K. Mallick, VSM (Retd), 'Military Civil Fusion in China', Vivekananda International Foundation, 1 August 2022. Available at: https://www.vifindia.org/article/2022/august/01/military-civil-fusion-in-china.

11 Ibid.

12 Ibid. Op cit 9.

13 'Full Text: China's National Defense in the New Era', The State Council, The People's Republic of China, 24 July 2019. Available at: https://english.www.gov.cn/archive/whitepaper/201907/24/content_WS5d3941ddc6d08408f502283d.html.

14 Ibid.

15 'Full Text: China's National Defense in the New Era 'Xinhua, 24 July 2019. Available at: https://english.www.gov.cn/archive/whitepaper/201907/24/content_WS5d3941ddc6d08408f502283d.html. PLA Army (PLAA) has five territorial army commands, the Xinjiang Military Command and the Tibet military command. PLAA is transitioning to trans-theatre operations. PLA Navy (PLAN) has been expanded greatly. It has been restructured into Eastern Theatre Command (ETC) Navy (Donghai Fleet), the Southern Theatre Command (STC) Navy (Nanhai Fleet), Northern Theatre Command NTC Fleet (Beihai Fleet) and the PLAN Marine Corps. Theatre Commands of the Navy have acquired naval bases, submarines, surface ships, aviation brigades. PLAN is undertaking operations in the near as well as far sea while improving strategic deterrence and counter attacks, maritime manoeuvre operations, maritime joint operations, etc. PLA Air Force (PLAAF) also has five Theatre Commands and one Airborne Corps. It is acquiring

capability for strategic early warning, air strike, air and missile defence, information countermeasure, etc.

The former Second Artillery of the PLA has been reorganised into PLA Rocket Force (PLARF). It comprises of nuclear, conventional missile and support system. It is acquiring nuclear deterrence and counterattack capabilities. PLA Strategic Support Force (PLASSF) is a new combat force in-charge of providing support in battle field environment, information, communication and new technologies. PLA Joint Logistic Support Force (PLAJLSF) has been set up to provide logistic support to other forces in inventory and warehouse, medical services, transport, oil pipelines areas, etc. It has five joint logistic support centres spread across the contrary.

People's Armed Police (PAP) is responsible for internal security. While it is not a part of the PLA, it reports to the CMC and is responsible for border defence as well. The Chinese coast guard has been transferred from State Oceanic Administration to the PAP. PAP is enhancing its capabilities in emergency response, counterterrorism, maritime rights protection, disaster relief etc. PAO is extensively used in South China Sea, East China Sea where China claim Islands, riff reefs and rocks. Cutting edge technologies are being introduced in the military in a big way. For instance, Tianhe-2 super computer is used to plan military strategy and give information support to defence forces. China has taken a lead in developing the military applications of artificial intelligence, quantum computing and other emerging technologies.

16. George Wright, 'Li Shangfu: Chinese defence minister sacked', BBC, 24 October 2023. Available at: https://www.bbc.com/news/world-asia-china-67207353.
17. 'Major Issues in Economic Work', Xi Jinping's speech at the Central Economic Work Conference, 15 December 2022, *Qiushi Journal*, Chinese edition, No. 4, 2023.
18. In August 2023, Evergrande filed for bankruptcy protection in the US. China's biggest developer Country Garden defaulted in October 2023 on repayment of dollar-denominated bonds. The IMF has warned that the turmoil in the property sector could spread to the financial sector and local governments. See: Ralph Jennings, 'China's real estate, debt crises prompt IMF warning of widening economic damage', *South China Morning Post*, 10 October 2023. Available at: https://www.scmp.com/economy/china-economy/article/3237417/chinas-real-estate-debt-crises-prompt-imf-warning-widening-economic-damage.
19. 'China's top economic planner begins preliminary study of 15th Five-Year Plan', *People's Daily*, 19 December 2023. Available at: http://en.people.cn/n3/2023/1219/c90000-20111917.html.
20. 'Xi calls for more efforts to shoulder new cultural mission in congratulatory letter to forum on building up nation's cultural strength', *Global Times*, 8 June 2023, Available at: https://www.globaltimes.cn/page/202306/1292132.shtml.
21. 'Spending on R&D in China Hits New High', *China Daily*, 21 January 2023. Available at: http://english.www.gov.cn/archive/statistics/202301/21/content_WS63cb3422c6d0a757729e5fl3.html.

22 'Sci-tech advancement to benefit Chinese people, whole world', Xinhua, 31 May 2023.
23 Xi Jinping, 'Heightening Historical Consciousness and Strengthening Confidence in Chinese Culture Through the Study of the History of Chinese Civilisation'. This speech was delivered at the thirty-ninth group study session of the Politburo of the 19th CPCCC on 27 May 2022 and was published in *Qiushi Journal*, Chinese edition, No. 14, 2022. The English translation was carried in the English edition of *Qiushi Journal* updated on 25 October 2022.
24 Ibid.
25 Xi Jinping, 'Secure a Decisive Victory in Building a Moderately Prosperous Society in All Respects and Strive for the Great Success of Socialism with Chinese Characteristics for a New Era', report delivered at the 19th National Congress of the Communist Party of China, 18 October 2017. Available at: http://www.xinhuanet.com/english/download/Xi_Jinping's_report_at_19th_CPC_National_Congress.pdf.
26 'Report to the 20th National Congress of the Communist Party of China', Ministry of Foreign Affairs of the People's Republic of China, 16 October 2022. Available at: https://www.fmprc.gov.cn/eng/zxxx_662805/202210/t20221025_10791908.html.
27 Ibid.
28 Ibid., Op cit 1, p. 479.
29 Ibid., Op cit 1, p. 479.
30 Ibid., Op cit 1, p. 480.
31 Ibid., Op cit 1, p. 480.
32 Ibid., Op cit 1, p. 480.
33 Ibid., Op cit 1, p. 273. Speaking at the third group study session of the Politburo of CPC Central Committee, Xi Jinping said that while China would pursue peaceful development, 'no foreign country should expect China to trade off its core interests or swallow bitter fruit that undermine China's sovereignty, security or development interests'. He advised the UN of developing 'clear-cut criteria of right and wrong so as to advance the fight against terrorism in all form.' (p. 275).
    In a speech delivered at the Moscow State Institute of International Relations on 23 March 2013, Xi Jinping declared that China and Russia 'should live in everlasting amity and never be enemies … stand tall and look far' (p. 302). He declared that China and Russia will 'forever be good neighbour, good friends and good partners' (p. 302).
    In a meeting with the US President Barack Obama on 7 June 2013, Xi Jinping spoke about the Chinese Dream of 'peace, development, cooperation and mutual benefit' and proposed a 'new model of major country's relationship between China and the US' emphasising that the two sides should expand cooperation and control dispute (p. 308).
    In April 2014, speaking at the college of Europe in Bruges, Belgium, he emphasised the need for building the 'China-EU Comprehensive Strategic Partnership' of global significance (p. 309). Speaking at Nazarbayev University, Astana on 7 September 2013, Xi Jinping proposed the idea of building Silk Road Economic belt. In October, he proposed to the ASEAN nations that a twenty-first-century Maritime

Silk Road be built (p. 320). He also proposed 'diplomacy with neighbouring countries characterised by friendship, sincerity, reciprocity and inclusiveness' (p. 325).

In a speech at the Julius Nyerere International Convention Centre, Dar es Salaam, Tanzania, he promised assistance to Africa 'with no political string attached', announcing more investment and finances. He also visited Latin America and promised to launch the forum of Latin America and the Caribbean Cooperation. In the other states, he promised to promote the Silk Road spirit and spoke about 'One Belt One Road' or Silk Road Economic Belt and the Maritime Silk Road of the 21st century (p. 348).

34 Ibid., p. 550.
35 'Chair's Statement of the Third Belt and Road Forum for International Cooperation', Beijing, 18 October 2023. Available at: https://www.mfa.gov.cn/eng/zxxx_662805/202310/t20231020_11164505.html.
36 'China-initiated GDI seeing sound implementation: Report', Xinhua, 21 June 2023. Available at: http://en.qstheory.cn/2023-06/21/c_896672.htm.
37 'The Global Security Initiative Concept Paper', Xinhua, 21 February 2023. Available at: https://english.news.cn/20230221/75375646823e4060832c760e00a1ec19/c.html.
38 Ibid.
39 President Xi Jinping Meets with the US President Joe Biden, Ministry of Foreign Affairs of the People's Republic of China, 16 November 2023. Available at: https://www.fmprc.gov.cn/mfa_eng/zxxx_662805/202311/t20231116_11181442.html. The two sides have agreed on a series of steps to start their dialogues on a number of strategic issues.
40 According to a White House statement issued after the meeting, the two sides have agreed to continue with 'high-level diplomacy and interactions ... in key areas, including on commercial, economic, financial, Asia-Pacific, arms control and non-proliferation, maritime, export control enforcement, policy-planning, agriculture, and disability issues.' Available at: https://www.whitehouse.gov/briefing-room/statements-releases/2023/11/15/readout-of-president-joe-bidens-meeting-with-president-xi-jinping-of-the-peoples-republic-of-china-2/#:~:text=He%20stressed%20that%20the%20United,or%20a%20new%20Cold%20War.

Part Two

Decoding China's Strategic Ambitions

3

Russia and China in the Post-Cold-War World

P.S. Raghavan

In May 2024, Russian President Vladimir Putin made a state visit to China. It was his first foreign visit after his inauguration for a fifth presidential term. In March 2023, China's President Xi Jinping had also chose Russia for his first foreign visit after his re-election.

In their joint media appearance in 2024, the two leaders reiterated their mutual support for the core interests of their countries. Xi called for a political resolution of the Ukraine crisis, that would aid in shaping a 'new balanced, effective and sustainable European security architecture'. Putin, in turn, stressed the need for a 'reliable and appropriate security architecture in the Asia-Pacific Region, without 'harmful' and 'counterproductive' closed military–political alliances (with reference to Quad and AUKUS). Xi also declared that the bilateral relationship promoted 'emergence of a multipolar world and economic globalisation based on genuine multilateralism', and brought a win-win approach to a new architecture of mutually beneficial cooperation, strengthening cooperation in trade, research, technology, manufacturing and supply chain management.[1]

Their joint statement declared that bilateral relations had reached the highest level in history, transcending the military–political alliance model of the Cold War.[2]

The clear public message conveyed by the visit, the statements and documents was of a continued robust relationship between the two countries, with no daylight between their respective assessments of global geopolitical challenges. In the backdrop of western warnings about China 'back-filling' economic sanctions on Russia, the joint statement does not shrink from hailing the 'steadily advancing' defence cooperation and the upsurge in trade and energy cooperation. The bilateral trade turnover surged to US$240 billion in 2023, making Russia China's fourth largest trade partner.

A Chequered Inheritance

Over the centuries, Russia–China relationship has seen indifference, accommodation, bonhomie and turbulence, before arriving at the harmony that recent statements project.

Until the 17th century, the two countries were separated by nomadic groups which populated Siberia. In the mid-17th century, Russian settlers moved towards the Amur River and came up against Chinese opposition, which pushed them back. After a few decades of skirmishes, they agreed on a line of division, formalised by the Treaty of Nerchinsk in 1689. However, creeping Russian advances beyond this line continued, moving up to the Amur River and beyond. In the mid-19th century, when China was bogged down in domestic problems and weakened by wars with Britain and France, Russia forced the beleaguered Chinese government to accept a new border on the Amur, established by the Treaty of Aigun, in 1858. Russia went on to annex land up to the Pacific coastline, where a naval base was set up in Vladivostok. This annexation was formalised by the Treaty of Peking in 1860. These 'unequal treaties', which resulted in China ceding over 900,000 square kilometres of resource-rich territory, have not been forgotten by the Chinese: they have caused friction between the two countries in the later years.

Relations remained fraught for decades thereafter, with military skirmishes and cross-border interference – including in the Xinjiang region of China, where Soviet agencies tried to spread anti-China sentiments among the Uyghur population.

The emergence of the People's Republic of China (PRC) in 1949, under the Communist Party of China, ushered in a decade-long period of cordiality with the communist leadership of the Soviet Union. In the 1950s, USSR extended extensive assistance to China to bolster its industrial and defence capabilities. But this bonhomie was short-lived. Mao Zedong's personality clashes and ideological differences with Soviet leaders resulted in a deterioration in relations, resurfacing of border tensions and a schism in the socialist movement across the world, opening up strategic space for the US–China rapprochement of the early 1970s. Border disputes in the Xinjiang province developed into military skirmishes in 1969 and resumed Soviet cross-border influence operations among Uyghurs, threatening to blow up into a full-fledged war. At one stage, the Soviet Union was reported to have contemplated a pre-emptive nuclear strike on China. This widely known fact among historians was corroborated by declassified US State Department documents.[3]

China accepted the invitation by the US to acquiesce in its Soviet containment strategy, in return for US articulation of the One-China policy and opening of new areas of cooperation. The two countries strengthened intelligence cooperation, including establishment of US listening posts on Chinese territory to monitor Soviet troop movements and strategic nuclear deployments. The US stepped up transfers of military and dual-use technologies to China, with the declared objective of helping to reduce its technology gap with Russia.

After the Soviet invasion of Afghanistan in 1979, US–China relations received a major fillip. The two countries collaborated closely to extend military support to Pakistan and supply weaponry to the Afghan Mujahideen. The CIA purchased rifles, grenade launchers and anti-aircraft weapons from China for supply to Pakistan. Chinese and US weaponry were regularly supplied through the Karakoram Highway. Training camps were set up on Chinese territory for Afghan rebels. Deng Xiaoping was reported to have told the Americans that China and the United States should unite to 'turn Afghanistan into a quagmire for the Soviets'.[4]

Post-Cold War Reset

The violent events on Tiananmen Square in 1989 terminated US–China military and intelligence cooperation. Recognising that China's utility to the US as a counterpoise to the USSR had receded, the Chinese leadership braced itself for a new phase of competition with the US, when partnership with Russia would once again become important.

After the disintegration of the Soviet Union, China was concerned about the increasing western orientation of the Yeltsin government of Russia and the potential threat of American influence in the newly independent Central Asian Republics. Deng's China moved quickly to resolve the knotty border conflicts with Russia and the Central Asian countries (largely on generous terms). This paved the way for the multilateral initiative of the Shanghai Cooperation Organization (SCO) with Russia and the Central Asian countries. It served the multiple objectives of securing Russian accommodation of Chinese security interests in Central Asia (a region contiguous to Xinjiang), checking the American footprint there, accessing its abundant energy and other natural resources, and opening a land transit route for Chinese exports to West Asia and Europe.

This détente with Russia opened up its market for exports from a rapidly expanding Chinese economy. Russia offered a valuable opportunity for China to diversify its sources of energy supplies. Another critical interest of China was in the sophisticated Russian weapons and technologies, which the West had denied it since the Tiananmen Incident. The potential of Russian–China relations was well beyond what the US and its allies were willing to transfer to China, even at the height of their cooperation.

The Yeltsin government's gradual shift away from the West and the subsequent transfer of Russia's leadership to Vladimir Putin consolidated the partnership, which was formalised in a Treaty of Good Neighbourliness, Friendship and Cooperation in July 2001. This treaty, whose validity was extended in 2021, continues to be invoked as the legal basis of the Russia–China strategic partnership.

At the time, the Chinese were careful to underplay the accelerating rapprochement with Russia, until they normalised US–China trade relations in 2000.⁵ A furtive glance at US reactions continues to attend every major development in Russia–China relations even today.

The Putin–Xi Tango

The new millennium witnessed an intensification of relations – deeper defence cooperation, stronger energy partnerships and closer political consultations.⁶ There was greater accent on working together for a multipolar world order, developing platforms such as the Russia–India–China dialogue and BRIC (later BRICS), and coordinating activism in G20 and other economic forums.

Xi Jinping's ascension to power in China in 2013 gave further thrust to the relationship. From his first visit to Russia, he has been steadfast in his assertion of the importance of the Russia–China strategic partnership.

The core complementarities of the partnership have been implicitly or explicitly reiterated over the years. They share opposition to the western ideas of democracy propagation, humanitarian interventions and regime change. They advocate for a multipolar world and 'genuine multilateralism' (though their definitions of these terms and their vision of their roles in the processes are not identical). They believe that the 'rules-based order' propagated by the West is self-serving, discriminatory and hegemonistic. Russia and China find common cause in seeking a greater role in the global economic and financial architecture.

For China, Russia is a geopolitical counterweight to the United States. Considering that its tensions with the West will endure, keeping Russia close is important for the security of its continental flank – even more so if (as the Chinese believe) the India–US strategic partnership could act against Chinese interests. China needs Russia's cooperation to advance its interests in Eurasia and Russian acquiescence to access the Arctic. Their common intent to limit western political influence in Central Asia is pursued through an informal arrangement by which Russia provides a security umbrella over the region, while China wields increasing economic influence. For China, overland access to Russia's energy supplies and natural resources provides insurance against potential disruption of supplies from vulnerable sea routes. Russia is the only country that China classifies as a 'Comprehensive Strategic Partnership of Coordination for a New Era', characterised by 'cooperation on all issues, including international affairs, military and technological development'.

For Russia too, the obvious complementarities make the partnership with China an important element of its external strategy. Its importance increased progressively with the rapid deterioration in Russia–West relations from 2014 onwards, and even more steeply after Russia's invasion of Ukraine in 2022. As the US and its allies sought to isolate Russia politically and economically, China's support in international forums as well as trade and investment links with China acquired greater salience. As Europe drastically scaled down energy imports from Russia, China offered an alternative market.

Defence cooperation continues to be a major area of bilateral interest. It includes Chinese acquisitions of major weapons platforms, like the S-400 air defence system and Su-35 aircraft, as well as the joint development and manufacture of other military platforms.[7]

This cooperation has experienced challenges over the years. There have been periodical complaints against China for reverse engineering high-tech Russian systems, as well as high-profile espionage cases in Russian courts. Reports have surfaced that Russia had refused supplies of sophisticated platforms out of apprehensions of copying and onward transmission. The Russian military–industrial complex has publicly called out Chinese infringements of intellectual property rights (IPR).[8] The deterioration in the global political environment led the two countries to resolve differences over this issue.

Meanwhile, intensive investment and indigenous research and development (R&D) have been enhancing the capabilities of China's military–industrial complex. Its dependence on Russia for defence assistance has been decreasing over the years, though in some niche sectors like high-end aerospace and satellite technologies, the dependence is likely to continue in the foreseeable future.[9] According to SIPRI's 2023 fact sheet on international arms transfers, 77 per cent of China's arms imports 2019–2023 came from Russia. China was the second most important market for Russia (after India, which accounted for 21 per cent of Russia's exports).[10]

At the same time, China's global arms exports are rising: SIPRI's fact sheet shows that in 2019–2023, China has risen to become the world's fourth largest arms exporter. It may increasingly compete with Russia for markets in Asia and Africa.

To demonstrate solidarity against western actions in their respective neighbourhoods, China and Russia have held joint naval exercises in the South China Sea and the Baltic Sea. Their joint military exercises are increasingly extensive in scope and sophistication, involving advanced equipment and joint command and control systems. As external tensions intensify, peaceful and undisputed borders provide both countries with a stable 'strategic rear', enabling their military and security establishment to focus on major threats elsewhere.

Over the years, while they focussed on their bilateral and multilateral complementarities, they refrained from being drawn into the external disputes of each other. This was true of Russia's differences with the West in the 2000's or China's friction with ASEAN countries in the South China Sea. China did not endorse Russia's annexation of Crimea; in fact, it expanded its economic and military ties with Ukraine after 2014. Russia did not endorse China's territorial claims in the South China Sea. Putin continued to woo Indian, Japanese and Korean investment in the Russian energy sector and in its Far East region, with the obvious objective of balancing the Chinese presence. Russia also deepened cooperation with China's strategic rivals. Its partnership with Vietnam included sale of sophisticated weaponry, a Free Trade Agreement (with the Russia-led Eurasian Economic Union), joint exploration for energy in the South China Sea and plans to reopen a Russian naval base in Cam Ranh Bay. Its defence cooperation with India includes sales of high-technology weapons systems, their co-development and transfer of technologies.

But with the US moving towards a dual containment strategy, they developed a closer association with their respective external concerns. In their joint statement issued during Putin's visit to Beijing in February 2022, China expressed opposition to NATO's enlargement, calling upon it to respect the sovereignty, security and interests of other countries. It also supported Russia's proposals for 'long-term legally binding security guarantees in Europe'.[11] Russia too has become more strident in its criticism of Indo-Pacific initiatives like the Quad and AUKUS, as reflected in the May 2024 Joint Statement.

The Ukraine Effect

Since the commencement of Russia's war in Ukraine, the Russia–China relationship has been subjected to intense scrutiny. Most of the analyses and consequent policy prescriptions are ideologically driven, selectively drawing on evidence to justify conclusions and recommendations. They serve narratives that support the US/NATO approach to the Russia-Ukraine war.

The much-quoted 'no limits friendship' declaration in the Russia–China joint statement of February 2022 has been asserted to be a turning point in the relationship: 'the new inter-State relations ... are superior to political and military alliances of the Cold War era. Friendship between the two States has no limits, there are no "forbidden" areas of cooperation.'[12] The fact is that similar formulations have routinely figured in Russia–China statements since at least 2014 (the Putin-Xi era), with bilateral strategic ties described as being 'at their best point in history'. The most recent (prior to 2022) was a 2021 joint statement, in which Xi and Putin declared that relations 'have reached the highest level in their history ... not a Cold War-type politico-military alliance, but exceeding this form of interstate interaction.'[13]

With the war dragging on, political leaders and analysts have looked for signs of daylight between Russian and Chinese positions. President Putin's public remarks at his meeting with Xi on the sidelines of the Shanghai Cooperation Organization (SCO) Summit in Samarkhand (Uzbekistan) in September 2022 noted that he understands the latter's concerns about the war in Ukraine and will explain Russia's perspectives, was taken as an indication. Similarly, Xi was reported to have agreed with visiting German Chancellor Olaf Scholz in November 2022 that threats or use of nuclear weapons was unacceptable. These remarks have attracted the deduction that China was uneasy over Russia's prosecution of the war.[14]

On the contrary, the totality of publicly available evidence shows a strong Chinese endorsement of Russia's (and specifically, Putin's) behaviour (without directly endorsing the invasion of Ukraine). At every interaction, Xi has gone out of his way to advertise his great personal friendship with Putin and to commend the latter's contribution to bilateral relations. At their meeting in May 2024, he added an endorsement of Putin's leadership of Russia: 'I am convinced that you will certainly lead Russia to great achievements in national development and revival.'[15] On his visit to Moscow in March 2023, Xi expressed gratitude to Putin for his positive attitude and support for the 'development and construction of China'.

China has steadfastly voted against or abstained on every resolution in international organizations which seeks to criticise Russian actions in Ukraine or elsewhere. After the Russian invasion of Ukraine, the two countries' coordination of positions in BRICS (Brazil, Russia, India, China, and South Africa), SCO (Shanghai Cooperation Organisation) and other regional structures has intensified. US and European leaders and Ukrainian President Volodymyr Zelenskyy have been unsuccessful in their strenuous efforts to draw China into international meetings on Zelenskyy's 'peace formula'; China has refused participation at any level.

China has routinely denied or ignored allegations that it continues to export military or dual-use items to Russia. But the surge in bilateral trade turnover in 2023 does indicate that China has stepped into the breach created by Russia's loss of trade with the West. Reports indicate that Chinese supplies have replaced European exports of products like computer chips, smartphones and raw materials needed for military equipment, also corroborated by the fact that Russia has risen to the fourth place among China's trade partners in 2023 (or sixth, if Taiwan and Hong Kong are counted separately).

Exports of Russian agricultural products to China have also flourished in recent years. China's food self-sufficiency has recently been falling. With the US, Canada and Australia being its main suppliers, China has every incentive to divert as much of its demand as possible to a less hostile supplier.

Just a few days after the commencement of Russia's military operations in Ukraine, the Russian gas major, Gazprom, announced that it would construct a gas pipeline, which would annually deliver 50 billion cubic metres (bcm) of gas to China. This would compensate for the loss of the 55 bcm supply to Europe, which the now blown-up Nord Stream pipeline would have delivered from Russia to Germany. It was also reported that the China National Petroleum Corporation (CNPC) signed a contract with Russian oil company Rosneft for the supply of 100 million tonnes of oil to China through Kazakhstan over 10 years. The dual containment policy of the West has heightened for China the strategic importance of reducing dependence on imports by sea lanes through the Strait of Malacca.[16]

Over the years, therefore, Russia could make a bigger contribution to China's energy and food security – a reorientation that has been one of the consequences of Russia's war in Ukraine. Another consequence is also that over 90 per cent of bilateral trade is now transacted in roubles and yuan.

It has been reported that big Chinese companies and banks have shown some hesitation in engaging with Russia for fear of punitive western sanctions. This may be to avoid regulatory complications in their operations in the US and Europe. However, though the US and European leaders have been 'warning' China against helping the Russian war machine, implying that they may attract sanctions, no major Chinese company has actually been sanctioned. This is simply because Chinese companies have extensive links with western investors and are part of intricate supply chains across geographies. Sanctions against them would cause collateral damage to commercial interests in unanticipated quarters. The US learnt this from experience in 2018, when sanctions on Russian aluminium major Rusal impacted downstream industries and investors across the western world and shook global aluminium prices. A face-saving way had to be found to withdraw the sanctions.

The Ukraine war has not disrupted the regular participation of Russia and China in military drills of each other. In 2022, the Chinese army, navy and air force participated in a major Russian strategic exercise, Vostok 2022, which included land and naval drills. In 2023, Russian forces participated in elaborate Chinese strategic drills in the Sea of Japan.

The May 2023 EPRS briefing to the European Parliament also argues that Russia's shrinking geopolitical influence in Central Asia encourages China to directly deal with Central Asian countries, as it did in the China–Central Asia summit in May 2023.[17] In fact, both countries have supported this development. Their joint statement of May 2024 says that both sides emphasized the potential for multifaceted cooperation between the Collective Security Treaty Organization (CSTO) – the politico-military alliance of Russia and three Central Asian countries – and China, to maintain peace and security in Eurasia and jointly counter external challenges.[18] In the current climate of heightened tensions with the West, Russia's military commitments on its western flank, and a shared paranoia about the West exploiting a security vacuum in the region, it is as much pragmatism as Russian weakness that would dictate putting turf considerations aside.

Alongside these developments, one area of past dissonance that has now turned into a shared interest is the Arctic. When a Chinese white paper in

2018 declared China as a 'near-Arctic state', all members of the Arctic Council, including Russia, rejected this term. Russia maintained this position until as late as 2021, when it was chairing the Council. The Arctic littorals forming the Council have for long been united in keeping the governance of the Arctic to themselves. The eight members of the Council are now sharply divided between seven NATO countries and Russia. This has enabled China to insert itself into the region through participation in infrastructure, energy and connectivity projects. Russian concerns about letting China into the region have been subjugated to the imperative of countering NATO advance.

Much has been written and said about Chinese 'mediation' and its so-called peace plan for a 'political settlement of the Ukraine crisis', articulated in February 2023.[19] Presumably in the hope that China could restrain Russia, criticism of this plan has been muted. In effect, though, it protects Russian interests, while including formulaic references to sovereignty and international law. It calls for rejecting double standards; abandoning cold war mentality; accepting that security is indivisible; ceasing hostilities, gradually deescalating and eventually reaching a comprehensive ceasefire; resuming peace talks; ensuring safety of nuclear power plants; lifting all unilateral sanctions and ensuring stable supply chains; and supporting post-conflict reconstruction. Russia could not have asked for more.

Analytical Pitfalls

Much of the scholarship on Russia–China relations comes from western strategic analysts. Their discourse on the actions of Russia and China, their objectives and ambitions, is invariably based on ideological and strategic stereotypes, rarely factoring the context of external movements and trends that shape them. Particularly striking is the characterisation of Russian (specifically Putin's) and Chinese approaches to the world order after the Russian invasion of Ukraine. The US National Security Strategy (October 2022) describes Russia as a threat to the free and open international system, 'recklessly flouting the basic laws of the international order', whereas China is a 'competitor with the intent and power to reshape the international order'.[20] Other descriptions of Putin are more vicious – compulsive rule-breaker, anarchist, representing 'a paradigm shift in Kremlin thinking ... from a belief in great power accommodation to unapologetic rule-breaking'. Bobo Lo has described Putin's invasion of Ukraine as an atavistic mission to recover historically Russian lands, which happens to be an inaccurate description.[21] China, on the other hand, is uniformly described as a serious systemic participant in the global order, seeking to reshape it to its advantage but from within – a revisionist rather than a revolutionary state.

Even before Russia's invasion of Ukraine, this distinction between Russian and Chinese approaches has been baked into analyses of much of the US strategic community. In their treatise on Russia–China relations, Bolt and Cross write, '... while China has asserted its maritime interests, it is relatively cautious in its foreign policy ... Russia has been more willing to violate traditional rules ... and defy US preferences ...'[22]

It is a narrative that consistently projects Russia as a major threat to US security and geopolitical interests because of its nuclear weapons arsenal and aggressive policies. This thesis validates the raison d'etre of NATO, sustains the US military–industrial complex and keeps the transatlantic alliance together. It ignores – without evaluation – the motivations behind Russia's aggressive actions (for example, in Georgia or Crimea) in the context of what it sees as its core security concerns and, most relevant from an analytical perspective, the relevant historical backdrop.

China, on the other hand, gets an easier pass. As the US's economic interdependence with China has grown in the last decade or so, Chinese actions have drawn less critical scrutiny. In addition to China's attraction for Wall Street, Silicon Valley and Hollywood, there is the strategic reality that the South China Sea and Southeast Asia do not have the same compelling strategic significance to the US, and particularly to its European allies, as the Black Sea and Ukraine. Hence China's unilateral enforcement of its territorial claims, converting almost an entire sea into its territorial waters, its harsh, unilateral economic sanctions on Japan, Korea and Mongolia for actions that it deems to be contrary to its national interests, and the exploitative template of its Belt and Road Initiative, can all be conveniently portrayed as lesser infractions or even as China broadly playing within the rules of the international order. It is a self-serving argument that has sustained Western hostility towards Russia, even while keeping lines of communications and business with China.

Putin has led Russia for over two decades and the western alliance has dealt with him, in summit meetings and at other levels, as a serious leader, albeit with strong disagreements on major bilateral and global issues. After his meeting with Putin in June 2021, US President Joe Biden acknowledged that their discussions had reflected their respective perceptions of their national interests.[23] More recently, Biden has spoken of Putin in harsh terms. While this is understandable as political propaganda in wartime, it should not spill over into sober academic analysis.

These skewed perceptions feed into policy prescriptions for decision-makers and into assessments of the state of Russia–China relations. They have led to suggestions that China is embarrassed by Russia's wanton rule-breaking and would like to find a way to reconcile its support for Russia with its desire to uphold principles of sovereignty and territorial integrity. The foregoing description of China's (and specifically Xi's) support for Russia and Putin suggests that China is less concerned by Russia's rule-breaking than by its impact on developments of China's political and economic interests.

In an effort to create some daylight between Russian and Chinese positions, the EU and the US have engaged with China in discussions on Ukraine. It has been suggested in various official and unofficial circles that the US and China could cooperate to mediate between Russia and Ukraine, after the latter's bargaining position improved. The narrative has also been put out that this would suit China's interests and enable it to rebuild its reputation in Europe. Again, there is no evidence that China is responsive to these overtures. The US's pressure on its European allies to put economic pressure on China has been partially successful. But major European leaders visiting China – of the European Commission, France, Germany, Italy and Poland, among others – were principally pursuing their commercial interests, though they may have added the exhortation not to assist Moscow's war efforts through exports of dual-use items. However, China's comfort level with Vladimir Putin does not appear to have dimmed because of their efforts.

Another prevalent narrative is of the international isolation of Russia, through economic sanctions, UN resolutions, the International Criminal Courts' (ICC) arrest warrant against Putin and the banning of Russian participation in international political, cultural and sports events. This is projected to be hastening Russia's descent into becoming a vassal of China.

The reality, as now acknowledged even by mainstream western media, is that this isolation has not extended much beyond the western world. Many democracies did not condemn Russia after its invasion or join the US-led sanctions on it. Many Asian and African countries did not support the UN resolutions condemning the invasion. Germany's Chancellor Olaf Scholz acknowledged that the democracies invited to the outreach meeting of the G7 (June 2022) – India, Indonesia, Senegal, South Africa and Argentina – all have perspectives on the Ukraine war that differ from that of the G7. This was again demonstrated at the G20 meeting in New Delhi in September 2023, when non-western participants succeeded in diluting the language that the US and its allies wanted to insert in the summit communique. Russia continues to participate in G20, BRICS and SCO meetings, and Organization of the Petroleum Exporting Countries Plus (OPEC+) continues to involve Russia in its decision-making. It is in the public domain that when Saudi Arabia wanted to join BRICS, its Crown Prince telephoned Putin for support and subsequently thanked him for his assistance in the matter.

Russia's influence in Africa has been recently illustrated by the images, seen on every international news channel, of West African countries spurning French influence and inviting the Russians. Russia and China both collaborate and compete in the political and economic spheres in West Asia and Africa but find common cause in resisting western efforts to sideline their influence.

At the same time, Putin has continued to demonstrate his 'strategic autonomy' from China by visiting Vietnam (where the red carpet was rolled out for him) in

June 2024 and later receiving Indian Prime Minister Narendra Modi in Moscow in July. There was an earlier instance in 2020, just after the breakout of hostilities across the India–Tibet border, when India's defence minister visited Moscow and was assured by his Russian hosts that the deliveries of contracted military equipment would be fast-tracked. These included the air defence system S-400. This provoked angry comments in the Chinese media, which were publicized in the Indian, Russian and western media, that Russia was double-crossing its strategic partner, China, by helping its adversary.

The narrative of the Russian economy going into freefall due to western sanctions is also overblown, as reported from time to time by the western media. In April 2024, the International Monetary Fund raised Russia's growth forecast for 2024 to 3.2 per cent from 2.6 per cent as projected in January, attributing it to strong government spending and investment into the war economy, higher consumer spending and continued robustness of oil exports. While the Chinese GDP is over ten times that of Russia, it is useful to remember that Russia's per capita GDP in 2024 is higher than that of China (US$14,400 vs US$13,100), according to IMF data. The gap in per capita GDP by purchasing power parity (PPP) is wider – US$38,300 to US$25,000.[24]

The economic sanctions, particularly technology denial, will eventually take their toll on Russia's competitiveness and technological prowess, but this has not yet happened. On the contrary, the war seems to have spurred technological innovations for the battlefield. This is, of course, equally true of Ukraine.

These facts are relevant for evaluating the impact of 'asymmetry' in the Russia–China relationship. There is an asymmetry of economic strength and global reach, but it is not yet so extreme as to reduce Russia to a Chinese vassal and to bury Putin's ambition of making Russia a great power again. The strong mutuality of their interests in the current geopolitical situation would restrain either side from letting periodical jarring notes disturb the equilibrium of their relationship.

The Way Ahead

Western analysts are split between two main assessments about the Russia–China relationship. One is that the relationship will eventually be limited by historical animosities, asymmetry of power and divergent strategic ambitions, thereby providing strategic opportunities to dilute their solidarity. The other is that it is rapidly morphing into an unshakeable alliance that necessitates a dual containment strategy by the US against Russia and China.

The weight of history is undeniable. There will always be an undercurrent of apprehension in Russia that China could reopen the territorial settlement. There is basis for this concern. Though the border settlement in the early 2000s was projected as China finally renouncing all claims to the land ('Outer Manchuria') lost to Russia in the 'unequal treaties' of the 19th century, it is an issue that recurs in the Chinese media, particularly social media. Russian officials have privately mentioned seeing Chinese maps, even in government offices, with the Russia–China border reflecting country boundaries as in the early 19th century. When Russia celebrated the 160th anniversary of the founding of Vladivostok in 2020, the Chinese social media reacted indignantly. Irate Chinese netizens, including diplomats and journalists, recalled that it was Chinese territory, lost by an unequal treaty; some declared that this historical wrong would be corrected one day. The Chinese government did not comment.

On its part, the Russian government declares that the border settlement was final and irrevocable. Speaking at their videoconference in the run-up to the 20th anniversary of the signing of the bilateral Treaty of Good-Neighbourliness and Friendly Cooperation in June 2021, Putin stressed that the treaty confirms the 'absence of mutual territorial claims' and the mutual determination to make the Russia–China border a 'belt of eternal peace and friendship', adding that years of jointly working on the border issue had yielded a result acceptable to both.[25] Xi did not respond to this comment. Significantly, China's 'standard map', published in August 2023 by the Chinese Ministry of Natural Resources, showed Bolshoi Ussuriysky Island (Heixiazi Island for the Chinese), at the confluence of the Ussuri and Amur rivers, as Chinese territory. The 2004 border settlement had agreed on arrangements for shared sovereignty over this island.

In the current external environment, it is obviously pragmatic for both countries to avoid any dispute. But there could well be circumstances in the future that might tempt or compel China to reclaim its lost territories – for strategic depth and huge mineral wealth.

There are also other potential irritants. There are reports about Chinese officials and businesspersons being patronizing with their Russian counterparts in bilateral and multilateral forums. Russians complain that despite Putin's strong support for the Belt and Road Initiative (BRI), most China–Europe connectivity projects have taken a southern route through Central Asia and the Caucasus. These irritants have not touched the leadership of the two countries.

More broadly, there is a power differential, but (as elaborated in the foregoing) it has not yet reached a stage where it is impacting the interests of the two countries.

In the present circumstances, the two countries have a strong stake in the success of each other. China would be severely threatened by a strategic defeat of Russia that may result in regime change, external interference in its politics, or even a break-up of the country. At the same time, the West's continued focus on confronting Russia in Ukraine affords China the space to expand its political and economic outreach and reinforce its military capacities. Equally,

Russia needs strong Chinese political and economic support, with the steadfast solidarity offered by Xi Jinping. The political, economic, energy and security complementarities are important in the face of hostility with the West, but they will remain important even if the hostility reduces, as an insurance for the future. In sum, China has a stake in Putin's continuation in power and will, therefore, give him the leeway to assert a level of strategic autonomy. Equally, to sustain China's strong support for his regime, Putin will have to make concessions to China's interests in Central Asia or the Arctic.

The Grey Rhinos

Two factors could profoundly influence the framework within which the Russia–China relationship operates. The first is the way in which the current conflict in Ukraine plays out. The second, and not unrelated, is the way in which the US handles its strategic approaches to Russia and China, whenever the war draws to an end.

The publicly articulated western objective is to hand Russia a strategic defeat in the war. The subtext is that the confrontation of the more formidable strategic challenge from China, while simultaneously being pursued, would take on a more frontal position thereafter. What the eventual nature of this strategic defeat will be, how possible or proximate it is, and whether American political will and European unity can be sustained sufficiently to see this process through, are all unknown unknowns at the time of this writing. How China would respond to prevent the destruction of its cosy arrangement with Russia is another unknown. The approach of the Trump Administration, which will assume office in January 2025, remains shrouded in a web of contradictory statements. Finally, given the constant probing of red lines by both belligerents, the breakout of an unintended conflagration, with unimaginable consequences, cannot be ruled out, as long as the war continues.

On the other hand, if Russia emerges with a settlement that enhances its political and economic standing – most western analysts would term this a low-probability, even a black swan, event – this would alter some of the dynamics of the Russia–China relationship, particularly if it presages a reduction in the tensions between Russia and the West.

The Third Arm

The other factor, which has always been consequential in Russia–China relations in recent decades, is the US's approach to each of them. China tilted away from the USSR at least partially because of the United States. It tilted towards it in the 70s and more pronouncedly in the 80s to counter the USSR. The correction in the 90s was to withstand US pressures, with the Putin-Xi tango following the same logic.

In the early 2000s, both China and Russia valued their political and economic relations with the US and its allies. The economic engagement of each with Europe and the US was far more significant than their bilateral economic relations. Also, self-image as a great power drove the aspiration of each to have independent relations with the US and Europe. Russian and Chinese efforts to promote multipolarity and democratisation of the global financial architecture were carefully projected as an expression of non-West, rather than anti-West, perspectives. Hence, while on one plane, they saw their bilateral relations as balancing the US, each also saw any sign of improvement in the relations of the other with the US as potentially diminishing its importance to the US.

The dynamics changed after 2014, when Russia's annexation of China sent its relations with the West into a nosedive. Western sanctions, exclusion of Russia from various international forums and widening proxy conflicts across geographies, from the Caucasus to the Caspian, West Asia and Afghanistan, pushed Russia into a much closer embrace of China. In return for its political and economic support of Russia, China extracted concessions on hydrocarbons supplies and advanced military technologies. At the same time, China continued to be deeply engaged with the West, riding on the resilience of its economy, which helped to cushion some of the impact on the West of the financial crisis of 2008.

In 2016, veteran Chinese diplomat Fu Ying wrote in *Foreign Affairs* that relations among China, Russia and the United States 'resemble a scalene triangle, in which the greatest distance between the three points is between Moscow and Washington'. The China–Russia arm was the shortest, indicating 'positive and stable relations'. The US–Chinese side of the triangle was, in her estimation, of intermediate length.[26] The unstated message from Fu Ying's essay was that this is the configuration that suits China best: US–Russia hostility, making Russia more dependent on Chinese support, while China deals with the US on an equal footing on bilateral and global issues.

The Trump administration altered the shape of the triangle by identifying China as the principal threat to US global dominance and ratcheting up economic and political pressure on China, including by the robust reactivation of the Quad grouping. At the same time, it also unleashed the harshest sanctions regime seen against Russia until then, including secondary sanctions aimed, inter alia, at severing energy links between Europe and Russia and the defence cooperation between India and Russia. This lengthening of both the US–China and the US–Russia arms resulted in a considerable shortening of the Russia–China arm.

Early in its term, the Biden administration signalled a course recalibration. Biden invited Putin for a meeting in Geneva in June 2021 to explore a modus vivendi with Russia that would free the US to focus more strongly on China as its principal strategic challenge. Putin appeared to reciprocate but made the point that, for such a geopolitical rebalance to be sustainable, it should incorporate suitable security guarantees for Russia. Russia views NATO's expansion and weapons deployments, as well as other US policies across Europe and Asia, as threatening its territorial integrity and its influence on its periphery. It wanted some assurances on these matters. Substantive bilateral discussions followed in subsequent months, covering strategic stability, transborder cybercrimes, security guarantees in respect of Ukraine and their respective interests in the Arctic.

In candid remarks to the media, Biden conveyed his impression from the conversation with Putin, that Russia needs a modus vivendi with the US, because it is being squeezed by China. Its flagging economy and surging Chinese power are in danger of denting its great power ambitions, by reducing it to a junior partner of China.[27] On the US side, a modus vivendi with Russia offers the sound geopolitical logic of making peace with a lesser challenger to prevent it from strengthening the principal adversary by strengthening alliance with it.

A logical corollary of this approach would be an American strategy aimed at weakening some of the Russia–China bonds. Writing in *Foreign Affairs*, Charles Kupchan of the Council on Foreign Relations (CFR) elaborated on the elements of such a strategy. He suggested that the US's efforts to 'tame' China should aim at luring Russia away from it. This should start with the US jettisoning its 'democracy versus autocracy' narrative, which unites Russia and China. Washington should encourage India to help wean Russia away from China, by waiving sanctions on purchase of the S-400 system. Further, America and its allies should help reduce Russia's economic dependence on China by restraint in the use of sanctions and by working towards a diplomatic resolution of the conflict in eastern Ukraine. The US and Russia should also lead the strategic stability dialogue towards an arms control arrangement, that eventually pushes China to accept limits on its missiles, which should be in Moscow's interest as well. Finally, the US and Russia should thwart Beijing's creeping ambition in the Arctic and check its growing influence in Central Asia, Middle East and Africa. Kupchan argued that the present US policy leaves China free to pursue its expansion in the Pacific, confident of Russia's support. Putting the China–Russia relationship 'back into play' would divert some of China's attention to its continental flank. It would be an important step towards thwarting China's ambitions for a 'Sinocentric international system'.[28]

A US–Russia detente that could bring the Russia–China relationship 'into play' makes geopolitical sense but would involve a deviation from the course that the US and NATO have set in recent years, and in which stakeholders in the US and in Europe have made heavy political and economic investments. US's strategy over two decades has been to wean western Europe away from dependence on, and engagement with, Russia. Meanwhile, the US has encouraged NATO's Central European members, whose political ambitions and economic priorities are strongly influenced by their troubled history with Russia. In trying to promote accommodation with Russia, replacing the traditional hostility, Biden was trying to make NATO reverse a course in which many of its members were invested. In the event, Biden's rebalancing effort could not proceed to its apparent conclusion.

Besides the headwinds in the US and Europe, it should also be recognised that there are limits to the wedge that Washington can insert between Russia and China under the present circumstances. Recent history has created deep mutual suspicions, which are not easily eradicated. Russia and China are unlikely to give up the insurance that their partnership provides against external hostility. Therefore, it would be unrealistic to expect that Washington could significantly disrupt the Sino–Russian partnership by attempting to move dramatically closer to either Moscow or Beijing.[29] But if the US were to reach some accommodation with Russia on a European security architecture, it would increase Russia's leverage vis a vis China and circumscribe China's freedom of action. It would then reduce the intensity of a Russia–China alliance.

Implications for India

India views the Russia–China relationship from the perspective of its relations with the two countries. Hostility with the US has increasingly pushed Russia closer to China, India's biggest strategic challenge. Worsening US–Russia relations have increased US pressures on India to dilute its dependencies on Russia. The draconian sanctions authorized by the US legislation CAATSA (Countering America's Adversaries Through Sanctions Act) seek to prevent India from buying sophisticated weapons systems from Russia. This has inevitably impacted India–Russia defence cooperation. US–China rivalry lends further warmth to the Russia–China embrace. India–China tensions and the power differential have led India to partner with the US and its Asian allies as external balancing. This further accentuates Chinese hostility to India and also Chinese pressure on Russia to dilute its relations with India.

The bilateral element of India's relations with Russia is important, but there is also broader strategic consideration. The Eurasian landmass from Central Asia to the Caspian and beyond is India's near neighbourhood. It is bound on the north and northwest by China and Russia. India's security interests dictate an active presence there and prevention of a Russia–China axis acting against India's interest. A lowering of the temperature of Russia–US relations and a firm approach of the US towards China (stopping short of military tensions) is the best form of external influence on Russia–China relations that Indian policymakers could wish for.

P.S. Raghavan is a former diplomat, now chairman of the National Security Advisory Board of India. The views expressed here are personal.

Notes

1. Official Internet Resources of the President of Russia, 'Media statement following Russia-China talks,' 16 May 16 2024, http://en.kremlin.ru/events/president/news/74049.
2. Official Internet Resources of the President of Russia, 'Joint Statement by the Russian Federation and the People's Republic of China on Deepening Relations of Comprehensive Partnership and Strategic Cooperation, Entering a New Era in the Context of the 75th Anniversary of the Establishment of Diplomatic Relations between the Two Countries,' trans. Google, 16 May 2024, Новости · Президент · События · Президент России.
3. Memorandum for the President from Secretary of State William Rogers, 'The Possibility of a Soviet Strike Against Chinese Nuclear Facilities,' 10 September 1969, sino.sov.19.pdf.
4. Hugo Meijer, 'Balancing Conflicting Security Interests: U.S. Defense Exports to China in the Last Decade of the Cold War,' *Journal of Cold War Studies* (2015): 4–40, https://sciencespo.hal.science/hal-03459494.
5. Vijay Gokhale, *After Tiananmen* (HarperCollins India, 2021), 86–88.
6. Official Internet Resources of the President of Russia, 'Press Statements Following Russian-Chinese Talks,' 4 July 2017, http://en.kremlin.ru/events/president/news/54979.
7. Ethan Meick, *China-Russia Military-to-Military Relations: Moving Toward a Higher Level of Cooperation*, (US–China Economic and Security Review Commission, 20 March 2017) https://www.uscc.gov/sites/default/files/Research/China-Russia%20Mil-Mil%20Relations%20Moving%20Toward%20Higher%20Level%20of%20Cooperation.pdf.
8. China Power Team, 'How Deep Are China-Russia Military Ties?,' *China Power Project*, 10 May 2022, updated 9 November 2023, https://chinapower.csis.org/series-china-russia-relations/.
9. Ibid.
10. Pieter D. Wezeman et al., *Trends in International Arms Transfers, 2023* (SIPRI Fact Sheet, March 2024), https://www.sipri.org/sites/default/files/2024-03/fs_2403_at_2023.pdf.
11. Official Internet Resources of the President of Russia, 'Joint Statement of the Russian Federation and the People's Republic of China on the International Relations Entering a New Era and the Global Sustainable Development,' 4 February 2022, http://www.en.kremlin.ru/supplement/5770.
12. Ibid.
13. Official Internet Resources of the President of Russia, 'Joint Statement of the Russian Federation and the People's Republic of China on the Twentieth Anniversary of the Treaty of Good Neighbourliness and Friendly Cooperation between the Russian

Federation and the People's Republic of China,' 28 June 2021, http://static.kremlin.ru/media/events/files/en/Bo3RF3JzGDvMAPjHBQAuSemVPWTEvb3c.pdf.

14 See, for example, Bobo Lo, 'The Sino-Russian Partnership: Assumptions, Myths and Realities,' The French Institute of International Relations (IFRI), No. 42, (March 2023): https://www.ifri.org/en/studies/sino-russian-partnership-assumptions-myths-and-realities.

15 Official Internet Resources of the President of Russia, 'Beginning of the conversation with President of China Xi Jinping' May 16, 2024, http://en.kremlin.ru/events/president/transcripts/74046.

16 Ulrich Jochheim, 'Russia–China relations: a quantum jump?,' European Parliamentary Research Service, May 2023, https://www.europarl.europa.eu/RegData/etudes/BRIE/2022/729349/EPRS_BRI(2022)729349_EN.pd.

17 Ulrich Jochheim, 'Russia–China relations: a quantum jump?,' European Parliamentary Research Service, May 2023, https://www.europarl.europa.eu/RegData/etudes/BRIE/2022/729349/EPRS_BRI(2022)729349_EN.pdf.

18 Official Internet Resources of the President of Russia, 'Joint Statement by the Russian Federation and the People's Republic of China on Deepening Relations of Comprehensive Partnership and Strategic Cooperation, Entering a New Era in the Context of the 75th Anniversary of the Establishment of Diplomatic Relations between the Two Countries,' trans. Google, 16 May 2024, Новости · Президент · События · Президент России.

19 Ministry of Foreign Affairs, The People's Republic of China, 'China's Position on the Political Settlement of the Ukraine Crisis,' 24 February 2023, https://www.fmprc.gov.cn/eng/zy/gb/202405/t20240531_11367485.html.

20 The White House, 'US National Security Strategy,' October 2022, https://www.whitehouse.gov/wp-content/uploads/2022/10/Biden-Harris-Administrations-National-Security-Strategy-10.2022.pdf.

21 Bobo Lo, 'The Sino-Russian Partnership: Assumptions, Myths and Realities,' The French Institute of International Relations (IFRI), No. 42, (March 2023): https://www.ifri.org/en/studies/sino-russian-partnership-assumptions-myths-and-realities.

22 Paul J. Bolt and Sharyl N. Cross, China, Russia and Twenty-First Century Global Geopolitics (Oxford University Press, 2018).

23 The White House, 'Remarks by President Biden in Press Conference,' 16 June 2021, https://www.whitehouse.gov/briefing-room/speeches-remarks/2021/06/16/remarks-by-president-biden-in-press-conference-4/.

24 Steady but Slow: Resilience amid Divergence, World Economic Outlook (IMF), April 2024, https://www.imf.org/en/Publications/WEO/Issues/2024/04/16/world-economic-outlook-april-2024.

25 Official Internet Resources of the President of Russia, 'Conversation with President of China Xi Jinping,' 28 June 2021, http://en.kremlin.ru/events/president/news/65940.

26 Fu Ying, 'How China Sees Russia: Beijing and Moscow are Close, but Not Allies,' Foreign Affairs, 14 December 2015, https://www.foreignaffairs.com/articles/china/2015-12-14/how-china-sees-russia.

27 The White House, 'Remarks by President Biden in Press Conference,' 16 June 2021, https://www.whitehouse.gov/briefing-room/speeches-remarks/2021/06/16/remarks-by-president-biden-in-press-conference-4/.
28 Charles A. Kupchan, 'The Right Way to Split China and Russia,' *Foreign Affairs*, 4 August 2021, https://www.foreignaffairs.com/articles/united-states/2021-08-04/right-way-split-china-and-russia.
29 Paul J. Bolt and Sharyl N. Cross, *China, Russia and Twenty-First Century Global Geopolitics* (Oxford University Press, 2018).

4

Biden Administration's Responses to the China Challenge

Arun K. Singh

Perception and Defining of the Challenge

The Interim National Security Strategy,[1] released in March 2021, within two months of the Administration's inauguration, began with an explicit acknowledgment of the US concerns. It stated, 'we face a world of rising nationalism, receding democracy, growing rivalry with China, Russia, and other authoritarian states, and a technological revolution that is reshaping every aspect of our lives.' Evaluating the nature of the China challenge, it elaborated: 'It (China) is the only competitor potentially capable of combining its economic, diplomatic, military, and technological power to mount a sustained challenge to a stable and open international system.'

In the National Security Strategy (NSS),[2] eventually released on 12 October 2022 (delayed on account of Russia's invasion of Ukraine in February 2022), a distinction was specifically drawn between the challenges posed to the US by Russia and the PRC. It says,

> Russia poses an immediate threat to the free and open international system, recklessly flouting the basic laws of the international order today, as its brutal war of aggression against Ukraine has shown ... Russia poses an immediate and ongoing threat to the regional security order in Europe, and it is a source of disruption and instability globally but it lacks the across the spectrum capabilities of the PRC.

The strategy affirmed that 'PRC presents America's most consequential geopolitical challenge.'

The Biden administration also laid out a three-fold strategy to respond to China in its NSS: investing in the foundations of strength at home; aligning efforts with a network of allies and partners, acting with a common purpose and cause and competing with the PRC to defend the US interests, and build a vision for the future.

Earlier, the NSS, released under the Trump administration in December 2017, had stated that China is a 'revisionist power' that seeks to 'displace the United States in the Indo-Pacific region, expand the reaches of its state-driven economic model, and reorder the region in its favor'. In January 2018, the administration had put out its National Defence Strategy asserting that China is a 'strategic competitor' that uses 'predatory economics' and 'military modernization' to 'erode American security and prosperity'. These documents outlined a competitive strategy towards China, based on 'principled realism' and 'peace through strength' principles. The Trump administration also published a report in 2020, titled 'United States Strategic Approach to the People's Republic of China', which detailed a whole-of-government approach to protect American interests and values from the 'Chinese Communist Party's malign actions and policies'. The report identified four pillars of the US strategy: protecting the American people, homeland and way of life; promoting American prosperity; preserving peace through strength and advancing American influence.

They had marked a noted shift from the Obama administration (2009–2016), which had started by initially talking of 'strategic reassurance' to China, signalling a strategy to accommodate some of its interests, but then shifted first to a 'pivot' and then to 'rebalancing' in Asia to deal with the growing economic, technological and military challenge from China. Even the 'rebalancing' was not carried out effectively, due to continued US preoccupation with Europe on account of Russia's action in Ukraine in 2014, and continued instability in West Asia.

Aligning

The China Challenge in the Indo-Pacific Region

An Indo-Pacific Strategy was released in February 2022 by the Biden administration, recognising the more immediate China challenge in the region.[3] It explained the 'intensifying American focus' as

> due in part to the fact that the Indo-Pacific faces mounting challenges, particularly from the PRC. The PRC is combining its economic, diplomatic, military, and technological might as it pursues a sphere of influence in the Indo-Pacific and seeks to become the world's most influential power. The PRC's coercion and aggression spans the globe, but it is most acute in the Indo-Pacific.

Later, explaining how China is seeking to create an 'enhanced sphere of influence' in the Indo-Pacific region, the NSS elaborated:

> Beijing frequently uses its economic power to coerce countries. It benefits from the openness of the international economy while limiting access to its domestic market, and it seeks to make the world more dependent on the PRC while reducing its own dependence on the world. The PRC is also investing in a military that is rapidly modernizing, increasingly capable in the Indo-Pacific, and

growing in strength and reach globally – all while seeking to erode US alliances in the region and around the world.

The Interim NSS had talked about the role of allies in organising a common front against China. Terming them 'America's greatest strategic asset', the Administration postulated: 'We will work with allies to share responsibilities equitably while encouraging them to invest in their own comparative advantages against shared current and future threats.' To achieve this end, the US would position itself 'diplomatically and militarily' to defend its allies in the event of Chinese coercion or undue influence.

An action plan was mapped out in the Indo-Pacific Strategy, identifying ten core lines of effort aimed to be accomplished in the next twelve to twenty-four months: drive new resources to the Indo-Pacific; lead an Indo-Pacific economic framework; reinforce deterrence; strengthen an empowered and unified Association of Southeast Asian Nations (ASEAN); support India's continued rise and regional leadership; deliver on the Quad; expand US–Japan–Republic of Korea (ROK) cooperation; partner to build resilience in the Pacific Islands; support good governance and accountability and, finally, support open, resilient, secure and trustworthy technologies.

Joe Biden made his inaugural trip to Asia on 20–22 May 2022, on the heels of the president hosting ASEAN leaders in Washington for a special summit on 13 May 2022.[4] Biden made his first stop in Seoul, where both countries reiterated the 'iron-clad' nature of the bilateral relationship and emphasised the goal of transforming it into a 'global, comprehensive, strategic alliance'.[5] The next halt was in Tokyo for Biden's participation in the second Quad leaders' in-person meeting.[6]

On the eve of the Tokyo Quad summit, Biden launched an Indo-Pacific Economic Framework (IPEF),[7] fleshing out a blueprint for the US's reenergised economic engagement in the region. IPEF brings together fourteen countries, including India, which contribute about 40 per cent to the global GDP. The framework has four pillars: trade, supply chain resilience, decarbonisation and infrastructure and anti-corruption and tax. Though the framework was quite broad, the trade pillar[8] was seen as weak as it did not deal with market access issues.[9] The political strategy was to project the US re-engagement with the region after Trump administration had walked out of the earlier negotiated Trans-Pacific Partnership.

The first in-person ministerial meeting of IPEF was held in Los Angeles on 10 September 2022.[10] It set out the negotiating objectives for each pillar.[11] From 10 to 15 December 2022, the US met with all IPEF partners for the first full IPEF negotiation round in Brisbane, Australia. The round saw the introduction of the initial text for all four pillars.[12] Then India hosted the special negotiations round for IPEF in New Delhi from 8 to 11 February 2023.[13] The round covered IPEF Pillars II (Supply Chains), III (Clean Economy) and IV (Fair Economy). Officials from the US, Australia, Brunei, Fiji, India, Indonesia, Japan, the Republic of Korea, Malaysia, New Zealand, the Philippines, Singapore, Thailand and Vietnam attended. It was announced on 28 May that the negotiations on the supply chain pillar of IPEF had been substantially and successfully concluded.

The Joint Statement issued on 16 November 2023, following the third IPEF ministerial meeting held in San Francisco, announced the substantial conclusion of the negotiations of the IPEF Clean Economy Agreement under Pillar III and the IPEF Fair Economy Agreement under Pillar IV, as well as of the Agreement on the Indo-Pacific Economic Framework for Prosperity, which seeks to establish a ministerial-level council and commission to formalise and ensure ongoing cooperation. Moreover, following the substantial conclusion of the negotiations on the IPEF Supply Chain Agreement in May 2023, the IPEF Ministers signed the IPEF Supply Chain Agreement during the Ministerial Meeting.

Progress could not be made on the trade pillar largely on account of continued political challenges in the US on market access issues and trade agreements in general.[14]

The US hosted the first-ever Pacific Islands Summit at the White House in September 2022, inviting twelve Pacific Island countries, including the Solomon Islands, which had previously signed a security agreement with China in April 2022.[15] Ten countries sent their leaders, while Nauru and Vanuatu sent representatives. The declaration issued at the summit spoke of deepening cooperation on issues such as climate change and maritime security, advancing economic growth and protecting the Blue Pacific. The summit came at a time when concerns had arisen, inter alia, in the US, Japan, New Zealand and Australia regarding the signing of a security pact between China and Solomon Islands, with potential for allowing Chinese naval vessels to replenish there.[16] A follow-up US–Pacific Islands Forum Leaders Dialogue was held in Port Moresby, Papua New Guinea, on 22 May 2023, wherein Secretary of State Antony Blinken and leaders of Pacific Island Countries reaffirmed their commitment to the US–Pacific Partnership issued in September 2022.[17] President Biden was supposed to attend the meeting in Papua New Guinea. However, he had to pull out of the visit due to debt ceiling negotiations in Washington.

The US also formally upgraded its relationship with the ASEAN to a comprehensive strategic partnership during the 10th ASEAN–US summit in November 2022 in Phnom Penh, Cambodia.[18] Biden visited Vietnam in September 2023, where he elevated the US–Vietnam relationship to the status of a comprehensive strategic partnership.[19] During Indonesian President Joko Widodo's visit to the US in November 2023, both countries announced a US–Indonesia Comprehensive Strategic Partnership.[20]

Efforts to Bolster Security Partnerships

In mid-December 2022, the cabinet of Japanese Prime Minister Kishida approved the most ambitious and rapid expansion of military power in Japan since the country's Self-Defense Forces (SDF) were created in 1954. In December 2022, Japan adopted a new National Security Strategy[21] and released its National Defense Strategy[22] and Defense Buildup Programme,[23] including a counterstrike capability that marked a departure from the country's exclusively self-defense-only post-war principle. The US National Security Advisor Jake Sullivan issued a statement on 16 December, acknowledging the 'bold and historic step' by Japan to strengthen and defend the free and open Indo-Pacific.[24]

In January 2023, the US announced that it planned to reorganise its Marine Corps units based in Japan's Okinawa Island by 2026, and signed new agreements with Tokyo to cooperate on space and advanced military technologies to deter China's military.[25] The US indicated plans to arm its Okinawa Marine Littoral Regiment (MLR) with missiles and lighter gear, enabling easier manoeuvrability. The change came as Tokyo and Washington had been projecting efforts to beef up deterrence and response capabilities in southwestern Japan, near Taiwan—a self-ruled democratic island that Beijing regards as a breakaway province to be reunified with the mainland; by force, if necessary.

The Biden administration actively pushed for reconciliations in Japan and South Korea's relationship. The administration realised that South Korea and Japan's complex history and negative perceptions of each other have inhibited closer trilateral cooperation between them and the US. Therefore, the Indo-Pacific Strategy specifically spoke about the importance of promoting cooperation between Japan and ROK. On 16 March 2023, Japanese Prime Minister Fumio Kishida held a summit meeting in Tokyo with the President of the Republic of Korea Mr Yoon Suk Yeol. During the summit, both countries agreed to a settlement of dispute over the issue of compensation demands from South Koreans about wartime labour that had strained their relationship.[26] The US was quick to acknowledge the effort and welcomed their decision.[27] Fumio Kishida visited Seoul in May,[28] the first such bilateral visit by a Japanese leader in more than twelve years, returning the trip the South Korean president had made to Tokyo in March. The reciprocal visits were indicative of the speed of progress being attempted in their countries' relationship. On 18 August 2023, Biden hosted the Japanese and South Korean leaders for a 'historic' trilateral summit at Camp David.

The US, under Joe Biden, also set up a new marine base in Guam in January 2023 as part of the broader US strategy to disperse and strengthen its forces around the Pacific.[29] During Secretary of Defense Lloyd J. Austin's visit to the Philippines in February 2023, the Biden administration announced the establishment of additional military bases in the Philippines Sea.[30] The expanded access would potentially fill a crucial gap in the US positioning in the region. In February 2023, after a Chinese coast guard ship reportedly hit a Philippine patrol vessel, the US promptly issued a statement of support saying that 'the PRC's conduct was provocative and unsafe'.[31] The 13 February statement further stated,

> the United States stands with our Philippine allies in upholding the rules-based international maritime order and reaffirms an armed attack on Philippine armed forces, public vessels, or aircraft, including those of the Coast Guard in the South China Sea, would invoke US mutual defense commitments under Article IV of the 1951 US Philippines Mutual Defense Treaty.

Overall, the administration has kept up its effort to deepen security alliances with China's neighbours. The Biden administration revealed plans to supply Australia with nuclear propulsion submarines by signing the Submarine Rotational Forces-West agreement in March 2023.[32] The AUKUS partners – Australia, the United Kingdom and the United States – unveiled plans to provide Australia with conventionally armed, nuclear-powered attack submarines by the early 2030s to counter China's ambitions in the Indo-Pacific. The submarines would be able to operate further and faster than the country's existing diesel-engine fleet and Australia will also be able to carry out long-range strikes against enemies for the first time. This move would enable Australia to play an increasingly critical role in supporting the US military operations as part of a strategy of collective deterrence.

At the Madrid Summit, 28–29 June 2022, the NATO countries adopted the 2022 NATO Strategic Concept. Identifying China as a systemic challenge, the document stated, 'the PRC employs a broad range of political, economic and military tools to increase its global footprint and project power, while remaining opaque about its strategy, intentions and military build-up.' The document also outlined a comprehensive approach to address the challenges posed by China, including strengthening deterrence and defence, enhancing resilience, deepening partnerships and engaging in dialogue.[33]

Similarly, the G7 Hiroshima Leaders' Communiqué released during the summit on 20 May 2023 asserted that the leaders were determined to work together to 'support a free and open Indo-Pacific and oppose any unilateral attempts to change the status quo by force or coercion'.[34]

Competing

Setting the tone for how the US–China relationship would evolve under the Biden administration, Secretary of State Antony Blinken said, 'the United States' relationship with China will be competitive where it should be, collaborative where it can be, adversarial where it must be', during the first high-level gathering of the US and Chinese officials in Alaska in March 2021. A year later, speaking at the George Washington University in May 2022, Antony Blinken articulated the US's approach as: 'invest, align, and compete' to manage the 'complex and consequential' US–China relationship,[35] similar to the articulation in the NSS subsequently released in October.

Marking the Biden administration's initial moves against China, the US telecom regulator blacklisted five Chinese companies in March 2021, including Huawei Technologies, stating that they posed a threat to the US national security under a 2019 law.[36] In the following month, the US Senate approved the Strategic Competition Act, mandating diplomatic and strategic initiatives to counteract Beijing.[37] The move reflected a hardline bipartisan sentiment on dealings with China. Expanding on the Trump-era blacklist, the Biden administration also issued an executive order in June 2021, seeking to bar American investment into Chinese firms with purported ties to defense or surveillance technology sectors.[38] The same month, the US Senate passed the Innovation and Competition Act intended to boost domestic semiconductor manufacturing by allowing for funding for scientific research and subsidies for chipmakers in the US as part of its overall aim of outcompeting China.[39]

The US Department of Commerce implemented export controls on advanced computing and semiconductors to China in October 2022. The official release from the Bureau of Industry and Security states that the move intends to 'protect US national security and foreign policy interests' and will 'restrict the People's Republic of China's (PRC's) ability to both purchase and manufacture certain high-end chips used in military applications'.[40] The export controls require companies to receive a license to export US-made advanced computing and semiconductor products to China. The new export controls have been assessed as one of the strictest US actions against China in recent years. The US chip measures have also been coordinated with important partners, including Japan[41] and the Netherlands,[42] the two other key players in the advanced semiconductor ecosystem. When the Republicans took control of Congress in 2023, with bipartisan support, they created a new Congressional Select Committee on competition with China. The committee focuses on issues surrounding the rivalry between the US and China, including technological capability, intellectual property protection and research security.

An executive order was issued by President Biden on 9 August 2023 that addressed the US's investments in certain national security technologies and products in countries of concern. The order identified China as a country of concern that seeks to develop and exploit sensitive or advanced technologies or products critical for military, intelligence, surveillance or cyber-enabled capabilities. The draft regulations subsequently issued an aim to establish a new programme to prohibit or require notification of certain types of outbound investments by the US persons into certain entities located in or subject to the jurisdiction of China and certain other entities owned by persons of China involved in specific categories of advanced technologies and products.[43]

The CHIPS and Science Act, passed in August 2022 by the Biden administration, aimed to remedy the US's overseas dependence on China.[44] The bill allocated about $53 billion in federal funding to manufacture semiconductor chips in the US.

Towards the end of its first year in office, in December 2021, the administration passed the Uyghur Forced Labor Prevention Act, which banned imports from China's Xinjiang region.[45] The Act came into effect in June 2022. Taking a firm step to show its disapproval of China's treatment of minorities in the Xinjiang region, the US Treasury Department also put eight Chinese technology firms on the investment blacklist for their alleged support of the 'biometric surveillance and tracking of ethnic and religious minorities in China, particularly the predominantly Muslim Uyghur minority in Xinjiang'.[46]

Cooperating

While the emphasis on Washington's growing competition with Beijing comes across clearly in the US's strategy documents and actions, the Biden administration has also highlighted the possibility and need for cooperation with China. For instance, the Interim NSS says,

> we also recognize that strategic competition does not, and should not, preclude working with China when it is in our national interest to do so. Indeed, renewing America's advantages ensures that we will engage China from a position of confidence and strength. We will conduct practical, results-oriented diplomacy with Beijing and work to reduce the risk of misperception and miscalculation.

In a speech on 20 April 2023 at John Hopkins University in Washington, the US Treasury Secretary Janet Yellen insisted that since the US and China are the largest and second largest economies, respectively, and are deeply integrated, a 'decoupling' of both economies 'would be destabilizing for the rest of the world'. Hence, she hinted at the possibility of toning down of some of the US's rhetoric related to China, and defining more narrowly the scope of economic and technology restrictions to when they were relevant to national security considerations and not aimed at gaining just economic advantage. However, she also expressed concern about China's 'recent uptick in coercive actions targeting US firms', especially at a time when China states that it is reopening for foreign investment. These comments were in response to the Chinese actions against the US firms such as Micron, due diligence firm Mintz and consulting firm Bain. China has also expanded its anti-espionage law to tighten State control over a wider range of data and digital activities, causing concern to foreign businesses.[47] In April this year, the US Chamber of Commerce issued a statement in response to Beijing's crackdown on some US businesses in China. The statement mentioned, 'we encourage the Chinese government to consult with the foreign business community on the revised law and then issue implementing regulations that provide reasonable clarity and address the practical questions investors have.'[48] Chinese actions have been seen as response to US measures, aimed at getting US business to lobby the US government to soften some of the restrictions imposed, and show greater openness to European businesses to drive a wedge in any broader Western coordination on China.

Speaking at Brookings on 27 April 2023, the US National Security Advisor Jake Sullivan, while elaborating on the 'Biden Administration's International Economic Agenda', said, 'We've implemented carefully tailored restrictions on the most advanced semiconductor technology exports to China. Those restrictions are premised on straightforward national security concerns … And we're making progress in addressing outbound investments in sensitive technologies with a core national security nexus.' He added that, 'we are for de-risking and diversifying, not decoupling. We'll keep investing in our own capacities, and in secure, resilient supply chains. We'll keep pushing for a level playing field for our workers and companies and defending against abuses.'[49] The reference to 'de-risking' rather than 'decoupling' was seen as an effort to align the US and EU positions.

The US–China relations have seen many instances of heightened friction during this period. Following Speaker of the House of Representatives Nancy Pelosi's visit to Taiwan in August 2022, Beijing launched military exercises around the island and suspended or cancelled eight official military-level dialogues and cooperation channels with the US.[50] When Biden and Xi held their first in-person meeting on the sidelines of the G20 Summit in Bali in November 2022, it was agreed, however, that channels of communication would be kept open and that the Secretary of State would visit Beijing to continue the process. There was a subsequent fallout in relations due to the 'balloon incident', when a US fighter jet shot a Chinese spy balloon that had flown across a large swathe of the US territory.[51] Secretary of State Antony Blinken, who was scheduled to visit China in February 2023, had to postpone his trip and eventually went there in mid-June. Earlier, then Chinese foreign minister Qin Gang had met the US ambassador to China, Nick Burns, in

Beijing on 8 May 2023, wherein he emphasised the need for stabilising the relationship between the two countries.[52] The US National security adviser Jake Sullivan met with top Chinese official Wang Yi in Vienna on 11 May 2023,[53] in Malta in September and in Bangkok on 26–27 January 2024. These meetings were, inter alia, described as 'part of ongoing efforts to maintain open lines of communication and responsibly manage competition'.

On 25 May 2023, the US Commerce Secretary Gina Raimondo met with Minister of Commerce of the People's Republic of China Wang Wentao in Washington, DC.[54] This bilateral meeting came amid planned US actions to curb American investments into China in certain high-technology sectors. The following day Wang Wentao met with the US Trade Representative Katherine Tai on the margins of the APEC Ministers Responsible for Trade Meeting in Detroit.[55] According to the official statement, Tai 'discussed the importance of the US–China trade relationship in the global economy and the need for both sides to continue engaging with one another.'

Xie Feng, the newly appointed Chinese Ambassador to the US, who arrived in Washington DC on 23 May 2023, during his meeting with the US Under Secretary of State Victoria Nuland, said that 'it is important to uphold the principles of mutual respect, peaceful coexistence and win-win cooperation, enhance dialogue, manage differences and promote cooperation, so as to bring the China–US relationship back to the right track.'[56] A Sunnylands common position was developed on 14 November 2023 on climate change between the chief negotiators of the US and China, John Kerry and Xie Zhenhua, in the run-up to the COP28 in the UAE later that month.

During the G7 meeting in Hiroshima on 19–21 May 2023, the member countries had also expressed concerns about the economic challenges posed by China. Articulating their collective stance on China, the joint statement states, 'We are not decoupling or turning inwards. At the same time, we recognize that economic resilience requires de-risking and diversifying.'[57] In response, China's Ministry of Foreign Affairs spokesperson issued remarks under the title 'Hyping up of China-related Issues' and stated that the G7 is 'hindering international peace, undermining regional stability and curbing other countries' development'.[58]

The US President Biden and Chinese President Xi had a summit meeting in Woodside, California on 15 November 2023, on the margins of the APEC summit. The US readout of the meeting stated that 'President Biden emphasized that the United States and China are in competition, noting that the United States would continue to invest in the sources of American strength at home and align with allies and partners around the world.'

It went on to stress the 'importance of responsibly managing competitive aspects of the relationship, preventing conflict, maintaining open lines of communication, cooperating on areas of shared interest'.

The future pathway was described as 'continued high-level diplomacy and interactions, including visits in both directions and ongoing working-level consultations in key areas, including on commercial, economic, financial, Asia-Pacific, arms control and nonproliferation, maritime, export control enforcement, policy-planning, agriculture, and disability issues'.

The US projection of the meeting was that Biden maintained his position on issues but was able to stabilise the China relationship with revival of across-the-board communications, including at the highest levels. There are also subsequent reports of less aggressive Chinese manoeuvres around the US ships and aircraft moving through or over the South China Sea.

The Chinese readout, however, claimed that Xi argued that 'major power competition cannot solve the problems facing China, US and the world'.

Clearly, structural challenges in the relationship remain. However, one can expect both countries to try and maintain guardrails in 2024, in the run-up to the US presidential elections in November. For China, Biden would be a more predictable adversary than Trump.

Conclusion

There is bipartisan recognition in the US that it needs to compete vigorously with China in trade, investment and technology if it wants to sustain its leadership position in the global system. It also needs to develop a response to the growing Chinese economic and security footprint in different regions, especially the Indo-Pacific. Various US efforts domestically, and to rebuild relationships around the world, are aimed at responding to the China challenge. At the same time, the US wants to keep channels of communication open with China to signal its intent at competition and pushback, but prevent the relationship from 'veering towards conflict'. It would also not like to have to deal with a two-front major conflict situation, in view of the ongoing Russia–Ukraine conflict in the European theatre. It is also attempting to prevent China from providing major lethal supplies to aid the Russian war effort. However, economic and technology competition and striving for greater influence in defining global rules and norms are here to stay for the foreseeable future in the US–China relationship.

Notes

1 'Interim National Security Strategic Guidance', The White House, 2021, https://www.whitehouse.gov/briefing-room/statements-releases/2021/03/03/interim-national-security-strategic-guidance/.
2 'The Biden-Harris Administration's National Security Strategy', The White House, 2022, https://www.whitehouse.gov/briefing-room/statements-releases/2022/10/12/fact-sheet-the-biden-harris-administrations-national-security-strategy/.

3. 'Indo-Pacific Strategy of the United States', The White House, 2022, https://www.whitehouse.gov/briefing-room/speeches-remarks/2022/02/11/fact-sheet-indo-pacific-strategy-of-the-united-states/.
4. 'ASEAN-US Special Summit 2022, Joint Vision Statement.' The White House, 2022, https://www.whitehouse.gov/briefing-room/statements-releases/2022/05/13/asean-u-s-special-summit-2022-joint-vision-statement/.
5. 'Remarks by President Biden and President Yoon Suk Yeol of the Republic of Korea in Joint Press Conference', The White House, 2022, https://www.whitehouse.gov/briefing-room/speeches-remarks/2022/05/21/remarks-by-president-biden-and-president-yoon-suk-yeol-of-the-republic-of-korea-in-joint-press-conference/.
6. 'Quad Joint Leaders' Statement', The White House, 2022, https://www.whitehouse.gov/briefing-room/statements-releases/2022/05/24/quad-joint-leaders-statement/. The first-ever leadership summit was held virtually on 12 March 2021. On 24 September 2021, President Biden hosted Prime Minister Scott Morrison of Australia, Prime Minister Narendra Modi of India and Prime Minister Yoshihide Suga of Japan at the White House for the first-ever in-person Leaders' Summit.
7. 'Fact Sheet: In Asia, President Biden and a Dozen Indo-Pacific Partners Launch the Indo-Pacific Economic Framework for Prosperity', The White House, 2022.
8. Ken Moriyasu, 'Biden's IPEF Trade Pact Lacks Core Policy: CSIS Head', NIKKEI Asia, 21 October 2022, https://asia.nikkei.com/Politics/International-relations/Indo-Pacific/Biden-s-IPEF-trade-pact-lacks-core-policy-CSIS-head.
9. Han-Koo Yeo and Wendy Cutler, 'Strengthening Regional Supply Chain Resiliency Through the Indo-Pacific Economic Framework (IPEF)', Asia Society Policy Institute, 2023, https://asiasociety.org/policy-institute/strengthening-regional-supply-chain-resiliency-through-indo-pacific-economic-framework-ipef#how-can-ipef-contribute-to-supply-chain-resilience--15658.
10. 'Indo-Pacific Economic Framework Ministerial Summit Concludes in Los Angeles', *Business Standard*, 10 September 2022, https://www.business-standard.com/article/international/indo-pacific-economic-framework-ministerial-summit-concludes-in-los-angeles-122091000061_1.html.
11. 'Joint USTR and Department of Commerce Readout of the First Indo-Pacific Economic Framework Negotiating Round', Office of the United States Trade Representative, 15 December 2022, https://ustr.gov/about-us/policy-offices/press-office/press-releases/2022/december/joint-ustr-and-department-commerce-readout-first-indo-pacific-economic-framework-negotiating-round.
12. Ibid.
13. 'India Hosts the Special Negotiation Round for Pillars II-IV of Indo-Pacific Economic Framework (IPEF) from 8 to 11 February 2023 in New Delhi', Press Information Bureau, 13 February 2023, https://pib.gov.in/PressReleasePage.aspx?PRID=1898768#:~:text=India%20hosted%20the%20special%20negotiating,and%20IV%20(Fair%20Economy).
14. Joint Statement from Indo–Pacific Economic Framework For Prosperity Partner Nations, US Department of Commerce, 16 November 2023.

15 'US–Pacific Island Country Summit: 28–29 September 2022 in Washington, D.C.', US Department of State, https://www.state.gov/u-s-pacific-islands-country-summit/.
16 Zongyuan Zoe Liu, 'What the China-Solomon Islands Pact Means for the US and South Pacific', Council on Foreign Relations, 4 May 2022, https://www.cfr.org/in-brief/china-solomon-islands-security-pact-us-south-pacific.
17 'US–Pacific Islands Forum Leaders Dialogue in Port Moresby, Papua New Guinea', The White House, 22 May 2023, https://www.whitehouse.gov/briefing-room/statements-releases/2023/05/22/u-s-pacific-islands-forum-leaders-dialogue-in-port-moresby-papua-new-guinea/.
18 'ASEAN–U.S. Leaders' Statement on the Establishment of the ASEAN-U.S. Comprehensive Strategic Partnership', The White House, 12 November 2022, https://www.whitehouse.gov/briefing-room/statements-releases/2022/11/12/asean-u-s-leaders-statement-on-the-establishment-of-the-asean-u-s-comprehensive-strategic-partnership/.
19 'Remarks by President Biden and President Yoon Suk Yeol of the Republic of Korea in Joint Press Conference', The White House, 21 May 2022, https://www.whitehouse.gov/briefing-room/speeches-remarks/2022/05/21/remarks-by-president-biden-and-president-yoon-suk-yeol-of-the-republic-of-korea-in-joint-press-conference/.
20 'Fact Sheet: President Joseph R. Biden and President Joko Widodo Announce the US–Indonesia Comprehensive Strategic Partnership', US Embassy and Consulates in Indonesia, 13 November 2023, https://id.usembassy.gov/fact-sheet-president-joseph-r-biden-and-president-joko-widodo-announce-the-u-s-indonesia-comprehensive-strategic-partnership/#:~:text=The%20United%20States%20and%20Indonesia,on%20quality%20investments%20through%20the.
21 'National Security Strategy of Japan', Ministry of Foreign Affairs, December 2022, https://www.cas.go.jp/jp/siryou/221216anzenhoshou/nss-e.pdf.
22 'National Defense Strategy', Ministry of Defense, 16 December 2022, https://www.mod.go.jp/j/approach/agenda/guideline/strategy/pdf/strategy_en.pdf.
23 'Defense Buildup Programme', Ministry of Defense, 16 December 2022, https://www.mod.go.jp/j/approach/agenda/guideline/plan/pdf/program_en.pdf.
24 'Statement by National Security Advisor Jake Sullivan on Japan's Historic National Security Strategy', The White House, 16 December 2022, https://www.whitehouse.gov/briefing-room/statements-releases/2022/12/16/statement-by-national-sescurity-advisor-jake-sullivan-on-japans-historic-national-security-strategy/.
25 Nike Ching, 'US, Japan Deepen Alliance to Deter Rising Chinese Military Threats', VOA, 11 January 2023, https://www.voanews.com/a/us-and-japan-deepen-alliance-to-deter-rising-chinese-military-threats/6913426.html.
26 Jean Mackenzie and Nicholas Yong, 'South Korea to Compensate Victims of Japan's Wartime Forced Labour,' BBC, 6 March 2023, https://www.bbc.com/news/world-asia-64858944.
27 'Statement from President Joe Biden on Japan-ROK Announcement', The White House, 5 March 2023. https://www.whitehouse.gov/briefing-room/statements-releases/2023/03/05/statement-from-president-joe-biden-on-japan-rok-announcement/.

28 'PM Kishida Arrives in Seoul for First Visit by a Japanese Leader in 12 years', *The Indian Express*, 8 May 2023, https://indianexpress.com/article/world/japan-pm-south-korea-visit-8597194/.

29 Nancy A. Youssef, 'New US Base on Guam Is Aimed at Deterring China', *The Wall Street Journal*, 26 January 2023, https://www.wsj.com/articles/new-u-s-base-on-guam-is-aimed-at-deterring-china-11674731857.

30 Jim Garamone, 'Austin Visit to Philippine Base Highlights Benefits of US–Philippine Alliance', US Department of Defense, 1 February 2023, https://www.defense.gov/News/News-Stories/Article/Article/3284587/austin-visit-to-philippine-base-highlights-benefits-of-us-philippine-alliance/.

31 'U.S. Support for the Philippines in the South China Sea,' US Department of State, 13 February 2023, https://www.state.gov/u-s-support-for-the-philippines-in-the-south-china-sea-3/.

32 'Fact Sheet: Trilateral Australia–UK–US Partnership on Nuclear-Powered Submarines', The White House, 13 March 2023, https://www.whitehouse.gov/briefing-room/statements-releases/2023/03/13/fact-sheet-trilateral-australia-uk-us-partnership-on-nuclear-powered-submarines/.

33 'NATO 2022 Strategic Concept' adopted by the heads of state and government at the NATO Summit in Madrid, 29 June 2022, https://www.nato.int/nato_static_fl2014/assets/pdf/2022/6/pdf/290622-strategic-concept.pdf.

34 'G7 Hiroshima Leaders' Communiqué', The White House, 20 May 2023, https://www.whitehouse.gov/briefing-room/statements-releases/2023/05/20/g7-hiroshima-leaders-communique/.

35 Antony J. Blinken, Speech: 'The Administration's Approach to the People's Republic of China', US Department of State, 26 May 2022, https://www.state.gov/the-administrations-approach-to-the-peoples-republic-of-china/.

36 David Shepardson, 'Five Chinese Companies Pose Threat to US National Security–FCC', Reuters, 13 March 2021, https://www.reuters.com/article/us-usa-china-tech-idUSKBN2B42DW.

37 Patricia Zengerle and Michael Martina, 'US Lawmakers Intensify Bipartisan Efforts to Counter China', Reuters, 21 April 2021, https://www.reuters.com/world/asia-pacific/us-lawmakers-look-advance-sweeping-bid-counter-china-2021-04-21/.

38 'Fact Sheet: Executive Order Addressing the Threat from Securities Investments that Finance Certain Companies of the People's Republic of China', The White House, 3 June 2021, https://www.whitehouse.gov/briefing-room/statements-releases/2021/06/03/fact-sheet-executive-order-addressing-the-threat-from-securities-investments-that-finance-certain-companies-of-the-peoples-republic-of-china/.

39 Thomas Franck, 'Senate Passes $250 Billion Bipartisan Tech and Manufacturing Bill Aimed at Countering China', CNBC, 8 June 2021, https://www.cnbc.com/2021/06/08/senate-passes-bipartisan-tech-and-manufacturing-bill-aimed-at-china.html.

40 'Commerce Implements New Export Controls on Advanced Computing and Semiconductor', Bureau of Industry and Security, US Department of Commerce, 7 October 2022, https://www.bis.doc.gov/index.php/documents/

about-bis/newsroom/press-releases/3158-2022-10-07-bis-press-release-advanced-computing-and-semiconductor-manufacturing-controls-final/file.
41 Annabelle Liang, 'US–China Chip War: Japan Plans to Restrict Some Equipment Exports', BBC, 31 March 2023, https://www.bbc.com/news/business-65134017.
42 Pieter Haeck, 'The Netherlands to Block Export of Advanced Chips Printers to China', Politico, 8 March 2023, https://www.politico.eu/article/netherlands-impose-restrictions-chips-export-to-china-asml/.
43 'Executive Order on Addressing United States Investments in Certain National Security Technologies and Products in Countries of Concern', The White House, 9 August 2023, https://www.whitehouse.gov/briefing-room/presidential-actions/2023/08/09/executive-order-on-addressing-united-states-investments-in-certain-national-security-technologies-and-products-in-countries-of-concern/.
44 'Fact Sheet: Chips and Science Act will Lower Costs, Create Jobs, Strengthen Supply Chains, and Counter China', The White House, 9 August 2022, https://www.whitehouse.gov/briefing-room/statements-releases/2022/08/09/fact-sheet-chips-and-science-act-will-lower-costs-create-jobs-strengthen-supply-chains-and-counter-china/.
45 'Uyghur Forced Labor Prevention Act', US Customs and Border Protection, https://www.cbp.gov/trade/forced-labor/UFLPA.
46 'Treasury Identifies Eight Chinese Tech Firms as Part of The Chinese Military-Industrial Complex', US Department of the Treasury, 16 December 2021, https://home.treasury.gov/news/press-releases/jy0538.
47 'China: Anti-Espionage Law Heightens Risks for Foreign Firms', DW, 5 May 2023, https://www.dw.com/en/china-anti-espionage-law-heightens-risks-for-foreign-firms/a-65528537#:~:text=China's%20rubber%2Dstamp%20parliament%20last,deemed%20related%20to%20national%20security.
48 'US Chamber Statement on Concerns Over PRC Investment Climate', US Chamber of Commerce, 28 April 2023, https://www.uschamber.com/international/u-s-chamber-statement-on-concerns-over-prc-investment-climate.
49 'Remarks by National Security Advisor Jake Sullivan on Renewing American Economic Leadership at the Brookings Institution', The White House.
50 'The Ministry of Foreign Affairs Announces Countermeasures in Response to Nancy Pelosi's Visit to Taiwan', Ministry of Foreign Affairs of the People's Republic of China, 5 August 2022, https://www.fmprc.gov.cn/eng/zxxx_662805/202208/t20220805_10735706.html.
51 James Palmer, 'How a Chinese Spy Balloon Blew Up a Key US Diplomatic Trip', Foreign Policy, 3 February 2023, https://foreignpolicy.com/2023/02/03/china-spy-balloon-surveillance-montana-us-nuclear-blinken/.
52 Nectar Gan, 'China Says Relations with US on "Cold Ice", but Stabilizing Ties a "Top Priority"', CNN, 8 May 2023, https://edition.cnn.com/2023/05/08/china/china-us-qin-gang-nicholas-burns-meet-intl-hnk/index.html.
53 'Readout of National Security Advisor Jake Sullivan's Meeting with Chinese Communist Party Politburo Member and Director of the Office of the Foreign Affairs Commission Wang Yi', The White House, 11 May 2023, https://www.whitehouse.

gov/briefing-room/statements-releases/2023/05/11/readout-of-national-security-advisor-jake-sullivans-meeting-with-chinese-communist-party-politburo-member-and-director-of-the-office-of-the-foreign-affairs-commission-wang-yi/.
54 'Readout of Secretary Raimondo's Meeting with Ministry of Commerce Minister Wang Wentao', US Department of Commerce, 25 May 2023, https://www.commerce.gov/news/press-releases/2023/05/readout-secretary-raimondos-meeting-ministry-commerce-minister-wang.
55 'Readout of Ambassador Katherine Tai's Meeting with Minister of Commerce of the People's Republic of China Wang Wentao', Office of the US State Representative, 26 May 2023, https://ustr.gov/about-us/policy-offices/press-office/press-releases/2023/may/readout-ambassador-katherine-tais-meeting-minister-commerce-peoples-republic-china-wang-wentao.
56 'Ambassador Xie Feng Met with US Under Secretary of State Victoria Nuland', Embassy of the People's Republic of China in the United States of America, 25 May 2023, http://us.china-embassy.gov.cn/eng/dshd/202305/t20230526_11084020.htm.
57 'G7 Hiroshima Leaders' Communiqué', The White House, 20 May 2023, https://www.whitehouse.gov/briefing-room/statements-releases/2023/05/20/g7-hiroshima-leaders-communique/.
58 'Foreign Ministry Spokesperson's Remarks on G7 Hiroshima Summit's Hyping up of China-related Issues', Ministry of Foreign Affairs of People's Republic of China.

5

China's Foreign Policy Under Xi Jinping
Transformations and Problems
Srikanth Kondapalli

China's foreign policy under President Xi Jinping has been undergoing transformations since he took over the reins of administration in 2012. While in the Communist Party–state system of China there is a certain continuity between policies under different leaderships, many changes have emerged during Xi's tenure. Xi had presided over three Communist Party (CPC) Congresses, in 2012 (18th), 2017 (19th) and 2022 (20th), with important directives on foreign policies of the country. In addition, Xi also presided over three central conferences on work relating to foreign affairs (中央外事工作会) 28–29 November 2014, 22–23 June 2018 and 27–28 December 2023, the 4th, 5th and 6th meetings respectively, where the guidelines for the diplomatic corps of the country were laid down. Xi also travelled abroad hundreds of times during his tenure of over a decade, making several speeches and remarks on foreign policy. These suggest a gradual transformation from Deng Xiaoping's *taoguang yanghui* (韬光养晦 or 'keep a low profile') to *fenfa youwei* (奋发有为 or 'accomplish something'), with greater emphasis, recently, on national security than on the economy. Significantly, a grand strategy is also evolving to include preparations for two centennials (the Communist Party in 2021 and the People's Republic in 2049), realising the 'China Dream' and 'China Rejuvenation'; building a 'community of common destiny'; implementing 'socialism with Chinese characteristics under the new era' and outlining global strategies on security, development and civilisation (referred to as its Global Security Initiative, GSI; Global Development Initiative, GDI and Global Civilisational Initiative, GCI). This has coincided with the 19th Communist Party Congress agenda in 2017 of 'occupying the centre stage', or acquiring hegemony at the global and Asian regional levels. With these, China's foreign policy acquired new dimensions, such as focusing on 'major power relations', 'wolf warrior diplomacy (战狼外交)', 'core interests' and an outreach programme of Belt and Road Initiative (BRI). With the formation of a new Central Foreign Affairs Commission in February 2018, the foreign policy establishment was further centralised. Cumulatively, these were termed 'Xi Jinping Thought on Diplomacy' at the 18th CPC Congress.

It is argued in this chapter that by following the above guidelines under Xi, China's foreign policies achieved many successes but also relative losses. Its main achievements in the last decade include China's global outreach in terms of the BRI projects, which attracted more than eighty countries; bracing international sanctions on Xinjiang and other areas; nudging the US–North Korea talks in Hanoi and Singapore; China–Central Asia Summit meetings; 'limitless partnership' with Russia and enhanced influence in Africa and South America. However, China also faced setbacks with economic decline and the COVID-19 pandemic, which negatively affected China's soft power across the world; the US–China 'decoupling' process that seemingly brought China under Cold War 2.0 conditions and sanctions; getting labelled as a 'systemic rival' by the European Union that followed a 'de-risking' strategy and tensions with India, Japan, Vietnam, the Philippines and others over sovereignty issues. Significantly, though the Party organisations have strengthened in foreign policy under Xi, his handpicked foreign minister Qin Gang disappeared in mid-2023 and has been missing since.

Introduction

In China, the CPC's dominance pervades all walks of life, including foreign policy. The leadership of the party and its ideology is binding on the matter of its establishment. Since the elevation of Xi Jinping to the top leadership position since the 18th CPC Congress in 2012, over-centralisation of Party authority has become the norm.[1] These are expressed in the labelling of Xi as the 'core of the leadership' and his thought as the guiding philosophy in diplomacy and other areas.[2] Xi's term since 2012 was called the 'new era' to distinguish it from the tenures of previous leaders, such as Mao Zedong and Deng Xiaoping. Xi's Party Congress injunctions, foreign affairs work conference reports and his speeches and visits abroad and responses to the ground reality form the oeuvre of China's foreign policy.[3]

As the third largest country in the world by area, having the largest population until July 2023, second largest economy in the world since 2010,[4] largest trading partner for more than half of the countries across the world, a permanent member of the United Nations Security Council since 1971 and a major nuclear and conventional military power, China holds considerable heft in the international domain. Mao Zedong once called China the 'centre of gravity' in Asia. But Xi's China initiated plans that went even beyond Asia – such as the transcontinental BRI in 2013, Global Development Initiative, Global Security Initiative, Global Civilisational Initiative and multilateral initiatives with Central and East Europe, Africa, South America and others. China's inherent strengths and aspirations have coalesced under Xi to provide an expanded agenda in the country's foreign policy.[5]

Party Perspectives

The enlarged agenda of Chinese foreign policy in the recent times is seen in the Party and other documents. For instance, the 18th CPC in 2012, when Xi became the General Secretary of the Party, emphasis was laid on relations with major powers, reforms in global governance, multilateralism, core interests, good neighbourliness, building soft power, etc.[6] The previous Party Congresses had advocated 'three pillars' (relations with major powers, neighbours and developing countries) and 'five pillars' (relations with major powers, neighbours, developing countries, multilateralism and soft power). Soon after taking the reins of the Party into his hands, Xi stated that core interests are more important than developmental interests.[7] The core interests were mainly related to China's perceived national sovereignty and territorial integrity issues.

A year later, in June 2013, China unveiled a 'new type of major power relations' with the US (and Russia and Europe) that mentions 'non-conflict, non-confrontation, win-win' relations. This is to prevent competition between China and the US from going out of hand and to steer relations that facilitated China's rise, stability in Taiwan Straits, etc. China also began its ambitious BRI in 2013, with three summit meetings being held till 2023, and over $956 billion in investments in 'five connectivities' (policy coordination, physical connectivity, trade promotion, renminbi internationalisation and people-to-people contacts) across most continents.[8] Despite criticism and a slowdown in the BRI projects due to the spread of the pandemic and other factors, China did garner considerable diplomatic mileage out of these projects.

At the 19th CPC Congress in 2017, Xi made the most audacious announcement that China wished to move to the 'centre stage' of global politics with a concrete roadmap till 2049 (to build a 'well-off society' by 2021, a 'well-off society with socialism' by 2035 and 'socialist modernisation' by 2050), coinciding with the 200th anniversary of the People's Republic. 'China Dream', 'China Rejuvenation', 'community of common destiny', a new type of international relations, 'Five Principles of Peaceful Coexistence', independent foreign policy, good neighbourhood and other goals were mentioned in this context. BRI was inserted into the Party constitution, aligning it to China's cross-century projects. Xi also stated that multipolarity phenomenon is 'rapidly accelerating'– a euphemism for the self-assertion and defensive response and anti-US postures taken by several countries. With the core interests in mind, Xi declared a 'six Nos' policy, that is, to 'anyone, any organisation, any political party, at any time or in any form, to separate any part of Chinese territory from China'. While this was mainly meant for Taiwan scenarios, it is potentially applicable to all sovereignty claims that China has raised, including in Japan, Southeast Asian countries and India. Xi suggested that the country should 'maintain sufficient ability to defeat any form of Taiwan independence'. For this, a major reorganisation of the armed forces was called for, including ushering in joint operations by 2020, completing mechanisation and informationisation by 2035 and raising a 'world-class' military by 2050. The burgeoning State-owned enterprises were asked to 'expan[d] state capital … [and become] globally competitive world class firms'.[9] Unlike in the 1990s, when Chinese companies faced hostile environments abroad, they have now expanded owing to increasing mergers and acquisitions.[10]

The 20th CPC Congress held in October 2022 is a remarkable departure from the previous Party Congresses, with its emphasis on national security rather than on economic growth. This came against the background of all-round disruptions caused by the COVID-19 pandemic, the Russia–Ukraine war, technological disruptions, relative economic decline of China in the wake of US–China tensions and also the domestic political churning process.[11] The wording of the Congress report is also strong. For instance, the report noted the ways of 'effectively responding to grave, intricate international developments and a series of immense risks and challenges', condemning 'external attempts to blackmail, contain, blockade, and exert maximum pressure on China'. It was critical of 'mechanisms for countering foreign sanctions, interference', and ascertained that 'long-arm jurisdiction will be strengthened', alluding to 'intricate' and 'grave' international developments, involving 'global changes of a magnitude not seen in a century' that present 'a series of immense risks and challenges' for China. While it called for building a 'peaceful … [but] fortified China', it suggested that China 'must take the people's security as our ultimate goal, political security as our fundamental task, economic security as our foundation, military, technological, cultural and social security as important pillars, and international security as a support'. Significantly, it also declared that 'national security is the foundation of national rejuvenation, and social stability'. It suggested taking 'strategic initiative for China's complete reunification' without ruling out the 'use of force'. Emphasis on national security implied that China's diplomats were under watch for any potential breach of secrecy or deviating from the Party line on diplomacy. The case of Qin Gang's dismissal led to several speculations, ranging from leaking nuclear secrets to his alleged links with journalists.[12]

Xi Jinping also presided over three apex central conferences on work relating to foreign affairs in 2014, 2018 and 2023 with all Politburo members and diplomats attending. While the Party Congress provides overall guidelines to different stakeholders for the next five years, the foreign affairs work conferences are specifically addressed to the foreign ministry and diplomats. Xi addressed the November 2014, 4th Central Conference on Work Relating to Foreign Affairs (中央外事工作会), stating that the diplomatic corps 'must never give up our legitimate rights and interests'. Given the current status of the rise of China, other countries were to recognise these 'legitimate rights and interests' of the nation and adapt to these demands, and China's diplomats were tasked with drilling this aspect into the minds of the countries they dealt with. They 'must resolutely safeguard territorial sovereignty and maritime rights and interests' and oppose 'the arbitrary use or threat of force'. They were to make efforts to 'seek other countries' understanding of and support for the China Dream, which is about peace, development, cooperation and win-win outcomes', 'protect China's overseas interests and continue to improve our capacity to provide such protection'.[13] At the 5th Central Conference on Work Relating to Foreign Affairs in 2018, Xi reiterated 'Socialism with Chinese Characteristics in the New Era', to build 'strategic self-confidence and maintain strategic determination, adhere to innovation in diplomatic theory and practice, adhere to strategic planning and global deployment; community of common destiny'.[14] The 6th Central Conference on Work Relating to Foreign Affairs in 2023 saw Xi suggest that China should 'coordinate development and security, and effectively safeguard national sovereignty, security, and development interests with firm will and tenacious struggle'. Further, he stated:

> We must establish a systematic concept, grasp the general trend with a correct view of history and the overall situation, make overall plans and take the initiative … We must carry forward the spirit of struggle, resolutely oppose all power politics and bullying, and effectively defend national interests and national dignity.[15]

In brief, the sum total of the Party Congresses, foreign affairs work conferences and other injunctions under Xi is that foreign policy has been elevated to Xi Jinping Thought on Diplomacy[16] alongside his elevation to the core of the leadership, with heavy centralisation of the decision-making process.[17] Many fundamentals of China's foreign policy inherited from the previous period also came under this rubric, such as independent foreign policy,[18] strategic autonomy, protecting sovereign and territorial integrity and modernisation,[19] while Socialism with Chinese Characteristics under the New Era, China Dream, China Rejuvenation, community of common destiny, major-country diplomacy,[20] multipolarity, BRI, GDI, GSI, GCI and others were added during Xi's term.[21]

Diplomatic Concepts

One of the frequently cited thoughts of Xi's is about the China Dream (中国梦),[22] which was promoted during his tour of an exhibit titled 'Road to National Rejuvenation' at the National Museum of China in November 2012. The stated objective is for China to become a 'modern socialist country that is prosperous, strong, democratic, civilised, and harmonious'. Xi said that young people should 'dare to dream, work assiduously to fulfil the dreams and contribute to the revitalisation of the nation'. It was the China Dream that inspired the BRI and the Made in China 2025 campaign.[23] Linked to this is China Rejuvenation (伟大复兴), which is said to be concerned with restoring China to its former greatness as a global power. This includes building both economic and military strength, as well as cultural influence. A 19th-century concept of 'rich country, strong army' (富国强兵) was revived as a part of this rejuvenation campaign. The implication of this concept on international relations is that it exposes irredentist claims of China on 'lost territories', with serious consequences for Senkaku Islands, South China Sea Islands and India–China border areas. It is surprising that a day before Xi visited Moscow in March 2023, China had changed the names of places in Siberia, including Vladivostok's, to Chinese names without so much as a murmur from a dependent Russia after the Ukraine conflict broke out.

Another is the 'community of common destiny' [人类命运共同体], which Xi invoked in October 2013 at a Workshop on Diplomatic Work with Neighbouring Countries. In 2015, Xi addressed the UN General Assembly, where he cited five components, namely, political partnership, economic development, security, cultural exchanges and environment. In September 2023, China's foreign ministry released a paper which listed the countries that had agreed to the Chinese version of this community of common destiny. The thirteen countries with a 'common understanding' included Pakistan, Laos, Cambodia, Myanmar, Indonesia, Kazakhstan, Tajikistan, Uzbekistan, Thailand, Mongolia, Turkmenistan, Malaysia and Kyrgyzstan. It also stated that China has an agreement to build a community of common destiny with five Lancang–Mekong countries, Cambodia, Laos, Myanmar, Thailand and Vietnam. It also outlined its decision to build such a community with countries in Central Asia, including Kazakhstan, Kyrgyzstan, Tajikistan, Turkmenistan and Uzbekistan.[24] This new concept suggests the emergence of a grand strategy of China that would have implications for its power transitions at global and regional levels. In conjunction with the Chinese leaders' stress on realising 'strategic opportunities', and other initiatives such as BRI, the Asia Infrastructure Investment Bank (AIIB), GDI, GSI and GCI, China's imprint abroad is set to expand in the near future.

Given its status as the second largest economy and trading nation, and its influence in the UN and other bodies, China is consolidating its position with its Global Development Initiative. In September 2021, Xi suggested that China prioritise development. The GDI, according to Xi, upholds the view that development is the master key to solving all problems. It is also said to have a people-centred approach, that is, the GDI puts people first and aims to promote their well-being and all-round development. It is said to benefit all as it seeks to leave no country and no person behind in the pursuit of sustainable development. It is an innovation-driven initiative, recognising innovation as a key driver of sustainable development. It also promotes green development and sustainable lifestyles, and emphasises the importance of concrete actions and measurable results in achieving sustainable development goals. In pursuance of this, a 'Group of Friends' comprising about seventy countries was formed by China in the UN on 20 January 2022. While the avowed focus of this is to further the UN's Sustainable Development Goals, the actual focus turned out to be on China's own development priorities. Besides, these goals were not well aligned with other global development initiatives, nor were any major funds allocated for this purpose.[25] GDI provides China with an alternative economic framework in the longer term – compared to the Bretton Woods institutions – even though China is a beneficiary of the latter framework. In addition, China's State-owned enterprises tend to garner contracts from other countries.

Global Security Initiative is another scheme of China's grand strategy in the security domain. As has been the Chinese practice, many initiatives that the leadership began several years ago are amalgamated into new schemes. For instance, the principles of GSI include 'common, comprehensive, cooperative and sustainable security'.[26] Some of these were mentioned earlier in the 'New Security concept' in the early 21st century, when China cobbled up with Southeast Asian countries. Other principles include respecting the sovereignty and territorial integrity of all countries, abiding by the purposes and principles of the UN Charter, taking the legitimate security concerns of all countries seriously, peacefully resolving differences and disputes between countries through dialogue and consultation and maintaining security in both traditional and non-traditional domains. China's leaders mention these ad nauseam, even though in practice they are mainly rhetorical; for example, the case of the South China Sea Islands dispute, where repeated negotiations do not yield desired outcomes, and the India–China territorial dispute in Galwan, where, despite twenty Corps Commanders meetings, 'disengagement and de-escalations' were not ushered in, violating all agreements in this regard.

Implementing GSI will cover formulating a 'new agenda for peace'; building a major-country relationship; preventing nuclear war and avoiding arms races; facilitating peace talks; implementing the five-point proposal on realising peace and stability in the Middle East; resolving conflicts in Africa and the Latin American Zone of Peace; taking up concerns of the Pacific Island countries; maritime dialogues and strengthening its role in the UN. The preferred mechanisms for addressing these security issues are through multilateral processes involving the UN, Shanghai Cooperation Organisation (SCO),

BRICS (comprising Brazil, Russia, India, China, South Africa, Iran, Egypt and Ethiopia), the Conference on Interaction and Confidence Building Measures in Asia (CICA), the 'China + Central Asia' mechanism, Meeting of Foreign Ministers of the Neighbouring Countries of Afghanistan, China-Horn of Africa Peace, Governance and Development Conference, China–Africa Peace and Security Forum, the Middle East Security Forum, the Beijing Xiangshan Forum, the Global Public Security Cooperation Forum and others.

China's Global Civilisation Initiative aims to dominate the global cultural domain, which is currently dominated by the Western ethos. In the light of Samuel Huntington's 'clash of civilisations' debate and the US Director of Policy Planning Kiron Skinner's observations that Chinese are 'not Caucasian',[27] China began preparing for conflict in the new domain of culture. Beijing advocated dialogue, or even an alliance of civilisations. It organised mega conferences to allow for this by inviting mainly non-Western civilisational representatives. It advocated for respecting the diversity of civilisations; common values of humanity (to promote China's own values and interests); emphasised the importance of inheritance and innovation of civilisations; argued for robustness in international people-to-people exchanges and cooperation and, in its current 14th Five Year Plan, proposed and implemented its objective of becoming a 'Socialist Cultural Power'.

While the above concepts have been put across in an innocuous manner and many a time did not ruffle feathers of global and regional orders, a phenomenon under Xi that became controversial was 'wolf warrior' diplomacy [战狼外交], which drew inspiration from a film series by the same name. The first film in the series ended with the slogan 'Whoever attacks China will be killed no matter how far away' [犯我 中华者，虽远必诛].[28] The sequel to this film ended with a message onscreen: 'Citizens of the People's Republic of China. When you encounter danger in a foreign land, do not give up! Please remember, at your back stands a strong motherland.' Clubbed with the revival of the 'middle kingdom' syndrome in China, with its 'barbarian versus civilised' discourse and rise of nationalism within the country, 'wolf warrior' diplomacy resulted in its 'assertive' approach to international relations in the last decade. Many foreign ministry officials were associated with this school of thought, including Zhao Lijian, Lu Shaoye, Liu Xiaoming, Wang Wenbin and Hua Chunying.

Zhao Lijian, for instance, criticised the US military for allegedly introducing bioweapons at Wuhan military sports events in October 2019. The foreign ministry was also critical of the US and Western sanctions on issues related to Xinjiang,[29] Tibet, Taiwan, South China Sea and Huawei and ZTE as companies. Australia raising the issue of the COVID-19 virus originating in Wuhan at the World Health Assembly in May 2020 also raised hackles among China's diplomats.³⁰ In December 2020, Zhao Lijian tweeted a digitally altered image of an Australian soldier holding a bloodied knife to the throat of an Afghan child. Then Australian prime minister Scott Morrison retorted, 'The Chinese government should be totally ashamed of this post. It diminishes them in the world's eyes.'³¹ Further, in April 2020, China's ambassador to France Lu Shaye criticised the West's criticism of China's handling of the COVID-19 outbreak. In March 2021, the Chinese embassy in Paris warned against French lawmakers meeting officials during an upcoming visit to Taiwan, and the embassy described Antoine Bondaz of the Foundation for Strategic Research as a 'small-time thug' and 'mad hyena'.

Even though Xi Jinping observed at a study session on 31 May 2021 that diplomats should present an image of a 'credible, lovable and respectable China to the world … [and that it] is necessary to make friends, unite and win over the majority, and constantly expand the circle of friends [when it comes to] international public opinion', 'wolf warrior' diplomacy had cost China much of its soft power across the world. For instance, an internal report by the China Institute of Contemporary International Relations, a think tank affiliated with the Ministry of State Security, reportedly warned of anti-China sentiment rising due to the coronavirus outbreak.³² A Pew survey conducted from June 2020 to August 2020 found that unfavourable views of China had reached historic highs in 2020.³³ Also, the Portland Soft Power Index placed China at twenty-seven out of thirty countries in its global rankings.³⁴

Assessment

The new concepts and phenomenon in China's diplomatic practice outlined above suggest a major transformation in China's diplomatic practice under Xi's tenure, referred to as the 'new era'. There is definitely a shift from Deng Xiaoping's taoguang yanghui to fenfa youwei, as mentioned earlier, as the emphasis has move away from the economy to national security.³⁵ One of the consequences of this transformation is the adoption of a more assertive foreign policy approach by Xi, which is reflected in challenges to the West-dominated institutions like the Bretton Woods institutions, and in efforts to enhance multipolar trends in conjunction with Russia and other countries. Xi's assertive policy is also apparent from his comments soon after he ascended to the crucial Party-state post in 2012, that core interests were more important than developmental interests, along with his hard stance on China's sovereignty and territorial disputes with Taiwan, Japan, Southeast Asian countries, India and others.³⁶

Another feature of China's diplomacy under Xi is the recent rise in high-profile visits, summit meetings and strategic partnerships with the US, Russia, European, African and Latin American countries, India and others. Also, the three BRI summit meetings garnered publicity for China, as did multilateral fora like the BRICS, SCO and Forum for Cooperation between China and Africa (FOCAC). In order to tell China's stories to the rest of the world, it extensively utilised forums of digital diplomacy with Twitter (now X), Weibo and other social networking sites; opened CCTV channels for Africa and engaged the global public to promote China's interests. Even though China is one of the major polluters of the world, it was able to rebrand itself as a 'developing country'; continued 'united front' tactics with developing countries on 'equal but differentiated responsibilities' and declared its intention to achieve carbon neutrality by 2060.[37]

Clearly, under Xi, China has indicated a desire and will to play greater role in global and regional orders – which taoguang yanghui policies under Deng Xiaoping may have constrained. The domestic and external balancing efforts under Xi are indicators of such a direction. It is reflected in the grand strategy formulations such as unveiling pan-continental projects such as BRI, AIIB, GDI, GSI, GCI and others. BRI, despite drawing criticism for its lack of transparency, debt diplomacy, riding roughshod on sovereignty claims of other countries and the like, did attract a number of developing countries that received diversified funding for infrastructure projects. While it will perhaps take time to see positive outcomes of China's recent cobbling up of the Saudi Arabia–Iran deal, the twelve-point 'position paper' on resolving the Ukraine war, Middle East Peace Proposals, inputs on the Israel–Palestine conflict, Code of Conduct in South China Sea and various other issues, it is clear that China has stepped up its diplomatic manoeuvres in the recent times. China's 'greater diplomacy' is attracting global attention. It also made gains on the climate change and sustainable development fronts.

However, there are problems galore for China's diplomacy under Xi. While Xi clarified during a US Congressional member delegation visit in 2023 that China is *not* trying to replace the US, his statements and preparations to the contrary led to a cascading effect – the 'de-coupling' process with the US and 'de-risking' with Europe. The US had also made preparations for 'Build Back Better World' to counter the BRI, and made efforts to build Quad partnerships in addition to strengthening alliances and arms transfers to Taiwan, the Philippines and other nations.

Deng's taoguang yanghui allowed China's position in the international system to rise, while Xi's fenfa youwei pitted China prematurely against the Western countries and major countries in Asia. While China had pursued multipolarity to ward off being labelled as the 'next Soviet Union', the going is getting tough for China. Its geopolitical rivalries have sharpened due to its hostile policies; 'weaponisation' of trade, tourism and other coercive measures against South Korea, Taiwan, Australia, Thailand, Malaysia and other countries have also had a negative impact. Second, the obsession with 'core interests' and the resolve to address these challenges immediately – unlike during Zhou Enlai's and Deng Xiaoping's times – soured China's relations with its neighbours, despite the other projects and initiatives. Xi's extreme 'One China' narrative shone through his comments at the CPC's 100th anniversary celebrations in July 2021, that he 'will break the heads' of those who split China, and fuelled the world's negative perceptions of China.

Third, China's lack of transparency in investigating the origins of the COVID-19 virus in Wuhan and the millions of deaths and massive destruction the pandemic caused across the globe, in addition to supply-chain disruptions and major economic losses has brought its responsibility and accountability into question. China's export of its Party-state-backed 'China model' abroad raised concerns everywhere, despite an increase in mergers and acquisitions of Chinese businesses. Its inability to provide 'net security' – public goods and services – during humanitarian crises or natural disasters is also tarnishing its 'responsible country' image.

While Xi claimed leadership of globalisation in his Davos speeches, China's trade and investment protectionist trends have alienated the US, EU, India and other countries who have been critical of its reluctance to open up its markets. Finally, despite strengthening of the CPC leadership's role in foreign policy under Xi to unprecedented levels – reflected in the refurbishing of the Central Office of Foreign Affairs in 2018 and other national security measures – Foreign Minister Qin Gang's dismissal brought into question the effectiveness of such a centralisation process.[38]

Notes

1. Steve Tsang and Men Honghua (eds.), *China in the Xi Jinping Era*, The Nottingham China Policy Institute Series (Palgrave Macmillan, 2016); Richard McGregor, *Xi Jinping: The Backlash* (The Lowy Institute for International Policy–Penguin Random House, 2019) and Bates Gill, *Daring to Struggle – China's Global Ambitions under Xi Jinping* (New York: Oxford University Press, 2022).
2. John S. Van Oudenaren, 'Xi Jinping Thought on Diplomacy: Roadmap to Global Leadership?', *China Brief* 22, no. 18 (4 October 2022), https://jamestown.org/program/xi-jinping-thought-on-diplomacy-roadmap-to-global-leadership.
3. People's Daily, Department of Commentary, *Narrating China's Governance Stories in Xi Jinping's Speeches* (Singapore: Springer, 2020).
4. Lorenzo Bencivelli and Flavia Tonelli, *China's International Projection in the Xi Jinping Era: An Economic Perspective* (Switzerland: Springer, 2022).
5. Robert D. Blackwill and Kurt M. Campbell, 'Xi Jinping on the Global Stage Chinese Foreign Policy Under a Powerful but Exposed Leader', Council on Foreign Relations Special Report No. 74, February 2016.

6 'Firmly March on the Path of Socialism with Chinese Characteristics and Strive to Complete the Building of a Moderately Prosperous Society in All Respects', Report to the Eighteenth National Congress of the Communist Party of China, 8 November 2012, http://www.china.org.cn/china/18th_cpc_congress/2012-11/16/content_27137540.htm.

7 Wang Yi, 'Peaceful Development and the Chinese Dream of National Rejuvenation', *CIIS*, 11 March 2014, https://www.ciis.org.cn/english/COMMENTARIES/202007/t20200715_2843.html; Rosemary Foot and Amy King, 'China's World View in the Xi Jinping Era: Where do Japan, Russia and the US fit?', *The British Journal of Politics and International Relations* 23, no. 2 (2021): 210–227; and Zeng Jinghan, Xiao Yuefan and Shaun Breslin, 'Securing China's Core Interests: The State of the Debate in China', *International Affairs* 91, no. 2 (March 2015), https://www.researchgate.net/publication/274197129_Securing_China%27s_core_interests_The_state_of_the_debate_in_China.

8 Srikanth Kondapalli and Hu Xiaowen (eds), *One Belt, One Road – China's Global Outreach* (New Delhi: Pentagon Press, 2017).

9 'Secure a Decisive Victory in Building a Moderately Prosperous Society in All Respects and Strive for the Great Success of Socialism with Chinese Characteristics for a New Era', Full Text of Xi Jinping's Report at 19th CPC National Congress, Xinhuanet, 18 October 2017, http://www.xinhuanet.com/english/special/2017-11/03/c_136725942.htm.

10 'China M&A 2022 review and 2023 outlook', February 2023, https://www.pwccn.com/en/services/deals-m-and-a/publications/ma-2022-review-and-2023-outlook.html; and 'China's Mergers and Acquisitions Market: Latest Trends', *China Briefing*, 31 May 2022, https://www.china-briefing.com/news/china-mergers-and-acquisitions-market-latest-trends/. However, the US–China decoupling process and sanctions could negatively impact this sector.

11 'Hold high the great banner of socialism with Chinese characteristics and strive in unity to build a modern socialist country in all respects'. 'Full text of the report to the 20th National Congress of the Communist Party of China', Xinhua, 16 October 2022, https://english.news.cn/20221025/8eb6f5239f984f01a2bc45b5b5db0c51/c.html.

12 Kawashima Shin, 'Major Changes at China's Foreign Ministry', *The Diplomat*, 26 November 2023, https://thediplomat.com/2023/11/major-changes-at-chinas-foreign-ministry/.

13 'Xi Jinping attended the Central Foreign Affairs Work Conference and delivered an important speech', www.12371.cn, 29 November 2014, https://news.12371.cn/2014/11/29/ARTI1417254669280703.shtml. Xi stated: 'we must not be blinded by random flowers or obscured by floating clouds. Instead, we must look at the world carefully through the telescope of historical laws. Based on comprehensive judgment, our country's development is still in an important period of strategic opportunities where much can be achieved. Our biggest opportunity is to continue to grow and develop. At the same time, we must pay attention to various risks and challenges, and be good at turning crises into opportunities and dangers into safety.'

14 'Xi Jinping emphasised at the Central Foreign Affairs Work Conference that we should adhere to the guidance of socialist diplomacy with Chinese characteristics for a new era and strive to create a new situation for major-country diplomacy with Chinese characteristics', www.12371.cn, 23 June 2018, https://news.12371.cn/2018/06/23/ARTI1529759038219530.shtml.

15 'The Central Foreign Affairs Work Conference was held in Beijing and Xi Jinping delivered an important speech', www.12371.cn, 28 December 2023, https://www.12371.cn/2023/12/28/ARTI1703764696024461.shtml; and 'The Central Conference on Work Relating to Foreign Affairs was Held in Beijing Xi Jinping Delivered an Important Address at the Conference', Chinese People's Institute of Foreign Affairs, 2 January 2024, https://www.cpifa.org/en/article/2596.

16 According to Qiushi, this includes ten aspects, viz., (1) upholding the authority of the CPC Central Committee as the overarching principle and strengthening the Party's centralised, unified leadership over external work; (2) advancing major country diplomacy with Chinese characteristics to fulfill the mission of the great rejuvenation of the Chinese nation; (3) building a community with a shared future for mankind with a view to defending world peace and promoting common development; (4) enhancing strategic confidence based on the foundation of socialism with Chinese characteristics; (5) promoting Belt and Road cooperation under the principle of extensive consultation, joint contribution and shared benefits; (6) pursuing peaceful development on the basis of mutual respect and win-win cooperation; (7) fostering global partnerships by pursuing a broad-based diplomatic agenda; (8) steering the reform of the global governance system under the principle of fairness and justice; (9) upholding national sovereignty, security and development interests with China's core interests as a red line; (10) developing a distinctive Chinese style of diplomacy by both drawing on fine traditions and adapting to the changing times. See 'Ten core principles of Xi Jinping Thought on Diplomacy', *Qiushi*, 16 July 2021, http://en.qstheory.cn/2021-07/16/c_643502.htm.

17 Chih-heng Yang, 'The impact of China's diplomatic trends on the international situation after the 20th National Congress of the Communist Party of China', The Prospect Foundation, 10 November 2022, https://www.pf.org.tw/tw/pfch/12-9750.html.

18 Deng Hongbo, 'Firmly Pursue an Independent Foreign Policy of Peace', *Guangming Daily*, 14 November 2022, http://theory.people.com.cn/n1/2022/1114/c40531-32565498.html.

19 Xu Bu and Chen Wenbing, 'Xi Jinping Thought on Diplomacy Research Center: Persisting in promoting the construction of a community with a shared future for mankind', China Institute of International Studies, 19 March 2023, https://www.ciis.org.cn/yjcg/sspl/202303/t20230319_8894.html.

20 Yang Jiemian, 'Xi Jinping Thought on Diplomacy and Enlightenment from the Experience of Major Power Diplomacy with Chinese Characteristics in the New Era', China Diplomacy, 11 November 2022, http://cn.chinadiplomacy.org.cn/2022-11/15/content_78520185.shtml.

21 Wang Yi, 'Study and Implement Xi Jinping Thought on Diplomacy Conscientiously and Forge Ahead on a Momentous Journey of China's Diplomacy in the New Era', Chinese People's Institute of Foreign Affairs, *https://www.cpifa.org/en/cms/book/352*.
22 James C. Hsiung (ed.), *The Xi Jinping Era -His Comprehensive Strategy Towards China Dream* (New York: CN Times Books, 2015).
23 David Arase, 'The Geopolitics of Xi Jinping's Chinese Dream: Problems and Prospects', *ISEAS Trends in Southeast Asia*, No. 15, 2016, pp 1–31.
24 The State Council Information Office of the People's Republic of China, 'A Global Community of Shared Future: China's Proposals and Actions', Ministry of Foreign Affairs of the People's Republic of China, September 2023, https://www.fmprc.gov.cn/eng/zxxx_662805/202309/t20230926_11150122.html
25 Centre for International Knowledge on Development, 'Progress Report on the Global Development Initiative 2023', June 2023, https://www.mfa.gov.cn/eng/topics_665678/GDI/wj/202306/P020230620670430885509.pdf.
26 'The Global Security Initiative Concept Paper', Chinese People's Institute of Foreign Affairs, 22 February 2023, https://www.cpifa.org/en/article/2391
27 Skinner's comments are as follows: '[Competition with China] is different as an adversarial dyad than in the 20th century with the Soviet Union in the sense that … when we think about the Soviet Union and that competition, in a way it was a fight within the Western family. Karl Marx was a German Jew who developed a philosophy that was within the larger body of political thought … that has some tenants even within classical liberalism … You could look at the Soviet Union – part West, part East – but it had some openings there that got us the Helsinki Final Act of 1975 which was a really important Western concept that opened the door to undermine the Soviet Union – a totalitarian state – on human rights principles. That's not really possible with China. This is a fight with a really different civilization and a different ideology, and the United States hasn't had that before. Nor has it had an economic competitor the way that we have. The Soviet Union was a country with nuclear weapons, a huge Red Army, but a backwards economy. … In China we have an economic competitor, we have an ideological competitor, one that really does seek a kind of global reach that many of us didn't expect a couple of decades ago. And I think it's also really striking that it's the first time that we'll have a great power competitor that is not Caucasian.' As cited by Abraham N. Denmark, 'Problematic Thinking on China from the State Department's Head of Policy Planning', War On the Rocks, 7 May 2019, https://warontherocks.com/2019/05/problematic-thinking-on-china-from-the-state-departments-head-of-policy-planning/.
28 Chun Han Wong,Chapter 7, *Party of One – The Rise of Xi Jinping and China's Superpower Future* (New York: Avid Reader Press, 2023), pp. 524–604.
29 In March 2021, the United States, the European Union, Britain and Canada imposed sanctions on Chinese officials for human rights abuse in Xinjiang. Chinese Foreign Ministry retaliated by sanctioning several European nationals, including French Member of the European Parliament Raphaël Glucksmann, Adrian Zenz, MERICS Reinhard Butikofer, Michael Gahler, Ilhan Kyuchyuk, Miriam Lexmann of the European Parliament and others.

30 Michael P. Senger, *Snake Oil – How Xi Jinping Shut Down the World* (Plenary Press, 2021).
31 Chen Kung and He Jun, 'Australia-China Economic and Trade Relations Are Heading for a Hard Reset', *The Diplomat*, 16 December 2020, https://thediplomat.com/2020/12/australia-china-economic-and-trade-relations-are-heading-for-a-hard-reset/.
32 'Internal Chinese report warns Beijing faces Tiananmen-like global backlash over virus – sources', Reuters, 5 May 2020, https://www.reuters.com/article/idUSKBN22G193/.
33 Laura Silver, Kat Delvin and Christine Huang, 'Unfavorable Views of China Reach Historic Highs in Many Countries', Pew Research Centre, 6 October 2020, https://www.pewresearch.org/global/2020/10/06/unfavorable-views-of-china-reach-historic-highs-in-many-countries/.
34 Jonathan McClory, *The Soft Power 30 Report – A Global Ranking of Soft Power*, Portland, https://portland-communications.com/pdf/The-Soft-Power_30.pdf.
35 Yan Xuetong, 'From Keeping a Low Profile to Striving for Achievement', *The Chinese Journal of International Politics*, Volume 7, Issue 2, Summer 2014, pp 153–184, https://academic.oup.com/cjip/article/7/2/153/438673?login=false.
36 Zhang Jian, 'The domestic sources of China's more assertive foreign policy', *International Politics*, Vol. 51, 2014, pp 390–397, https://doi.org/10.1057/ip.2014.11; Richard Q. Turcsányi, *Chinese Assertiveness in the South China Sea: Power Sources, Domestic Politics, and Reactive Foreign Policy* (Prague: Springer, 2017).
37 Yang Jiechi, former foreign minister and Politburo member, argued that China will overcome challenges from outside as 'five strategic conditions [are] in our favor, namely the strong leadership of the CPC, the significant institutional strengths of socialism with Chinese characteristics, the solid foundation laid by China's sustained and fast development, long-term and enduring social stability, and a powerful drive that fills us with confidence and strength.' Yang Jiechi, 'Studying and Implementing Xi Jinping Thought on Diplomacy in a Deep-going Way and Opening up New Horizons in China's External Work', *People's Daily*, 16 May 2022, https://www.fmprc.gov.cn/mfa_eng/wjdt_665385/zyjh_665391/202205/t20220516_10686371.html.
38 Meng Yan, 'The Basic History and Essential Characteristics of New China's diplomacy over the Past 70 years', *Studies on Marxist theory on Higher Education* 5, no. 3 (2019): 37–45, http://smthe.tsinghuajournals.com/article/2019/2096-1170/101349A-2019-3-037.shtml; and Wu Guoguang, 'Emergence of the Central Office of Foreign Affairs: From leadership Politics to "Greater Diplomacy"', *China Leadership Monitor*, 2 September 2021, https://www.prcleader.org/post/emergence-of-the-central-office-of-foreign-affairs-from-leadership-politics-to-greater-diplomacy.

6

Strategic Competition in Southeast Asia and the Indo-Pacific

Biren Nanda

Chinese History and Culture have played a key role in shaping China's external relations and its strategic agenda in the Southeast Asian region. The Cold War may have begun and ended in Europe but it was waged most fiercely in Southeast Asia. Today, there is a renewed recognition that developments in Southeast Asia and the Indo-Pacific will help shape the contours of international politics over the coming decades. The source of that certainty is the rise of China and related geopolitical consequences.

Many analysts[1] believe that China's history and culture have played a key role in shaping its external relations. According to this view, ever since 1949, China has been engaged in a drive to regain its 'rightful place' in the world. This drive has had two key components. The first was the drive for unity, which involved control over Taiwan, Tibet, Xinjiang and China's assertion of historical claims over territory and the waters on its periphery. The second drive was to restore China's 'traditional influence' on its neighbourhood. China appears to view Southeast Asia as potentially the most fruitful and receptive region for the projection of Chinese influence. China's relations with Southeast Asia have been described by some analysts as historically part of a traditional 'Confucian tribute system' and in the contemporary period as part of the Western concept of a 'sphere of influence'.

China's larger strategic agenda seems to be driven by the following regional objectives in Southeast Asia: (1) to maintain a stable political and security environment, particularly on China's periphery, that will allow its economic growth to continue; (2) to maintain and expand trade routes transiting through Southeast Asia; (3) to gain access to regional energy resources and raw materials; (4) to develop trade relationships for economic and political purposes; (5) to isolate Taiwan and (6) to gain influence in the region to defeat perceived attempts at strategic encirclement or containment.

What is the broader strategic picture in the Indo-Pacific? The defining nature of strategic developments since the Global Financial Crisis of 2007–08 has been a rising China making territorial assertions in the South and East China Seas and along the India–China border, as well as coercive manoeuvring by the PLA Navy off the coast of Taiwan—all part of a broader effort to supplant the US as the pre-eminent power in Asia. The trend has escalated after the COVID-19 crisis which broke out in November 2019.

Second, China continues to build a massive 'blue water navy'[2] that can defend its sealines of communication and become a dominant force in the Indian and Pacific Oceans. China's port-building activities in the Indian Ocean littoral have led to concerns that it is part of a larger strategy to bring about the strategic domination of the IOR.

Third, China's Belt and Road Initiative (BRI) is a grand strategy[3] unparalleled in scope and ambition and far exceeding anything the world has seen before. It is also a masterly blueprint to integrate China's markets, gain access to resources, utilise excess domestic capacity, strengthen China's periphery, gain strategic military access in the maritime domain and enlist 'all-weather friends'. Chinese BRI loans, given on usurious terms for projects that are not bankable, are leading countries along India's periphery into a debt trap.

Fourth, we must take note of the strategic and security underpinnings of the US–China 'trade war'.[4] On the surface, the tariffs imposed by the US seek to address the trade deficit and theft of intellectual property but, more broadly, they are a reaction to the rise of China as a challenger to the US' dominance in the prevailing capitalist, liberal and democratic order. The US actions reflect concerns that China's trade and industrial policies have been unfair and threaten the US advantage in high-technology sectors. The US tariffs and export controls have targeted a range of high-technology industries, especially in areas where China hopes to lead by 2025 or 2049.

Fifth, the strategic collusion between China and Pakistan and China and the Democratic People's Republic of Korea (DPRK) exacerbates security challenges for India, Japan, South Korea and the US. In South Asia, China's support to Pakistan – which in the past has included nuclear and missile proliferation – encourages the latter to support cross-border terrorism and indulge in nuclear brinkmanship with India. The US withdrawal from Afghanistan has also increased India's threat perception from terrorist groups operating in that country.

Sixth, in the Korean peninsula, China's unwillingness or inability to rein in the DPRK allows the latter to engage in nuclear brinkmanship with the ROK, Japan and the US. China has periodically displayed an ability to help defuse crises and bring the DPRK to the conference table, though without any lasting results. This gives China considerable leverage over those countries – Japan, ROK and the US – which are most affected by the DPRK's rogue state behaviour. Nuclear and missile proliferation activities between the DPRK and Pakistan are another dimension that has been seriously detrimental to India's national security.

How do we assess the achievements of the ASEAN-centric regional security architecture? Regional efforts at ASEAN institution-building have attempted to advance the security and prosperity of Southeast Asian states. The regional security architecture in East Asia has been characterised by regional frameworks centred around the ASEAN, the American bilateral alliance system, the US' strategic cooperation with non-allied countries, the growing bilateral defense relations between middle powers and the special relationships that continue to exist between former Communist bloc countries.

ASEAN-centric security institutions have largely failed to address the hard security issues that have come to the fore with China's assertive rise.[5] Economic interdependence between the ASEAN and China and China's soft coercion and offers of investment funds have induced many ASEAN countries to fall in line. As a consequence, ASEAN unity on Chinese claims on the Spratlys and Paracels in the South China Sea has broken down since 2012. Though the ASEAN has embraced the 'Indo–Pacific', there is a state of confusion where accommodation of China is writ large and questions are raised against the Quad. Expectations from the East Asian Summit (EAS) are fading. As such, ringing endorsements of ASEAN centrality to the broader Indo-Pacific would appear to be misplaced. Recent efforts at advancing regional economic integration through the Regional Comprehensive Economic Partnership (RCEP) will only serve to strengthen China's growing influence in the region.

The ASEAN Regional Forum (ARF) has achieved some success in confidence-building measures, anti-terrorist collaboration and humanitarian assistance and disaster relief (HADR), but made little progress in preventive diplomacy and conflict resolution.

The ASEAN Defense Ministers' Meeting (ADMM) and its Indo-Pacific extension, the ADMM Plus, were created to include defense officials in the dialogue and to move from a discussion of CBMs to tangible defense and security cooperation focusing on NTS issues. The ADMM and ADMM Plus have made some headway in practical security cooperation in HADR, military medicine, counterterrorism and maritime security through cooperative security exercises. The reported decision by the ADMM Plus in Malaysia in 2015 to scrap a planned joint statement reference to the South China Sea issue fostered the impression that the ADMM Plus could go the way of the ARF.

In the Joint Declaration issued[6] at the end of the seventeenth ADMM held in Jakarta on 15 November 2023, there was once again no direct reference made to the territorial disputes in the South China Sea. The participants did, however, stress the importance of maintaining and promoting the freedom of navigation and overflight and pursuing a peaceful resolution of disputes, without coercion, in accordance with international law, including the 1982 UN Convention on the Law of the Sea.

In assessing the future of the ADMM Plus, the most critical challenge is that while it has religiously kept to the NTS remit, it continues to face centrifugal forces pushing for an expansion to hard security issues.

Perhaps, the biggest threat to ASEAN centrality comes from ASEAN itself; particularly ASEAN's tendency to capitulate under Chinese pressure and bandwagon with China as Cambodia and Laos have done, and to join Chinese efforts at legitimising aggression in the South China Sea through the discussions on the 'Code of Conduct', which is essentially a derogation from international law. It is difficult to see how a 'code of conduct' can be effective if it merely ratifies the status quo.

What is China's vision for regional security architecture in Asia? China's vision involves building a security architecture[7] that embraces ASEAN centrality, albeit a weakened one, and is focused on partnerships, draws upon existing institutions like the Shanghai Cooperation Organisation (SCO) and the Conference on Interaction and Conference Building (CICA) and seeks to dilute the US influence in Asia. India's interest and that of its regional partners should be to nudge China towards a greater acceptance of multipolarity in Asia.

How is the US responding to an aggressive and assertive China? The US has focussed on its Indo-Pacific Strategy, strengthened its alliances and partnerships and established a web of trilateral and 2+2 dialogues for better policy coordination among the US, Japan, Australia and India. The Quad – now elevated to the summit level – sits at the apex of these dialogues. The Quad should be seen as part of the countervailing strategies adopted in the Indo-Pacific to counter an aggressive, assertive and expansionist China. China, on the other hand, regards the Quad and mini-laterals as quasi-alliances aimed at itself.

Under the Trump administration, America's National Security Strategy (NSS)[8] and 'principled realism' signalled an intent to reverse the US decline and reassert a 'neo-American' order. The US trade sanctions on China targeted key technologies vital for the realisation of China's 2025 and 2049 goals.

Though committed to continuing a vigorous policy to counter the Chinese challenge, President Biden has signalled important differences in his approach. Gone is the 'America First' paradigm. The US is committed to its 'historic partnerships' and to working with allies and partners. The strategic perspectives of the Biden administration are, however, largely similar to the Indo-Pacific strategy adopted by the Trump administration.[9]

Confrontation, competition and cooperation with China continue to be the paradigm for the US' strategic policy towards China and represent a tectonic shift from the pattern that has persisted since 1971. Chinese scholars increasingly believe that the current state of the US–China relations is the 'new normal'.[10] The strategic determination and resilience of both China and the US is being put to the test.

President Biden has announced the 'Build Back Better for the World' plan, an infrastructure-financing mechanism for medium- to low-income countries designed to offer an alternative to China's BRI. The initiative has the potential to mobilise the private sector and catalyse hundreds of billions of dollars in infrastructure investments in regional countries. Together with Japanese ODA, this strategic initiative can provide a viable alternative to countries seeking to build infrastructure, while avoiding the pitfalls of a BRI-induced debt trap.

Philippines President Ferdinand Marcos Jr was hosted by President Biden in Washington DC in May 2023. The latter also hosted the South Korean president in Washington DC in April 2023 and visited Vietnam himself in September 2023; he also welcomed President Joko Widodo of Indonesia to the White House in November 2023. These visits had significant outcomes aimed at countering Chinese territorial assertions in the South China Sea. The outcomes included the expansion of the Enhanced Defense Cooperation Agreement with the Philippines and Comprehensive Strategic Partnerships with Indonesia and Vietnam.

At the Trilateral Camp David Summit between the President Biden and the Prime Ministers of ROK, Japan and Australia, held in September 2023, the leaders agreed to institute high-level consultations, strengthen security cooperation, broaden cooperation in the Indo-Pacific and deepen economic, technological and security cooperation.

If the Biden administration has made greater efforts to attend ASEAN meetings and engage bilaterally with ASEAN countries, it is because it wishes to determine what ASEAN is prepared to do with the US to cooperate on China. Unless ASEAN members define clear parameters for what they are and are not prepared to do, ASEAN centrality will soon become irrelevant and the US will place even greater emphasis on the Quad. Without American attention, China will also take ASEAN for granted.

The US has previously described India as being central to its Indo-Pacific Strategy and an essential element in the Indo-Pacific Security Architecture. India and the US need to jointly evolve a common strategy that takes into account the growing strategic salience of the Indian Ocean, and the challenge that China presents in the region.

India's perspective within the Quad is quite distinct as it upholds multipolar stability and an equitable regional order based on cooperation and not dominance. Furthermore, despite the common embrace of the Indo-Pacific terminology, the US and its allies are mainly focussed on Asia Pacific security and their military deployments also correspond to this. India must meet its continental challenges on its own, while also providing net security across the IOR.

What are the defining features of the new Asian geopolitics? This new strain of geopolitics is markedly different from what existed during the Cold War. During the fight against Communism, the US extended its security umbrella and allowed ASEAN members to focus on economic growth and domestic stability. Now, China has displaced Japan as Asia's largest economy and its GDP is five times than that of the ASEAN. ASEAN's capacity to offer a combined response to this new geopolitics is thus under challenge. Membership expansion from the original five states has made reconciling national positions even more difficult.

Since the onset of the COVID-19 crisis, China has behaved in an aggressive and dangerous manner, first by hiding the deadly nature of the virus and then by allowing it to spread to other countries. The Chinese leadership appears to have reckoned that if the pandemic was to damage China, it might as well level the playing field by infecting the whole world.[11]

Second, China took advantage of the COVID-19-induced distraction and inward focus of major powers to renew its territorial assertions in the South and East China Seas, and along the Sino-Indian border. In doing so, China was conforming to its historical pattern of behaviour. In 1962, China attacked India in the midst of the Cuban Missile Crisis.[12] More recently, it aggressively pursued its territorial assertions in the South China Sea in the aftermath of the Global Financial Crisis, when the US was preoccupied with its economy and the two wars in Afghanistan and Iraq.

The COVID-19 crisis exacerbated tensions between China and the US and accelerated, rather than changed, existing geopolitical trends. Chinese state behaviour suggests an inexorable push to replace the US as the dominant power in Asia. 'Southeast Asian countries are pieces on a strategic chessboard that China has every intention to dominate.'[13]

The US finds its strategic gaze once again diverted away from the Indo-Pacific. It will inevitably have to divert its resources away from the region and lean heavily on its regional allies in Asia to continue countering China amidst ongoing conflicts in Ukraine and the Middle East. What is currently occurring has echoes from the past. In 2011, the US under President Obama announced the 'pivot to Asia', but very soon found itself entangled with the fight against global terrorist groups.

How did China become a problem for ASEAN and India? During the 1990s, China made immense progress in forging new economic links with Southeast Asia. China's support to Southeast Asian countries during the Asian Economic Crisis in 1997–98, and its substantive trade and investment links in the region made China the major Asian player in the region.[14]

The geo-economic trends in Southeast Asia over the past few decades were being driven by the individual rationality of investors seeking to benefit from the economic opportunity in China, but whose cumulative effects were generating major geopolitical consequences.

Conventional geopolitical wisdom holds that states will engage in power balancing against rising powers. This line of reasoning suggested that states would engage in 'containing' or 'hedging' against China's rise. This did not happen in the 1990s because multinational firms seeking to access market opportunities in China were willing to do whatever it took to get in. The cumulative effect of these decisions helped build up a formidable strategic competitor and simultaneously undermined the long-term interests of other nations. In fact, substantial Foreign Direct Investment (FDI) into China came from three countries and regions most concerned about China's rise: Taiwan, Japan and the US.[15]

The tensions between the geopolitical and geo-economic pressures in Southeast Asia were mediated by the interdependence created by cross-border production networks. These cross-border networks, while speeding up economic growth in Southeast Asian countries, made them less resilient and more vulnerable to Chinese pressure.

For long, Southeast Asian countries focussed their attention on trade and development and neglected defense spending. Today, they are unable to counter the massive Chinese arms buildup, and taking advantage of the situation, Beijing has expanded its military presence in the disputed areas of the Taiwan Straits and the East and South China seas.

Writing in *The Foreign Affairs* on 21 November 2023, John Lee says,

> Strategically important countries such as Malaysia, the Philippines, and Thailand have spent, on average, just 1.0 to 1.5 per cent of GDP each year on defense for the last decade. Indonesia spends even less; its defense budget has remained below one per cent of GDP every year since 1998. Among the major maritime players in Southeast Asia, only Singapore and Vietnam seem to take defense seriously. Their annual spending has averaged between 2.0 and 2.5 per cent of GDP, respectively, over the past few decades.

China has absorbed the regional value chains and hollowed out the US industrial base. China's predatory market practices have adversely impacted its trading partners. The BRI has made neighbours dependent on and submissive to China. China also seeks to reduce the US presence in Asia.

The resurgence of territorial disputes in the South China Sea over the past two decades had clearly signalled a return to the imperatives of geopolitics in the region. President Obama's pivot to the region, Washington's effort to rebalance its foreign policy in order to focus on the strategic challenge posed by China's rise and the Trump administration's 'Indo-Pacific Strategy' gave Southeast Asian countries an opportunity to hedge against China's more opaque intentions. In all this, ASEAN countries risked becoming pawns in the geopolitical clash between China and the US. The ASEAN as a collective body appeared to be divided on how it should deal with China's increasing assertiveness. The prosperity of the region had for long rested upon the foundation of good relations between ASEAN's main economic partner (China) and its major security partner (US). With strategic competition between China and the US, this balance has fallen apart.

While the US participation in the EAS was expected to counter the growing Chinese clout in East Asian affairs, there was a risk that regional states would get caught up in the US–China rivalry, and would eventually be forced to choose sides. Indeed, the US–China tensions within the EAS prevented it from functioning effectively as a forum for discussing the resolution of hard security issues in East Asia.[16]

As a consequence, countries in the region have strengthened their individual military capabilities and augmented bilateral defense cooperation with regional partners. Southeast Asian countries have also continued to comprehensively engage China bilaterally and in multilateral institutions in an effort to balance conflict and competition with economic cooperation.[17] What was the thought process behind ASEAN's reluctant embrace of the Indo-Pacific? On 23 June 2019, ASEAN finally – albeit reluctantly – embraced the Indo-Pacific concept.[18] The ASEAN's reluctance to embrace the Indo-Pacific concept as a framework to conduct regional policymaking stemmed from a number of reasons.

First and foremost, there were fears that the adoption of the framework would invite an adverse Chinese reaction. The Chinese interpretation of the Quad as a budding alliance and its association with the US' Indo-Pacific Strategy also added to ASEAN's fears and reluctance. Second, in the ASEAN view, there was a lack of clarity on what the 'Free and Open Indo-Pacific' exactly stood for. This was because the Indo-Pacific geopolitical construct was a work in progress and there continued to be nuanced differences in the articulation of the concept between Quad members themselves. Third, there were growing ASEAN fears – so clearly articulated by the Singapore Prime Minister in his address at the Shangri La Dialogue in 2019 – that prolonged the US–China tensions and the pushback against globalisation would undermine the economic prosperity of the region.

Indonesia was the first ASEAN member to embrace the Indo-Pacific[19] as the new paradigm and framework for policymaking in the region. Indonesia's vision for the region is balanced and inclusive, and links itself to President Joko Widodo's characterisation of the archipelago as the 'Global Maritime Fulcrum'. The emphasis is on giving a maritime orientation to Indonesia's foreign and domestic policy and focusing on the creation of maritime infrastructure, attracting investment and promoting trade. The security dimension is accorded a lower priority.

The ASEAN Outlook on the Indo-Pacific (AOIP) was a giant leap. ASEAN had finally taken a step forward, albeit hesitantly, to embrace the Indo-Pacific – but in the 'ASEAN way at a pace comfortable to all'. The following are some of the key takeaways from the statement:

ASEAN does not see the Indo-Pacific as a single strategic geography, but rather as a 'seamless maritime space' and a 'region of dynamic economic integration' comprising the wider Asia Pacific and Indian Ocean regions. It perceives the Indo-Pacific as lying at the centre of geopolitical and geostrategic shifts, which present unprecedented opportunities for economic growth as well as risks of miscalculation and conflict due to the rise of 'material powers' in the region.

Placing itself at the centre of these two maritime regions and 'acting as a conduit and portal', ASEAN will seek to shape the political and security architecture and work towards keeping the region peaceful and stable. To this end, ASEAN will strengthen existing ASEAN-led mechanisms, and particularly the EAS, as platforms for dialogue and implementation of Indo-Pacific Cooperation. ASEAN centrality will continue to be the guiding principle for the economic and security architecture of the broader Indo-Pacific Region.

ASEAN has set for itself the lofty objective of helping shape the regional security architecture in the wider Indo-Pacific. However, it needs to be cautious on three counts. First, it does not have the political heft to shift the region's focus from strategic competition to a development-oriented approach or act as an 'honest broker' to defuse tensions between great powers in the wider Indo-Pacific region. Second, ASEAN is mistaken if it believes it has the capacity to harmonise competing connectivity initiatives of great powers because these rely on underlying strategic drivers for achieving their objectives. Third, the current impasse between the US and China is about which country will be the dominant power in the Indo-Pacific. ASEAN may, for a while, try its best to stand aside, but eventually it will be forced to pick sides.

What was ASEAN's response to the AUKUS pact? When the news of the AUKUS agreement broke on 16 September 2021, ASEAN was taken by surprise. It has failed to reach a consensus to date, but sees AUKUS as increasing geopolitical risks in the region and bypassing all notions of ASEAN centrality. Indonesia and Malaysia in particular have expressed concerns on the impact of AUKUS in fuelling and escalating power projection and undermining nuclear non-proliferation in the region. Singapore, on its part, has expressed the hope that AUKUS will strengthen regional peace and security, with FM Balakrishnan stating: 'AUKUS … was not really the centrepiece of concern. The real strategic question remains the relationship between the US and China, and how they manage this strategic realignment, rebalancing and recalibration of that relationship'.

Vietnam and the Philippines see the AUKUS as a welcome step to restore the strategic balance in the region.

How did ASEAN countries craft responses to increasing Chinese assertiveness in the region? Since the normalisation of relations in 1991, Sino-Vietnamese relations[20] have developed into one of normalised or mature asymmetry. This is a relationship in which China seeks acknowledgement of its primacy and

Vietnam seeks recognition of its autonomy. Maritime disputes in the South China Sea have emerged as the major irritant in bilateral relations because of the salience of conflicting claims to sovereignty. Vietnam's leaders have attempted to prevent maritime boundary disputes from spilling over and impacting Vietnam's comprehensive strategic cooperative partnership with China negatively. At the same time, Vietnam has attempted to manage its maritime disputes with China through government-to-government negotiations, and in times of crisis through party-to party channels.

In the late 1980s and early 1990s, Vietnam began to reconceptualise how it framed its foreign policy and elevated the importance of national interests over socialist ideology in its relations with China. Vietnam pursued a policy of 'multi-lateralising and diversifying' its external relations with all major powers. In this context, it is important to note Vietnam's active diplomacy in seeking closer ties with the US to balance China. China is Vietnam's largest trading partner. Vietnam's decision to join the Trans-Pacific Partnership (TPP)[21] was an attempt to diversify economic relations away from China. At the same time, Vietnam has taken major steps to develop a robust capacity through force modernisation to resist maritime intervention by China.

Under former President Benigno Aquino III, the Philippines had been the Southeast Asian claimant to the Spratlys most willing to challenge China through arbitration and increasing its military cooperation with the US. His successor President Duterte had repeatedly expressed interest in attracting Chinese investment to the Philippines and favouring bilateral negotiations and joint development of resources. President Duterte pursued a more independent policy, balancing alliance security commitments with the US, with the desire to restore ties with China. However, the arbitration award in favour of the Philippines,[22] and China's muscular bullying response, reduced his ability to find middle ground. While the Philippines was restrained in its public response to the ruling, China continued its aggressive actions against the Philippines in the South China Sea. After spending five years trying to placate China, the Philippines seems to have realised that Chinese belligerence has not diminished. Chinese PLAN ships have continued to encroach upon the Philippine's Exclusive Economic Zone (EEZ) to harass and intimidate Philippines' fishing vessels. Tangible economic benefits from Chinese infrastructure investment in the Philippines have also not been forthcoming. President Ferdinand Marcos has taken a tougher position towards Beijing and embraced the Permanent Court of Arbitration (PCA) ruling; at the same time, he seeks 'stronger and multifaceted relations with all partners'.

China's 'Nine Dash Line' claim includes parts of Indonesia's EEZ off the Natuna Islands.[23] In a March 2016 confrontation with Indonesia, a Chinese coast guard ship rammed a previously detained Chinese fishing boat to free it from Indonesian custody. The incident took place near the Indonesia's Natuna Islands, close to the southern end of the South China Sea. While China claimed that the boat was on China's traditional fishing grounds, Indonesia holds that the concept of traditional fishing grounds is not recognised by international law.

President Joko Widodo initiated a muscular policy to defend Indonesia's maritime rights in the EEZ off the Natuna Islands. At least one large Chinese fishing vessel was destroyed by the Indonesian Navy as a punitive measure in April 2016. Confrontations between Indonesian naval and coast guard vessels and Chinese fishing vessels have been a regular feature in recent years. On the other hand, since Indonesia values its economic engagement with China and courts Chinese investment, it treats the issue with China to be primarily concerning unauthorised fishing, and not involving sovereign rights and Indonesia's EEZ. In order to assuage concerns regarding China's aggressive behaviour in its neighbourhood, Indonesia upgraded its relations with the US to a 'Comprehensive Strategic Partnership' during the visit to Washington DC in November 2023.

Myanmar's position between South Asia and Southeast Asia is of geostrategic importance to its neighbour China, and is viewed by some in China as the key to preventing its encirclement by the US. Myanmar also has the potential to give China greater access to the Indian Ocean and to the oil-rich Middle East. This is particularly valuable to China as it seeks to raise levels of development in its western interior, which has experienced much lower rates of economic growth than China's eastern coastal areas.

China has helped Myanmar build a road linking Yunnan Province with a port on the Irrawaddy River. Chinese companies are also developing Myanmar's hydrocarbon resources. The isolation of the military regime in Myanmar due to its record in human rights terms has had the unintended consequence of encouraging ties with China. China has gained key strategic and economic access to the Indian Ocean, which in turn has had an impact on the geopolitical balance with India.[24]

The China–Myanmar Economic Corridor (CMEC) – a spur of the BRI – will connect Yunnan Province with the Bay of Bengal. A major 'pillar of the CMEC' is the $1.3 billion investment in the Kyaukphyu Port and Special Economic Zone being built with Chinese assistance. By developing and eventually leasing ports like Hambantota and Kyaukphyu, China has diminished its vulnerability in the Malacca Straits.

After the initiation of reforms by the military-backed government in Myanmar in 2011, the dominant trend had been opening up to the West and a gradual reduction in dependence on China. However, Myanmar needs China's cooperation to settle ongoing ethnic conflicts in the country. Despite suspended projects and domestic resentment against it, China remains a major economic partner for Myanmar. The overthrow of an elected government, the reimposition of its rule by the military junta and the consequent imposition of Western sanctions has once again thrust Myanmar into the Chinese embrace.

Thailand appears to be relatively comfortable with its expanding ties with China. It also has shared geopolitical interests with China on limiting Vietnamese influence in Cambodia. Thailand has a well-integrated Sino-Thai ethnic minority. Its prompt offer of financial assistance in the wake of Thailand's financial difficulties in 1997 and the lack of territorial disputes between China and Thailand have also helped. Thailand has a long tradition of balancing its relations with major powers and, since its 2014 coup, has been shifting the balance of its relations towards China. Two factors explain why China has become Thailand's friend. First, we note Beijing's lack of criticism of political developments in the Kingdom. Second has to do with the great attention China has given to Thailand's leaders. In contrast, Western leaders and diplomats struggled in their interactions with the Thai authorities as part of their efforts to remind Thailand to uphold the principles of 'liberal democracy'.[25]

China views Singapore as part of a group including Japan, South Korea, Taiwan and Australia that are closer to the US than ideal.[26] It is concerned that such a ring of countries in the region could be used to encircle it. Singapore, on the other hand, sees in its relationship with China the potential for mutual gain and seeks to emphasise the economic element of their relationship while underplaying the strategic challenges. Thus, Singapore seeks to develop a constructive relationship with China while hedging against it.

What are the trends in the evolving geopolitics of Asia? The US and China have been engaged in a struggle to control the narrative around COVID-19 and the heightened maritime and strategic competition in the South China Sea.[27]

Southeast Asian countries which have been heavily dependent on China for infrastructure and other developmental needs – like Cambodia and Laos – are likely to become even more prone to Chinese influence as the economic and health crisis unfolds over time. Even the larger Southeast Asian countries like Indonesia and Malaysia have been significant recipients of Chinese medical aid[28] and loans for infrastructure development. These countries may appear to be pushing back against Chinese assertions, but their actions always remain within bounds of 'managing' their relationship with their most powerful neighbour.

The chaotic initial response of the US to the COVID-19 pandemic reinforced the image of a superpower in decline.[29] The US was seen to have failed to live up to its global role when, in the initial phase, it struggled to tackle the pandemic at home, even cutting off funding for the WHO. Taking advantage of the situation, China pushed the narrative that its political system allowed it to perform better. China was able to project itself as a global healthcare leader. However, China's image has eventually been somewhat dented by the 'Zero-COVID' strategy, which has attracted criticism abroad and public censure at home, while failing to stem the spread of COVID-19.

Southeast Asian countries do not want to be in a position of having to choose between China, their major trading partner, and the US, which has been their major partner in security in the region. Singapore Prime Minister Lee Hsein Loong, in an article published in the *Foreign Affairs*' June 2020 issue, wrote that despite China's growing military strength, it would be unable to assume the role played by the US in Asia. Lee had added that Asia Pacific countries do not wish to be forced to choose between the US and China and that they wanted to cultivate good relations with both.

Vietnam, ASEAN's 2020 Chair, tried and failed to forge a consensus approach in dealing with a more assertive post-COVID China. It would appear that Vietnam and some maritime members of ASEAN wish to push a collective approach against China's territorial assertions. However, mainland ASEAN countries fear the punitive economic costs China may impose as a consequence of this approach. Some ASEAN members like Vietnam are now seeking to advance their strategic autonomy by enhancing cooperation with middle powers in the Indo-Pacific.[30]

The ASEAN's consensual approach leaves it ill-equipped to lead in the task of forging a regional strategy. The ASEAN requires change and renewal to enable it to serve as the third pole in the new geopolitics of Southeast Asia. This can give ASEAN the capacity to mitigate the consequences of the strategic contest between China and the US, and retain a role in determining the future of the region.

It is possible to discern a number of regional trends. First, China's assertive behaviour in the South China Sea will likely continue over time. Second, there will continue to be concerns over the reliability and consistency of the US as an ally or a partner. The US must frame the narrative around realising the goal of a 'Free and Open Indo-Pacific' rather than the objective of 'containing China'. Third, the ability of the US and its partners to offer an alternative to the BRI will be a key factor in influencing outcomes which will determine which country will be the pre-eminent power in Asia. Fourth, middle powers in the region – Japan, India and Australia – have a vital role to play in maintaining the regional power balance. The heightened profile and policy coordination within the Quad, mini-laterals and 2+2 Dialogues is a positive development, and so is the deterrent symbolism of naval exercises like the Malabar Exercise.

What is the current state of the Quad's agenda? Over time, the Quad agenda has focussed on providing global goods—the Quad Vaccine Partnership, cooperation on climate change, the peaceful uses of outer space, infrastructure, education and critical and emerging technologies. The Quad has also focused on addressing regional challenges, HADR cooperation, maritime security, counterterrorism, countering disinformation, cyber security and supporting international law and the rules-based order.

On Myanmar, the Quad nations have called for an end to violence, the release of all those arbitrarily detained and unhindered humanitarian access. They have expressed their support for ASEAN's efforts to seek a solution in Myanmar. Quad countries have criticised North Korea's destabilising ballistic missile launches in violation of the UN Security Council resolutions, and reaffirmed their commitment to the complete denuclearisation of North Korea.

In May 2022, the Biden administration launched its first major trade initiative, the Indo-Pacific Economic Framework (IPEF). The IPEF is billed as an effort to expand the US economic leadership in the Indo-Pacific region, and is seen by some as the economic counterpart of the Quad. This was also the objective of the TPP, a trade deal that was negotiated during the Obama administration. President Trump withdrew from the TPP in 2017, and the Biden administration has made it clear that it does not intend to reenter that trade pact, which is now renamed the Comprehensive and Progressive Agreement for Trans-Pacific Partnership or CPTPP. Thirteen countries have joined the IPEF framework talks with the US. Collectively, the IPEF participants account for about 40 per cent of the global economy.

The IPEF negotiations are organised into four pillars: (1) Higher standards and rules for digital trade, such as cross-border data flows; (2) resilient supply chains that will withstand unexpected disruptions like the pandemic; (3) green energy commitments and projects and (4) fair trade, including rules targeting corruption and effective taxation. There has been slow progress in these four areas.

How are supply chain resilience and economic security risks shaping the contours of global trade? With the outbreak of the COVID-19 pandemic, supply chain resilience has emerged as a policy priority for all countries. The issue of supply chains has also raised the profile of emerging economies that offer possible alternatives to China as production platforms for multinational firms. All major emerging economies – Vietnam and India being prime examples – are attempting to take advantage of this new focus on supply chain resilience, while (to varying degrees) balancing the economic security risks posed by China's rise. The challenge is to craft trade, investment and technology policies in ways that promote mutual economic security and enhance international economic rules and norm.

What is the cost-benefit analysis of India's engagement with the ASEAN when it comes to China? The imperative of bringing in India to balance the overwhelming weight of China in regional affairs has been a significant strand of strategic thinking amongst some ASEAN countries. It was no surprise, therefore, that as far back as 2005, on the eve of India's participation in the inaugural East Asia Summit, Singapore Senior Minister Goh Chok Tong[31] said:

> I like to think of new Asia as a mega jumbo jet that is being constructed. Northeast Asia, comprising China, Japan and South Korea, forms one wing with a powerful engine. India, the second wing, will also have a powerful engine. The Southeast Asian countries form the fuselage. Even if we lack a powerful engine for growth among the 10 countries, we will be lifted by the two wings.

The importance ASEAN nations have begun to attach to relations with India is reflective of their collective search for ways to balance China's coercive behaviour and territorial assertions in the South China Sea.

The India–ASEAN Dialogue Partnership has progressed steadily over the years. Significant achievements of the partnership include closer political and security cooperation, particularly through dialogue within the ASEAN-centric regional architecture, cooperation in maritime security, counterterrorism, HADR, trade liberalisation through the ASEAN–India FTA in goods and services; cooperation in human resource development and steadily growing people-to-people links and connectivity.

India has strengthened bilateral defense and security cooperation with Vietnam, Malaysia, Philippines, Singapore and Indonesia at a time when these countries are seeing rising tensions and territorial disputes with China. India's bilateral defense cooperation with individual ASEAN countries has been institutionalised through the signing of bilateral defense Cooperation Agreements or MoUs. Three forms of cooperation have gained momentum—cooperation between navies, the maintenance and supply of equipment and assistance for training.

China does not feel threatened by India's Dialogue Partnership with the ASEAN, nor does it feel threatened by its military cooperation with individual ASEAN countries. But China does feel threatened by India's inclusion in the Quad, which it views as a quasi-alliance directed at itself, as mentioned before.

The Realist Perspective of International Relations gives us some useful insights into geopolitics in Asia and the likely future of Sino-US relations. Offensive realism put forward by Professor John J. Mearsheimer holds that the anarchic nature of the international system is responsible for the promotion of aggressive state behaviour in international politics. According to the theory of offensive realism, the ultimate goal of every great power is to maximise power and dominate the system. As a corollary, if China continues to grow, it will eventually dominate Asia the way the US dominates the western hemisphere. As a reaction to China's rise, therefore, the US will go to enormous lengths to prevent China from asserting regional hegemony. If China does achieve regional hegemony in Asia, it will dictate the boundaries of acceptable behaviour and sanction against those who break the rules. China will have its own version of the Munroe Doctrine and try to push the US out of Asia.

Notes

1. Marvin Ott, 'US–Indonesia Society and The Sigur Center for Asian Studies' conference on 'China–Indonesia Relations and Implications for the United States' in Washington, D.C., US on 7 November 2003, as quoted in the CRS Report for Congress entitled 'China–Southeast Asia Relations: Trends, Issues, and Implications for the United States'.
2. James Maclaren, 'With Its New Aircraft Carrier, Is China Now a Blue Water Navy?' *The Diplomat*, 25 January 2020, https://thediplomat.com/2020/01/with-its-new-aircraft-carrier-is-china-now-a-blue-water-navy/.
3. Michael Clarke, 'The Belt and Road Initiative: China's New Grand Strategy?', *Asia Policy*, National Bureau of Asian Research 24 (July 2017): 71–79, https://muse.jhu.edu/article/666556/pdf.
4. Marianne Schneider-Petsinger, Jue Wang, Yu Jie and James Crabtree, 'US–China Strategic Competition: The Quest for Global Technological Leadership', Asia-Pacific Programme and the US and the Americas Programme, November 2019, https://www.chathamhouse.org/sites/default/files/CHHJ7480-US-China-Competition-RP-WEB.pdf.
5. Joshua Kurlantzick, 'ASEAN's Future and Asian Integration', Council on Foreign Relations Working Paper, November 2012, https://www.cfr.org/sites/default/files/pdf/2012/10/IIGG_WorkingPaper10_Kurlantzick.pdf.
6. Joint Declaration by the ADMM-Plus Defense Minister's meeting on Defense Cooperation to Strengthen Solidarity for a Harmonized Security, ASEAN, 23 November 2022, https://asean.org/joint-declaration-by-the-admm-plus-defence-ministers-on-defence-cooperation-to-strengthen-solidarity-for-a-harmonized-security/.
7. Alice Ekman, 'At the 2016 Xiangshan Forum, China Outlines a Vision for Regional Security Governance', *The Diplomat*, 15 October 2016, https://thediplomat.com/2016/10/at-the-2016-xiangshan-forum-china-outlines-a-vision-for-regional-security-governance/.
8. Trump Administration National Security Strategy of the United States of America, Trump White House, December 2017, https://trumpwhitehouse.archives.gov/wp-content/uploads/2017/12/NSS-Final-12-18-2017-0905.pdf.
9. Dr Monika Chansoria, 'Elements of Change and Continuity in the Future of the Indo–Pacific', Fondation pour la Recherche Strategique, Note de la FRS no. 3, 2 March 2021.
10. Shannon Tiezzi, 'Do the Anchorage Talks Represent a New Normal for US-China Relations?', *The Diplomat*, 19 March 2021, https://thediplomat.com/2021/03/do-the-anchorage-talks-represent-a-new-normal-for-us-china-relations/.

11. Bob Woodward, 'US Deputy National Security Adviser Matt Pottinger Was amongst the First Senior Trump Administration White House Officials Who Held This View', Prologue, *Rage* (Simon and Schuster UK, 2021).
12. Bruce Riedel, *JFK's Forgotten Crisis: Tibet, the CIA and the Sino-Indian War* (Harper Collins India, 2015), 303–05.
13. Elizabeth Becker, 'Southeast Asia is the Ground Zero in the New US–China Conflict – and Beijing is Winning', Foreign Policy, 29 August 2020, https://foreignpolicy.com/2020/08/29/southeast-asia-china-book.
14. John Kirton, 'The G7 and China in the Management of the International Financial System', Department of Political Science, Centre of International Studies, University of Toronto, https://tspace.library.utoronto.ca/html/1807/4865/china4.htm.
15. Chunlai Chen, 'China's 40 Years of Reform and Development: 1978–2018', Australian National University, http://press-files.anu.edu.au/downloads/press/n4267/html/ch29.xhtml.
16. Sebastian Strangio, 'At ASEAN Meetings, US, China Spar Over Maritime Disputes', *The Diplomat*, 10 September 2020, https://thediplomat.com/2020/09/at-asean-meetings-us-china-spar-over-maritime-disputes/.
17. Arief Subhan, 'Defence and Security cooperation in ASEAN', The ASEAN Post, 12 May 2018, https://theaseanpost.com/article/defence-and-security-cooperation-asean.
18. Prashanth Parameshwaran, 'Assessing ASEAN's New Indo–Pacific Outlook', *The Diplomat*, 24 June 2019, https://thediplomat.com/2019/06/assessing-aseans-new-indo-pacific-outlook/.
19. The first official reference to the Indo-Pacific in a document adopted by Indonesia and India was in the 'Shared Vision of India–Indonesia Maritime Cooperation in the Indo–Pacific' released during the visit of Prime Minister Modi to Indonesia in May 2018. In that vision document, both leaders agreed to strengthen maritime cooperation for the promotion of peace, stability and bringing robust economic growth and prosperity to the Indo–Pacific Region.
20. Huong Le Thu, 'Rough Waters Ahead for Vietnam China Relations', Carnegie Endowment for International Peace, 30 September 2020, https://carnegieendowment.org/2020/09/30/rough-waters-ahead-for-vietnam-china-relations-pub-82826.
21. In January 2018, the remaining eleven countries agreed on a revised TPP, now renamed the 'Comprehensive and Progressive Agreement for Trans-Pacific Partnership' (CPTPP); Khahn Vu, 'Vietnam Becomes Seventh Country to Ratify Trans-Pacific Trade Pact', Reuters, 12 November 2018, https://www.reuters.com/article/us-trade-tpp-idUSKCN1NH0VF.
22. Ridderhof R. (2016. July 12), *The South China Sea Arbitration (12 July 2016) PCA Case No. 2013-19*. The Peace Palace Library, The Hague Netherlands, https://www.peacepalacelibrary.nl/2016/07/pca-award-south-china-sea-12-july-2016/.
23. Ankit Panda, 'Indonesia's Latest Natuna Islands Spat with China Should Be a Wake-Up Call for Southeast Asia', *The Diplomat*, 28 January 2020, https://thediplomat.com/2020/01/indonesias-latest-natuna-islands-spat-with-china-should-be-a-wake-up-call-for-southeast-asia/.

24 Marvin C. Ott, 'Myanmar in China's Embrace', Foreign Policy Research Institute, United States, 24 January 2020, https://www.fpri.org/article/2020/01/myanmar-in-chinas-embrace/.
25 Sasiwan Chingchit, 'The Curious Case of Thai–Chinese Relations: Best Friends Forever?', The Asia Foundation, 30 March 2016, https://asiafoundation.org/2016/03/30/the-curious-case-of-thai-chinese-relations-best-friends-forever/.
26 Felix K. Chang, 'The Odd Couple: Singapore's Relations with China', Foreign Policy Research Institute, The United States, 3 December 2019, https://www.fpri.org/article/2019/12/the-odd-couple-singapores-relations-with-china/.
27 Lindsey W. Ford and Julian Gewirtz, 'China's Post-Coronavirus Aggression Is Reshaping Asia', Foreign Policy, 18 June 2020, https://foreignpolicy.com/2020/06/18/china-india-aggression-asia-alliances/.
28 Esther N.S. Tamara, 'US, China Virus Aid: Who Gives More to SEA?', The ASEAN Post, 31 August 2020, https://theaseanpost.com/article/us-china-virus-aid-who-gives-more-sea.
29 Richard Wike, Janell Fetterolf and Mara Mordecai, 'US Image Plummets Internationally As Most Say Country Has Handled Coronavirus Badly', Pew Research Center, United States, 15 September 2020, https://www.pewresearch.org/global/2020/09/15/us-image-plummets-internationally-as-most-say-country-has-handled-coronavirus-badly/.
30 Ambassador Chau Phan Sahn, 'Vietnam Plans a Major Outreach in India: Ambassador Chau', *The Tribune*, 4 November 2019, https://www.tribuneindia.com/news/archive/nation/vietnam-plans-a-major-outreach-in-india-ambassador-chau-856258.
31 Keynote address by Senior Minister Goh Chok Tong of the Republic of Singapore at the Singapore Conference, London, 15 March 2005.

7

An Assessment of Chinese Inroads in South Asia

Sreeradha Datta

With international attention riveting on the Indo-Pacific, the Indian Ocean and the Bay of Bengal, the South Asia region has also seen an increasing salience in recent years. Given the quick-paced developments taking place in the region, the extra-regional players had established engagement with the region in one way or the other. In the backdrop of new emerging international realignments and multilaterals, the extra-regional powers found more reasons to engage, but it was China that established the most significant partnerships in the South Asian region.

Background

Post the 1947 partition of the Indian subcontinent, China's interests in South Asia were evident in its various trade, strategic and defence issues with Sri Lanka, Pakistan, Nepal and Bangladesh, though it has only been in the past three decades that it has made significant inroads into the region. The last decade especially has seen a significant thrust of Chinese engagement, encompassing a plethora of political, economic, developmental partnerships, defence cooperation as well as involvement in the social sector with its South Asian neighbours. Whether in Bangladesh, Nepal, Sri Lanka or Maldives, the growing Chinese footprint is evident; even in Bhutan, despite the nation having no formal association with China, has seen it increase its overtures. The bilateral ties in South Asia were taken to a higher level with China's launching of the One Belt and One Road project (OBOR, later BRI) in 2013, that included seventy-one countries from Southeast Asia to Eastern Europe and Africa, and almost the entire South Asian neighbourhood – except Bhutan.

A foothold in South Asia via physical connectivity would not only boost bilateral trade and commerce, but also reduce China's dependency on the Malacca Straits by constructing alternative overland routes to ensure its access to the Indian Ocean and a secure energy supply.[1] It is not just the connectivity corridors that link China to the Indian Ocean but many of the Chinese infrastructure projects including building an airport and ports in Sri Lanka, and the China–Maldives Friendship Bridge along with expansion of the international airport, all of which lend China more room for manoeuvre in the region.

Apart from enhancing its strategic presence, China has been able to raise its political stakes in the region through several layers of engagement, including bilateral engagements. While China's relationship with India and Pakistan predates its bilateral ties with the rest of its South Asian neighbourhood, post the partition of Pakistan and the dilution of the Cold War that cast its shadow on the region, it gradually developed strong ties with many of them. In the 1970s, South Asian states did receive some attention from China but post the 1980s the bilateral relationship added many different aspects. The beginning was different for many. China supported the Maldives in its struggle for national independence and the two countries established diplomatic relations in October 1972. For Bangladesh, Sino-Pakistani ties dictated non-recognition of Bangladesh, ignoring its first Prime Minister Mujibur Rahman's overtures, finally recognising Dhaka only after the assassination of Bangabandhu Mujibur. It was in 1978 that Chinese Vice Premier Li Shien-Nien, accompanied by Foreign Minister Huang Hua, visited Bangladesh, which was followed by a reciprocal visit in March 1978, that led to the beginning of several initiatives, including training Bangladeshi Air Force personnel, supplying Bangladesh with military supplies and helping with its development projects.[2] Year 1957 saw the establishment of diplomatic relations with Sri Lanka, the two sides signing the first agreement on economic and technological cooperation in 1962. But it was Sri Lankan Prime Minister Sirimavo Bandaranaike's visit to China in 1972 that proved a turning point in the Sri Lanka–China relationship.[3] Although the military relationship between Nepal and China was minimal in the initial years, China raised its investment from $19 million to $38 million in 2014, in major infrastructure and energy projects ensuring greater proximity with the Himalayan kingdom. More importantly, the opening of four additional overland routes (apart from Lhasa–Kodari Highway); outreach to political parties after the demise of monarchy; involvement in domestic politics; launching of Confucius Institutes and other influence operations; offering Nepal alternative transit routes; hydel and other projects like Pokhara Airport; exerting pressure on Nepal for the Tibetan refugee issue, etc. have ensured deeper bilateral ties between the two nations. Economic packages for each of the neighbours were rolled out by China to gradually expanding its engagement to establishing strong defence and military ties.

Defence Cooperation

Indeed, 'Beijing is the leading supplier of Pakistan's conventional weapons and strategic platforms, and the dominant supplier of Pakistan's higher-end offensive strike capabilities and 'increasingly compatible arms supply chains and networked communications systems could allow the countries to aggregate their defense capabilities'.[4] Similarly, Bangladesh's military uses hardware supplied essentially by China. Bangladesh has spent $3 billion on Chinese military equipment over 2011–2020.[5] Prime Minister Sheikh Hasina inaugurated the Chinese-built $1.2 billion six-slot submarine base named BNS Sheikh Hasina at Pekua in Cox's Bazar in 2023. This project appears to be part of the Bangladesh Army's 'Forces Goal 2030' programme, a defence plan that Bangladesh had outlined in 2009, seeking to expand and modernise the country's armed forces. A Chinese company, Vanguard, has reportedly been chosen as a partner for the FM-90 missile maintenance centre to be established in Bangladesh. At the moment, Bangladesh's air force, navy and army are all armed with this missile.[6]

Traditionally, China's inroad into Bangladesh's and Sri Lanka's defence sector was always considerable, and China is considering setting up a radar base in the jungles near Dondra Bay of Sri Lanka, which is likely to give it an overview of the Indian Navy in the Indian Ocean Region (IOR) and the US military activities in Diego Garcia. To recall briefly, India in 2022 had raised its apprehensions over Chinese 'research' vessel Shi Yan 6, given broader concerns that China will gradually utilise ports at Hambantota and Colombo to support operations of PLAN vessels and support vessels in the region. For now, Sri Lanka has brought in a moratorium for a year on any similar Chinese vessel entering Sri Lanka's territorial waters. Chinese military delegation visited the Maldives, Sri Lanka and Nepal in March 2024, which reflects the importance of this sector. China has even offered non-lethal weapons for free as well as conducting training of the Maldivian security forces.

While China and Nepal established stronger military cooperation in 2018, in recent times, it saw a further thrust.[8] Some media reports have emerged regarding China's plans to recruit Nepali Gorkha soldiers into its People's Liberation Army (PLA) since the annual routine intake of some 1,400 Gorkha soldiers into the Indian Army remains suspended after the Agnipath scheme was introduced. It appears that China 'is waiting in the wings and India cannot afford to forsake this diplomatic leverage'.[9] There have been reports of the Nepal Army planning to buy armoured personnel carriers from a Chinese firm blacklisted by the US.[10]

Since 1988, China has assisted the Myanmar military. It had supplied them with arms amounting to $1–2 billion in the early 1990s, followed by another $400 million worth of arms in 1994.[11] Through training, exercises and defence supplies, China has become an important military partner for Myanmar. According to UN data, transfer of arms and other goods from China, including raw materials for Myanmar's domestic arms production, was around $267 million (as of 2023).[12]

Recent Developments

Chinese engagement in the South Asian region has gathered momentum through various infrastructure and connectivity projects. Interestingly, some of the earlier projects and those underway or in the pipeline in the region have now been brought under China's Belt and Road Initiative (BRI), including the Bangladesh, China, India, Myanmar (BCIM) corridor which has not seen any progress. With the launch of BRI, the scope for engagement broadened for the South Asian partners. The interest was evident, with five South Asian countries agreeing to join the BRI initiative: Sri Lanka (December 2014), Maldives (December 2014), Bangladesh (October 2016), Pakistan (May 2017) Nepal (May 2017) and Myanmar (2018). In July 2018, the Bhutanese government was also invited though they had declined to join the BRI.

Infrastructural Support

A quick glance at some of the agreements, proposals and ongoing projects suggests that Pakistan has been the recipient of the largest funds from China ever since the BRI project was first announced in 2013. The China–Pakistan Economic Corridor (CPEC) launched in April 2015 has received $62 billion from China. But it has been beset with corruption, delays and other issues, including environmental and security concerns and, as pointed out, the Gwadar port remains underutilised.[13]

Sri Lanka is also a recipient of substantial funds from China with projects like the Hambantota Port and airport, which were subsumed in the BRI. Apart from the Colombo Port City, China has also invested heavily in the development of other infrastructure projects here, including Colombo–Katunayake Expressway, Moragahakanda Project – which is the biggest reservoir in Sri Lanka – Southern Railway and Expressway linking Colombo and Hambantota, and also energy projects.

With regard to Bangladesh, China included a large number of projects in its MoU list. Some recent estimates are of $7.07 billion in investments from China. In addition, Chinese companies have received construction contracts worth $22.94 billion in different sectors. In the last ten years, China has released $4.45 billion for thirty-five projects under the BRI, according to Yao Wen, the Chinese Ambassador to Bangladesh.[14] Apart from 'The 12 highways and 21 bridge projects', and the '$2.5 billion at the Pyra power plant,' according to Yao Wen, 27 power and energy projects, municipal initiatives, manufacturing, and agricultural ventures as 'lighthouses' are guiding the enduring cooperation between the two nations.[15]

The year 2023 marks the harvest season of the BRI cooperation between China and Bangladesh. Fourteen mega-infrastructure projects have been completed or advanced within the year. Prime Minister Sheikh Hasina inaugurated the Bangabandhu Sheikh Mujibur Rahman Tunnel; China's investment stock in Bangladesh has increased to nearly $1.4 billion. Approximately 700 Chinese companies are operating in Bangladesh, creating over 550,000 job opportunities for local people.[16]

Smaller projects like Establishing Digital Connectivity have been initiated with $1 billion, and China's annual FDI stands at 13.5 per cent. In 2015, FDI from China was only $56 million, growing by 11.5 times since. However, Bangladesh has cancelled the Sonadia deep-sea project and has not agreed to any of China's port development proposals as yet.[17] Presumably owing to Indian pressure.

Maldives began on a high note, signing a slew of agreements that resulted in the building of the Sinamale Bridge, but with the changes in its domestic political situation, the BRI projects were trimmed down. However, the situation has significantly changed after President Muizzu took over, who travelled to Beijing in January 2024 and signed twenty agreements that included cooperation on infrastructure, trade, economy, green development, grants and other development projects – including about $127 million in aid to develop roads in the capital Male, and build 30,000 social housing units.[18] While Maldives and China have forged a strategic partnership, Muizzu was described descrieds an old friend, China's interference in Male's internal issues were evident through the 'Out India' street protests held there.

The status of BRI is slightly different in Nepal. Post the signing of the BRI six years ago, the inauguration of the Pokhara international airport in May 2023 was the only project that has been completed with a $215 million loan. It was also in mid-2022 that China and Nepal got around to discussing the Trans-Himalayan infrastructure project, with China promising to undertake a project feasibility study of a China–Nepal cross-border railway project and pledging $118 million in grant assistance.[19] The Trans-Himalayan Economic Corridor is centred around this proposed railway line, which will connect to the Tibetan railway, ensuring China's access to South Asia via that side of Nepal.[20] Apart from the strategic contours implied in this project, the debate around it is also centred on the technical/technological difficulties. This is also because Nepal wants grants and not loans, and Kathmandu has different expectations from the relationship than Beijing. China has provided a grant of $300 million for a feasibility study, although the projected cost of a rail line is now estimated to have increased from $3 billion to $8 billion.

Given the domestic changes and upheavals in Myanmar, the status of China's projects there has been uneven. Myanmar subsequently signed the memorandum of understanding on BRI in 2018 and the China–Myanmar Economic Corridor (CMEC) became a key project under the BRI banner. In 2019, the two sides signed thirty-three MoUs during Xi's visit. China's BRI projects in Myanmar focus on hydropower, cross-border industrial zones and connectivity such as through the high-speed railway networks and the Kyaukphyu deep seaport. These projects have grappled with delays, barring the Myanmar–China oil and gas pipeline that started operations in 2013.[21] While China has lent its support to the Junta, the status of its projects in the country is in a state of flux now.

With the large number of Chinese infrastructural projects underway in the region, it faces a huge balance of payments deficit. As of 2022, this stands at $42 billion.

Bilateral Trade Gap and Debt Issues

While the COVID-19 pandemic and the Russia–Ukraine conflict has impacted adversely on the global economy as well as the South Asian region, China continues to pursue its objectives in the South Asia region. Since 2013, the volume of goods traded between China and South Asian countries has increased from less than $100 billion to nearly $200 billion, with an average annual growth rate as high as 8.3 per cent.[22] Indeed, China's bilateral trade ties with each of its South Asian neighbours shows the significant trade gap in China's favour. Bangladesh's export to China is less than $1 billion a year, though the bilateral trade is $25 billion – thus there exists a trade gap pf nearly $24 billion (as of 2022). Nepal had a trade deficit of $3 billion in 2022, while the Maldives' trade deficit amounted to around $3.12 billion. Similarly, Sri Lanka recorded a deficit of $412.1 million as in March 2023. While the trade gap with China is an economic reality that many of the economies will not be able to address in near future, the issue of foreign debts that these states are facing are also linked to projects funded by China. Given its high rate of interest, strict payment schedules, alongside some severe conditionalities, Nepal and Bangladesh have been reconsidering some of its proposals. In recent times, the economic meltdown in Sri Lanka and Pakistan has been instructive for other neighbours.

Pakistan owes China $67.2 billion for the period from 2000 to 2021, and $28.4 billion of Pakistan's loans from China were in the energy sector.[23] Given the economic crises Pakistan was faced with, the International Monetary Fund (IMF) approved a $3 billion bailout programme for it in July 2023. Its external debt still stands at $100 billion, with one third of it owed to China.[24] Beijing has also agreed to finance and upgrade the rail track from Peshawar to Karachi at the reduced cost of $6.7 billion and to invest $1.5 billion in Pakistan Refinery.[25]

Similarly, China is the biggest bilateral creditor to Sri Lanka as well, having lent it about $7 billion. Sri Lanka's economic issues are associated with being highly export-dependent. Since gaining political independence in 1948, they have been forced to seek IMF bailouts seventeen times. The latest crisis occurred in mid-2022 when Sri Lanka faced external debt service payments of $6 billion against foreign reserves of $1.9 billion, inevitably leading to defaulting of payment. Apart from other multilateral agencies and bilateral partners, it was seen that Sri Lanka owed more than 52 per cent of its overall debt of $46.9 billion to China.[26] Colombo's debt basket had several sources, but China's loans with high interest rates and strict and short timelines, unviable projects at commercial interest rates and inflated project costs contributed to the country's economic crisis significantly. Subsequently, the IMF bailout and other bilateral support, including from India, gave Sri Lanka some breathing room, but China's hard balling during the crisis period did not go unnoticed. However, Colombo secured a second tranche of a $2.9 billion from the IMF earlier this year. The World Bank agreed to a $600 million loan in 2022.[27]

The Sri Lankan crises sent a strong message to other nations in the region, with Nepal and Bangladesh officially announcing that they were able to manage their debt crises in the face of the growing concerns being raised about the state of their economies. Some facts and figures do point to the fact that Nepal is feeling the pinch of the huge loans –multilateral as well as bilateral ones – including those taken from China, which is now its largest creditor.[28] Its foreign debt to China has increased by six times in the past few years. Nepal's total outstanding external debts stood at 934.14 billion Nepali rupees ($7.82 billion) at the end of 2020–21 fiscal year ending in mid-July; it owes 87.89 per cent of its foreign debts to multilateral donors, and the remaining to bilateral donors.[29]

In fact, the lack of clarity surrounding the future commercial usage of Pokhara Airport has also been a cause for consternation in Nepal. This has led to Nepali experts pointing out that the Pokhara International Airport adds unusual debt burden to the nation. The high wage rates for Chinese contractors, as compared to the government rates, high interest rates, only Chinese contractors being allowed to work on the project, etc. are some of the issues rankling Nepal. Moreover, Nepal has bought six airplanes from China on loan, which remain grounded for many years now due to economic unviability, high operating costs, pilot training challenges, insurance issues and unavailability of spare parts, adding to the Kathmandu's debt burden.[30] Nepal cancelled a $2.5 billion ($3.4 billion) deal with China's Gezhouba Group Corporation for the construction of the Budhi Gandaki hydroelectric project, citing lapses in the award process.[31]

Bangladesh in recent months has also faced an economic downturn. While many factors have led it to that slippery slope, Dhaka owes about $4 billion, or 6 per cent of its total foreign debt, to Beijing.[32] Bangladesh's foreign exchange reserves reached $48 billion in August 2021, declining over the past seventeen months to $24 billion in January 2023 as per IMF calculations.[33] It needs to be noted here that despite years of being funded by Beijing, Dhaka had long steered clear of any debt burden, but cumulative factors have led to the ongoing problems cropping up.³⁴ The unravelling of the economic crises has also led to many in Bangladesh questioning the efficacy of big projects with China. Data from the Bangladesh Bank shows that the country's yearly growth in FDI from China stood at 13.5 per cent. In 2015, FDI from China was only $56 million, which in seven years has increased by 11.5 times.³⁵

Although Dhaka had earlier agreed, it subsequently cancelled the Sonadia deep sea project and has not agreed to any of China's port development proposals as yet. Dhaka's concern was evident when Mustafa Kamal, the Bangladeshi finance minister, mentioned that, despite the problems Sri Lanka was facing, China was not addressing the issue adequately.³⁶ Bangladesh has also raised concerns about the terms and conditions of Chinese agreements which do not allow for the selection of contractors through an open-tender process, but rather allows only Chinese contractors to participate.³⁷ The nation has received a $1.4 billion loan from IMF to tide over its present crisis.

By 2018, Chinese loans had saddled Male with nearly $1.5 billion in debt – a high figure for a nation with a GDP of less than $9 billion. While the earlier Solih government had reviewed several projects, the present Muizzu government has signed up for new ones. The World Bank has warned Maldives since the $1.37 billion it already owes Beijing represents about 20 per cent of its public debt.³⁸

Ironically, Colombo, which faced flak over its debt crises, has still gone ahead and acquired $1.2 billion from China recently for the development of the port city of Colombo, specifically for the International Financial Centre project.³⁹ Despite recent crises, it was learnt when the issue was raised in the parliament that the government had given 14 acres of valuable land in Colombo city to China without calling for tenders. This land belonged to the port authorities.⁴⁰ The Chinese company (CHEC Port City Colombo) has secured an agreement to build, operate and transfer a warehousing hub within the port as per its latest deal, bringing its total investments in Sri Lanka to over $2 billion, and making the company the single largest foreign investor in the island nation.⁴¹

While Nepal faces rising debt owed to China, politically Beijing is able to exert influence over the elites in Kathmandu. On 16 August 2022, Kathmandu's Tribhuvan University inaugurated Nepal's second Confucius Institute; more than 30,000 learners have already registered with the Confucius Institutes. Sri Lanka has two such institutes, as does Bangladesh. The Chinese government also gives out annual scholarships for students in these South Asian states and these fundings are on the rise.

In Nepal, China has begun to interfere in political affairs; in Sri Lanka, China has converted unsustainable infrastructure investments into long-term leases, impinging on sovereignty; in Bangladesh, it is becoming apparent that China's promised grants are, in effect, costly loans.⁴² Myanmar civil society has expressed its dissatisfaction with China, but in spite of all this the Chinese geopolitical influence has increased within the Indian neighbourhood.

Chinese Continued Engagement

India is predicted to be the third largest economy in the next few years, which will have relevance in global politics and an impact especially on its immediate neighbourhood. But China will continue to find ways and means to engage with South Asian countries. And, as mentioned by Wang Yi, 'As China's close neighbour, South Asian countries are welcome to get on board the "express train" of China's development to share the dividends brought by it.'[43]

It is also equally true, as seen in wake of Taiwan's 2024 general elections, that several of the South Asian countries sensitive to China have endorsed its claim to Taiwan.[44] China has reinforced its own narrative of being a leader of the Global South – 'a country that is supportive of developing countries and one that understands and responds to their needs.'[45]

Indian fear and apprehension about China's intentions and its ability to influence the South Asian political situation will continue. A particular report about Chinese cyber espionage linked to the BRI has warned about Beijing using its huge infrastructure projects to spy on companies and countries as well as to dampen dissent. Although the report cites only Maldives in South Asia amongst the other states across the globe, it's a possibility in the region as well, given the large infrastructure network that China is building here.[46] This indeed has been a recurring fear in India and elsewhere.

China has been able to develop domestic constituencies in many of the South Asian polities. Some of the developments in Maldives, including the former President Abdulla Yameen's anti-India and anti-Solih positions, have been nurtured by such external influences. President Muizzu has removed Indian military personnel, replacing them with civilian to maintain the Indian aircrafts that were gifted to them. Muizzu while working on putting in place a 'China–Maldives Comprehensive Strategic Cooperative Partnership', he is also accusing the Solih regime of compromising the country's sovereignty.[47] China seems to be closely engaging with many of the domestic issues and increasingly becoming vocal about some policy choices being made by South Asian leadership. The Chinese Ambassador to Dhaka Li Jiming warned Bangladesh against joining the Quad, a US-led initiative, or Dhaka's relations with Beijing would 'substantially get damaged' – a case in point.[48] Such an outburst was not only uncharacteristic but has also set a rather unpleasant precedent in the diplomatic sphere, receiving strong domestic reactions from within Bangladesh.

Although Dhaka has not officially confirmed it is going forward with the proposal, Ambassador Li Jiming has expressed his country's intention to implement the Teesta River Comprehensive Management Project.[49]

However the last visit of Sheikh Hasina to Beijing in July 2024 did not go as well as anticipated and there were speculations about the differences over this project may have been one of the major factors. But, China continues to be seen supporting Bangladesh over the Rohingya refugee repatriation.[50] In opportune situations, China never fails to reiterate, 'Bangladesh's adherence to the one-China principle and believes that Bangladesh will continue to firmly support China on issues concerning China's core interests, such as Taiwan, Tibet and Xinjiang.'[51] Bangladesh, while continuing to engage robustly with China, has also shown its independent policy choices; its announcement of the Indo-Pacific outlook recently reflects Dhaka's fine-balancing of all its important foreign relations.

While many have questioned the future of Gwadar port in Pakistan, China has continued to support it even though its commercial viability seems presently uncertain; however, given the strategic importance, Chinese interests in the region will never flag.

Concerns Exist

Despite debt issues and other concerns, South Asian states' willingness to engage with China is evident, although some chinks in the armour are also visible. While the neighbourhood enjoys the dividends and the pitfalls of engagement with China, India's 'Neighbourhood first' policy also offers them the confidence to counter China publicly. For the first time, a Nepali high-ranking leader has openly criticised China and its obstructionist trade policy. The Minister for Industry, Commerce and Supplies, Lekh Raj Bhatta has accused China of imposing an 'undeclared blockade-like situation' at Tatopani and Rasuwagadhi to Nepal's detriment, also questioning whether Nepal should trade with China at all under the given circumstances. Trade across the land border has almost entirely stopped since the outbreak of COVID-19 a year ago. It is estimated that about US$200 million worth of goods, transported in about 1,500 containers and imported by Nepali businessmen from or via China, have been stranded between these two border points during 2021.[52]

In 2022, a Sri Lankan Tamil parliamentarian did not mince words when expressing his concern over China's interference in 'internal affairs of Sri Lanka'. The ensuing Twitter war between him and the Chinese embassy was once again a reflection of the strong and controversial positions China is not hesitating to take.[53] While in all the South Asian states there have always been constituencies with sharp views about China and its engagement with policies in the region, the articulation has become more pronounced recently and so has China's reactions.

The humongous Chinese infrastructure initiatives have also raised concerns and apprehensions about large infrastructure and its impact on the ecosystems and communities whose livelihood depends on it in these countries.[54] Myanmar civil society has raised such issues and other nations as well, in all likelihood, will be facing similar issues shortly if they are not already. Pakistan has also periodically seen local protests over the CPEC projects including the Gwadar port infrastructure, but irrespective of local people's sentiments as cited above the governments in South Asia continue to show their willingness to work with China.

Future Trends and Implications for India

The 2024 India–China patrolling agreement over the Line of Actual Control reflects the two neighbours' willingness to review and bridge their bilateral issues. Given the quick paced global developments and growing Indian external outreach, pragmatism led to this bilateral breakthrough. At the same time, India will have to internalise China's growing presence in the region and, as has been rightly said, China is a non-resident South Asian power. This is unlikely to change in the next decade. As a political commentator have pointed out, India continues to be the state with the most influence on the choices, interests and conduct of the countries under study. However, the balance is gradually shifting towards China for the role it can play as a developmental partner as well as a balancing factor against the regional power, India.[55]

While China envisions assuming a primary global position, South Asia is critical for it to do so, not only because of the available resources in the region, but also because of India and its rapid growth. China's engagement in South Asia will always have an Indian context; even if Sino-Indian cooperation unfolds in the future, China is not going to take its eyes off India.

Secondly, China has several advantages in South Asia. The lack of expectation from China is perhaps its largest advantage vis à vis India in the neighbourhood. Given Indian primacy in the region, there is an underlying expectation from India; thus, Indian ability to manage the perception becomes rather crucial. India's engagement in the region, unlike that of China's, works at several levels. State to state, elite leadership and people to people often are not on the same page. Evidently, good state–state ties may not reflect the actual state of bilateral ties. India constantly has to manage the perceptions that exists in the region. China on the other hand has no such issues; not only are the expectations limited from it, also the bilateral engagement China pursues with the South Asia region is often linear without the complications that geographical proximity lends to India and its relationship in the neighbourhood.

Thirdly, while India is fully cognisant about how the South Asian neighbours have leveraged from the existing narrative of Sino-Indian competition in the region, wary of over dependence on India, the neighbours will continue to reap the dividends from China's interest in South Asia. No neighbour is likely to place all its eggs in the India basket, and many have taken balancing to a fine diplomatic art and India will have to accept, internalise and play along too.

Fourthly, India will need to articulate the red lines to the neighbours and the implication for overstepping certain core, especially security concerns. The neighbourhood is going to be dynamic so even stable ties with Bhutan will see some changes in the days to come and India needs to prepare for that. The goodwill about Indian support will run out of its steam at some point. Many domestic issues affect the bilateral ties in the region. As a case in point, the Agnipath policy could have been addressed differently, just as international border closures cannot be an option either. They leave a lasting impression that feeds negative perceptions. However, the question is what will India do when the neighbours ignore the Indian redlines?

Fifthly, because of China's increased engagement in the region, there is a popular perception that Indian initiatives pales in comparison in most cases. But India will always remain a vital neighbour for each of South Asian countries (with the exception of Pakistan) one that they love to hate but at the same time one none will desire to completely delink from. They also understand the value of India when they negotiate with China; how India's views and leverages from that ground reality will also impact on China's increasing/diminishing weight in the region.

Sixthly, China's attempt to move from bilateral to regional relations through the BRI has not borne very substantial fruits as yet but China will persist with its outreach to maintain and strengthen its bilateral ties with the South Asian states. China's engagement is crucial for them as well as they tend to believe India is not a toothless power. The neighbours see value in balancing their two large Asian neighbours. India and China.

India has strengthened its partnership with the neighbours but prioritising few issues/aspects in each neighbouring state that has greater visibility and emotive quotient is essential. While bilateral ties remain India's priority, pushing regional initiatives will strengthen Indian position. The energy trade between Nepal and Bangladesh through India is going to reap great benefits for the subregion. The beginning of regional energy trade is going to reap great benefits for India as well as others. It needs to be replicated in cross border connectivity and commerce. The lack of Bangladesh-Bhutan-India-Nepal (BBIN) subregionalism implementation reflects the limitation of such initiatives. China will continue to be the bigger cause for Indian concerns in the neighbourhood (as elsewhere) and India as a better option will have to be showcased constantly.

To conclude, the region will see each South Asian state desiring to increase its political and military options while pursuing their developmental agenda through engagement with both India and China. While India is initiating cross border transport infrastructure in the BBIN region and attempting to develop economic corridors with its neighbours, China's continued presence in the region will continue to pose problems for India. Irrespective of neighbourhood policies being undertaken by India, continued dialogue with various stakeholders and regular management will be the key to ensuring Indian prominence in the region.

Notes

1. James Tunningley, 'Special Report: Can China Overcome Malacca Dilemma through OBOR and CPEC?', *Global Risk Insight*, 8 March 2017, https://globalriskinsights.com/2017/03/china-overcome-malacca-dilemma-obor-cpec/.
2. G.P. Deshpande, 'The Long Years of China's South Asia Policy', *China Report* 46, no. 3 (2011): 193–199.
3. Saman Kelegama, 'China–Sri Lanka Economic Relations,' *China Report* 50, no. 2 (2014): 131–149.
4. Sameer P. Lalwani, 'A Threshold Alliance: The China–Pakistan Military Relationship', USIP Special Report, 22 March 2023, https://www.usip.org/publications/2023/03/threshold-alliance-china-pakistan-military-relationship.
5. 'Bangladesh Dissatisfied with China's Military Supplies Quality: Reports,' *The Print*, 13 August 2022 https://theprint.in/world/bangladesh-dissatisfied-with-chinas-military-supplies-quality-reports/1081037/
6. Sakshi Tiwari, 'China to Set Up a Massive Missile Facility in Bangladesh as Beijing Continues to Encircle India, Arm Neighbours,' *Eurasian Times*, 19 February 2022, https://eurasiantimes.com/china-to-set-up-a-massive-missile-facility-in-bangladesh-india/
7. Naseer Jamal, 'China's Sri Lanka Radar Plan Likely to Threaten India's', *Economic Times*, 7 April 2023.
8. Anil Giri, 'Nepal, China to Resume Joint Military Drills', *The Kathmandu Post*, 18 August 2023, https://kathmandupost.com/national/2023/08/18/nepal-china-to-resume-joint-military-drills.
9. Rahul Bedi, 'Why India Should Be Worried About Chinese Army's Plans to Recruit Nepali Gorkhas,' *The Print*, 10 May 2023 https://thewire.in/world/india-china-army-nepali-gorkhas-worry Rahul Bedi.
10. 'Nepal Army Plans to Buy Armoured Personnel Carriers from Chinese Firm Blacklisted by US,' ANI, 27 May 2023, https://www.aninews.in/news/world/asia/nepal-army-plans-to-buy-armoured-personnel-carriers-from-chinese-firm-blacklisted-by-us20230527215033/.
11. H. Shivananda, 'Sino-Myanmar Military Cooperation and Its Implications for India', *Journal of Defence Studies* 5, no. 3 (July 2011).
12. Simon Lewis, 'UN Expert Says Russia, China Sending Deadly Aid to Myanmar's Military', Rueters, 15 May 2023, https://www.reuters.com/world/un-expert-says-russia-china-sending-deadly-aid-myanmars-military-2023-05-17/.
13. Suranjana Tewari, 'China's Roads Win Hearts in South Asia – But at a Cost,' BBC, 15 October 2023, https://www.bbc.com/news/world-asia-66981742.
14. Abbas Uddin Noyon, 'How China's Belt and Riad Changing Bangladesh's Economy and Structure', *The Business Standard*, 10 May 2023, https://

www.tbsnews.net/economy/how-chinas-belt-and-road-changing-bangladeshs-infrastructures-709826.

15 Ibid. As was proposed, $24.45 billion was designated for infrastructure projects as assistance, while $13.6 billion was allocated for joint venture investments. Additionally, China pledged to provide $20 billion in loans for various development projects. Also in 2016 same year, Bangladesh signed agreements for eight projects, with a total of more than $9.45 billion financed by China. These projects included the Padma Bridge rail link (valued at $3.3 billion), the Payra 320 MW coal-powered thermal power plant (worth $1.56 billion), an investment in the Development of National ICT Infra-Network for the Bangladesh Government project (with a budget of $1 billion), and a power grid network strengthening project (valued at $1.32 billion).

16 Yao Wen, *China-Bangladesh Relations in 2023: Laying Solid Foundation for Splendid Future*, annual publication of Diplomatic Correspondent Association of Bangladesh (DCAB), 31 Dec 2023, embassy.gov.cn/eng/dshd/202401/t20240103_11216212.htm

17 Adam Pitman, 'What One BRI project Shows Us About China's Investment in Bangladesh,' *Dhaka Tribune*, 27 June 2022, https://www.dhakatribune.com/longform/2022/06/27/what-one-bri-project-shows-us-about-chinas-investment-in-bangladesh

18 Helen Regan, 'Maldives Signs China Military Pact in Further Shift Away from India', CNN, 5 March 2024, https://edition.cnn.com/2024/03/05/asia/maldives-china-military-assistance-pact-india-intl-hnk/index.html

19 'China, Nepal Agree to Build Trans-Himalayan Network,' *The Times of India*, 12 August 2022, http://timesofindia.indiatimes.com/articleshow/93508407.cms?utm_source=contentofinterest&utm_medium=text&utm_campaign=cppst.

20 Anu Anwar, 'South Asia and China's Belt Road Initiative: Security Implications and the Way Forward,' *Asia Pacific Centre for Security Studies*, 9 October 2020, https://dkiapcss.edu/wp-content/uploads/2020/09/10-Anwar-25thA.pdf.

21 Moe Thuzar, 'How Has China's Belt and Road Initiative Impacted Southeast Asian Countries Myanmar?' *Carnegie Endowment for Peace*, 5 May 2023, https://carnegieendowment.org/2023/12/05/how-has-china-s-belt-and-road-initiative-impacted-southeast-asian-countries-pub-91170

22 Wang Yi, 'Strengthen Solidarity and Coordination and Pursue Common Development in Asia', Opening Ceremony of the 7th China-South Asia Expo 17 August 2023, https://www.mfa.gov.cn/eng/wjdt_665385/zyjh_665391/202308/t20230831_11136146.html; https://www.fmprc.gov.cn/mfa_eng/wjdt_665385/zyjh_665391/202308/t20230831_11136146.htm.

23 Adnan Aamir, 'China Loaned Pakistan $21bn More than Reported, Study Finds', Nikkei Asia, 9 November 2023, https://asia.nikkei.com/Spotlight/Belt-and-Road/China-loaned-Pakistan-21bn-more-than-reported-study-finds

24 Suranjana Tewari, 'China's Roads Win Hearts in South Asia – But at a Cost,' BBC, 15 October 2023, https://www.bbc.com/news/world-asia-66981742

25 Naseer Jamal, 'Seeking Fresh Growth under BRI', *Dawn*, 23 Oct 2023, https://www.dawn.com/news/1782976 z

26. Archana Shukla and Mariko Oi, 'Sri Lanka Crisis: Colombo Reaches Debt Deal with China,' *BBC News*, 13 October 2023, https://www.bbc.com/news/business-67097443
27. Ibid.
28. Kamala Thiagarajan, 'Nepal's Economic Woes, Following Sri Lanka's Crisis, Turn up the Heat on China's Belt and Road Loans,' *South China Morning Post*, 19 April 2022, https://www.scmp.com/comment/opinion/article/3174453/nepals-economic-woes-following-sri-lankas-crisis-turn-heat-chinas.
29. Hari Prasad Shrestha, 'Time to Be Alert to the Debt Trap for Nepal', *South Asia Journal,* 9 June 2022, https://southasiajournal.net/time-to-be-alert-to-the-debt-trap-for-nepal/
30. Ibid.
31. 'Nepal scraps $3.4 billion hydropower plant deal with Chinese company,' *Strait Times*, 14 November 2017, https://www.straitstimes.com/asia/east-asia/nepal-scraps-34-billion-hydropower-plant-deal-with-chinese-company
32. 'Bangladesh Finance Minister Warns Developing Nations of Chinese Loans Strapped with Debt-Trap,' *Economic Times*, 10 August 2022, https://economictimes.indiatimes.com/news/international/world-news/bangladesh-finance-minister-warns-developing-nations-of-chinese-loans-strapped-with-debt-trap/articleshow/93470044.cms?utm_source=contentofinterest&utm_medium=text&utm_campaign=cppst.
33. Sufian Siddique, 'Bangladesh Has a Resilient Economy, Will Not Collapse Like Pakistan; Is Streets Ahead of It in All-Round Development,' *South Asia Monitor,* 9 March 2023, https://www.southasiamonitor.org/perspective/bangladesh-has-resilient-economy-will-not-collapse-pakistan-streets-ahead-it-all-round
34. For details read, Sreeradha Datta, 'Dhakaracy', *The Telegraph,* 4 June 2023.
35. Abbas Uddin Noyon, 'How China's Belt and Riad Changing Bangladesh's Economy and Structure', *The Business Standard*, 10 May 2023, https://www.tbsnews.net/economy/how-chinas-belt-and-road-changing-bangladeshs-infrastructures-709826
36. 'Bangladesh Finance Minister Warns Developing Nations of Chinese Loans Strapped with Debt-Trap', *Economic Times*, 10 August 2022, https://economictimes.indiatimes.com/news/international/world-news/bangladesh-finance-minister-warns-developing-nations-of-chinese-loans-strapped-with-debt-trap/articleshow/93470044.cms?utm_source=contentofinterest&utm_medium=text&utm_campaign=cppst.
37. Jahangir Shah, 'Bangladesh Set to Take Chinese Loan on Hard Conditions', *Prothom Alo*, 28 March 2023.
38. 'Maldives and China Sign 20 Agreements, Vow Greater Cooperation on Belt and Road Initiative,' Scroll.in, 11 January 2024, https://scroll.in/latest/1061953/maldives-and-china-sign-20-agreements-vow-greater-cooperation-on-belt-and-road-initiative
39. 'Sabry Brings $1.2 billion from China to the Port City of Colombo in Sri Lanka,' *Mawrata News,* 27 June 2023.
40. 'A Valuable 14-acre Plot of Land in Colombo was Given to China', *Mawrata News*, 23 May 2023.

41. CHEC Port City Colombo (Pvt) Ltd is a wholly owned subsidiary of China Harbour Engineering Company (CHEC), which in turn is a subsidiary of China Communications Construction Company Limited (CCCC), a majority state-owned enterprise with headquarters in Beijing (*Asia Times*, 17 February 2023).
42. Ibid. Op cit 24.
43. Wang Yi, 'Strengthen Solidarity and Coordination and Pursue Common Development in Asia,' *Foreign Ministry of Peoples Republic of China*, https://www.fmprc.gov.cn/mfa_eng/wjdt_665385/zyjh_665391/202308/t20230831_11136146.html.
44. Shantanu Roy-Chaudhury, 'South Asia Sides with China after Taiwan's elections', *East Asia Forum*, 9 March 2024, https://eastasiaforum.org/2024/03/09/south-asia-sides-with-china-after-taiwans-elections/.
45. Ibid. Op cit 43.
46. 'China Accused of Using Belt and Road Initiative for Spying: Report,' *The Straits Times*, 16 August 2018, https://www.straitstimes.com/asia/east-asia/china-accused-of-using-belt-and-road-initiative-for-spying-report
47. Mimrah Ghafoor, 'Damaging and Disingenuous: Evaluating the "India Out" Campaign in Maldives', *The Diplomat*, 10 May 2023, https://thediplomat.com/2023/05/damaging-and-disingenuous-evaluating-the-india-out-campaign-in-maldives/
48. 'If Dhaka Joins Quad, It'll Harm Ties with Beijing', *Daily Star*, 11 May 2021 https://www.thedailystar.net/frontpage/news/beijing-wants-dhaka-not-join-quad-2091529.
49. 'Envoy: China Serious About Implementing Teesta Project', *Dhaka Tribune*, 14 October 2022, https://www.dhakatribune.com/bangladesh/2022/10/14/envoy-china-serious-about-implementing-teesta-project
50. Ingyin Naing, 'Rohingya Refugees Wary as China Develops Plan for Repatriation,' *VOA*, 3 August 2023, https://www.voanews.com/a/rohingya-refugees-wary-as-china-develops-plan-for-repatriation-/7211192.html.
51. 'China and Bangladesh Hold the 12th Round of Diplomatic Consultation', Ministry of Foreign affairs of People's Republic of China, 29 May 2023, https://www.fmprc.gov.cn/eng/wjbxw/202305/t20230531_11086323.html.
52. Achyut Wagle, 'What's Cooking in Nepal–China Relations?', *Kathmandu Post*, 3 February 2021, https://www.straitstimes.com/asia/whats-cooking-in-nepal-china-relations-kathmandu-post-contributor.
53. N. Sathiya Moorthy, 'Sri Lanka: How Chinese 'Interference in Internal Affairs' Provoked Tamil MP's Ire', *First Post*, 31 December 2023, https://www.firstpost.com/opinion/sri-lanka-how-chinese-interference-in-internal-affairs-provoked-tamil-mps-ire-11906541.html.
54. Blake Alexander and Rebecca Roy, 'How the Belt and Road Impacts Oceans and Coasts', *Asia Times*, 11 December 2022, https://asiatimes.com/2022/12/how-the-belt-and-road-impacts-oceans-and-coasts/.
55. Deep Pal, 'China's Influence in South Asia', *Carnegie Endowment for Peace*, 31 October 2021, https://carnegieendowment.org/2021/10/13/china-s-influence-in-south-asia-vulnerabilities-and-resilience-in-four-countries-pub-85552.

8

Pakistan–China Relations[1]

Tilak Devasher

The leadership of Pakistan and China has variously described their friendship as 'all-weather', 'higher than the mountains', 'deeper than the oceans', 'sweeter than honey', 'stronger than steel' and 'Iron brothers'. In March 1969, Chinese president Liu Shao-chi used the term *mujahidana dosti* (friendship between fellow fighters in a jihad) when he visited Pakistan,[2] though that moniker has not been used now for quite some time for obvious reasons. It is indeed a unique relationship relationship between a communist giant and an Islamic country, between a godless nation state and a God-obsessed one.

An editorial in the *Dawn* rationalised Islamic Pakistan's alliance with Communist China as follows: For the preservation of our Islamic state and to minimise the risk of Hindu Bharat's aggression against it, we must now turn to China, and this we can do with no risk to our Islamic ideology. In Hindu Bharat, Islam is hated because it is Islam and Muslims are periodically butchered in large numbers because they are Muslims. In Red China religion as such may be decried, but of all religions only one, namely Islam, is not singled out for denigration and of all communities only one, namely the Muslims, are not singled out for violent persecution.[3]

Continued commonality of interests has bridged differences in language, culture, history and ideology. For China, Pakistan continues to be the hub of its South Asia policy; for Pakistan, China is the pole star in its national security strategy. Irrespective of the nature of the governments in Pakistan – civilian or military – and irrespective of the party – Pakistan People's Party (PPP), Pakistan Muslim League Nawaz (PML-N) or Pakistan Tehreek-i-Insaf (PTI) – there is a basic understanding that the relationship with China is sacrosanct.

Till recently, China's interest in Pakistan was not bilateral per se, but a combination of two interrelated stakes that had more to do with its regional interests. The first was the mutuality of interests with Pakistan vis-à-vis India. The second was the spillover of terrorism and Islamic radicalisation from Pakistan and Afghanistan into Xinjiang, adversely impacting the 8 million ethnic Uyghurs. Pakistan's motivation has been to use 'borrowed power' from China to balance its inferiority with India. To this end, it has seen in China a friend that would bail it out politically and militarily. The new bilateral element in the relationship is economic—the China–Pakistan Economic Corridor (CPEC) that has been billed as a game changer.

Background

The Pakistan–China relationship dates back to the 1950s, when Pakistan was one of the first states to recognise the People's Republic of China and the first Muslim nation to do so. However, it was only in the 1960s, especially after the 1962 Indo-China war, that the relationship started taking off. The first sign of this was the two countries resolving their boundary issue in Kashmir. A high point of the budding Pak–China relationship (as also of the Pak–US relationship) was Pakistan facilitating the secret visit of the US Secretary of State Henry Kissinger to China in July 1971.

A thumbnail sketch of the growth of bilateral relations would include: establishment of diplomatic relations in 1950; resolving border issues in 1963; beginning of military aid in 1966 and beginning of economic cooperation in 1979s.

There are a host of examples where China has served as a key ally for Pakistan. Some of these include providing diplomatic support to Pakistan's position on Kashmir in the United Nations; vetoing proposals in the UN that were harmful to Pakistan and lobbying against bringing any proposal to the UN Security Council (UNSC) that would hurt Pakistan's interests. For years, China vetoed or held up the UNSC resolutions banning jihadi groups like the Jamaat-ud-Dawa (JuD), dropping its resistance only after the terror attacks in Mumbai in November 2008. In response to the US raid that killed Osama bin Laden, Chinese Prime Minister Wen Jiabao issued a statement in support of Pakistan; China put on hold India's complaint in the UN about Zakiur-Rehman Lakhvi, the Lashkar-e-Taiba (LeT) mastermind behind the Mumbai attacks, and the banning of Masood Azhar, the Jaish-e-Mohammad (JeM) chief, in March 2016. Earlier, China had even vetoed Bangladesh's entry into the UN since it regarded it to be a rebellious province of Pakistan.

On its part, Pakistan has refrained from taking up the issue of the persecution of Muslim Uyghurs in China, though it has been very vociferous about the status of Muslims like the Rohingyas and the Kashmiris. Equally, it has ensured that the issue was not taken up during the Organization of Islamic Cooperation (OIC) meetings, which was acknowledged by China too.[4] Pakistan also showed solidarity with China when the then PM Imran Khan visited the Beijing Winter Olympics 2022 that was boycotted by countries led by the US and the UK leaderships.[5] Pakistan has also gone out of its way to secure Chinese interests within its borders. The attack on the Lal Masjid in 2007 was in part meant to assuage Chinese concerns since some Chinese nationals had been held hostage there. It is believed that the brutal crackdown in Balochistan and the 'kill and dump' policy adopted there is meant to protect Chinese interests.[6]

Defence Cooperation

Even more than the political, the key element of the Pak–China relationship has been, and is, defence cooperation. For China, militarily equipping Pakistan has been a low-cost option to keep India bogged down and threatened with a potential two-front war.

China has become Pakistan's most important defence partner and is the leading supplier of its conventional weapons and strategic platforms and higher-end offensive strike capabilities. Additionally, China and Pakistan have accelerated holding of complex joint military exercises and interoperability. Hence, compatible arms supply chains and networked communications systems could allow the countries to aggregate their defence capabilities.[7] This also indicates a drawing down of reliance of the Pakistan military on Western sources, despite quality issues with some Chinese systems. Among the defence equipment supplied have been the Chinese F-7 aircraft, JF-17 Thunder fighter aircraft, J-10 medium-role combat aircraft, F-22P frigates with helicopters, K-8 jet trainers, T-85 tanks, small arms and ammunition. Recent acquisitions include Chinese-made VT-4 battle tanks (April 2020) and the Wing Loong II UCAVs. China has also helped Pakistan build its heavy mechanical complex, aeronautical complex and several defence production units.[8] On 19 April 2015, China concluded the sale of eight conventional submarines worth $5 billion. The basic reason for why Pakistan, over the decades, has emerged as the largest recipient of China's defence exports and how the relationship has grown to include co-production and transfer of technology, as also nuclear cooperation, is the mutuality of their interests to keep India under check.

Moreover, unlike the US, China has never cut off supplies of weapons or imposed sanctions on Pakistan. An example of the close defence cooperation is the general impression that the Chinese engineers were allowed to examine the wreckage of the US stealth helicopter that had crashed in Abbottabad during the raid to kill Osama bin Laden.[9]

A further sign of the deepening military relationship is the growing numbers of China–Pakistan military exercises. These included a joint exercise close to the Line of Actual Control (LAC) against the backdrop of the Galwan clash between India and China. The Shaheen series of joint exercises between the two air forces is a regular feature.[10]

According to a recent study by a US think tank, the United States Institute of Peace (USIP), carried out by Sameer Lalwani, the deepening China–Pakistan military partnership over the past decade is approaching a 'threshold alliance' (a state of military relations short of a formal treaty alliance but much more advanced than 'defense cooperation agreements'). Despite this, a military alliance is not, however, inevitable.

Lalwani makes the significant point:

> The latent capacity of the China–Pakistan military partnership—measured in terms of arms transfers, military exercises and basing prospects—advances both countries' peacetime interests, but also allows the option of burden sharing and interoperability in a crisis. If either country's political calculus changes, most of the material and technical conditions for an alliance may already be in place.[11]

Pakistan's inability to meet its defence requirements due to the persisting economic crisis could make Islamabad more dependent on China in the coming years. Concessionary Chinese financing could enable Pakistan to procure advanced weapons systems deemed essential for its national security interests.

Nuclear Cooperation

The key element in this relationship has been nuclear cooperation. As Andrew Small puts it, 'if the military relationship lies at the heart of China–Pakistan ties, nuclear weapons lie at the heart of the military relationship.'[12] There is fairly well-documented evidence that transfer of Chinese technology and expertise to Pakistan in the 1980s and 1990s helped operationalise Pakistan's nuclear weapon and missile programme. This included supplies of low-enriched uranium, nuclear warhead design from its 1966 nuclear test and 5,000 ring magnets for use in gas centrifuges to enrich uranium.[13] On missiles, China is reported to have supplied Pakistan with thirty-four short-range ballistic M-11 missiles, built a turnkey ballistic missile manufacturing facility near Rawalpindi and helped Pakistan develop the 750-km-range solid-fuelled Shaheen-1 ballistic missile.[14]

On the civil side, China helped Pakistan build two nuclear reactors at Chashma in 1990s before joining the Nuclear Suppliers Group (NSG). It signed a deal in 2009 to build two more, under the 'grandfather' clause—namely, that these two new reactors were part of the earlier deal (for Chashma 1 and 2), which China had already declared as part of its commitments when it joined the NSG.[15] Subsequently, China launched/committed additional nuclear power projects – Chashma 3,4 and 5 – all grandfathered under the NSG.

Economic Relations

Pakistan has been one of China's major trading partners. It, however, has an enormous trade deficit with China. Out of the total trade of around $12.35 billion between the two countries in 2014, only around $2.76 billion were exports from Pakistan. According to Urumqi Customs, the total trade between Xinjiang and Pakistan in the year 2014 was worth only $319 million. Bilateral trade volume exceeded $20 billion for the first time in 2017 according to China

Customs. In 2017, China's exports to Pakistan increased by 5.9 per cent to $18.25 billion. Economic cooperation between Pakistan and China has recently increased and a free trade agreement has been signed.[16]

The primary reason for trade between Pakistan and China being at a low ebb is that Pakistan's exports to China are basically low-value raw material and commodities, since it is not in a position to export high-tech goods. This, together with minimal people-to-people contacts, detracts from the high-sounding epithets of the political and military relationship. China is also uncomfortable with Pakistan seeking large bailouts from it and has invariably pushed it towards multilateral institutions like the IMF. For Beijing, the risk of Pakistan's default is simply too high. China would not want to be the only country shoring up Pakistan financially.

China–Pakistan Economic Corridor (CPEC)

President Xi Jinping's two-day visit to Pakistan in April 2015 marked the formal launch of the CPEC that was part of the president's pet project of the Silk Road Economic Belt and the Twenty-first-Century Maritime Silk Road (also referred to as One Belt One Road or OBOR, and now as the Belt and Road Initiative or BRI). The original route linked Gwadar in Balochistan with Kashgar in Xinjiang via Balochistan and KPK, although subsequently the route was changed to go via Punjab. When conceived, China was to provide an investment-cum-loan package of $45.65 billion over the next ten to fifteen years for Pakistan's energy and infrastructure. This would involve about $34 billion in private sector investment by Chinese companies, insurers and banks. The remaining $11 billion will be in the shape of 'very concessional loans' and some grants, according to Planning and Development Minister Ahsan Iqbal.[17] The amount was subsequently hiked up to $62 billion. The biggest chunk of the investment, about $35 billion, was for energy projects including coal-fired power plants, a dam, a solar power park and a gas pipeline to Iran. Together, these projects were expected to create about 17,000 megawatts (MW) of power.

The moot question is whether CPEC would take the economic and strategic relationship between the two countries to a new level. When launched, CPEC was seen as series of projects that would potentially alter Pakistan's developmental trajectory, generating new jobs, investment and sustainable growth. While CPEC has addressed some infrastructure challenges, it has not delivered sustainable growth, while saddling Pakistan with enhanced debt.[18]

China's interest in an economic corridor from Gwadar to Kashgar in Xinjiang is understandable. With about 80 per cent of Chinese oil imports arriving via sea routes from the Middle East and Africa, any alternative route to the 'choke-point' of the Malacca Straits would be appealing. Rerouting part of the supplies to Xinjiang from the Persian Gulf via Gwadar shortens the distance by over

7,500 km. In terms of time, China would gain over ten days in transport time for goods and energy. Currently, it takes twelve days to ship goods and fuel from the Middle East, whereas the corridor would cut this down to thirty-six hours.[19] The corridor would also open up Xinjiang, since the distance between the province and Gwadar is 2,500 km; compared to 4,500 from China's eastern seaboard.

However, there is considerable skepticism about the economic viability of the corridor given the uneconomic costs for China of using Gwadar as a transit point for even part of its crude shipments. The cost of transporting a barrel of oil through the Malacca Straits would be just a fraction of transshipping costs for it via Gwadar and thence to Kashgar. This being so, quite clearly for the Chinese the significance of the CPEC has to be more strategic than economic. Gwadar gives China a vantage point in the Arabian Sea that could serve as a look-out point and over the years develop into a naval facility if not a base.

Be that as it may, for Pakistan, what the CPEC signifies is a huge Chinese commitment and an expansion and upgradation of the relationship from the political and military to the economic sphere. The crucial question, however, is whether Pakistan can keep up its end of the bargain.

Theoretically, if all the envisaged projects materialised, Pakistan would get a network of roads, railways and energy pipelines linking Gwadar to Kashgar. All this potentially would be a shot in the arm for Pakistan's faltering economy and consolidate a decades-old strategic partnership.

To provide security to the 3,000 km long CPEC, the Pakistan Army created a Special Security Division (SSD) consisting of nine composite infantry battalions (9,000 personnel) and six wings of civilian armed forces (6,000 personnel) to be headed by a serving major general of the army.

Several Pakistanis have noted with concern the adverse effects on their resources. For one thing, Islamabad simply isn't able to pay China back, given its own precarious economic condition. In fact, quite frequently, Pakistan has had to seek rollover of debt payments and deposits to boost its foreign exchange reserves. Pakistanis are conscious of the Sri Lanka example, where the Chinese have taken over the port of Hambantota after it was unable to pay its debts. In contrast, neither the US nor the IMF has ever taken over territory as payment for a loan. Gwadar has the potential to become a new Hambantota. According to Pervez Hoodbhoy, a noted commentator, CPEC was built around the fatally flawed premise that infrastructure – roads, bridges and electricity – alone would create growth and jobs. What was not factored in was the crucial input—human capital. He argues that China was probably guilty of short-selling Pakistan: most Independent Power Producers (IPP) deals were considered a scam, as were tax exemptions to Chinese companies, duty-free imports from China that have driven many local manufacturers to bankruptcy.[20]

In Pakistan, the ongoing economic, security and political crises have, on the one hand, led to a slowdown in the execution of CPEC; on the other, this makes it even more likely for Pakistan to become more reliant on Chinese support, especially against the backdrop of the growing strategic competition between the US and China. According to Uzair Yunus, 'Negotiations to either ease conditions or access additional debt to ease the balance of payments crisis may lead to increased Chinese demands in the economic and security domains.'[21] According to IMF data, China holds roughly $30 billion of Pakistan's $126 billion total external foreign debt. This is thrice its IMF debt ($7.8 billion) and exceeds its borrowings from the World Bank and Asian Development Bank combined.[22]

Gwadar

At the centre of the CPEC project is the port of Gwadar, located near the mouth of the Strait of Hormuz as the corridor's gateway that opens up access for China to the Middle East and Africa. China had financed the construction of the Gwadar Port in the early years of the 21st century. It was inaugurated in 2008 and, for several years, operated by a Singaporean company PSA International. In February 2013, the operation of the port was taken over by the state-run Chinese Overseas Port Holdings Company (COPHC).

The fly in the ointment are the street protests in Gwadar due to lack of access to clean drinking water, loss of livelihood due to Chinese deep-water fishing and limited access to jobs in key projects being undertaken in and around Gwadar. In 2022, the *Haq Do Tehreek* (Gwadar Rights Movement) staged sit-in protests for over fifty days in Gwadar. The protests included blocking the Gwadar East Bay Expressway and demanded that the Chinese leave the city. Similarly, attacks on Chinese personnel in recent months have seen an escalation. The Baloch Liberation Army (BLA), the Tehreek-e-Taliban Pakistan (TTP) and Sindhi nationalist groups have carried out these attacks. Further attacks could lead to increased demands for the presence of Chinese personnel to provide security to Chinese citizens and projects. While Pakistan has so far resisted these demands, a worsening economic and security situation will increase Chinese pressure that Pakistan would find difficult to resist, especially such demands as made part of a broader economic and security package to stabilise the country's economy.[23]

One of the key reasons for China continuing CPEC is that none of the groups have been able to target any major Chinese project in Pakistan. Quite possibly, they lack the capacity to launch major attacks and so have focussed on softer individual targets. Despite the targets being soft, the impact has been quite severe in that they create panic and raise questions about the ability of Pakistan to protect the Chinese, and serve to erode Beijing's confidence in

Pakistan's security system. This, in turn, could lead to China contemplating deploying, covertly or overtly, their own security agencies in Pakistan to look after the security of their nationals.[24]

Chinese Influence in Pakistan

The *China Index 2022*, published by the China in the World (CITW) Network, an initiative of Doublethink Lab, a Taiwan-based non-profit entity, has placed Pakistan at the top of the list of countries beholden to Chinese influence. The Index focuses on eighty-two countries that are seen to be within the Chinese sphere of influence. Interestingly, while Pakistani media and academia is said to be less beholden to Chinese influence, Pakistan is considered a frontrunner in the so-called 'dependence cluster'. This 'cluster' refers to Chinese influence over Pakistan's economic, technological and domestic politics domains. Pakistan has also been placed first under the 'rulemaking cluster' that implies that China exerts significant influence over Pakistani military, law enforcement and foreign policy domains as well.[25]

In January 2016, due to the wrangling and discord between Pakistani politicians over the CPEC route, there was an unprecedented intervention and admonition by the Chinese embassy in Islamabad. In a statement it said:

> We hope that relevant parties could strengthen communication and coordination, solve differences properly, so as to create favourable conditions for the CPEC. We are ready to work with Pakistani side to actively promote construction of the CPEC projects, and bring tangible benefits to the peoples of the two countries.[26]

The delays in implementation of CPEC have not gone unnoticed by the Chinese. Reading between the lines of media reports, it would appear that the Chinese are getting increasingly frustrated with the failure of the political leadership to provide inter-ministerial and inter-provincial coordination. It has been suggested in the media that the Chinese have even suggested that the government formally rope in the Pakistan Army to ensure the management and smooth execution of CPEC.[27]

That all was not well between the 'Iron Brothers' was manifested during a December 2022 meeting between the Chinese Ambassador to Pakistan Nong Rong and Special Assistant to Prime Minister on Coordination Syed Tariq Fatemi in Islamabad. The ambassador acknowledged that Chinese companies in Pakistan had opted for a 'go-slow' policy due to delay in payment to the Independent Power Producers (IPPs), rising exchange rate and 'unhelpful behaviour of the National Electric Power Regulatory Authority (Nepra) with its companies'. He also recalled that President Xi had offered to deploy Chinese experts in Pakistan to help establish Special Economic Zones (SEZs) and underlined that it was high time that Pakistan follow-up on the outcome of that decision.[28]

Significantly, China's role in Pak domestic politics has also been evident. For example, the outgoing Chinese Consul General in Lahore, Long Dingbin, in a letter dated 25 January 2021, heaped praise on the then incarcerated Leader of Opposition in National Assembly Shehbaz Sharif. He stated Sharif's contributions as Punjab's chief minister for CPEC projects was 'impressive'. He described Sharif as an 'old friend of China' and added that he was impressed by his devotion for the CPEC projects. He underlined that the PML-N would always remain a 'great friend' of China, whether 'it's in power or as an opposition party'. These were unusual remarks of an accredited diplomat about an opposition leader and party and would not have gone unnoticed by the Imran Khan government.[29]

There have also been reports that Beijing has been trying to convince Islamabad since 2015 to get rid of the eighteenth Constitutional amendment of 2010 that had given the provinces substantial autonomy. Beijing would rather deal only with Islamabad than have the provinces meddling in its projects.[30]

Pakistan's dilemma of trying to walk a tightrope between China and the US was revealed in the Discord Leaks, a veritable treasure trove of secret communication files released by a US military whistleblower on Discord, a popular free chat platform for the video gaming community. One of the memos leaked was titled 'Pakistan's Difficult Choices', in which Hina Rabbani Khar, Caretaker Minister of State for Foreign Affairs, wrote about Islamabad needing to avoid giving the appearance of appeasing the West. She averred that Pakistan's efforts to preserve its ties with the US could seriously harm the benefits of the country's 'real strategic' partnership with China and that Islamabad could 'no longer … maintain a middle ground' between China and the US.

The memo quite possibly underlines that Pakistan is no longer trying to adhere to the 'middle ground' between China and the US but has made a fundamental and perhaps permanent shift in its foreign policy to tilt towards China. Clearly, Pakistan now believes that its relationship with China is far too important to be jeopardised on the altar of US apprehension of China's increasing power.[31] Despite this, Pakistan is also trying hard to keep its relations with the US going and even increase its scope beyond military cooperation. China would not mind this so that it is not left to do the heavy-lifting and propping up Pakistan on its own.

Problems in the Relationship

The key problems that have come to the fore in the relationship have been terrorism in Xinjiang linked to jihadi training camps in Pakistan and Afghanistan, and the issue of th safety of Chinese workers in Pakistan.

While Pakistan has cracked down on Uyghurs in its territory, even handing over some periodically to China, its failure to completely stop Uyghurs from getting trained and returning to Xinjiang is a source of growing unease in China's relationship with Islamabad. Such incidents have even provoked rare Chinese criticism of Pakistan. It was acknowledged in Pakistan that other such attacks could have adverse implications for Pak–China ties.[32] Chinese concern about the role of Islamic militancy in Pakistan and its spread to China's Xinjiang province is clear from the fact that China withdrew its objections over the banning of the Jamaat-ud-Dawa (JuD) – a front organisation of the Lashkar-e-Taiba – in 2008.[33]

The second issue is regarding the safety and protection of about 10,000 Chinese workers in infrastructure and energy projects all over Pakistan and the increasing number that would start working on the CPEC. There have been several attacks on them in the past by Baloch separatists as well as jihadis in Gwadar, Peshawar and Islamabad. The Jamaat-ul-Ahrar, a splinter group of the TTP, has warned Beijing against persecuting the Muslim population in Xinjiang; otherwise 'the centres of Chinese economic interests' would be targeted in ways beyond the imagination of the Chinese government.[34] According to Andrew Small, senior Chinese leaders such as former President Hu Jintao had asked Pakistani leaders to increase protection of Chinese workers. China had even threatened to cut funding from projects and withdraw its workers from the country.[35] That Pakistan is aware of this is obvious from its commitment to create a 'special security division' of 12,000 specially trained personnel, as mentioned earlier.[36] While this should address some Chinese concerns, the fact remains that the security of the CPEC's network of pipelines, highways and railway lines will require almost constant attention. Given Pakistan's track record of protecting its own Sui gas pipelines, the jury is out whether such protection will be foolproof.

Conclusion

The friendship between Pakistan and China has stood the test of time since the 1960s to a large extent because of their mutual hostility towards India. Chinese support of Pakistan, especially military support, has been a low-cost option of diverting Indian attention from China and making sure it remains bogged down in squabbles with Pakistan.

Since the initial years, the economic content of the relationship has not been prominent. The CPEC has the potential to be a game changer through greater connectivity and greater Chinese investment in infrastructure projects. Whether it will be so or not, however, remains to be seen. It has a chance of success not so much because of Pakistan's efforts, but owing to the Chinese push, especially under President Xi Jinping.

For Pakistan to really benefit from the opportunity that has come its way, it will have to realise that China would be as concerned about jihadi terrorism emanating from Pakistan as is the US. If Pakistan remains in the old groove of using non-state actors as instruments of state policy, and does not focus on its own economic development, it faces the risk of alienating the Chinese as seriously as it has alienated the US. In all probability, Pakistan would find the Chinese far harder task-masters than the US, especially since they share a common border. Thus, Pakistan would need to do some serious introspection about the costs of exporting terror as also the economic costs of the CPEC.

The bottom line is that the deteriorating economy of Pakistan is likely to increase Chinese leverage over the country, forcing the former to yield to Chinese requests. Such requests could increase Chinese influence in the Arabian Sea (Gwadar) and also in the Himalayas (Gilgit Baltistan).[37]

Notes

1. Ideas for parts of the article have been taken from the author's book, *Pakistan: Courting the Abyss* (New Delhi: HarperCollins Publishers, 2016).
2. Abdul Sattar, 'Foreign Policy: Relations with the West, China and the Middle East', in Hafeez Malik (ed.), *Pakistan: Founders' Aspirations & Today's Realities* (Karachi: Oxford University Press, 2001), 370.
3. Editorial, *Dawn*, 26 April 1963. Cited in Aparna Pande, *Explaining Pakistan's Foreign Policy: Escaping India* (London: Routledge, 2011), 120–21.
4. Sajjad Malik, 'Pakistan saved China from embarrassment on Xinjiang violence', *The Daily Times*, 5 September 2009.
5. Munir Ahmed, 'Of Sino-Pak Business and Brotherhood', *The Daily Times*, 10 February 2022, https://dailytimes.com.pk/882940/of-sino-pak-business-and-brotherhood/.
6. Siegfried O. Wolf, 'China's Role in Pakistan: International and Domestic Implications', in Sylvia Mishra (ed.), *Studies on Pakistan* (New Delhi: Paragon Publishers, 2014), 131.
7. Sameer P. Lalwani, A Threshold Alliance: The China-Pakistan Military Relationship, USIP Special Report 517, March 2023, https://www.usip.org/publications/2023/03/threshold-alliance-china-pakistan-military-relationship.
8. Lisa Curtis and Derek Scissors, 'The Limits of the Pakistan–China Alliance', Backgrounder #2641 on Asia and the Pacific, 19 January 2012 (Washington DC: The Heritage Foundation), https://www.heritage.org/asia/report/the-limits-the-pakistan-china-alliance.
9. Mark Mazetti, 'US Aides Believe China Examined Stealth Copter', *The New York Times*, 14 August 2001, https://www.nytimes.com/2011/08/15/world/asia/15copter.html#:~:text=American%20spy%20agencies%20have%20concluded,elude%20radar%2C%20the%20officials%20said.

10 Rajeswari Pillai Rajagopalan, 'The China-Pakistan Partnership Continues to Deepen', Observer Research Foundation, 10 July 2021, https://www.orfonline.org/research/the-china-pakistan-partnership-continues-to-deepen/.
11 Ibid. Op cit 7.
12 Andrew Small, *The China Pakistan Axis: Asia's New Geopolitics* (Gurgaon: Random House India, 2015), 29.
13 Lisa Curtis and Derek Scissors, 'The Limits of the Pakistan–China Alliance'; Andrew Small, ibid, 33–35.
14 Lisa Curtis and Derek Scissors, op cit; Andrew Small, op cit, 33–35.
15 Lisa Curtis and Derek Scissors, op cit; Andrew Small, op cit, 33–35.
16 Syed Ali Nawaz Gilani, 'China-Pakistan Relations: New Dimensions', *Business Recorder*, 22 May 2022, https://www.brecorder.com/news/40174762/china-pakistan-relations-new-dimensions.
17 Khaleeq Kiani, 'Issues in China's offer for investment', *Dawn*, 17 November 2014, https://www.dawn.com/news/1144932.
18 Ibid. Op cit 5.
19 Syed Shoaib Hasan, 'Pakistan and the Chinese Century', *Dawn*, 14 December 2014, https://www.dawn.com/news/1150780.
20 Pervez Hoodbhoy, 'Don't Blame the Chinese', *Dawn*, 18 February 2023, https://www.dawn.com/news/1737793/dont-blame-the-chinese.
21 Uzair Younus, 'With Pakistan's Economy in Freefall, Chinese Economic and Military Influence Is Likely to Grow in the Country', Atlantic Council, 9 March 2023, https://www.atlanticcouncil.org/blogs/southasiasource/with-pakistans-economy-in-freefall-chinese-economic-and-military-influence-is-likely-to-grow-in-the-country/.
22 Ibid. Op cit 20.
23 Ibid. Op cit 21.
24 Salman Rafi Sheikh, 'China's Pakistan Infrastructure Initiative's Continuing Problems', Asia Sentinel, 27 October 2022, https://www.asiasentinel.com/p/china-pakistan-infrastructure-problems.
25 Syed Mohammad Ali, 'China's Influence in Pakistan', *The Express Tribune*, 23 December 2022, https://tribune.com.pk/story/2392359/chinas-influence-in-pakistan.
26 Obaid Abrar Khan, 'Pak Political Parties Must Hammer Out Rifts: China', The News, 10 January 2016, https://www.thenews.com.pk/print/89216-Pak-political-parties-must-hammer-out-rifts-China.
27 'Who Controls the CPEC?,' Editorial, *The Nation*, 19 July 2016.
28 Mushtaq Ghumman, 'Chinese Firms have Adopted Go-Slow Policy?', *Business Recorder*, 24 December 2022, https://www.brecorder.com/news/40216416/chinese-firms-have-adopted-go-slow-policy.
29 'Chinese Envoy Heaps Praise on Shehbaz for "Punjab Speed" in CPEC projects', *The Express Tribune*, 26 January 2021, https://tribune.com.pk/story/2281447/chinese-envoy-heaps-praise-on-shehbaz-for-punjab-speed-in-cpec-projects.
30 Ibid. Op cit 24.
31 'Difficult Choices', Editorial, *The News*, 2 May 2023, https://www.thenews.com.pk/print/1066138-difficult-choices; 'Decision time', Editorial, *Dawn*, 2 May 2023,

https://www.dawn.com/news/1750464/decision-time; Dr Qaisar Rashid, 'Pakistan on Discord Leaks', *Daily Times*, 2 May 2023, https://dailytimes.com.pk/1089101/pakistan-on-discord-leaks/.

32. Jason Dean and Jeremy Page, 'Beijing Points to Pakistan after Ethnic Violence', *The Wall Street Journal*, 1 August 2011, https://www.wsj.com/articles/SB10001424053111903341404576481312937363114; 'Kashgar Must Not Mar Ties', *Dawn*, 8 August 2011, www.Dawn.com/news/650312/kashgar-must-notmar-ties.
33. Zhang Li, 'To Manage Conflict in South Asia: China's Stakes, Perceptions and Inputs', Institute for Security and Development Policy, Asia Paper, Stockholm, October 2009, https://www.isdp.eu/publication/manage-conflict-south-asia-chinas-stakes-perceptions-inputs/.
34. Tahir Ali, 'Taliban Group Threatens to Attack Chinese Interests', *The Nation*, 17 November 2014, https://www.nation.com.pk/17-Nov-2014/taliban-group-threatens-to-attack-chinese-interests.
35. Andrew Small, 'Intensifying China–Pakistan Ties', Interview by Jayshree Bajoria, Council on Foreign Relations, New York, 7 July 2010, https://www.cfr.org/interview/intensifying-china-pakistan-ties.
36. Zahid Gishkori, 'Economic Corridor: 12,000-Strong Force to Guard Chinese Workers', *The Express Tribune*, 30 March 2015, https://tribune.com.pk/story/861078/economic-corridor-12000-strong-force-to-guard-chinese-workers.
37. Ibid. Op cit 5.

9

China and West Asia
A Solid Trajectory
Anil Trigunayat

China is hoping to be the next US in the Middle East (West Asia) through its geoeconomic engagement, geostrategic calculations and geopolitical machinations. It is true that in recent decades, since it embarked on its economic revival courtesy, the US and West opening up in 1970s, Beijing has strategically been engaging the West Asian, especially the Gulf Cooperation Council (GCC) countries, to secure energy supplies and maritime routes and choke-points, while deepening ties at all levels, yet remaining under the radar. Ironically, in the 21st century, the US's shift to the Indo-Pacific and partisan behaviour during the Russia–Ukraine War and Israel–Hamas war is intricately linked with the growing global Chinese influence, especially in Africa and the Middle East. In West Asia, there is a general perception and even fear that the US is in gradual retraction mode or at least becoming ineffective or inactive in the region, even though Washington may wish to claim otherwise. This was again clearly borne out by the deepening mistrust towards the US during the Israel–Hamas War (October 2023 onwards) when its role was seen only through the Israeli prism and lack of sympathy for the Arabs and Palestinians, despite the shuttle diplomacy by Secretary Antony Blinken.

The Arab–Islamic Summit outcomes and the visits of Foreign Ministers' delegation led by the Saudi Foreign Minister to P5 (permanent five, viz., the US, the UK, France, Russia and China) countries to urge for immediate ceasefire fell on deaf ears in Washington DC, as the very next day, the US vetoed the UN Security Council (UNSC) Resolution piloted by UN Secretary General Guterres under the rarely invoked powers granted by Article 99 of the UN Charter. Such US patterns provided a significant opening to both the regional powers as well as China to encash on that opportunity, especially since 2013 when Beijing launched its Belt and Road Initiative (BRI), currently encompassing the whole region, irrespective of the intra-regional rivalries between Saudi Arabia and the Sunni world, with Shia Iran or the nuclear Iran and Israel suffering from a mutually assured destruction syndrome. China's engagement with the region has acquired a unique dependency and trust quotient because of its developmental and non-prescriptive and non-interventionist policies, which are often value-neutral – in direct contrast to the West – and help it navigate the competing regional powers as well. Khashoggi saga is one such example. China during the Israel–Hamas war maintained a mostly pro-Arab stance without provoking Israel beyond a point, even as it chaired the rotational presidency of UNSC in November 2023 when the war and destruction was at its peak. It perhaps does look at its economic interests and key investments in Israel pragmatically.

China's politically value-neutral approach suits the West Asian powers and their leaders, who often prefer their own style of the autocratic democracy model and feel duly endorsed by the Chinese leadership, economic heft and prowess. Some of the GCC countries assessing the geopolitical and geo-strategic shifts have also embarked on their 'Act East Policy' to reach out and have closer partnerships with their major markets and clients, like China, India, Japan, South Korea, etc. since the economic pivot has also moved towards Asia. In this, China remains the main pivot for these countries. Take for example the visit of President Xi Jinping to Riyadh in December 2022, when he held three summits with regional leaders and signed many strategic agreements, calling it a 'New Era for China and the Arab world. China's recent diplomatic overtures have led to a rapprochement between Riyadh and Tehran as both have agreed to respect each other's sovereignty and territorial integrity and mutual concerns (March 2023).

Advancing its role as a mediator, China seems to have emerged as a reliable facilitator and sort of guarantor on cantankerous issues between Saudi Arabia and Iran. This was another feather in President Xi Jinping's furry cap as he embarked on his third term as president. China has also flashed out its alternative models of security and development through Global Security Initiative (GSI); Global Development Initiative (GDI) and Global Civilizational Initiative (GCI). Xi Jinping noted how his trip to Saudi Arabia heralded a 'new era' in the China–Arab partnership, as mentioned earlier, and invited the Gulf States to join the Global Security Initiative (GSI) 'in a joint effort to uphold regional peace and stability'. He further added that 'China will continue to firmly support GCC countries in safeguarding their security, and support the efforts by regional countries to resolve differences through dialogue and consultation and to build a Gulf collective security architecture'.[1]

It would, however, be premature to say that China has emerged as a credible alternative to the US in the region as, in the near future, it is unlikely to command the requisite heft and capability to be the regional security arbiter; but in a diffused regional and dysfunctional global order, Beijing will continue to exploit the crevices; sometimes even in collusion with Russia at the expense of the US.

Therefore, an attempt has been made in this essay to look at diverse contours and direction of the China's extensive and deepening engagement with West Asia or Middle East and North Africa (MENA) region that needs to be carefully watched and India would do well to continuously analyse trends to work newer alternatives and viable choices, as the regional countries do not wish to opt for either one at the expense of the other.

Please note that 'West Asia' and 'Middle East' have been used interchangeably in this essay.

Geo-strategic and Geopolitical Context

In a recently released report, prior to the China–Arab Summit in Saudi Arabia (December 2022), Beijing reiterated its long-standing position with regard to the region. Describing the summit as a milestone event, the Chinese Foreign Ministry said in the report that Beijing will take it as an opportunity to promote the building of the China–Arab community with a shared future in the new era so as to bring benefits to the two peoples, promote unity and cooperation between developing countries and safeguard the peace and development of the world. Again, Foreign Minister Wang Yi, while visiting Cairo for the Arab League Meet on 14 January 2024, said that Chin will host the tenth meeting of China–Arab States Cooperation Ministerial Forum (CACSF) which was held on May 29–30 in Beijing. Calling Arab states 'true friends and good partners' of China, he also said that China will continue to support Arab countries in seeking strength through unity and upholding strategic independence.[2]

Beijing has actively followed a policy of dealing with the regional powers on 'as is where is' basis. Usually, they prefer not to pass value judgements or dictate what should be the political contours of the local governance or socio-economic management, but rather engage and enhance partnerships and exploit the economic potential and opportunities strategically, without being prescriptive, which has generated confidence in the Chinese intent and its capacity to be a useful partner. An equanimous approach towards the region which is based on geo-economic and strategic interests has been adopted, which has paid off dividends from Tehran to Tel Aviv through wealth creation on a mutually beneficial basis. At least that is how it is perceived by the West Asian countries. Since they avoid getting entangled into the regional rivalry matrix, Beijing has kept its interests afloat by being a bilaterally dependable market and investment and technology provider as well as destination. Likewise, the regional powers are also following a multi-aligned matrix and avoiding a binary order while navigating the competing commands. As rivalry between large powers has mounted, small- and medium-sized states have increasingly found themselves subjected to competing demands – such as requests from China to support its policies towards Hong Kong and Taiwan, Uyghurs, One China Policy or from the US to shun Chinese infrastructure investment and 5G technology. Being seen by both sides as a plausible partner makes it more likely that a given state will be the target of suasion rather than sanctions, allowing it to mollify one solicitous great power at a relatively low cost while not provoking the other.[3]

A recent Washington Institute survey confirms that at the grassroots level, support to diversifying relationship from the US towards China and Russia has increased significantly, especially due to the US's active engagement and support to Israel in the ongoing Israel–Hamas war. Washington Institute survey, conducted between 14 November and 6 December 2023, show that the past several months have had an impact on popular perceptions of global powers' regional roles. A majority of respondents in the UAE (66 per cent), Saudi Arabia (67 per cent), Kuwait (62 per cent), Egypt (57 per cent), Bahrain (68 per cent), Qatar (63 per cent) and Lebanon (72 per cent) agree with the following statement: 'We can no longer count on the United States, and therefore must look more to other nations like Russia and China as partners.' The percentages who agree with that sentiment have notably increased in every country, including an eleven-point jump in Bahrain (up from 57 per cent in July 2022).[4]

In 2013, China launched its comprehensive One Belt One Road (OBOR) initiative with connectivity and economy at its heart, also underscoring the Chinese strategic outreach to West Asia. Nearly all the Arab and Middle Eastern countries have signed up to it, which is a significant achievement for Beijing and some cause of worry for the US and India. Later, in 2016, just before the visit of President Xi Jinping to Riyadh, Cairo and Tehran, an Arab Policy Paper outlining the Chinese vision and interactive paradigm shift was released.[5] They also celebrated the sixtieth anniversary of diplomatic relations with the Arab world. The strategy comprising wide-ranging consultations, joint enterprise and contribution and shared benefit and prosperity further underscored peaceful development, solidarity and mutually beneficial cooperation in a win-win scenario based on openness, transparency and trust. They sought to achieve this through 1+2+3 cooperation matrix, with the first one encompassing energy cooperation and related core infrastructure; second, construction, trade and investment facilitation and the third aimed at harnessing innovative technologies in nuclear energy, space and satellite and renewables. This also marked the centrality of energy and economic cooperation of China in the region. It blended very well with the 2015 announcement for jointly building Silk Road Economic Belt and 21st-century Maritime Silk Road initiatives and projects.

China's quest for strategic infrastructure, ports, roads and Special Economic Zones (SEZs) and Industrial Parks across the whole geographical spectrum are creating the requisite structures for regional connectivity and footprints of the Dragon across the Middle East, providing it with a unique and rather powerful stakeholder-ship as a prelude to increased security cooperation and engagement. Richard W. Carney argues that countries in which political leaders rely more heavily on clientelism coupled with greater control over the corporate sector have a higher demand for Chinese infrastructure spending.[6] It is evident in the growing periphery of collaboration in space, nuclear, cyber, tech transfer, defence, digital standards, spread of Chinese 5G and 6G and new and renewable energy as the host countries diversify their economies away from hydrocarbons. Chinese investments in these sunrise sectors has increased significantly. The petrodollars that China provides by being the largest buyer of the Middle East oil and gas are providing the capital for modernisation of the Gulf economies, infrastructure and society.

This is further supplemented by the desire of the regional satraps like Saudi Arabia, UAE, Turkey, Qatar, Iran and Egypt to play a more independent and assertive role in the emerging regional and global dynamic. In this strategy, the role of alternate power centres like China, Russia and India acquires greater salience. Beijing has been quick to avail of such opportunities as its strategic choice, knowing too well that at the present time it or even the Sino-Russian axis does not have the requisite heft and wherewithal to provide a desired security cover and confidence to the region, as has been done by the US for decades. But incrementally they are getting there as the defence and military cooperation moves apace. Besides, China has the capacity to convert and transform its economic heft into military assets should it need them.

China has expanded and deepened its footprints through high-level contacts and various levels of the strategic partnerships with major powers in the region. Over the past decade, China has forged a variety of 'strategic' partnerships with a host of countries in the region – 'comprehensive strategic partnership' with Saudi Arabia, the UAE, Iran, Egypt and Algeria; 'strategic cooperation' with Turkey and 'strategic partnerships' with Qatar, Kuwait and Oman. Further, Saudi Arabia and the UAE are 'pivot states' crucial to 'China's global network politically and economically' and Turkey is a 'node state' – a bridge to facilitate Chinese interests.[7] Israel has been designated as an Innovative Strategic Partner. These strategic arrangements provide it with the required frameworks for protection and sustenance of its BRI projects as well as economic and energy as well as territorial interests. It has already set up base in Djibouti in Horn of Africa and has full access to Duqm Port in Oman. Khalifa Port in UAE over which the US raised concerns, Jizan Port in Saudi Arabia, Port Said in Egypt and Ain Sokhna in Djibouti and even a likelihood of Socotra in Yemen in collaboration with UAE could provide China with the key strategic levers as and when it needs them for ensuring stability and security of the region, or even its own offensive maritime use in the Red Sea, Indian Ocean and Mediterranean. It has also been reported that as a result of signing of a comprehensive partnership agreement with Iran and proposed $400 billion in investments, China may get access to the Iranian ports for use and development of Jask in the Strait of Hormuz. China has also been actively involved in the anti-piracy operations through which it claims to provide security and stability in Africa and the world, while protecting its own commercial ships and securing maritime routes. However, on the Houthis attacking commercial ships, Beijing's approach was circumspect.

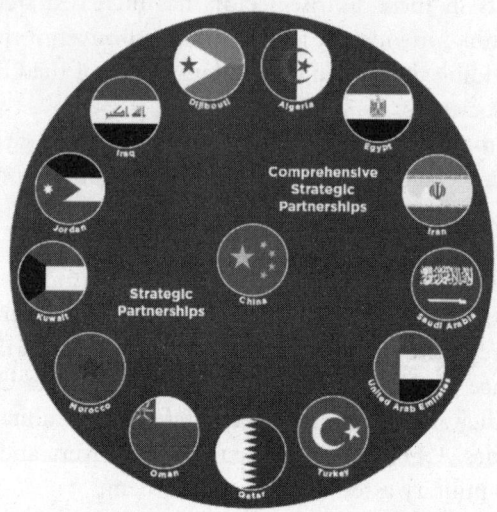

Source:

Likewise, knowing too well the limitations of its Malacca Straits choke-points, from where most of its trade passes, China embarked on another offshoot of its maritime artery through amenable and ever-so-pliant Pakistan, via the China Pakistan Economic Corridor (CPEC) and the Gwadar Port, which will ensure access to Gulf energy more smoothly. Given its primary consideration for safeguarding and promoting its own economic interests, it is exploring and deploying tactics that include conflict 'management' instead of 'resolution' and promoting a 'non-conflictual' relationship between China's strategic partners in the region, especially in the Gulf, who are deeply divided and involved in proxy wars. This strategy is directly linked to the BRI, which links China's energy and trade ties with the rest of the world, including South Asia, and is assuming a security dynamic. This smart gaming was also witnessed during the recent Israel–Hamas conflict (Palestine War) of 2023, when China was omnipresent yet doing very little on the ground. On 14 January 2024 in Cairo, a joint statement with the Arab League noted that China and the Arab side support the holding of an inclusive dialogue participated in by all Palestinian factions, which is committed to achieving Palestinian's reconciliation. It called for holding an international peace conference with broad participation as soon as possible to promote the implementation of the two-state solution, and on such basis resuming peace talks between Palestine and Israel. China has taken the Arab position in toto. It also held a unity meeting of the Palestinian factions in Beijing including Hamas and Fatah to bring about reconciliation (April 2024).[8]

Many Middle East countries are keen to join BRICS (Brazil, Russia, India, China and South Africa) and SCO (Shanghai Cooperation Organization), where China, India and Russia are the key players. Iran has already joined the SCO as a full member when India held the presidency in 2023. Saudi Arabia, Egypt and Qatar have joined as dialogue partners. Likewise, several Middle East countries including Saudi Arabia, UAE, Turkey, Egypt, Algeria and Qatar had expressed their interest in joining the BRICS. Saudi Arabia, Egypt, Iran and UAE joined at the Johannesburg BRICS summit in 2023. Turkey is expected to join during Russian Presidency in 2024. Several of them are already the founding members of the Chinese Asia infrastructure Bank (AIIB) as well as the BRICS New Development Bank, which will provide it much-needed financial heft and the ability to function as BRICS Plus mull over a new currency and greater reliance on national currencies in trade and investments which might acquire further salience during the Russian presidency in 2024, which could be seen as an alternate, even if a nascent, attempt at de-dollarisation of the financial landscape and the US dollar hegemony with perhaps a greater 'Yuanisation'. UAE and Saudi Arabia and Iran and Russia already prefer bilateral trade in Yuan and their own currencies.

As the great power rivalry intensifies in the region, Chinese designs will become clearer and the political and strategic capital invested in the region will begin to pay off dividends. It will of course depend on how the US and Western bloc plays their cards and how fast, if at all, their interest in the region wanes. However, the energy and food crisis due to Russia–Ukraine war may have reoriented the Western focus towards the oil- and gas-producing countries to meet their demands away from Russia. Outcome of the Russia–Ukraine war as well as that of the Israel–Hamas war and polarisation of power blocs – in which one pole is most likely to be governed by China – could cause dilemma of choices among the various West Asian actors, who for now are trying to leverage the bilateral relationships with all partners to their advantage. Meanwhile, along with Russia, China continues to block the UNSC resolutions on Syria, Libya, Iraq, Palestine, Iran and Yemen, while urging peaceful resolution through dialogue which gains it more traction in the region. Likewise, both with Russia and UAE, and Brazil and Malta, it has worked closely for the various proposed and even passed UN resolutions, while criticising and expressing regrets and disappointment at the US veto.

Expanding Security, Technology and Defence Partnership

Middle East has always been a zone of geopolitical contestations. The hydrocarbons have been the mainstay, along with maritime and strategic trading routes. During the Cold War era, US–Soviet competition prevailed with the major regional powers being Egypt, Iraq and Syria. Iran, until the advent of 1979 Islamic Revolution, and Israel and the Sunni Arab and Gulf countries were mainly in the US camp during the Cold War era. But the Gulf and Iran–Iraq and the US invasion of Iraq to remove Saddam Hussein and existential confrontation between Tel Aviv and Tehran under Ayatollahs, and several hotspots post Arab Spring in Libya, Syria, Yemen, Iraq and Palestine, have defined the volatile nature of the region. The US has remained a major arbiter of security and stability, especially for the Arab and GCC countries, and Israel has tried to bring about security-oriented rapprochement between Israel and some Arab countries like UAE, Bahrain, Morocco and Sudan under the aegis of Trump-driven Abraham Accords. For President Biden, after a slow start and gradually making up with Saudi Arabia, the efforts were directed to bring about a rapprochement and formal diplomatic relations between Riyadh and Tel Aviv, which also became a major reason for the 7 October Hamas terrorist attacks and killing of 1,200 Israeli citizens and nearly 245 hostages. At the same time, the Palestinian issue remains cantankerous, and no serious effort is being made to resolve it. Some fatigue even among the Arab countries is quite evident in this regard as they are moving to shield their own economic and security interests. China supported the Abraham Accords while sticking to its position on Palestine.

With the US becoming a competitor in the oil and gas sector, and after the ignominious exit from Afghanistan as well as its perceived withdrawal from the region, it has caused a paradigm shift in the partnership choices of the major powers – especially GCC countries. China has emerged as their favourite. For decades, China continued to predicate the relationship on ensuring its energy security and safety of the trading routes towards Malacca Straits but, with the US policy shift into the Indo-Pacific, Beijing is trying to strengthen its security and connectivity relationships through strategic initiatives with key partners in the region. It has followed a policy of friendship with all, preference for none; at least overtly. That is why Beijing has been able to garner full participation of the region in its BRI project which has been expanded through the Maritime Silk Road, Digital Silk Road and Health Silk Road initiatives encompassing critical and crucial areas of partnership which will have long-term benefits and repercussions for its entrenchment in the region.

China has successfully gained a strong foothold in the strategic domain in the region by capitalising on the opportunities thrown up by geopolitical contestations and developments. During the COVID-19 pandemic, several West Asian countries not only depended on Chinese assistance but were the first to introduce and administer Chinese vaccines as well as produce them locally. UAE, Egypt and Morocco were the key partners to begin with. Saudi Arabia, UAE and Qatar provided significant aid and assistance to China in its fight against the pandemic and stood with it against the American onslaught. Likewise, the Chinese 5G technology and networks, Huawei and ZTE, are well ensconced in the region, much to American discomfort. Chinese satellite navigation system Bei Dou has much greater acceptance in the region as far as its application in telecommunications, maritime security and weather – especially with regard to agriculture – are concerned. China is the biggest supplier of the drones to the Arab world and manufacturing locally adds to its heft. Similarly, the Chinese missiles and other defence equipment are gaining currency in the region, mainly as they find the US and Western conditions and restrictions on supplies rather constricting and compromising their sovereignty.

According to reports, in March 2017 itself, Saudi Arabia's King Abdulaziz City for Science and Technology and China Aerospace Science and Technology Corp. signed a partnership deal to produce China's CH-4 Unmanned Aerial Vehicle (UAV), which is similar to the US-made MQ-1 Predator drone. Saudi Arabia has been in possession of such drones since 2014, as has Iraq. This Saudi facility will likely operate as a hub 'for manufacturing and servicing for other CH-4 operators in the Middle East, including Egypt, Iraq and Jordan'. Likewise, the UAE, a coalition partner in the Saudi-led air campaign against Houthi rebels in Yemen since 2015, imported Chinese-made Wing Loong I drones in 2011, and became the first customer of the Wing Loong II drone in 2017. Stockholm International Peace Research Institute (SIPRI) estimated that China's weapon exports to Arab world increased by 7 per cent during 2016–20, with Saudi Arabia, UAE, Egypt and Iraq being the main importers. China's exports grew by 290 per cent to Saudi Arabia and by 77 per cent to the UAE between the 2012–2016 period and the 2017–2021 period as per SIPRI. According to the US Defence News, China has been exporting armed drones to Saudi Arabia, the UAE, Egypt, Iraq and Jordan. The website notes that these drones have been used in conflict zones in countries, including Libya and Yemen. China's projected impressive economic performance and growing involvement in regions outside its borders have resulted in strengthened military-security ties (arms deals and weapons co-production) with some Middle Eastern countries (particularly Persian Gulf nations) as one dimension of its overall Middle East strategy.[9]

China has continued with concerted efforts to expand its Middle East defense relationships in recent times. In early November, the US officials sounded the alarm on talks between China and Oman to establish a Chinese military base in the country, similar to the military facility China built in Djibouti in 2017 – its first and only overseas base today. And then the UAE on 13 November 2023 announced it had finalised a deal with China's National Aero-Technology Import & Export Corporation to purchase a fleet of L-15 advanced jet trainers, with technical support included.[10]

A sanction-hit, embattled Iran, after its comprehensive strategic partnership in 2020, does expect a much greater result-oriented cooperation, even as Beijing tries to follow an equanimous policy with its rivals Saudi-led Sunni group as well as with Israel. However, the agreement signed by both countries called for 'cooperation mechanisms in the fields of … equipment and technology [in the security and defence domain]'. This was clearly evident during the visit of late President Ebrahim Raisi to Beijing (in February 2023) when he impressed upon China to do more in keeping with the commitments. Tehran was also miffed by the Chinese stance on the China–GCC Summit Declaration (November 2022) in Riyadh regarding the status of three disputed islands in favour of the GCC. Some Iranian media even spoke of Taiwan's independence to convey the message. Even though Beijing does not like a nuclear Iran, it has been a key factor in facilitating the Joint Comprehensive Plan of Action (JCPOA) negotiations as well as in the subsequent efforts to revive it after President Trump walked out of it. Indeed, Beijing will have to tread cautiously with its balancing policy as it works behind the scenes to bring about some semblance of dialogue and a modus vivendi among competing actors in the region. Meanwhile, China continues to be the arbiter of the Saudi–Iran deal, with the most recent meeting of Wang Yi with Deputy Foreign Ministers in Beijing ensuring understanding and the continuity of diplomatic ties. During the talks with Saudi Deputy Foreign Minister Waleed Elkhereiji and his Iranian counterpart Ali Bagheri Kani (November 2023), Wang urged that Middle Eastern countries should work to 'eliminate external interference' while renewing Beijing's call for 'an immediate ceasefire' in the Israel–Gaza war.[11] President Raisi had also recently visited Riyadh for the Arab–Islamic Summit in the context of ongoing Israel–Hamas war. In the wake of the death of President Raisi in a helicopter crash (20 May 2024), Saudi and all Arab countries stood in concert with Iran and even offered assistance to locate the crash site which is indicative of the modus vivendi the regional majors are working for.

Saudi Arabia and the UAE – the biggest importers of the US defence equipment – were quite disenchanted with the failure of the US protective shields and the responses during the missile and drone attacks by the Iranian-backed Houthis. Even the US's non-predictive policy with regard to the Iran Nuclear deal (JCPOA) has caused enough security concerns with regard to the US's geopolitical intent, and occasional prodding on human rights issues and democracy etc. annoys them. This was evident during the Russia–Ukraine war, when the Saudi Crown Prince Mohammed bin Salman (MBS) and the UAE's ruler Sheikh Mohammad bin Zayed al Nayahan (MBZ) declined to take calls from President Biden, let alone the exceptionally warm reception of President Xi Jinping. The UAE, representing the Arab Seat in 2023 at the UNSC, abstained on the Resolution condemning Russia. This was further evident when the

Organisation of Petroleum Exporting Countries (OPEC+) countries in concert with Russia refused to follow the US diktat to increase production of oil to ease the pressure caused by weaponisation of energy supplies by Russia. Moreover, they have refused to go along with the sanctions against Russia and , in fact, the UAE has emerged as a major entrepot for Russian trade in Rouble–Dirham modality. The quest for strategic autonomy, especially that of major powers in the region, is evident as they pursue strategic autonomy oriented foreign policy with diversification as the mantra for international discourse.

Visit of President Xi Jinping, immediately after the lifting of pandemic restrictions, to Riyadh in December 2022, was iconic and instructive not only in the shape of the grand reception but also the outcomes of the Comprehensive Strategic Partnership. It also provided an opportunity for him to meet over thirty regional leaders across three summits and became one of the most powerful pushes to reiterate China's strategic interests and overt heft in the region.

As the shape of the new global order becomes imminent in the form of Cold War 2.0 post the Eurasian war, the alternative financial architecture will surely be an integral part of it, which will compete against the existing US-led SWIFT and Brettonwoods-governed Western system as the global discontent with the US financial hegemony grows. China being the lead at the other pole is well placed to take advantage of that opportunity. It has already established an alternate financial bank, AIIB, with $100 billion capital and the $40 billion New Silk Road Fund to promote private investments. Several infrastructure projects, including the power sector in Egypt and the UAE, are being funded. Currency swap arrangements have been set up by regional central banks with their Chinese counterpart. Another alternative is the proposed BRICS currency, and the joining of the UAE, Saudi Arabia, Iran and Egypt will further enrich that alternative, and consequently expedite de-dollarisation. In 2023, at Davos, Saudi Finance Minister Mohammed al-Jadaan revealed Riyadh's willingness to trade in not just the Yuan, but also a variety of other currencies. The UAE already has a similar mechanism with China. Likewise, Iraq became the latest to distance itself from dollar dominance, announcing that it plans to regulate foreign trade from China directly in yuan. Thus, yuanisation is becoming a reality in the Middle Eastern financial discourse. Even Egypt, a longtime friend of China, is diversifying its currency basket away from the US Dollar, 'Since Egypt is a non-oil exporter, there was no need to peg its local currency to the US dollar,' as Hassan Abdalla, the Governor of the Central Bank of Egypt (CBE), said at a major economic conference in Cairo. 'It is for the sake of the idea of pegging – and I'm not talking about the price, I'm speaking about the idea,' he said. 'America is not my major trading partner. I don't know why people are always fixated on the dollar.'[12]

While de-dollarisation may still be way off, the Middle Eastern countries, especially the oil-producing ones, realise that their petrodollars added to the US financial muscle since 1974, and the US has scored a self-goal against its currency when it cut Russia off from the SWIFT payment system and froze over $350 billion of its gold and foreign exchange reserves. Critics argue that that act alone massively reduced trust in the dollar-based monetary system amongst many countries, especially those in the Global South, which have long been skeptical of the US hegemony, causing them to further question the viability and risk of holding their reserves in the mighty dollar. China sees an opportunity in this as a viable alternate choice amidst the ongoing currency warfare that would become an integral part of the new financial architecture. Russia has already decided yuan as major currency of exchange[13] and stopped trading in dollars and euros as a result of even more sanctions announced at G7 Summit in Italy in June 2024.

More importantly, China is aligning and synergising its BRI philosophy with the regional developmental roadmaps like Vision 2030 of Saudi Arabia, Egypt, the UAE and others. Special attention is being paid as China uses the economic toolkit to achieve its geopolitical objectives. It has also emphasised on creating institutional interactive frameworks to follow on its initiatives which include the Forum on China–Africa Cooperation (FOCAC), the China–Arab States Cooperation Forum (CASCF) and the China–Gulf Cooperation Council (C-GCC) Strategic Dialogue. FOCAC's relationship with MENA is based on the North African members of the Arab League: Algeria, Djibouti, Egypt, Libya, Mauritania, Morocco, Somalia, Sudan and Tunisia have membership in CASCF and FOCAC. Moreover, China has also appointed two special envoys for the region.

In early January 2022, the foreign ministers of Saudi Arabia, Kuwait, Oman, Bahrain and the Islamic Republic of Iran travelled to China within the span of a week to strengthen their ties with the Chinese Communist Party. Then the leaders of Egypt, Qatar and the UAE were the stars at the Beijing Olympics, along with President Putin of Russia in February, when the West was politically boycotting the games due to the treatment of Muslims and Uyghurs. The Arab leaders were also able to have face-to-face meetings in Beijing since the Qatar blockade began in 2017. The trend continued during the China–Arab Forum and the BRI Forum – organised to mark its tenth anniversary – when special emphasis was placed on the Middle East.

Last meeting of the CACSF and C-GCC was held during the remarkable visit of President Xi Jinping to Riyadh in 2023. The high-profile visits of President Xi Jinping to Saudi Arabia and the welcome he received are often compared with the drab fist shake between President Biden and Crown Prince Salman.

China's comprehensive strategy for the region is to 'achieve win-win cooperation, common development, and a better future of the China–Arab strategic and cooperative relations'. It also specifically mentions the need to intensify China's military cooperation with the Arab countries, and also to 'deepen cooperation on weapons, equipment and various specialized technologies, and carry out joint military exercises'. Arab Policy Paper further adds that China 'will continue to support the development of national defence and military forces of Arab States to maintain peace and security of the region'. In 2019, China also expressed its desire to be part of the Gulf security architecture, especially in the Strait of Hormuz. These indicate the continued focus on securitisation of its West Asian policy. However, Jonathan Fulton argues that China has a diverse set of relations across the region and a clear preference for the Middle East status quo, as fragile as that may be.[14]

The Geo-Economic Calculations

China has sought to ensure its energy security and supplies from the Middle East and has used its economic clout to subserve its geopolitical and strategic interests by nurturing economic engagement with all Gulf and regional countries while avoiding entanglement in their regional rivalries and disputes. It has been able to keep both Saudi Arabia and Iran content and waded cautiously the fault lines between these two major protagonists, and even tried to bridge them. All key actors seem to accept this since the Chinese policy overtly remains for mutual benefit on an equal basis and due respect to local political hierarchy and system. No wonder the BRI has expanded beyond original contours and the trade and investment and technological collaboration has moved ahead at a confident pace. Besides, Beijing's inability to be cowed down by Western pressure has provided them with the requisite comfort level as it defies the Western unilateral sanctions, be they against Iran or Russia.

Energy has been the prime mover for China in the region. Oil accounts for over 40 per cent of Arab exports to China. Since 2019, China has emerged as the largest importer of hydrocarbons in the world and nearly half of it came from the Arabs. Interestingly, China started importing oil for the first time in the region from Oman and even currently Oman's 80–90 per cent exports go to China. China's most important energy partners remain Saudi Arabia, Iraq, Oman, the UAE, Qatar, Kuwait and Libya. Even though in defiance of Countering America's Adversaries Through Sanctions Act (CAATSA) sanctions of the US, Beijing continued to import Iranian oil, the overall imports went down. These will continue to increase as the Chinese economy comes out of the shadows of the pandemic and the Russia–Ukraine War. As such, the IEA (International Energy Agency) has estimated that by 2035, the exports of oil from the region to China will double. This indicates the interdependent trajectory of relationship.

China is also engaging in developing assets in the regional oil fields, especially in Iraq, where it acquired substantial stakes to ensure uninterrupted supplies. Saudi investments in refineries in China and CPEC strategic port in Gwadar, Pakistan, are to ensure the trouble-free transportation of Gulf oil. During the visit of President Xi Jinping in 2016, nearly $70 billion in investments was committed, of which a major part was in the energy sector. Estimates indicate that Saudi Arabia may even surpass Russia to become the biggest supplier of crude oil to China.

It is indeed an interesting fact that even though Saudi Arabia was the last country to establish diplomatic relations with People's Republic of China (1990) and had even opposed its entry to the UN in 1971, it has become the most important pivot and driver for Chinese heft in the region.

Trade and investments have seen an unprecedented upswing, given the fact that China is a late actor in the region. In 2018, China's bilateral trade with the Arab world stood at $244 billion and China emerged as the second largest investor. Overall investment crossed $177 billion of which $70 billion went to GCC countries. Four years later in 2022, China's trade with the Middle East reached $507.152 billion, up 27.1 per cent year-on-year, and China remained the largest trading partner in the Middle East. Chinese have brought their trade basket to the region as they established a huge marketing enterprise in Dubai, with over 3,000 Chinese companies displaying their products at the China–Middle East Investment and Trade Promotion Centre. Likewise, it has created specialised markets and Arab-speaking marts in Beijing, Shanghai and most prominently in Yiwu – the largest commodity market buzzing with Arab traders. In 2020, China was among the top four export markets for ten MENA countries, and among the top four source of imports for every country in the region. Its trade relationships follow a predictable pattern, with much higher values of trade with the energy exporters of the Gulf. Since 2020, its top five MENA trade partners were Saudi Arabia, the UAE, Iraq, Turkey and Oman. The economic corridor between China and the Middle East, North Africa and Türkiye (MENAT) region is set to see business and investment flows accelerate substantially in the coming five years, according to a recently released HSBC report titled 'The China–MENAT Corridor: Unlocking Growth Potential'. HSBC noted $178 billion in 'untapped trade potential' between China and MENAT until 2027.[15]

Some of the key strategic projects where China has been participating are the iconic and futuristic NEOM (Special Economic Zone with a New Future) city in Saudi Arabia; reconstruction in Syria; China–Egypt Suez Economic and Trade Cooperation zone with over $20 billion; industrial zone in Duqm strategic port of Oman; Silk City in Kuwait and Sino-Jordanian University in Amman. Apart from that, under various BRI initiatives, China is creating trade, transport, renewable energy and connectivity infrastructure across the region through focused investments. Iraq was the largest beneficiary from China's BRI in 2021, with about $10.5 billion in construction contracts. Syria became the last country to sign the BRI in 2021.

Strong shift towards the Middle East in BRI investments and projects was noticed as per several studies. African and Middle Eastern countries picked up an increasingly large share of Chinese engagement, up from 8 per cent in 2020 to about 38 per cent of BRI engagement in 2021. Arab and Middle Eastern countries increased investment by about 360 per cent and construction engagement by 116 per cent compared to 2020.[16]

Several Middle Eastern countries and their sovereign wealth funds are planning to invest more in China in 2024 according to Deutsche Bank Middle East. State-owned investors in Bahrain, Kuwait, Oman, Qatar, Saudi Arabia and the UAE invested more than $2.3 billion into Greater China in 2023 compared with about $100 million in 2022 according to Global SWF.[17] Investments into Chinese companies in areas including electric vehicles (EVs), batteries, energy storage, renewables and industrial technology will be 'a big focus' for investors as the sovereign wealth funds evaluate Chinese large corporates as quite attractive. A $533 million deal between the AMR ALuwlaa and Zhonghuan International Group from Hong Kong to set up an iron ore factory, and a $500 million-agreement between Saudi Arabia's ASK Group and China National Geological & Mining Corporation for the Arabian Shield copper mining project were among the major businesses-to-business deals during the 10th China–Arab Business Forum and, likewise, the government-to-business agreements included a $5.6 billion deal between the Saudi Ministry of Investment and Chinese developer of autonomous driving technology, Human Horizons, to set up a joint venture for the research, development, manufacturing and sale of electric vehicles.

In 2023, China continued its regional economic expansion, making concentrated progress with energy and development deals. In early November, Egypt's General Authority for the Suez Canal Economic Zone (SCZONE) signed a $15.6 billion deal with multiple Chinese companies for eleven different projects in the zone, including green fuel and manufacturing projects. This deal echoes a similar agreement between SCZONE and China Energy Investment group in October, worth $6.75 billion, which likewise promised numerous green hydrogen and green ammonia projects. Following the third Belt and Road Forum held in Beijing in early October 2023, the China Development Bank disbursed a $957 million loan agreement to Egypt's central bank in an effort to finance projects agreed upon at the forum.[18]

Through its economic engagement, China has successfully steered the conflictual relationships, be it between Algeria–Morocco or, for that matter, Saudi Arabia–Iran or Tehran–Tel Aviv. Despite its close partnership with

Israel which is predicated on the US designs, China remains committed to the Palestine cause and a two-state solution. However, it may have to face headwinds in times to come when the die is really cast.

Knotting the Soft Power

In order to harness the P2P advantage to sustain the strategic contours of the relationship in recent times, China has also embarked on a soft power projection mission. In the modern-day international discourse, one often subscribes to the idea that the China–Arab relations are a recent phenomenon. Nothing can be farther than the reality and Chinese leadership is not only rediscovering and reemphasising on this P2P dimension, but also finding a new cultural corridor and more sharpened toolkits of influence to supplement their strategic outreach commensurate with the changing geopolitics in the region.

China has advanced its soft power projection in the region with a number of humanitarian initiatives, recognising that soft power is essential for its status as a great power. Such initiatives included medical aid during the COVID-19 pandemic, cultural promotion with a focus on strengthening people-to-people relations, mainly through tourism, which has seen a surge in the recent years, educational initiatives through university exchanges and cooperation and the establishment of Confucius institutes in the Middle East (numbering fifteen as of 2021).[19] It has been learnt that more centres have been established since then. Chinese language is also being taught in schools in several countries in the region.

Islam and treatment of Uyghur Muslims and their human rights in China are often the talking point for the West. But for the Arab and Muslim world, it has remained under the warps and wraps as barely any public discussion on the issue generates any disconcert in the region. Economic propensity and interdependence have undermined the religious discourse as only occasional voices of criticism like that of Turkey are heard. Even the Organisation of Islamic Cooperation (OIC) remains muted and satisfied with the explanations rendered by the official Chinese media. The treatment by the Chinese is often accepted at face value; that they are fighting against extremism and terrorism. Most recently, the Joint Statement between China and Arab League (on 14 January 2024) remained silent and appeared to support the status quo. Turkiye which has over 100,000 Uyghurs sent its Foreign Minister Hakan Fidan to Beijing and the Xinjiang Autonomous Region (June 2024) Urumqui and Kashgar after conferring with Chinese leaders in Beijing and subtle messaging was conveyed as both sides are working to enrich ties.[20]

China is making renewed efforts to reach out to the Arab world at grassroots level by enforcing and highlighting religious, cultural, linguistic and culinary components of diplomacy in their relationship.[21] Efforts are being made to revive the past history and interactions even during the past with famous Admiral Zheng – he (fourteenth century) who played a critical role in forming the original Silk Road's cultural connectivity dimension; Yuan and Qing dynasties, or for that matter, readings, travels and writings of various Chinese-Arabic scholars such as Mohamed Makin and Wang Jingazi. Mosques have been built and refurbished for Arabs to feel at home in China. Chinese language and culture are being taught in Saudi schools, in addition to the twenty-one Confucius Centres spread across the Arab world. The relationship with Al Azhar University in Egypt for deradicalisation has been given a renewed focus, since China's earliest formal contacts had been with the Egyptians. Essentially, efforts are being made for reviving the 19th- and 20th-century religious interface between China and the Arab world to provide a historical context. In modern days, the Xinhua Chinese news agency is present in every country in the Middle East trying to create new narratives, as organisations like Islamic Association in China help create a more palatable Islamic narrative for the CPC and the regime.

In the MENA region, it is evident that China's public diplomacy has been effective, with data from the Arab Barometer in 2021 showing that China compares favourably with the US across several categories.

Conclusion

It is clear that China has been able to successfully entrench itself as a desirable economic partner and an alternate choice for the Middle East through its value-neutral, economic cooperation-driven, strategically oriented, non-interventionist and overtly non-prescriptive policies. Its engagement revolves mainly around energy, trade, arms sales, cultural relations and active political engagement. It wishes to ensure its energy security at all costs and, while trying to play a constructive role in defusing tensions in the region, it has stayed clear of regional conflicts. In the larger geopolitical Sino-US competition matrix, while it is not yet ready or capable to displace the US as a major player and security provider, it is getting there much faster given the penchant of the major Gulf and Middle Eastern countries that see great merit in diversifying their foreign policy choices.

In times to come, it could become the US+1 or more. Incidentally, India's policy in the region has not been vastly different, and quite successful too under PM Narendra Modi. But the scale and intent of Chinese engagement is rapid and enormous, and that could be a challenge for India in its extended neighbourhood, especially under the recrowned President Xi Jinping. Perhaps we would need to reorient yet again towards speedy 'Act West' policy with a more focussed region-centric approach as compared to rather staid 'Link West' terminology. Ipso facto China will become a challenge for India in West Asia.

Notes

1. Mordechai Chaziza, 'The Global Security Initiative: China's New Security Architecture for the Gulf', *The Diplomat*, 5 March 2023, https://thediplomat.com/2023/05/the-global-security-initiative-chinas-new-security-architecture-for-the-gulf/.
2. 'China Ready to Work with Arab League to Build Community with Shared Future', CGTN, 15 January 2024, https://news.cgtn.com/news/2024-01-15/China-to-work-with-Arab-League-to-build-community-with-shared-future-1qnFX0vvXfW/p.html. In keeping with his tradition, Wang Yi undertook his first visit to Africa – including to Egypt, Tunisia, Togo and Cote d'Ivoire – from 13–18 January 2024.
3. Michael Singh, 'The Middle East in a Multipolar Era: Why America's Allies Are Flirting With Russia and China', *Foreign Affairs*, 7 December 2022, https://www.foreignaffairs.com/middle-east/middle-east-multipolar-era.
4. Ana Estrada Hamm, Rebecca Redlich and Frances McDonough, 'With Attention on Gaza, Russia and China Continue Economic and Military Inroads in Arab States', Fikra Forum, 4 January 2024, https://www.washingtoninstitute.org/policy-analysis/attention-gaza-russia-and-china-continue-economic-and-military-inroads-arab-states.
5. 'Full text of China's Arab Policy Paper', Xinhua, 13 January 2016.
6. Richard W. Carney, *Chance to Lead: Acquiring Global Influence via Infrastructure Development and Digitalization* (Cambridge: Cambridge University Press, 2023).
7. Dr N. Janardhan in Anil Trigunayat (ed.), *Evolving Security Dynamic in West Asia and India's Challenges* (Delhi: Pentagon Press, 2022), 24.
8. 'With Second Meeting in June, China Finds Opportunity in Hamas-Fatah Talks', Al-Monitor, (AQ:Date)
9. M.M. Papageorgiou, 'China's Growing Presence in the Middle East's Arms Race and Security Dynamics', M. Eslami, A.V. Guedes Vieira (eds), *The Arms Race in the Middle East, Contributions to International Relations*, Springer, 2023, https://doi.org/10.1007/978-3-031-32432-1_16.
10. Tony Osborne, 'UAE Finalizes L-15 Jet Trainer Deal With China's CATIC', Aviation Week Network, 13 November 2023, https://aviationweek.com/shownews/dubai-airshow/uae-finalizes-l-15-jet-trainer-deal-chinas-catic.
11. Zhao Ziwen, 'China Urges Iran and Saudi Arabia to Work Together to "Avoid Miscalculation" as Diplomats Meet on Restoration of Ties', *South China Morning Post*, 17 December 2023, https://www.scmp.com/news/china/diplomacy/article/3245358/china-urges-iran-and-saudi-arabia-work-together-avoid-miscalculation-diplomats-meet-restoration-ties?firstTimeRegister=true.
12. 'Egypt to Develop New Currency Indicator to Wean People Off U.S. dollar', Reuters, 24 October 2022, https://www.reuters.com/markets/currencies/egypt-develop-new-currency-indicator-wean-people-off-us-dollar-2022-10-23/.
13. Huileng Tan, Russia Adopts Chinese Yuan-to-Ruble as Benchmark Exchange Rate after US Sanctions Force a Further Move Away from the Dollar, Yahoo News, 14 June 2024, https://ca.news.yahoo.com/russia-adopts-chinese-yuan-ruble-070215837.html?guccounter=1

14 Dr Jonathan Fulton, 'Testimony before the US-China Economic and Security Review Commission: Hearing on "US-China Relations in 2020: Enduring Problems and Emerging Challenges"', 9 September 2020.
15 Li Qiyu, 'China Middle East to explore cooperation: CIFTIS forum', China Economic Net, 6 September 2023, http://en.ce.cn/Insight/202309/06/t20230906_38703348.shtml#:~:text=The%20economies%20of%20Middle%20East%20countries%20and%20China,the%20largest%20trading%20partner%20in%20the%20Middle%20East.
16 Christoph Nedopil Wang, 'Brief: China Belt and Road Initiative (BRI) Investment Report 2021', Green Finance & Development Center, 2 February 2022, https://greenfdc.org/brief-china-belt-and-road-initiative-bri-investment-report-2021/.
17 Yuke Xie, 'Middle East Investments in China to Bloom in Amount, Scope in 2024 as Sovereign Wealth Funds Aim to Diversify: Bankers', 15 January 2024, https://www.scmp.com/business/banking-finance/article/3248475/middle-east-investments-china-bloom-amount-scope-2024-sovereign-wealth-funds-aim-diversify-bankers.
18 Ibid. Op cit 4.
19 Mohammad Eslami and Maria Papageorgiou, 'China's Increasing Role in the Middle East: Implications for Regional and International Dynamics', *Georgetown Journal of International Affairs*, 2 June 2023, https://gjia.georgetown.edu/2023/06/02/chinas-increasing-role-in-the-middle-east-implications-for-regional-and-international-dynamics/.
20 Have Turkey, China hit reset button on Uyghurs as Fidan visits Xinjiang? - Al-Monitor: Independent, trusted coverage of the Middle East
21 Fazzur Rahman Siddiqui, 'China and the Arab World: Past and Present', Indian Council of World Affairs, 2022.

10

A Decade of the Belt and Road Initiative

Commodore Gopal Suri

The One Belt One Road (一带一路), now officially called the Belt and Road Initiative (BRI), has become synonymous with China's ambitions of expanding its footprint across the globe. No longer is China 'hiding its strength and biding its time' as it sheds the garb of reticence of the Deng era. In many ways, the One Belt One Road signifies a China which is no longer the sleeping giant, but a nation which keeps in step with the changes in the world and often is the cause of much of these changes. The 'One Belt One Road', when conceived in 2013,[1] and rolled out officially in 2015 with the publishing of its 'Visions and Actions',[2] raised a number of eyebrows across the globe as the perception of its unilateral approach gained traction. China was quick to realise this sentiment and consequently changed the term to make it a more acceptable – 'Belt and Road' – since the 'One' appeared to indicate a sort of Chinese imposition on its partners. True to form, the BRI has undergone a substantial shift from its early days of trillion-dollar investment ambitions to a more sedate approach in recent times.

A Decade of the BRI[3]

It has been ten years since President Xi Jinping laid out his vision of the BRI in Kazakhstan and seven years since the People's Republic of China (PRC) enunciated its Action Plan for the BRI. The PRC, therefore, claims that the BRI is in its tenth year of operation.[4] The Communist Party of China (CPC) has also incorporated pushing for Belt and Road development into its Constitution, according to a resolution approved by the 19th CPC National Congress in October 2017. The interim period has also seen a gradual rise in the profile of the BRI from 2015 to 2019, with the pandemic causing a sharp drop in activity in the years 2020 and 2021. The year 2022 saw a rise in BRI activity, especially in investments from the PRC, in the partner countries of the BRI. Buoyed by this rise as also the completion of a decade of the BRI, the PRC conducted the third Belt and Road Forum (BRF) in October 2023. A snapshot of the BRI over the last decade in some important domains can aid in understanding the current status of the major Chinese initiative.

Agreements with Partner Countries

The PRC claims that it has signed cooperation agreements with 147 countries across all continents, barring North America and Australia.[5] While verification of this claim is difficult – considering that not all of the PRC's partner countries publish such details and may in fact do not agree on projects being under the BRI – the BRI does have a substantially large geographical coverage. Nearly all countries in regions like Southeast Asia, Central Asia, Africa and Latin America are signatories of the BRI, either in its entirety or for specific projects under its umbrella. Countries like Indonesia, Saudi Arabia, Kuwait and others are also, increasingly, signing agreements with the PRC for dovetailing their national development plans with the BRI. All five countries in Central Asia have signed such documents with Turkmenistan signing an MoU to 'enhance the synergy between the initiative to revive the Great Silk Road and the BRI' on 6 January 2023.[6]

Chinese Investments under BRI

Investment is a good indicator of activity under the BRI, though the actual disbursement for agreed projects with partner countries is difficult to monitor. The initial enthusiasm for the BRI saw a sharp spike in investment in 2015, the year when the 'Vision & Action Plan' was rolled out. However, the subsequent years did not see the same level of commitment although investments rose till about 2018, peaking at $51 billion that year. Consequently, till the pandemic struck, the level of investments fell with recovery picking up from 2021, though they have yet to reach the pre-pandemic levels. Year 2022 saw a distinct rise in investment to about $29 billion. This was also the highest share of investments, which accounted for about 48 per cent of engagement under BRI as compared to 29 per cent in 2021. The Green Finance Development Centre of the Fudan University highlights the fact that the average deal size for investments has increased from about $444 million in 2021 to $650 million in 2022, which is the highest since 2019. However, as compared to the peak of 2014, the investment deal size is 21 per cent smaller.

Chinese Contracts

Chinese companies, both state-owned and private, have undertaken contracts in various parts of the world under the aegis of the BRI. The volumes of these contracts (in USD terms) have witnessed a trend similar to that of Chinese investment in these regions. These volumes peaked in 2017 at about $74.5 billion and have since been reducing with 2022 witnessing the lowest, at about $38 billion, the lowest since the inception of the BRI. The average deal size for construction projects was also the smallest since 2013, dropping from $496 million in 2021 to $330 million in 2022. The energy and transport sectors saw huge involvement of Chinese enterprises and accounted for nearly 70 per cent of Chinese contracts under the BRI. Chinese companies have also been involved in real estate construction, which accounts for about 10 per cent of these contracts.

Regional Engagement

The two figures below illustrate Chinese engagement across the globe (as a percentage of total Chinese engagement in that domain) under the BRI from 2014 to 2023.[7]

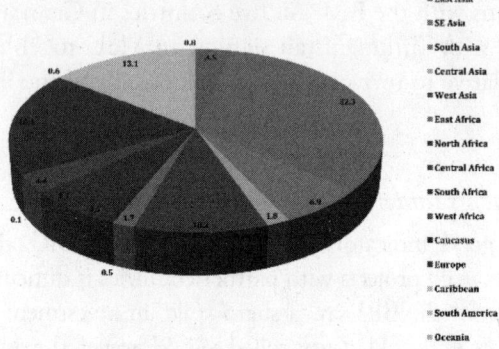

Figure 1. Chinese Investment

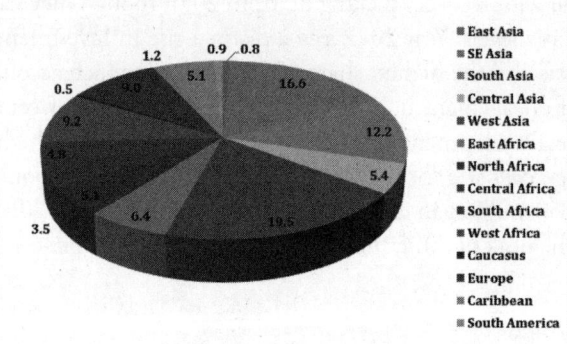

Figure 2. Chinese Contracts

Southeast Asia, Europe and West Asia have been the recipients of the largest chunk of Chinese investment under the BRI over the last decade, accounting for more than 57 per cent of investment under the BRI. However, investment in Europe has halved from a peak of $7 billion in 2019 to just about $3.75 billion in 2022. While Chinese investment in West Asia has been clearly focused on the energy sector, Southeast Asia has witnessed Chinese investment across a variety of sectors. The finance sector saw a huge jump in investment in 2022, largely due to the agreement between China's Silk Road Fund (SRF) and Indonesia's sovereign wealth fund, the Indonesia Investment Authority, for a joint investment fund with the SRF providing $2.9 billion. The increasing Saudi–China bonhomie also led to a distinct spike in Chinese investment in energy in this country, up from $1.2 billion in 2021 to $5.4 billion in 2022.

Southeast Asia and West Asia also had the largest number of Chinese contracts, accounting for more than 35 per cent of all contracts under the BRI over the last decade. Much of these contracts have been in the energy sector, which accounts for nearly 40 per cent, with West Asia cornering nearly a quarter of these. South and Southeast Asia have also utilised Chinese companies in the energy sector and together account for another 33 per cent of these contracts. Chinese companies have been involved across the globe in building transport infrastructure across the spectrum of ports, airports and railroads. A large part of this effort, nearly 55 per cent, has been focused on Southeast Asia, South Asia, West Asia and West Africa. Singapore and Malaysia also saw extensive involvement of Chinese companies in rail projects in the wake of the pandemic. The real estate sector has been another big player in getting contracts under the umbrella of the BRI (10 per cent).

Bangladesh, Pakistan and Sri Lanka have had substantial Chinese engagement under the BRI in South Asia, accounting for nearly $26 billion over the last decade (refer to the figures below). However, Chinese investments have been waning in the region, especially with Pakistan witnessing a significant drop in these levels over the last five to eight years. A similar trend has been seen in Chinese contracts in the region, with the value of contracts dropping substantially from $2.4 billion in 2021 to about $1.2 billion in 2022.

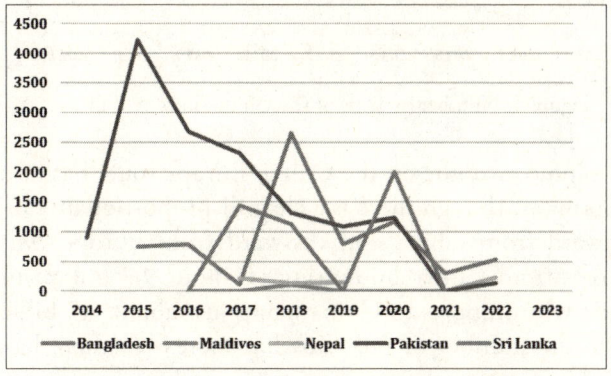

Figure 3. Chinese Investment (in Million USD)

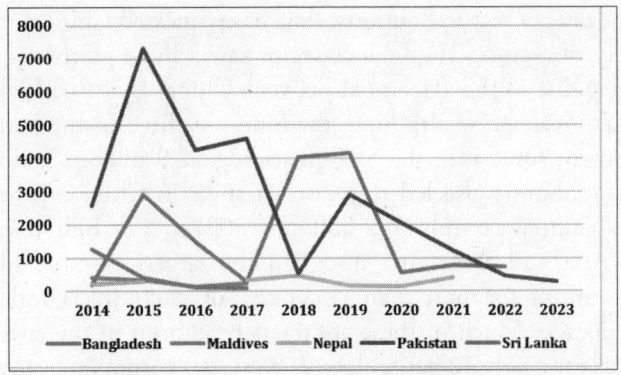

Figure 4. Chinese Contracts (in Million USD)

Rail Connectivity
The China–Europe rail is an important symbol of the overland connectivity brought about by the BRI. The number of trips from China to Europe and back has been rising steadily since the inception of this service, with 2022 seeing an all-time high of 16,000 trains plying along the route.

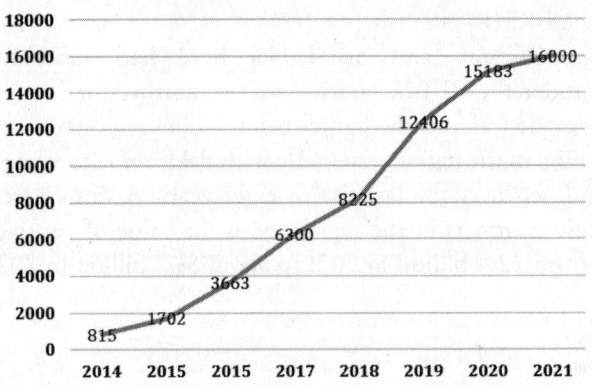

Figure 5. Number of Trips of the China–Europe Rail[8]

The highest volume of traffic on the China–Europe route has been between China and Germany, though there is a clear disproportionality in the traffic flowing westward from China and eastward from Europe. Much of the traffic is exports from China amounting to about 9.7 billion tonnes over the last decade with imports to China being just about 4.7 billion tonnes. Further, while the number of rail trips has increased, there has not been a proportional increase in the freight – as seen from the two figures given below – of freight between China and its top six partners in the railroad trade. On the other hand, freight has reduced from 2021 onwards. While these statistics reflect China's position as a primary supplier in the global value chains and a manufacturing hub, the economic viability of the rail connectivity may be suspect, considering the extremely low volumes of freight on the eastward trips from Europe to China.

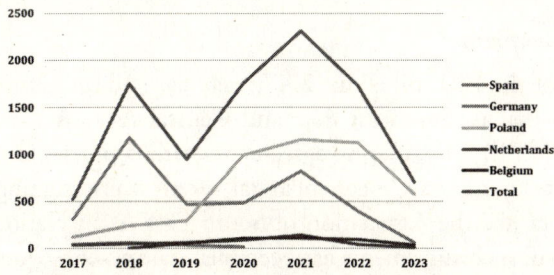

Figure 6. China to Europe (Freight in Thousand Tonnes)

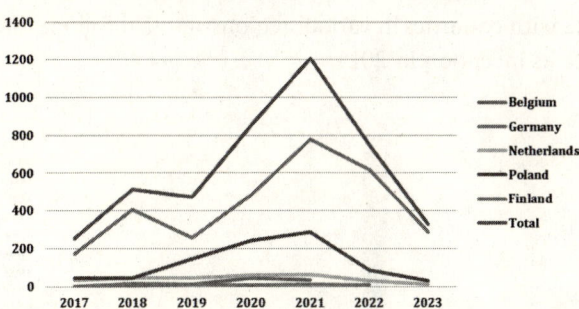

Figure 7. Europe to China (Freight in Thousand Tonnes)

The clear drop in freight volumes on the China–Europe route in 2022 has been largely due to the Ukraine conflict, as traders no longer want their goods to pass through Russia on account of the sanctions imposed by the US and EU in the wake of the war.[9]

In other regions, like South Asia, proposed rail connectivity under the BRI has not had the same success as in Europe. The trans-Himalayan rail across the Sino-Nepal border is still at a pre-feasibility stage while the China–Myanmar link has been stalled, largely because of the instability in Myanmar. Pakistan's ambitious plan to upgrade the existing Peshawar–Lahore–Karachi rail line has yet to see the light, with China still remaining tenuous about the funding for this project. On the other hand, Chinese firms are heavily involved in various rail projects in Southeast Asia, like the Thailand–Myanmar line and the Jakarta–Bandung high-speed rail.

Trajectory of BRI

The overview of Chinese investment and contracts under the BRI and the overland connectivity provides an indication of the direction of Chinese engagement under President Xi's pet project.

Geographical Footprint

The early years of the BRI, till about 2017, were focused on China's immediate neighbourhood, that is, Southeast Asia and Central Asia, as also Central and Eastern Europe (CEE) for garnering agreements with countries in these regions. All of these agreements have been bilateral, even whilst signing agreements with regional fora like the Association of South East Asian Nations (ASEAN). Implementation of such agreements has been bilateral and consequently overland connectivity initiatives like the Silk Road Economic Belt (SREB) through Eurasia have been implemented through bilateral agreements with countries like Russia and Kazakhstan. The chart below depicts the number of year-wise agreements signed by China with countries in various regions across the globe under the aegis of the BRI since its inception in 2014.

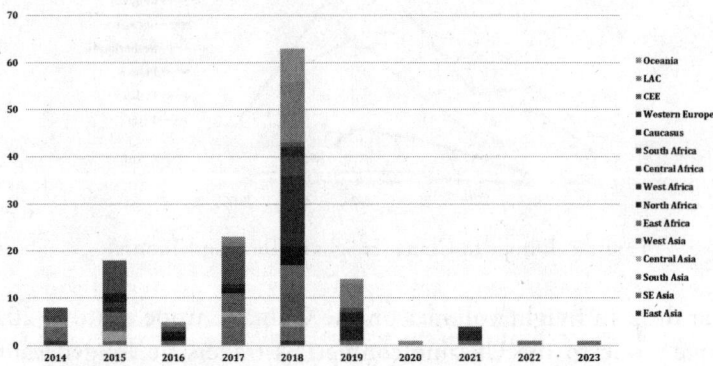

Figure 8. Agreements Signed by China under the BRI[10]

The BRI has now expanded to most regions of the world, almost 140 countries, barring North America and a large part of Western Europe. While Italy had signed on to the initiative in 2018, the agreement has lapsed without any forward movement. Interestingly, Russia, an important strategic partner, has not signed on to the initiative, though agreements have been signed between China and Russia on projects for the overland Eurasia rail network from China to Europe.

Many of these countries, especially in Africa and the Pacific islands, are very small economies and on the lower scale of development (income), with higher-income countries constituting less than one-third the number. In fact, many of the higher-income countries, especially in CEE, LAC and West Asia, are very small economies (in terms of GDP).

BRI expansion into Europe, especially in Western Europe, has almost come to a standstill, on account of increasing frictions due to issues of reciprocal market access, fears of illegal Chinese stealing of technology, Chinese economic coercion as witnessed with Lithuania and, of course, American pressure on Europe.

The engagement with Africa and the LAC countries has been largely confined to the domain of energy and mineral resources insofar as investment is concerned, while Chinese companies have mainly undertaken contracts in the energy and transportation sectors in these regions. The table below provides a summary of Chinese engagement in these sectors in the regions as a percentage of total Chinese engagement in each of these domains (investment and contracts).

	Chinese Investment		Chinese Contracts	
	Energy	Minerals	Energy	Transport
Africa	17 per cent	50 per cent	31 per cent	38 per cent
LAC	42 per cent	45 per cent	49 per cent	31 per cent

Increasing Political Alignment

The post COVID-19 years have seen China ramping up its engagement with West Asia and Central Asia. In consonance with these moves, China has signed agreements with all the five countries of Central Asia, as also Saudi Arabia and Kuwait, to dovetail the BRI with their national development plans. Indonesia has also recently agreed to enhance synergy between its Global Maritime Fulcrum national development plan and the BRI. The China Pakistan Economic Corridor (CPEC) and the China Myanmar Economic Corridor (CMEC) are clear examples of national development plans of countries being enmeshed with the BRI to the extent that these are treated as integral parts of the Chinese initiative. Inclusion of the BRI, to enhance its synergy with national development plans of various countries, is likely to receive further impetus as China steps up its engagement across the globe, especially in West Asia, Africa, Pacific and Latin America.

Synergy with Regional Development Initiatives

The BRI has also been enmeshed with the development plans of various regional organisations. The 'ASEAN-China Joint Statement on Synergising the Master Plan on ASEAN Connectivity (MPAC) 2025 and the Belt and Road Initiative (BRI)' adopted in 2019 has ensured the imprint of the BRI umbrella over many road and rail projects in Southeast Asia. Similarly, the Forum for China Africa Cooperation (FOCAC) has agreed to 'synergise' the African Union's Agenda 2063 and national development strategies of African countries with the BRI and the Global Development Initiative (GDI). Such agreements will ensure Chinese participation in a host of ventures of these partner countries, thereby, providing political leverage over development activity.

Regional Priorities

Investment is an important measurable parameter for judging the focus of the BRI. A look at the investment pattern over the last decade shows a distinct downward trend in China's global investment since 2018 which has been further accentuated by COVID-19 in 2020 and 2021. China appears to have re-calibrated its approach to the BRI after the second Belt and Road Forum held in 2019, possibly on account of issues like the takeover of the Hambantota Port and other such events termed as 'bad debts' across the world. Consequently, Europe has witnessed a sharp reduction in Chinese investment with the focus remaining on SE Asia, West Asia and South America. South Asia, apart from the initial years of CPEC till 2015, has witnessed diminishing investments, with the last two years witnessing less than $1 billion.

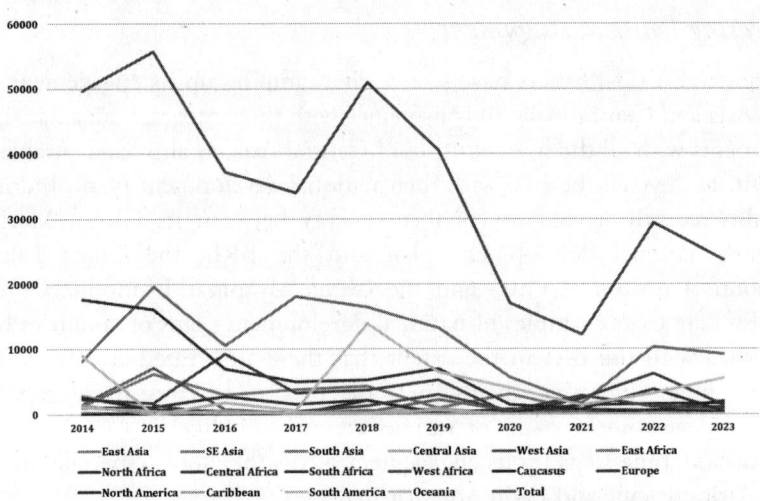

Figure 9. Chinese Investment under BRI (in Million USD)

In summary, Southeast Asia has been the recipient of the largest Chinese investment while West Asia, in recent times, has gained prominence. The recent Chinese attention towards West Asia, possibly on account of a perception of American withdrawal from the region, appears to be dictating the destinations for future Chinese investment even as China continues to keep its periphery of Southeast Asia under a sharp watch.

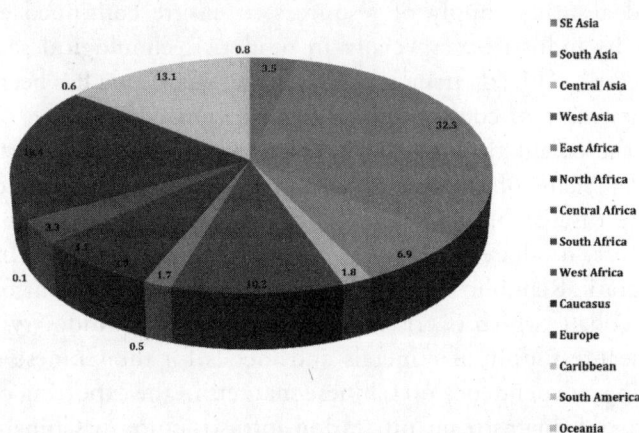

Figure 10. Regional Chinese Investment under BRI (2014–2023) (per cent of Total Investment)

Sectoral Investment

Analysis of the sectors of investment under the BRI clearly reveals the preponderance of the energy sector which accounts for nearly 35 per cent of the cumulative investment under the BRI over the last decade. The other major sectors for investment are minerals and the transport sector, which together account for about 33 per cent. These are discussed in detail subsequently. The spread of Chinese investments is displayed in the chart below to provide the expanse of such investment across various sectors.

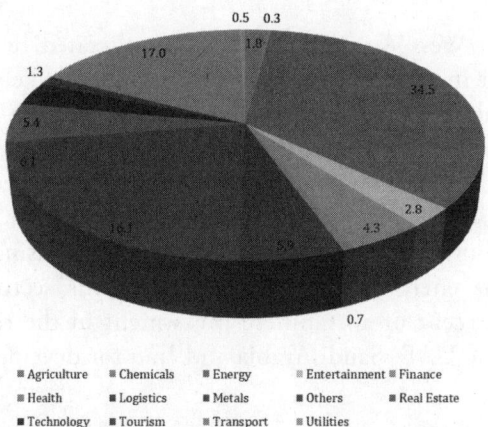

Figure 11. Sectoral Investment (2014–2022) (in per cent of Cumulative Investment)

Resource Security

China's agreements with various countries under the BRI framework has ensured a steady supply of resources to ensure continued economic progress of its industries, especially in modern technological sectors like telecom, electric vehicles, artificial intelligence, etc. China has been steadily increasing its share of copper exports from countries like Chile, Peru and Mexico to the extent that it gets 60–80 per cent of their exports. China has a similar share of exports of chromium from Pakistan and others, while in the case of niobium and other ores which are used in telecom and IT sectors, its share is 40–70 per cent from countries like Indonesia. The Democratic Republic of Congo supplies nearly 90 per cent of China's imports of cobalt, which is critical for modern telecom industry. This has ensured a secure supply of minerals and metals for the Chinese economy while creating a dependency on Chinese markets in the exporting countries. The presence of downstream processing infrastructure in China for these minerals has further exacerbated such dependencies. A look at the trends of these exports/imports, along with China's advances in modern technologies like telecom and AI, indicates that China will remain a primary market for these countries, at least in the near future.

Copper   Chromium

Niobium   Cobalt

Figure 12. Exports of Minerals to China (in per cent of Total Exports of that Mineral)[11]

Energy Security

China's focus on West Asia has been largely dictated by its dependence on the region for its supplies of oil and gas, which is likely to remain well into the foreseeable future. While the initial years of the BRI did not see much Chinese investment in this region, the last few years have seen a ramping-up of Chinese activity, especially in the energy sector. This region now accounts for more than 20 per cent of Chinese investment in the energy sector. South America is another region increasingly coming into Chinese focus as energy becomes important. This sector also accounts for nearly 70 per cent of all Chinese investment in the region with large investments in the UAE, Saudi Arabia and Iraq for development of oil and gas fields.

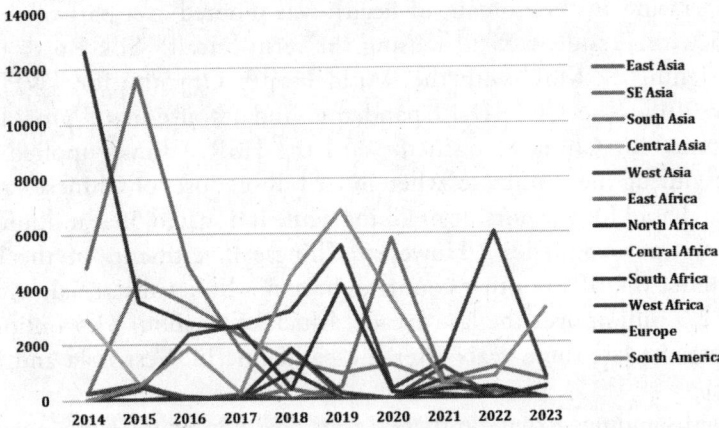

Figure 13. Chinese Regional Investment in the Energy Sector under BRI (in Million USD)

Quantum of Engagement

The BRI, both in terms of investments and contracts undertaken by Chinese companies, shows a distinct downward trend since 2019, which has further accentuated in the post-pandemic period. China appears to have become more cautious in its investments in terms of size as also returns. The majority of its investments are focused on securing its needs for resources and energy as also for utilising its industrial capacities in sectors like transport and technology to further its national interests. The hesitation in committing to large projects like the trans-Himalayan railway from Nepal to China and to Pakistan for its ML-1 railway project is clearly indicative of this approach. Considering the current state of the Chinese economy, it is unlikely that this trend will be reversed.

New Sectors of Engagement

The BRI has expanded to non-traditional sectors of engagement, especially in the socioeconomic development and the health domains. The CPEC is one clear example with the CPEC Long-Term Plan (LTP) talking about agricultural development and poverty alleviation. Notwithstanding the fact that projects/activities in this domain are difficult to monitor even as the quantum of such activity remains small, some projects like the hospital and vocational training institute in Gwadar stand out. Another ongoing activity is the provision of 'smart classrooms' in Afghanistan and Pakistan. MoUs between Chinese universities and those in Africa, Pakistan and development of agricultural technology are furthering the goals of increased people-to-people contact under the BRI.

Cooperation in the domain of health was mooted as a part of the BRI in 2015 with President Xi first using the term 'Health Silk Road' (HSR) whilst signing an MoU with the World Health Organization (WHO) in January 2017. The COVID-19 pandemic and its aftermath provided an opportunity for China to push forward the HSR. China supplied many vaccines during the pandemic, wherein 1.2 billion doses of Chinese vaccines were purchased for use outside of China while it donated 58.2 million doses to ninety-three countries.[12] However, Chinese investments in the health sector under the BRI in other countries have not been substantial, with just about $2.9 billion over the last decade. Much of it, about $1.4 billion, has been over the last three years after the pandemic in West Asia and South America.

Notwithstanding, activity in these sectors does not require large investment but has the benefit of accruing disproportional returns in terms of goodwill generated for China amongst the local populace, which is also reflected in the positive image witnessed in some of the local surveys conducted in these countries.

Integration of Maritime Logistic Chains

China continues to remain at the top of the Liner Shipping Connectivity Index.[13] State-owned enterprises like the China Ocean Shipping Company (COSCO) are driving this growth. The impetus for this activity has been provided by the 21st-century Maritime Silk Road (MSR) under the BRI, which clearly prioritises alignment of strategies of countries along the BRI to 'jointly build unobstructed, safe and efficient maritime transport channels'.[14] This has led to a slew of agreements with Myanmar, Pakistan, Sri Lanka, the UAE, Greece, Turkey and Morocco, amongst others, wherein Chinese companies have acquired stakes to build and operate ports, services and attendant transport linkages. Most of these ports, like Hambantota, Djibouti, Piraeus and others are situated at critical junctions of important commercial maritime routes. These ports also sit astride geostrategically vital maritime straits like the Bab-el-Mandeb and Suez Canal, which have historically been used to control maritime trade. State-owned companies like COSCO have been at the forefront of such activity, providing an integrated and uninterrupted maritime logistics chain, stretching all the way from China through the Indian Ocean Region (IOR) to markets in Europe.

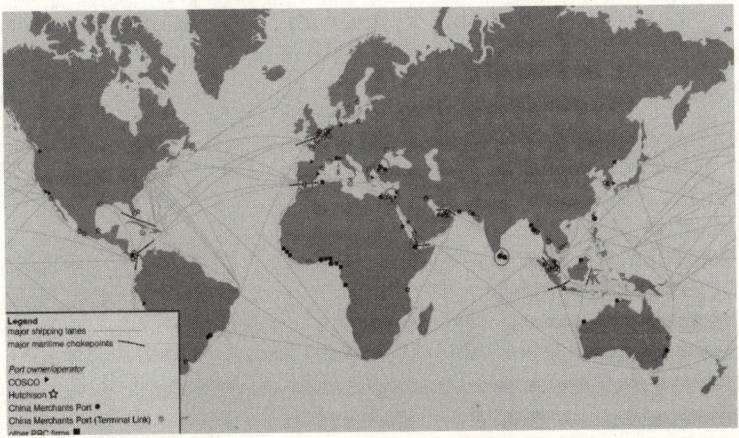

Figure 14. Location of Ports with Chinese Involvement[15]

In addition, forums like the Silk Road Maritime International Cooperation Forum has been held regularly to push forward issues of port integration, adoption of new technologies and green practices with the involvement of stakeholders of ports with Chinese involvement. China has used its pervasive presence in this sector to push forward its National Public Information Platform for Transportation and Logistics (LOGINK), a logistics management platform that aggregates logistics data from domestic and foreign ports, and foreign logistics from across the globe. This platform provides China with the potential to monitor and leverage the international logistics market, increase dependency on itself and exploit the vulnerabilities of LOGINK users for economic and geostrategic purposes.[16]

Military Maritime Advantage
The locations of many of these ports also provide China with military advantage, especially in areas of Chinese maritime interest, like the Indian Ocean and the Mediterranean. The People's Liberation Army (Navy) (PLAN) has also frequented many of these ports, either on port calls or whilst conducting joint exercises with the host nations. PLAN's anti-piracy escort force deployed in the Indian Ocean regularly calls at many ports in the northern Arabian Sea like Salalah, Karachi and other ports in the Persian Gulf. Some reports of the twenty-five-year strategic partnership deal between China and Iran talk about the establishment of Chinese military facilities on the Iranian coastline in the vicinity of the strategic Strait of Hormuz. The Pakistani port of Gwadar has long been thought of as a long-term strategic asset for the PLAN, especially when viewed in the context of the commercial unviability of this project. Chinese military presence in these areas allows monitoring of adversaries in peace and

has the potential to provide the PLAN with in-theatre operational support in times of conflict. Consequently, China stands to gain, both militarily and commercially, from control of these vital ports. A quick look at some of the ports with Chinese involvement across the globe, and their potential for naval use, provides a clear picture of the expanding Chinese footprint in this domain.

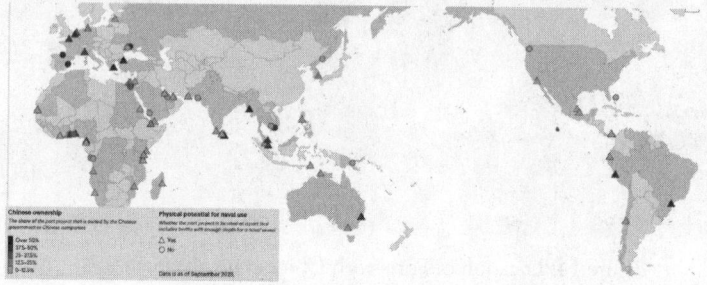

Figure 15. Ports with Potential for Chinese Naval Presence[17]

Financial Integration

Building a 'currency stability system, investment and financing system and credit information system' is one of the priorities of the BRI. Much of this jargon is plain speak for internationalisation of the Chinese currency, which has been a goal for China as part of its ambitions to become a global power. The BRI and its attendant agreements with various countries has become a useful platform for the furtherance of this Chinese goal. While the RMB accounts for only 3.71 per cent of the world's currency activity,[18] its share has been gradually increasing in no small measure due to the BRI.

According to the People's Bank of China, in 2021, cross-border RMB settlement between China and countries along the Belt and Road registered RMB 5.42 trillion yuan, a year-on-year increase of 19.6 per cent. China also has currency swap agreements with thirty-three countries, many of them BRI partners, like Hungary, Sri Lanka, Nepal and Chile among others. China has been dealing in the RMB as also national currencies with countries like Russia and Iran to bypass Western sanctions in the wake of the Ukraine conflict. This has served the dual purpose of the internationalisation of the Yuan as also the push to substitute the USD as a medium of international monetary exchange.

A Belt and Road Initiative Tax Administration Cooperation Mechanism (BRITACOM) was also launched in 2019 to facilitate tax administration cooperation and building a growth-friendly tax environment in partner countries. This forum put out an 'Improving Tax Environment Action Plan 2023–2025' at the BRI Forum in October 2023. However, assessing the actual effect of such fora may not be feasible considering that much of the actions need to be undertaken by countries on a bilateral basis.

Proliferation of Chinese Technology

The construction of cross-border optical cables and other communications trunk line networks to improve international communications connectivity and create an Information Silk Road (now termed Digital Silk Road or DSR) is another professed goal of the BRI. This has been premised on the growing appeal of Chinese technology, especially in the communication and 'smart city' segment, primarily due to the lower costs as also availability of latest advances in the field of AI.

China has fully funded and laid the China–Pakistan cross-border optical fibre cable (OFC) and is currently in the process of upgrading this infrastructure. Chinese undersea cables laid by firms like Huawei Marine Technology (HMT) are spread across the world's oceans. BRI investments in telecom accounted for nearly 50 per cent of all investments in the technology sector since 2015. Smart city development initiatives under BRI are finding traction with countries like Kyrgyzstan, Uzbekistan and Kazakhstan, that are utilising Chinese surveillance and data processing equipment to implement these programmes. The telecom infrastructure in these countries as also many others in Africa and South Asia has been supplied by Huawei, some under Chinese loans. This spread of Chinese technology, coupled with Chinese initiatives like the Global Initiative on Data Security and China's push for global technology standards, has the potential to create a Chinese 'technology sphere' as an alternate to the existing globalised world of technology. A look at the map below, of the global presence of Chinese telecom operators, provides a glimpse into the possible geography of Chinese influence in the near future.

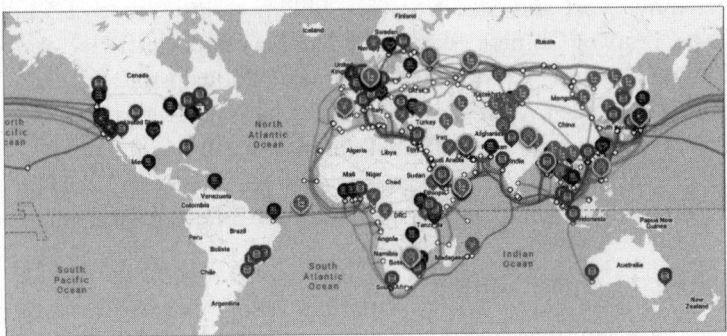

Figure 16. Overseas Presence of Chinese Telecom Companies[19]

Setting Standards

China has been pushing for acceptance of its national standards in many global bodies in various domains like telecom and emerging technologies. Acceleration of the 'internationalisation of Chinese standards' is a stated objective of the Made in China 2025 (MIC 2025).[20] The BRI has consequently become a platform for this internationalisation of Chinese standards.

China has signed a host of agreements with a number of countries in SE Asia, West Asia, Eastern Europe, Africa and Russia, as also with organisations like the UNIDO for standards in domains like infrastructure, hydropower and aircrafts. It has also signed a 'Joint Initiative on Strengthening Standards Cooperation and Building the Belt and Road'. The Standardisation Administration of China is at the forefront of this activity and works with similar bodies in other countries for taking forward this objective with countries like Russia. Other BRI institutions like the Belt and Road Accounting Standards Cooperation Mechanism have launched dedicated initiatives to promote cooperation in their respective domains among the participating countries.

Headwinds

Over the last decade, the BRI has faced quite strong headwinds spanning the spectrum of debt, violation of environment and labour regulations, public opposition and human rights violations. Chinese projects like the Myitsone Dam and the Letpadaung copper mine in Myanmar, Rempang Eco-City in Indonesia, Gwadar in Pakistan and many others have faced public opposition due to insensitivity to local interests and inadequate compensation for acquired land. Many governments have also learnt from the lessons of Hambantota and limited their ambitions like Myanmar, where it scaled down the cost of the Kyaukphyu Port and SEZ from $10 billion to just about $1.3 billion to avoid debt. Fears of Chinese takeover of Zambia's state electricity company in 2018 due to ballooning Chinese debt became a national issue. While such fears have gradually receded, China also appears to have reduced the average size of investments from a peak of about $570 million in 2014 to about $444 million in 2022, possibly to mitigate these fears. Nevertheless, the fear of debt to China remains, especially in countries of Africa, more so after the pandemic.

Other Allied Chinese Initiatives

China, in the recent times, has put forward a number of global initiatives which appear to be complementary to the BRI in many aspects. These initiatives are clearly aimed at enhancing China's role as a global player and even offer alternatives to existing international governance structures. Some of the professed objectives of these initiatives, while complementing the BRI, may subsume the BRI in due course.

Global Community of Shared Future

President Xi has been pushing his concept of 'Community with a Shared Future for Mankind', since he first proposed it in the 71st session of the United Nations General Assembly (UNGA) in January 2017. The concept has since been published by China in the form of a white paper called 'A Global Community of Shared Future: China's Proposals and Actions' in September 2023.[21] It is credited with being the fount for the launch of all Chinese global initiatives, including the BRI, as also the GDI, GSI and GCI. Xi again stressed on this concept at the Belt and Road Forum in October 2023, when he talked about humankind being 'a community with a shared future' and the BRI aiding in this concept.

Global Development Initiative

At the general debate during the 76th Session of the UNGA on 21 September 2021, President Xi Jinping proposed the Global Development Initiative or GDI in the context of revitalising the global economy.[22] The GDI proposes to accord higher priority to development needs, especially those of developing countries. It professes fostering of a more equal and balanced global partnership for acceleration of attainment of the goals of UN Sustainable Development Goals (SDG) 2030. It aims to use the advances in modern technology to boost productivity, while also emphasising the need to respond to climate change. China has formed a Group of Friends of the GDI in the UN to push forward this initiative and, in September 2022, announced a list of fifty projects under the initiative, largely pertaining to socioeconomic issues like poverty alleviation, food security and climate change. The GDI and the BRI have a mutual overlap, especially in the domain of development. Currently, the projects under the GDI appear to be addressing socioeconomic issues of poverty reduction, pandemic response and food security in developing and least-developed countries in SE Asia, Latin America and the like. On the other hand, BRI continues on its earlier trend of investment for connectivity and infrastructure in these regions. It appears that the GDI is largely directed at the global south while the BRI has a much larger worldwide footprint.

Global Civilisation Initiative

Xi Jinping, while attending the 'Dialogue with World Political Parties High-level Meeting' on 16 March 2023, talked about the BRI and the need to accelerate the implementation of the GDI to build a 'global community of development', and proposed a Global Civilisation Initiative (GCI).[23] While the GCI is yet to be clearly etched out by China, it appears to be aimed at enhancing the people-to-people exchanges and building a 'global network for inter-civilisation dialogue and cooperation'. Much of this overlaps with the BRI, which also has similar aims, though all these initiatives are definitely intended for furthering Chinese aspirations of becoming a global player, if not a power.

Advantage China?

Global Influence

The expansion of the BRI has clearly helped China in increasing its influence in many regions like Africa, Asia and the Pacific. While quantifying the influence may be difficult, it is of import that China has come to be a major player in many of these regions. South Asia, especially Pakistan, is a clear example—as witnessed in the increasing Chinese role in Afghanistan in consonance with Pakistan, especially in the wake of the US withdrawal in August 2021. Another case study is the rapprochement between Iran and Saudi Arabia, apparently mediated by China in March 2023. The growing Chinese influence is evident in the large number of ministers present for the Ministerial Meeting of the Group of Friends of the GDI in September 2022 from Asia and Africa. China has also garnered influence at the United Nations with the UN's Department of Economic and Social Affairs (DESA) launching a project in cooperation with it to assess the 'macroeconomic implications of the Belt and Road Initiative' for the countries along the Belt and Road.[24] Even as Chinese investment, BRI or otherwise, helps China build influence, it is not immune to opposition, especially from the public in many countries of its engagement, as highlighted earlier in this chapter. Nevertheless, the reality of growing Chinese influence is a trend that is likely to see an upward trajectory.

Regional Security Order

China's focus on its periphery is evident in the huge investments it has made under the BRI in Southeast Asia. Southeast Asia is an extremely important neighbourhood for China, especially when considering its strategic military importance coupled with the existent maritime disputes in the region. Control over the maritime regions of the South China Sea not only ensures protection of China's territorial claims but also furthers its military strategy of projecting power beyond the First Island Chain. China has leveraged its economic engagement with ASEAN, and bilaterally with countries like Indonesia, Vietnam and Malaysia, which has ensured the preservation of a degree of stability, despite its own aggressive maritime posturing in the region.

Countries like Indonesia have gradually toned down their rhetoric around China's maritime aggression over the last couple of years, even as China is pushing for the acceptance of a code of conduct that is possibly more favourable to its own position. Many of the countries, including American allies like Singapore, have unequivocally expressed their discomfort with American military posturing that has the potential to raise tensions with China in the region. Consequently, China appears to be gradually reshaping the security dynamics of the region for the furtherance of its own territorial and military interests.

Global Military Presence

The 21st century Maritime Silk Road has aided expansion of China's maritime presence to many regions of the world, providing the potential for its naval presence in areas of its interest around the globe. Djibouti's evolution from a Chinese commercial port to a military base is intended to consolidate Chinese military presence in the northern Arabian Sea and Africa. Other such commercial ventures in the Mediterranean and in the Atlantic also have the potential to accommodate future Chinese military facilities, in consonance with China's ambitions of becoming a global maritime power by the middle of this century.

Chinese Technosphere

The spread of Chinese technology, especially in the telecom domain in Africa and Central Asia, in consonance with the adoption of Chinese standards in many of these regions, has the potential to create a Chinese 'technosphere'. The continued adoption of digital initiatives in many countries in these regions, like the development of smart cities, has made Chinese technology an economically viable choice – as witnessed in Central Asia, where Huawei has signed a number of deals for provision of surveillance equipment under the umbrella of the DSR.[25] The spread of Chinese undersea cables like the Pakistan and East Africa Connecting Europe (PEACE) cable is another domain where countries looking for economically viable technology solutions are increasingly looking to Chinese technology firms to provide solutions. Considering the pervasive presence of the Chinese state in all such engagement, the development of a Chinese-dependent technosphere in the near future is likely to become a reality.

Overseas Market Expansion

The spread of the BRI as seen over the last decade has opened up many new markets for China. While Africa had always been a focus of Chinese foreign policy, the BRI has helped expand Chinese presence all over the continent. China is now among the top three trading partners of 114 BRI partner countries, and the largest trading partner for sixty-eight BRI participant countries. It is also the largest source of import for seventy-four and the largest export market for thirty-five BRI participants.[26]

Bad Debt

The BRI has been plagued by perceptions of bad debt from its nascent years. The most glaring example was that of Hambantota, where the Sri Lankan government signed a $1.1 billion ninety-nine-year lease agreement in 2017 with China Merchant Port Holdings for a 70 per cent stake in the strategic port to offset accumulated debt. A recent study by the Rhodium Group suggests that the debt issue continues to bedevil Chinese investment, with figures of about $78 billion under renegotiation by China with various countries. The study also cast doubt on China's claims that it has attempted rescue-lending over the last decade. China's lending banks have also been blamed for their recalcitrance in reducing the debt stress on borrowing countries. Nevertheless, much of this debt is a cause of concern for not just the countries that have taken the loans, but also for China and the rest of the world who need to deal with this issue.

Implications for India

India has not participated in the BRI and has voiced its objections to the initiative on account of its unilateral approach, which is in contradiction to India's collective and cooperative approach towards regional development. India's position on the BRI was clearly articulated on the eve of the first BRF in May 2017, when it underlined that connectivity initiatives should be based on 'universally recognized international norms, good governance, rule of law, openness, transparency and equality' and must follow 'principles of financial responsibility to avoid projects that would create unsustainable debt burden for communities'.[27] Further, the absence of transparency and non-adherence to accepted international norms of finance, highlighted by India, have come to haunt many of the deals under the BRI. The lack of sensitivity shown by China towards India's territorial integrity in the charting of the CPEC has also been reflected in other regions of the BRI. Consequently, India has not taken part in the BRI, even as it has continued its engagement with China in other domains. India's stand did not find much traction with the world in the early days of the BRI, but many of the issues it highlighted have now come to symbolise the many problems of the BRI, which are of growing concern for China and the world. Nevertheless, India has maintained a close watch on the BRI, especially in South Asia and other areas of interest.

Even as the BRI appears to have lost some steam over the past few years, it remains a pet project of the Chinese leadership and hence it will continue to receive attention and impetus as a tool to further Chinese interests. South Asia remains an important area of interest, especially Pakistan, as it provides a foothold for China to secure its resource and energy interests in the littoral of the IOR, as also for expanding its influence in West Asia. China is likely to remain invested in Pakistan through the CPEC, albeit on an economically smaller scale, for the distant future. Stability in Afghanistan will boost Chinese investment in the country, which could be included under the CPEC, as has been touted by some Chinese analysts and officials for the past two years. Chinese promises to Bangladesh, stemming from President Xi's visit to that country in 2016, have not been realised in their entirety even as projects like the Mongla Port continue to whet an appetite for Chinese investment. Political instability as also Chinese economic caution seems to have dictated the pace of investment in Nepal. Nevertheless, South Asia remains an area of major interest for China, being on its periphery, and future opportunities may beckon the Chinese to re-prioritise their investments in this region.

Southeast Asia is of critical importance to China and that is reflected in its investment in the region under BRI. This sentiment is also complemented by the dependence of this region as reflected in agreements of Indonesia, Singapore, Laos and Cambodia with China under the BRI. Philippines, under the new administration, has been much more cautious in its engagement with China, largely due to the latter's aggressive maritime posturing in the disputes of the South China Sea. Notwithstanding, China remains the preferred partner of choice in the economic domain for the foreseeable future for the region, even as American and European initiatives for the Indo-Pacific region gather steam. India's espousal of the centrality of ASEAN for the Indo-Pacific, therefore, needs to be translated into perceptible reality in the near, rather than mid-term, for its interests to be furthered in Southeast Asia.

The criticality of energy resources and perceptions of American 'withdrawal' have led to West Asia garnering much attention under the BRI in the recent past. China has grown to become the largest economic partner for most countries of the region. A complementary need for investment and infrastructure has propelled the growth of this partnership. China has leveraged these advantages to consolidate its foothold in this region with increased arms sales to the UAE, Saudi Arabia and some others. The purported twenty-four-year strategic partnership deal with Iran is also likely to push forward Chinese connectivity initiatives, especially railroads, from Central Asia to this region and the Persian Gulf.

Chinese involvement in maritime infrastructure development in Duqm (Oman) and Khalifa (UAE) coupled with increasing naval deployments and exercises has the potential to expand Chinese military presence to this vital region. Chinese ambitions to be a major geopolitical actor, if not leader, in the region have manifested in the Iran–Saudi rapprochement, as also attempts to mediate in the Israel–Palestine dispute. While many of these initiatives have not found much traction with countries of the region, the growing footprint of the BRI has the potential to provide China with leverage to further its interests. The region is also of vital importance to India. Growing Chinese influence, especially in the energy sector, has the potential to create a competition for resources which can be detrimental to Indian interests. India's historical and traditional relationships with countries of the region have the capacity to withstand the vicissitudes of such competition. Nevertheless, bilateral and regional initiatives like the International North–South Transport Corridor (INSTC) and others should continue to receive the necessary impetus to ensure their relevance in the changing dynamics of this region.

Africa has remained a major focus area for the BRI, though the investments have been relatively smaller when compared to Southeast and West Asia. China has concurrently remained invested in Africa, not just through the BRI but also in the diplomatic and military realms. Africa, especially East Africa, has also seen complementary Chinese military activity like increased arms sales and the setting up of the base at Djibouti to expand influence in the region. Consequently, it has been able to exercise influence on the geopolitics of the region through initiatives like the 'China-Horn of Africa on Security, Governance and Development' held in June 2022.

The growing prevalence of Chinese technology in the telecom sector in South and West Asia is a cause of concern, especially when viewed in context of the push for wider acceptance of Chinese standards and initiatives like the Global Initiative on Data Security (GIDS). The DSR, which is intended to expand this presence, needs to be looked at anew and a suitable alternative explored.

Prognosis

The BRI appears to be set for a continued albeit stunted future as China recalibrates its approach to the world amidst the changed realities of an intensified competition with the US and a slowing economy. China's initial enthusiasm for the BRI has been tempered by the reality of the individual aspirations of participant countries over the past decade. As a major platform for Chinese international engagement, the BRI is likely to retain its primacy even as other initiatives like the GDI and GCI gain traction in the Chinese foreign policy pantheon. Branching away from traditional sectors like transport and real estate to the socioeconomic realm appears set to continue with the size of the projects reducing to financially viable dimensions. Considering the profusion of proposals put forward by China to the world in the recent past, the BRI, while continuing, may also be repositioned to reflect changed Chinese priorities in the near future.

Notes

1. President Xi Jinping Proposes to Build a Silk Road Economic Belt with Central Asian Countries, 07 Sep 13. https://eng.yidaiyilu.gov.cn/p/1849.html. Accessed on 16 Oct 15.
2. Vision and Actions on Jointly Building Silk Road Economic Belt and 21st-Century Maritime Silk Road, 28 Mar 15. http://2017.beltandroadforum.org/english/n100/2017/0410/c22-45.html. Accessed on 10 April, 2017.
3. Collated using data from the American Enterprise Institute's China Global Investment Tracker, Fall 2022. https://www.aei.org/china-global-investment-tracker/; Christoph Nedopil, *China Belt and Road Initiative (BRI) Investment Report 2022*, Green Finance & Development Center, FISF Fudan University, Shanghai, January 2023.
4. 'China Expands BRI Cooperation, signing deals with five countries in 2022: ministry', *The Global Times*, 10 January 2023. https://www.globaltimes.cn/page/202301/1283557.shtml.
5. 'Countries of the Belt and Road Initiative'. Green Finance and Development Center, Fudan University https://greenfdc.org/countries-of-the-belt-and-road-initiative-bri/.
6. Ibid.
7. Data available up to June.
8. Statistics collated by author from the United Transport Logistics Company – Eurasian Rail Alliance (UTLC ERA). https://www.utlc.com/en/ (for data from 2017 onwards).
9. Kristian Schmidt, Director Land Transport European Commission, as quoted in Hanne Cokelaere and Sarah Anne Aarup, 'Ukraine War Shakes Up China-Europe Railway Express', Politico, 25 July 2022. https://www.politico.eu/article/ukraine-china-silk-road-railway/.
10. Collated by author using data from the Green Finance & Development Centre, Fudan University; Christoph Nedopil, 'Countries of the Belt and Road Initiative'; Shanghai, Green Finance & Development Center, FISF Fudan University (www.greenfdc.org). CEE stands for 'Central and Eastern Europe', LAC stands for Latin America and Caribbean.
11. Data collated from the International Trade Centre's Trade Map. https://www.trademap.org/.
12. 'New Analysis Finds Large-Scale Role of Chinese COVID-19 Vaccine Developers in Addressing Global Demand for Doses and Technology', Global Health Centre, 27 October 2021. https://www.graduateinstitute.ch/Vaccines-China.
13. *The Liner Shipping Connectivity Index* is maintained by UN Trade and Development (UNCTAD) and indicates how well countries are connected by global shipping networks based on the status of their maritime transport sector.
14. 'Full Text of the Vision for Maritime Cooperation Under the Belt and Road Initiative', Xinhua, 20 June 2017. http://english.gov.cn/archive/publications/2017/06/20/content_281475691873460.htm.
15. Isaac B. Kardon and Wendy Leutert, 'Pier Competitor: China's Power Position in Global Ports', *International Security*, Vol. 46, No. 4, Spring 2022, pp. 9–47.

16. Gabriel Collins and Jack Bianchi, 'China's LOGINK Logistics Platform and Its Strategic Potential for Economic, Political, and Military Power Projection', Baker Institute for Public Policy, 25 April 2023. https://www.bakerinstitute.org/research/chinas-logink-logistics-platform-and-its-strategic-potential-economic-political-and.
17. Zongyuan Zoe Liu, 'Tracking China's Control of Overseas Ports', Council on Foreign Relations, 6 November 2023. https://www.cfr.org/tracker/china-overseas-ports.
18. SWIFT RMB Tracker offers monthly reports and statistics on Renminbi's (RMB) progress towards becoming an international currency. https://www.swift.com/our-solutions/compliance-and-shared-services/business-intelligence/renminbi/rmb-tracker/rmb-tracker-document-centre.
19. Fergus Ryan, Audrey Fritz and Daria Impiombato, 'Mapping China' Tech Giants: Reining in China's Technology Giants', Australian Strategic Policy Institute. https://www.aspi.org.au/report/mapping-chinas-technology-giants-reining-chinas-technology-giants.
20. 'Made in China 2025', State Council, 7 July 2015. http://www.cittadellascienza.it/cina/wp-content/uploads/2017/02/IoT-ONE-Made-in-China-2025.pdf.
21. 'A Global Community of Shared Future: China's Proposals and Actions', The State Council Information Office of the PRC, September 2023. https://www.fmprc.gov.cn/mfa_eng/zxxx_662805/202309/t20230926_11150122.html.
22. 'Xi Jinping Attends the General Debate of the 76th Session of the United Nations General Assembly and Delivers an Important Speech', Ministry of Foreign Affairs PRC, 22 September 2021. https://www.fmprc.gov.cn/mfa_eng/zxxx_662805/202109/t20210923_9580033.html.
23. 'Xi Jinping Attends the CPC in Dialogue with World Political Parties High-level Meeting and Delivers a Keynote Speech', Ministry of Foreign Affairs PRC, 16 March 2023. https://www.fmprc.gov.cn/mfa_eng/zxxx_662805/202303/t20230317_11043656.html.
24. 'Jointly Building the "Belt and Road" towards the Sustainable Development Goals', UN Department of Economic and Social Affairs https://www.un.org/en/desa/jointly-building-%E2%80%9Cbelt-and-road%E2%80%9D-towards-sustainable-development-goals.
25. 'China's Growing Influence in Central Asia through Surveillance Systems', Policy Brief by The Caspian Policy Center. https://api.caspianpolicy.org/media/uploads/2020/09/PB-Chinas-growing-influence-in-CA-through-surveillance-systems.pdf.
26. 'Trade index between China, BRI partners rises to 165.4 in 2022 from 100 in 2013', *Global Times*, 13 October 2023. https://www.globaltimes.cn/page/202310/1299798.shtml.
27. 'Official Spokesperson's response to a query on participation of India in OBOR/BRI Forum', Ministry of External Affairs, Government of India, 13 May 2017. https://www.mea.gov.in/media-briefings.htm?dtl/28463/Official+Spokespersons+response+to+a+query+on+participation+of+India+in+ OBORBRI+Forum.

Part Three

Decoding China's Domestic Preoccupations

11

China after the 20th Party Congress
Political, Economic and Technological Developments

Ananth Krishnan

In March 2023, Xi Jinping began an unprecedented third term as China's president following the conclusion of the first session of the 14th National People's Congress (NPC) in Beijing. Xi's third term was essentially confirmed in October 2022, when the Communist Party of China (CPC) convened its once-in-five-years National Congress. Xi emerged from the congress securing a third term as CPC General Secretary and achieving a clean sweep by filling the party's seven-member Politburo Standing Committee (PBSC) with his allies.

Despite this political success, Xi's third term did, however, begin with the Chinese leader on the back foot and with the party confronting serious challenges on several fronts: unprecedented public protests in several cities against the draconian 'Zero-COVID' policy; an increasingly dire economic scenario as a result of both the pandemic control measures and larger structural issues plaguing the Chinese economy, from debt to real estate slowdown and a looming strategic challenge from worsening China–US tensions, a trade and technology war and measures by Washington to cripple some of China's emerging high-tech industries.

This chapter will analyse the state of play on these challenges that will likely loom over Xi's third five-year term as well as the party's ongoing attempts to address them. If achieving a level of technological self-sufficiency, particularly in critical and strategic sectors, is likely to remain the abiding priority for Xi and the Communist Party in this critical period until the next congress in 2027, this mission faces serious obstacles, especially with a renewed effort by the US and its allies to limit Chinese access to critical technologies such as advanced chips. Moreover, a plethora of economic challenges at home are further complicating this effort, with the country facing a vicious cycle of depressed economic sentiment, falling investment and rising joblessness especially among the youth – matters that are likely to occupy the minds of the Chinese leadership in the third Xi term even as it unfolds against the backdrop of a worsening geopolitical contest with the US. This chapter argues that even beyond the range of economic problems, the party faces an increasingly widespread sentiment among the Chinese – arguably for the first time in the reform era – of pessimism about their future prospects, a sense of 'a new national stasis', dubbed by Chinese writers as a feeling of 'neijuan' or 'involution'. Xi, in contrast, appears to be seeking to form a new social contract that is no longer predicated on the party delivering growth to secure public support but is centred on rallying the public by turning to ideology and appealing to national sentiment. Whether he is able to do so remains an open question but is one that will likely determine the success or failure of Xi's China.

Political State of Play: From Clean Sweep to COVID-19 Protests

The 20th National Congress of the CPC, which was convened in Beijing, concluded on 22 October 2022 confirming Xi's third term, defying the precedent of the previous two Jiang Zemin and Hu Jintao generations of the party's leadership. The political outcomes of the congress also paved the way for Xi's complete domination of elite Chinese politics not only for the coming five years but for the next decade as no apparent successor was anointed who would be in a position to assume any of Xi's titles at the next congress in 2027.

The day after the congress concluded, the newly appointed Central Committee convened its first sitting to choose the next PBSC. As many as four Xi allies with, as we will see, long-standing ties to the Chinese leader were appointed to join two others who continue, thus making for an unprecedented clean sweep. This was made possible by the apparently forced early retirement of two officials despite their being under the unofficial retirement age of sixty-eight – former second ranked leader and premier Li Keqiang and former PBSC member Wang Yang, both of whom share close ties with Hu Jintao, Xi's predecessor. The other major talking point of the congress, a usually carefully choreographed event, was the unexpected escorting offstage of a frail-looking Hu Jintao while voting was under way. Chinese state media later explained his removal for health reasons, although online speculation suggested Hu may have been unhappy with the treatment of his two protégés.

The political clean sweep underlines how Xi has re-engineered party politics in a manner that even Mao Zedong, who had to contend with political rivals and factions, was unable to despite his extraordinary accumulation and exercise of power culminating in the Cultural Revolution (1966–1976), which itself was engineered to oust rivals who had begun to challenge Mao's authority. A decade into his term, Xi has appeared to face no such challenge, decimating factional networks, such as those linked to Hu Jintao and Jiang Zemin, which had played vital roles in party politics for decades. The party congress also approved amendments to the party constitution further underlining Xi's 'core' status by calling on the party to 'establish his core position and the guiding role' of his ideology and 'uphold his core position and the centralized, unified leadership' of the party, called the 'two establishes' and 'two upholds'.

The new leaders all have ties to Xi.[1] Second-ranked Li Qiang was appointed outgoing premier Li Keqiang's successor despite the widespread criticism, during the time he served as the party chief in Shanghai, of a draconian and ill-handled lockdown that led to shortages of food and medicines. He worked as Xi's chief of staff in Zhejiang province where he was party chief in the mid-2000s. Third-ranked Zhao Leji, like Xi, has roots in Shaanxi province. He later helped lead Xi's anti-corruption crackdown, which also eliminated many political rivals as head of the powerful anti-corruption authority. Fourth-ranked Wang Huning has served as Xi's key ideological czar. Fifth-ranked Cai Qi also goes back a long way with Xi, having worked as the director of Xi's office when he served in the province of Fujian. Finally, Ding Xuexiang, the youngest member of the new PBSC, had served as Xi's chief of staff and as director of the General Office of the Party Central Committee, its key nodal body. He had also served as Xi's chief of staff when he was the party secretary of Shanghai province and in the past term regularly accompanied Xi on all his foreign visits.

If this clean sweep of the PBSC was no doubt an unprecedented political success for Xi, only weeks after his coronation he quickly came back down to earth, facing an extraordinary political crisis. Protests spilled out onto the streets in the very first month of Xi's third term as party chief with the public having enough of three years of the draconian anti-COVID-19 measures. Many in China were banking on the October 2022 party congress to mark an end to COVID-19 lockdowns that had extracted heavy social and economic tolls. Yet Xi would emphasise the policy's success at the congress, where he strongly defended the Zero-COVID policy as the right choice for China which showed that the government 'put people's lives first'. For months, party media had criticised the West – particularly the US – for its lax approach to COVID-19 and the millions of deaths. This focus had, however, led to a self-imposed narrative trap that the party could not easily get out of.

China's leaders were well aware that no country in the world had managed a transition to living with COVID-19 without huge costs. These costs had been used to justify the continuation of the Zero-COVID approach. The question of continuing with it had also become intensely political. The problem for the leadership was that public tolerance for a policy that many initially supported was declining rapidly. As lockdowns grew harsher, as seen in Shanghai, to control new variants such as Omicron, the broad expectation was that the conclusion of the congress would herald an easing. By July 2022 the COVID-19 policies had weighed down on economic growth and led to over 20 per cent unemployment as businesses stopped hiring.

However, one of the first policies announced after the congress, named '20 easing measures', in early November 2022, ended up causing only confusion and further tightening rather than the widely expected easing. The vaguely framed measures called on local authorities to shorten quarantine periods but at the same time asked them to 'adhere unwaveringly' to Zero-COVID and stamp out outbreaks – hardly an easing.

This built-up frustration exploded into public anger on 24 November 2022, when news broke online of ten people being killed in an apartment complex fire in the city of Urumqi in the western Xinjiang region. Videos widely circulating on Chinese social media showed fire trucks appearing to try to douse the fire by spraying from outside the gates of the compound. For millions in China who had similarly been locked down in apartment complexes, the tragedy struck a nerve. Two days later, dozens of people gathered for a memorial to the victims on Shanghai's Urumqi Road, where they chanted for an end to lockdowns and mass testing. Videos showed some even calling for Xi to step down. The protests then spread to Beijing and dozens of Chinese college campuses. In Beijing, a large crowd of mostly young people took to the streets in the central Liangmaqiao area – home to many embassies – and called for an end to the Zero-COVID policy. Within days, a rattled government announced an end to the policy.

There were also compelling economic reasons for the government to wind down Zero-COVID. Indeed, even before the street protests, migrant workers had protested against the restrictions and working conditions in Zhengzhou at the world's biggest iPhone assembly plant – a protest that made global headlines and was damaging to the Chinese leadership's assertions about the success of Zero-COVID ensuring the stability of the Chinese economy and industry in apparent contrast to the rest of the world. Workers at the iPhone assembly plant were seen clashing with police, and some were even seen climbing over factory walls to flee a lockdown and walking for miles along national highways to return home – images that were damning about how Zero-COVID was working. From migrant workers to residents in Urumqi in the far western Xinjiang region protesting the fire, to young students in campuses across China complaining that the COVID-19 restrictions had stolen their future, the protests had unlikely taken on a national character, arguably the first protests that saw 'nationwide, broad-based, and combine[d] popular anger over multiple issues in a manner unheard of since Tiananmen Square in 1989'.[2] The protests were certainly unprecedented in recent Chinese history for their spread across the nation's campuses and in several cities. China sees thousands of localised protests every year, but a challenge to a national policy – that too one with associated with the country's leader – was unprecedented. The protests were in some quarters in Beijing seen as giving the government much-needed political space to walk back a high-level policy endorsed by the central leadership – one that was extracting increasing economic tolls. The protests may have offered an off-ramp to Xi, who acknowledged to visiting European officials that the measures had left the youth frustrated.[3]

Yet when the U-turn finally came, the suddenness and lack of preparation stunned even the country's own health experts. For months, the Xi government had ignored calls by Chinese public health experts for an orderly transition out of Zero-COVID and to prepare the groundwork through a mass vaccination campaign. With the party fixated on the party congress, those calls went unheeded. The result was two months of chaos and an extraordinary burden on hospitals in December 2022 and January 2023, and an estimated one million deaths, mostly of unvaccinated elderly Chinese.[4] In December, even the Chinese capital – the city with the most medical resources – saw overwhelmed hospitals and up to two-week-long waits at crematoria. The National Health Commission (NHC) estimated in an internal meeting that the total number of cases by 20 December 2022, two weeks after the formal lifting of Zero-COVID, was as high as 248 million, although the publicly announced official numbers were far lower.[5]

The deaths could have been avoided with a planned exit. At the time of the exit from Zero-COVID, China had 12 million people above the age of eighty who were yet to complete three doses of Chinese vaccines needed to prevent large-scale hospitalisation and death, and 80 million above the age of sixty who had not been fully vaccinated. Only in September, China's Center for Disease Control and Prevention (CDC) had urged the government to carry out a vaccination booster campaign, describing it as a prerequisite for a safe exit strategy. That warning was not heeded. Contrary to popular perception, the problem was not with Chinese vaccines, which were shown to be very effective in preventing hospitalisation and death after three doses in Hong Kong. The problem was the vaccination strategy. Instead, China's limited medical resources had remained focused on conducting regular mass testing, resources that could have been used for a speedy vaccination campaign.[6]

Despite the extraordinary winter of 2022, the leadership appeared to emerge politically unscathed as the country opened up and returned to pre-COVID-19 normalcy in early 2023. The excess deaths among the elderly did not cause any widespread public backlash. Instead, the dominant mood in early 2023 was a sense of relief at the lifting of restrictions and the resumption of economic activity, with widespread public expectations of an economic boom in 2023 following three years of the pandemic. Yet the leadership would soon face another challenge, as deep-rooted structural problems would come to the fore, extinguishing all hopes of a major Chinese rebound after three challenging years.

The Economic State of Play and the Road Ahead: Slowdown, Stagnation, Self-Sufficiency

In 2022, China's economy grew 3 per cent, the second-slowest growth rate since the final year of Mao Zedong's Cultural Revolution in 1976. If the weight of Zero-COVID policies had played a factor in depressing growth, the economy was also facing headwinds from a number of deep-rooted lingering problems, including a slowdown in the real estate sector, rising local government debt and the costs from a worsening trade-and-technology war with the US.

The NPC March 2023 work report, which listed the priorities for government policy and the challenges facing China for the coming five years, acknowledged these problems, declaring that 'a number of prominent issues and problems – some of which had been building for years and others which were just emerging – demanded urgent action'. 'China's economy was beset by acute structural and institutional problems. Development was imbalanced, uncoordinated, and unsustainable, and the traditional development model could no longer keep us moving forward. Some deep-seated problems in institutions and barriers built by vested interests were becoming more and more apparent,' the report said. 'We have accelerated efforts to build our self-reliance and strength in science and technology, with nationwide R&D spending rising from 1 trillion yuan to 2.8 trillion yuan, the second highest in the world.'[7]

The work report outlined a 'two-step strategic plan' for 2035, a key year for the Communist Party marking the halfway point between its centenary in 2021 and the People's Republic of China marking its centenary in 2049. The two steps called to 'basically realize socialist modernization from 2020 through 2035' and to 'build China into a great modern socialist country that is prosperous, strong, democratic, culturally advanced, harmonious, and beautiful from 2035 through the middle of this century'.

As for China's development objectives for 2035, the plan called to 'significantly increase economic strength, scientific and technological capabilities, and composite national strength; substantially grow the per capita GDP to be on par with that of a mid-level developed country; join the ranks of the world's most innovative countries, with great self-reliance and strength in science and technology; build a modernized economy; form a new pattern of development; basically achieve new industrialization, informatization, urbanization, and agricultural modernization; become a leading country in education, science and technology, talent, culture, sports, and health; and significantly enhance national soft power'. To work towards these rather lofty goals, the plan also listed short-term objectives for the 2023–2028 period, noting that 'the next five years will be crucial' for China to 'make breakthroughs in promoting high-quality economic development; achieve greater self-reliance and strength in science and technology; make major progress in creating a new pattern of development and building a modernized economy'.

Indeed, the push for self-reliance was one of the main takeaways from the Communist Party's once-in-five-years congress in 2022, during which Xi made a call to 'significantly increase economic strength, scientific and technological capabilities, and comprehensive national strength' and pledged that by 2035 China 'will join the ranks of the world's most innovative countries with great self-reliance and strength in science and technology'.[8] The broader context for this self-reliance push was what Xi described at the congress as an increasingly grim external environment facing China. Xi described a world in a state of flux where 'backlash against globalisation is rising' and 'unilateralism and protectionism are mounting'. He blamed unnamed countries in an thinly veiled attack on the US for 'the erection of fences and barriers, decoupling disruption of industrial supply chains, and unilateral sanctions'. 'External attempts to suppress and contain China may escalate at any time,' he said, warning that currently 'the capacity for scientific and technological innovation is not yet strong enough'.[9]

Achieving a technological leapfrogging in this current geopolitical context is arguably the abiding priority for the Communist Party. This mission does, however, face tall obstacles, particularly with a renewed focus by the US to limit Chinese access to critical technologies, especially advanced chips required for Beijing to develop a world-class semiconductor industry. China's slowing economy, coupled with what are expected to be growing Western curbs on investing in high-tech Chinese industries, is imposing serious limitations on how much financial firepower Beijing can put into this effort, not to mention constraints in know-how for an industry still depending 'heavily on imported technical know-how and core technologies'. Beijing also has to undo the self-inflicted damage from its regulatory interventions harming its private sector – the most innovative part of the Chinese economy – even as it funnels resources to more inefficient state-led enterprises.[10]

By the middle of 2023, the Chinese economy appeared trapped in a vicious cycle with no easy way out. Domestic demand remained depressed, domestic and foreign investment declined and deflation fears grew as various policy measures announced – although the government eschewed a major stimulus plan – failed to have the desired impact.[11]

Unemployment among young Chinese in 2023 reached record levels crossing 20 per cent, prompting the government to announce it would stop publishing unemployment numbers.[12]

Reports from China suggested the unemployment problem was widespread. In the eastern manufacturing heartland province of Jiangsu, a report from the provincial development and reform commission, the top economic planning body, found that by the end of June 2023 employment by manufacturing enterprises 'fell by 119,000 compared to the same period last year, and the actual working hours of front-line workers decreased, while wages also declined'. The report, that was later taken down, added that from January 2023 to June 2023 'nearly 70 per cent of large-scale foreign trade oriented companies reported falling export orders, which was the highest in recent years' while 'the number of employees also dropped by 130,000 and 147,000 for foreign trade and foreign invested companies at the end of June, respectively, compared to the same period last year'. A combination of international and domestic headwinds, the report said, had left a grim economic situation in the province that creates the most jobs in China, with the unemployment situation worsened by 'the mismatch between the [wishes of] the youth, and the labour market demand, the structural unemployment challenges, as well as the underemployment of highly educated graduates, which crowded out vocational school and junior college graduates'.[13]

A beleaguered private sector, which has faced the brunt of regulatory restrictions in the Xi Jinping era amid a return of the dominance of state-run companies, has further complicated the economic situation. In the first five months of 2023, profits of private sector industrial companies were down by close to 22 per cent year-on-year. In July 2023, the Communist Party launched a belated effort to boost depressed sentiment in the private sector, which accounts for an estimated 80 per cent of urban jobs, by announcing thirty-one new measures to create a more 'favourable environment'. The measures were, however, seen as too little too late after years of regulatory tightening. The plan pledged to give the private sector equal treatment and to better protect legal and intellectual property rights. Some Chinese economists remained sceptical as to whether it would give the economy the required boost, warning that core problems such as 'a lack of capital and confidence' needed to first be tackled.[14]

Beyond the range of economic problems is a widespread sentiment among the Chinese of pessimism about their future prospects, a sense of 'a new national stasis', a feeling of 'neijuan' or 'involution', the opposite of progress and growth and a turn inward. Deepening this sentiment is the renewed focus by the leadership on what it calls 'political security', an ideological hardening and an inward turn for the first time in the reform era that is leading to a 'sense of stagnation' especially among elites and the young, who saw an increasingly open and globalised China as the key to a prosperous future.[15]

Xi, however, appears to want to form a new social contract that is centred around rallying the public by turning to ideology and appealing to national sentiment. He has urged the youth to 'chi ku' – literally, 'eat the bitterness', a Chinese saying that refers to soldiering on through difficult times – and to contribute to the nation as patriots, slamming the in-vogue sentiments of 'involution' and 'lying flat', another ubiquitous phrase referring to young people choosing to opt out of the rat race – a stark contrast to the party's messages of 'striving hard'.[16]

Whether Xi's message will resonate remains an open question, yet it is a hugely important one. As Xi embarks on his unprecedented third term, the increasingly dire economic situation at home has no doubt been the focus both abroad and at home, including in Politburo meetings, as the party grapples with how it can revitalise a beaten-down private sector and create jobs for the record number of unemployed youth. Meanwhile, a worsening rivalry with the US is likely to dominate China's geopolitical focus. Yet arguably, it is the challenge of reversing this sentiment of stasis at home – even more than the economic and geopolitical problems – that will mark the sternest test for Xi as he looks to galvanise the country to address multiplying challenges on numerous fronts. Whether he is able to do so will likely determine the success or failure of both his term at the helm and of China's quest for global supremacy.

Notes

1. Verna Yu and Emma Graham-Harrison, 'Who's Who in Xi Jinping's China as Leader Cements Power', *The Guardian*, 23 October 2022, accessed on 1 February 2024, https://www.theguardian.com/world/2022/oct/23/whos-who-in-xi-jinping-china-as-leader-cements-power.
2. Yuan Yang, 'China's Zero-COVID Protests Create a Rare Nationwide Coalition of Interests', CAN, 28 November 2022, accessed on 1 February 2024, https://www.channelnewsasia.com/commentary/china-zero-COVID-protest-lockdown-urumqi-shanghai-beijing-xi-jinping-3105271.
3. Xiaofei Xu, Steven Jiang and Rob Picheta, 'China's Xi Acknowledges COVID Frustration Caused Protests And Hints at Relaxing Rules, EU Official Says', CNN, 2 December 2022, accessed on 1 February 2024, https://edition.cnn.com/2022/12/02/china/china-xi-eu-meeting-COVID-protests-intl/index.html).
4. Julie Steenhuysen and Deena Beasley, 'New COVID Model Predicts Over 1 Million Deaths in China', Reuters, 17 December 2022, https://www.reuters.com/world/china/new-COVID-model-predicts-over-1-mln-deaths-china-through-2023-2022-12-17/.
5. Bloomberg, 'China Estimates COVID Surge Is Infecting 37 Million People a Day', 23 December 2022, accessed on 1 February 2024, https://www.bloomberg.com/news/articles/2022-12-23/china-estimates-COVID-surge-is-infecting-37-million-people-a-day.
6. Ananth Krishnan, 'Focus on Vaccination, Return to Normalcy: China's CDC Scientists', *The Hindu*, 22 September 2022, accessed on 1 February 2024, https://www.thehindu.com/news/international/chinas-cdc-scientists-urge-beijing-to-step-up-vaccinations-return-to-normalcy/article65922520.ece.
7. Full Text of the Report on the Work of the Government, Delivered to the First Session of the 14th National People's Congress of the People's Republic of China on 5 March, and Adopted on 13 March. Xinhua, 15 March 2023, accessed on

1 February 2024, http://english.www.gov.cn/news/topnews/202303/15/content_WS64110ba2c6d0f528699db479.html.
8 Full text of the Report to the 20th National Congress of the Communist Party of China, Ministry of Foreign Affairs of China, 25 October 2022, accessed on 1 February 2024, https://www.fmprc.gov.cn/mfa_eng/zxxx_662805/202210/t20221025_10791908.html.
9 Ibid.
10 Ralph Jennings, 'China's Hi-tech Self-sufficiency Quest Faces 3 Barriers – But 1 Potential Huge Pay-off', *South China Morning Post*, 6 August 2023, accessed on 1 February 2024, https://www.scmp.com/economy/global-economy/article/3229999/chinas-hi-tech-self-sufficiency-quest-faces-3-barriers-1-potential-huge-pay.
11 Andrew Mullen, 'China Inflation: 4 Takeaways As Deflation Worries Grew in July, But Is the Worst Over?', *South China Morning Post*, 10 August 2023, accessed on 1 February 2024, https://www.scmp.com/economy/economic-indicators/article/3230530/china-inflation-4-takeaways-deflation-worries-grew-july-worst-over.
12 Mariko Oi and Nick Marsh, 'China Suspends Youth Unemployment Data After Record High', BBC, 15 August 2023, accessed on 1 February 2024, https://www.bbc.com/news/business-66506132#.
13 Luna Sun, 'China's Eastern Economic Powerhouse Provides National Snapshot; Declining Workforce, Demand and Wages Plague Jiangsu', *South China Morning Post*, 12 August 2023, accessed on 1 February 2024, https://www.scmp.com/economy/economic-indicators/article/3230826/chinas-eastern-economic-powerhouse-provides-national-snapshot-declining-workforce-demand-and-wages.
14 Frank Tang, 'China's 31-Point Plan Vows Private Firms, Like State Brethren, Will be "Bigger, Better and Stronger"', *South China Morning Post*, 20 July 2023, accessed on 1 February 2024, https://www.scmp.com/economy/china-economy/article/3228308/can-chinas-new-action-plan-lift-economy-out-deep-rooted-malaise-bring-market-peace-mind?module=inline&pgtype=article.
15 Ian Johnson, 'Xi's Age of Stagnation', *Foreign Affairs*, September/October 2023.
16 Li Yuan, 'China's Young People Can't Find Jobs. Xi Jinping Says to "Eat Bitterness"', *New York Times*, 30 May 2023, accessed on 1 February 2024, https://www.nytimes.com/2023/05/30/business/china-youth-unemployment.html

12

China's Economic Trajectory
Politics in Command
Manoj Kewalramani

On 12 December 2023, grey skies blanketed Hanoi when Chinese president Xi Jinping and his wife Peng Liyuan walked down the red-carpeted stairs from their jet on a state visit to Vietnam. Prime Minister Pham Minh Chinh greeted Xi on the tarmac. The visit would result in both sides agreeing to build a 'China–Vietnam community with a shared future that carries strategic significance'.[1] In Beijing, Chinese foreign ministry officials described the visit as 'extraordinarily successful'.[2]

On the front page of the *People's Daily*, reports and visuals from the trip competed for space with the readout of the two-day-long Central Economic Work Conference (CEWC). The CEWC, usually held in December, is an annual meeting that charts the priorities for and direction of economic policy for the subsequent year. The readout of the 2023 meeting in the *People's Daily* was accompanied by an image of Xi delivering a speech. What was unsaid, however, was that something truly remarkable had taken place. For the first time since the era of Mao Zedong, China's top leader had publicly skipped part of the conference.[3] The two months preceding this development were also norm-shattering in a sense. Autumn had gradually given way to winter but the much-anticipated third plenary session of the 20th Central Committee of the Communist Party of China (CPC) had not come to pass.[4] Historically, third plenary sessions have focussed on issues of economic policy and reform.

Were these shifts signs of Xi's confidence in China's economic trajectory, despite persistent challenges? Or were they indicators of the lack of any significant political challenge to his preferred policy direction going ahead? Perhaps it was a bit of both, and what this implies is that the days of high GDP growth rates, easy money and pro-business policy environment are well in the rearview mirror. The Party-state is likely to continue to maintain a domineering grip over the direction of money flow and economic operations. Politics and strategic ends, in other words, will continue to supersede economic rationale.

Twists and Turns

In its mid-year review of China's economic development in 2023, the Politburo had concluded that the economy had been experiencing 'undulating development and twists and turns'.⁵ The year 2023, however, had begun with high expectations of a return to rapid growth in China. In early January, the harsh and eventually unsustainable Zero-COVID policy formally came to an end. The unravelling of the Zero-COVID policy from November 2022 onward was as sudden and abrupt as the lockdowns that the policy had generated. The policy, which had been championed by Xi Jinping, had led to serious setbacks across sectors.⁶ From an economic perspective, by the end of 2022, repeated disruptions and what appeared to be an ideologically motivated adherence to a policy that had outlived its utility had eroded the predictability, reliability and efficiency of economic policy.⁷

In mid-December 2022, the Communist Party's leadership met for the annual Central Economic Work Conference (CEWC). Quarter-on-quarter GDP growth had fluctuated wildly through the year owing to lockdowns. By the end of the year, the Chinese economy had wound up growing by just 3 per cent, well short of the official target of 5.5 per cent.⁸ 'The meeting pointed out that the foundation of China's economic recovery is not yet solid, pressure on three fronts—shrinking demand, supply shocks and weakening expectations—is still large, the external environment is turbulent and unstable, with a deepening impact on our economy,' the official readout after the meeting assessed. 'Economic stability' was the 'top priority' for 2023, it added.⁹

The broad pathway to achieve this, as per the CEWC, was to focus on improving psychological expectations and boosting confidence in development. In terms of key policy initiatives, the CEWC indicated increased fiscal spending. This was reflected in the March 2023 work report presented by then Premier Li Keqiang. Li indicated that the deficit-to-GDP ratio in 2023 would increase from 2.8 per cent to 3 per cent for 2023. He also expanded the annual quota of special-purpose bonds by 150 billion yuan to 3.8 trillion yuan for 2023.

The 2022 CEWC also identified five key areas of action. Let us next explore the developments within this context through the year.

Expansion of Domestic Demand

This is a long-term strategic objective for Beijing, particularly with external demand weakening and developed countries erecting new barriers to limit market access. Official data showed that from January to November, China's foreign trade was basically flat on a year-on-year basis, at 37.96 trillion yuan. Trade with the European Union and the US fell by 2.2 per cent and 6.9 per cent respectively.¹⁰ China's foreign trade-to-GDP ratio is well over 33 per cent; as exports become further strained, the Chinese leadership has been emphasising the importance of boosting domestic consumption.

Chinese leaders tend to define domestic demand as including consumption demand and investment demand.¹¹ In other words, there is a significant supply-side element to the tabulation of consumption. These two types of demands are then further segmented into state investment in major projects, private enterprise investment and residents' final consumption, such as housing, vehicles and services.

Just prior to the 2022 CEWC, the government issued two key documents. The Outline of the Plan for the Strategy to Expand Domestic Demand (2022–2035)[12] and the NDRC's plan to implement the strategy of expanding domestic demand during 2023–2025.[13] These discussed boosting traditional consumption, services consumption, new types of consumption and green and low-carbon consumption. A key component of this effort, as per the plans, was to boost spending to support the manufacturing sector; investments in transportation, energy infrastructure, logistics, water conservancy, environmental protection and livelihood-related infrastructure and development of new infrastructure—such as digital infrastructure to support 5G networks, Artificial Intelligence (AI) and Internet of Things (IoT). Other elements were to boost incomes, support supply of high-quality products and services and build a unified national market to boost domestic circulation. In July, the NDRC issued measures to restore and expand consumption.[14] These covered sectors ranging from automobiles, charging infrastructure for new energy vehicles, affordable rental housing, furniture and home appliances, tourism, catering and sports and health services, etc.

This increased government support did not truly spur domestic consumption. As per official data, retail sales for the January to November period hit 42.8 trillion yuan, up 7.2 per cent year-on-year.[15] This might appear robust but was well below expectations and is inflated owing to the low base effect. Meanwhile, fixed asset investment for the January to November period increased by 2.9 per cent year-on-year to around 46.08 trillion yuan. Few noteworthy data points in this context are the decline in property development investment, which fell by 9.4 per cent year-on-year during the January to November period and in private investment, which fell by 0.5 per cent from a year earlier.[16] That said, it is worth noting that excluding the property sector, private investment recorded 9.1 per cent expansion. On the one hand, this is indicative of the weakness of the real estate sector, which looms large over the broader economy and has played a role in fuelling deflationary winds.[17] China's consumer inflation began slowing in February before turning negative in July. It recovered briefly thereafter, before again tumbling towards the end of the year. On the other hand, the private investment data is also testament to the Party-state's ability to continue to guide capital in priority domains.

Construction of a Modern Industrial System

In this context, Beijing's policy agenda has consistently focused on building a modern industrial system that is 'independently controllable, secure, and reliable'.[18] The process to do so has entailed upgrading traditional industries, supporting the development of new and emerging technologies and building strategic material reserves, among other things. In September 2023, speaking at the National New Industrialization Promotion Conference, Xi Jinping stressed on the need to 'organically combine the construction of a manufacturing powerhouse with the development of digital economy and industrial informatization to establish a strong material and technological foundation for Chinese-style modernization.'[19] In other words, the goal of this strategy is to achieve industrial advancement and technological self-reliance by improving the resilience and security of industrial and supply chains, accelerating the upgrading of industrial innovation capability, promoting the optimisation and upgrading of industrial structure, the deep integration of digital technology and the real economy and green industrial development.[20] In order to boost this effort, in March, the new plan on reforming Party and state institutions included the establishment of a Central Science and Technology Commission to coordinate the construction of the national innovation system and reformation of the science and technology system.[21]

In terms of the success with regard to building a modern industrial system and technological advancements, official data informs that over the course of the year, fixed-asset investments in high-tech industries grew by 10.5 per cent year-on-year, of which the investment in high-tech manufacturing and high-tech services grew by 10.5 per cent and 10.6 per cent respectively. In the January to November period, the growth rate of industrial and manufacturing value-added output averaged 4.3 per cent year-on-year. In fact, the 'three new'—solar cells, lithium-ion batteries and electric vehicles—have dominated China's exports this year.[22]

Another significant data point in this regard is the comparison between lending to the real estate and manufacturing sectors. As of the end of September, outstanding real estate loans fell by 0.2 per cent year-on-year while manufacturing sector lending jumped by 38.2 per cent.[23]

In addition, there has been an evident easing of the tone and approach with regard to enterprises within the platform economy, after a nearly two year-long regulatory campaign. This had wiped out significant market valuation and market confidence.[24] A key decision that emerged from the 2022 CEWC was the call to improve 'regular oversight' over the digital economy and support for platform enterprises to lead development, create jobs and participate in international competition. In July 2023, Chinese Premier Li Qiang met with representatives of leading platform companies. Praising them as 'trailblazers of the era', Li promised support and urged them to better 'empower the development of the real economy'.[25] But instead of being indicative of a hands-off approach, this phrase suggested a continued push by the government to direct private capital towards what it considers to be strategically significant domains. Earlier in the year, Chinese media reported about 'green-light investment cases' involving platform enterprises to empower the real economy. These covered fields such as semiconductors, autonomous vehicles, new energy and agriculture.[26] Toward the end of the year, the National Press and Publication Administration issued new rules placing spending limits and banning certain in-game measures that could induce high spending. The move wiped off tens of billions of dollars from the valuations of major players.[27]

Effective Implementation of the 'Two Unswervings'

At the 2022 CEWC, the leadership emphasised state-owned enterprise (SOE) reform to ensure that they 'truly operate them according to market-oriented mechanisms' along with support for 'equal treatment of state-owned and private enterprises' to ensure the growth and development of the private economy and private enterprises. This, the meeting said, was the leadership's 'unambiguous' attitude amid recent 'incorrect comments' on the CPC's views about the role of the private sector in the economy. This message was further underscored by Xi Jinping during the National People's Congress (NPC) session in March 2023, when he described private entrepreneurs as 'family'.[28] Likewise, through 2023, steps were taken to indicate support for the private sector. In July, the State Council issued a policy document promoting the development and growth of the private sector. Finally, by September, the NDRC announced that it had set up a Bureau for the Development of the Private Economy. Two key functions of this bureau are to promote the growth of private investment and maintain a mechanism for regular communication with private enterprises.[29]

While there is clearly some narrative and policy course correction taking place, one should not view these actions as a fundamental shift in the approach to the private sector. Beijing's perspective remains that private enterprises do not have a carte blanche to pursue profits. They must be restrained by strategic, social and ideological goals. This was clearly stated by Han Zhifeng, deputy director of the Department of Fixed Assets Investments at the NDRC, in a press briefing in August, when discussing the low levels of private investment. Among other reasons, he attributed it to the lack of a clear view of the development trends and investment directions among private players.[30]

The genesis of this changed approach to the private sector can be traced back to the 19th Party Congress. Back then, Xi Jinping had announced a shift in the principal contradiction facing Chinese society, away from the need for higher growth to the contradiction between 'unbalanced and inadequate development and the people's ever-growing needs for a better life'. In essence, this meant a shift away from a rapid GDP growth-centred model towards high-quality development. The leadership argued that this was necessary to meet the needs of society and to ensure the competitiveness of the Chinese economy going forward. This is a strategic decision, which the CPC believes impinges not just on China's future development and national power, but also the Party's ruling legitimacy. Therefore, one should not expect any rollback.

The concept of high-quality growth implies de-prioritising GDP growth rates, while focussing on improving the quality and efficiency of growth in the process of development. This entails focusing on total factor productivity, innovation-driven growth, optimal resource utilisation, environmental sustainability, livelihood issues such as employment, education and health, improving access to economic opportunities, directing capital towards national priorities, addressing inequalities and uneven regional development. In practice, this ambitious shift has proven difficult to implement. For instance, the spooking of investors amid the common prosperity push and anti-monopolies regulatory action in late 2021 and 2022 is a case in point, as is the energy crisis of the winter of 2021, which was the product of steps taken to meet carbon emission targets.[31] Moreover, implementing this agenda has resulted in greater CPC influence over enterprise decision making, intensified support for SOEs and tighter regulatory action to ensure compliance by the private sector. Entrepreneurs in Xi's new era have been called on to demonstrate patriotism, professionalism, innovation and social responsibility.

While the 2022 CEWC and Xi's remarks at the 2023 NPC indicate greater breathing room for private players, this perspective on the role of the private sector in the broader goal of national development is unlikely to change.[32] Xi's expressions of support for the private sector did not imply a return to the way things used to be. Rather, they indicated that there will likely be standardised regulation keeping in mind the objectives of high-quality development and common prosperity.[33] For instance, he called on private entrepreneurs to 'strengthen their sense of family and country' and 'enhance their sense of responsibility and mission to promote common prosperity'. In addition, inviting private capital to participate in the construction of major national projects and key industrial and supply chain projects, he also stressed that it was 'necessary to standardise and guide the healthy development of all kinds of capital' and 'create an environment for fair competition'.

Preventing and Resolving Major Risks

In this context, the leadership identified the real estate market, local government debt[34] and the systemic challenges facing the banking sector as key risks that needed to be addressed. These risks are, of course, interlinked and systemic in nature, and addressing them requires changes in the political economy. The real estate sector contributes nearly one-third of China's economy and accounts for around 70 per cent of household wealth. It is also critical from the perspective of local government revenues. The real estate sector has witnessed phenomenal growth over the years, with credit expansion since the 2008 global financial crisis fuelling property speculation. Not only did this fuel economic growth but it also made housing expensive for the ordinary Chinese. Local governments, in fact, leveraged this situation to raise revenue through land financing and land-use rights sales. Given the nature of the local political economy, banks were therefore incentivised to continue lending.

However, the tide did seemingly begin to turn around late 2016. This is when Xi Jinping first spoke about houses needing to serve the purpose of living rather than speculation. This was a mantra that he reiterated at the 19th Party Congress. Subsequently, the CPC identified financial risks as one of the three critical battles that the Party must address. In essence, the leadership was suggesting that while growth mattered, there was a need to bring order and market discipline. This, from the leadership's perspective, was critical to address risks and ensure that capital was directed to productive outcomes benefiting the real economy. These moves also indicated a greater willingness to address the moral hazard that underpins China's financial system, that is, the implicit guarantee of a central government bailout for banks and local governments, owing to the need to limit financial, social and political stability challenges.

In August 2020, the central government outlined new 'red lines' for property developers, limiting their credit-raising ability. These consisted of hard limits on a company's debt-to-asset ratio, its debt-to-equity ratio and its cash-to-short-term-debt ratio. If developers failed to meet these red lines, their access to capital would be restricted. The policy led to a cash crunch, as most developers were unable to qualify as per the red lines. Consequently, they struggled to pay off vendors and employees and project delays worsened. This, in turn, led to protests and mortgage boycotts by home buyers. The China Index Academy estimated that in 2022, China's hundred largest property developers ended up with US $1.1 trillion in sales—down by 41.3 per cent year-on-year.[35] Another indicator of the extent of the weakness in the sector was the fact that local government revenue from land transactions fell around 31 per cent, to $697.3 billion in 2022.[36] These challenges led to some policy easing.

In his remarks in Davos in January 2023, Liu He explained that the government had focussed its efforts on ensuring that purchase contracts are honoured, with the delivery of pre-sold but unfinished housing projects being prioritised. He added that along with this, the government had conducted massive 'blood transfusion' to the real estate sector through bank lending, bond issuance guarantee and equity financing. And that it was also moving ahead to facilitate 'blood formation' by relaxing restrictions that were introduced to address the overheating in the property market. Through the year, a slew of fiscal and other measures were announced to support the property market.

These included offering buyers the option to renegotiate their mortgage interest rates, down payment reductions, tax breaks, support for urban renewal projects, etc.[37] These measures have had limited impact. From January to November, funds raised by property enterprises fell by 13.4 per cent year-on-year; property sales by floor area fell by 8.0 per cent; new construction starts measured by floor area tumbled by 21.2 per cent and key developers like Country Garden and Evergrande still continue to face financial stress.[38] The property sector, in fact, has turned from a driver of Chinese growth to now weighing it down.[39] Estimates for 2024, in this regard, are not optimistic either.[40]

This is a purposeful effort by Chinese policymakers to shift the drivers of China's economic growth. However, it has significant implications for financial stability given banks' exposure to the real estate sector, the erosion in the wealth of China's middle class[41] and the capacity of local governments to deliver on their tasks. According to reports, China's local government debt reached 92 trillion yuan (about $12.58 trillion), or 76 per cent of the country's economic output in 2022; up from 62.2 per cent in 2019.[42]

In July, the Politburo meeting referenced the need to prevent and resolve local government debt risks through a comprehensive debt package plan.[43] Since then, Beijing reportedly dispatched financial experts to examine the books of local governments and find ways to cut their debts, including arranging more debt swaps and credit support from state banks. Central authorities have also reportedly asked banks to roll over much of this debt with longer-term loans at lower interest rates.[44] In addition, in late October, the People's Bank of China announced that it will issue an additional 1 trillion yuan ($137.4 billion) worth of special treasury bonds in the final quarter of 2023 and first quarter of 2024 to support local governments to meet expenditure goals across eight specific areas.[45] In late October 2023, the leadership held the Central Financial Work Conference. This hinted at continued support for local governments through the call to 'establish a long-term mechanism to prevent and resolve local debt risks, establish a government debt management mechanism that is compatible with high-quality development, and optimize the debt structure of central and local governments.'[46] At the same time, it emphasised the importance of tightening central oversight over regional financial risks while directing capital towards technological innovation, advanced manufacturing, green development and small, medium and micro enterprises. The meeting also committed to support large state-owned financial institutions to become better and stronger, serve as the main force in serving the real economy and the ballast for maintaining financial stability, strictly enforce access standards and regulatory requirements for small- and medium-sized financial institutions, conduct specialized operations based on local conditions, strengthen the functional positioning of policy-based financial institutions and give full play to the functions of the insurance industry as an economic shock absorber and social stabilizer.[47]

A few weeks later, the new Central Financial Commission—whose mandate is to figure out the execution of the agenda outlined by the financial work conference—emphasised the priorities of finance supporting the real economy and the need to manage local risks.[48] In fact, in early December, Moody's Investors Service changed its outlook for China's sovereign debt to negative. This, it argued, reflected 'rising evidence that financial support will be provided by the government and wider public sector to financially stressed regional and local governments and SoEs.'[49] These steps are significant but it is unclear whether they can immediately address what is a structural challenge intrinsic to China's political economy.

Attract and Utilise Foreign Capital

While the 2022 CEWC highlighted the need to accelerate building the new development pattern, or dual circulation, there was an emphasis on the need to attract foreign investment while continuing to ensure 'high level of openness to the outside world'. In order to do this, the meeting called to 'expand market access', open up the services sector further, 'implement national treatment for foreign-funded enterprises', 'guarantee equal participation of foreign-funded enterprises in government procurement, bidding, and standard setting' and 'protection of intellectual property rights and the legitimate rights and interests of foreign investors'.[50]

Despite geopolitical tensions with the West worsening and the concerns around the Zero-COVID policy, Foreign Direct Investment (FDI) in China remained robust through the pandemic, but the rate of growth slowed in 2022 before inflows sharply turned downward in 2023. Official data records FDI increasing from 1.034 trillion yuan in 2020 to 1.149 trillion yuan in 2021 and 1.23 trillion yuan in 2022.[51] However, for the January to November period in 2023, the number fell to 1.04 trillion yuan, down to 10 per cent year on year.[52] In the third quarter, or Q3, China recorded an FDI deficit of $11.8 billion—the first such instance since the records began in 1998.[53] FDI in manufacturing also fell 2.1 per cent year-on-year during that period. However, FDI in high-tech industries, such as artificial intelligence, big data, biomedicine, aerospace, new materials and new energy, grew by 1.8 per cent.[54]

Since late 2022, the Chinese leadership has taken a series of steps to attract and incentivise foreign capital. In October 2022, the NPC Standing Committee carried out inspections identifying gaps in the enforcement of the Foreign Investment Law and proposing solutions.[55] Towards the end of the year the Foreign Trade Law was amended to simplify registration procedures for foreign trade operators.[56] In January 2023, the State Council announced new measures to encourage foreign investors to set up R&D centres in the country.[57] In March 2023, Li Qiang promised more opening in a meeting with key foreign CEOs.[58]

The government also launched a new 'Invest in China' campaign.[59] In June, Premier Li Qiang visited France and Germany. In a bid to shore up investor confidence, he talked up China's economic resilience and pushed back against the trend of de-risking. Failure to cooperate is the biggest risk, and failure to develop is the biggest insecurity, Li told German businesses.[60] Likewise, during his visit to San Francisco, Xi too sought to assuage concerns of American businesses.[61] In August, the State Council issued a twenty-four-point guideline on boosting foreign investment. The document indicated a desire to work more actively through specific incentives – such as preferential tax policies, data transfer easing and support—for R&D investments—and mobilising foreign missions and local governments to attract foreign investment in key areas.[62]

Despite these steps, policy unpredictability along with the increased awareness of the need for supply chain resilience and geopolitical tensions continue to weigh heavily on investor sentiment. Foreign holdings of Chinese stocks and bonds fell by 17 per cent in 2022, and this trend of declining foreign investment in Chinese markets worsened in 2023.[63] Surveys of foreign firms in China also reflect the weakening sentiment. For example, a March 2023 survey by the American Chamber of Commerce found that 55 per cent of American companies did not rank China among their top three investment destinations.[64] Another report by the Chamber in September concluded that 'China is becoming more challenging for foreign investors'.[65] Likewise, the EU's Chamber of Commerce in China reported in June that 64 per cent of European firms claimed that doing business in China had become more difficult in the past year.[66] In addition, 11 per cent of European firms had shifted existing investments out of China, and another 8 per cent of them were expected to move future investments away from the mainland.

Yet, it is worth keeping in mind that foreign companies are not exiting China en masse as some had predicted. For instance, the March report by the American Chamber of Commerce referenced above also found that a 'majority of members are not considering relocating their supply chain', although there was a 10 per cent increase among those who are considering that option. Decoupling, therefore, is yet to be seen in any substantial terms. Regardless of the political, market and geopolitical challenges, most foreign companies appear to be largely remaining in China, although new investments are being reconsidered. In other words, at the enterprise level, there is a process of de-risking through diversification that appears to be taking place and, increasingly, geopolitical tensions are playing a role in these decisions with developed countries adopting a carrot-and-stick approach to shaping enterprise decisions.

The one area where this is likely to have the sharpest and earliest effect is in critical and emerging technologies. Export controls, investment screening and legislative changes like the US CHIPS and Science Act are cases in point. In its rhetoric, Beijing has decried these efforts as going against the trend of the times and tide of history. Yet, in its actions, it seems to have acknowledged that the trend of de-risking is here to stay. Renewed engagement with the US and EU on trade and export controls through the establishment of formal dialogue mechanisms in 2023 is also indicative of this.[67]

More importantly, the Chinese leadership's own new outlook and approach to security under Xi Jinping's comprehensive national security concept are creating uncertainties for foreign enterprises and inhibiting their potential growth. The first Politburo study session for 2023 saw Xi Jinping stress on boosting security when it came to development and security through development.[68] This meant expanding domestic demand, securing key industrial and supply chains, pursuing scientific and technological innovation and breaking through key chokepoints and vulnerabilities. This is part of an increasingly difficult balance that the Party-state is attempting to strike between opening and attracting greater foreign capital and expertise while addressing its security concerns. More frequently, this balance has tilted in favour of the security agenda. For instance, from March to May 2023, reports emerged of raids targeting Western consultancy and due diligence firms as part of a nationwide anti-espionage crackdown.[69] In late April, Chinese lawmakers approved broad amendments to the country's anti-espionage law. This expanded the definition of espionage and banned the transfer of any information related to national security.[70]

Later in the year, the NPC began the process for amending the Law on Guarding State Secrets, with a specific focus on information security.[71] Further on, the new National Data Administration was established. In October 2023, the NDA's chief Liu Liehong underscored that while the agency will establish standards and mechanisms to smooth data sharing, 'under the current international situation, security issues remain a top priority for China'.[72] The Ministry of State Security's December 2023 campaign to crack down on those expressing critical or pessimistic views on the economy as individuals with 'ulterior motives' is a measure of how intertwined economic and security issues have become from Beijing's perspective.[73] Another example is the hosting of the first China International Supply Chain Promotion Expo in November 2023, which is part of Beijing's proactive efforts to integrate itself into key industrial chains where it enjoys competitive advantages.[74] Maintaining the balance between development and security is likely to remain a seminal challenge for Xi's China.

Staying the Course in 2024

In mid-December, the Chinese leadership met for the 2023 CEWC. A few days before that, Communist Party's Politburo had discussed the economic situation. The Politburo meeting's readout offered a rather positive assessment of the economy by the top leadership.[75] The meeting held that despite the challenges experienced through the year, China's economy had 'shown signs of recovery', with progress being achieved in high-quality development, building of a modern industrial system, scientific and technological innovation and secure development.[76] It also emphasised the need to adhere to 'the general principle of seeking progress while maintaining stability', seek progress through stability, 'effectively improve the quality of the economy and promote its growth within a reasonable range' and pursue Chinese-style modernisation.[77] The meeting also briefly listed key priority areas going forward.

The CEWC reiterated the key principles articulated by the Politburo, while detailing the agenda 2024. The CEWC said that in the next year:

> it is necessary to adhere to the general principle of seeking progress while maintaining stability, promoting stability through progress, and establishing the new before abolishing the old. It will be essential to implement policies that are conducive to stabilizing expectations, growth, and employment. More efforts will be needed when it comes to taking proactive measures in transforming methods, adjusting structures, raising quality, and increasing efficiency, with a view to continuously strengthening the foundation for stability and improvement. It is imperative to strengthen counter-cyclical and cross-cyclical adjustments of macroeconomic policies, continue to implement proactive fiscal policies and prudent monetary policies, and enhance policy innovation and coordination.[78]

This paragraph was indicative of the decision by the leadership to stay the course on its development agenda despite the downward pressure on growth. The key components of this agenda are:
- Adhering to the 'new development philosophy' which involves making growth more innovative, coordinated, green, open and equitable;
- building a 'new development paradigm', which emphasises high-quality development, reform and opening up to build linkages while reducing dependencies and building self-reliance and strength in high-level science and technology;
- persisting with supply-side structural reform and focussing on coordinated efforts to expand effective demand;
- ensuring a balance between high-level development and high-level security, using the former to promote the latter, and the latter to secure the former;
- improving people's well-being and social stability and
- pursuing Chinese-style modernisation as the top political priority.

In essence, this implies a continued tolerance for lower GDP growth in favour of pursuing structural changes that boost future development and social and environmental policy objectives. Official data showed that average GDP growth across the first three quarters of 2023 was 5.2 per cent, which was well above the 5 per cent target. In November, the International Monetary Fund (IMF) upgraded its forecast to predict 5.4 per cent GDP growth for China in 2023. Investment banks UBS and Goldman Sachs estimated China's 2023 growth to be around 5.2 per cent and 5.3 per cent respectively. However, these estimates slide sharply downward for 2024. The IMF, UBS and Goldman Sachs' estimates for 2024 range between 4.4 per cent and 4.8 per cent.[79] The CEWC's discussion on fiscal and monetary policies suggests that Beijing is likely to continue to hold the line, regardless of GDP growth slipping below 5 per cent in 2024.

While calling for 'proactive fiscal policies', the readout stressed on the need to 'improve the efficiency of funds and the effectiveness of policies', along with strengthening financial support for 'major national strategic tasks' and 'reasonably expanding' the scope of local government special bonds for capital purposes. Delivering a rather ominous message on financial discipline, the meeting said that 'general expenditures should be strictly controlled. Party and government departments should get used to working within a limited budget'.[80] When it came to monetary policy, the readout emphasised the need to be 'flexible, moderate, precise, and effective' while calling on financial institutions to 'increase support for technological innovation, green transformation, small and micro enterprises, and the digital economy'.

At this point, it is important to stress that tolerance for slower growth and maintaining a tight grip on money supply does not imply that growth is not important for Beijing. In fact, growth remains key to the overall development agenda. Two specific references from the CEWC readout underscore this. First, the emphasis on the principles of 'promoting stability through progress' and 'establishing the new before abolishing the old' entail a signal to the bureaucracy that progress in new areas and industries must not come at the cost of disruptions in certain critical domains, which might have implications for social stability. Consequently, they mustn't act too quickly or too harshly. Second, the call to 'strengthen coordination in fiscal, monetary, employment, industrial, regional, technological, and environmental policies, and include non-economic policies in the evaluation of the consistency of macroeconomic policy orientation' implies a desire to mitigate unintended consequences of policies across different domains on the broader economic agenda.[81]

The readout also sheds light on what the leadership views as the drivers of China's future economic growth. These are captured across nine priority areas:[82]
- Promote technological innovation to support the development of a modern industrial system.
- Expand domestic demand; under which it discussed the need to ensure 'sustained expansion' and 'foster and expand new types of consumption, including smart homes, entertainment and tourism, sports events, as

well as domestic products and China-chic goods'. It also mentioned new energy vehicles and electronic products and promoting large-scale upgrading of equipment and the replacement of old consumer goods with new ones. It also talked about the need to 'give full play to the multiplier effect of government investment, focus on supporting research in key and core technologies, new infrastructure, energy conservation, emission and carbon reduction'. In addition, it called for supporting private capital's participation in new infrastructure and other areas.
- Deepen reform in key areas, such as strengthening core functions and core competitiveness of SOEs; supporting small and medium enterprises (SMEs) and pursuing reforms in market access and access to factors of production, fair law enforcement, and protection of rights and interests to support private enterprises, building a unified national market, etc.
- Expand high-level opening up; expand trade; relax market access in telecoms and healthcare; implement the agenda of the Belt and Road Initiative (BRI) and promote 'Invest in China' brand, etc.
- Prevent and defuse risks in the real estate sector, local government debt and financial sector. It calls to 'speed up the building of a new development mode for the real estate market' and balance 'addressing local government debt risks and stable development'.
- Do a good job in the work related to agriculture, rural areas and farmers. This was indicative of policy continuity with regard to rural areas.
- Promote integrated development of rural and urban areas and coordinated regional development.
- Strengthen ecological conservation and pursue green and low-carbon development.
- Do everything 'within our capacity and our means' to make sure that people's livelihoods are secured. Employment should be given priority to ensure jobs for key groups.[83]

The 2023 CEWC readout also shed light on the key challenges in pursuing this agenda. It said that:

> … Some difficulties and challenges must be tackled to achieve further economic recovery. Those include a lack of effective demand, overcapacity in some industries, weak social expectations and many hidden risks. There are bottlenecks in the domestic economic flow, and the external environment is increasingly complex, severe and uncertain. It is necessary to be vigilant against potential risks and effectively address these problems. Generally speaking, the favorable conditions for China's development outweigh the unfavorable ones, and the overall trend of economic recovery and long-term improvement remains unchanged. Confidence and determination must be boosted.[84]

Conclusion

In summary, the scrapping of the Zero-COVID policy has created positive momentum for the Chinese economy in 2023. There was anticipation that pent-up consumer demand, increased fiscal spending and efforts to boost market confidence and signal openness and predictability will result in growth rebounding. The recovery, however, has been rather tepid. Exports have not gained strength. De-risking by the West is now truly underway. Domestic demand has remained weak. The real estate sector continues to remain in a flux, weighing on the overall economy. Local government debt risks remain largely unresolved. And the private sector doesn't seem terribly enthused by the government's outreach.

However, there are clearly advances being made in securitising economic development, boosting technological innovation, market diversification, building a modern industrial base to move up the manufacturing value chain, enhancing resource efficiency and curtailing environmental damage, along with breaking down barriers of local protectionism to further balance growth. In order to achieve these objectives, there is a profound change taking place in the role of the Party-state in the economy. It is likely to continue to be far more interventionist in its approach in order to guide capital and labour to serve what it views as political and national objectives.

This is a purposeful effort to reorient the drivers of China's future development. For the moment, it appears that Beijing is willing to bear the costs of this approach in terms of slower and lethargic GDP growth, weak market sentiment and lowered private sector and foreign investor confidence. The question, however, is how long will it be able to do so? Moreover, it is unclear whether such a shift in the economic structure can be achieved without the required fiscal and tax reform, hukou reform, boosting of consumption through demand-side incentives. In addition, certain structural challenges—such as local market protectionism, weakening external demand and the moral hazard at the heart of China's banking sector—are likely to persist.

Notes

1. 'China, Vietnam Agree to Build Community with Shared Future That Carries Strategic Significance', Xinhua, 13 December 2023, https://english.news.cn/20231213/553904f268594b4ea9c0999df3c7208b/c.html.
2. Hua Chunying 华春莹 (@SpokespersonCHN), 13 December 2023, 4.20 p.m., Twitter, https://twitter.com/SpokespersonCHN/status/1734888618072920131?s=20.
3. 'China's Xi Publicly Skips Day 2 of Economic Event for First Time', Bloomberg, 13 December 2023. https://www.bloomberg.com/news/articles/2023-12-13/china-s-xi-publicly-skips-day-2-of-economic-event-for-first-time.

4   Legu Zhang, 'China's Third Plenum Day in "Uncharted Territory"', VOA, 4 December 2023, https://www.voanews.com/a/china-s-third-plenum-delay-in-uncharted-territory-/7384506.html.
5   'The Political Bureau of the CPC Central Committee Held a Meeting to Analyze and Study the Current Economic Situation and Economic Work', *People's Daily*, 25 July 2023, http://paper.people.com.cn/rmrb/html/2023-07/25/nw.D110000renmrb_20230725_1-01.htm.
6   For a deeper understanding of the zero-COVID policy, read: Manoj Kewalramani, Testimony before the US–China Economic and Security Review Commission, 'Hearing on Challenges from Chinese Policy in 2022', 3 August 2022, https://www.uscc.gov/sites/default/files/2022-08/Manoj_Kewalramani_Testimony.pdf.
7   European Union Chamber of Commerce in China, 'European Business in China: Position Paper 2022/2023', https://europeanchamber.oss-cn-beijing.aliyuncs.com/upload/documents/documents/European_Business_in_China_Position_Paper_2022_2023[1068].pdf.
8   'China's Economy Expands 3% in 2022 after Zero-COVID Policies Hit Growth', Financial Times, 16 January 2023, https://www.ft.com/content/ebe63075-32c1-46a0-8d49-570dfb654547.
9   'The Central Economic Work Conference was held in Beijing. Xi Jinping, Li Keqiang and Li Qiang made an important speech. Zhao Leji, Wang Huning, Han Zheng, Cai Qiding, Xue Xiang and Li Xi attended the meeting', Xinhuanet, 16 December 2022. http://www.news.cn/politics/leaders/2022-12/16/c_1129214446.htm.
10 'China's Foreign Trade Up 1.2 Pct in November', Xinhuanet, 7 December 2023, https://english.news.cn/20231207/42fa5b4d05fc4c42983cda547cf048a7/c.html.
11 Liu He, 'Organically combine the implementation of the strategy of expanding domestic demand with deepening supply-side structural reform (scientiously study, publicize and implement the spirit of the 20th National Congress of the Communist Party of China)', *People's Daily*, 4 November 2022. http://paper.people.com.cn/rmrb/html/2022-11/04/nw.D110000renmrb_20221104_1-06.htm.
12 'The Central Committee of the Communist Party of China and the State Council issued the Outline of Strategic Planning for Expanding Domestic Demand (2022-2035)', *People's Daily*, 15 December 2022, http://paper.people.com.cn/rmrb/html/2022-12/15/nw.D110000renmrb_20221215_4-01.htm.
13 'Implementation Plan of the "14th Five-Year Plan" Strategy for Expanding Domestic Demand', National Development and Reform Commission, Notice, https://www.ndrc.gov.cn/xxgk/zcfb/tz/202212/t20221215_1343551.html.
14 'The General Office of the State Council Forwarded to the National Development and Reform Commission: Notice on the Resumption and Expansion of Consumption Measures Letter of the State Council [2023] No. 70', Central Government of the People's Republic of China, 31 July 2023, https://www.gov.cn/zhengce/content/202307/content_6895599.htm.
15 'Total Retail Sales of Consumer Goods in November 2023', National Bureau of Statistics of China, 16 December 2023. https://www.stats.gov.cn/english/PressRelease/202312/t20231221_1945707.html.

16 'Update: China's Fixed-Asset Investment up 2.9 percent in First 11 Months', Xinhuanet, 15 December 2023, https://english.news.cn/20231215/ea5b94760b07471ba6b58f10ba8b6fdc/c.html.
17 'Deflation in China: The Spillover Effects for Global Markets', J.P. Morgan, 28 September 2023, https://www.jpmorgan.com/insights/global-research/international/china-deflation.
18 Xi Jinping, 'Certain Major Issues for Our National Medium- to Long-Term Economic and Social Development Strategy', Qiushi, 1 November 2020, https://web.archive.org/web/20201111020608/http:/www.qstheory.cn/dukan/qs/2020-10/31/c_1126680390.htm
19 'Xi Jinping Made Important Instructions on Promoting New Industrialization and Emphasized: "Put the Requirements of High-Quality Development Throughout the Whole Process of New Industrialization. Build a Strong Material and Technological Foundation for Chinese-Style Modernization"', *People's Daily*, 24 September 2023, http://paper.people.com.cn/rmrb/html/2023-09/24/nw.D110000renmrb_20230924_1-04.htm.
20 Ibid.
21 'China Releases Plan on Reforming Party and State Institutions', Xinhua, 16 March 2023. https://english.www.gov.cn/policies/latestreleases/202303/16/content_WS6413be82c6d0f528699db58e.html.
22 You Xiaoying, 'The "New Three": How China Came to Lead Solar Cell, Lithium Battery and EV Manufacturing', Dialogue Earth, 7 November 2023, https://chinadialogue.net/en/business/new-three-china-solar-cell-lithium-battery-ev/
23 'With Manufacturing Loans Rising, Can China Avoid a New Supply Glut?', *The Hindu*, 13 November 2023, https://www.thehindu.com/business/with-manufacturing-loans-rising-can-china-avoid-a-new-supply-glut/article67529027.ece.
24 Rogier Creemers, 'The Great Rectification: A New Paradigm for China's Online Platform Economy', SSRN Electronic Journal, 2023, https://dx.doi.org/10.2139/ssrn.4320952.
25 Zhang Hongpei and Xiong Xinyi, 'China Sends Strongest Signal to Support Platform Forms as Premier Li Meets with Industry Representatives', Global Times, 12 July 2023, https://www.globaltimes.cn/page/202307/1294243.shtml; Evelyn Yu and Jackie Cai, 'China Premier Meets Major Tech Companies, Vows More Support', Bloomberg, 12 July 2023, https://www.bloomberg.com/news/articles/2023-07-12/china-premier-meets-major-internet-companies-vows-more-support-ljznb85o.
26 Fan Feifei and Mo Jingxi, 'Key Growth Role Seen for Platform Firms', chinadaily.com.cn, 13 July 2023, https://global.chinadaily.com.cn/a/202307/13/WS64af0389a31035260b8160b2.html.
27 Wayne Chang and Laura He, 'New draft rules targeting in-game spending wipe billions from China's tech giants', CNN business, 22 December 2023, https://edition.cnn.com/2023/12/22/business/chinese-tech-giants-shares-plunge-online-gaming-ban-intl-hnk/index.html.
28 'Xi Jinping emphasized when visiting members of the China Democratic National Construction Association, Industry and Commerce Joint Committee who attended the CPPCC meeting: Correctly guide the healthy development of the private

economy and high-quality development', *People's Daily*, 7 March 2023. http://paper.people.com.cn/rmrb/html/2023-03/07/nw.D110000renmrb_20230307_1-01.htm.

29 'China establishes bureau for private economy development amid strong policy support'. Xinhua. 4 September 2023, https://english.www.gov.cn/news/202309/04/content_WS64f56d99c6d0868f4e8df14a.html.

30 Reporter Liu Zhiqiang, 'The National Development and Reform Commission Issued a Notice to Mobilize the Enthusiasm of Private Investment. Promote Private Investment with Practical Recruitment and Implementation (Policy Interpretation)', *People's Daily*, 8 August 2023, http://paper.people.com.cn/rmrb/html/2023-08/08/nw.D110000renmrb_20230808_1-02.htm.

31 Orange Wang, 'China's Power Crisis "Man-Made", and Miscalculations by Beijing Serve as "a Very Painful Lesson", Coal Insiders Say', *South China Morning Post*, 10 November 2021, https://www.scmp.com/economy/china-economy/article/3155584/chinas-power-crisis-man-made-and-miscalculations-beijing.

32 Max J. Zenglein and Jacob Gunter, 'The Party Knows Best: Aligning Economic Actors with China's Strategic Goals', Mercator Institute of China Studies, 12 October 2023, https://merics.org/en/report/party-knows-best-aligning-economic-actors-chinas-strategic-goals.

33 Ibid.

34 As per the IMF at the end of 2022, on-the-books debt of local governments in China was 35 trillion yuan. Implicit debt, however, likely amounted to around 70.4 trillion yuan. This figure includes 56.7 trillion yuan of LGFV debt and 13.7 trillion yuan of debt tied to government-guided funds and special construction funds. See Zhang Yukun and Cheng Siwei, 'China's Local Governments Struggle with Hidden Debt', Nikkei Asia, 8 May 2023, https://asia.nikkei.com/Spotlight/Caixin/China-s-local-governments-struggle-with-hidden-debt.

35 Elise Mak, 'Top 100 Chinese Developers Saw Sales Plunge 40 Per Cent in 2022 as Property Crisis Deepened', *South China Morning Post*, 4 January 2023, https://www.scmp.com/business/china-business/article/3205513/top-100-chinese-developers-saw-sales-plunge-40-cent-2022-property-crisis-deepened.

36 Zhang Huimin, 'China's Local Govts Need New Sources of Revenue as Land Use Payments Slump 31%', Yicai Global, 10 January 2023, https://www.yicaiglobal.com/news/china-local-govts-need-new-sources-of-revenue-as-land-use-payments-slump-31.

37 'China Unveils More Measures to Support Property Sector', Xinhua. 25 August 2023, http://english.scio.gov.cn/pressroom/2023-08/25/content_107593161.htm; Lulu Yilun Chen, 'Here's Everything China Is Doing to Save Its Property Market', Bloomberg News, 31 August 2023. https://www.bnnbloomberg.ca/here-s-everything-china-is-doing-to-save-its-property-market-1.1965968.

38 'Investment in Real Estate Development from January to November 2023', National Bureau of Statistics of China, 16 December 2023. https://www.stats.gov.cn/english/PressRelease/202312/t20231221_1945706.html.

39 'China Property Crisis in Charts: Spillover Spreads Across Economy', Bloomberg News, 22 December 2023. https://www.bloomberg.com/news/

articles/2023-12-21/10-charts-that-show-how-china-s-property-crisis-is-spreading-across-economy.

40 'Outlook Report: China Property Developers Outlook 2024', FitchRatings, 27 November 2023. https://www.fitchratings.com/research/corporate-finance/china-property-developers-outlook-2024-27-11-2023.

41 'China's Real Estate Meltdown Is Battering Middle Class Wealth', Bloomberg News, 18 December 2023. https://www.bloomberg.com/news/articles/2023-12-17/china-s-shrinking-household-wealth-families-strive-to-save-nest-eggs.

42 'Exclusive: China tells banks to roll over local government debts as risks mount – sources', Reuters, 17 October 2023, https://www.reuters.com/world/china/china-instructs-banks-roll-over-local-government-debt-sources-2023-10-17//

43 'The Political Bureau of the Central Committee of the Communist Party of China Held a Meeting to Analyze and Study the Current Economic Situation and Economic Work. Xi Jinping, General Secretary of the Central Committee of the Communist Party of China, Presided over the Meeting', Xinhuanet, 24 July 2023, http://www.news.cn/politics/leaders/2023-07/24/c_1129765310.htm.

44 Ibid.

45 Arendse Huld, 'China to Issue RMB 1 Trillion in Special Treasury Bonds to Local Governments in Q4 2023 and Q1 2024', China Briefing, 8 November 2023, https://www.china-briefing.com/news/china-treasury-bonds-issued-to-local-governments-in-q4-2023.

46 'Central Financial Work Conference Held in Beijing. Xi Jinping and Li Qiang Delivered an Important Speech, Zhao Leji, Wang Huning, Cai Qiding, Xue Xiang, and Li Xi attended', *People's Daily*, 1 November 2023, http://paper.people.com.cn/rmrb/html/2023-11/01/nw.D110000renmrb_20231101_1-01.htm.

47 Ibid.

48 Mandy Zuo, 'Chinese Premier Li Qiang Puts Financial Risk at Forefront as Head of New Communist Party Body', South China Morning Post, 21 November 2023. https://www.scmp.com/economy/china-economy/article/3242334/chinese-premier-li-qiang-puts-financial-risk-forefront-head-new-communist-party-body.

49 Rob Garver, 'Moody's Changes Outlook for China's Debt to "Negative"', VOA News, 5 December 2023. https://www.voanews.com/a/moody-s-cuts-china-credit-outlook-citing-lower-growth-property-risks/7384771.html.

50 'The Central Economic Work Conference was held in Beijing. Xi Jinping, Li Keqiang and Li Qiang made an important speech. Zhao Leji, Wang Huning, Han Zheng, Cai Qiding, Xue Xiang and Li Xi attended the meeting', Xinhuanet, 16 December 2022, http://www.news.cn/politics/leaders/2022-12/16/c_1129214446.htm.

51 'China's FDI inflow up 6.3 pct in 2022', Xinhuanet, 18 January 2023, https://english.news.cn/20230118/e48132caa312457bb5a11c7a950e7550/c.html.

52 'China's FDI Inflow Reaches 1.04 Trln Yuan in First 11 Months', Xinhua, 21 December 2023, https://english.www.gov.cn/archive/statistics/202312/21/content_WS65842437c6d0868f4e8e26a3.html.

53 Amanda Lee and Mandy Zuo, 'China's FDI Inflow up 6.3 Pct in 2022', *South China Morning Post*, 9 November 2023, https://www.scmp.com/economy/

china-economy/article/3240805/chinas-foreign-investment-boon-years-past-has-ended-economists-say-all-hope-not-lost-fdi.

54 'China's FDI in High-Tech Manufacturing Sector Realizes 11-Month-Increase in 2023', *Global Times*, 21 December 2023, https://www.globaltimes.cn/page/202312/1304087.shtml.

55 'Strengthen Confidence, Work Together, Work Hard, and Move Forward Courageously. The Broad Masses of Cadres and the Masses Conscientiously Study and Implement the Spirit of the 20th National Congress of the Party', *People's Daily*, 25 October 2022, http://paper.people.com.cn/rmrb/html/2022-10/25/nw.D110000renmrb_20221025_1-06.htm.

56 Arendse Huld, 'China Cancels Foreign Trade Operator Registration, Simplifying Import and Export Procedures', China Briefing, 11 January 2023, https://www.china-briefing.com/news/china-cancels-foreign-trade-operator-registration-simplifying-import-and-export-procedures/

57 'MOFCOM Holds Press Briefing on Measures for Encouraging Foreign Investment in Establishing Research and Development Centers', Ministry of Commerce People's Republic of China, 19 January 2023, http://english.mofcom.gov.cn/article/newsrelease/press/202301/20230103380451.shtml.

58 'Chinese Premier Calls for Global Efforts on Economic Risks, Challenges', Xinhua, 28 March 2023. https://english.news.cn/20230328/dcc50b1e74bc4c26a94d7ca5287db87a/c.html.

59 Shen Weiduo and Qi Xijia, 'China Launches Yearlong Campaign in Strong Move to Attract Foreign Investment', *Global Times*, 28 March 2023, https://www.globaltimes.cn/page/202303/1288131.shtml.

60 'Chinese Premier Calls for Upholding Economic Globalization, China–Germany win-win cooperation', Xinhua, 20 June 2023, https://english.www.gov.cn/news/202306/20/content_WS6490df38c6d0868f4e8dd016.html.

61 Gavind Bade and Phelim Kine, 'Chinese President Xi's 'Siren Call' to US Business Hits Great Wall of Skepticism', Politico, 16 November 2023, https://www.politico.com/news/2023/11/16/china-us-xi-biden-california-00127708.

62 Manoj Kewalramani, 'Seeking Foreign Investment—Wang Yi on US's "Evil Claws" in South China Sea – Warning Japan on NATO Expansion—July Data Shows Greater Weakness – NBS Suspends Youth Unemployment Data   Gwadar Attack', Tracking People's Daily, 15 August 2023. https://trackingpeoplesdaily.substack.com/p/seeking-foreign-investment-wang-yi.

63 'Investment into China Picks Up in January After Late 2022 Drop', Bloomberg News, 21 February 2023, https://www.bloomberg.com/news/articles/2023-02-21/investment-into-china-picks-up-in-january-after-late-2022-drop; Hudson Lockett, 'Over 75% of foreign money invested into Chinese stocks in 2023 has left', *Financial Times*, 21 November 2023, https://www.ft.com/content/20c5d5c8-dd64-4c22-a3fc-60d4a8336aeb.

64 Tim Zhang, '2023 China Business Climate Survey Report', AmCham China, 5 March 2023, https://www.amchamchina.org/2023-china-business-climate-survey-report/

65 '2023 China Business Report', AmCham Shanghai, 19 September 2023, https://www.amcham-shanghai.org/en/article/amcham-shanghai-releases-report-business-climate-china
66 'European Chamber Report Finds Significant Deterioration of Business Confidence in China', The European Union Chamber of Commerce in China, 21 June 2023, https://www.europeanchamber.com.cn/en/press-releases/3529.
67 'EU Calls for Greater Market Access and Fair Competition at EU–China High-Level Dialogue', European Commission, 25 September 2023, https://ec.europa.eu/commission/presscorner/detail/en/ip_23_4609; Manoj Kewalramani and Amit Kumar, 'Biden-Xi Summit: Challenge is to continue US-China engagements despite tensions', Moneycontrol, 15 November 2023, https://www.moneycontrol.com/news/opinion/what-to-expect-from-the-joe-biden-xi-jinping-summit-11742331.html.
68 'Xi Jinping Emphasized During the Second Collective Study Session of the Political Bureau of the CPC Central Committee. Accelerate the Construction of a New Development Pattern and Enhance the Security Initiative of Development', *People's Daily*, 2 February 2023, http://paper.people.com.cn/rmrb/html/2023-02/02/nw.D110000renmrb_20230202_1-01.htm.
69 Engen Tham and James Pomfret, 'Consultancy Firms in China Tested Limits before Beijing's Crackdown', Reuters, 15 May 2023, https://www.reuters.com/world/china/consultancy-firms-china-tested-limits-before-beijings-crackdown-2023-05-15/.
70 Ananth Krishnan, 'Explained: What are the Amendments to China's Anti-Espionage Law?', *The Hindu*, 1 May 2023, https://www.thehindu.com/news/international/explained-what-are-the-amendments-to-chinas-anti-espionage-law/article66801316.ece.
71 Vanessa Cai, '"Worried and Fearful": China's Move to Amend State Secrets Law Fuels Concern Among Businesses', *South China Morning Post*, 20 October 2023, https://www.scmp.com/news/china/politics/article/3238712/worried-and-fearful-chinas-move-amend-state-secrets-law-fuels-concern-among-businesses.
72 Jan Cai and William Zheng, 'China Launches New Data Agency as Ambitions in AI and Digital Economy Soar', *South China Morning Post*, 20 November 2023, https://www.scmp.com/news/china/politics/article/3242067/china-launches-new-data-agency-ambitions-ai-and-digital-economy-soar.
73 'Prominent Chinese Business Analysts are Starting to Disappear from Social Media', CNN Business, 22 December 2023, https://edition.cnn.com/2023/12/22/business/respected-chinese-economists-disappear-from-social-media-intl-hnk/index.html.
74 Luna Sun, 'China Manufacturing: Tech Can Keep Supply Chain Risks in Check, Expo Panellists Say', *South China Morning Post*, 30 November 2023, https://www.scmp.com/economy/china-economy/article/3243263/china-manufacturing-tech-can-keep-supply-chain-risks-check-expo-panellists-say.
75 'CPC Leadership Holds Meeting on 2024 Economic Work, Anti-Corruption Work, Party Discipline', Xinhua, 9 December 2023, https://english.news.cn/20231209/1a3fda9ed9d64c55ab74df3db5091dd4/c.html.
76 Ibid.

77 Ibid.
78 'Xi Delivers Important Speech at Central Economic Work Conference', Xinhua, 14 December 2023, https://english.news.cn/20231214/4f94c9806822484283c3d304a0ad0042/c.html.
79 'Graphics: What Can Be Expected from China's Economic Work Conference?', CGTN, 10 December 2023, https://news.cgtn.com/news/2023-12-10/Graphics-What-can-be-expected-from-China-s-economic-work-conference--1pqDdqkV9Zu/index.html.
80 'Xi Delivers Important Speech at Central Economic Work Conference', Xinhua, 14 December 2023, https://english.news.cn/20231214/4f94c9806822484283c3d304a0ad0042/c.html.
81 'CPC Leadership Holds Meeting on 2024 Economic Work, Anti-Corruption Work, Party Discipline', Xinhua, 9 December 2023. https://english.news.cn/20231209/1a3fda9ed9d64c55ab74df3db5091dd4/c.html.
82 Ibid.
83 Employment remains a key risk for Beijing. In June, the unemployment rate for urban workers aged sixteen to twenty-four reached a record 21.3 per cent. Subsequently, the National Bureau of Statistics suspended the publishing of data regarding youth unemployment. See 'China Stops Publishing Youth Unemployment Data Amid Slump', DW, 15 August 2023, https://www.dw.com/en/china-stops-publishing-youth-unemployment-data-amid-slump/a-66532954.
84 Ibid.

13

Science and Technology Innovation in China
Group Captain Chandan Sharda

China's transformation from a predominately agrarian economy to a significant player in science and technology innovation (S&TI) took place over time. Following the Cultural Revolution (1966–1976), the Chinese government started to give science and technology (S&T) higher emphasis, sparking a period of explosive development and modernisation. It began spending extensively in S&T research and development (R&D) in the 1980s and 1990s, opened to more foreign investment and commerce and developed many technology parks and special economic zones (SEZs) that were intended to draw foreign capital and promote technical innovation.[1] China maintained its significant investment in this area in recent years, concentrating particularly on specialised technologies like artificial intelligence (AI), quantum, blockchain, 5G and biotechnology. As a result, China has become one of the world's leading centres for innovation and is today leading the world in thirty-seven out of forty-four critical technologies. This chapter will look at China's technological development over time and its evolution as a major player in S&TI.

State Support

In terms of developing regulations, restructuring the S&T structure and providing funds to state-owned enterprises (SOEs) or private businesses, the Chinese government has significantly contributed to supporting and fostering innovation.

At the beginning of the 21st century, China changed its stance from *kejiao xingguo* (revitalising the nation through science, technology and education) to *rencai qiangguo* (empowering the nation through talent). In addition to including these themes in its Five-Year Plans (FYPs), the Chinese government has occasionally unveiled important initiatives or programmes. Some of these which have made a significant impact on its innovation capabilities are listed below:

(a) Made in China 2025: This national policy aims to modernise China's manufacturing industry and increase its competitiveness in the international scene. It focuses on ten important industries, including biotechnology, robotics, advanced information technology and aerospace.

(b) **National Strategy for Development Driven by Innovation:** This strategy was aimed at transforming China into an innovation-driven economy by 2020 and being recognised as a world innovator by 2049.
(c) **National Medium- and Long-Term Plan for the Development of Science and Technology (MLP) (2006–2020):** The MLP outlines a thorough plan for fostering S&T development and designated eight frontier technologies (biotechnology, information technology, advanced materials technology, advanced manufacturing technology, advanced energy technology, magnetic contained fusion technology, marine, lasers and aerospace technology) which represented China's comprehensive high-tech innovation capability. It also identified sixteen Mega-Engineering Programmes (MEPs) (but only thirteen were made public) and four Mega-Science Programmes (two more added later) as priorities for support.[2]
(d) **S&TI 2030 Mega-Programmes:** The 13th Five-Year Plan for S&TI introduced the 'S&TI 2030 Mega-Programmes' which mentions ten MEPs and six Mega-Science Programmes. These appear to have been developed on MLPs and the then-current MEPs, and it is likely that they will be incorporated into the MLP (2021–2035),[3] which has not yet been made public.
(e) **China Standards 2035:** This ambitious 15-year-plan, which was unveiled in 2020, outlines China's goals for establishing the world's norms in the niche technologies. This was expected to open the door for Chinese industries to dominate the world market and exert systemic influence.
(f) **Long-Term Goals for 2035:** The Long-Term Goals for 2035 were mentioned in the 14th FYP, which was published in 2021. It also mentioned twenty-three priority areas, including BeiDou, AI, Quantum, Brain science and brain-inspired research, new energy vehicles, etc. The 14th FYP defined the following Long-Term Goals for 2035:
   (i) Become an S&T superpower.
   (ii) Make significant advancements in fundamental technologies.
   (iii) Lead innovation-oriented nations.
   (iv) Establish a modernised economy to achieve 'new type' industrialisation, informatisation, urbanisation and agricultural modernisation.
(g) **R&D Tax Incentives:** The Chinese government offers tax breaks to entice businesses to spend money on R&D. This comprises a corporate income tax rate reduction for businesses involved in high-tech R&D and a tax deduction for R&D expenses.

The Chinese government's initiatives and policies were essential in fostering and advancing innovation in the nation. They promoted collaboration between business, academia and government investment in R&D. A culture of innovation was promoted by encouraging schools to prioritise science, technology, engineering and mathematics (STEM) education and establishing innovation centres and incubators to support start-ups and emerging businesses. The government also ensured a conducive business environment by streamlining regulations, cutting back on red tape and supporting start-ups.

Reorganising S&T Infrastructure

In 2006, when the MLP started, there were two types of National Science &Technology Programmes (NSTPs) in China: basic programmes and MEPs. The State provided financial support for the basic programmes which included five components[4] administered by some thirty government agencies. Due to problems with the funding system (lack of top-level design, unified planning, ineffective coordination, lack of transparency in funding distribution and accountability in spending[5] in 2014, the State Council reorganised NSTPs into five types:
(a) National Natural Science Foundation of China (NSFC)
(b) MEPs managed by twelve ministries along with the military, two provinces, three SOEs and one university
(c) National Key R&D Programmes
(d) Special Fund for Guiding Technology Innovation
(e) Special Fund for S&T Bases and Talent[6]

At the Two Sessions of March 2023, the State Council announced the restructuring of the Ministry of Science & Technology wherein it would be divested of several responsibilities and related funding management authority which would be transferred to other departments.[7] The creation of a Central Science and Technology Commission, which is allegedly intended to organise and coordinate S&T activities at the central level, will strengthen the party's position regarding S&T issues. Additionally, nearly 40 per cent of the Central Committee members, the elite body that decides major policies, are from technical backgrounds. Of the twenty-four-member Politburo, the core of the Central Committee, the number of members who may be considered 'S&T savvy' has increased from two to eight.[8]

China has made significant investments in R&D in the S&T field since it views this as a strategic area that will benefit many sectors in the long-term. Support for R&D efforts in the nation has been provided by both government financing and private investment.

The Chinese government has made a significant investment in R&D, both in direct funding of research projects and the creation of research institutions. Its policies and programmes like offering tax incentives, subsidies and grants have been with the aim of encouraging private companies to invest in R&D,

particularly in the areas of advanced manufacturing, information technology and biotechnology.

Private companies in China have also made significant investments in R&D, both in their own businesses and through partnerships with academic institutions. For example, companies like Huawei, Baidu and Tencent have established research centres to develop new technologies and products and have invested heavily in cutting-edge technologies such as AI, 5G and the Internet of Things (IoT). Through the Golden Shares,[9] the government exercises control over these companies in terms of direction for R&D, control over content the company broadcasts among other things. The government also exercises control over companies through the 'political officers' on the company's board, who have a say in the government funding to that company.

In May 2023, at a press conference, Minister of Science and Technology Wang Zhigang emphasised the need for increased investment in basic research in fields where China is coming under increasing pressure from the US and other Western nations, such as AI, big data, energy storage, semiconductors, biotechnology and clean energy transition.[10] Overall, China's spending on R&D has increased from 2.1 per cent to more than 2.5 per cent of gross domestic product (GDP) over the past five years. S&T funding is expected to continue to rise and is projected to reach $48 billion in 2023 (an increase of 2 per cent on 2022 levels based on the Chinese yuan).

Talent Development

China has an education and training system in place that is quite well-developed to encourage innovation. These are some of the crucial elements of this system:
(a) Strong vocational education system.
(b) A sturdy higher education system wherein China has several top-ranked universities, including Tsinghua University and Peking University, which are known for their established programmes in S&T.
(c) Research institutes or academies like Chinese Academy of Sciences, which provide opportunities for scientists and researchers to collaborate and pursue cutting-edge research in a range of technology fields.
(d) Corporate training by private companies like Huawei, Tencent and Baidu which establish training programmes and research centres to support the development of new technologies or products and to provide opportunities for employees to develop new skills and knowledge.
(e) International collaboration wherein China has established collaborations with other countries to support S&TI. This includes partnerships with academic institutions, government agencies and private companies to exchange knowledge and technologies and supporting joint research projects.

(f) To overcome the existing talent shortage especially in the niche technologies, in 2008, the Organization Department of the Central Committee of the Communist Party of China had implemented the Thousand Talents Programme (TTP) with the aim of attracting about 2,000 leading scientists and professionals from around the world, mostly ethnic Chinese, below the age of fifty-five. Two years later, an affiliated programme for young talents was introduced targeting overseas scholars forty years old or younger.

Due to limited success in these initiatives, China still faces a severe shortage of elite academics and other professionals and is seeing a new outflow of top scientists. This could seriously jeopardise its aspirations of developing a nation focused on innovation which was the primary objective of the MLP. The TTP courted controversy when the US government began to target Chinese scholars and high-tech professionals working there, making it challenging for China to send students and scholars abroad, particularly in some high-technology disciplines. Nonetheless, the allure of fund availability for research programmes and the availability of facilities will continue to draw scientists from other nations to China.

Industry Structure

The structure of China's technology industry, which includes the SOEs, private companies and the academia is complex and evolving. The succeeding paragraphs explain the same concisely.

(a) SOEs: The Chinese government has a controlling stake in these companies and provides them with financial support, technology transfer and access to markets. SOEs, which collaborate closely with academic institutions to develop new technologies and products, receive support and resources from the government. They are an important part of the technology landscape in China and contribute significantly to the country's innovation and competitiveness.

(b) Private Businesses: In recent years, the number of private companies in the technology industry in China has grown rapidly. These companies have been instrumental in driving innovation in areas such as e-commerce, mobile technology and the IoT. Some private companies like Huawei, Tencent and Alibaba, with backing from the State, have grown to become major global players. Private companies have played a critical role in enhancing innovation in China by driving competition, fostering entrepreneurship, investing in R&D and collaborating with universities or research institutes. These collaborations have aided transfer of technology and knowledge between industry and academia and supported the development of new products and services.

(c) Industry-Academia Collaboration: In China, the connection between business and academia is strong and entrenched. Universities and research institutes collaborate closely with companies on R&D projects, technology transfer and commercialisation of new products and services. The government established S&T parks to encourage collaboration and promote joint research projects between industry and academia.

(d) Military-Civil Fusion (MCF): The importance of this aggressive state-led and -directed national strategy became apparent on establishment of the Central Commission for Military Civilian Fusion Development in 2017. MCF aims to establish seamless flow of knowledge, technology, resources, materials and talent back and forth between the military, industry and academia.[11]

Niche Technologies

Artificial Intelligence

Significant support policy for AI can be traced back to China's 2006 National Medium- and Long-Term Plan for the Development of S&T (2006–2020) which laid the foundation for future R&D in this field. This was followed by the State Council identifying AI as one of eleven priority areas in 2011, the New Generation AI Development Plan in 2017, National New Generation of AI Standardisation Guidance in 2020 and more. The disruptive nature of AI appeals to China which expects AI to account for an increase of 26 per cent of China's GDP by 2030 and automate 51 per cent of its work activity. AI is expected to play a major role in industrial automation which, to a great extent, will overcome the disadvantage China anticipates due to its aging population. However, barriers to accessing public data, uncertain data quality, lack of data diversity and protectionist data policies are significant challenges that China must overcome to truly adopt AI.[12]

(a) Civil Applications: Currently, AI is playing a major role in unmanned vehicles, agriculture, medical diagnostics, robotics, smart manufacturing, natural language processing and Social Credit System. China has been exporting AI-enabled facial recognition systems to many regimes which support authoritarian form of governance thereby enhancing its geopolitical influence. The AI industry in China is a rapidly developing multibillion industries with its market worth likely to reach $60 billion in 2025 from about $23 billion in 2021.

(b) Military Applications: While China has been studying the feasibility of incorporating AI in many fields in the military, it has achieved some degree of success in unmanned ground, air or sea vehicles, imagery or intelligence analysis, war – gaming simulation, camouflage, converting commercial satellites to espionage platforms and decision-making. The progress that China has made in AI also will give it the ability to use this in offensive and defensive operations in cyberspace and space.[13]

Quantum

Research in this domain has been ongoing in Chinese Academy of Sciences since 1998 but it was Jian-Wei Pan, China's 'father of quantum', the youngest ever member of Chinese Academy of Sciences in 2011, who truly transformed the R&D in this field. In September 2017 China launched Micius, a quantum satellite, which made it possible to have a secure quantum enabled video conference between Beijing and Vienna. The high computing speeds that a quantum computer promises will result in less time needed to solve problems and simulations, while the secure communications and encryption afforded by quantum will result in the loss of intelligence for adversaries. While it has been the pioneer in the R&D in this field and has achieved some progress in the fields of quantum communications (achieved twin field Quantum Key Distribution over an 833 kilometre optical fibre line) and computers (built the world's first light based quantum computer and also designed the 62 qubit quantum processor), it is still in nascent stage in quantum radars (technology claimed to be proven at limited ranges but not commercially or militarily viable as yet) and quantum navigation.

5G

China realised the potential offered by 5G early and set up a $724 billion fund in 2019 to commercialise it. It announced the 5G Industry Development Plan (2019–22) for complete 5G network coverage in and around Beijing and identified other cities wherein infrastructure was to be set up and funds allotted to integrate with 5G. In 2019, it came out with Tiangang 5G chip, used during the 7th Military World Games and established the first 5G checkpoint at Yunfeng Reservoir with the aim of stemming the flow of refugees from North Korea. China's 5G Application Set Sail Action Plan (2021–23) identified key industries (media, transportation, agriculture) where there was room for improvement and set a target of 560 million 5G users in the country by 2023. Chinese researchers, analysts and policymakers see a connection between the rollout of 5G networks and economic planners' aim of upgrading nations manufacturing base and promoting a more technologically advanced economy. However, higher power demands and inefficient distribution of spectrum monopolies have slowed the adoption of 5G. To provide network access to its troops located in remote border areas, the PLA has been known to collaborate with civil enterprises to launch 5G base stations.[14] These high speed 5G signals will not only be a morale booster for the soldiers but will also enable faster military data transmission.

6G

Chinese analysts refer to 6G technology as having the potential to realise seamless 'air-space-earth-sea-integrated systems' which implies significantly increased digital surveillance.[15] Even as it took a clear lead in 5G, China started investing in 6G which was expected to be ten times faster than 5G. It established the IMT-2030 6G which comprised thirty-seven different research bodies and industry representatives in 2019, kick-starting a centralised push to drive China's 6G R&D process. The results were apparent when it succeeded in sending 1TB of data over 1 kilometre in 1 second and by December 2021 had managed a 6G wireless transmission speed of 206.25 Gbps. China claims to have launched Tianyan-05, the world's first so-called 6G satellite.

Blockchain

In October 2019, President Xi Jinping exhorted adoption of Blockchain technology to promote innovation, but it was during the COVID-19 pandemic that the technology was truly exploited by tracking the health status of citizens. It has currently found application in international trading, subway electronic invoices, verifying contracts, health data, supply chain financing, food origin tracking, judiciary and smart prison. China set up the National Blockchain & Distributed Accounting Technology Standardisation Technical Committee in April 2020 to establish standards and the state backed Blockchain-based Service Network[16] is planning its first major international expansion in South Korea and Asia Pacific. In the military domain, use of this technology is currently restricted to tracking logistics and maintaining personnel records.

Semiconductors

The US-led western embargo on sale of high-end semiconductors (or chips) to China has forced China to re-strategise its homegrown chip capacity and capability. The embargo will have an adverse effect on China's efforts at progressing in niche technologies (smart weapons, space, etc.), but will not affect sectors which do not need sub 14 – 21 nanometre chips (cars, washing machines and TVs). Chinese semiconductor firms which focus on legacy technologies (those used in power management, microcontrollers and sensors) will continue to be critical to the overall supply chain. However, China remains especially weak on CPUs with the x86 architecture, for which the US firms have a captive customer base.

China has the biggest advantage in the semiconductor supply chain due to its unrivalled dominance in key raw material markets including silicon (which generated around 70 per cent of the world's silicon material in 2021), germanium, tungsten (a large producer), gallium and fluorite. It also has a robust assembly, testing and packaging industry after Taiwan and is the second largest in the world for outsourced semiconductor assembly and test (OSAT); it is also making advances in design and manufacture, albeit with government assistance. The major areas where it is currently lacking are trained manpower and production inputs such as core intellectual property (IP), electronic design automation, semiconductor manufacturing equipment and specific manufacturing materials.

Semiconductor sectors have high capital requirement and recovering the investment can take a long time which requires an appetite for risk and patience which the Chinese lack. China's earlier efforts to gain self-reliance in this field did not produce the desired results because funds were not allocated effectively, and actual investment was less than stated. This resulted in the latest efforts wherein select semiconductor companies will be provided easier access to funds, without having to achieve performance goals, and these companies will play a bigger role in state-backed research projects.[17]

Strength of China's S&T Ecosystem

Strengths, some of which are described below, will determine China's competitiveness in the global technological industry:

(a) Large and Growing Market: China has a rapidly growing domestic market which provides a large customer base for technology companies. This has helped attract investment and build a strong ecosystem of technology companies, startups and investors.

(b) Skilled Workforce: China has a large and skilled workforce, particularly in areas such as engineering and manufacturing. This provides a strong foundation for the development of new technologies and products.

(c) Government Support: The Chinese government has played an important role in supporting and promoting innovation; through initiatives such as subsidies, tax incentives and investment in R&D.

(d) Manufacturing Infrastructure: China has a well-developed manufacturing infrastructure which provides a strong foundation for the development of new technologies and products. This includes a large pool of skilled workers and a supportive business environment.

Challenges to China's S&T Ecosystem

China faces some challenges before it can truly unleash the full power of its S&T innovation system. Some of the major challenges are listed below:

(a) IP Concerns: China is often criticised for its weak IP protection regime, which has led to concerns about the theft of IP and the infringement of patent and trademark rights. This resulted in US-led sanctions or tech embargo resulting in slowing down of China's rise in these fields.
(b) Competition from West: China is facing increased competition from established technology companies in the US and Europe which have been dominant in the global technology market for many years. This gets exacerbated by the US plans to revive its own domestic semiconductor and rare earth mining industries.
(c) Lack of Innovation Culture: Although China has made significant investments in R&D, there is still a lack of a culture of innovation and risk-taking which is essential for the development of new technologies and products. For example, AI developers in China struggle to create AI applications that produce value for China's traditional industries due to low rates of digitisation among the Chinese enterprises and lagging cloud adoption.[18]
(d) Funding: While the Chinese government has invested heavily in innovation of these technologies, but corruption, ineffective coordination, lack of transparency in funding distribution and accountability in spending have resulted in funds not filtering down to the companies and organisations that are working on these technologies.
(e) Impact of COVID-19: Due to COVID-19's adverse impact on its economy, China will face a major challenge in ensuring that R&D investment levels do not drop amid a slowing economy. This will be especially critical since it faces increasing denial of technology from the West.

Future Trajectory

Given the disruptive nature of these technologies, it is difficult to accurately determine China's future trajectory in these fields, but some major developments may be anticipated based on the trends that China has followed:
(a) Setting Standards: China Standards 2035 made it clear that China had aimed at setting global standards for emerging technologies like 5G and IoT. Providing these technologies to Third World countries at a cheap price not only spreads use of Chinese equipment, but it also helps China to garner votes at the standards setting organisations.
(b) Militarisation of Technologies: China has been working on exploring military applications of these technologies like AI-enabled missiles, surveillance technologies, power grid cybersecurity, biotechnology and quantum radar. However, the difference between 'making breakthroughs' and 'operationalising' of these technologies must be factored in while assessing the time frames.

(c) Exporting Technologies: China has already started exporting smart city technologies to select countries around the world. Third World countries which cannot afford high priced technologies from the West are most susceptible to procuring these technologies from China. This trend will increase, given that unlike the West, China has no hesitation in building relations with non-democratic governments openly. In addition to enhancing its influence in regions around the world, this also provides China access to data collected from these countries.

(d) Integration of Technologies: China's Ministry of Science and Technology declared its intention to integrate AI with new technologies and accelerate the application of AI in 2022. In March 2023, the ministry in collaboration with National Natural Science Foundation of China, announced 'AI for Science' with the aim of promoting the use of AI in frontier sciences like drug development, gene research and biology breeding.[19] China also set up the 'Quantum AI for Science & Technology' to develop cutting edge interdisciplinary research in applications of quantum technology including quantum AI. These provide an indication that China will continue to integrate these niche technologies with the aim of realising their true disruptive nature.

(e) Integration of AI in Space: China will continue the integration of AI in its space programme. While the offensive element has already been discussed earlier, China has also announced use of AI for space debris removal.

(f) Quantum: China will continue its work on developing a quantum radar and quantum-based navigation system. It has already announced plans for completing a Quantum Communication System by 2025, establishing a mid to high orbit Quantum satellites and creating Quantum simulators for solving difficult problems.

(g) Blockchain: For the PLA, China is exploring use of this technology for ensuring secure communication, interpretation of large amount of data through various sensors and for enabling de-centralisation of weapon systems based on different platforms and ships.

(h) Semiconductors: The US-led ban on export of high-end semiconductors to China will slow down the speed at which it has been undertaking progress in niche military fields, but if the new policies are implemented correctly then it will result in China innovating the same and becoming a major exporter, eating into the market that is currently with the West.

Conclusion

China's transformation from a predominately agrarian economy to a leading innovator in S&T is a testament to the nation's dedication to modernising its economy and expanding its technological capabilities. The push by successive governments in terms of policies, funding, obtaining technology from the West and training personnel has been consistent. The major challenges China faces are from the increasing restrictions on technology from the West and implementation of its own policies down to the grass root level. China realises that its future economic growth will, to a large extent, be dictated by the breakthroughs in these technologies and hence is continually refining its organisation setup and policies to ensure that innovation in S&T is maintained.

Notes

1. J.L. Gaida, 'ASPI's Critical Technology Tracker'. *The Wall Street Journal* wsj.com/articles/chinas-xi-stacks-government-with-science-and-tech-experts-amid-rivalry-with-u-s-11668772682.
2. Meyers, Michael, and Andrea S. Graham. 'Table 2: Common Language Effect Sizes'. *Nature Communications* 12, no. 1 (2021): 895. https://www.nature.com/articles/s41599-021-00895-7/tables/2.
3. Yutao Sun and Cong Cao, 'Planning for Science: China's "Grand Experiment" and Global Implications', *Humanities & Social Science Communications* 8, no. 215 (2021), accessed in March 2023. https://doi.org/10.1057/s41599-021-00895-7.
4. The five components were the National Key Basic Research Programme ('973') including Mega-Science Programs under MLP and the National Naturel Science Foundation of China (NSFC) Program, the National High Technology R&D Programme ('863'), the National Key Technology R&D Program, the newly-established National S&T Infrastructure Platform Programme and other policy-oriented S&T programmes.
5. Ibid.
6. The programmes listed at (c), (d) and (e) are under the administration of Ministry of Science & Technology.
7. Huang Yanhao and Han Wei, 'The remaking of China's Science and Technology Ministry', *Nikkei Asia*, 15 March 2023, https://asia.nikkei.com/Spotlight/Caixin/The-remaking-of-China-s-Science-and-Technology-Ministry.
8. Karen Hao, *The Wall Street Journal* (2022), accessed on 10 April 2023(AQ: article name needed).
9. Also known as 'special management shares', these usually involve a one per cent share that gives special rights over certain business decision.
10. Smriti Mallapaty, 'China Is Mobilizing Science to Spur Self-Reliance', *Nature*, 615 (2023): 570–571, accessed on 6 April 2023, https://doi.org/10.1038/d41586-023-00744-4.
11. Major General P.K. Mallick, 2022. 'Military Civil Fusion in China'. *Vivekananda International Foundation*, 01 August 2022, accessed on 21 March 2023, https://www.vifindia.org/article/2022/august/01/military-civil-fusion-in-china.
12. William A. Carter and William D. Crumpler, 'Smart Money on Chinese Advances in AI'. Centre for Strategic and International Studies, Technology Policy Program,

September 2019, accessed on 02 April 2023, https://csis-website-prod.s3.amazonaws.com/s3fs-public/publicatin/191023_SmartMoneyChinaAdvancesInAI.pdf.
13. China demonstrated use of AI-enabled three hunter satellites to capture a high value target in space in 2022.
14. PTI, 'China Opens 5G Signal Station at the World's Highest Radar Location near Tibetan Border', *The Economic Times*, 12 April 2021, https://m.economictimes.com/news/defence/china-opens-5g-signal-station-at-worlds-highest-radar-location-near-tibet-border/amp_articleshow/82034052.cms.
15. E. Chen, 'Challenges and Progress in China's Development of 5G and 6G'. *China Brief* 21, no.17 (2021), https://jamestwon.org/program/challenges-and-progress-in-chinas-development-of-5g-and-6g.
16. Blockchain-based Service Network or BSN is a Chinese initiative common hosting platform for its small and large companies engaging in blockchain technology.
17. Qianer Liu, 'China Gives Chipmakers New Powers to Guide Industry Recovery', *Financial Times*, 21 March 2023, https://www.ft.com/content/d97ca301-f766-48c0-a542-e1d522c7724e.
18. Ibid.
19. Yang Yang, 'China Launches Special Deployment of AI for Science', Asia News Network, 29 March 2023, https://asianews.network/china-launches-special-deployment-of-ai-for-science/.

14

Impact of Zero-COVID Policy on China

Santosh Pai

The travel bans and accompanying lockdowns imposed on the city of Wuhan in the Hubei province on 23 January 2020 marked the beginning of the Zero-COVID policy in China.[1] Emergency measures included contact tracing, mass testing, border quarantine, lockdowns and mitigation software. These were later extended across the country, modified periodically and implemented with varying degrees of strictness. Such a strategy to Find, Test, Trace, Isolate and Support (FTTIS) has been described as a complex adaptive system akin to a game of snakes and ladders that requires massive capacities and rapid response.[2]

China abruptly abandoned its Zero-COVID policy on 7 December 2022, when a set of new measures was announced that signalled significant relaxations.[3] China was not the only country to implement such a strategy but the scale and duration of implementation in comparison with other countries made it unprecedented.[4] The Zero-COVID policy had far-reaching implications for Chinese society. It left behind a legacy of significant setbacks in domestic politics, economic management and external environment, which might be irreversible.

Domestic Politics

China's GDP growth has averaged over 9 per cent a year since 1978, when reforms were launched.[5] It is the central pillar of the Party's social contract with Chinese citizens. When Xi Jinping came to power in 2012, China had overtaken Japan to become the world's second largest economy. With the economy in good shape, Xi could afford to make consolidation of political power his foremost priority. The 'tigers and flies' campaign against corrupt officials and repression of dissent was the highlight of his first term.[6] The second term was characterised by efforts to prolong his ideological and political longevity. 'Xi Jinping Thought' was embedded in the Constitution and presidential term limits were abolished. Despite neglect of the economy during this transition from 'collective leadership' to 'leader for life' model, China continued to post an average growth rate of 6.7 per cent for ten years due to economic forces that earlier reforms had unleashed by embracing globalisation.[7]

Xi Jinping's continued attempts at centralising power amidst the mounting costs of the US–China trade war, the Hong Kong protests and increased global scrutiny of Xinjiang made 2019 a particularly challenging year for the

Communist Party.[8] When COVID infections first broke out in early 2020, the Communist Party was due for a political pushback. On 15 February 2020, it became apparent that Xi was going to co-opt China's response to the pandemic for political ends. A copy of his speech purportedly delivered two weeks ago on 3 February 2020 was published in the Party's *Qiushi* journal. It contained a chronology of Xi's efforts to fight the pandemic starting from 7 January 2020.[9] After the initial wave subsided and lockdowns were relaxed, a white paper released by the publicity department of the Party on 7 June 2020 characterised the pandemic as 'a crisis and a major test for China' and confirmed that Xi 'assumed full command over the control efforts'.[10] In the same week, internal differences between Party leaders on the pandemic response began to emerge in the public domain. When Premier Li Keqiang, whose role included supervision over the economy, promised government support for street vendors to ease the pressure caused due to unemployment,[11] the Party quickly shot it down, labelling such stalls as 'unhygienic and uncivilised'.[12] Li Keqiang's death on 27 October 2023, shortly after stepping down as Premier in March 2023, prompted surprising reactions around the world.[13]

By December 2020, dire concerns about food security were competing for attention on the agenda for the Central Economic Work Conference (CEWC). 'Effectively resolving the problems of seeds and cultivated land' was identified as one of eight key missions alongside self-sufficiency in strategic technology and control over supply chains.[14] With a paltry 2.3 per cent growth in GDP to report for 2020, the annual work report presented to the People's Congress in March 2021 stuck to basic goals such as 'people's lives, compulsory education and basic medical care' as part of its Common Prosperity narrative. As the pandemic raged and vaccination rates climbed across the world, China escaped with relatively small disruptions throughout 2021. The Party rejoiced in its centenary celebrations and commemorated the year with a third historic resolution that crowned Xi Jinping as a successor to Mao Zedong and Deng Xiaoping to lead the country towards national rejuvenation in the New Era.[15]

When Beijing hosted the Winter Olympics in February 2022, it served as a perfect platform for Xi, sitting with his guest Vladimir Putin, president of Russia, to trumpet the Party's narrative that China's political system had proved to be superior to those of Western democracies in handling the pandemic.[16] Few weeks later, as Putin's tanks rolled into Ukraine, the Omicron virus triggered China's longest lockdown in Shanghai.

April witnessed record unemployment (6.1 per cent) and year-on-year slump in retail sales (11.1 per cent growth) since March 2020.[17] With citizens mired in food shortages, and schools, exhibition centres and residential buildings being converted into quarantine centres, dissent began to seep into popular culture.[18] Politics could no longer distract from economic pain. Amidst the gloom, many politicians grabbed the opportunity to demonstrate their loyalty to the Party and its leader. One among them was Li Qiang, then Shanghai's Party Secretary and now China's Premier. Incidents of civil unrest followed the trail of lockdowns across the country over the next few months as the Party strictly enforced the Zero-COVID policy, which had become a proxy for Party legitimacy.

In November, when frustrated workers vented their anger it was their employer Foxconn which apologised to the Party for fear of recrimination.[19] It later emerged that Foxconn's Founder Terry Gou had warned China that the government's Zero-COVID stance would threaten the position of the world's second-largest economy in the global supply chain.[20] Later in the month, when a fire broke in a locked-down building in Xinjiang, the protestors were unequivocal in demanding an end to the Zero-COVID policy.[21] Shortly after, protesters in Beijing took to the streets with blank placards in solidarity.[22] A Politburo decision in November cautioned against 'excessive policy steps' and 'one-size-fits-approach' while emphasising the need for 'people to continue with their work and life'.[23] This was an early indicator of flexibility in the Party's position. On 7 December 2022, without any preparation for a vaccination drive or expansion in hospital capacities, a non-binding circular containing 'New Ten Points' was published.[24] The decisions of how and when to lift control measures were left open to interpretation by local governments. The Central leaders needed plausible deniability. Pressure from a complex set of external and domestic sources had reached a critical level, which made it increasingly difficult for the authorities to justify the continuation of the Zero-COVID policy.

Post-facto justification for abandonment of Zero-COVID policy figured in the 2022 CEWC report published in December, which – in sharp contrast to the 2021 edition – was less ideological, spoke of market confidence, connected the need to raise income levels to boost demand, reduced references to Common Prosperity, assured the private sector that the Party was not hostile, deleted the reference to 'disorderly expansion of capital' in relation to the technology sector, pointed to return of normality in the real estate sector, reduced urgency of action on climate change and reinstated economic growth as a priority, instead of merely concerning itself with public health.[25] It was an admission that politics at the cost of economic performance no longer made sense.

The Chinese economy expanded by only 3 per cent in 2022, the lowest since 1976, if 2020 is excluded, and well below the government target of 5.5 per cent.[26] The conservative target of 5 per cent for 2023 offers further evidence that the Party has reconciled itself with a period of slower growth. Projections for China's growth have been revised downwards significantly from pre-COVID levels of 6 per cent to roughly 3 per cent by 2030 and 2 per cent by 2040.[27] Xi's flawed priorities during the implementation of the Zero-COVID policy have deeply undermined the Party's social contract with Chinese society. An important outcome of China's Zero-COVID policy has been an expansion of the state's surveillance apparatus, using digital tools such as cameras and QR codes. Tools and technologies deployed to advance the strategy of FTTIS have been normalised in many areas even after exiting the 'Zero-COVID' stance. The exodus of expatriates from China during the pandemic and the conspicuous absence of foreign tourists even a year after the end of Zero-COVID reflects a loss of confidence across the world in China's domestic governance, which is likely to translate to reduced foreign direct investment flows.

Economic Management

China's post-1978 economic rise is inextricably linked to its performance in foreign trade. In the last decade, domestic drivers of economic growth have emerged in the form of the real estate and technology sectors. Each of these drivers of growth were impacted during the Zero-COVID period.

Foreign Trade

In May 2020, during a Politburo meeting, perhaps anticipating decoupling tendencies from Western countries amid calls for resilience in global supply chains, Xi Jinping resurrected the idea of a dual circulation strategy, which was touted earlier to cope with the US–China trade war.[28] It immediately became the new peg for economic reform in China with academics and policymakers chiming in about the need to boost domestic consumption, accelerate supply-side reforms, reform state-owned enterprises and so on. The primary cause for concern was China's excessive reliance on global trade for growth.

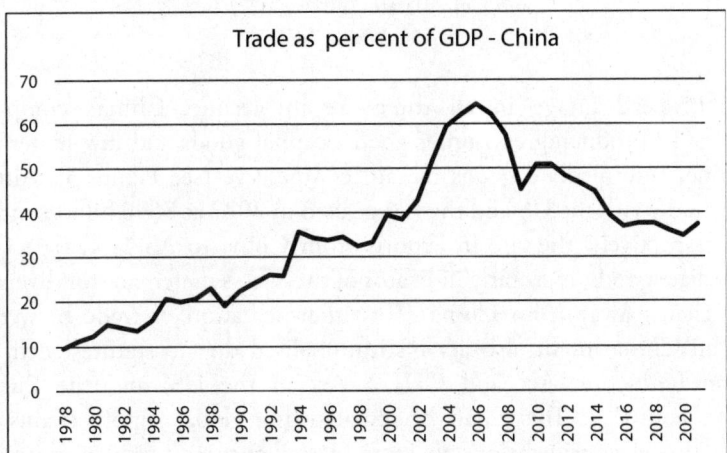

Figure 1: Trade (% of GDP) of China 1978–2020
Source: World Bank

Although China posted topline growth in exports and imports during the Zero-COVID period, a closer look at trade data reveals far-reaching and possibly irreversible changes in trade patterns. First, the contribution of global trade to China's GDP has been in long-term decline since it peaked in 2006 (see Figure 1). Second, the geographical composition of China's trade changed during the Zero-COVID period. ASEAN has emerged as China's largest trading partner, surpassing the European Union and the United States (see Figure 2).

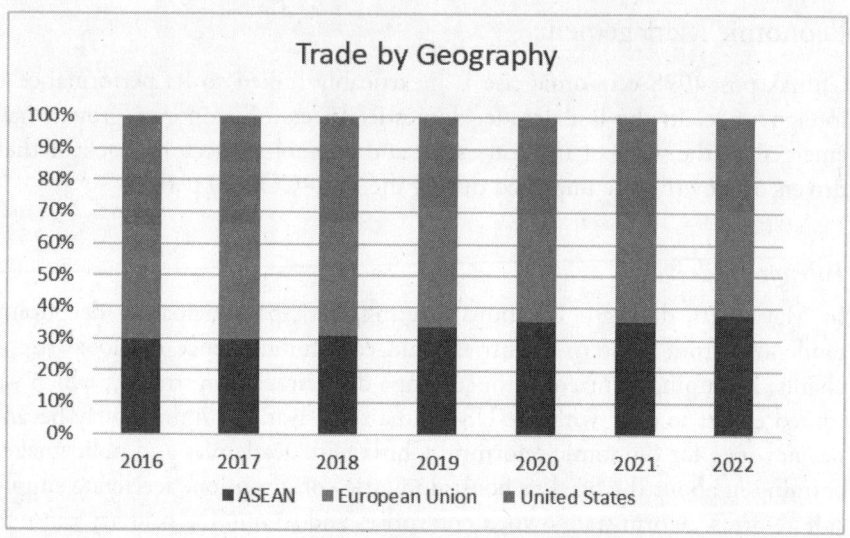

Figure 2: Region-wise Statistics Trade between China and ASEAN, European Union and United States (2016–2022)

Source: NBS, China

Competitive advantage in all three are in decline. China's comparative advantage in producing consumer goods, capital goods and raw materials are in decline. Intermediate goods remain competitive (see Figure 3). Although China's trade with the US and the EU peaked in 2022 at $690 billion and $850 billion respectively, the rise in exports from China to ASEAN, especially in intermediate goods, is an early indicator of the West's preference for diversifying supply chains away from China. This intermediation of trade between the West and China might also get institutionalised due to statutes such as the Inflation Reduction Act and CHIPS Act in the US, and the European Supply Chain Act. This trend of restructuring global supply chains based on geopolitical considerations to increase resilience and reduce centrality of China is likely to gain momentum during the post-war reconstruction period in Ukraine.

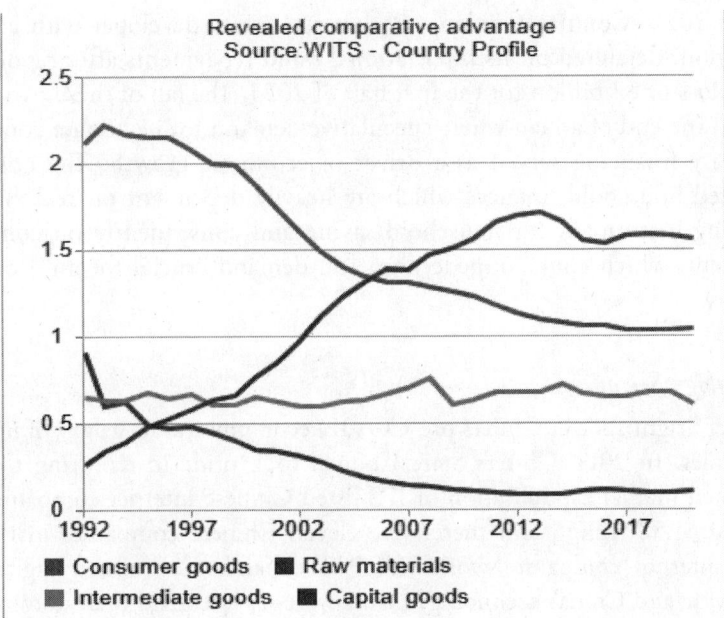

Figure 3: Revealed Comparative Advantage of China's Exports 1992–2020
Source: World Bank

Real Estate Sector

Starting from a low base in the early 2000s, China's real estate sector expanded to become a relatively large component of GDP with support from the triumvirate of local governments, private developers and banks. Local governments resorted to reckless levels of land sales to offset revenue loss caused by the centre-province tax reforms. Private developers capitalised on the demand caused by rapid urbanisation and growth in the savings of migrant workers. Banks that were used to obeying instructions of Party leaders on lending to State Owned Enterprises connived with local governments to finance real estate projects. By international standards, China's real estate sector contributes an exceptionally large part of the country's GDP. In 2021, the sector (including direct and indirect contributions) accounted for 22.5 per cent of China's GDP and 25.4 per cent, including imported content.[29]

Between early 2021 and mid-2022, evidence of overbuilding in Tier 3, Tier 4 and Tier 5 cities was evident as prices for residential housing dropped by nearly 20 per cent.[30] The crisis at Evergrande, one of China's largest builders, came to a boil in December 2021 when it defaulted on interest payments to bondholders.[31] When investors resorted to street protests, the regulators interjected in an unprecedented manner, later forcing the company to restructure.[32] Shortly after Evergrande filed for bankruptcy in the US in

August 2023, Country Garden, another real estate developer with a better reputation, defaulted on its international bond repayments after reporting a record loss of $7 billion for the first half of 2023. The fall of these two giants marked the end of an era where speculative demand for real estate combined with easy financing served as a driver of economic growth. The crisis has impacted household finances which are heavily dependent on real estate as a leading instrument for household saving and consequently on consumer sentiment, which could impede domestic demand crucial for an economic recovery.

Technology Sector

Another bright spot in China's pre-COVID economy was its galaxy of internet companies. In 2019, China's State Council took pride in reporting that the combined market capitalisation of 172 listed Chinese internet companies had touched $1.52 trillion and there were eleven Chinese companies in the top thirty internet companies worldwide.[33] The pandemic boosted digitisation worldwide and China's technology giants were set to extend their domination. Unfortunately, this opportunity to grow profits placed the internet industry in direct conflict with the Party – which was trying to encourage citizens to have more kids and boost domestic consumption that was essential for the success of the dual circulation policy.

Abolishment of the one-child policy in 2015 had failed to spur population growth.[34] Results of the Seventh National Census prompted the announcement of a three-child policy in May 2021.[35] In 2022, China registered a zero per cent growth in population for the first time in its history (see Figure 4). Policymakers realised that expenditure on education was rising in tandem with the proliferation of online education (edtech) companies that had found a booming market among middle-class parents during the pandemic. This presented a perfect opportunity for the Party to rein in the 'disorderly expansion of capital' and cure the 'stubborn malady' which the tutoring industry had become. Xi Jinping gave a prominent position to the excesses of the technology industry during the Two Sessions in March 2021. With this, the series of regulatory measures, that began with the cancellation of the Ant Group's initial public offering (IPO) in November 2020 as a purported retaliation against Jack Ma, was shaped into a wider crusade against the entire industry.[36] Several ministries joined forces in unleashing a barrage of curtailment measures including a ban on online tutoring, time limits on online gaming and a curb on overseas listings.[37]

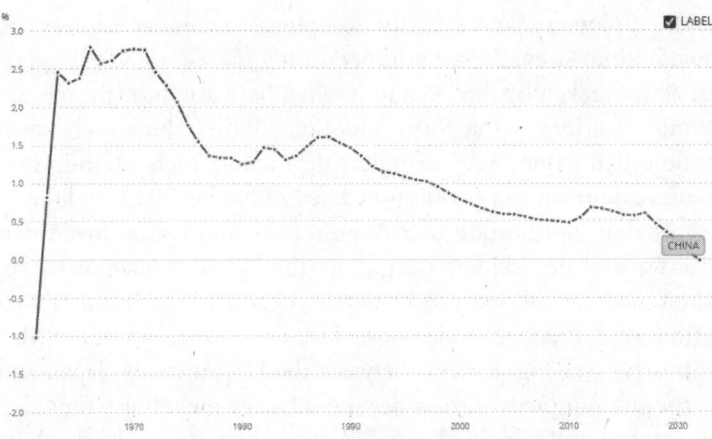

Figure 4: China's Annual Population Growth Rate (1960–2022)
Source: World Bank

The cumulative impact of growing distrust in China's dominance of global supply chains, a subdued real estate sector and a clampdown against the technology sector will undoubtedly translate to a lower GDP growth rate. China is yet to articulate a sound strategy to replace these growth drivers. Li Keqiang's parting work report presented during the Two Sessions in March 2023 focused more on 2022 than the future. With Xi's new team of economic advisors – Premier Li Qiang, along with Vice Premiers Ding Xuexiang and He Lifeng – reflecting loyalty more than experience, there is little hope for bold economic reforms to undo the damage caused by the Zero-COVID policy. A number of legacy systemic issues such as an ageing population, declining productivity, accumulated debt, excessive weightage of the real estate sector in the economy, over-reliance on exports and investment, low domestic consumption and underdeveloped financial markets will make policymaking more complex. Finally, policy missteps under Xi – characterised by his statist preferences and growing interference of the Party in the economy and corporate affairs – will offer little elbow room for bold decisions.

External Environment

During China's self-imposed isolation under Zero-COVID policy, decoupling tendencies that first took root in the form of economic sanctions under the US President Donald Trump crossed over firmly into geopolitics. Despite expectations that tensions will ease under President Joe Biden, there was bipartisan consensus in Washington behind extending the US–China rivalry into areas beyond trade. Buoyed by America's resolve to project power in the

Indo-Pacific, diplomatic and security groupings to combat China's influence have grown both in strength and number during the Zero-COVID period.

Several actions taken by the US and its allies have also brought the construct of 'economic security' to the fore. Adoption of the Chips and Science Act and Inflation Reduction Act, secondary legislation such as the Commerce Department's export control notification dated 7 October 2022, and the Treasury Department's draft notification of 9 August 2023 on overseas investment have triggered a wave of de-risking strategies by the US allies such as the EU and Japan. The Quadrilateral Security Dialogue (Quad) is one illustration of such coordination. After President Biden hosted the first virtual summit in May 2021, regular ministry-level engagements between the US, Australia, Japan and India have kept the grouping active on a wide range of issues including national security, pandemic control and supply chains.[38] A more focused grouping on military capabilities is the AUKUS – comprising the US, the UK and Australia – which is aimed at equipping Australia with nuclear submarines and other technologies.[39] Even a pre-COVID grouping such as the G7 was refashioned in 2021, when Boris Johnson invited leaders of India, South Korea, South Africa and Australia to join.[40] In contrast, despite recent expansion of the BRICS grouping, China's isolation appears to be growing.[41]

China responded by doubling down on efforts to extend the Comprehensive National Security doctrine (first articulated by Xi in 2014) into sixteen arenas.[42] This 'securitisation of everything' approach is another legacy of the Zero-COVID period that will weigh down China's diplomatic efforts in the West. The Ukraine war and China's proximity to Russia has further contributed to its isolation. China's multiple adjustments of its policy towards the war make it clear that its overarching objective remains maintaining and maximising CPC's power at home, which brings it in direct confrontation with Western democracies.[43]

When the US announced a sweeping set of export controls on 7 October 2022, to prohibit sale of semiconductor chips manufactured anywhere in the world using American tools or technology, it was clear that there was global consensus on the need to restrain China – from a national security viewpoint. In response, China has managed to hold naval exercises with South Africa and Russia for the second time since 2019, just days before the first anniversary of the Ukraine war.[44] China also scored a small victory by brokering a rapprochement between Iran and Saudi Arabia.[45] However, the sustainability of such diplomatic wins is doubtful in the face of tangible Western commitments such as America's $2 trillion budget backing the Inflation Reduction Act, CHIPS and Science Act and Bipartisan Infrastructure Law (BIL); Germany's commitment to increase defence spending by $100 billion as part of its Zeitenwende policy; NATO's expansion to include Finland and Japan's largest year-on-year defence budget increase of 26 per cent since 1952.

The Belt and Road Initiative, Xi's flagship initiative with overlapping foreign policy and economic objectives, has also suffered setbacks during the Zero-COVID period. The debt crisis in Sri Lanka and Pakistan have highlighted the inherent risks of a lending mechanism that operates on political whims rather than transparent risk measurement criteria. China's reputation in the West also suffered due to its mishandling of the early phase of the outbreak of COVID-19 and its stonewalling of any objective investigation into the origin of the pandemic. High-level participation at the third edition of the Belt and Road Forum hit a new low in 2023, when only twenty-three heads of state or government participated. The notable decline in European participation underlined the widening chasm between China and the West.[46]

Implications for India

The relationship between India and China deteriorated significantly during the Zero-COVID period. It took a catastrophic hit when troops from both countries clashed in the Galwan Valley during the first few months of the pandemic.[47] In retaliation, India, which had already implemented a FDI screening mechanism[48] to deter opportunistic Chinese investments, extended the economic war by banning more than 300 internet applications with links to China.[49] It became the first country to ban Tiktok – which then caught on as a trend in several countries.[50] It also imposed curbs on participation of Chinese companies in public procurement.[51] While China protested these steps vehemently, it soon became clear that this was the beginning of a larger global backlash against China so there were no specific countermeasures taken.

Disruptions caused to global supply chains by the continuation of the Zero-COVID policy due to political factors rather than public health reasons angered the global business community. Zero-COVID policy extracted a heavy toll when China's long-held dominance as a manufacturing destination became a source of risk. India's positioning as a low-cost manufacturing destination made it a natural alternative for global corporations seeking to diversify their supply chains away from China. Vietnam and other ASEAN countries had a head-start in this race. India unveiled an ambitious Productivity-Linked Incentive (PLI) scheme to entice foreign investors with the potential size of its domestic market. There is only one glitch – India's trade dependency on China.

Trade between India and China has expanded throughout the Zero-COVID period. India's bilateral trade deficit with China crossed the $100 billion mark for the first time in 2022.[52] It was earlier believed that growth in Chinese investments could help reduce trade dependency on China due to localisation, but it did not materialise. India has shortlisted 102 items (at the eight-digit

Harmonised System Code level) where expansion of domestic capacity can reduce its import bill.[53] China has a share of more than 50 per cent in fourteen of these items, with a 38.62 per cent increase in the value of imports from 2017–18 to 2021–22.[54] Reducing dependency on China for products for which domestic capacity and alternate sources both don't exist will be India's biggest challenge in preventing weaponisation of trade ties by China.

In foreign policy, India has been quick to capitalise on anti-China sentiments during the Zero-COVID period but has stopped short of explicitly criticising Russia over the Ukraine war. America's tilt towards the Indo-Pacific will certainly benefit India. While India has made headway with a few European countries during the pandemic, it remains to be seen whether Europe's economic dependency on China will soften its political stand – especially after a resolution is found to the Ukraine war.

Conclusion

The pandemic accelerated several trends which were already visible in China, including its inward turn, strong surveillance by the Party-State, slowdown of the economy and selective de-risking vis-à-vis the West to reduce vulnerabilities. The situation has been compounded by the sharp deterioration in relations with the US-led West and the geopolitical headwinds. The sudden abandonment of the Zero-COVID policy has demonstrated that the lofty promise of Common Prosperity cannot be a substitute for actual economic growth. Sources of economic growth that provided legitimacy to the Party at home and diplomatic power abroad have been stunted. Efforts of the West to reduce trade dependency on China will make other countries, which seek to position themselves as alternate manufacturing destinations, more dependent on China. This might inadvertently give China more bargaining power with countries in Southeast Asia.

The list of structural challenges facing China has grown during the Zero-COVID period and the Party is yet to formulate concrete solutions. The communique issued at the second plenum in March 2023 highlights the need for reform of both Party and state institutions. It also refers to a five-sphere integrated plan (a blanket reference to coordinated progress in the economic, political, cultural, social and environmental fields) and the four-pronged comprehensive strategy (which dates back to Xi's formulation in 2014). With the resolution of the Ukraine war and normalisation of the US–China ties both looking distant, India will need to walk a tightrope as it capitalises on opportunities that have arisen due to setbacks suffered by China, even as it reduces its own dependency on the nation.

Notes

1. 'In Unprecedented Move, China Locks Down Megacity to Curb Virus Spread', Xinhuanet, 23 January 2020, http://www.xinhuanet.com/english/2020-01/23/c_138729430.htm.
2. Selina Rajan, Jonathan Cylus and Martin McKee, 'Successful Find-Test-Trace-Isolate-Support Systems: How to Win at Snakes and Ladders', *Eurohealth* 26, no. 2 (2020), https://apps.who.int/iris/bitstream/handle/10665/336292/Eurohealth-26-2-34-39-eng.pdf.
3. 'China Focus: COVID-19 Response Further Optimized with 10 New Measures', Xinhuanet, 7 December 2022, https://english.news.cn/20221207/ca014c043bf24728b8dcbc0198565fdf/c.html
4. Neils Graham, 'The Numbers That Drove China's Zero-COVID Policy', Atlantic council, 8 December 2022, https://www.atlanticcouncil.org/blogs/econographics/the-numbers-that-drove-chinas-zero-COVID-policy/.
5. The World Bank in China, World Bank, 11 April 2023, https://www.worldbank.org/en/country/china/overview#1.
6. Celia Hatton, 'China's Xi Jinping: What has He Achieved in His First Year?', BBC News, 9 March 2014, https://www.bbc.com/news/world-asia-china-26463983.
7. Laura He, 'China's economy is "in deep trouble" as Xi Heads for Next Decade in Power', CNN Business, 15 October 2022, https://edition.cnn.com/2022/10/14/economy/china-party-congress-economy-trouble-xi-intl-hnk/index.html.
8. Minxin Pei, 'Xi Jinping Can Blame His Centralisation of Power for a Rotten 2019 – and Maybe an Even Worse 2020', *South China Morning Post*, 17 December 2019, https://www.scmp.com/comment/opinion/article/3042392/xi-jinping-can-blame-his-centralisation-power-rotten-2019-and-maybe.
9. Xi Jinping, 'Speech at the Meeting of the Standing Committee of the Political Bureau of the Central Committee to Study the Response to the Novel Coronavirus Pneumonia Epidemic', QS Theory, 15 February 2020, http://www.qstheory.cn/dukan/qs/2020-02/15/c_1125572832.htm.
10. White Paper: 'Xu Lin Introduces China's Response to COVID-19', State Council of Information Office, PRC, 7 June 2020, http://english.scio.gov.cn/aboutscio/2020-06/07/content_76228596.htm.
11. Mattew Walsh, 'Premier Promises Government Support for Street Vendors', Caixin Global, 2 June 2020, https://www.caixinglobal.com/2020-06-02/premier-promises-government-support-for-street-vendors-101562239.html.
12. Li Yuan, 'China's Street Vendor Push Ignites a Debate: How Rich Is It?', *The New York Times*, 11 June 2020, https://www.nytimes.com/2020/06/11/business/china-street-vendors-stall-economy.html.
13. 'Reactions to Death of Chinese Ex-Premier Li Keqiang', Reuters, 27 October 2023, https://www.reuters.com/world/china/reactions-death-chinese-ex-premier-li-keqiang-2023-10-27/
14. 'China's Central Economic Work Conference Outlines 8 Key Missions for 2021', China Banking News, 21 December 2020, https://www.chinabankingnews.

com/2020/12/21/chinas-central-economic-work-conference-outlines-8-key-missions-for-2021/

15. Yew Lun Tian, 'Xi clinches third term as China's president amid host of challenges', Reuters, 10 March 2023, https://www.reuters.com/world/china/chinas-parliament-elects-xi-jinping-chinas-president-2023-03-10/

16. Nectar Gan, 'Zero-COVID was Supposed to Prove China's Supremacy. How Did It All Go So Wrong for Xi Jinping?', CNN, 28 December 2022, https://edition.cnn.com/2022/12/27/china/china-2022-zero-COVID-intl-hnk-mic/index.html.

17. Evelyn Cheng, 'China's Economic Data Disappoint in April as COVID Controls Weigh', CNBC, 15 May 2022, https://www.cnbc.com/2022/05/16/china-economy-COVID-lockdowns-weigh-on-retail-industrial-production-data.html.

18. Sarah Cook, 'China's Censors Aim to Contain Dissent During Harsh COVID-19 Lockdowns', *The Diplomat*, 18 May 2022, https://thediplomat.com/2022/05/chinas-censors-aim-to-contain-dissent-during-harsh-COVID-19-lockdowns/

19. Joe McDonalds, Associated Press, 'Foxconn Apologizes for Pay Dispute that Sparked Factory Protests in China', PBS, 24 November 2022, https://www.pbs.org/newshour/world/foxconn-apologizes-for-pay-dispute-that-sparked-factory-protests-in-china.

20. 'Apple Supplier Foxconn's Founder Pushed China to Ease COVID Curbs – WSJ', Reuters, 9 December 2022, https://www.reuters.com/world/china/apple-supplier-foxconn-pushed-china-ease-COVID-curbs-wsj-2022-12-08/.

21. Yew Lun Tian, 'Protests Erupt in Xinjiang and Beijing After Deadly Fire', Reuters, 26 November 2022, https://www.reuters.com/world/china/huge-COVID-protests-erupt-chinas-xinjiang-after-deadly-fire-2022-11-26/.

22. Matt Murphy, 'China's Protests: Blank Paper Becomes the Symbol of Rare Demonstrations', BBC News, 28 November 2022, https://www.bbc.com/news/world-asia-china-63778871.

23. 'Xi Jinping Presides over Meeting of Standing Committee of Political Bureau of CPC Central Committee on COVID-19 Prevention and Control', Xinhua, 11 November 2022, https://english.www.gov.cn/news/topnews/202211/11/content_WS636e27a2c6d0a757729e2e60.html.

24. Zhuoran Li, 'How Beijing Accidentally Ended the Zero COVID Policy', *The Diplomat*, 7 January 2023, https://thediplomat.com/2023/01/how-beijing-accidentally-ended-the-zero-COVID-policy/.

25. 'China's Political-Economy, Foreign and Security Policy: 2023', Asia Society, 17 January 2023, https://asiasociety.org/policy-institute/chinas-political-economy-foreign-and-security-policy-2023.

26. Kevin Yao and Ellen Zhang, 'China's 2022 Economic Growth One of the Worst on Record, Post-Pandemic Policy Faces Test', Reuters, 17 January 2023, https://www.reuters.com/world/china/chinas-economy-slows-sharply-q4-2022-growth-one-worst-record-2023-01-17/.

27. Roland Rajah, Alyssa Leng, 'Revising Down the Rise of China', Lowy Institute, 14 March 2022, https://www.lowyinstitute.org/publications/revising-down-rise-china.

28. Frank Tang, 'Explainer: What is China's Dual Circulation Economic Strategy and Why Is It Important?', *South China Morning Post*, 19 November 2020,

https://www.scmp.com/economy/china-economy/article/3110184/what-chinas-dual-circulation-economic-strategy-and-why-it.

29 Kenneth S. Rogoff and Yuanchen Yang, 'A Tale of Tier 3 Cities', Working Paper, National Bureau of Economic Research, Massachusetts, US, September 2022, https://www.nber.org/system/files/working_papers/w30519/w30519.pdf.

30 'Tier 3 Cities: A Hotbed of Trouble in China's Property Sector?', Standford Center on China's Economy and Institutions, Stanford University, 15 December 2022, https://sccei.fsi.stanford.edu/china-briefs/tier-3-cities-hotbed-trouble-chinas-property-sector.

31 'Timeline: Snowballing crisis at Evergrande, world's most indebted developer', Channel News Asia, 29 July 2022, https://www.channelnewsasia.com/business/timeline-snowballing-crisis-evergrande-worlds-most-indebted-developer-2845751.

32 Clare Jim and Xie Yu, 'China Evergrande Races Court Deadline on Debt Restructuring Terms – Sources', Reuters, 9 March 2023, https://www.reuters.com/world/china/china-evergrande-races-court-deadline-debt-restructuring-terms-sources-2023-03-09/.

33 The State Council, PRC, Press release: 'Listed Chinese Internet Companies See Market Capitalization Surge in Q1', Xinhua, 14 April 2019, https://english.www.gov.cn/news/top_news/2019/04/14/content_281476608153188.htm.

34 David McKenzie, China's One-Child Policy Ends – But Is It Too Little, Too Late?', CNN, 29 October 2015, https://www.cnn.com/2015/10/29/china/china-one-child-policy-ends-mckenzie/index.html.

35 'China to Support Couples Having Third Child', Xinhua, 31 May 2021, http://www.xinhuanet.com/english/2021-05/31/c_139980774.htm.

36 Raymond Zhong, 'In Halting Ant's I.P.O., China Sends a Warning to Business', *The New York Times*, 24 December 2020, https://www.nytimes.com/2020/11/06/technology/china-ant-group-ipo.html.

37 'China's Big Tech Crackdown: A Complete Timeline', The China Project, 2 August 2021, https://thechinaproject.com/big-tech-crackdown-timeline/.

38 'Quad Joint Leaders' Statement', The White House, 24 May 2022, https://www.whitehouse.gov/briefing-room/statements-releases/2022/05/24/quad-joint-leaders-statement/.

39 'FACT SHEET: Trilateral Australia-UK-US Partnership on Nuclear-Powered Submarines', The White House, 13 March 2023, https://www.whitehouse.gov/briefing-room/statements-releases/2023/03/13/fact-sheet-trilateral-australia-uk-us-partnership-on-nuclear-powered-submarines/.

40 'The UK Hosted the G7 Summit As Part of Its 2021 G7 Presidency', Government of UK, https://www.gov.uk/government/topical-events/g7-uk-2021.

41 Heribert Dieter, 'First Summit of the Anti-China Coalition', *SWP Comment*, 2021, C 36, 10 June 2021. doi:10.18449/2021C36, https://www.swp-berlin.org/en/publication/first-summit-of-the-anti-china-coalition.

42 Kajata Drinhausen and Helena Legarda, '"Comprehensive National Security" Unleashed: How Xi's Approach Shapes China's Policies at Home and Abroad', MERICS, 15 September 2022, https://www.merics.org/en/report/comprehensive-national-security-unleashed-how-xis-approach-shapes-chinas-policies-home-and-

43 Guoguang Wu, 'Interpreting Xi Jinping's Shifting Strategy on the Russia–Ukraine War', 11 October 2023, https://asiasociety.org/policy-institute/interpreting-xi-jinpings-shifting-strategy-russia-ukraine-war.

44 Ann M. Simmons, 'Russia, China to Hold Joint Naval Drills as Moscow and Belarus Vow to Cement Ties', *The Wall Street Journal*, 19 December 2022, https://www.wsj.com/articles/russia-and-china-to-hold-joint-naval-drills-11671457894?mod=article_inline.

45 Parisa Hafezi, Nayera Abdallah and Aziz El Yaakoubi, 'Iran and Saudi Arabia Agree to Resume Ties in Talks Brokered by China', Reuters, 10 March 2023, https://www.reuters.com/world/middle-east/iran-saudi-arabia-agree-resume-ties-re-open-embassies-iranian-state-media-2023-03-10/.

46 Shannon Tiezzi, 'Which World Leaders Came to China's 3rd Belt and Road Forum?', *The Diplomat*, 18 October 2023, https://thediplomat.com/2023/10/which-world-leaders-came-to-chinas-3rd-belt-and-road-forum/.

47 Simon Scarr and Sanjeev Miglani, 'Satellite Images Suggest Chinese activity at India's Himalayan Border before Clash', Reuters, 19 June 2020, https://www.reuters.com/graphics/INDIA-CHINA/BATTLE/yxmvjkzxwpr/.

48 Press Note no. 3 (2020 Series): 'Review of Foreign Direct Investment (FDI) Policy for Curbing Opportunistic Takeovers/Acquisitions of Indian Companies Due to the Current COVID-19 Pandemic', Department for Promotion of Industry and Internal Trade, Ministry of Commerce & Industry, Government of India, 17 April 2020, https://dpiit.gov.in/sites/default/files/pn3_2020.pdf.

49 Amit Mukherjee, 'Govt Move to Ban over 230 Apps Linked to China "on Immediate Priority Basis"', *The New Indian Express*, 5 February 2023, https://www.newindianexpress.com/business/2023/feb/05/govt-move-to-ban-over-230-apps-linked-to-china-on-immediate-priority-basis-2544612.html.

50 Amanda Aronczyk, 'A Look at the Fallout of TikTok Ban in India', NPR, 15 January 2021, https://www.npr.org/2021/01/15/957371287/a-look-at-the-fallout-of-tiktok-ban-in-india.

51 Public Procurement Division, Ministry of Finance vide OM No. 6/18/2019-PPD, 23 July 2020, https://wbxpress.com/files/2021/03/OM-6.pdf.

52 'India–China Trade Climbs to USD 135.98 Billion in 2022, Trade Deficit Crosses USD 100 Billion for the First Time', *Economic Times*, 13 January 2023, https://economictimes.indiatimes.com/news/economy/foreign-trade/india-china-trade-climbs-to-usd-135-98-billion-in-2022-trade-deficit-crosses-usd-100-billion-for-the-first-time/articleshow/96969775.cms.

53 Department of Commerce: Economic Division (Epl-1), 'Analysis of Import Items at HS 8 Digit Level for Domestic Production Opportunity', 2022, p. 5, https://commerce.gov.in/wp-content/uploads/2022/04/Domestic-production-opportunity-Public-document_disseminated.pdf.

54 Based on five years' data.

15

COVID-19 and Public Health Crisis in China
Central and Local Responses
Madhurima Nundy

In the advent of COVID-19, the capacities and resilience of public health systems and governments to respond to the crisis have been tested. There have been a range of responses by governments to meet the demands on health services and bridge gaps during the course of the pandemic. While it was important that countries build their response systems from the local to the central level to protect its population, it was equally important that cooperation at global and regional levels be fostered. The COVID-19 experience reinforces the fact of human lives being intricately connected globally, and that organisation of health services and the way they have evolved is as deeply political as it is linked to the social, economic, environmental, demographic and epidemiological context.

I critically look at China's response to the crisis with the caveat that there was no perfect response to mitigate the impact of COVID-19 globally. Public health responses were determined by science, technology, capacities of health services, economic wherewithal and politics. I do not discuss why the pandemic started in the first place because there are debates on its origins – one end of the spectrum puts the blame solely on China and on the other end are those stating the complexity of emerging diseases that are linked to structural entanglements of state, science and technology and global capitalism. But there is consensus on the larger context of environmental degradation, increase in human–wildlife interface and unplanned urbanisation that leads to outbreaks of new infections with pandemic potential. The fact that China was viewed as the place where COVID-19 originated brought every action and response of the Communist Party of China (CPC) under constant scrutiny. At the national level, China's initial response during the onset of the outbreak till the time it reached pandemic proportions, and later the Zero-COVID policy, drew considerable criticism globally. China's response to cooperation at the global level also elicited debates between what entailed nationalism and what entailed diplomacy. China has had a history of epidemics in the past and there is much that is expected from it when it comes to pandemic preparedness, response and cooperation at the regional and global level in times of public health crisis.

These insights have implications for public health, especially future epidemics, globally. Much of the data on China for the COVID-19 years is opaque; whatever information we get is from Western sources. But what can be said with conviction is that China has undergone consistent health service reforms over the last two decades to address inequities in access to health services – addressing both demand and supply concerns. While they have made significant progress, COVID-19 brought forth the entrenched path dependencies due to resistance to change, which stems from systemic and political challenges.

In this chapter, I look at the responses and actions of the CPC to COVID-19 in different stages of the pandemic in the last three years. I attempt to analyse these responses at all the stages – which include the onset of the pandemic from late 2019, the Zero-COVID policy that lasted for almost three years and the opening up in December 2022 – what these responses meant and why they were taken in their context and their implications from a public health perspective.

Early Stages of the Pandemic

After China's weak response to severe acute respiratory syndrome (SARS) in 2003, the reconstitution of a public health emergency response system was on the agenda of the Chinese government. Post SARS, China has been grappling with several infectious diseases and outbreaks that have been effectively contained by reducing mortalities – these have been linked to influenza viruses like H1N1 (swine flu), dengue, hepatitis, HIV/AIDS and tuberculosis. China invested in rebuilding its epidemic surveillance and response stations, and initiated several public health and medical reforms to strengthen health services that had dismantled post the economic reforms of the 1980s. These outcomes are visible in improved health infrastructure, increasing access to health services and better health outcomes, but at the same time there are challenges and contradictions in the way the health services have evolved. Some of these include: the commercial nature of public institutions, weak primary-level services, greater burden and overdependence on hospitals, regional inequities and high out-of-pocket expenditure. Moreover, low levels of accountability and transparency at the level of the local government and the dynamics between the centre and local governments have added to the existing challenges.

The virus that originated in the Chinese province of Wuhan in late 2019 was declared a public health emergency of international concern by 30 January 2020 and a pandemic by 12 March 2020 by the World Health Organization (WHO). There was enough chaos and confusion in the initial months. There were lapses in reporting from Wuhan on several counts – the Chinese authorities delayed the public announcement of the outbreak and the sharing of information with the WHO; they downplayed the severity of the disease and the risk of human-to-human transmission and there was a delay in implementing timely and effective containment measures, such as lockdowns, travel restrictions and contact tracing. They silenced the whistleblowers who tried to warn the world about the new virus and accused them of spreading false rumours.

The case of Dr Li Wenliang, an ophthalmologist who raised an alarm on social media about the nature and intensity of the spread in early January, was reprimanded by the government and there were attempts to censor him on the grounds of disturbing social order. His death from COVID-19 created a furore not only in the community but globally with *The New York Times* investigating details leading to his death.[1] The CPC also lacked transparency and accountability in its response and communication with the public and the international community. The nature of centre–province dynamics led to criticisms. In most circumstances, the local government officials hesitate to communicate directly with the centre and, without the permission of the centre, they are unable to give out information unless they receive a green signal. A similar scenario played out during this time and in this case the delay by even a few days was critical.

In the early stages, the reporting of newer infections to the Centre for Disease Control (CDC) in China was delayed. Once the cases started rising, limited hospital capacities and shortage of medical staff became apparent. The hospitals were slow in connecting with the local authorities and disease control and prevention systems. This led to delays in reporting as well as in accurate counting of cases and deaths. These initial responses would have been critical in halting or mitigating the spread of the virus.[2] But once the central government responded, things started moving as the centre–local collaboration was put into action. Significant measures and protocols like lockdown, quarantines and travel restrictions were initiated only on 23 January 2020 when the crisis had already escalated. This was akin to 'closing the stable doors after the horses had bolted' at a time when there was maximum mobility due to the onset of the Chinese New Year celebrations. By now, cases had started emerging in the US, Japan, South Korea, Thailand and Italy that faced the initial brunt and devastating effects of the virus. Apart from the usual administrative and communication delays, this slow response by China could also be attributed to low investments in preventive and promotive public health services, fragmented systems of governance that lacked coordination and weak local capacities that were still not geared towards outbreak response and management, despite past experiences. All this made China's relationship with the world tenuous, even though the WHO lauded them for their cooperation. The information coming from China lacked transparency and enquiries related to the origins of the virus were met with contempt. The world found it difficult to trust China's reported numbers of infections and deaths. Some leaked documents from the Hubei Provincial Centre for Disease Control and Prevention revealed that Chinese officials were giving the world more optimistic data. The documents also revealed that a history of underfunding, understaffing, poor morale and bureaucratic models of governance hampered China's early warning system.[3]

Initially, Xi Jinping was missing but, once the severity of the outbreak was recognised by the CPC, the centre and Wuhan province acted to contain the spread. The government implemented strict containment measures in Wuhan, the epicentre of the outbreak. The entire city and surrounding areas were locked down and quarantined from the rest of China with sealed borders. Public health measures within Wuhan included establishing makeshift hospitals, mobilising over 40,000 human resources from provinces all across to move to Wuhan and mass testing was conducted on all residents. In other cities too mobility was restricted, along with mass testing. At the national level, the production of masks, testing kits and research on sequencing the genome of the new virus was also underway. At the global level, the CPC shared data of the virus with the WHO and other countries, which helped in understanding the nature of the virus and contributed to early countermeasures like development of vaccines, preventive measures and treatments.

During the period of lockdown in Wuhan that lasted for seventy-six days (23 January to 8 April 2020), the city came to a standstill with only frontline workers on a war foot to deliver services to citizens. Ordinary citizens who complained about the lapses were checked by the Party and blocked from communicating further. This is observed in the banning of *Wuhan Diary* by Fang Fang early on. Fang Fang was maintaining an online diary detailing the challenges faced by ordinary people on a day-to-day basis throughout the Wuhan lockdown.[4]

Following the initial response, once the cases came down, China reopened again in April, but by this time the cases around the world were increasing. While China opened domestic travel with strict vigilance, it turned around and sealed its borders for the rest of the world as new infections were now entering from beyond its border. Meanwhile, the Chinese government collaborated with other countries and international organisations to control the spread of the virus, including sharing information and expertise. To improve its image, China had also started sending out medical kits, masks and protective suits, medical supplies and equipment and medical teams to other countries. While China was at the forefront of providing aid to countries, it was criticised for its nationalist propaganda. The early success of containing the spread of the virus in Wuhan gave it the confidence to continue with what came to be known as the 'Zero-COVID policy', by sealing its borders to the world and enforcing strict local lockdowns across China (mostly cities) as and when cases would emerge.

Zero-COVID Policy and Its Implications

Zero-COVID is a public health strategy that stresses the use of contact monitoring, border restrictions, mass screening and periodic lockdowns to effectively shut down all avenues for COVID-19 to propagate. It is an elimination technique, not a mitigation strategy. The goal is to reduce active cases to zero as much as possible. There are several countries that experimented with Zero-COVID strategy, and most of these countries had the economic wherewithal that was important to sustain this strategy for a long period of time, including Singapore, New Zealand, Australia and China. These countries did very well in the initial phases. Since there was no perfect response to mitigating COVID-19, this strategy also seemed logical in order to buy time for vaccines to be made available, strengthen health services and then gradually open up. But enforcing Zero-COVID can induce maximum disruption to the economy, society and lives. It also involves tremendous costs as there is a large dependency on human resources (especially frontline workers) and other facilities to sustain this strategy. Most of the countries who started with Zero-COVID policy lifted the policy and opened up their economies by early 2021. There was a growing consensus globally by then that one had to learn to live with the virus but strategies to mitigate the spread of the virus had to continue actively. This was also the time when vaccines had been rolled out worldwide. But China continued with its Zero-COVID policy for three full years, starting in early 2020, through 2021 and 2022.

While the world went through the devastating second wave in mid-2021, the impact on China, as reported, seemed low. They attributed it to their governance, strict Zero-COVID policy and administration of the vaccine. They took a moral high ground by stating that every human life was important to China unlike the other democratic countries who were allowing people to die by not enforcing lockdowns. China also had its homegrown vaccines whose efficacy ranged from 51 to 79 per cent.[5] Almost 86 per cent of the population was vaccinated by early 2022. China also distributed these vaccines to African countries and refused to import any of the other vaccines with greater efficacy for its own population – techno-nationalism at play with Beijing resisting purchase of foreign vaccines. The CPC used the vaccine as a weapon for nationalism and diplomacy. China till date has approved seven homegrown vaccines, with the traditional inactivated vaccines being made available earlier. China's vaccines accounted for almost half of the 7.3 billion COVID-19 vaccine doses delivered globally by October 2021.[6] The efficacy of Chinese vaccines and the long-term protection they offer have been questioned by experts, even though the WHO had given its approval.

As the world seemed to be getting back to some normalcy and countries lifted travel restrictions gradually, while emphasising on mitigation strategies, China was the only country unwilling to forgo its Zero-COVID policy. China lauded its governance ('authoritarian' in the Western eyes) since it wished to convey that it was the main reason the nation was able to minimise and eliminate infections as opposed to the response by other countries, especially the Western ones. China's ability to control and limit the outbreak after initial missteps and its V-shaped economic recovery (unlike other major economies) was touted as evidence of systemic superiority, but it also created a narrative trap which made exit from Zero-COVID more difficult.[7]

Although lockdown as an emergency response was used in varying intensities across the world, China implemented it relatively aggressively. There were billions spent on digital tracking, mass testing and maintaining an army of cadres – policemen, health workers and delivery men – for monitoring, surveillance and state propaganda. This policy impasse rolled into the next crisis when Shanghai and other eastern cities started reporting cases of COVID-19 in February 2022. They went on to conduct mass testing and contact tracing, and imposed strict quarantine measures. Shanghai, a city of 25 million, went through a phased lockdown around end of March 2022, when cases were already rising, and was partially free from total imprisonment only by end of May. Massive human resources were needed to implement a Zero-COVID policy. The People's Liberation Army (PLA) dispatched more than 2,000 medical personnel to Shanghai. About 38,000 healthcare workers from provinces such as Jiangsu, Zhejiang and the capital Beijing were dispatched to Shanghai.[8] This shows that to manage a city like Shanghai one required a massive number of workforce at different levels – for testing, treatment, delivery, social assistance and the rest.

Zero-COVID policy came with high costs of sustenance despite China's capacities. Government medical and health spending on the national and local levels totalled ¥730.3 billion ($110 billion) for the first four months of 2022, up 7.5 per cent from 2021 and 22 per cent from 2019.[9] Beijing's decision to continue with the Zero-COVID strategy was criticised worldwide during this time. This was not only affecting the lives of ordinary Chinese people and the economy, but also global supply chains linked to the Chinese economy. Shanghai is a city where over 30 per cent of the population is over sixty years old. There were several deaths reported during this time, especially among the older population, a significant proportion of whom still remained unvaccinated and confined to homes and care homes and, therefore, left vulnerable.[10] The lockdown also witnessed loss of income, difficulty in accessing basic amenities like food and regular healthcare services. There were instances of solidarity and community support through local neighbourhood committees but largely people coped in isolation as with all cities that underwent lockdown in other countries before this. Everyone wondered when and what would be the exit strategy that China would adopt because, at this point, a Zero-COVID policy seemed exaggerated from a public health and epidemiological perspective. While at one end, the Shanghai lockdown was assumed to be unnecessary, the everyday participation of the residents in this scenario helped sustain the lockdown for a long duration, akin to a ritual by participants who are used to performing it. At the same time, there was discontentment expressed on social media in various forms and there were polarised views on the same.[11] In all lockdowns, governance across cities at various points was heterogenous and dynamic. Old and new mechanisms were put to action. Traditional mechanisms like neighbourhood committees helped in implementing central policies with some degree of flexibility to address needs of the residents[12] and newer mechanisms like digital technologies were put to action for various purposes apart from surveillance.

While Xi consolidated his power in the 20th Party Congress held in October 2022, the world, especially Chinese citizens, waited to hear that there would be relaxation in COVID-19 restrictions but the leadership further reinforced the 'long' Zero-COVID policy that was to continue. There was difference in opinion regarding the policy within CPC. The increased internal tensions and anticipating further internal conflicts, CPC started easing restrictions from early November 2022. Following this, a series of events made the frustrations among citizens palpable. To mention some instances, these included delays and long lines when getting tested, deaths due to delays in seeking care and frustration – especially among the younger people – due to loss of income.

There were two events that precipitated large-scale protests that led to the almost abrupt and final withdrawal of the Zero-COVID policy. One was the imprisonment of Foxconn factory workers within the factory walls so as to keep them quarantined, which occurred on 22 November 2022 in Zhengzhou, Henan Province. The labour protests against this imprisonment turned violent. This was followed by a series of protests by citizens, especially students, across Beijing, Shanghai and beyond. The second event was the death of ten residents in Urumqi in a building that caught fire, and delays that ensued in evacuating the residents due to the intense lockdown on 24 November 2022. This was the turning point that intensified the protests across Chinese cities, mostly by young people demanding the government do away with draconian COVID-19 policies. Over the weekend after the Urumqi incident, protests spread rapidly across fifteen cities. The CPC started detaining protestors as demonstrations increased, but by 7 December it abruptly lifted many of the restrictions defined by the Zero-COVID policy. The complete restrictions were finally ended officially on 8 January 2023. While the mass protests might have been a trigger to lift the three-year policy, the Zero-COVID policy was simply becoming unsustainable for the economy and society. There was huge financial pressure on the local governments for the cost of implementing the policy. Even before Beijing announced easing of restrictions, some local government officials across China – fearing protests and not getting any clear instructions from the centre – had started easing the stringent rules. For instance, Guangzhou ended the citywide lockdown and mandatory mass COVID-19 tests on 1 December 2023.[13]

The removal of restrictions led to a surge of cases and deaths, especially of older people. Till date, China has reported approximately 100 million cases of COVID-19 and about 121,000 deaths due to COVID-19 in the last three years.[14] The number of deaths reported were less as the cause of death due to COVID-19 was restricted to only those who were directly linked to COVID-related pneumonia. The rest of the deaths, where the primary cause was a comorbidity which had aggravated due to COVID-19, were not reported as COVID-related deaths. There was also deliberate underreporting. Estimates of 'excess deaths' range from 1 to 1.8 million.

The major issue of the last upsurge of cases after some of the restrictions were lifted in December 2022 in China was that there was no well-thought-out exit strategy in a phased manner. The abrupt removal of restrictions was almost like a reaction to the protests. Hospitals were still unprepared to bear the load of cases, people were still not vaccinated with the third dose, especially those above eighty years of age, and the government had not communicated to its citizens in any proper manner what the exit or mitigating strategies would be. The three years of draconian policy had worn down people and many were probably no longer interested in adhering to any restrictions.

Implications for China and Lessons for the Future

Sustainability, equitability and ethicality of any policy is important and there are calculated risks to be taken, the trade-offs being measured in terms of human, social and economic costs. Policies also have to be dynamic, determined by changing behaviour of the virus, human adaptability to the virus, vaccine development and efficacy, capacities of states and so on. A Zero-COVID policy is the most prone to neglecting health disparities. At the same time, mitigation could also falter when it loses sight of overall population health. But in the long run, a Zero-COVID policy was unsustainable with heavy economic and social costs.

In China, COVID-19 made Xi's authoritarianism visible to the world. Many see that Xi's policy over the COVID-19 years had little to do with public health and more to wield and consolidate his own power. The CPC now takes the credit for leading China successfully through the COVID-19 years but, as with many countries, China's response to COVID-19 has not been responsive to the needs of the population but has been akin to using a whip to keep children in order in a classroom. This is clearly not a prudent public health response. At the same time, China's initial response, though delayed, was eventually effective in containing the virus, but the long-term Zero-COVID policy came at a great economic and societal cost and reinforced the surveillance state.

There is much that is expected of a nation as big as China, not only for its response to domestic challenges, but also its actions at the regional and global levels. China did respond to global calls for aid, but there needs to be more sustained collaborations in research and development and public health strategy for responding to future epidemics. Most countries who have the capacities to address such public health crises need to underplay nationalistic politics and work towards collaborative engagements to arrive at informed scientific responses – not just to pandemics, but to other public health challenges as well.

Notes

1. M. Xiao, I. Qian, T.W. Liu and C. Buckley, 'How a Chinese Doctor Who Warned of COVID-19 Spent His Final Days', *The New York Times*, 6 October 2022, https://www.nytimes.com/2022/10/06/world/asia/COVID-china-doctor-li-wenliang.html.
2. C. Xing and R. Zhang, 'COVID-19 in China: Responses, Challenges and Implications for the Health System', *Healthcare*, Issue 9, No. 82, 2021, https://doi.org/10.3390/healthcare9010082.
3. N.P. Walsh, 'The Wuhan Files', 1 December 2020, https://edition.cnn.com/2020/11/30/asia/wuhan-china-COVID-intl/index.html.
4. Fang Fang, a writer and Wuhan resident, was writing her diary online every night since the days leading to the lockdown. It was an eyewitness account of the unfolding of the events, challenges faced by ordinary citizens regarding lack of information and the harsh consequences of the lockdown. Fang Fang, *Wuhan Diary: Dispatches from a Quarantined City*, tr. Michael Berry (New York, US: HarperVia, 2020).
5. S. Mallapaty, 'China's COVID Vaccines Have Been Crucial – But Now Immunity Is Waning', *Nature* 598, no. 7881(2021): 398–399. doi: 10.1038/d41586-021-02796-w.
6. Ibid.
7. According to economists, while examining recessions and recoveries of economies, a V-shaped recovery involves a sharp rise back to a previous peak after a sharp decline in these metrics.
8. 'China Sends Military, Doctors to Shanghai to Test 26 Million Residents for COVID', Reuters, 4 April 2022, *Wion News,* https://www.wionews.com/world/china-sends-military-doctors-to-shanghai-to-test-26-million-residents-for-COVID-468219.
9. 'Xi's Infamous Zero-COVID Policy Takes Toll on Cash-Strapped Local Government', *Business Standard,* 9 June 2022, https://www.business-standard.

com/article/international/xi-s-infamous-zero-COVID-policy-takes-toll-on-cash-strapped-local-govt-122060900139_1.html.

10   'Xi's COVID Authoritarianism Meets Red Line at Vaccine Mandates', Bloomberg, 12 July 2022, https://news.yahoo.com/xi-COVID-authoritarianism-meets-red-100000268.html?soc_src=social-sh&soc_trk=tw&tsrc=twtr.

11   J. Zhang, 'From Lockdowns (*Fengcheng*) to Silence (*Jingmo*): Zero-COVID Politics in China', *HAU: Journal of Ethnographic Theory*, Issue 13, No. 2, 2023, pp. 272–278.

12   X. Nie, Z. Huang and L. Wu, 'Community Governance During the Shanghai COVID-19 Lockdown I: The Roles and Actions of Residents' Committees', *Urban Geography* (2024): 1-21, doi: 10.1080/02723638.2024.2333217.

13   Z. Li, 'How Beijing Accidentally Ended the Zero-COVID Policy', *The Diplomat*, 7 January 2023, https://thediplomat.com/2023/01/how-beijing-accidentally-ended-the-zero-COVID-policy/.

14   China, WHO, 2023, https://COVID19.who.int/region/wpro/country/cn.

16

Further Decline of Human Rights Scenario in Xinjiang Under COVID-19 Restrictions

Debasish Chaudhuri

Brazen display of the destructive capacity of transnational terrorism originating from the Muslim world in the 9/11 incidents has thoroughly changed the perception of threat to territorial sovereignty, national security and social stability across the countries. The global war on terrorism (GWT) led by the US created opportunity for the governments of all the countries – irrespective of ideological orientation and political culture – to pursue politicisation of national security, design stringent public security policies and intensify coercion of marginalised groups within the national boundaries, often at the cost of basic civil and human rights. This marked the decline of liberal forces, rise of far-right illiberal populists and emergence of neo-liberal discourse in the world.[1]

The GWT slowly blurred the distinction between just and unjust war and legitimised measures against terrorist groups and those supposedly engaged with them.[2] The notion that radical Islam was the greatest civilisational challenge in the international political discourse, and 'spirit of revenge' and 'simplistic script of good vs. evil' in post-9/11 global politics put moderate forces of Islam and Muslim communities in a disadvantageous position.[3] This has directly or indirectly given impetus to make harsh minority policies, frame discriminating legal provisions and take disproportionately intimidating and provocative measures towards Muslim minorities in many majoritarian states, irrespective of their political culture.

The Chinese leadership categorised ethnic separatists, religious extremists and transnational terrorists from Xinjiang Uyghur Autonomous Region (XUAR) as 'three evil forces' and introduced 'strike hard' campaign as early as the mid-1990s. The category was already broad enough to include a large section of Uyghur society comprising religious minded traditionalists, activists, right conscious youths, intellectuals as well as people from other professions and business circles. The changing international dynamics in the post-9/11 world created opportunity for China to project itself as a victim of transborder terror groups in Xinjiang and engage in anti-terrorism cooperation at the multilateral as well as bilateral level. In the new scenario, the central leadership gave the then regional Party Secretary complete authority to handle growing separatist tendency and resentment among common Uyghur Muslims. Unmitigated grievances among ordinary people and increasing discrimination towards the major minority group of XUAR led to deadly riots in the regional capital Urumqi in 2009. Inter-ethnic tensions after the riots became even more acute and number of Uyghur-led violence occurred in other parts of China, including the capital Beijing in 2013 and 2014.

It was this time that there was drastic change of political culture and state–society relationship under Xi Jinping's grand narrative of the 'China Dream', national rejuvenation and the launch of the global outreach programme 'Belt and Road Initiative' (BRI).[4] To further restrict the life of minority groups like the Uyghur and Tibetan people, Xi Jinping gave it an ideological twist by making religions to 'adapt to the socialist society', 'manage religious affairs in line with laws', 'merge religious doctrines with Chinese culture' and 'devote themselves to China's reform and opening up drive and socialist modernization'.[5] The securitisation process in various parts of China, including minority areas, was underway since the end of the first decade of the 21st century, which enhanced Party-state's capacity to build extensive and effective surveillance systems. To ensure 'everlasting' social stability and create an atmosphere for fulfilling Xi Jinping's ambitious BRI programme in Xinjiang, Chen Quanguo, – a hardliner who won accolades from the central leadership for pacifying Tibet after the 2008 riots – was specially brought in to handle the situation in 2016.

The five years of Chen's rule have been marked by the intensification of physical, digital and biological surveillance in the name of de-extremisation particularly of the Uyghur society and the entire Xinjiang Muslim community at large. Deterioration of the overall humanitarian conditions worsened following the outburst of the COVID-19 pandemic and subsequent restrictions. This chapter highlights the situation of Xinjiang prior to the pandemic and focuses on the difficulties of the people in the region under COVID-19 restrictions and internal political developments after Chen was replaced in the face of severe criticism by the international community for his draconian policies. It concludes with details of the total disregard of basic human rights of the minorities in Xinjiang, and how India could not stand up against China on the human rights issue in the international arena.

Overview of the Conflict

China confronted the danger of terrorism for the first time in the early 1990s in Xinjiang, when it was exposed to various currents of extremist ideologies and religious orthodoxies as well as training and resources for violent activities from the Muslim world. In order to tackle new geopolitical developments in the

region and a possible nexus between the radical Uyghur factions and transborder terror groups, China took the following measures by the mid-1990s:
1. Defining the rise of Uyghur-led violence as well as any form of resistance by the community as an act of 'three evil forces' under the spell of ethnic separatism, religious extremism and transnational terrorism.
2. Launching of various strike-hard measures and restricting social, cultural and religious practices.
3. Cooperating with the newly established countries in Central Asia by setting up Shanghai Five, which eventually developed into the Shanghai Cooperation Organisation (SCO).
4. Developing clandestine relations with the Islamic regime of Taliban in Afghanistan to dissuade them from providing training to the Uyghur militants.[6]

China's repressive policies against the poverty-stricken, religious-minded rural population as well as aspiring, educated, ordinary people belonging to the Uyghur Muslim community under the pretext of fighting the perpetrators of violence in Xinjiang got validation when the country joined in the GWT. China took full advantage of this situation and jumped on the bandwagon for getting moral and material support from the US and its allies. In fact, every passing year after 2001, especially prior to the 2008 Beijing Olympics, the local authority sharpened physical and verbal assaults on the entire Uyghur community without proper assessment of the root cause of their discontent and the depth of their alienation. To the surprise of the central leadership, eruption of violent riots in the regional capital between two largest ethnic groups – the Han and the Uyghur in Urumqi on 5 July 2009, revealed the social cost of the coercion of the largest minority group in Xinjiang for over a decade.[7]

In the couple of years after the July riots, some sort of introspection by the central Party leadership regarding the appropriate way of handling the issues relating to the ethnic minorities and the governance of Xinjiang followed. However, the central leadership had neither the capacity to break away from 'hundred years of entanglement' between the Party and ethnic minorities, nor the intention to bring any fundamental changes in its policies towards Xinjiang. Just to clear the mess created in the course China's fight against 'three evil forces' since the mid-1990s, Zhang Chunxian, a moderate leader, was sent to Xinjiang to serve as Regional Party Secretary. Zhang took a nuanced approach by delinking religious observances or cultural practices and extremist ideas, while promoting 'de-extremisation' and reducing interethnic tension. He mingled with people from all walks of life and adopted a relatively balanced approach by emphasising on the improvement of people's livelihood and toning down the caustic verbal campaign against separatism and terrorism.[8] The central leadership became impatient with Zhang's style of reducing interethnic tensions when the number of violent attacks in the region and other parts of China by the Uyghur radical groups increased between 2013 and 2014.

Apparently, to revitalise the time-tested culture of manufacturing internal enemies and encouraging security forces and citizens to wage 'people's war' against antagonistic forces detrimental to the elusive inter-ethnic unity, Xi Jinping visited Xinjiang in April 2014. During his stay in the region, he himself used harsh rhetoric and called for combating terrorism with an iron hand. This visit was deliberately orchestrated to exhibit an image of a strong and decisive central leadership which unequivocally advocated taking a firm stand against terrorism and maintaining stability in the region. Xi's apparently successful tour was marred by the incident of knife attacks and a bomb explosion at the Urumqi Railway Station a few hours after the conclusion of the President's visit on 30 April. The process of further hardening of policies started in the Second Xinjiang Work Forum held at the end of May 2014, which called for long-lasting political stability in Xinjiang and the core ideas of governing Xinjiang (*zhijiang*) evolved.[9]

With the appointment of hardliner Chen Quanguo in August 2016, it was clearly indicated that the central leadership was determined not to tolerate any kind of moderation in dealing with the troubles in Xinjiang or the slightest alteration of their counter-terrorism discourse; and completely eradicate traces of resistance – be it mute, peaceful or violent. Moreover, majoritarian biases against Islam across the world and particularly the Uyghur community in China made for a conducive atmosphere for Chen Quanguo to carry out his programme of silencing the Uyghur and other target groups without worrying about the reactions of the larger society.

Governing Xinjiang

There have been certain fundamental changes in the style of governance since Xi Jinping climbed to the top leadership position in Chinese politics. He gave a new twist to Deng Xiaoping's 'four modernisations', which, according to him, are socialisation, legalisation, intelligentisation and specialisation, and rely on 'three-dimensional prevention and control system': full utilisation of internet, network information technology and cyber security for advancing social control mechanism. For over a decade, the central authorities took up the task of securitisation across the country through grid social management, strict censorship on social media and monitoring online activities of netizens, utilisation of big data for the collection of information about individual citizens and introduction of the social credit system.[10] Broadly speaking, most of these processes have been underway in Xinjiang for some time, but new meaning has been imbued into them under Xi Jinping's leadership, whose intention is to permanently resolve ethnic problems by minimising inter-ethnic tensions, uprooting extremism and decisively crushing and controlling the entire Muslim community in Xinjiang.

The then Party Secretary Chen Quanguo set his agenda in Xinjiang based on President Xi's core idea of handling relations between stability and development; adhering to make concerted efforts of the Party, government, military, police, Xinjiang Production and Construction Corp (XPCC) and common masses and effectively carrying out 'combination punches' (*zuhe quan*) on the enemy. Chen treated the region as an experimentation site for new social control technologies, innovative methods of repression, onslaught against Islamic faith and religious practices and Sinicisation of indigenous culture.[11]

A series of new laws and amendments, namely, the National Security Law, the Criminal Law and Criminal Procedure Law, Counter-terrorism Law, Regulations of Implementation of the Counter-terrorism Law in Xinjiang, De-extremisation Regulations, Regulation on Religious Affairs and Regulation on Banning Burqa in Public Places legally armoured the local authorities and strengthened Chen Quanguo's position to take some drastic steps in the region. Under his leadership, counter-terrorism, stability maintenance and de-extremisation were all integrated within a single social control system and surveillance mechanism in Xinjiang.

Chen took stern steps against all elements suspected of providing any kind of support to such radical forces or any activity seen as going against the interests of the state. Besides terrorists and 'three evil forces', the regional administration increased vigilance and propaganda against 'two-faced cliques' (*liangmianpai*) and 'two-faced people' (*liangmianren*). These included the people who were part of the Party and government system in the region and were suspected of providing vital support to the perpetrators of terror, violence and crime against the state and the people. To eliminate them, the regional leadership enhanced disciplinary measures within the Party and the administration.

A whole range of surveillance measures were adopted after Chen assumed charge of the region. These included:
1. Physical control through 'convenience police stations' within existing urban grid-management infrastructure
2. Electronic monitoring using advanced surveillance products and services like highly sophisticated surveillance cameras, face and voice recognition software, big data 'police cloud platform', Wi-Fi sniffer and mandatory installation of Beidou (a Chinese version of GPS) in all vehicles

3. Genetic codification by collecting DNA samples on a large scale, mainly of the Uyghur population in Xinjiang, and the creation of a biometric database of the population
4. Restrictions on foreign travel and confiscation of passports
5. Deploying Party cadres to the countryside in order to influence institutions from the grassroots, to create a base for mass mobilisation for official campaigns against religious extremism, and penetrate into the day-to-day lives of the Muslims in Xinjiang
6. Recruitment of many Uyghur youths in the security forces at the local level. To increase self-surveillance, 'Double-linked household' system was introduced for mutually monitoring individual families
7. Psychological control through so-called vocational training, physical torture, indoctrination, brainwashing and psychological experiments, Maoist-style socialist education and self-criticism sessions in the detention centres
8. Crackdown on local religious or cultural symbols, and even expressions of Uyghur pride.

A list of seventy-five signs of religious extremism and related reading materials were circulated among the grassroots cadres and officials in some parts of Xinjiang in late 2014. Some of the signs of extremist tendency included showing disrespect to the village Party Secretary or cadres; abstinence from alcohol; growing and colouring beards; wearing short trousers; standing with legs wide apart, etc. According to these guidelines, persons having these characteristics or tendencies was to be reported to the police. After the regional government began the large-scale detention of the Uyghur and other Muslims, the authorities in certain areas of Xinjiang began to refer to the aforementioned list to tighten security in and around mosques in search of people showing such behaviour. Civilians were rewarded for keeping vigil on such people on behalf of the authorities and reporting their observations.

It would appear that perhaps there was consensus among the authorities at the centre as well as in the region over how the use of an advanced technology-driven social governance system, superior surveillance mechanisms, invasive and intrusive social monitoring techniques and forced-assimilation would ultimately ensure peace, stability and security in Xinjiang.

Under COVID Restrictions

While the social control mechanism under Chen Quanguo increased the vulnerability of the Uyghur and other Muslim groups of Xinjiang, they were plunged into complete despair when the COVID-19 pandemic broke out at the end of 2019, leading to the imposition of regular lockdowns and restrictions across the entire society. Life of the common people in every part of the world came to standstill and became extremely uncertain during this time. While it was one of the most challenging times for the ruling powers in all countries around the world, the state authorities also took full advantage of the situation to expand their role in the personal matters of the citizens and surveillance. It is implicit that the degree of suffering for a particular section of population in any country depended on their overall vulnerability as well as the capability, agility, intent and sensibility of the authorities towards that section. It is understandable that Chen Quanguo fully utilised this opportunity, but ineffectiveness of technology-driven surveillance mechanism and limitation of totalistic control over any section of society in emergency-situation of handling pandemic became exposed in the end of his rule in Xinjiang.

Following the SARS epidemic in 2003, the Hu-Wen administration put forward the idea of 'being vigilant in peace time' and developed comparatively robust crisis management centres and surveillance mechanism to handle incidents ranging from epidemic and natural calamities to man-made disasters including terrorism. This is the reason why China was able to take much more prompt measures after initial hiccups since the COVID-19 outbreak in Wuhan for the first time.[12] However, the tendency of denial or suppression of information regarding the positive cases and overall repressive atmosphere caused greater confusion, causalities and fear among people, especially from minority areas.

It appeared as if the Xinjiang authorities lacked a sense of priority even during the pandemic, as all their efforts were focused on de-extremisation. The local officials considered the information about the spread of the disease as a 'state secret' and often remained tight-lipped about the pandemic, and in this regards the region's highest court notified them about the strict punishments for spreading rumours related to affected cases, violation of COVID protocols and social restrictions and intervention in the works of medical and other government personnel.

To the best of our knowledge, Xinjiang Uyghur Autonomous Region Health Commission (XUARHC) began to release information regarding confirmed COVID-19 cases within the region, and in Urumqi as well as other places including the western-most prefecture of the region, Yili. These reports started appearing on its official website from the last week of January 2020.[13] According to an unverified report, as many as 13,000 people from Wuhan entered Xinjiang before the local authorities imposed ban on intercity transportation.[14] By March, cases were being reported in Urumqi, Turfan, Bayangol, Aksu, Ili, Kashgar and various divisions of *bingtuan* (corps) were spread across the region. According to an official release, there were a total of seventy-six confirmed COVID-19 infections – fifty-two from various provinces and twenty-four belonging to *bingtuan* divisions – three deaths and sixty-four recoveries were reported from the region.[15]

The official *People's Daily* reported on 12 March that there had been no hospitalisations due to COVID-19 in Xinjiang. Despite widespread fear and uncertainty, in the end of March, the regional government claimed that things were returning to normal in the construction sector, oil fields, garment factories, agricultural activities and schools. The programme of transferring Uyghur and other Muslim-minority labour forces in various parts of Xinjiang as well as rest of China resumed as before. According to some foreign sources, it was estimated that about 50,000 people were transferred within and outside the region under said programme, most of whom were likely former inmates of Xinjiang's detention centres.[16]

Based on some Chinese and English sources, it may be inferred that the county and lower-level administrations in Xinjiang began to take measures against the spread of COVID-19 by sealing off the area, setting up quarantine facilities near or within the detention camp sites, restricting people's movements and imposing home confinement. By the first week of June, the regional government had issued two lists of around 230 COVID-19 testing service centres and healthcare institutes across the prefectures.[17]

The locals were still worried about the spread of virus in the testing centres and prisons as the region has the highest number of such facilities in the country. Some of the COVID-19 restrictions made the life of the Uyghur and other minorities even more difficult and in some areas they even faced the risk of starvation when the inflow of goods was disrupted due to lockdown.

As feared by many officials and civilians, the number of cases started increasing again in July 2020. Reports about new cases continued to surface from different parts of Xinjiang and the regional authorities imposed rigorous medical surveillance and remained on high alert to ensure that no cases went unnoticed. The prolonged lockdowns, coupled with the ongoing de-extremisation, Sinicisation of Islam, culturalisation efforts and the systematic imposition of Chinese language, celebration of Han social customs and habits as well as socialisation of Xinjiang with the Chinese not only inundated the minorities but also isolated the Han population from their ethnic neighbours in the region.

Finally, the news regarding a COVID-19 outbreak in factories linked with forced labour began to appear in late October. According to a report in the *Guardian*, more than 180 cases of coronavirus were detected in a factory established in 2018 in Shufu County, Kashgar Prefecture, Southwest Xinjiang. This compelled the local bodies to take urgent action and test about 4.5 million people living in the area by the first week of November. It was claimed by the authorities that only 183 people had been affected by the virus and 138 of them were asymptomatic.[18] The limited research into the actual situation of the pandemic in China has resulted in the lack of reliable sources being available, other than partial and unverified information from spurious Chinese and Western sources. As the county governments set about conducting COVID-19 testing at a large scale, the number of cases emerging from the bordering areas of Xinjiang increased and reports of new cases continued to appear in various media for over a year.[19]

While tackling the pandemic situations in Xinjiang, the regional authorities fully utilised medical surveillance and lockdown to accomplish their goal of silencing and taming an entire ethnic community into loyal subjects. The disproportionately high-handed, coercive mechanisms made for a convenient tool. In the face of international criticism, however, China released that just an official declaration of the success of its de-extremisation process and a visual display of over-gratified multi-ethnic congregations was not enough to establish efficacy and benign nature of Chen's 'innovative' style of governance. The central and local authorities felt the urgent need to promote tourism to dispel any fears of terrorism from the minds of Chinese citizens, and reiterate that the region had remained largely unaffected by the pandemic. This was also considered as an ideal means of showcasing the 'superior' lifestyle of the indigenous population and the human rights situation under President Xi Jinping's rule.[20]

Xi himself spoke highly of China's success in the battle against the pandemic in September 2020, causing the local leaders of Xinjiang to take the situation even more lightly, and encouraging unrestricted entry of tourists into the region (Tan 2020, 8 September). Xinjiang began to offer cheap travel packages and launched various tourism activities throughout its fourteen prefectures during the national holidays in 2020 and 2021. The region became a lucrative tourist destination despite being in the midst of the uncertainty due to the mysterious strains of the coronavirus and their unpredictable consequences for public life. To promote tourism, COVID-19-related restrictions were relaxed for tourists from other provinces. They were neither required to take mandatory tests nor quarantine at the time of entering and leaving the region.

It is questionable how far China was able to convince international critics of the improved human rights situation or promote positive public opinion about the government's pandemic strategy through State-sponsored visits for foreign delegates and promoting patriotic tourism in Xinjiang amidst the worldwide pandemic. In fact, the surge of domestic tourism in Xinjiang further increased the vulnerability of its local population and soon the spread of coronavirus in the region compelled Chen Quanguo's administration to impose harsh Zero-COVID policies.[21] It is generally observed by commentators on the Xinjiang situation that Chen successfully accomplished most of his innovative policy goals as far as the governance of minorities was concerned, and found permanent solutions to address the longstanding problem of maintaining everlasting peace, social stability and national security in this troubled region.

Chen was relieved from his responsibilities in December 2021 amidst international criticism because he was the only visible face of China's Xinjiang policy in the recent years. This, however, did not dent his image and status in the CPC in any way. In fact, when the new Regional Party Secretary Ma Xingrui took charge of the region, his job was to just follow the rules, regulations and practices put in place by Chen, and convey to the local population that he was not going to make any major departures from these policies.[22]

Mastery, Mistrust and Misfire

This totalitarian project of the Party-state was challenged from the initial stage of the COVID-19 pandemic because of suppression of news related to imminent spread of an unknown disease and inefficient handling of the emergency situations. However, people adjusted to the aggressive policies to combat the spread of COVID-19 across China simply because they were able to aid in keeping casualties much lower than most countries. Detection of the Delta variant and then the Omicron strain in August 2021 and December 2021, respectively, shattered Xi Jinping's assertion of China's unparalleled success in its fight against the pandemic, and the visibly shaken state leadership decided to intensify and prolong Zero-COVID policies. They paid no heed to the basic civic rights, fate of economic activity and the livelihoods of the common masses. This continued until the Zero-COVID policies were abruptly jettisoned, and coexisting with the virus became a way of life in the world following mass vaccination.

As the time for the decision regarding Xi Jinping's third five-year term in the 20th Party Congress was approaching, the president was hellbent on proving that China's Zero-COVID policy had seen significant success and was a glowing testament to the superiority of their political ideology over the West.

The shortage of food and necessary amenities for daily use created survival crisis even in Shanghai, Beijing and other provincial cities because of draconian Zero-COVID policies. The common people everywhere developed a deep-rooted distrust in the wisdom of the top leadership, causing widespread resentment against the Party's authority. This resulted in a series of protests in most major cities in October–November 2022. Students from about fifty universities in China were involved in the lockdown demonstrations and Chinese students from various universities overseas also expressed their solidarity without any fear of consequence. The protests are also known as White Paper Protests or the A4 Revolution because demonstrators held up blank white papers to evade censorship. The COVID-19 lockdown protests took a critical turn after a fire in a building killed ten people and injured nine in a Uyghur residential area in Urumqi on 24 November.

Like other big cities, stringent and disruptive Zero-COVID restrictions were imposed in every corner of Xinjiang since the spread of Omicron in 2022. Nevertheless, the region was brought under special scrutiny because of the Western countries' efforts to improve the human rights situation in the region through the UN and other bilateral and multilateral forums since 2016. The Chinese leadership considered this as a direct attack on its internal matters and an attempt of the Western democracies to tarnish its image as a proponent of an alternative development model.

In 2022, the first major lockdown was imposed in Urumqi and, slowly, the whole region faced strict restrictions from the first week of August, despite the decrease in the number of positive cases and deaths from the virus. On 10 August, Urumqi City Epidemic Control Headquarter decided to execute temporary close-off (static) management measures (*linshixing jingtai guanli cuoshi*) in six districts for five days. This was followed by maintaining strict vigil on people's movements, tough restrictions on key work units, severe traffic regulations, stern implementation of individual responsibilities and safeguard supplies of citizens living in confinement.[23] The entire region gradually came under the static management of Zero-COVID restrictions. This time there was no official announcement for citywide lockdowns, but every district and all residential complexes – from high-risk to low-risk areas – were sealed off and people were ordered to stay home. Lack of financial and bureaucratic capacity at the level of the municipal government had a huge impact on lockdown implementation across the region. With no scope of income, the common people found it difficult to live solely on their savings in the face of food scarcity and in some places rise in the prices of daily amenities and, if infected with virus, to be taken forcefully to substandard quarantine facilities or hospitals.[24]

Getting information about the region was almost impossible because of the de-extremisation measures. Home to over 25 million people, Xinjiang remained isolated and dropped off the radar of the people from other parts of the country. Without being noticed by the Chinese and international media, the region experienced over four months of lockdown at a stretch from August 2022. In fact, the international critics were so preoccupied with the repressive de-extremisation measures that they missed out on taking stock of the tragic consequences of the Zero-COVID restrictions in the region, though lockdown reports from Shanghai regularly featured in headlines across the world.

The problem started with the categorisation of COVID-19 as one of the most infectious diseases in human history, akin to the bubonic plague and cholera, by the international authorities, when it is classified as a Category-B infectious disease in China, which includes HIV, viral hepatitis and H7N9 bird flu. This helped the Party-state to empower the local governments to take strong measures and made the violators of lockdown protocols liable to criminal offence. This also justified the continuation of their draconian Zero-COVID policies until, as recently as 2022, when the majority of the population was infected by Omicron, which was much less infectious than the original strains.[25] This ambiguous categorisation was the main reason for people's suffering in the Zero-COVID period across China. In addition to be subjected to the criminalisation of their ethnicity, the Uyghur in Xinjiang were also treated as offenders for violating pandemic norms even when they were in dire need of a meal or medicine. The situation was so critical that following the relaxation of the Zero-COVID policies, the Supreme Court of China had to declare explicitly that going against COVID-19-related restrictions would no longer be treated as a criminal offence.[26]

Among the many loopholes of Zero-COVID policies and their implementation, cruel measures such as sealing off entire neighbourhoods, work units and housing complexes with only one exit, blocking fire escapes and firm monitoring at the public exits were also taken by municipal administrations across the country during lockdown, which led to the tragedy in Urumqi. According to a report by the Associate Press, in some places, the doors of some houses were even chained; rumours among suspicious locals said that this had been the case at the time of the fire as well.[27] The official sources report ten deaths and nine injuries – apparently much less than the actual figures – and all of them were Uyghur.

The incident became a rallying point for the ongoing protests against the Zero-COVID restrictions across the country. Huge spontaneous protests erupted in different parts of Urumqi on 25 November, and spread to most of the big cities over the weekend. Like other parts of China, the majority of protesters in the Xinjiang capital belonged to the majority Han community, and the Uyghur and other Muslim minorities were too scared to take to the streets despite their fury, because of fear of detention and imprisonment. These protests were a testament to the solidarity between the Uyghur and Han populations in Xinjiang, which is quite rare in view of the continuous propaganda being spread in the region against indigenous Muslim populations (ABC 2022, 27 November).

Conclusion

The nation-wide protests against the Zero-COVID policies were considered a direct threat to the regime's political stability. One report suggests that Xi Jinping allowed Li Qiang, his long-term ally who became Premier in March 2023, to take responsibility to tackle the situation. Soon after taking charge of Party's central COVID-19 taskforce, he decided to take modest measures to loosen restrictions on 11 November 2022.[28] Protests demanding the revoking of Zero-COVID policies after a deadly fire in Xinjiang accelerated the process of their withdrawal and, on 7 December, China ended lockdown, local travel restrictions and mass testing. Finally, in the next year, on 17 February, Xi Jinping declared 'decisive victory' over COVID-19, and emphasised the correctness of China's pandemic strategy.[29] While highlighting their achievements in the fight against the deadly virus, the leadership's failure to show enough sensitivity towards the masses and depriving them of basic human rights to life, work and social security was completely overlooked.

Given China's protracted struggle against 'three evil forces' and incessant crackdowns on the local Muslim population in name of de-extremisation, the central and local leadership were caught off-guard by the protests in Xinjiang, which triggered a series of protests and demonstrations in other parts of the country. Therefore, it became imperative for the highest leadership to reiterate the ideological standing of the Party-state on the Xinjiang problem, and vowed to continue its all-round struggle against extremist forces and local suspicious individuals. Some fundamental changes also happened in Xinjiang between Xi Jinping's embarrassing first visit to the reopening of the region for Han tourists at the end of Zero-COVID policy. It was also during this period that the Xinjiang issue repeatedly occupied focus in the debate on UN Human Rights Council and attracted international criticism from the West. The US and some of its European partners even imposed punitive sanctions on sixty Chinese companies and thirty-five officials and government agencies for human rights violation in this Muslim-dominated regions (UHRP 2024, January). Against this backdrop, Xi Jinping made his second visit to Xinjiang on 26 August 2023 on his way back from the BRICS Summit in South Africa. While interacting with the cadres of the regional party committee, government officials and Corp members, he recapped his ideas on governing Xinjiang (*zhijiang*) according to the concepts of rule of law, unity, stability, prosperity and development. As he reminded officials to adhere to the time-tested policies designed by the central party leadership Xi – which included emphasis on positive propaganda, dissemination of the story of modern Xinjiang, focused and purposeful refutation of all sorts of false media reportage, negative public opinion and harmful discourse (Xinhua News Agency 2023, 26 August).

Takeaway for India

Unlike China, India never questioned its obligations to keep to the universal human rights norms and generally did not accept violations anywhere in the world as a mere spectator. At the same time, it refused to downrightly rally behind the US and other Western democracies to hold any country responsible for the violation of human rights within its territories, and impose restrictions including economic sanctions. It primarily observed principles of non-interference in the internal issues of another sovereign country. The Indian foreign policy establishment valued collective interest, international law and the principles of the United Nations' Charter, while fulfilling its international responsibilities on issues pertaining to human rights without sacrificing its national interests.

The increasing number of India's abstentions from voting on several resolutions at the UN Security Council, the UN General Assembly and the UN Human Rights Council (UNHRC) in the recent years raises a volley of questions regarding its international posture and basic principles of foreign policies. Broadly speaking, abstention from voting in the UN hardly augured well to the status of a large democratic country like India among international communities. This might be interpreted as a concern for national interest, disregard for the human rights in other countries and unprincipled neutrality; retaliation and giving priority to one country over others; concealed support or opposition to the resolution; balancing act between major powers in the conflict-riddled world and maintaining balanced diplomatic relationships with both parties; ideological positions; indecisiveness of the political dispensation against taking a hard decision in global affairs. It also includes an expectation for reciprocity from certain countries in a similar situation. A case-by-case study of India's abstention might reveal some rational choice in its foreign policy, but it is totally incomprehensible as to why India abstained from voting in a draft resolution in the UNHRC regarding the deteriorating human rights situation in Xinjiang since 2016 and the deplorable humanitarian crisis during the pandemic years in October 2022.

India mostly considers the problems in Xinjiang as China's internal matters and does not try to take advantage of ethno-national separatist movements in the region. On the contrary, China never spares any opportunity to undermine India's standing on the issue of Kashmir and terrorism, and always advocates in favour of Pakistan. In January 2016, China was the only country among the fifteen-member UN Security Council to oppose the US's proposal of labelling the dreaded Pakistani national Masood Azhar as a 'global' terrorist. It was quite a setback for India's diplomatic efforts not to be able to get him banned by the UN. However, the cancellation of the visas of the Uyghur exiled leader Dolkun Isa and two Chinese dissidents under PRC's pressure, in April 2016, was an embarrassment for India's political leadership and an affront against its sovereignty. China appears to have been emboldened by some unknown reasons to repeatedly attack India's strategic interests in the union territories of Jammu & Kashmir and Ladakh since the clashes in the Galwan Valley in June 2020. Against this backdrop, India's decision of not casting its vote on the matter of human rights violations in Xinjiang in the UNHRC is self-defeating and harmful to its status as the largest democracy and rising economic power in the world.

In this connection, it is important to note here that on the next day of the vote the UNHRC on the issue of Xinjiang, the Indian Ministry of External Affairs justified its abstention by stating India's 'long-held position that country-specific resolutions are never helpful' and its preference for 'dialogue to deal with such issue' (Ramachandran 2022, 20 October). Both these phrases are problematic—the first indicates the inflexibility of India's foreign policy, and the second reveals a poor understanding of how China engages in human rights debates with international interlocutors. While the intention of the US and its allies to back this resolution is questionable, it is also not true that India refrains from voting for country-specific resolutions.

In my opinion, this is an opportune occasion to have a more nuanced discussion on whether Indian foreign policy should be more flexible in dealing with country-specific resolution in the international forums, in its consideration of its commitment to human rights as well as national interests. While tit-for-tat is not the ideal diplomatic stance, India should learn to say 'no' when dealing with China.

Notes

1 Liberal intellectual forces were discredited when the principle of American interventionism for making a better world was hijacked and wars against Afghanistan and Iraq were unleashed by the Bush administration following 9/11 incident, in the name of fighting against terrorism and accumulation of weapons of mass destruction. In the face of expansionist Russia and increasingly powerful and ambitious China, international liberal politics have practically taken a backseat. The rise of far-right populist leaders in the US and many European countries posed a challenge to the liberal politics on the domestic front as well (Zack Beauchamp, 'The war on terror and the long death of liberal interventionism', Vox, 8, September 2021).
2 Tim Dunne, 'Liberalism, International Terrorism, and Democratic Wars', *International Relations*, Vol. 23, No. 1 (2009): 110–111.
3 Joseph Stieb, 'The vital center reborn: Redefining liberalism between 9/11 and the Iraq War', *Modern American History*, Vol. 4, Issue 3 (2021): 295–297.
4 Debasish Chaudhuri, 'Countering Internal Security Challenges of Xinjiang: Rise of the Surveillance State', Monograph, The Institute of Chinese Studies, Delhi, No. 7 (March 2021): 28–30.
5 'Xi's call for improved religious work', Xinhua net (23 April 2016).

6   Debasish Chaudhuri, *Xinjiang and the Chinese State: Violence in the Reform Era* (New York: Routledge, 2018): 171–174 & 215–216.
7   Guojun Zhao, 'Normalization of "East Turkestan" terrorist activities and its governance', *Guoji zhanwang*, No. 1 (2015): 110.
8   Chaudhuri, 'Countering Internal Security Challenges of Xinjiang: Rise of the Surveillance State', 15–18.
9   Some of broad themes include creation of socialist Xinjiang with Chinese character; Sinicisation of Islam and local culture; and inculating 'modern habits' among people (Chaudhuri, 'Countering Internal Security Challenges of Xinjiang: Rise of the Surveillance State', 50–53, 65–66 & 119).
10 Lianbin Qing, 'General Secretary Xi Jinping innovates new thinking and new ideology on social governance', *Frontline* (17 August 2017).
11 Chaudhuri, 'Countering Internal Security Challenges of Xinjiang: Rise of the Surveillance State', 52–53.
12 An interim report of an independent panel appointed by the WHO criticised China for not being able to forcefully apply public health measures during the initial phase of COVID-19 breakout. The authorities took strict measures once they acknowledged the problem. By January 2021, though harsh restrictions and rigid enforcement came at a significant cost, they proved to be a highly successful method of tackling the virus. In one year, there were just under 100,000 recorded infections with only 4,800 deaths linked to COVID-19 (Andreas Illmer, et al, 'Wuhan lockdown: A year of China fight against the COVID pandemic', BBC, (22 January 2021)).
13 'Increase of one pneumonia infected COVID patient – total cases increased to three', *People's Daily* (Online), (25 January 2020).
14 'China Seeks to Divert Attention From Virus Mishandling With Dancing Xinjiang Minorities: Uyghur Exiles', Radio Free Asia, (14 February 2020).
15 XUAR Health Commission, '1 March: 24-hour latest reports on Xinjiang's (including corps areas) COVID-19 pandemic situation', (2 March 2020).
16 Austin Ramzy, 'Xinjiang returns to work, but coronavirus worries linger in China', *The New York Times*, (30 March 2020).
17 'Latest policies on measures against pandemic in Xinjiang', XUAR govt. website, (10 July 2020).
18 'Large COVID outbreak in China linked to Xinjiang forced labour', *The Guardian*, (29 March 2020).
19 Apparently, more than 180 cases of COVID-19 were documented in Shufu county (Kashgar) in the last week of October 2020 ('Large COVID outbreak in China linked to Xinjiang forced labour'). According to a similar new released by CNN's Beijing bureau, health officials in Xinjiang reported 183 (22 symptomatic and 161 asymptomatic) COVID-19 infections after completing mass testing programme on 27 October. The XUAR Health Commission claims that authorities completed a mass testing programme for 4.74 million people in the city of Kashgar ('China reports 183 cases in Xinjiang after testing nearly 5 million', CNN Beijing Bureau, (28 October 2020)).

20. 'China uses tourism to smother Xinjiang's culture', *The Economist*, (2 January 2021); Thomas Peter and Cate Candell, 'Wider image in China's new patriotic tourism, riot police and minders', Reuters, (17 June 2021).
21. Jack Lau and Coco Feng, 'Coronavirus cases upend holiday plans in a corner of China's Xinjiang region', *South China Morning Post*, (4 October 2021).
22. Ma Xingrui, 'Firmly pledging to fulfil works towards social stability and everlasting peace', *People's Daily* (Online), (21 April 2022).
23. 'Temporary static management measures are implemented in key urban areas of Urumqi, Xinjiang', CCTV News, (10 August 2022).
24. Jessie Yeung, et al, 'China bans residents from leaving Xinjiang just weeks after its last COVID lockdown', CNN, (6 October 2022).
25. William Zheng, 'China to reopen borders, drop COVID quarantine from January 8', *South China Morning Post* (26 December 2022).
26. Phoebe Zhang, 'China's removal of criminal sanctions for spreading COVID-19 prompts calls for previous cases to be reviewed', *South China Morning Post* (1 February 2023).
27. 'China's Xinjiang region loosens some restrictions after pandemic lockdown demonstrations', Associated Press, (26 November2022).
28. After implementing the stringent Zero-COVID policy for two months in Shanghai, one of China's largest municipalities, and directly witnessing impact of strict lockdown on the economy, Li apparently became more open to the idea of living with COVID than his colleagues.
29. Julie Zhu, et al, 'Insight: How China's No. 2 hastened the end of Xi's Zero-COVID policy', Reuters, (3 March 2023).

References

Andreas Illmer, Yitsing Wang, and Tessa Wong, 'Wuhan Lockdown: A Year Of China Fight Against The Covid Pandemic', BBC, 22 January 2021. https://www.bbc.com/news/world-asia-china-55628488.

Austin Ramzy, 'Xinjiang Returns To Work, But Coronavirus Worries Linger In China', *The New York Times*, 30 March 2020. https://www.nytimes.com/2020/03/30/world/asia/china-coronavirus-xinjiang.html.

'China's Xinjiang Region Loosens Some Restrictions After Pandemic Lockdown Demonstrations,' Associated Press, 26 November2022. https://www.cbc.ca/news/world/china-COVID-lockdown-xinjiang-1.6665483

'China Reports 183 Cases In Xinjiang After Testing Nearly 5 Million', CNN Beijing Bureau, 28 October 2020. https://edition.cnn.com/world/live-news/coronavirus-pandemic-10-28-20-intl/h_a170c3adb39a3b02edd780e1bddc6705.

'China Uses Tourism To Smother Xinjiang's Culture', *The Economist*, 2 January 2021. https://www.economist.com/china/2021/01/02/china-uses-tourism-to-smother-xinjiangs-culture.

'China's Covid-Zero Lockdown In Xinjiang Hits 100 Days', *Straits Times*, 17 November 2022. https://www.straitstimes.com/asia/east-asia/china-s-COVID-zero-lockdown-in-xinjiang-hits-100-days.

Debasish Chaudhuri, *Xinjiang and the Chinese State: Violence in the Reform Era* (New York: Routledge, 2018).

Debasish Chaudhuri, 'Countering Internal Security Challenges Of Xinjiang: Rise Of The Surveillance State', Monograph, The Institute of Chinese Studies, Delhi, No. 7, March 2021.

Guojun Zhao, 'Normalization Of "East Turkestan" Terrorist Activities And Its Governance', *Guoji zhanwang*, No. 1, 2015, pp. 104–117.

Hotan Online, 'Latest Policies On Measures Against Pandemic In Xinjiang', Sohu, 10 July 2020. https://www.sohu.com/a/406918983_727669.

'Increase Of One Pneumonia Infected Covid Patient – Total Cases Increased To Three', *People's Daily* (Online), 25 January 2020. https://web.archive.org/web/20200305220701/http:/xj.people.com.cn/n2/2020/0125/c186332-33743867.html.

Jack Lau and Coco Feng, 'Coronavirus Cases Upend Holiday Plans In A Corner Of China's Xinjiang Region', *South China Morning Post*, 4 October 2021. https://www.scmp.com/news/china/science/article/3151177/COVID-cases-upend-holiday-plans-corner-chinas-xinjiang-region.

Jessie Yeung, Yong Xiong and Nectar Gan, 'China Bans Residents From Leaving Xinjiang Just Weeks After Its Last Covid Lockdown', CNN, 6 October 2022. https://edition.cnn.com/2022/10/05/china/xinjiang-china-COVID-lockdown-intl-hnk-mic/index.html.

Joseph Stieb, 'The Vital Center Reborn: Redefining Liberalism Between 9/11 And The Iraq War', *Modern American History*, Vol. 4, Issue 3, 2021, pp. 285–304.

Joshua Lipes, 'China Seeks To Divert Attention From Virus Mishandling With Dancing Xinjiang Minorities: Uyghur Exiles', Radio Free Asia, 14 February 2020. https://www.rfa.org/english/news/uyghur/dancing-02142020171104.html.

Julie Zhu, Yew Lun Tian and Engen Tham, 'Insight: How China's No. 2 Hastened The End Of Xi's Zero-Covid Policy', Reuters, 3 March 2023. https://www.reuters.com/world/china/how-chinas-new-no2-hasteed-end-xis-zero-COVID-policy-2023-03-03/.

'Large Covid Outbreak In China Linked To Xinjiang Forced Labour', *The Guardian*, 29 March 2020. https://www.theguardian.com/world/2020/oct/29/large-COVID-outbreak-in-china-linked-to-xinjiang-forced-labour.

Lianbin Qing, 'General Secretary Xi Jinping Innovates New Thinking And New Ideology On Social Governance', *Frontline*, 17 August 2017 http://theory.people.com.cn/n1/2017/0817/c83859-29476974.html.

Ma Xingrui, 'Firmly Pledging To Fulfil Works Towards Social Stability And Everlasting Peace', *People's Daily* (Online), 21 April 2022. http://politics.people.com.cn/n1/2022/0421/c1001-32404316.html.

Phoebe Zhang, 'China's Removal Of Criminal Sanctions For Spreading Covid-19 Prompts Calls For Previous Cases To Be Reviewed', 1 February 2023. https://www.scmp.com/news/china/politics/article/3207553/chinas-removal-criminal-sanctions-spreading-COVID-19-prompts-calls-previous-cases-be-reviewed.

'Shanghai Hit By Protests As Anger At Zero-Covid And Urumqi Fore Spreads Across China', ABC, 27.

November 2022. https://www.abc.net.au/news/2022-11-27/shanghai-hit-by-COVID-protests-as-anger-spreads-across-china/101703980.

Sudha Ramachandran, 'India Abstains On Xinjiang Resolution At Unhrc', *The Diplomat*, 20 October2022. https://thediplomat.com/2022/10/india-abstains-on-xinjiang-resolution-at-unhrc/.

Tan Dawn Wei, 'China Paving The Way Out Of Covid-19 Doldrums: Xi', *Straits Times*, 9 September 2020. https://www.straitstimes.com/asia/east-asia/china-paving-the-way-out-of-COVID-19-doldrums-xi.

'Temporary Static Management Measures Are Implemented In Key Urban Areas Of Urumqi, Xinjiang', CCTV News, 10 August 2022. https://news.cctv.com/2022/08/10/ARTIkc2NeOQgSoFlv0jNbV28220810.shtml.

Thomas Peter and Cate Candell, 'Wider Image In China's New Patriotic Tourism, Riot Police And Minders', Reuters, 17 June 2021. https://www.reuters.com/world/china/wider-image-chinas-new-xinjiang-patriotic-tourism-riot-police-minders-2021-06-17/.

Tim Dunne, 'Liberalism, International Terrorism, And Democratic Wars', *International Relations*, Vol. 23, No. 1, 2009, pp. 107–114. https://www.researchgate.net/publication/49513439_Liberalism_International_Terrorism_and_Democratic_Wars.

Uyghur Human Rights Project, 'U.s. Sanctions Tracker', January 2024. https://uhrp.org/sanctions-tracker/.

William Zheng, 'China To Reopen Borders, Drop Covid Quarantine From January 8', 26 December 2022, *South China Morning Post*. https://www.scmp.com/news/china/science/article/3204601/china-reopen-borders-drop-COVID-quarantine-january-8.

'Xi's Call For Improved Religious Work', Xinhua net, 23 April 2016. http://news.xinhuanet.com/english/2016-04/23/c_135306131.htm.

'Xi Jinping Called For Firmly Grasp Strategic Position Of Xinjiang In The Perspective Of China's Overall Situation And Build Beautiful Xinjiang In A Better Way In The Course Of Modernisation With Chinese Characteristics', CNR, 26 August 2023. https://news.cnr.cn/native/gd/sz/20230826/t20230826_526397084.shtml.

XUAR govt., 'Latest policies on measures against pandemic in Xinjiang), 10 July 2020. https://www.sohu.com/a/406918983_727669.

XUAR Health Commission, '1 March: 24-Hour Latest Reports On Xinjiang's (Including Corps Areas) Covid-19 Pandemic Situation', 2 March 2020. https://web.archive.org/web/20200302015853/http:/www.xjhfpc.gov.cn/info/1495/19322.htm.

Zack Beauchamp, 'The War on Terror and the Long Death of Liberal Interventionism', Vox, 8 September 2021. https://www.vox.com/22639548/911-anniversary-war-on-terror-liberal-interventionism.

17

The Tibet Question
Jayadeva Ranade

Tibet, China and India are areas of ever-present latent tension with the potential for serious geostrategic consequences for the Indo-Pacific region. It has become volatile since the Chinese intrusion in April 2020. Tensions have been rising since April 2013.

Tibet, with its vast resources of rare earth elements and minerals estimated at over $8 billion[1] and its central location is particularly important for China. Tibet, also known as the 'Water Tower' of Asia, is important for India and the region as it is the source of most major river systems in Asia. The region also encapsulates the areas of India–China rivalry, namely the undemarcated land border, India's integral position in the global Buddhist community, the reincarnation of the 14th Dalai Lama and the assurance of the flow of water in Tibetan glacier-fed rivers. China has been using its growth in economic and military strength and its diplomatic influence in international forums such as the United Nations Security Council (UNSC) and international financial institutions like the World Bank and the Asian Development Bank to steadily increase pressure on India.

China's Occupation of Tibet and Its Implications for India

Ever since the communists captured power in Beijing in October 1949 and proceeded to occupy Tibet under Mao's orders, India's northern borders have been troubled. Mao disregarded the fact that Tibet had been independent from 1912 to 1951 and instructed the Second Field Army, with Liu Bocheng as the commander and Deng Xiaoping as the political commissar, to invade and occupy Tibet.

From 1949 to 1966, Deng Xiaoping was second-in-command of China's Southwest Military Command, stationed in Chengdu. Under Marshal Liu Bocheng, Deng Xiaoping was responsible for the invasion and 'liberation' of Tibet, which began in 1949, and oversaw the widespread destruction of monasteries and the arrests of the Tibetan Buddhist clergy. The Chinese communist regime, while it discarded most of erstwhile Imperial China's policies and practices, chose to retain and perpetuate the expansionist policies of the predecessor dynasties. They considered the decision of the Chinese representative to the 1914 Simla Convention, Ivan Chen, not to sign the Simla Agreement as binding. That he had initialled the agreement but said it would need to be ratified by Beijing was ignored. Once the Chinese communist regime had occupied, or as they describe it 'liberated',

Tibet, they soon advanced claims on Aksai Chin, Ladakh, Arunachal Pradesh, pockets of Himachal Pradesh and Uttarakhand, claiming that the regions had been under Tibetan rule. Mao had described Tibet as China's palm and Ladakh, Nepal, Sikkim, Bhutan and Arunachal Pradesh as the five fingers of Tibet.

Contested Narrative on the Tibet Question

The conflict between China and Tibet centres on differing views of history. China claims it has ruled Tibet for over 700 years[2] while Tibetans say they were independent until China invaded in 1959[3]. China's current stance that Tibet was always part of China only developed in the 20th century. This narrative intensified after the People's Republic of China (PRC) was formed in 1949.[4] Before that, Chinese writers saw Tibet as a subordinate state, not an integral part of China.

After China's Qing dynasty fell in 1911, the new government claimed Tibet as part of China and sent troops there. The 13th Dalai Lama, who had fled to India to live in exile due to a potential threat of invasion by the Qing dynasty, had just returned in 1912. Upon his return, he decided to make Tibet a 'truly' independent modern nation. Learning from experience, he denied the new government's offer of Chinese titles and instead decided to exercise both temporal and ecclesiastical rule in Tibet.[5]

The Chinese observers are of the understanding that the stationing of Qing officials or ambans (governors), the size of the Qing garrison and the entry of Qing armies into Tibet are part of the larger 'Chinese central government's normal revisions of its policies for a region that has been part of the Chinese state for centuries'.[6]

The Tibetan narrative argues that the relationship between China and Tibet is based on the concept of the 'priest–patron' relationship (Tibetan: Mchod-yon) and this concept differs from the Westphalian notion of sovereignty-based rule between a state and its subject. Despite the ambiguity regarding the structuring of Tibet's status in the Westphalian sense, the Tibetan delegations in the Simla Convention were armed with documents and records indicating Tibet's historical status as an independent nation, its territorial extent and boundaries.

Zhou Enlai's Visit to India

When Chinese Premier Zhou Enlai visited India in November 1956, Indian Prime Minister Jawaharlal Nehru raised the question of the McMahon Line. Zhou Enlai said the line was not fair, but since it was an accomplished fact and because of the friendly relations which existed between China and the countries concerned – India and Myanmar – the Chinese government believed they should give recognition to the McMahon Line. However, in November 1958 in a memorandum to the Indian Embassy, the Chinese wrote that the India–China border had never been formally delimited, that the McMahon line was illegal as the Simla Convention was never recognised by the Chinese central government and that there were differences on the boundary between the two sides. In a letter to Nehru in January 1959, Zhou Enlai questioned the boundary between India and China. The border problems between India and the PRC, therefore, started well before the 14th Dalai Lama escaped and found sanctuary in India in March 1959.[7]

Boundary talks began in December 1981 and continued until November 1986. In 1988, after Prime Minister Rajiv Gandhi's visit to Beijing, the Joint Working Group (JWG) was set up to discuss the border with the understanding that the political leadership would provide impetus where necessary. The JWG met 15 times between July 1989 and 2005 but failed to make any tangible progress. In 1993 the 'Agreement on the Maintenance of Peace and Tranquility along the LAC in the India–China Border Areas' was signed during Prime Minister Narasimha Rao's visit to China in September 1993. Since 2003 a new mechanism, ostensibly to raise the level of discussions, was instituted, namely the Special Representative-level talks. It has met 22 times thus far with negligible progress. Meanwhile, notwithstanding these talks, the Chinese undertook military action to alter the ground situation in May 2020.

The establishment of the People's Liberation Army's (PLA's) Western Theatre Command in 2016 was a significant move by China. It is China's largest theatre command and is designed to facilitate the outward flow of China's military power and potentially coordinate operational plans with Pakistan.[8] Its stated responsibilities include safeguarding China's borders with Afghanistan and Pakistan, safeguarding Chinese investments and projects in the China–Pakistan Economic Corridor (CPEC), protecting China's 4,057 km land frontier with India and focusing on 'threats in Xinjiang and Tibet as well as Afghanistan and other states that host training bases for separatist and extremists'.[9] Its tasking shows that a potent role is envisaged for it in the region.

The Western Theatre Command's formation saw the flow of Chinese military power across India's entire northern border. The increase in military strength deployed along the India–China border became evident even earlier from the increase in the number of generals in the then Chengdu and Tibet Military Regions. The number of major generals and lieutenant generals in the Chengdu Military Region rose from fifty-four to seventy and from eight to ten respectively from 2005 to 2009. Similarly the Tibet Military Region which had eight major generals in 2005 had one lieutenant general and twelve major generals by 2009.

Two articles by Chinese scholars authored in August and October 2020 make the Chinese position evident. One of the articles is by Hu Shisheng, director of the Institute for South Asian Studies at the China Institutes of Contemporary International Relations (CICIR). Hu Shisheng is considered CICIR's leading expert on South Asian affairs, especially India and Pakistan. CICIR is one of China's most influential institutes and is directly under the Ministry of State Security (MoSS), China's external intelligence establishment.

In his 33-page article titled 'The Behavioural Logic behind India's Tough Foreign Policy towards China'[10] and published in *Contemporary International Relations* (*CIR*), the CICIR's official publication, Hu Shisheng was categoric that the 'conflict was not incidental' but the 'inevitable' result of the 'high risk, high yield' policy followed by the Modi administration. He attributed this policy to 'a desire to seek revenge' prompted by 'India's long-term pursuit of absolute security and dominance in the regional order' and the Modi government's ambition to 'overtake China by taking advantage of India's favourable external strategic environment'. Hu Shisheng assessed that 'India's geo-value' has risen to its highest since Independence because of the demands of the US and the West to contain China, particularly in the context of intensifying China–US confrontation, adding that this has given the Modi administration 'more courage and confidence to be tough on China'. Describing the conflict at the Galwan Valley as 'anything but the end', Hu Shisheng said the contest over the border is highly likely to move to a new stage featuring 'contention for control with real power', which will inevitably give rise to border standoffs and clashes.

He assessed that India and China 'were doomed to have a serious collision of interests or even military conflict from the very beginning of their independence and since establishing frontier and regional order'. He asserted this was inevitable 'as one newly born state is a denier of the colonial order, while the other one is its successor'. He clarified this as China resenting humiliation by foreign colonial powers while India, on the contrary, had accepted colonial rule and felt it had benefited from this. Explaining that India perceives itself as a 'successor' to the colonial power and continues to pursue its policies, he said that because of this 'Tibet-related issues and border disputes between China and India continued to intensify and even today, from time to time, these two problems still threaten the stability of China–India relations'. More significantly and pointing to continuing tensions in bilateral ties, he asserted that more complicated than border issues are the contention for influence and dominance and 'order in the region involving relations among China, India and their neighbours'. As the respective national strengths of India and China grow, 'the two major regional powers would have an increasing overlap of interests in the same area'.[11]

In another paper named 'From Donglang to Galwan River Valley: Beware of Three Changes in the Sino-Indian Border Issue'[12] reproduced in the Paper on 29 August 2020, Dr Tongyu Tao stated there would be frequent clashes on the border between India and China because the balance of power between the two in the border area has changed. He referred to improvements in border and defence infrastructure by India and said, 'The recent confrontation in East Ladakh was caused by India's infrastructure construction in the actual control zone. In the Galwan area, the dispute was the construction of the Daulat Beg Oldi [DBO] road in India.' He observed, 'In the past few decades, India has built a large number of facilities on the Sikkim section of the Sino-Indian border, deployed a large number of troops, and even built military installations such as bunkers in some places, constantly changing the border areas' status quo.' He said, 'In the future, as the comprehensive national strength of China and India increases, infrastructure construction activities in border areas will inevitably increase.' He underscored that 'the two sides have huge differences on the actual line of control. Delineating the actual line of control is not easier than delimiting the formal boundary line. Therefore, there is no solution to the actual line of control for the time being'.[13]

In the meanwhile and despite ongoing talks between the border commanders, there has been no reduction in troop deployments or the induction of new modern weaponry by China. More airports have been built in the Tibet Autonomous Region (TAR), and J-10, J-11 and the latest J-20 jet aircraft have been noticed deployed in airfields like Hotan, Gongga and Shigatse. Monitoring developments in TAR has become even more important after India's 4,057-km undemarcated border with China witnessed intensified military activity along its entire length since at least July 2021, when the clash at Galwan Valley resulted in the deaths of Indian soldiers. The higher TAR authorities have been noticed paying unusually increased attention to the border prefectures and counties. Reports have disclosed the presence of Red Arrow-12 missiles in the Xinjiang Military Region. PLA Rocket Force (PLARF) and the PLA's erstwhile Strategic Support Force (PLA SSF) units are present in the PLA Western Theatre Command close to the LAC. Satellite imagery of mid-October 2023 shows that China is constructing new underground military facilities at Lhoka in TAR. Multiple underground facilities already exist at Lhoka. Satellite images on 31 October showed PLA construction activities in Seti Chu and Chupda Chu valleys opposite Tulung La sector in Arunachal Pradesh, confirming reports that the Chinese are building major defence infrastructure projects and roads in the region. Since April 2023, China's Ministry of Civil Affairs has announced a 'standardised' list of geographical names of places within the Indian state of Arunachal Pradesh while referring to it as 'Southern Tibet'. These were published in Chinese, Tibetan and Pinyin. The building of logistics infrastructure and the 'xiaokang' (model border defence well-off villages) has accelerated. The PLA has also increased patrolling activities especially in the Metok region (opposite Upper Siang District, Arunachal Pradesh). On 10 May 2024 the PLA authorities announced bidding for the construction of oxygen supply systems in Shigatse, Nyalam and Chamdo in TAR. The project is estimated to cost around 3 billion yuan and was to be completed in 50 calendar days. The oxygen supply will help the troops stationed in remote areas of TAR to easily access oxygen without travelling back to Lhasa or other big cities. These activities by China along the LAC need to be viewed against the backdrop of Beijing's overall unfriendly attitude towards India and its unyielding stance at the 19 rounds of the border commanders' conference.[14]

Sinicisation of Tibetan Buddhism: The Politics of Reincarnation and the Enhanced Role of the China-appointed Panchen Lama

While India granted asylum to the 14th Dalai Lama and the other religious heads of Tibetan Buddhist sects, in keeping with its tradition, it took care not to provoke China by requesting the Dalai Lama to eschew any anti-China activity or comment on Indian soil. He was also facilitated and permitted to look after the welfare of Tibetans who escaped to India and to preserve their religion, customs and traditions. The Dalai Lama has abided by this undertaking.

A trove of ancient Indian religious and other texts from the ancient Nalanda University, which had been kept safely by the Tibetans, was brought to India by the Tibetans and preserved. They are now being translated.

Since the early 2000s, Buddhism has, however, become another area of contention with China claiming it as an 'ancient Chinese religion'. Beijing sees Buddhism as a way of strengthening its relationship with Southeast Asian nations. Conscious that the heads of all Tibetan Buddhist sects are in India, China started organising the World Buddhist Forum in 2006 to bolster support for Gyaltsen Norbu, its pick as the Panchen Lama, to show that it means to preserve the religious and cultural practices of the Tibetan Buddhist people who have sought refuge in India, and in preparation for garnering support when the time is due to select the 14th Dalai Lama's reincarnation.

Tibetan Buddhism is central to the Tibetan national identity and has been a key historical rallying and unifying point. Monks and nuns have been at the forefront of the Tibetan struggle against China's rule. There was a significant number of monks and nuns who participated in the 1959, 1987 and 2008 protests, and a large number of self-immolators against Chinese rule included monks and nuns. The Chinese communists, therefore, consider Tibetan Buddhism to be an ideological challenge to Chinese communism.

The Chinese communist state has been preparing for the Dalai Lama's succession since as early as 2007 when it passed Order Number 5 – 'Management Measures for the Reincarnation of Living Buddhas in Tibetan Buddhism'.[15] This order gives the China Buddhist Association and the Chinese Communist Party's State Administration of Religious Affairs (SARA) the authority to recognise and identify reincarnations including that of the 14th Dalai Lama's successor. Pursuant to this the CPC has been increasing the visibility and profile of Gyaltsen Norbu, the China-appointed Panchen Lama, who is also the vice president of the China Buddhist Association and the president of the Tibet Branch of China Buddhist Association. The CPC authorities have orchestrated yearly visits for him to the TAR and other parts of Tibet and, gradually overcoming popular resistance, he conducted his longest tour of the TAR from 5 June to 6 December 2023. He toured Chamdo, Lhasa and Shigatse this time and engaged in cultural and religious activities and, for the very first time, ordained monks at Tashilhunpo Monastery, the traditional seat of the Panchen Lamas, between 6 October and 7 November. The CPC is systematically preparing the China-appointed Panchen Lama Gyaltsen Norbu for his important historical role as preceptor to the reincarnate 15th Dalai Lama.

The CPC has been simultaneously pressurising and enticing the monastic and religious circles of Tibet to accept the CPC's stance on reincarnations and to adapt Tibetan Buddhism to 'socialism with Chinese characteristics'.[16] For example, the Institute of Socialism in Tibet and the Tibet Buddhist Association called more than one hundred Tibetan monks from the Sera, Ganden and Drepung monasteries for an intensive ten-day training session in 2019.

Meanwhile, China's communist regime gradually stepped up its efforts to undermine the 14th Dalai Lama's influence. Successive campaigns were launched in the TAR and adjacent Tibetan-dominated areas to portray the Dalai Lama as a 'separatist'. A former TAR party secretary Zhang Qingli said the Dalai Lama is 'a sheep in wolf's clothing and with the heart of a beast'!.[17] On 21 October 2017, at a press conference on the sidelines of the 19th Party Congress, the vice minister and executive deputy head of the CPC Central Committee's (CC's) United Front Work Department (UFWD), Zhang Yijiong, who was promoted at the 19th Congress to become a full member of the CPC CC, reaffirmed China's opposition to the Dalai Lama's visits to foreign countries. Asserting that 'the 14th Dalai Lama is not only a religious figure, but also a political one', Zhang Yijiong made a remark with implications for India. He stated: 'After fleeing China in 1959, he established a so-called government-in-exile, whose goal and core agenda is the independence of Tibet and to separate [from] China. For decades, the group headed by the 14th Dalai Lama has never stopped such attempts. As head of the group, the 14th Dalai Lama has never stopped his activities in this regard over the past decades.' The statement suggests potentially increasing pressure on India with regard to the activities of the Central Tibetan Administration in Dharamshala. In an apparent toughening of the current policy, Zhang Yijiong warned foreign officials against meeting the Dalai Lama saying they 'can't get away by saying they were meeting the exiled Tibetan leader in a personal capacity as they still represent their governments'. Announcing that '[any] country, or any organisation of anyone, accepting to meet with the Dalai Lama, in our view, is a major offence to the sentiment of the Chinese people', he expressed the Chinese government's 'firm opposition' to such meetings and added, '[we] consider such visit as a severe insult to the feelings of the Chinese people'. Interestingly, amid reports of restrictions imposed by authorities on the movement and teachings especially by Tibetan Buddhist monks and nuns inside China, Zhang Yijiong observed that Tibetan Buddhism was a special religion 'born in our ancient China'. 'It's a Chinese religion. It didn't come in from the outside.'[18]

Zhang Yijiong, who had worked in the TAR from 2006 to 2010 as a deputy party secretary, hinted that China's policy towards Tibetan Buddhists would endure and that the authority of the Chinese government would prevail in all religious matters concerning Tibetan Buddhism. Meanwhile, Chinese President Xi Jinping strengthened the CPC CC's UFWD, which has expanded its activities. The UFWD with its increased personnel strength and larger budget has enlarged the Seventh Bureau which looks after matters relating to Tibet and Tibetans.

Available information[19] is that since at least 2016, China's 'united front' activities have increased in India, some European countries, Australia, the US and countries along the Belt and Road Initiative. In addition to targeting Tibetan groups and supporters, the UFWD is reaching out to opinion-makers and 'influencers' by offering cash incentives, scholarships through its 'front' organisations and trips to China. This was accompanied by an increase in security measures across the TAR. The number of individuals employed by the Public Security Bureau to eavesdrop on telephone and internet communications increased appreciably. Domestic spending on security in the TAR between 2007 and 2016 increased by 404 per cent.[20] Since the 2008 pan-Tibet national uprising, China has allotted TAR the highest per capita domestic security budget of all provinces and regions. These figures are in addition to the billions of dollars spent on security-related urban social stability and governance and surveillance technology initiatives. China invested $197 million in 2017, an increase of six times that of the previous year, on the domestic security budget.

Chen Quanguo, a former soldier turned CPC cadre, was appointed the TAR party secretary in 2011 on the recommendation of the then vice president of China Xi Jinping. He introduced a new surveillance and control system, known as the 'Grid-Style Social Governance Management' system, making the security apparatus in the TAR more stringent. This divided urban communities into geometric zones for closer and easier surveillance of the people. It entailed the establishment of police stations and checkpoints stationed 300 to 500 meters apart, and which were equipped with sophisticated, integrated, high-tech facial recognition surveillance systems. Party cadres were also stationed in monasteries.

The Chinese authorities appear to have accelerated efforts to impose 'socialism with Chinese characteristics' on the Tibetans. Tibetan history has been replaced by one authorised by the CPC and it is being taught in schools in the TAR and Tibetan regions.[21] More insidious and damaging are the moves intended to impose CPC control over Tibetan Buddhism and to get the Tibetan people to learn Chinese (Mandarin) instead of Tibetan. The policy that ethnic minorities could study in their respective languages in local schools was revised and it was mandated that all instruction must be in Chinese.[22] The move will have deleterious long-term effects as it means that Tibetans will not be able to access their history, classics or scriptures. It effectively implies the erasure of a civilisation that has existed for well over a few centuries.

Nepal, a country that China deems a potential tool to be used by 'hostile foreign powers'[23] – an oblique reference to the United States and India – to stir trouble in Tibet, has become a country of importance for China. China, facilitated by the installation of a communist government in Nepal, is using Buddhism to expand its regional influence in Nepal. Its interest in Nepal is primarily because of the nearly 20,000 Tibetans residing there. Additionally, many people of Tibetan origin live in the northern fringes of Nepal bordering Tibet.

China has expanded its influence in Nepal, and its embassy interacts directly with Nepal's politicians and police to restrict the activities of Tibetans resident there. China has a specific interest in Lumbini, the birthplace of the Buddha, which lies in Nepal just across the border with India. As a high-ranking Chinese official once told a Nepali reporter, 'We visit Nepal because you have Lumbini, the birthplace of the Buddha.'

Nepal has been the site of ongoing efforts by Beijing to oversee or at least influence the selection of Tibetan Buddhist religious leaders. It has successfully blocked the Dalai Lama from visiting Nepal. In fact, in 2012, Nepal's then culture minister, Minendra Rijal, said the Dalai Lama might visit Lumbini sometime in the future after 'the leadership of China will find ways to deal with His Holiness the Dalai Lama, which will be respectful of the Chinese people'.[24]

In the close neighbourhood too, Beijing has initiated steps that are potentially fraught. China is positioning Tibet as the fulcrum for its strategic policy in the sensitive Himalayan region thus directly and adversely impacting India. The importance of the Himalayan region cannot be overestimated, especially at a time when the Tibetan Buddhists – predominant in this region – are entering a sensitive period with succession to the current 14th Dalai Lama being the central issue. China's foreign policy objectives are aimed at enveloping the Himalayan states in the region, which are on India's northern periphery, into a

China-dominated grouping. While it will be wrapped in the guise of preserving the ecology and environment, the main objective will be to advance Beijing's strategic agenda.[25]

Two events held in the TAR and the TAR party secretary's trip to Nepal, Sri Lanka and Singapore earlier this month need to be viewed against this backdrop. Beijing held two important, though less noticed, events – the '3rd China–Tibet "Rim of the Himalayas" International Cooperation Forum for International Cooperation' in Nyingchi, TAR, on 4 and 5 October 2023, and the '2023 Annual Conference of the China South Asia Society', which held a seminar on the 'Intersection and Integration of Regional Country Studies and Frontier Studies' in Lhasa on 4 November 2023.

There have been a series of high-level visits by CPC officials to the TAR and Nyingchi Prefecture. Their speeches included references to strengthening border defence, increasing the number of 'model' border defence villages and completing the strategic G-219 highway on time.

On 4 and 5 October 2023 China convened its '3rd China–Tibet "Rim of the Himalayas" International Cooperation Forum for International Cooperation' in Nyingchi. Significant among the 280 representatives from over 40 countries, regions and international organisations attending the conference were: Pakistan's acting foreign minister, Jalil Abbas Jilani; the interim foreign minister of Afghanistan, Amir Khan Muttaqi; the vice chairperson of the National Assembly of Nepal, Urmila Ayal; the secretary of the Ministry of Energy and Natural Resources of Bhutan, Karma Tshering; the deputy prime minister of Mongolia, S. Amarsaikhan; and Sri Lanka's minister of sports and youth affairs, Roshan Ranasinghe.

While many attendees have companies working on mining and other projects in Tibet, the presence of representatives from Pakistan, Afghanistan, Nepal and Bhutan indicates that Beijing intends to involve them in its policies for the Himalayan region. China has, for some years, been talking of a Trans-Regional Himalayan Corridor (THRC) and might offer trade and connectivity to the aforementioned countries.[26] Sri Lanka's presence appears intended to draw another South Asian country that already has close ties with China even closer.

The speech by TAR Party Secretary Wang Junzheng outlined China's aims for this forum. He said that cooperation and exchange are the only ways to prosperity and development of the Himalayan region. He said, 'Tibet is an important node on the Southern Silk Road and an important channel for China to open up to South Asia.'[27] It has obvious locational advantages in strengthening cooperation with neighbouring countries around the Himalayas.

A grouping of so-called Himalayan states, which are actually countries like Pakistan and Sri Lanka with close ties to China, will reinforce China's determination to build the world's largest dam on the Great Bend on the

Brahmaputra ignoring the concerns of lower riparian states like India, Myanmar and Bangladesh.

The Yarlung Tsangpo, or the Brahmaputra, courses through the TAR for 2,900 km before it reaches the Great Bend in Nyingchi. The Great Bend, where the Brahmaputra turns south and flows into India and onwards through Bangladesh into the Bay of Bengal, is the site of China's proposed largest dam in the world. The construction of this mega-dam will directly and adversely impact India and Bangladesh. An official announcement in December 2020 confirmed earlier reliable reports that China planned to erect a series of dams on the Brahmaputra and divert the river to irrigate its arable but water-starved north. China claims that the proposed mega-dam, which will be three times the size of the world's largest, the Three Gorges Dam, will supply adequate hydropower for China's entire southwest. Construction work related to the dam is already underway and the Motuo road link, vital for the proposed mega-dam on the Brahmaputra has been completed. Construction of the dam also has military implications for India. Of concern is also the dam that China is building on the Arun River, a tributary flowing from Tibet and feeding the Ganges.

Displaying Beijing's support for this foreign policy initiative,[28] CPC CC Politburo member and Chinese foreign minister Wang Yi emphasised that China has engaged in 'extensive and profound cooperation with other countries in the Himalayan region, continually building consensus on cooperation, actively supporting green development, and enhancing capacity building'.[29] He pointed out that the 'Himalayan countries are geographically connected, share cultural similarities, and are intertwined by destiny. They hold highly similar views on ecological protection and are partners in the modernization process'.[30] Two of the five suggestions he proposed envisage major connectivity projects, trade and cultural exchanges.

The development indicates that Beijing is intent on setting up a grouping of Himalayan states and drawing them into its economic, diplomatic and if possible cultural–religious sphere, and at the same time confront India. The construction of roads will facilitate Chinese exports and people travelling to these countries, offer them alternate routes and gradually overwhelm their economies. Though the plan would take some years to take shape, China might start focusing on growing its economic, political and military influence in these countries. The development implies, as indicated by the presence of the deputy prime minister of Mongolia S. Amarsaikhan, that China will make strenuous efforts to ensure that its nominee succeeds the 14th Dalai Lama.

Finally, as Chinese President Xi Jinping gives no indication of easing tensions and trying to restore normal ties with India by getting the PLA to withdraw to its pre-April 2020 positions, China is increasing pressure points on India. It is persuading international financial institutions like the World Bank and the Asian Development Bank to denote Ladakh, Arunachal Pradesh and other areas as disputed territories. It has already persuaded them not to grant loans to India for even poverty alleviation projects in these areas.[31] India can expect Beijing to maintain sustained pressure.

Notes

1. According to the Chinese state-operated website, China–Tibet Information Network, China had conducted extensive geological surveys of the Qinghai–Tibet Plateau by Chinese researchers since 1999 and had uncovered (by 2007) 16 major mineral deposits in half of Tibet's territory, with an estimated value of $8 billion. The discoveries include copper, iron, lead and zinc. Given that half of Tibet's 2.6 million km² area remains unexplored, these findings suggest that Tibet could potentially become one of China's most mineral-rich regions if the results are confirmed. *Asia News*, 'Train to Lhasa to Take Out Tibet's mineral riches', 2007, https://www.asianews.it/news-en/Train-to-Lhasa-to-take-out-Tibet's-mineral-riches-8577.html
2. 'White Paper 1992: Tibet – Its Ownership and Human Rights Situation'.
3. Brenton Sullivan's review of Sam van Schaik's 'Tibet: A History', in *The Journal of Asian Studies*, 71(4), November 2012, pp. 1135–39.
4. Sperling, E., 2007, *The Tibet–China Conflict: History and Polemics*, Washington, DC: East–West Centre.
5. Stanley K. Hornbeck's review of Charles Bell's Tibet, Past and Present, in *The American Historical Review* 30(4), 1 July 1925, p. 827.
6. Sperling, E., 2007, *The Tibet–China Conflict: History and Polemics*, Washington, DC: East–West Centre.
7. The meeting between Zhou Enlai and Nehru during the former's visit to India largely focused on the legitimacy of the McMahon Line. Nehru stated that the McMahon Line was the accepted border based on the 1914 Simla Convention while Zhou's stance was that China did not recognise the McMahon Line as a legal boundary. The talk did not result in a resolution.
8. U.S. Department of Defense, 2023, 'Military and Security Developments Involving the People's Republic of China', https://media.defense.gov/2023/Oct/19/2003323409/-1/-1/1/2023-military-and-security-developments-involving-the-peoples-republic-of-china.pdf
9. https://ccasindia.org/BRIEF-SINO-PAK-Implications.pdf
10. Shisheng, H. and W. Jue, 2020, 'The Behavioural Logic behind India's Tough Foreign Policy towards China', *Contemporary International Relations*, 30(5).
11. Ibid.
12. https://ccasindia.org/CCAS-Chinese-Thinking-on-Border.pdf
13. Tao, T., 'From Donglang to Galwan River Valley: Beware of Three Changes in the Sino-Indian Border Issue'.
14. https://chinapower.csis.org/china-tibet-xinjiang-border-india-military-airport-heliport/

15. https://www.cecc.gov/resources/legal-provisions/measures-on-the-management-of-the-reincarnation-of-living-buddhas-in-0
16. https://www.hindustantimes.com/world-news/panchen-lama-says-buddhism-in-tibet-will-be-sinicised-adopt-socialist-traits-101615439553367.html; https://www.vifindia.org/print/9152
17. At a press conference on the sidelines of the 19th Party Congress, Zhang Yijiong – the vice minister of the CPC CC's UFWD and its executive deputy head at the time – expressed China's continued disapproval of the Dalai Lama's international travels. Zhang, who received a promotion to full CC member at the Congress, used the press conference to reinforce China's stance on the matter, https://ccasindia.org/CCAS-19th%20CC-TIBET.pdf
18. https://news.cctv.com/2017/10/22/ARTIgqCtJIh3K0KskNvZJ0jH171022.shtml; https://v.cctv.com/2017/10/21/VIDEu1MALMUEfPFgAuGqeovs171021.shtml
19. https://ccasindia.org/CCAS-19th%20CC-TIBET.pdf
20. https://jamestown.org/program/chinas-domestic-security-spending-analysis-available-data/
21. https://ccasindia.org/CHINA-CAMPAIGN-ETHNIC-MINORITIES.pdf
22. https://ccasindia.org/CHINA-REPLACES-ETHNIC-LANGUAGES-WITH-MANDARIN-A.pdf
23. https://archive.claws.in/559/china-against-any-country-interfering-in-sino-nepalese-ties-jayadeva-ranade.html
24. https://carnegieendowment.org/research/2017/03/buddhism-a-new-frontier-in-the-china-india-rivalry
25. https://ccasindia.org/TIBET-THE-FULCRUM-OF-CHINAS-STRATEGIC-POLICY-IN-THE-HIMALAYAS.pdf
26. https://www.vifindia.org/article/2023/december/05/tibet-the-fulcrum-of-china-s-strategic-policy-in-the-himalayas
27. https://bianba.changdu.gov.cn/bbxrmzf/c105705/202407/ce144d5df3df4881acbd7a5ac97e694d.shtml
28. https://baijiahao.baidu.com/s?id=1778890770704704364&wfr=spider&for=pc
29. Ibid.
30. Ibid.
31. https://timesofindia.indiatimes.com/world/china/china-suggests-it-blocked-indias-loan-efforts-at-adb-due-to-border-dispute/articleshow/4401348.cms

Part Four

Decoding China's Military Universe

18

Instrument of the Chinese Dream
A Military Appreciation of the 'New Era' People's Liberation Army

Lieutenant General Gautam Banerjee

'When the pace of change accelerates, the militaries that change and adapt are likely to gain massive advantage over potential enemies who are less agile.'
— Lt Col Scott Stephenson

As the principal bulwark of the Communist Party of China (CPC) autarkic rule over the People's Republic of China (PRC), the People's Liberation Army (PLA) has been of much interest. In the global strategic discourse, that interest turns into matters of serious concern when it comes to the CPC's assertion of the PRC's superior entitlements in what it sees as a Sino-centric environment. Here is a formidable economic, technological and political power that seeks to repudiate the post-Second World War codes of international conduct in favour of its self-arrogating versions of global order. The PLA, an integral organ of the party, is the CPC's prime instrument for achieving that end. This essay takes stock of the milestones of the PLA's processes of modernisation of combat hardware, force restructure of battle formations, reforms in higher defence organisation and the implications thereof. This undertaking is proposed to be attended to in two parts as follows:
- Part I: PLA as an Instrument of the CPC's Dream
- Part II: PLA's Service-Specific and Joint Services Empowerment.

Part I: PLA As Instrument of the CPC's Dream

PLA's Pivotal Role

In its essence, the CPC's mandate to the PLA can be summarised as: one, absolute subordination to the party and to 'win wars'; two, 'unification' of the motherland;[1] three, protection of PRC's 'new domains' of the acquired overseas interests and, four, establishment of PRC's exclusive hegemony in the Asia-Pacific Region while preventing 'interference' from the US-led proponents of the existing rule-based order.[2]

The PLA is being built up to extend its reach far into China's western and eastern areas of interest that would eventually lead to its military tentacles enjoying global presence.[3] To that end, the Chinese military is fast building up to deter – even oust – the US alliances' so far unchallenged military power in the Indo-Pacific region. PLA's modernised military arsenal is stated to match, even exceed in sheer numbers – though definitely not in quality – that of the US and its allies.[4] That build-up is also expected to subsume any regional resistance to PRC's hegemonic entitlements. Thrust on military diplomacy permits China to enter into the political and military systems of its client states through sale of hardware and training of personnel.

A defining ideology of the CPC is the congruence of military and economic power. During the first decade and a half of its assumption of power, it had committed to build a robust 'people's army' with nuclear weapons, even if that came at the cost of great hardships to its people. Having secured itself, the thrust was then shifted in the later 1970s to the nation's economic and technological modernisation. That in turn permitted China to pick up its pace in modernising its land, sea, air and nuclear forces. The restructuring of its military organisation in compatibility with its strategic goals followed a process which continues unhindered by any resource limitations.[5] As stated, China has also mastered military diplomacy to enter the political and military systems of its client states.[6]

Presently, China is gearing to back up its overseas economic interests in the backdrop of military heft.

The PLA: Concepts and Policies

PLA's 'new era' force restructure, modernisation and military reforms are dictated by the PRC's hegemonic ambitions as discussed above. It would, therefore, be apt to preface the discussion about the PLA's current concepts and policies with a brief mention of its background.

The Process of PLA's Modernisation

Aimed at absorption of advancements in the field of military affairs, the process of conceptualisation of the PLA's modernisation and restructuring commenced in the early 1980s at the instance of the PLA General Staff headed by Deng Xiaoping. On ground, the process was given added impetus in the early 1990s after the PRC was well on its way to achieving the other parts of its 'four modernisations'. Since then, the PLA has continued with the upgrade of its equipment profile and corresponding reconfiguration of its field forces. By 2015 or thereabouts, the process at the tactical and operational levels was well entrenched across all the echelons of the PLA.

As a natural corollary to the previous parts of its military modernisation process, the CPC – its highest political-military decision making as well as command and control body, the Central Military Commission (CMC) to be precise – formally switched over between late 2015 and early 2016 to implement the next phase of its apex level military reforms and restructure. In definite terms, this part involved integration of the PLA General Headquarters (GHQ) into the structure of the CMC, and corresponding restructuring of its regional commands into joint theatre commands. This stage also witnessed a surge in the PLA's investments on development of the various components of information warfare (IW), including intelligence, surveillance and reconnaissance (ISR), unmanned weapons systems, space and cyber operations and the latest digital tools for the military's systemic enhancements like power algorithms and artificial intelligence (AI).

During the following years and till date, China's CMC has continued to implement the reforms and restructuring in China's apex-level national defence organisation. The objectives are: one, effective management of the PLA's modernised and restructured military, paramilitary and defence-dedicated establishments, and two, building a reformed CMC's expertise in the exercise of effective command and control over a joint services PLA and operational training of the PLA's modernised field forces. Significantly, the process is also meant to establish absolute control of the party over its military institution in conformity with the core ideology of CPC.

Pushed relentlessly by a select group of hardline communist autocrats, headed by an obdurate Chairman of the CMC, modernisation of the PLA has been China's priority national effort. Slated to be functional by the end of 2020, this integration of apex-level defence decision-making system and corresponding field training is the final step in China's landmark endeavour to modernise and restructure the PLA from top to bottom. Though by and large both the steps of China's military modernisation and restructure schemes are said to have reached their productive stage, the process must necessarily be an unremitting one. Indeed, military schemes are never 'complete' in the absolute sense and require continuous readjustments and upgrades in addition to occasional reorientations.

PLA's 'New Era' Military Force Restructure, Modernisation and Reforms

The preceding brief sets the stage for the PLA's current outlines of conceptual and policy matters under the following heads:
- PLA's 'new era' force restructure
- Modernisation and restructuring of the PLA
- PLA's apex-level reforms, 2016–22
- Strategising and war preparedness

PLA's 'New Era' Force Restructure

PLA's new era force restructure has allowed it to 'right-size' its establishment of 3 million personnel to 2 million – presently, it stands at 2.2 million. To do so, 25 per cent across-the-board rationalisations have been applied at the military's formation headquarters and the rear echelon levels, while the bloated non-combat elements have been pruned by 50 per cent. The PLA's overall force structure has thus been optimised by trimming the PLA Army (PLAA) through mechanised, manoeuvre and firepower enhancements and corresponding discarding of its baggage of non-combat redundancies. That process is complemented by quantum enhancements in the PLA's overall joint operational strength through modernisation and restructure of the PLA Navy (PLAN) and the PLA Air Force (PLAAF).

PLA's new era force structure includes two new services: the PLA Rocket Forces (PLARF) and the PLA Strategic Support Forces (PLASSF). The joint force structure is complemented by the Joint Logistics Support Forces, integrated IW capabilities, induction of state-of-the-art weaponry like the 'aircraft carrier, radar killer' and hypersonic missiles (DF-17), scram jet high-velocity systems (Xingkong-2) and expanding inventories of Unmanned Aerial and Sea Vehicles (UAV, USV). PLA's regular force structure is further complemented by the half a million-strong military reserve forces and 660,000 paramilitary forces placed directly under the CMC.

PLA's policy of Military–Civil Fusion (MCF) is aimed at developing an integrated approach to defence research, technology, industry and dual-use infrastructure developments. Mobilisation of civil talent and adaptation of civil educational, logistic and administrative systems for military purposes are some other aspects of the MCF.[7]

All such apex-level reforms have recently been conferred with façades of legislative backing through promulgation of various laws and regulations related to military legislation, defence transportation, border security, security of military installations, enforcement of military discipline, management of civilian personnel and administration of MCF. That, of course, is but a cosmetic exercise against the Communist regime's arbitrary, dictatorial powers and is meant for assuaging democratic sensitivities.

Modernisation and Restructuring of the PLA

Military upgrades have been a regular feature in the CPC's rule since it assumed power in 1948. In its post-1979 version, brisk measures to prepare foundations for the eventual modernisation of the PLA's fighting forces – like refrain from non-combat ventures, structural rationalisations, unit-level weapon and equipment upgrades, military training and technical education – had continually progressed, albeit against much tug-of-war amongst the modernist and orthodox factions. By mid-1990s, the process had firmed and, by mid-2000s, modernisation and restructuring at the tactical unit level was well on its way across the core echelons of the PLA. The ambit of the effort was then extended to operational-level restructuring of field formations and conducting service-specific as well as joint operational-level training exercises. That process has continued through 2015 and thereafter.

Hardware modernisation and organisational restructuring have been complemented by regularly conducting proficiency training in training establishments, and collective exercises in training fields. A key aspect of the PLA's military modernisation has been the salience it has accorded to the science and technology education of its personnel, both at the officer and junior leadership levels. Accordingly, the PLA's seventy-seven services, universities and colleges – including the premier ones like the National Defence University (NDU), the National University of Defence Technology (NUDT) and the Academy of Military Sciences (AMS) – have been reorganised into forty-four training institutions.

Insights into the PLA's inventories and force capabilities are widely available and therefore not in the focus of this discussion. It suffices to point out that PLA's war-waging assets are massive in number, and as a corollary, permeation of modernisation and restructure schemes into the entire force would have to be a long and continuous process. Professional evaluations also suggest that the perfectionist claims of accuracy, lethality and battle functionalities of the PLA's modernised elements might need to be moderated somewhat. Similarly, claimed levels of proficiencies during training exercises and the exercising of chains of command and control seem to be somewhat overstated when tested under known war conditions. The PLA seeks to overcome these issues by regular conduct of joint field exercises with friendly foreign nations. These moderations are relevant in realist evaluation of the PLA's war-worthiness.[8]

PLA's Apex-Level Reforms, 2016–22

As mentioned earlier, having set the course for brisk implementation of the tactical and operational parts of its military modernisation and restructure schemes, the CPC formally switched over to implement the final part of it at the apex level of defence administration in 2015–16. By that stage, it had more or less reached the highpoint of its structural, hardware and procedural modernisation, and from thereon it was just a matter of pressing along towards wider permeation, routine course corrections and technological infusions, duly spaced by the decadal timelines of 2027, 2035 and 2049.

That stage would therefore be an appropriate start-point for a discussion over the PLA's current trends of operational pursuits.

In December 2015, through formal issuance of 'Guidelines on National Defence and Military Reforms', the apex-level command and control structure of the PLA, namely the PLA General Headquarters (GHQ), was subsumed into the PRC's highest political-military decision-making body, viz, the CMC. Constitutions of the PLA Rocket Force (PLARF), PLA Strategic Support Force (PLASSF), PLA Reserve Force, People's Militia and the People's Armed Police Force (PAPF) were also formalised under direct control of the CMC, the local control remaining vested upon the PLA. The end objective was to institute a 'seamless system in which the CMC takes charge of the overall administration of the PLA, the PAPF and the People's Militia and Reserve Forces, Battle Zone Commands focus on combat preparedness, and various military services pursue development'.[9] Significantly, the process was also meant to establish absolute control of the party over its military institution in conformity with the core ideology of the CPC.

PLA's Restructured Theatre Commands
Source: US DoD Annual Report to Congress, *Military and Security Developments Involving the People's Republic of China, 2020.*

The following years were devoted to structural integration of the PLA GHQ into the CMC. Executive orders were also promulgated to restructure the erstwhile seven regional commands into five joint theatre commands, and the process was given a two-year period to firm.[10] Besides battle formations from the PLAA, PLAN and PLAAF, varying numbers of air defence, rocket, special operations, aviation, airborne, air assault and amphibious forces as well as logistic regiments/brigades and establishments were grouped under the eastern, southern, western, northern and central joint theatre commands, and further affiliated with the recently reorganised group armies. It was only to be expected that such complex processes would be subject to a time spillover; according to a PLA report, restructuring of the western and central joint theatre commands was completed in June 2020, while others were 'following'.

The period 2016–20 was also marked by the PLA's accelerated systemic incorporation of various components of military Information Warfare (IW) including intelligence, surveillance and reconnaissance (ISR), unmanned weapons systems, space weaponisation and cyber operations. The already well-established joint operational and logistic communication networks were further reinforced through systemic integration of terrain acclimatisation processes and expanded coverages. Impetus was also given to the assimilation of the latest digital tools, like power algorithms, AI and psychological operations into the military's systemic enhancements. Like all military developments, these measures continue in the manner of routine, long-term features of military modernisation.[11]

In the final two years of this period, the goal was set to build the reformed CMC's professionalism in exercise of command and control over the PLA's joint services organisational structure. Conjointly, operational-level training of the PLA's modernised field forces was also focused upon. Thus, by the 2020 deadline, the reformed CMC was stated to have settled down in its apex-level military command and control functions. At the PLA's directive levels, modernised hardware and intra- as well as inter-service organisational restructures were also stated to have been well assimilated into a joint services system of warfare. Hereafter, building up a modernised arsenal and development of corresponding professional competence continue to permeate into the PLA's battle formations and units.[12]

Strategising and War Preparedness

The PRC has been reiterating its resolve to equip the PLA as a 'mechanised, informatised and intelligentised joint force with Chinese Characteristics' by 2027, consolidate the process by 2035 and build it into a 'world class' military by 2047. Obviously, these date-lines signify the stages of assimilation of modernisation and structural reforms into the PLA's war preparedness.[13] The aim is to strengthen the PLA in performing its foretasted mandates, particularly those related to unification of Taiwan and reclaim what are viewed as the PRC's 'lost territories'. The reiterated strategy is to win 'local wars' by recourse to 'active defence' – a subterfuge for preplanned aggression mislabelled as 'counter-attack in self-defence' – while preventing the US-led Western powers from coming to the aid of its victim(s) through 'Anti-Access-Area Denial' (AA/AD) campaigns. The PRC's two million military establishment is justified thus by its military-dependent hegemonic ambitions.[14]

In the context of promoting 'active defence', the PLA has recently propounded Multi-Domain Precision Warfare (MDPW) as its 'core operational concept'. The concept is but an updated reiteration of the PLA's post-1992 concepts of prosecuting full-spectrum, multidimensional warfare across the entire range of conventional, special and sub-conventional operations by the recourse to integrated networks of Command, Control, Communications, Computers, Intelligence, Surveillance and Reconnaissance (C4ISR). The MDPW further qualifies that concept with implied hints over militia, cyber and space enhancements to bolster its conventional and sub-conventional capabilities of striking at the opponent's systemic vulnerabilities. Utilisation of drone and cruise missile inventories is another thrust area for joint as well as service-specific operational usage.[15]

As in its preceding versions, there is a hint of 'all-out war' in the fundamentals of the MDPW. Muscle-flexing in Southeast China Sea, weaving a 'string of pearls' around the Indian Ocean, empowering irresponsible 'friends' in the region, hanging the Damocles sword over Taiwan, nonchalant diversion of river waters and global spread of cyber intrusions are some manifestations of the CPC-PLA's grand design. Given the glimpses of China's military strategy – which encompasses civilian, dual-use and purely military recourses to conduct operations at psychological, politico-economic and military levels – no nation that the CPC views as 'problematic' may afford to remain complacent to its forestated grand design.

In all that conceptualisation, amplification of the PLA's mandate from 'regional defence' to the recently added task of 'trans-theatre operations' is notable. Apparently, the latter task is meant to cover a growing need to protect the PRC's overseas assets, trade commitments and supply chains against possible disruption.[16] To hone battle proficiencies, the PLA has been regularly conducting joint services exercises – STRIDE-22 being the latest one – and participating in multinational military drills like the ZAPAD-21 series of exercises. However, while the mandate of regional defence is achievable by a mix of military coercion and aggression in a militarily modest neighbourhood, the PLA's trans-theatre force projection would need long-term building up to find fruition among powerful international stakeholders.

Comments

Analyses of formal as well as informal information on the PLA's assimilation of the modernisation schemes are, as expected, subject to variations and exaggerations on account of the observer's preconceptions. On that count, the vast range of inputs, mostly varying based on observer bias, have to be professionally analysed before the effective progress made so far may be adjudged.

While the processes of modernisation, restructuring and reforms may somewhat be forced to adhere to deadlines, permeation of these developments all across the PLA's massive military structure has to be a long-term and cyclic undertaking. Besides, it takes long years of practical experience, under battle conditions, to master the orchestration of revised systems of command, control, deployment, force application, logistics, etc. To that end, the PLA's apex-level command and control structure may require some years of hard training and field exercises to crystallise its proficiency in war waging.

On account of its high-end qualitative requirements, it would be farfetched at the present stage to anticipate application of MDPW at the tactical levels of the PLA to that degree as it was seen during the Coalition Force operations in the Gulf War – that level of grassroots integration is yet far. Indeed, there exists a large ambition–capability gap in China's strategy of integrated employment of all services at all levels. It is expected that this gap, given the right conditions, may become operationally manageable by the year 2030 or so. Till that happens, application of the concept would likely be limited to the theatre and area command levels. Meanwhile, for serious military operations, the PLA would mostly depend on partially automated execution of joint battle and weapon management functions.[17]

Notably, the ongoing reform, restructure and modernisation of the PLA do not, in any telling manner, restrict the CMC from tasking its field formations to undertake tactical-level localised and mid-intensity aggressions against its hopelessly outgunned neighbours – nations on the CPC's target list may note.

Part II: PLA's Service-Specific and Joint Services Empowerment

Service-Specific Modernisation and Force Structuring, 2016–23

The foregone discussion over the PLA's guiding concepts and policies sets the stage for delving further into certain salient aspects of the recent service-specific as well as joint services developments.

The PLA Army (PLAA)

In broad structural terms, the PLAA's frontline field formations consisting of eighteen group armies have been reorganised into thirteen combined corps or new joint services group armies, totalling approximately 975,000 personnel and orbatted under the five joint theatre commands. These group armies consist of up to six combined arms brigades (totalling eighty-one) and the usual complement of supporting arms brigades and logistic echelons. Significantly, the brigades consist of four to six battalion groups of integrated all-arm configuration. This is an immense improvement in the battle capabilities of the PLA's basic unit of combat.

Combined arms brigades are classified into light, medium and heavy according to their role and combat inventories. Additional punch is provided by the grouping of one or more of the fifteen Special Operations Forces (SOF) brigades. Notably, compositions of Xinjiang, Tibet, East Coast and possibly the Central Military Regional Commands have been retained in view of local operational sensitivities. Static Military Districts, with 'garrison' divisional formations and regiments/brigades under command, continue to be responsible for subsidiary combat operations, logistic support infrastructure, border management and internal security. Pending their turn for upgrade, these formations are equipped with legacy weapons and equipment.

Significant modernisations announced in April 2019 include induction of self-propelled anti-aircraft guns and precision weaponry, and upgrade of howitzers to support light tanks; both these weapons play key roles in operations in hilly and plateau areas. Induction of an advanced model of rifle, meant to turn soldiers into 'super soldiers', has commenced. The PLAA is building up its transportation by air and sea through tactical insertion manoeuvres and dismounted assault, and following up with logistic sustenance thereafter. Medium-lift helicopters and drones are being deployed to deliver explosives, ammunition and other items to support composite attack groups engaged in high-altitude and obstacle-breaching assaults. To that purpose, the thrust is on terrain-specific training in combined arms and joint operational formats. The Tibetan Plateau and island operations' scenarios astride the East Coast are the selected terrains for regular training. So far, results of such training under challenging conditions can be adjudged, both from the coverage of the PLA's in-house and foreign observers, to be dull somewhat.

Comments

The PLAA is briskly transforming into a trim, highly lethal and manoeuvrable ground force with adequate capabilities for joint operational roles in high-altitude plateau lands, coastal areas and near as well as distant lands. Its selected formations are training for inter- and intra-theatre sea and air transportation as well as overseas deployment on security and peacekeeping roles. The PLAA, PLAN and PLAAF are jointly operating in employ of the PLA's total numbers of seventeen army aviation air assault (helicopters), seven airborne and eight marine brigades for transportation, manoeuvres, force deployment and insertion operations. As the trend continues, the PLAA, grouped with the naval and air forces, could be expected to break free of its 'localised war' stipulation.

Deployment of the better part of the PLAA's thirteen group armies has to be terrain-dependent and therefore only partially effective on one terrain or the other – East Coast–China Seas–Taiwan on one end and Tibet–Xinjiang on the other. The PLAA's massive commitment to dominating the Indo-Tibetan border is an additional commitment. Massive development of air transportation capability for force re-deployment is aimed at covering up for such constraints. In its postmodernisation role, extension of the PLAA's operational deployment range beyond the PRC's borderlands to cover the PRC's areas of interest across the Asian landmass is expected to be in the CMC's agenda.

Amphibious, sea and air transportation and landing operations would enable the PLA to go beyond its current mandate of recovery of the so-labelled 'lost territories'. These would also play designated roles in the 'security' of the PRC's overseas economic ventures and assets. PLAA should also be expected to play larger roles in peace missions and disaster relief.[18]

Most significantly, as an integral instrument of the party, the PLA remains as a robust guarantor of the CPC's domestic rule.

PLA Army Navy (PLAN)

The 340-ship PLAN is, by numerical strength, the largest navy in the world. Of these, 125 ships are qualified as major surface combatants while more than 200 are stated to be of pre-modernisation design. The PLAN component of the theatre commands remains organised as before, into fleets and brigades or regiments. Under the PLAN's modernisation and restructuring schemes, PRC's massive marine industry is well-geared up to briskly replace older vessels with modern multi-role surface combatants and submarines.

In its 'new era' role, the PLAN is mandated to graduate from 'near sea defence' to 'far sea protection missions'.[19] Seizure of claimed islands and imposition of dominating control over the Southwest Pacific and Indian Oceans are intrinsic to that role. Notably, the Coast Guard and naval militia, even fishermen, are to be lead players in encroachment of the claimed islands as well as the title entitlements over marine resources. Considering the centrality of the Indian Ocean in the global political-economic order, the PRC seeks to extend the PLAN's reach further across the successive island chains, the Bay of Bengal and the Arabian Sea. The intent, as behoves a great power, is to protect its sea lanes of two-way energy and trade transportation as well as the expanding overseas commercial interests. In all that, inherence of hegemonic intent is evidenced by the PRC's gearing up with massive inventories of naval–air weaponry, long-range precision missiles, UAVs, USVs and ISR to prevent 'interference' from the global superpower under its AA/AD scheme.[20]

The PLAN is adapting to far-seas roles by sailing two partially operational aircraft carriers alongside the basic air and carrier battle groups. A third aircraft carrier is under construction and a fourth one is on the drawing board. Corresponding building up of composite battle groups is also underway through serial production of cruisers, frigates, guided missile destroyers, amphibious assault ships, mix of conventional, nuclear propelled and nuclear-armed submarines, patrol boats and ancillary ships from the PRC's many modern shipyards. As is the construction of amphibious transport aircraft, development of unmanned battleships and electromagnetic weaponry. For extended coverage of naval deployments, the PLAAF's modernised land-based H-6J maritime strike bombers are earmarked to be flown from inland and overseas bases. PRC's expanded naval reach is complemented also by expansion of the PLAN Marine Corps (PLANMC) from three to six (or eight) marine brigades (190,000 troops). Establishment of suitably located coastal bases for shipping maintenance facilities and force deployments all along the Indian Oceanic transportation lanes is also in focus.[21]

PLAN's training activities are in consonance with its modernisation and restructuring, the thrust being on far-sea sailing in the Pacific and Indian Oceans, passage of straits and amphibious manoeuvres and assault on islands. The obvious target areas are the Sea of Japan, Taiwan, the South China Sea and the Philippines Sea. PLAN's goal is to extend its strike capability in phases up to and beyond the PRC's immediate array of South China Sea islands, usually referred to as the 'first island chain' by 2027 or so. Naval exercises to meet that goal are being conducted regularly; 2021–22 saw the conduct of joint exercises in Philippines Sea, South China Sea, Java Sea, Celebs Sea, Sea of Japan, North Pacific-Alaskan waters and the Gulf of Aden. Building up on its thirteen years of counter-piracy experience, regular high-sea sailings and port visits, the PLAN is consolidating the PLA's joint services ISR capabilities and its hydrographic survey data base while mastering the art and science of oceanic sailing.

China's Maritime Geography: The Island Chains
Source: Zachary Fillingham, 'The PLA Navy: A Challenge to US Hegemony in East Asia?',
Geopolitical Monitor, 6 September 2015.

Comments

In the PLA's April 2018 Presidential Review, PLAN was commended for its 'brand new' image and for 'standing up in the East'. The obvious references were to its flag-bearing role spanning from West Pacific to Northern Indian Oceans, and forcible usurpations of China Sea islands. The trend of PLAN's hardware modernisation and fleet restructuring clearly indicates the CPC's intent of assuming ownership of the South China Sea and its islands and establishment of dominant control over the waters of the Indo-Pacific. Notably, the tactical trend points to grey-scale encroachment operations staged behind the frontages of civilian fishermen, naval militia and Coast Guard actions, all backed up by the PLAN's ready presence. Projection of their civilian fronts to such encroachments would pose serious hindrance to the victim nations in their efforts to resist the CPC's arbitrary territorial usurpations.

In firming its hegemony, the CPC's intent on preventing 'outsiders' – the US-led Western powers – from 'interfering' in regional affairs of what it considers as its own 'area of influence', as stated earlier, and thereby closing the dissenting nations' option of seeking succour from allies and partners. PLA's desire to extend the reach of its naval power to what are described as the 'second' and even a 'third island chains' is in tune with the said intent. PLAN's strategic presence across the globe in furtherance of the PRC's global economic interests is part of a longer-term objective.

PLA Air Force (PLAAF)

The PLA's air arm consists of nearly 2,800 military aircrafts, of which 2,250 are of the combat variety; 800 of these are of fourth-generation plus. Taking into account PLAN aviation, the PLAAF is the third-largest air force in the world. Like the other services, the modernised components of the PLAAF are reorganised into brigades and wings, and duly affiliated to various joint theatre commands, combined corps, group armies and naval fleets.

In PRC's recent White Paper, the PLAAF is mandated to graduate from 'territorial defence' to long-range 'offensive and defensive air power projection' across terrestrial as well as maritime domains.[22] Accordingly, the PLAAF is building up its fighter, bomber, air defence, air transportation and helicopter elements, supported by briskly building up communications, ISR and electronic warfare capabilities.[23] In the maritime domain, the PLAAF has more or less established its domination over both, the East and the South China Seas. It is now slated to be operative from the PRC-acquired overseas coastal bases to support PLAN operations all across the Indian-West Pacific Ocean.

Yet, to master frontier military aviation technologies, particularly in engines and avionics, the PLAAF is fast modernising to catch up with the Western air powers. PLAAF's modernisation schemes consist of upgrade of all 1,800 of its fighter aircrafts to fifth generation (J-20 version) capabilities and development of long-range and precision strike versions of its H-6 bombers. The PLA's overall strategies are complemented by development of long-range heavy lift air transportation capabilities (Y-20 variants) and air refuellers (H-6U and IL-78). In 2019, the PLAAF displayed its long-range refuellable nuclear capable bomber H-6N, which completes the PLA's nuclear triad. Induction of fleets of medium-lift utility helicopters (Z-20) for tactical transportation has also been reported.

The PLAAF possesses one of the largest inventories of long-range missiles and anti-missile defence systems. In 2021, a mid-course interceptor version – a component of its multi-tiered missile defence – was tested. Notably, massive force multiplication effect, in terms of electronic warfare and airborne early warning and control system (AWACS), is being built up simultaneously. Wide varieties of UAVs for combat (hunter, suicide and battlefield swarming drones), ISR and logistic roles are being integrated into the combat elements of all the three services.

PLAAF's airborne corps has been restructured into six combined arms brigades, besides being grouped with one each of SOF, air transport and logistic support brigades. Besides participating in multinational military exercises, these brigades regularly participate in joint training with the PLAA and PLANMC formations.

Comments

The trend is indicative of the PLAAF's growth into a strategic force with extra-regional reach. To that end, its air operational reach within the arcs of the China and Japan Seas are regularly demonstrated. However, true tactical efficacy of such demonstrative overflights may be apparent only when considered in terms of comprehensive force deployments – involving not only the packaging of air task forces, but also that of the matching components of the other two services, as well as operational logistic support.

For the attainment of extra-regional operational reach, the PRC's geographic situation calls for finding overseas air bases with integrated joint forces composition and logistics infrastructure along the ocean coasts. The PRC's quest for finding quasi-military overseas bases is aimed at addressing that hurdle. Herein, strength of India's geography makes it harder for it to flex its military muscles in the Indian Ocean region. It would therefore need many more years to attain the forestated objective.

Empowerment of the PLA's Support Services

The modernised PLA's objective is to perform multi-domain operational roles by favourably 'shaping' the battlefield before the decisive forces are committed to deliver the *coup de main*. To that end, the PLA has undertaken to organise its Rocket and Missile Forces (PLARF), Strategic Support Forces (PLASSF), Joint Logistics Support Forces, inventories of UAVs and USVs and IW capabilities. The last is being done through the establishment of cyber warfare cells at theatre command headquarters comprising nearly 50,000 personnel.

It is remarkable that the PLARF has expanded from twenty-six to thirty-nine brigades with various versions of antiship, cruise, siloed inter-continental as well as nuclear-conventional ballistic missiles, besides the development of hypersonic glide vehicles (HGV) - over 2,500 missiles in all. Among many other developments, special references may be made to long range reconnaissance-strike UAVs (Wing Loong II), scram jet high velocity systems (Xingkong-2), 'aircraft carrier and radar killer' missiles, hypersonic missiles (DF-17), laser beam weapon systems (LW-30) and Bei Dou transmission and satellite navigation systems. Battlefield efficacy of these developments may need to be evaluated.[24]

PLA's Operational Objectives

The processes of modernisation and reforms have not detracted the CPC from its foundational principle of 'barrel of gun' statecraft. Thus, while keeping its acts of military intimidation and territorial usurpations below the level of serious military conflagration, the CPC continues to – by subterfuge and deceit – proceed step-by-step towards its imperialist destination. In that, frivolous and vain claims in what it considers its 'region of influence' are being hardened over the years. When the CPC finds that the time is ripe, the sequence of assertive propaganda, military intimidation and incremental encroachments by border guard troops as well as militia and civilian villagers' or fishermen actions – backed up by a powerful PLA – is slated to be set in motion.

Reckonable parts of the South China Sea features and neighbouring borderlands have been occupied thus and the work remains incessant. Military arrogations against Vietnam, Taiwan, Japan, India, Philippines and Indonesia (Natuna Island) are some recent manifestations of that tactic.[25] Hapless targets of such arrogations are 'advised' against threats of debilitating retaliation and encouraged to resolve their issues through 'bilateral' mechanisms and keep away from the negative influences of 'interfering' outside powers. To that end, the PLA's operational objectives are to identify vulnerabilities in the Western military power network systems and exploit these by building its capabilities to deter, if not wipe out, 'outsider interference' in the West Pacific and Indian Ocean regions.

The PLA seeks to attain those objectives by covering its relative military weakness through creation of favourable tactical asymmetries. In that, conventional asymmetric methods are sought to be boosted by reliance on IW, swarming masses of manned and unmanned sea and air weapon platforms and sustained precision missile strikes, all aimed at deterring and denying the Western powers access to the PRC's areas of influence. PLA's modernisation, battle inventories and training are dedicated to those operational objectives.

When seen in the light of its military modernisation and reforms, the PLA's forcibly usurped islands, rising frequency of military intimidations over the Taiwan Strait, unilateral enforcements against the rightful international maritime activities in both the China Seas, aggressive posturing and incessant incursions across the Indo-Tibet Border and consolidation of military footholds all across the Indo-Pacific Region, the CPC's imperialist motivations become clear. Similarly indicative, when projected on a larger strategic canvas, are the PRC's solidarity with North Korean demon-dance and Russia's war strategy, intimidation of Japan, South Korea, Vietnam, Philippines and other neighbours and military provocations against international navigational freedom over the common waterways of the China Seas. These bellicosities conform to a worrisome rise of a hopelessly narcissist and innately overbearing power in the world's most happening Indo-Pacific region.

It cannot be but a matter of serious concern that all such militarist adventures are playing out in India's backyard.

In Perspective

Pushed relentlessly by a select group of hardline Communist autocrats headed by an obdurate Chairman of the CMC, modernisation of the PLA has been China's priority national effort. Having achieved the foundational goals of modernisation, the endeavour has graduated to accelerating the processes of integrating the PLA's 'mechanisation, informatisation and intelligentisation'. Professional analyses of inputs in that context suggest that even if the military modernisation and restructure schemes might have, by and large, reached a productive stage, effective integration of these schemes into the apex-level defence decision-making system as well as the conduct of field operations is yet to be realised as the final step in China's landmark endeavour to modernise, restructure and reform the PLA from top to bottom. The process is slated to be fully functional by the year 2027. Of course, military schemes are never 'complete' in the absolute sense and require continuous course corrections, readjustments and upgrades, besides the occasional reorientation. Indeed, the CPC is committed to that purpose.

Admittedly, possession of robust military power is a foundational condition for sustaining political and economic power across the globe. But the question arises as to why the CPC is intent on building such a disproportionately powerful military unless it anticipates a coalescence of strong resistance against its impending action plans of remodelling the existing order of usually accommodative global administration in tune with its hegemonic agenda. Considering that Communist China's ideology assigns a priority role to military power in securing its overbearing aspirations, that should be matter of grave concern among the regional stake-holders – Western as well as Asian ones.

The CPC's formal commitment to the 'recovery' of every inch of its so called 'lost' territories, and to bring near and far neighbourhoods into the grips of its hegemony – the 'Chinese Dream', in short – is so far working rather well. Its strategy of intermittent low-intensity territorial intrusions, creeping encroachments followed by permanent occupation, and finally subsuming its seizures, is insured by threats of massive military reaction should there be any attempt to resist or to recover any of the seized areas. The strategy has so far enabled China to occupy many South China Sea features, dominate good parts of the West Pacific Ocean and find military inroads into the Indian Ocean Region (IOR) – all without having to engage in any major battles. In the larger context, the Chinese juggernaut is committed to possessing all of its claimed territory spanning across land, islands and the vast expanse of common regional waters, either through arm-twisted 'agreements' or application of military force. Massive PLA build-up, chest-thumping over accomplishments in military exercises, brandishing of advanced weaponry and frequent indulgences in land-sea territorial probes are clear messages to that end.

The CPC views India as a serious contender to the 'Chinese Dream' and therefore an intransigent actor who needs to be kept impeded. The obvious purpose of the CMC hence is to seize territories deeper beyond the Indo-Tibet border, either by preemptive occupation of India's vast expanses of physically unheld areas, or by overwhelming India's modest counter-actions through deliberately planned, prepared and executed military operations. Over the decades past, this strategy has prompted the PLA to occupy nearly 2,000 square kilometre of additional territory across the Sino-India Line of Actual Control (LAC), over and above the 43,500 square kilometre it has occupied since its

1962 aggression. The trend suggests that the longer-term objective is to gain control, directly or through tributary patronages, over the entire periphery of the Himalayan highlands.

Similarly, in the maritime domain, the CPC's obvious purpose is to secure domineering control over the Indian Ocean and thus confine India's strategic outreach within her coastal fringes; finally, it comes down to barricading India's natural geo-strategic centrality in the Indian Ocean, thus leaving the waters to China's uncontested domination.

The point to remember here is that the CPC is never impressed enough by logic, laws or conventions to retreat from its usurpations unless there is liability of being evicted by force. But with the PLA's military power, backed up with Communist doggedness, that is an option unthinkable in the foreseeable future.

In sum, the CPC is committed to make the PLA an effective instrument in pursuant to its objectives – perpetuation of its autarkic regime, Taiwan's unification, territorial expansion – all underwritten by the achievement of regional hegemony and global economic monopoly. Depending on the political climate, the process may be recessed or diverted, but it would continue to feature in the CPC's 'Chinese Dream'.

Notes

1. The CPC's asserts its sovereign rights over huge parts of neighbourhood lands and seas through its arbitrarily drawn 'lines'; these lines are a testimony to the absurdity of its claims. Communistic 'unification' of Taiwan and assumption of sovereign control over the China Seas are the CPC's specific priorities.
2. *China's National Defence in a New Era*, 2021, http://www.xinhuanet.com/whitepaperonnationaldefence.doc.
3. The CPC's stated goal is to 'transform' the PLA into a 'world-class force' by mid-21st century. Recent official statements indicate that the interim target of military modernisation has been brought forward from the year 2035 to 2027 (the centenary of the CPC). Given its sloganeering propensities, such statements are to be sieved through the ruling clique's self-promoting bombast.
4. Office of the US Secretary of Defence, Annual Report to Congress, *Military and Security Developments Involving the People's Republic of China x China's Global Military Activities.*
5. China has adapted to Western-style military organisations 'with Chinese characteristics' in a vigorous manner.
6. *China's Global Military Activities,* op cit 2.
7. Anthony H. Cordesman and Grace Hwang, 'China: The Civil-Military Challenge: (Updated and Expanded) Volume One of a Graphic Net Assessment', Centre for Strategic and International Studies, 4 January 2022, https://www.csis.org/analysis/china-civil-military-challenge-updated-and-expanded-volume-one-graphic-net-assessment.

8   Ed Joel Wuthnow, et al (eds), *The PLA Beyond Borders: Chinese Military Operations in Regional and Global Context*, National Defence University, Washington DC, 2021.
9   *China's Military Strategy White Paper*, May 2015. Updates available on the official website of the state Council Information Office of the People's Republic of China, www.scio.gov.cn.
10 These measures had been incrementally introduced alongside widespread debate and discussions during the 2008–15 period.
11 James Char, 'The People's Liberation Army in its Tenth Decade: Assessing "Below the Neck", Reforms in China's Military Modernisation', *Journal of Strategic Studies*, 44(2), 2022, pp. 1–8.
12 'Full Text: China's National Defense in the New Era', The State Council Information Office of the People's Republic of China, 24 July 2019, https://english.www.gov.cn/archive/whitepaper/201907/24/content_WS5d3941ddc6d08408f502283d.html.
13 *China: Military Power; Modernising a Force to Fight and Win* (United States Defence Intelligence Agency Military Power Publications, 2020), www.dia.mil/Military-Power-Publications.
14 The much-hyped 'downsizing of the PLA to 1.7 million personnel, and maybe further' is to be viewed with due military insight. Herein, the bloated ranks of sundry entities of the regular army – militia, industrial, quasi-military, para-military and obsolescent elements, mostly manned by party apparatchiks – have been reorganised under distinct support units. Overall contribution of these elements to the modern warfare's subsidiary tasks, under the overall command and control of the PLA, remains equally if not more salient.
15 Institute for National Strategic Studies, *System Destruction Warfare and 'Multi-Domain Precision Warfare'*, https://indupress.indu.edu/
16 *NIDS China Security Report 2021: China's Military Strategy in the New Era* (Tokyo: National Institute of Defense Studies, Japan, 2020), https://www.nids.mod.go.jp/publication/chinareport/pdf/china_report_EN_web_2021_A01.pdf.
17 *China: Military Power*, op cit 14.
18 Institute of Strategic Studies, Islamabad, Open Military Studies 2, *China's People's Liberation Army: Restructuring and Modernization*, 2022, https://doi.org/10.1515/openms-2022.
19 PRC's Ministry of National Defence, China's New White Paper, *China's National Defence in the New Era*, 2022, https://eng.mod.gov.cn.
20 US DoD, 2022, China Power Report, *Military and Security Developments involving the PRC*, file:///C:/VIF%20Files%20in%20Kingston%20F-Copy/China%20Book/DoD_China-Report_2022.pdf.
21 Chinese bases/facilities are established at: Djibouti, Ream (Cambodia), Gwadar (Pakistan) and Hambantota (Sri Lanka). Reportedly, marine units are already deployed at Djibouti and Gwadar. The plan is to find more maritime base facilities in Myanmar, Maldives, the Africa Coast and Argentina.
22 China's New White Paper, op cit 16.

23. Lt Gen (Dr) V.K. Saxena (Retd), 'Growing Muscle of PLAAF, Perspectives on The People's Republic of China', Occasional Paper, The Vivekananda International Foundation, New Delhi, March 2016. https://www.vifindia.org/sites/default/files/growing-muscle-of-plaaf.pdf.
24. Lt Gen Gautam Banerjee, *The Course of China's Military Modernisation and Defence Reforms* (New Delhi: The Vivekananda International Foundation, 2021), https://www.vifindia.org/monograph/2021/april/28/The-Course-of-China-s-Military-Modernisation-and-Defence-Reforms.
25. Myanmar, India, Bhutan and Nepal, and littorals of the Western-Southern Pacific are the current targets.

19

India–China Border
Crystal-Gazing into the Foreseeable Future
Lieutenant General Rakesh Sharma

Setting the Stage

Historiography formulates interpretations, constructs and forms conclusions about the past and, with creative thinking, creates different versions of history. China through history considered itself the Middle Kingdom and its tributaries were expected to pay obeisance to the Emperor. The 19th-Century Opium Wars and the China Japanese Wars changed the internal environment within China. The 1911 Revolution ended the Qing Dynasty and the Republic of China came into being.

As a matter of course, the Chinese claim to have historic memories. Their history is singularly intricate. Lord Curzon had stated that 'the idea of a demarcated frontier is itself an essentially modern conception and finds little or no place in the ancient world'. He also tellingly remarked, 'it would be true to say that demarcation has never taken place in Asiatic countries except under the European pressure and by the intervention of "European Agents" … he would be a short-sighted commander who merely manned his ramparts in India and did not look beyond'.

Though the 1913–14 tripartite Shimla Conference had three plenipotentiaries – from Tibet, China and Britain – it was the British and Tibetan representatives who signed the convention settling the boundary east of Bhutan, under Article 9. Except the line Sir McMahon drew on the map, there was no accompanying description of this boundary.[1] China, in a formal statement, said that it did not recognise any bilateral agreement between Britain and Tibet.[2] Inexplicably, the contents of the convention were not published until the 1938 edition of Aitchison's compilation of treaties came out.

On the western side, trade caravans and explorers historically knew no political boundaries, except the mountain ranges. The ancient routes, the knowledge of which was passed from generation to generation, moved through the western Himalayas, traversing the Pamirs, Hind Kush, Kunlun, Karakoram, the Greater Himalaya and the Plateau of Tibet. There were exchanges of culture, ideas, thoughts and religious ideologies and, of course, trade. Eastern Ladakh (Ladakh is the land of High Passes) along the Shyok River Valley formed the corridor for trade with Punjab and Kashmir. The region also earned name with an informative character, originating from Yarkhandi (a Turkic dialect), Balti (Baltistan) and Ladakhi origins.

Suffice it to say that the border demarcation of Ladakh–Tibet border commenced with the First Sikh War and the Amritsar Treaty in 1846, when the British recognised Maharaja Gulab Singh of Jammu and Kashmir under their suzerainty. What followed was a history of 'lines' that attempted to delineate the boundary between Ladakh and Tibet by William Johnson, a bureaucrat with the Survey of India, the Johnson Line of 1865; the Ardagh–Johnson Line of 1897 and the Macartney–MacDonald Line of 1899. In the geopolitics of that era, the Karakoram Pass, a 5,540 metre or 18,176 foot mountain pass in the Karakoram Range, was formalised as a boundary between India and China in 1892, and has till now remained outside of controversy. The pass is 45 metres wide, devoid of vegetation and generally free of snow.

The Historical Baggage of Un-demarcated Border

After India's independence, the Ministry of States, headed by Vallabhbhai Patel, published two White Papers in July 1948 and February 1950. Both showed the entire northern boundary from the Indian–China–Afghan trijunction to the India–China–Nepal trijunction as 'undefined', in contrast to a clear depiction of the McMahon Line in the east. Prime Minister Jawaharlal Nehru, however, wrote to the Secretary-General of the Ministry of External Affairs on 1 July 1954:

> All our old maps dealing with the frontier should be carefully examined and, where necessary, withdrawn. New maps should be printed showing our northern and north-eastern frontier without any reference to any 'line'. These new maps should also not state there is any undemarcated territory ... this frontier should be considered a firm and definite one which is not open to discussion with anybody.[3]

Thus, in 1954, India published revised maps with the Johnson–Ardagh Line as the international border, extending the Indian frontier in the western sector to the Kunlun Mountains.

There is a protracted correspondence between Prime Minister Nehru and Premier Zhou Enlai on the vexed issues of the border. A letter written by Premier Zhou Enlai dated 7 November 1959 postulated '... each side withdraw 20 kilometres ... from the line up to which each side exercises actual control in the west (Ladakh)'. In a 17 December 1959 letter, Premier Zhou stated that

> the reason for the present existence of certain disputes over the Sino-Indian boundary is that the two countries have never formally delimited this boundary and that there is a divergence of views between the two countries regarding the

boundary. The Chinese Government holds that the so-called McMahon Line is wholly illegal ... it is known to the world that the Simla Convention itself is void of legal validity.[4]

The stark differences of opinion were evident in the exhaustive April 1960 talks in India between Nehru and Zhou, with the latter reiterating the matter of the Line of Actual Control (LAC), stating:

> ... the boundaries have to be defined in terms of latitude and longitude; but this was not done. The boundary line has to be fixed by negotiations. Although our boundary is not formally delimited or fixed, there exists a line of actual control. In the eastern sector, it is the McMahon line, and, on the western sector, the line is the Karakoram and Kongka pass.

India never accepted the so-called unilaterally defined 1959 LAC proposed by Premier Zhou. This position has been consistent and well known, even to the Chinese. Shivshankar Menon has written in his book *Choices: Inside the Making of India's Foreign Policy* that the LAC was 'described only in general terms on maps not to scale'[5] by the Chinese. China, however, has been insistent on the 1959 LAC proposed by Premier Zhou.

The foundation of the management of the LAC are the four formal agreements of 1993, 1996, 2005 and 2013. The Agreement on the Maintenance of Peace and Tranquility along the Line of Actual Control (LAC) in the India–China Border Areas in 1993 predetermined that there would be no use of force or a threat to use force, and the actual control line would be respected. Under this agreement, India formally accepted the concept of the LAC and the two sides signed the Agreement to Maintain Peace and Tranquillity. The reference to the LAC was unqualified to make it clear that it was not referring to the Premier Zhou LAC of 1959 but to the LAC as it stood at the time when the agreement was signed.

The 1996 agreement laid down confidence building measures (CBMs) and was like a no-war pact prohibiting the use of military capability against the other side, especially within 2 kilometres of the LAC. The 2005 Agreement on the Political Parameters and Guiding Principles for the Settlement of the India–China Boundary Question stated that if the border personnel on the two sides came face-to-face over differences on the alignment of the LAC or for any other reason, they should exercise self-restraint and not use force or threaten to use force against the other side, cease their activities in the area, not advance any further and simultaneously return to their respective bases. The India–China Border Agreement of 2013 laid down that neither side shall use military capability against the other side, and that their respective military strengths shall not be used to threaten or attack the other side. Given the multiple face-offs between the two sides over the years, a caveat was added that neither shall follow or tail patrols of the other side where there is no clear delineation of the LAC.

It had soon become apparent that the LAC was incurably faulty as a concept. This was largely because there was no formal delineation and demarcation, an issue studiously and deliberately avoided by the Chinese. Events in the following years further confirmed that the Chinese had deliberately ensured that the ill-defined nature of the LAC remained, in order to retain their leverage over India to engage in premeditated aggression at regular intervals alongside a well-planned psychological campaign.

Meanwhile, to reconcile their differences, the two countries agreed that there was a need for a Joint Working Group (JWG) to address the border issue. A total of fifteen meetings of this JWG were held between 1989 and 2005, with the last meeting on 30 and 31 March 2005. Meanwhile, a Special Representative (SR) mechanism on the India–China boundary question was constituted in 2003 to explore from the political perspective of the overall bilateral relationship the framework of a boundary settlement; this of course differed in scope from delineation of the LAC. The border issue remained unresolved. Over time, the Chinese developed extensive infrastructure in Aksai Chin. The travesty of this un-demarcated border was wrought at a tactical level, where the Indian units and formations deployed in eastern Ladakh faced the belligerent Chinese. Such 'transgressions' happened regularly and most were mutually amicably resolved under the provisions of the various agreements through 'banner drills' or Border Personnel Meetings (BPMs, without the matter ever being reported by the media). Since 2013, there have been gross violations of protocols in Raki Nalla, Chumar, Pangong Tso, Demchok and Doklam, and the 'stand-offs' have transcended to a new level where disengagement became impossible for a very long time – fistfights and brawls involving use of batons led to an adversarial atmosphere until resolved by BPMs. The Indian Army followed drills – weapons were always carried by the troops, albeit exercising restraint, in safe mode.

Dai Bingguo, then State Councillor, Director of the General Offices of Foreign Affairs and the National Security Group of the Chinese Communist Party's Central Committee and Special Representative (SR) for boundary negotiations with India from 2003 to 2013, had stated on 2 March 2013:

> … the disputed territory in the eastern sector of the China-India boundary, including Tawang, is inalienable from China's Tibet in terms of cultural background and administrative jurisdiction. Even British colonialists who drew the illegal McMahon Line respected China's jurisdiction over Tawang and admitted that Tawang was part of China's Tibet.[6]

Inexplicably, China did not consider the McMahon Line illegal while settling its boundary disputes with Myanmar!

Premeditated Expansionism by the People's Liberation Army (PLA) in 2020

In one stroke, in May 2020, thirty-two years of intensive negotiations, agreements, CBMs and protocols were discarded and put to waste. In many firsts, the PLA undertook premeditated expansionism on the LAC in eastern Ladakh in total contravention of the existing protocols and CBMs. First, military formations under exercise in early 2020 in the south of Kunlun Range were sidestepped to proximity of eastern Ladakh. Second, incursions were undertaken at multiple areas simultaneously. Third, despite well-established systems to avoid clashes, the PLA refused to vacate from the areas intruded. Fourth and most important, the routine fisticuffs and brawls turned violent at Galwan Valley and led to the death of twenty Indian soldiers, including a commanding officer, and an indeterminate number of PLA soldiers.

It is obvious that the entire schema of the Chinese belligerence has an overt and covert agenda, and involves a calculated obfuscation of facts. The chronology of events adds up to show that the PLA deliberately and in a well-planned manner broke down the systemic understanding and behaviour outlined in the various agreements, protocols and norms. There are two larger reasons for China's hostility in eastern Ladakh that commenced in May 2020. First, China's geopolitical aims and global ambitions are no secret. President Xi sees China as the most pre-eminent power in Asia and eventually the world, given its connectivity through transcontinental routes and waterways and assured political influence among the larger comity of nations through trade, commerce and infrastructural development. China has the most contested strategic geography of any major power in the world. Regional primacy hence has become the springboard for its global ambitions. Conventional wisdom indicates that this would require obtaining the subservience or at least the deference of its neighbouring countries. By achieving this, China will secure the dominant status in its territory through economic relationships, defence networks, diplomacy and cultural influence. Both coercion and inducement are being employed to shape the region to better accommodate Chinese leadership.

India is a geopolitical competitor for China despite the economic, military and technological asymmetry between the two nations. India has focused on steady growth, exhibited tremendous growth potential that it is constantly striving to achieve, immense soft power in the comity of nations, especially the Global South (without having to 'purchase likeability' like China), and political stability. India is a credible military power and a challenge in the geostrategic peninsular location at the head of the all-important Indian

Ocean. India is also becoming indispensable partner to the Western nations, especially the US. Indeed, China does not want security challenges to persist on its territorial periphery as it will then have to focus its energies on its own security rather than on creating global influence. For China, India has to hence be distracted from its growth path and embroiled in a web of inimical peacetime activities. Contextually, China would likely attempt to generate economic dependencies for India and create relationships with India's neighbours to promote an anti-India bias. Retaining the Damocles' Sword of an ambiguous, unresolved, live border and with a threat-in-being against India, it would greatly suit China.

Second, China has often stated that 'we cannot lose a single inch of the lands we inherited from our ancestors', and seeks to safeguard its sovereignty and maintain peace at the same time. It is another matter that there is no justification or historic authenticity backing the arbitrary 7 November 1959 line in eastern Ladakh or Arunachal Pradesh. China pursued a policy of maintaining a more favourable environment along the LAC since 2013, by altering the status quo using its increasingly varied toolkit – the most prominent strategy being the 'soft use' of 'hard power', well short of direct use of military force for fear of escalation to a conflict. This was followed by belligerence in Chumar in September 2014 and Doklam in 2017. It was PLA's use of 'hard power, softly' over a large frontage with major transgressions in eastern Ladakh in May 2020 that ultimately led to the tragic incident in Galwan on 15 June 2020. This time though the PLA surreptitiously moved to occupy key terrain features/locations and relied upon just sufficient backup of 'hard power' in the proximity to deter escalation.

What PLA had perhaps not anticipated was the robust and strong response by the Indian armed forces, launching eyeball-to-eyeball confrontations at all locations transgressed, and the ferociousness and tenacity of the Indian soldiers in Galwan on 15 June 2020 without the use of firearms. In an exemplary mobilisation, the Indian Army and the Indian Air Force picked up the gauntlet, brought in a strong force to Ladakh, accepted the challenge and even prepared for escalation. A quid pro quo operation was undertaken by the Indian military on the south bank of the Pangong Tso in the Kailash Range on 29 and 30 August 2020. All this while continuing twenty rounds of laborious negotiations at Chushul–Moldo and through diplomatic Working Mechanism for Coordination and Consultation (WMCC) to obtain a verifiable disengagement, de-escalation and return to status quo ante.

A significant change happened in the management of the LAC by the PLA and Indian Army following the tenth round of talks at Chushul, which led to phased, coordinated, verified and synchronised disengagement in the north and south of Pangong Tso. After the sixteenth round of China–India Corps Commander

Level Meeting in eastern Ladakh, consensus was reached on disengagement of the Chinese and Indian troops in the area of Jianan La (Daban), also designated at PP15. This followed the trend of previous disengagements with the creation of fixed distance of patrolling moratorium (buffer).

Inevitably, there is a changed character of LAC with differing distance buffer-land (moratorium on patrolling) agreed upon, creating a kind of belt of actual control. China's push for patrolling moratoriums at the key decision points along the LAC in Aksai Chin will suit the PLA as they had found the chance fisticuffs and stand-offs, difficult to deal with for over a decade. Evidently, the Chinese had conceived a strategic game plan for the entire eastern Ladakh border, and it was nothing like the simple salami-slicing in the South China Sea or targeting a few friction points. Eastern Ladakh and Aksai Chin will hereinafter be separated by a benign belt, laterally separating the PLA and the Indian Army troops.

The Future of India–China Border

This brings us to the inevitable question: what next? There is a need for a reality check before one can crystal-gaze into the foreseeable future, as inferred from studying four distinct trends. First is the issue of achieving status quo ante – a persistent demand of India's. The Chinese Foreign Ministry spokesperson Mao Ning, while calling PP15 consensus a 'positive development' on 9 September 2022, categorically reiterated that it would not accept India's demand to restore status quo prior to China's transgressions. She stated that, 'We don't accept the so-called status quo created by India's illegal crossing of the LAC, but that doesn't mean we don't attach importance to peace and tranquillity along the border. China and India hold different positions on the border issues'.[7]

The Chinese Foreign Minister Wang Yi had previously indicated the position that India and China 'need to take a long-term view, shift from emergency management to normal border management and control mechanisms, and prevent border-related incidents from causing unnecessary disruptions to bilateral relations'.[8] The statement plainly specifies the official Chinese position on the LAC in eastern Ladakh. A readout by the Chinese following the WMCC talks had stated the need to 'further ease the situation in the border area and strive to switch from emergency response to normalized management and control'.[9] Yang Shu, former Dean of Central Asian Studies at China's Lanzhou University, stated that soaring nationalistic sentiment had fuelled the latest clash and that 'I expect more brawls and even small-scale skirmishes will take place along the LAC if Beijing and New Delhi leadership fail to curb the irrational mood'.[10]

The inference is that where the forces exist today should be treated as firm dispositions and normal border management control should commence there. After the December 2022 clash at Yangtse near Tawang, it is apparent that the PLA probes to find weaknesses in the LAC management posture by the Indian Army units will continue, and the PLA might attempt to take advantage where feasible. Though the moratoriums of patrolling are deemed temporary, analysis of the present trends indicates that it is futile to expect PLA to withdraw to April 2020 status quo ante. The existing much escalated military dispositions will have to remain for a long time in the future.

There is fundamental divergence in the positions of the two sides. India believes that as long as peace and tranquillity is not restored in border areas and the state of borders remain 'abnormal', the overall India–China relations too cannot return to 'normal'. On the other hand, China is seeking to delink the issue of peace and tranquillity in border areas from the usual course of the development of international relations.

Second, modern borders must be precise, well demarcated and delineated, separating geographical, political and economic jurisdiction on either side of the line as correct symbols of sovereignty and territorial integrity. Frontier clarity is the entente cordiale between neighbours. The Chinese goalposts and motivations regarding India are clear and steady as if etched in stone. If borders are not precise and taken seriously, conflicts will continue to arise on transgressions by the PLA. It is becoming evident for India that building consensus on border resolution will remain elusive and the trust deficit will remain for a long time. At this juncture, forward movement on demarcating and delineating the currently flawed concept of LAC seems inconceivable. Similarly, with habitat constructed in proximity, expectations of de-escalation – that is repositioning of formations from opposite eastern Ladakh to permanent locations, say, in Urumqi, Hotan or Kashgar – does not seem likely.

Third, the feverish pace of improvement in infrastructure in Tibet and Xinjiang has ominous portends for the use of ground and air forces, missiles and rockets by China. The Lhasa Nyangchi rail line and the superhighways to Tibet and Xinjiang would make China's mobilisation cycles a lot faster and shorter. There have also been significant changes in the Tibetan and Xinjiang strategic geography. The newer strategic assets include planned construction or upgradation of roads in proximity to the LAC (G695), underground silos, blast pens in airfields, missile sites, positioning of Peoples Liberation Army Air Force aircraft, new road and rail structures and changing the demographics of border areas, thus expanding PLA's capacity to induct and maintain additional troop deployments. The execution of China's 14th Five-Year Plan for Economic and Social Development and Long-range Objectives Through the Year 2035 will witness the construction of the Chengdu–Chongqing world-class airport cluster and thirty more civilian transport airports.

Currently, Tibet and South Xinjiang have twelve airports operating or under construction. The 739-kilometre-long oil pipeline from Golmund to Lhasa will have a new 1,076 kilometre-long parallel Snow Mountain Oil Dragon Pipeline, increasing the oil depots in Tibet to ten. China has already installed central power grid connections across all sixty-six counties and eight districts in Tibet. These speedy and military-focused infrastructural upgradations cannot be overlooked.

Fourth, it is well-nigh impossible to outguess the Chinese trajectory forward. The Chinese are busy rewriting the rules-based international system to better reflect their own interests. Their attempts at ultra-nationalism are propelling them to seek more and more influence globally, and to dominate their region politically, militarily and economically. The balance of power has been severely disrupted in China's favour, and this unbalanced power has become a potential threat. Military prowess is now an important component of national strength, alongside other (more) important facets. The current force levels deployed by the PLA in Aksai Chin do not indicate significant conventional war threat along the LAC. However, with its sharp trends of national growth, immense potential and geostrategic location, India will soon be seen as an important geopolitical challenger to China's regional and global ambitions.

The Thrust for India on the Border Issue

So what should be India's policies to thwart China's long-term designs? There are six pathways that need to be considered. First, it is apparent that the architecture of LAC management with China will remain problematic. Invariably, peace will be guaranteed by the Indian Army retaining strong positional deployments and denying further incursions, while ensuring availability of strong reserves in proximity and deterrence by Indian Air Force and Indian Navy.

Second, the patrolling moratoriums or buffers in eastern Ladakh may stay on for substantive time. History does not promote confidence in any new agreements that India and China may negotiate in future, they may not bind China bilaterally and multi-nationally. There are bound to be serious repercussions on the infringement of these buffers, but it is necessary to create failsafe mechanisms to avoid escalation. With total distrust, the patrolling moratoriums and force posturing by the PLA necessitate Indian armed forces to maintain intense vigil, lest the PLA takes advantage and creates adverse situations and fait accompli.

Third, the LAC is based upon 'perceptions'. Perceptions are beliefs or opinions often held by officials at various rungs of decision-making and passed on as routine to the functional units and formations on ground. In regular press briefings too the word 'perceptions' finds a place, thereby, weakening India's stance and trust on the rationale of its own border. What China believes in or perceives is immaterial to India's firmness and convictions! Our 'perception' of the border and where the McMahon Line is must not be shaky and create ambiguity in people's minds about the truth. It is about our confidence in our truth that matters most. Truth and belief must not be victims within India. As a border resolution mechanism is not on the horizon, the word 'perceptions of the LAC' must be jettisoned from our lingo. India must believe in one LAC – from the top to the soldier on the front. The CPC/PLA's versions (or perceptions) of the border should be irrelevant to us till formal discussions at politico-diplomatic level commence to resolve it, if ever!

Fourth, tensions along the borders will evidently persist and, in fact, with increased military infrastructure and military build-up will remain 'threat in being'. While disengagement is part of the continued agenda, there is also need for giving primacy to de-escalation in various fora. Status quo of the escalated deployments may remain for a long time.

Fifth, it is obvious for India that being a strong nation in terms of comprehensive national power alone can ensure secure borders, and will be the recipe for peaceful coexistence with China. With China's continued geostrategic pressure, India needs to appreciate and plan out its border-management posture. India had mirrored induction along its northern border. It is imperative that modernisation thrusts for the armed forces include technological advancements in warfare like information warfare, space, cyber, artificial intelligence, quantum, robotics and disruptive technologies.

Sixth, as was evident in Yangste, the soldier still bears the burden of miscalculation. The bitter lesson most overlooked is: if we want to ensure territorial integrity of the land we call home, we need to be willing to put our sons and daughters in the mud, driving rain, heat and bitter cold and deep snow to defend it. Intricate machines cannot scuffle or fisticuff! The importance of human resource cannot be underplayed and, as is rightly said, quantity has a quality of its own.

Conclusion

It is well understood that China is the second largest global economy and the largest manufacturing hub and exporter. Despite some economic moderation and evident internal turmoil, China's current global trade and influence indicate resilience. India too has a burgeoning trade with China and they are politically/diplomatically linked through many global and regional organisations.

However, borders are inherent to sovereignty and territorial integrity, and border control is a quintessential exercise of sovereignty. Sovereignty represents the right of the Indian nation to govern its territory. Rightly, an international boundary should delineate the space between India and China as sovereign states. Within its borders, the Indian government has complete authority – an authority that cannot be impeded by other governments. The border serves to represent the limit; the furthest extent of a government's sovereignty. As a corollary, therefore, China has no plans or intentions to settle the border issue with India. The larger geopolitical environment in China does not indicate any war clouds on the horizon against India. Intentions of escalation or dominance cannot, however, be guaranteed in a situation devoid of trust. India must attempt to reach its immense potential and make advancements in modern hard power to thwart any inimical designs which may heighten the grey zone environment.

Notes

1. A.S. Bhasin, *Nehru, Tibet and China* (Gurgaon: Penguin Random House India, 2021), 14.
2. Bhasin, *Nehru, Tibet and China*, 13.
3. A.G. Noorani, 'Facts of History', *Frontline*, 30 August–12 September 2003, https://web.archive.org/web/20111002095213/http://frontlineonnet.com/fl2018/stories/20030912002104800.htm. This article traces in detail the treaties and engagements that have dealt with the status of the western sector of the Sino-Indian boundary in Jammu and Kashmir in the nineteenth century.
4. Claude Arpi, Notes, Memoranda and Letters Exchanged and Agreements Signed between the Governments of India and China, WHITE PAPER OIII, November 1959–March 1960, https://www.archive.claudearpi.net/maintenance/uploaded_pics/Corres_Nov59_Mar60.pdfhttps://www.archieve.claudearpi.net/maintenance/uploaded_pics/Corres_Nov59_Mar60.pdf.
5. Sushant Singh, 'Line of Actual Control (LAC), Where it Is Located, and Where India and China Differ', *Indian Express*, 01 June 2020, https://indianexpress.com/article/explained/line-of-actual-control-where-it-is-located-and-where-india-and-china-differ-6436436/.
6. Manoj Joshi, 'Is Tawang Becoming the Focus of Sino-Indian Relations', The Wire, 09 March 2017, https://thewire.in/external-affairs/tawang-china-india-relations.
7. Ananth Krishnan, India, China to Take up Remaining Lac Issues, *The Hindu*, 09 September 2022, https://www.thehindu.com/news/national/chinas-military-confirms-disengagement-at-lac-in-ladakh/article65869582.ece.
8. 'Border Row Must Not Be Allowed to Affect Ties', *The Times of India*, 16 July 2021, https://timesofindia.indiatimes.com/india/border-row-must-not-be-allowed-to-affect-india-ties-says-china/articleshow/84459425.cms.
9. 'China–India Border Situation Stable at the Moment: Chinese Vice FM Sun Weidong', *The Economic Times*, 26 January 2023, https://economictimes.indiatimes.com/news/defence/china-india-border-situation-stable-at-the-moment-chinese-vice-fm-sun-weidong/articleshow/97337540.cms?from=mdr.
10. Minnie Chan, 'China, India at Odds over Trigger for Troop Brawl at Disputed Himalayan Border', SCMP, 13 December 2022, https://www.scmp.com/news/china/diplomacy/article/3203155/china-india-odds-over-trigger-troop-brawl-disputed-himalayan-border.

20

Contest for the Heavens
China's Space Programme
Air Marshal Diptendu Choudhury

For centuries, the eternal wonder surrounding the stars and planets in the heavens helped nurture the thoughts about the possibility of human space travel. Thus, in the 20th century, when the Sputnik satellite was launched by the Soviet Union in 1959, it was the first foray into space. As the world watched closely, the politico-ideological Cold War rivalry between the two superpowers triggered the competition to prove their technological superiority. When Yuri Gagarin became the first human in space by orbiting the earth in the Vostok 1 capsule in April 1961, and Alan Shepard of the US followed suit less than a month later in the Mercury spacecraft, the race for space had officially begun. In the 21st century, with the enormous progress and potential in the space-related fields of science, technology, economy and military, it has become a major arena for showcasing national prowess and geopolitical power. Though many nations – including India – have emerged as serious stakeholders, China is committed to replace the US as the dominant player, if not the hegemon of the tiān táng or heavens. In the absence of international policies and regulatory mechanisms to ensure peace, the militarisation of space has already begun with the increasing contestation in the guise of national security interests and geopolitical leveraging. The future space security outlook and strategies of Beijing and Washington seem to have crossed the point of no return.

Journey to the Tiantang

China's space aspirations began with Mao Zedong's 'Two Bombs One Satellite' goal formulated way back in 1958. However, space was put on the back burner during the Cultural Revolution, and it was only in 1978 with Deng Xiaoping in office that China's space programme was revived.[1] In 1955, Qian Xuesen, who was a leading scientist in America's space endeavours, was deported back to China. He came to be considered the 'Father of China's Missile and Space Programme', and was pivotal in the negotiations with the Soviet Union for the development of nuclear weapons and the 'agreement on Moscow's assistance in the construction of civil and military facilities'.[2] Between the years 1953 and 1957, the Soviets signed several agreements of industrial support as part of a five-year plan. While this helped to establish the industrial base of China, Mao Zedong was keen on developing self-reliance and considered their continued reliance on the Soviets 'unacceptable'. As the political differences between the Soviet Union and China widened, Enlai Zhou and some other leaders who were convinced about the continued need for Soviet support, sought more industrial, technical and scientific assistance, especially for national defence and manufacturing.[3] 'During the early 1960s, the tensions between the two Communist Parties erupted into a public controversy so serious that it damaged the alliance between the two countries and disrupted all technology transfer efforts.'[4] This divergence led to the withdrawal of 1,400 Soviet technicians from the PRC and the cancellation of some 200 important joint scientific projects.

Soon after, China tested its ballistic missile in 1960, its nuclear weapon in 1964 and successfully tested the Dongfeng-2 medium-range ballistic missile carrying a nuclear warhead in 1966. In 1970, it launched the heaviest satellite of its time, the Dongfanghong-1, to become the fifth nation in the world to launch a satellite after USSR, US, France and Japan. The Richard Nixon-era détente between the US and China initiated by Henry Kissinger in 1971 was followed by the normalisation of diplomatic relations and the signing of the Cooperation in Science and Technology Agreement in 1979. This opened the window for Sino-European cooperation in science and space research, enabling China to launch its first intercontinental ballistic missile in 1980, followed by geosynchronous satellites in the mid-1980s. China thus established itself as a telecommunications satellite manufacturer and, with increasing reliability of its rockets, became an affordable commercial launch partner for a series of international space cooperation efforts.

The turn of the century saw China develop its Shenzhou series of space crafts and in 2003, with Chinese cosmonaut Colonel Yang Liwei of the People's Liberation Army Air Force carrying out fourteen orbits around Earth, it became the third nation to put a man independently into space. In 2007, it launched the Chang'e-1 lunar orbital spacecraft and also successfully tested its anti-satellite weapon capability when it destroyed a defunct satellite with a ballistic missile. More recently in 2019, China's Chang'e lunar probe landed on the 'far side' of the moon, followed by the landing of Zhurong rover on Mars. By 2021, China had commenced the construction of its 'Tiangong' space station or 'Heavenly Palace', which was declared operational when the three 'Taikonauts' or astronauts, replaced the construction crew in the space station in November 2022. Since the US law bans the National Aeronautics and Space Administration (NASA) from sharing data with China and prohibits Chinese astronauts from using the International Space Station (ISS), while a Chinese space station would possibly have been a long-term goal, the exclusion triggered the Chinese to expedite their indigenous programme. It expects the Tiangong to replace the ISS, which is due for decommissioning in 2031. With six docking ports, the Tiangong is expected to permit not only the docking of commercial spacecraft, but also enable tourist visits in the future.[5] Therefore, China's three decades of totally indigenous efforts underscores the country's self-reliance policy and endeavours, and has set the stage for its future ambitions in space. The enviable range and pace of its achievements can be measured from the following milestones:

- The completion and operation of the BeiDou Navigation Satellite System.[6]
- The high-resolution earth observation system.
- The conclusion of the three-step (orbit, land and return) lunar exploration programme.[7]
- Initiation of the space station.
- Reaching the mars orbit by Tianwen-1 and successful landing by Zhurong rover on the red planet.[8]
- Becoming the first country to establish a state-funded space-based solar power (SBSP) base plant.[9]

Other significant achievements include:
- The Zhuque-2[10] became the first liquid oxygen- and liquid methane (Methalox)-fuelled rocket to reach orbit.
- Planned launch of an extension module to upgrade the configuration and capacity of the space station.
- The Long March 9 super heavy reusable rocket transportation system and 13,000-satellite constellation of the Guo Wang network, which seeks to be the long-run game changer to the unprecedented challenge Elon Musk's SpaceX has presented before China.[11]

From a totally state-owned enterprise, the rapid transformation and leaps in space endeavours occurred in 2014, when China's National Development and Reform Commission published 'Document 60' to open the doors for commercialisation of its enterprise in space.[12] According to Statista Research Department, the government expenditure on space in 2022 has the US leading with US $61.97 billion, followed by China at almost $11.94 billion and India at $1.93 billion. When it comes to Chinese commercial space firms, the investments are expected to exceed $4.7 billion. Fuelled by an ever-rising demand for its commercial launch services, China expects to launch a staggering 4,000 satellites over the next decade, from the 400 currently in orbit.[13] As per a 2021 US National Intelligence assessment, '2030 Chinese space activities will increasingly erode the national security, commercial, and global influence advantages that the United States has accrued from its leadership in space'. The report also expects that China will continue to leverage its non-military and commercial space activities to expand its global influence.[14] Its ambition to be the world leader by 2045[15] is, however, not without its challenges.

The situation is not as rosy as projected, since despite the large demand and ample government support, the Chinese commercial space enterprise is not an easy market to access. This is essentially due to the contradiction that even though the government and industry are calling for international cooperation, the former is also simultaneously calling for greater production within the country. In the US, the absence of adequate regulatory space laws and policies allows private players like Elon Musk's SpaceX to achieve what it has. But in China, commercial enterprises cannot compete with the big state-owned China Aerospace Science and Technology Corporation (CASC) and the China Aerospace and Science Industry Corporation (CASIC), with their vast array of subordinate R&D, production complexes and specialised companies. However, in the recent years, at the smaller-scale end of manufacturing, 200 commercial space companies have been created with an outlay of ¥33 billion and the active support of the state-owned sector. Chinese start-ups are expanding at a rapid pace with commercial companies focusing on very specific technologies and partnering with foreign space-tech companies. China has twenty-five launch companies today, which enable satellite launches at a faster rate than other countries. Spacety – a commercial satellite manufacturer in partnership with several European component manufacturers – launches small satellites very regularly and competitively. Compared to the wait of over twelve to eighteen months for a European launch slot, Spacety offers one within three months.[16] The rapid proliferation of the commercial space sector driven by development and advances in science and technology is a sign of the salience given to space as the domain of the future. But China's engagement with space is much more than a venture for mere economic prosperity. It is the very pivot of its global leadership ambitions, and a long-term strategy is clearly at work.

An Unfolding Strategy

As a nation poised to dominate the space domain, China's rapid journey has been carefully crafted and executed with a strategic vision in place. It has issued white papers on space periodically in 2000, 2006, 2011, 2016[17,18] and 2021. Like its white papers on defence, the ones on space have been systematic stepping stones of a long-term vision, a vision of attaining a middle kingdom leadership on key elements of power across all domains. The serious transition of its space outlook is evident from 2016 onwards, with its first emphasis on 'space power'. A comparison of the 2011 white paper with that of 2016[19] brings to the fore several policy objectives.[20] Given the variety of the challenges in the wide field of space development, the emphasis on international cooperation was a pragmatic and strategic approach to piggybacking and leapfrogging on advances made by other nations, and to encourage an increased involvement of the private sector in the space programme. Another key aspect was the leveraging of its space programme across commercial, diplomatic and strategic objectives in the larger national interest. The Belt and Road Initiative Space Information Corridor, which includes earth observation, communications, navigation and positioning, satellite development, ground and application system construction and application product development was integrated into the larger One Belt, One Road framework to expand China's global connectivity and strategic cooperation. The satellite constellation construction programmes with the Brazil, Russia, India, China and South Africa (BRICS) and the Asia-Pacific Space Cooperation Organisation (APSCO) are initiatives to expand China's international strategic footprint and establish it as an alternative to the US, if not a world space leader.

Though the theme of peaceful development has been recurrent in its strategy, and was reiterated by Xi Jinping – 'China wants to enhance its cooperation with the international community in peaceful space exploration and development' – at the 2017 Global Space Exploration Conference in Beijing,[21] it is evidently in contradiction to its larger intent. In fact, the very emphasis that the space programme is intended to 'protect China's national rights and interests, and build up its overall strength' signalled the role of space in enhancing the country's 'zhonghe guoli' or Comprehensive National Power. Despite the ostensible focus on peaceful development of space for science, technology, social and economic growth, and while security goals and policies had been skirted, the document stated that the space programme was for national security and 'to build China into a space power in all respects, to have an advanced space science and technology industry, to provide a strong support for the realisation of the Chinese Dream of the renewal of the Chinese nation'.[22] There has been a clear duality in China's seemingly 'peaceful' approach to space. It is unfolding with a strikingly similarity to the erstwhile approach of *'Zhongguyo heping jueqi'* or China's peaceful rise[23] of the past, a term which it had swiftly revised to *'heping fazhan'* or peaceful development to allay international concerns. Its coercive actions in the South and East China Seas, Taiwan and on India's borders have been anything but peaceful. A closer look at its latest 2021 white paper brings out the evident strategy continuation of the previous papers, while unfolding its larger strategic outlook. Its mission is 'to meet the demands of economic, scientific and technological development, national security and social progress; and to raise the scientific and cultural levels of the Chinese people, protect China's national rights and interests, and build up its overall strength'. Its vision is 'to strengthen its space presence in an all-round manner: to enhance its capacity to better understand, freely access, efficiently use, and effectively manage space; to defend national security, lead self-reliance and self-improvement efforts in science and technology, and promote high-quality economic and social development' – which says it all.

The cost-intensive space domain is not easy to prioritise in a nation's developmental priorities. Especially in democracies, spending money on space remains a challenge when the heavy expenditure is weighed against agriculture, basic health, education, social security, infrastructure, etc. In the Cold War, it was the premise of the existential threat due to the ideological differences of Communism versus Capitalism between the USSR and the US, which was used to fuel the competition for space. Though advances in space science and technology contributed to the geopolitical status of a nation, post the ravages of the two World Wars, when food was scarce, jobs were few and economies were staggering under recession, it needed the support of the people of the nation to spend on space. Thus, in the US there has been a close connection between the two, as its space policies have often been consistent with and responsive to public opinion. China is no different and, despite an authoritarian one-party government, it has been very sensitive and discerning in carrying its people along when it comes to space. As per Hines,

> China's government is often highly concerned with domestic public opinion, particularly that of China's online population. Similarly, China's most ambitious projects, such as its human spaceflight programme, are often used as propaganda aimed at domestic audiences. Public support for China's space activities could, therefore, play an important role in influencing China's space policy.
> China, with a per capita GDP (2021) of $12,556 as compared to $70,248 of the US, has ensured that space policies of the Chinese Communist Party have the support of the people, who 'despite the steep costs, strongly support investments in human spaceflight, as well as lunar and Martian exploration'.[24]

The US still retains the position of the leader in space technologies and, in a world where space-based assets are becoming pivotal to information-age economies and power projection, the Chinese increasingly view the US as a competitor and a threat. Beijing's visionary strategy and initiatives for space, 'paired with its great power ambition, does not leave much to the imagination of the future trajectory, competition, and the inevitable militarisation of the global commons. The advances in Chinese technology, its economic heft, and its rapidly developing military capability and capacity, are heavily invested to bridge the gap with the US'.[25]

China's impressive demonstrated achievements has the US deeply concerned, and the report prepared for the US–China Economic and Security Review Commission assesses that 'capabilities China either currently possesses or is in the process of developing certainly pose a strategic risk to the United States' ability to operate in the Indo-Pacific region'. The key findings identify the following:

- China's presence in space underscores its status as a great power in the international system.
- Its PLA Strategic Support Force (PLASSF) Space Systems Department innovatively and effectively synergises China's space programme under a unified command structure.
- China's expanding infrastructure in space complements its rapidly advancing space-denial capacity and its growing kinetic and non-kinetic counter-space capabilities.
- And should the unique military-civil fusion-enabled and dual-use technology-driven Chinese space endeavours overtake the US, then its military ability against the PLA in the future would be at risk.
- 'China's zero-sum pursuit of space superiority harms U.S. economic competitiveness, weakens U.S. military advantages, and undermines strategic stability'.[26]

The Contested Heavens

To a significant extent, the threat the US perceives from China in all domains, and especially in space is possibly a creation of its own making. From the deportation of Qian Xuesen to the historical détente, where the US chose to mitigate the ideological Communist threat that the USSR and China presented by thawing towards Beijing, it created the conditions to propel China's economic and military rise, and inevitably its progress in space as well. The US was actively involved in fostering China's economic growth since its opening up to foreign trade, investment and implementation of free-market reforms in 1979. This ironically resulted in a market dependency in the US, where its highest trade deficit is with China standing at $310 billion in 2022. Over the past decade, there has been rising friction in all spheres in the great power contest between the US and China, which has expanded into space. The Wolf Amendment, which led to the formal Congressional blocking of China in 2011, prohibited the White House Office of Science and Technology Policy (OSTP) and NASA from coordinating any joint scientific activity with China.[27] Undeterred and taking a long view over the last decade, China's extensive international overt engagements and covert actions in the fields of science and technology played an active role in fuelling its indigenous military and space industry. Despite the US actions, 'The CPC's predatory space-related behaviour thrives in permissive environments that allow for the exploitation of uninformed U.S. decision makers at all levels'.[28]

The statement in the US Department of Defense Space Strategy of 2020 is as follows: 'The Department of Defense is taking innovative and bold actions to ensure space superiority and secure the nation's interest in space now and the future'[29] and underscores the current US approach. This strident attitude has emerged after years of a somewhat complacent approach to China's rise in the space realm. In the older US National Security Space Strategy of 2011, the outlook was:

> We seek to address the contested environment with a multi-layered deterrence approach. Our objectives are to improve safety, stability, and security in space; to maintain and enhance the strategic national security advantages afforded to the United States by space; and to energize the space industrial base that supports U.S. national security.[30]

In 2016, the US Space Subcommittee of the Committee for Science, Space and Technology conducted a hearing on 'Are We Losing the Space Race to China?', where its Chairman opened the proceedings with the statement: 'the ascendance of China as a leading space-faring nation'.[31] By 2020, the US priority towards space became distinctly military: 'Build a comprehensive military advantage in space; Integrate military space-power into national, joint, and combined operations; Shape the strategic environment; Cooperate with allies, partners, industry, and other U.S. Government departments and agencies.'[32]

The US articulated a definitive space security-centred outlook:

> Space underpins our national security and ability to respond decisively to crises around the world. Information collected from space informs national decision makers about evolving threats to U.S., allied, and partner interests. Space capabilities enable the U.S. military to protect and defend the U.S. homeland and to advance the national and collective security interests of the United States and its allies and partners.[33]

By the time the Biden administration took charge, the possibility of conflict in space escalated in the perception of the US: 'The Space Force stands on firmer political ground but is coming under pressure to deliver new technologies to counter threats from Russia and China.'[34]

On the other hand, the CPC's 'whole of society approach' strategy ensured the penetration of space across its commercial, private and academic spheres, and brought it closer towards realising its endeavour to dominate space in every way. The proactive engagement in all international space-related forums and synergistic cooperation with international space consortiums has enabled an irreversible strategic embrace of the space domain, much in the way the economies of most nations are today deeply enmeshed with that of China.

Its space cooperation initiatives based on global earth systems to distribute information in the fields of weather, agriculture, water management, public health and telecommunications have seductively drawn many nations into its fold. As per China's State Council Information Office, since 2016, it has signed forty-six space cooperation agreements and/or memoranda of understanding (MoUs) with nineteen countries and four international organisations.[35] China's cooperation with the erstwhile USSR in the Cold War era and the present day provides an interesting contrast. The resolution of the border issue between the two geographical giants in 1990 paved the way for greater cooperation.

After a phase of shallow cooperation in the early years, there has been a distinct convergence post Russia's annexation of Crimea in 2014. The increased cooperation which began over satellite communication paved the way for greater engagement. In 2017, the two countries established a five-year framework with the 'Outline of China-Russia Space Cooperation' for 2018–2022.[36] This allowed transfer sensitive space and missile defense technology, which allows China access to technologies dominated by the US and Russia. An MOU was signed in 2021 for the joint construction of an autonomous lunar permanent research base, the International Lunar Research Station (ILRS). The two are cooperating on developing a ballistic missile early warning system (BMEWS) which will provide advance information on potential incoming missiles' trajectory, speed, time-to-target and other critical information necessary for an effective interception.[37] Russia's space agency (Roscosmos) and the China National Space Administration (CNSA) inked a deal in November last year on bilateral space cooperation in 2023–2027, which includes the construction of the lunar station that is expected to be completed by 2035, and mutual accommodation of Glonass and BeiDou ground stations.

Two missions are planned during 2026–2030 to test the technologies of landing and cargo delivery, and the transportation of lunar soil samples to Earth. The plans envisage developing infrastructure in orbit and on the Moon's surface in 2031–2035 – in particular, communications systems, electrical power, research and other equipment. There is little doubt that Beijing is extensively using space programmes to bolster its foreign policy.

> It is actively pursuing its manned space programs and seeks to leverage the commercialization of space as a domain where it becomes the dominant player in the world. All these capabilities and activities have an embedded Chinese presence in practically every space-related field, much like its economic engagement with almost all countries of the world. This provides China with deterrent leverages in almost all domains.[38]

The larger concerns regarding China's outlook towards space emerge from two facts: It does not have separate civilian and military space programmes; its space programme has evolved out of its defence programme, with the CNSA being a part of the State Administration for Science, Technology and Industry for National Defense (SASTIND). The defence industrial enterprises that support military-related R&D, manufacturing and follow-on support come under the administration of SASTIND. It serves to qualitatively meet the PLA's requirements by infusing greater competition within the defence industry, encouraging greater military-civil fusion and providing policy guidance to the state-owned defence industry. Its responsibilities range from space and missiles, electronics, aviation, nuclear-related products, shipbuilding to other sectors.[39]

The Congressionally-mandated Pentagon Report of 2022 calls out China 'for plowing ahead with investments in advanced military space capabilities despite the regime's public rhetoric against the militarization of space' towards achieving 'space superiority'. The report also states that while China 'officially advocates for the peaceful use of space and is pursuing agreements in the UN on the non-weaponisation of space, it continues to improve its counter space weapons capabilities'.[40] The demonstrated coercive regional strategy and aggressive foreign policy are harbingers of a Chinese-dominant, if not dominated, space leadership. It undoubtedly sees space as the enterprise of its future:

> China aims to strengthen its space presence in an all-round manner: to enhance its capacity to better understand, freely access, efficiently use, and effectively manage space; to defend national security, lead self-reliance and self-improvement efforts in science and technology, and promote high-quality economic and social development; to advocate sound and efficient governance of outer space, and pioneer human progress; and to make a positive contribution to China's socialist modernization, and to peace and progress for all humanity.[41]

China is actively leveraging space for its Anti-Area/Access Denial along with sea-based and land-based space programmes for its regional power projection. Its sub-metric resolution satellite imaging capability, advanced space-based Command, Control, Communications, Computers, (C4) Intelligence, Surveillance and Reconnaissance (ISR), along with growing space-based military capabilities enhance its military capability significantly. Capability and capacity enhancements ranging from conventional and nuclear targeting, ground-air-sea operations, precision strike capabilities, missile defence, direct-ascent and co-orbital anti-satellite (ASAT) weapons, directed-energy weapons, cyber-ASAT capabilities[42] have the world and the US deeply concerned. While it unsurprisingly makes all the right noises about the peaceful 'use of outer space for peaceful purposes and opposes any attempt to turn outer space into a weapon or battlefield or launch an arms race in outer space'[43] in an attempt to allay fears, the underpinnings of its great power competition with the US and quest to be the world space leader is evident. The unclassified annual threat assessment of the US intelligence community states that: 'China is steadily progressing towards its goal of becoming a world-class space leader, with the intent to match or surpass the United States by 2045. Even by 2030, China probably will achieve world-class status in all but a few space technology areas'.[44]

Whither India – Strategic Implications

After decades of avowedly peaceful and civilian-driven Indian space endeavours – which have shown remarkable progress and gained international recognition – China's strides in space makes a review of India's space security a priority imperative. New Delhi's current approach to space has a more neo-realist outlook, considering the churn of the international system and world order, vis-a-vis China's attempts at creating an alternative system. Rajagopalan posits, 'India's approach to space is now driven by a sense of pragmatism and by national security concerns, as opposed to the morality- and sovereignty-related considerations that shaped the programme until the 1990s.'[45]

China's military rise and the evident inclusion of space in its geopolitical strategy has serious consequences on India's national security from two perspectives. The first is that the military use of space by India has become an unavoidable future security imperative. The Chinese Yaogan satellites are all dual-use satellites which have electro-optical, synthetic aperture radar and electronic intelligence capabilities. They significantly improve Beijing's target location accuracy, which in turn improves its anti-Ship ballistic Missile (ASBM) targeting capabilities and that of its sea-based forces. China's space-borne capability also aids in the precise location of targets for its Anti-Ship Cruise Missile (ASCM) capability.[46] The Gaofen satellites are high-resolution imagery satellites that can track and identify objects of interest, such as aircraft carriers, and therefore impact India's maritime domain. Future hypersonic weapons, such as space glide vehicles and fractional orbital bombardment systems, the BMEWS, ASAT capabilities – including co-orbital systems, directed energy weapons, high-powered lasers, and space-enabled electronic jamming, spoofing, cyber means, etc. – are a serious future threat. The second challenge is that as space rivalry grows between the US and China, along with their broader strategic contestation, it will increasingly put India in somewhat of an unenviable Hobson's choice situation, where space increasingly becomes the high ground of control between the US and China–Russia combine.

The evident growing competition between rival blocs will continue to pose difficult choices for India, as it has traditionally worked with both the US and Russia in space activities. India's deteriorated relations with China in the strategic context of intensified Sino-Russia nexus, and having joined the US promoted Artemis Accord, poses a challenge for India to be part of the

ILRS programme. The US–Russia relations in the current geopolitical climate will raise concerns in India's future cooperation with Russia in sensitive space sectors. Thus, India's future strategic pathway, when it comes to space, is akin to a situation of having to cross a fast-flowing river on wet and slippery stepping stones. It will need a fine combination of sure-footedness, deft balancing skills and bold foreign policy.

India's future national growth trajectory has led to a greater understanding and acceptance of the need to accelerate the integration of air and space domains, especially since there is little doubt that space is already weaponised; more so since China remains our long-term strategic rival in Asia and border-sharing military adversary, with whom future clashes remain a high-probability reality. The exhortation by India's Defence Minister for the Indian Air Force (IAF) to become an Aerospace Force and prepare to protect the nation from future challenges underscores this. It is a *realpolitik* call for technology evolution, gaining expertise and human resource management to defend the country against space-guided attacks and protect space assets.[47] While space significantly features in IAF's latest doctrine, the Service eschews any exclusive claim to space and firmly believes it to be a national commons. The doctrine states:

> While utilisation of space for economic and developmental purposes is likely to increase, the concurrent vulnerabilities of our country to hostile action seeking to destroy, degrade or deny our space capabilities as well as national capabilities through the medium of outer space are increasing. There is a requirement for the nation to have a robust defence mechanism for its space assets against threats from space. IAF, as an aerospace power, needs to be prepared for a greater role in space exploitation towards national objectives.[48]

It is time for a comprehensive and synergistic civil and military space vision to expand India's exclusively peaceful outlook towards space for a more future-relevant, national security-oriented one. A space vision which charts the nation's future in both civil and military domains and allows for inclusive capacity building and policy requirements is the way of the future. An expeditious execution of such a vision will provide the necessary context, direction and structure for a future-focussed strategic space enterprise. China has long stolen the march, and unless India leapfrogs over the asymmetric disadvantage to reduce the gap, it will be increasingly vulnerable to Beijing's space-enabled coercive strategies.

A synergistic strategy to 'space-map' India's space vision has the inherent advantage of overcoming the traditional silo-based approach towards space. Learning from others' best practices, some key considerations could uniquely define India's space map. The first is adopting a long-term civil-military integrated (CMI) approach. An approach that includes all aspects of space-related policies and strategies – from research and development to production and implementation, towards creating a common national enterprise for security and civil use – would best serve India's future interests. Integration of the civil and military space industries makes immense fiscal sense for a growing economy, especially as it allows for private investment. Space-faring nations face hurdles in managing their civil and military aspirations due to the inherent contradictions of a state-run space programme, with civil industry-led commercial ones. For India, a synergised programme will have several advantages:

- It will allow benefits of spin-off (conversion of military technologies in civil fields) and spin-on (civilian and commercial participation in military fields).
- It will enable better programme oversight.
- Importantly, it will permit much larger engagement between public and private industries.

Considering the strategic importance that space holds for the future, though every country would prefer an exclusively national programme, fiscal constraints make it unviable. India will find it increasingly difficult to balance its future budgetary commitments towards space given the strategic necessity for sustaining its current economic growth, while simultaneously meeting the enormous collective aspirations of the largest youth population. A pragmatic option for policy makers would therefore be to make space an area of collaborative international development with partner-nations, with whom their democratic ideals and values overlap with their strategic interests. India's mature and advanced civilian space programme will have to bridge the large gap to meet its future military needs of space smartly and securely. In light of the international acceptance of the reassertion of its independent foreign policy,[49] New Delhi's recent ultra-realist India-first approach will have to chart the path to the contested heavens very carefully.

Concluding Thoughts

China's space programme, having matured over decades, has picked up momentum in the recent years and is set to create new benchmarks of space capabilities. Its approach offers enormous opportunities for international cooperation but, at the same time, its larger national aspirations of becoming a dominant space power has caused it to leverage the Tiantang to cater to its future security interests. This has raised concerns amongst many nations, including India, and has hard-lined the US against what it perceives as a serious security threat of the future. The growing role of space in the economy will ensure its rising salience in geopolitics and international security. The enormous costs will foster greater interdependence amongst leading space nations and aspirational ones and, while it will make the global space sector more multipolar, China will certainly be a leading player. India's future growth, security and position in the world is inexorably linked to China's future trajectory; therefore, it will have to swiftly strategise its future space-map with a long-term vision. And while it does so, the role of space in a nation's comprehensive national power will continue to make the heavens an area of contest for the foreseeable future.

Notes

1. T.V. Fedorova and M.V. Novosyolova, 'Development of China's Space Programme in the Geopolitical Region of the Asia-Pacific', SHS Web of Conferences 134(2022), doi:10.1051/shsconf/202213400170.
2. Ibid.
3. Baichun Zhang, Jiuchun Zhang and Fang Yao, 'Technology Transfer from the Soviet Union to the People's Republic of China 1949–1966', *Comparative Technology Transfer and Society* 4, no. 2(August 2006):105–71.
4. Ibid.
5. Eytan Tepper, 'China's New Space Station Opens for Business in a Competitive Era of Space Activity', *Astronomy Magazine*, 13 December 2022.
6. 'BeiDou-3 Navigation Satellite System', Aerospace Technology, https://www.aerospace-technology.com/projects/beidou-3-navigation-satellite-system/.
7. 'Full Text: China's Space Program: A 2021 Perspective', Xinhua, 28 January 2022. https://english.www.gov.cn/archive/whitepaper/202201/28/content_WS61f35b3dc6d09c94e48a467a.html.
8. 'Tianwen-1 and Zhurong, China's Mars orbiter and rover', The Planetary Society, https://www.planetary.org/space-missions/tianwen-1.
9. Zhao Lei, 'Scientists Envision Solar Power Station In Space', chinadaily.com.cn, 27 February 2019, https://www.chinadaily.com.cn/a/201902/27/WS5c75c8b3a3106c65c34eb8e3.html.
10. Andrew Jones, 'Landspace Launches Third Methane Zhuque-2, Targets 2025 Launch of New Stainless-Steel Rocket', SpaceNews, 9 December 2023, https://spacenews.com/landspace-launches-third-methane-zhuque-2-targets-2025-launch-of-new-stainless-steel-rocket/.
11. Ling Xin, 'China Space Authorities Name Elon Musk's SpaceX an "Unprecedented Challenge"', South China Morning Post, 6 December 2023, https://www.scmp.com/news/china/science/article/3244086/china-space-authorities-name-elon-musks-spacex-unprecedented-challenge.
12. Blaine Curcio, 'China's Ascending Commercial Space Sector', *Space Symposium* 365, no. 2 (2021), https://room.eu.com/article/china's-ascending-commercial-space-sector.
13. Brian Waidelich, CNA, *China's Space Narrative*, East Asia Forum, https://eastasiaforum.org/2021/03/13/chinas-commercial-space-sector-shoots-for-the-stars/.

14. 'Chinese Space Activities Will Increasingly Challenge US Interests Through 2030', April 2021, Declassified by the Director of National Intelligence (DNI), https://www.dni.gov/files/ODNI/documents/assessments/NICM-Declassified-Chinese-Space-Activities-through-2030--2022.pdf.
15. Ma Chi, 'China Aims To Be World-Leading Space Power by 2045', chinadaily.com.cn, 17 November 2017, https://www.chinadaily.com.cn/china/2017-11/17/content_34653486.htm.
16. Baichun Zhang, Jiuchun Zhang and Fang Yao, 'Technology Transfer from the Soviet Union to the People's Republic of China 1949–1966', *Comparative Technology Transfer and Society* 4, no. 2 (August 2006): 105–71.
17. Andrew S. Erickson, 'China Defense White Papers – 1995–2019', Andrew S. Erickson Blog, 23 July 2019. https://www.andrewerickson.com/2019/07/china-defense-white-papers-1995-2019-download-complete-set-read-highlights-here/.
18. 'China's Space Activities in 2016: the 4th Version of White Paper', China National Space Administration, February 2017, https://www.unoosa.org/documents/pdf/copuos/stsc/2017/tech-01E.pdf.
19. 'China Issues White Paper on Space Activities', Xinhuanet, 27 December 2016. http://www.xinhuanet.com/english/2016-12/27/c_135936390.htm.
20. David Scott, 'Going Beyond the World. China Reaches for Outer Space'. https://dscottcom.files.wordpress.com/2019/04/china-space.pdf.
21. Ibid.
22. European Space Policy Institute, 'China's 2016 White Paper on Space: An Analysis', Executive Brief No. 7, 1 January 2017, https://www.espi.or.at/briefs/chinas-2016-white-paper-on-space-an-analysis/.
23. Sujian Guo, Introduction: 'Challenges and Opportunities for China's "Peaceful Rise"', *China's 'Peaceful Rise' in the 21st Century* (New York: Routledge, 2006).
24. R. Lincoln Hines, 'Heavenly Mandate: Public Opinion and China's Space Activities', *Space Policy*, Volume 60, May 2022. https://www.sciencedirect.com/science/article/abs/pii/S0265964621000527.
25. Air Marshall Diptendu Choudhury, 'Path to the Heavens (Part One)', *Blue Yonder: Journal for Aerospace Studies*, Inaugural Issue, January–June 2023.
26. Mark Stokes, Gabriel Alvarado, Emily Weinstein and Ian Easton, *China's Space and Counter-space Capabilities and Activities*, Report for the US–China Economic and Security Review Commission, 30 March 2020, https://www.uscc.gov/sites/default/files/2020-05/China_Space_and_Counterspace_Activities.pdf.
27. William Pentland, 'Congress Bans Scientific Collaboration with China, Cites High Espionage Risks', *Forbes*, 7 May 2011, https://www.forbes.com/sites/williampentland/2011/05/07/congress-bans-scientific-collaboration-with-china-cites-high-espionage-risks/.
28. Ibid., n. 16.
29. The US Defense Space Strategy Summary 2020, Department of Defense, June 2020, https://media.defense.gov/2020/Jun/17/2002317391/-1/-1/1/2020_DEFENSE_SPACE_STRATEGY_SUMMARY.PDF.

30 The US National Security Space Strategy, Unclassified Summary, DNI, January 2011, https://www.dni.gov/files/documents/Newsroom/Reports%20and%20Pubs/2011_nationalsecurityspacestrategy.pdf.
31 Ibid., n. 10.
32 Ibid.
33 The United States Space Priorities Framework 2021, The White House Washington, December 2021, https://www.whitehouse.gov/wp-content/uploads/2021/12/united-states-space-priorities-framework-_-december-1-2021.pdf.
34 Sandra Erwin, 'Space And National Security: What To Expect In 2022', SpaceNews, 19 January 2022. https://spacenews.com/space-and-national-security-what-to-expect-in-2022.
35 Blaine Curcio, 'China's International Collaboration in Space: An Evolving Approach from the Middle Kingdom', *Room: Space Journal of Asgardia* 1(31), 2022, https://room.eu.com/article/chinas-international-collaboration-in-space-an-evolving-approach-from-the-middle-kingdom.
36 He Qisong, 'Analysis of Space Cooperation Between China and Russia', *Russian Studies*, 2 August 2021, https://interpret.csis.org/translations/analysis-of-space-cooperation-between-china-and-russia/.
37 Vasily Kashin, 'Chinese–Russian Ballistic Missile Cooperation Signals Deepening Trust', *East Asia Forum*, 20 February 2021, https://www.eastasiaforum.org/2021/02/20/chinese-russian-ballistic-missile-cooperation-signals-deepening-trust/.
38 Ibid., n. 15.
39 Ibid., n. 16.
40 'Military and Security Developments Involving the People's Republic of China', US Department of Defense, 2022. https://media.defense.gov/2022/Nov/29/2003122279/-1/-1/1/2022-MILITARY-AND-SECURITY-DEVELOPMENTS-INVOLVING-THE-PEOPLES-REPUBLIC-OF-CHINA.PDF.
41 'China's Space Program: A 2021 Perspective', White Paper, The State Council Information Office of the People's Republic of China, 28 January 2022, http://www.cnsa.gov.cn/english/n6465645/n6465648/c6813088/content.html.
42 Anthony H. Cordesman, 'Chinese Space Strategy and Developments', Center for Strategic and International Studies, August 2016, https://www.csis.org/analysis/china-space-strategy-and-developments.
43 Ibid., n. 27.
44 Office of the Director of National Intelligence, *Annual Threat Assessment of the U.S. Intelligence Community*, 6 February 2023, https://www.dni.gov/files/ODNI/documents/assessments/ATA-2023-Unclassified-Report.pdf.
45 Rajeshwari Pillai Rajagopalan, 'India's Space Priorities Are Shifting towards National Security: Commentary', Carnegie Endowment for International Peace, 1 September 2022. https://carnegieendowment.org/2022/09/01/india-s-space-priorities-are-shifting-toward-national-security-pub-87809.
46 Kartik Bommakanti, 'India and China's Space And Naval Capabilities: A Comparative Analysis', Observer Research Foundation. https://www.orfonline.

org/research/42694-india-and-chinas-space-and-naval-capabilities-a-comparative-analysis.
47 Air National News, 5 May 2022 [video]. https://newsonair.gov.in/News?title=Rajnath-Singh-exhorts-Indian-Air-Force-to-become-Aerospace-Force-and-be-prepared-to-protect-country-from-future-challenges&id=440389.
48 'Doctrine of the Indian Air Force', IAP 2000–22: 3–4. https://indianairforce.nic.in/wp-content/uploads/2023/01/2MB.pdf.
49 Derek Grossman, 'Modi's Multipolar Moment Has Arrived', Foreign Policy, 6 June 2022, https://foreignpolicy.com/2022/06/06 modi-india-russia-ukraine-war-china-us-geopolitics-multipolar-quad/.

21

The Strategy of Military–Civil Fusion in China

Prerna Gandhi

> *'The kernel of good strategy contains three main components: diagnosis of a problem; an appropriate guiding policy; and a set of coherent actions.'*
> – Richard Rumelt, Good Strategy, Bad Strategy

Due to numerous geopolitical headwinds and economic challenges, the Chinese Party state has prioritised building the economy and defence capabilities simultaneously to optimise the resources available. The Communist Party of China (CPC) has closely studied the mistakes that resulted in the downfall of the Soviet Union, one of which was overextension exacerbated by excessive military spending. With both firms and local governments having spiralling levels of debt in recent years, China's debt-to-GDP ratio hit 286 per cent in 2023.[1] Further, with growing economic contention and technological containment by the US and the West, the strategy of Military-Civil Fusion (MCF) is seen as directly supporting China's ability to prevail in a long-term strategic competition. Supply-side Structural Reform (SSSR) announced by Xi Jinping in 2015 coincided with the rise of MCF in China. SSSR comprised five core policy objectives: cutting excess industrial capacity, reducing leverage in the corporate sector, de-stocking of property inventories, lowering costs for businesses and addressing 'weak links' in the economy. Both SSSR and MCF have had a large component of industrial upgradation and streamlining of productive forces. MCF received a further boost with the focus on 'new productive forces' involving new energy, new material and hi-tech manufacturing as a key driver of growth since September 2023.

China pursues MCF development strategy to 'fuse' its security and development strategies in support of China's national rejuvenation goals. MCF aims to create and leverage synergies between economic development and military modernisation so as to ensure free flow of dual-use technologies by allowing defence and commercial enterprises to collaborate and synchronise their efforts. With information superiority being seen as a prized goal, MCF also supports the shift in warfare approach by the People's Liberation Army (PLA) from 'informationised' to 'intelligentised' warfare. It also allows for bridging the gap in original innovation and disruptive technologies between China and other nations. As noted in the 2020 Annual Report to Congress on China in the US, the People's Republic of China (PRC) MCF development strategy encompasses six interrelated efforts: (1) fusing China's defence industrial base to its civilian technology and industrial base; (2) integrating and leveraging science and technology innovations across military and civilian sectors; (3) cultivating talent and blending military and civilian expertise and knowledge; (4) building military requirements into civilian infrastructure and leveraging civilian construction for military purposes; (5) leveraging civilian service and logistics capabilities for military purposes and (6) expanding and deepening China's national defence mobilisation system to include all relevant aspects of its society and economy for use in competition and war.[2]

Institutionalising of MCF Strategy

Since Mao Tse-tung, every Chinese leader has promoted a coordination and integration of civil and military efforts. This derives from the unique nature of civil-military relations in the PRC, wherein the PLA owes allegiance not to the state, but to the CPC. This subordination of the armed forces to the party has been the utmost priority of all top Chinese leaders. However, the structural organisation of the Central Military Commission (the same body serves as both party and state organ) has ensured not only the party's dominance in the state, but also strong military influence over the state that encourages fusion between military and civilian domains. The 'Two bombs, one satellite' project of the 1950s can be considered a precursor to the MCF. Under Deng Xiaoping, the PLA became a major stakeholder in China's opening up and economic liberalisation from 1978. Post Tiananmen crisis in 1989, the goal of economic development was established as the central task of the party and codified in the party constitution in 1992. This subverted ideological struggles within the party, making economic performance the legitimising factor for the party.

Civil–Military Integration (CMI) in the 1980s saw defence conversion of arms production lines to commercial manufacturing. This was seen as a means of both absorbing excess capacity in the arms-producing sector and also providing the PLA with additional revenue as the state had more engaging priorities. However, these CMI efforts did not add any growth to Chinese weapons development and production. By 1990, it was estimated that 80 per cent of defence output was civilian goods. But the Gulf War of 1991 shook China from its complacency and changed their entire strategic outlook. Jiang Zemin's Divestiture Act in 1998 was markedly significant to get the PLA to focus back on its core military activities. Hu Jintao, who assumed presidency in 2003, in his address at the 17th Party Congress mentioned 'path of development with Chinese characteristics featuring military and civilian integration'. In 2005, a key State Council policy document paved the way for the private industry's entry into the PRC's defence industrial base. Later in 2006, the 11th Five Year Plan transformed MCI into MCF with the objective of utilising all national resources to promote the defence industry.

Xi Jinping greatly raised the profile of MCF around 2014 and made it a key component of his national rejuvenation strategy, overseen by a new top-level body set up in 2017. In December 2014, at the All-Army Equipment Work Conference, President Xi noted the successes of MCF in the fields of defence technology and equipment development, but also highlighted the mindset challenges and vested interests in hindering further integration. This was notable since most developments under the MCF initiative had largely been confined to areas where there was little friction or vested interests. The solution, according to Xi, would be further consolidation of resources and breaking down of vested interests. In the plenary meeting of the PLA delegation at the Third Session of the 12th National People's Congress in March 2015, Xi called for MCF transition from 'early-state fusion' to 'deep fusion'. Xi remarked that a question he frequently pondered on was how to balance development and security in the formulation of overall national strategy, and stated that the elevation of MCF development into a national strategy represented an answer to his question.[3] On 21 July 2016, the 'Opinion on the Integrated Development of Economic Construction and National Defense Construction' (2016 Opinion) was released by the CPC Central Committee, State Council and the CMC.[4]

The National 13th Five-Year Plan for the development of strategic emerging industries released in November 2016 called for constructing a strategic emerging industry system for MCF. It emphasised promoting mutual compatibility and coordinated development of military and civilian science and technology innovation systems. In 2017, Xi established the Central Commission for Military–Civilian Fusion Development (CCMCFD) to promote MCF under the oversight of the CPC Central Committee. Four out of the seven Politburo Standing Committee members, ten out of twenty-five Politburo members and five out of the ten CMC members served on the committee. Several heads of the central Party organs and ministers of the State Council also represented on the Central Commission for Military–Civil Fusion Development. In his address to CCMCFD in June, he noted that 'we must accelerate the formation of a full-element, multi-domain, and high-return military-civil fusion deep development pattern, and gradually build up China's unified military-civil system of strategies and strategic capability'.[5] Later, in a five-year plan on promoting integrated military and civilian development in the science and technology sector released in the same year in August 2017, policymakers directed that a coordinated military-civilian innovation system for the sector should be put in place by 2020, and identified a new round of key sci-tech projects in military-civilian integration towards 2030.

Xi mentioned 'military-civilian integration' three times in his 19th Party Congress speech delivered on 18 October 2017. But in his 20th Party Congress address in October 2022, Xi did not reference MCF per se and spoke of better coordination of strategies and plans, aligning policies and systems and sharing resources and production factors between the military and civilian sectors. Since early 2022, the CPC appears to be deemphasising the term 'Military Civil Fusion' in public, in favour of 'integrated national strategic systems and capabilities'.

Many military research institutions in China, such as the National Defense University (NDU) and Academy for Military Sciences (AMS), have created research centres dedicated to MCF studies. AMS established its Military-Civil Fusion Research Center in 2011. According to a report by *PLA Daily*, this research centre has close working relationships with the Ministry of Industry and Information Technology (MIIT), including State Administration of Science, Technology and Industry for National Defense (SASTIND) that is under it, the CMC Equipment Development Department (EDD), the CMC Logistics Support Department (LSD), the CMC Strategic Planning Office, the Chinese Academy of Sciences (CAS) and the Chinese Academy of Engineering (CAE). The AMS research centre was also responsible for the organisation of a third-party assessment of the MCF strategy's level of implementation in 2015. In July 2015, the NDU unveiled its Research Center for Military Civil Fusion Deep Development in Beijing. This centre is responsible for compiling annual reports on MCF development in China and publishes the *Military-Civil Fusion Journal* which is an important platform to understand MCF policy priorities. Unfortunately, several key documents on MCF, including the 'Outline of the MCF Strategy' issued by Beijing, are not public.[6]

Reforming PRC Defence Industrial Complex into Market Entities

Nearly all of Chinese military industries are owned by ten major state-owned enterprises (SOEs). They are under the State-owned Assets and Administration Commission (SASAC) of the State Council, but SASTIND (under MIIT) is in charge of overseeing their business operations. These defence groups maintain military procurement relationships with the CMC EDD and service equipment procurement bureaus. In May 2007, Commission of Science, Technology and Industry for National Defense (COSTIND), National Development and Reform Commission (NDRC) and SASAC issued a guiding opinion to officially initiate the structural reform of ownership of the defence conglomerates. But the reform would gain currency in July 2017, when the State Council issued a notice for central SOEs to complete transition of centrally owned enterprises from 'people-owned' to 'wholly state-owned' by the end of 2017. The connotation of people-owned enterprises for the defence SOEs allowed for financial indiscipline and continuing with the erstwhile legacy of 'iron-rice bowl' where people were assured lifetime employment. On the other hand, the transition to wholly state-owned enterprises was to establish clear corporate governance and infuse new capital so as to turn them into independent market entities that bore their own profits, losses and risks.

Private Sector and MCF Strategy

The private sector contributes more than 50 per cent of total tax revenue, more than 60 per cent of GDP, more than 70 per cent of China's technological innovation, over 80 per cent of urban employment and makes up more than 90 per cent of market entities in China. However, it has been at the receiving end of numerous criticisms by the military – such as their being incapable of maintaining confidentiality, 'unreliable' products, 'non-guaranteed' wartime production, etc. Over the years, defence SOEs have deliberately set up obstacles to exclude participation of private enterprises. But with a slowing economy and changing labour force – especially in light of the issue of urban unemployment – has led policymakers to see MCF as creating numerous high-end jobs by opening business opportunities that were previously restricted to the broader economy through pent-up demand. Further, lack of genuine competition and strong vested interest have severely hindered technological innovation. Prior to 2017, civilian companies were required to obtain up to four licenses to take part in the defence supply chain, and the entire process took an average of four years.

In a move to further lower the entry barrier for civilian companies into the weapons and equipment R&D field, the CMC EDD in October 2017 announced that two of the licenses had been merged, reducing the total number of licenses required to three and shortening clearance time by six months. According to EDD data from 2019, the number of civilian companies that have obtained one of these permits had risen from 500 in 2013 to 2,300 in 2019. As of 2019, about 2 per cent (3,000 out of 150,000) of China's private high-tech companies are involved in the defence supply chain, primarily providing parts or material supplies. Between 2009 and 2019, 68 per cent of the private companies that entered this field specialised in information technology. While that represents significant progress for the PLA's informatisation drive, it is insufficient to address the problem of low self-sufficiency of 'core key technologies'. In 2018, Zhang Kejian, the deputy director of SASTIND, wrote that there are 'five bottlenecks' in military technologies: military-use electronics, critical materials, advanced propulsion technology, high-end manufacturing equipment and essential software (including operating systems).[7]

Reducing the dependence of the industrial base on imports of critical components and sophisticated technologies was an underlying pillar of the Made in China (MIC) 2025 strategy announced in 2015. The MIC 2025 targeted high-tech industries including aerospace equipment, communication equipment, power generation and transmission equipment, railways, etc. as areas where achieving self-sufficiency was important.

Logistics under MCF

The MCF Strategy seeks to shift the PLA towards modern streamlined logistics and support services through two planks. First, it seeks to harness the civilian sector through both public and private enterprises to improve the PLA's basic services and support functions – such as food, housing and healthcare services. Second, MCF aims to fuse the PLA Joint Logistic Support Force's (JLSF's) efforts to integrate the military's joint logistics functions with the PRC's advanced civilian logistics and infrastructure. This will provide the PLA with not only modern transportation and distribution, warehousing, information sharing and other types of support in peacetime and wartime, but also ensure a logistics system that is more efficient, with higher capacity, higher quality and global in its reach. JLSF's involvement in the 2020 coronavirus response in Wuhan saw it leverage China's civilian logistics. But numerous problems remain, including limited 'jointness' in the logistics system and possible delays caused by the need to shift JLSC assets to Theatre Command authorities in wartime.

In 2011, the total length of China's highways was 85,000 kilometres, but less than twenty sections had been reserved for use as emergency airstrips, which was far below the 500 mark which planners had deemed necessary. By 2023, China's total highways reached 169,100 kilometres, but it is unclear how many of the new emergency runways have been added. Airport sharing between the PLAAF and the Civil Aviation Administration of China (CAAC) dates to 1985. With the elevation of MCF to a national strategy, CAAC has reportedly established a joint working mechanism with the PLA Army, Navy and Air Force headquarters. Railways play an equally important role in Chinese economic and strategic goals linking Chinese producers with internal and region-wide markets. The trans-Eurasian Landbridge under the Belt and Road Initiative (BRI) provides more than 13,000 kilometres of railway lines connecting China with Europe through Central Asia and the South Caucasus. China also has more than 120,000 kilometres of navigable inland waterways that help connect production centres with the rest of the country.

MCF also plays a significant role in advancing the development of overseas logistical facilities. Currently, China has two national strategies that help advance its economic presence and interests abroad. The first is the 'Going Out' strategy initiated in the 1990s that promotes the overseas investment and international operations of Chinese companies. This was most evident in the hydrocarbons sector. The second is the BRI, which was launched in 2013 and promotes engagement through six major channels: policy agreements, infrastructure development, investment, trade, cultural exchange and supply chain cooperation. The 2019 China's National Defense in the New Era Defense White Paper emphasised overseas interests as a crucial part of China's national interests, and the strengthening mechanisms for protecting overseas interests as an important mission for China's armed forces. Today, Chinese entities own equity stakes or operational rights in nearly 100 ports worldwide.

Lawfare under MCF Strategy

In recent years, the PRC has implemented new laws strengthening the legal framework for national security and furthering MCF Strategy. Under Xi, economic growth has been replaced by national security as the public contract between the CPC and Chinese citizens. Many of the new laws impose broad obligations on citizens and corporations (domestic and foreign) to assist and cooperate with the Chinese government in its security actions. There is large emphasis on securing Chinese data. Many laws also focus on strengthening standards in the civilian sector that could assist with military objectives such as in maritime transportation. Civilian logistics capacity is seen as critical for any future military action against Taiwan. There are also legal efforts to ensure resilience and solidarity of Chinese entities against foreign pressure such as through economic sanctions. This is indicative that China foresees scenario of increased contestation with the US. Some of the salient laws are:

- **National Security Law**: Adopted in July 2015, the new law introduced a sweeping concept of national security into Chinese law for the first time. Though the law outlined that China must protect its national security interests from an ability to govern to outer space to cultural and social security, it wasn't augmented by particular detail about how specifically those goals will be achieved.
- **Counterterrorism Law**: Adopted in December 2015, the law gave China a legal definition of terrorism. It also laid down legal framework to allow China's armed forces to take part in counterterrorism operations abroad, provided approval is granted by the foreign country in question. Among its other provisions, the law required telecommunications operators and Internet service providers to provide information, decryption and other technical support to public and state security organisations 'conducting prevention and investigation of terrorist activities'.
- **National Defense Transportation Law**: Coming into effect in 2016, the National Defense Transportation Law covered the use of railways, waterways and air routes for defence purposes and will regulate the planning, construction, management and use of resources in transportation sectors for national defence.[8] Earlier, in 2015, China issued the Technical Standards for the Implementation of National Defence Requirements

for Newly Built Civil Ships. The standards apply to five types of ships: container, roll-on/roll-off, multipurpose, bulk carrier and breakbulk. It is estimated that a hundred civilian ships can be mobilised to support such a requirement. China's COSCO Shipping alone operates over 360 container ships – the third largest container fleet capacity worldwide.[9]

- ***Cyber Security Law***: The law, which went into effect in June 2017, promoted development of indigenous technologies and restricted sales of foreign ICT in China. The law also required foreign companies to submit ICT for government-administered national security reviews, store data in China and seek government approval before transferring data outside of China.
- ***Intelligence Law***: Adopted in June 2017, the law allowed authorities to monitor and investigate foreign and domestic individuals and organisations to protect national security. Specifically, it allowed authorities to use or seize vehicles, communication devices and buildings to support intelligence collection efforts.
- ***Anti-Foreign Sanctions Law***: Adopted at the 29th meeting of the Standing Committee of the 13th National People's Congress on 10 June 2021, the law formally allowed Beijing to take countermeasures against foreign individuals and entities involved in discriminatory measures that 'violate international laws and basic norms'. Steps available include denying visas and deporting culprits, as well as freezing an individual's assets. Under Article 11 and 12, no entity or person in the country is permitted to help another nation implement measures against China and are instead required to help Beijing carry out retaliatory measures. Article 14 states organisations and individuals who refuse to implement or cooperate with retaliatory measures will be 'subject to legal liability'.
- ***Data Security Law***: This law went into effect on 1 September 2021 and subjects almost all data-related activities to government oversight, as PRC officials grow concerned about the transfer of potentially sensitive data overseas. The law's most important contributions to data security are two new rules that did not exist before: companies considered as critical information infrastructure operators must store data collected in mainland China locally and must also undergo a security assessment to gain approval to send any of that data overseas.[10]
- ***Counterespionage Law***: On 26 April 2021, the PRC adopted a counterespionage law permitting the Ministry of State Security (MSS) authority to identify companies and organisations deemed susceptible to foreign infiltration or influence, and require these institutes to implement measures to prevent foreign infiltration. In July 2023, the PRC adopted an amended counterespionage with a broader scope. The revised law and its

implementation rules impose a set of stringent obligations on organisations. These include prohibitive requirements which forbid activities posing threats to national security, as well as general requirements aimed at enhancing vigilance, stressing reporting duties, facilitating cooperation with authorities, etc.[11]

Talent Cultivation under MCF Strategy

Under the MCF strategy, China aims to leverage its civilian education resources to complement and improve upon the military triad system of institutional education, unit training and military professional education. In addition to direct recruitment of college graduates, the PLA has also experimented with a variety of recruitment approaches and training programmes administered by civilian entities, including jointly administered Master's or PhD programmes, officer professional education and training programmes, NCO direct recruitment programme, civilian personnel programme, etc.

About 118 civilian institutions of higher education have a talent cultivation agreement with the PLA. In 2020, the US government banned students from the seven universities closely affiliated with the PLA to study in graduate programmes in the US. CPC operates more than 200 talent recruitment programmes that are overseen by central bodies, including the Central Coordination Group on Talent Work and the Overseas High level Talent Recruitment Work Group. The 2016 Opinion document elucidated the need to integrate defence mobilisation system and the state emergency management system to enable coordinated emergency responses and operations in the event of a national emergency.[12]

Innovation and MCF

Though China overtook the US in terms of the total number of published scientific papers in early 2018, it is still struggling to demonstrate its ability to bring original innovation. The innovation base's inability to produce original innovations and disruptive technologies and the defence industrial base's low self-sufficiency on 'core, critical technologies' remain concerning. Thus, the transfer of high-quality innovation resources and technologies from the military and defence industrial base to the civilian sector and vice versa under the MCF strategy is expected to stimulate innovation and accelerate the structural transformation of the Chinese economy. Chinese scholars and experts closely study MCI models used in other countries. Prominent scholars of MCF in China frequently reference American practices. While developing MCF or its earlier incarnation, MCI, China closely studied the Defense Advanced Research Projects Agency (DARPA) and Defense Innovation Unit

(DIU) programmes of the US and how America has systematically utilised its universities and businesses to develop dual-use technologies like the Internet, GPS, drones, vehicle navigation, blood banks, etc. The Manhattan Project to develop the first nuclear bomb during the Second World War was an early and successful example of MCI.

In 2015, SASTIND and the State Intellectual Property Office jointly published the first edition of the 'National Defense Science and Technology Industry Intellectual Property Conversion Catalogue' to promote the conversion of military technology to the civilian field. The General Office of MIIT and the Comprehensive Division of SASTIND jointly issued the 'Catalogue for Promoting Military Technology for Civilian Use' and 'Catalogue of Recommended Civilian Technologies and Products for Military Use' to promote the two-way transfer of military and civilian technological achievements. In June 2018, Ministry of Science and Technology (MOST), NDRC, SASTIND and the CMC EDD announced measures to promote resource sharing across a wide range of national scientific research facilities, including state key laboratories, national defence technology key laboratories, major military and defence industry test facilities and the over sixty facilities designated as 'national major scientific and technological infrastructure'. The degree to which this measure has been implemented is unclear, but state key labs and national defence key labs are both under SASTIND and CMC EDD.

Some Focus Priorities of the MCF Strategy

Hu Jintao's 18th Party Congress Report in 2012 put forward, for the first time, the strategic priority of building a Maritime Great Power. A decade later, in 2023, Chinese-owned shipping fleet reached 249.2 million gross tons, or 15.9 per cent of the market share, to edge ahead of Greece.[13] China today is one of only a handful of countries capable of building the large ocean-faring vessels that transport around 80 per cent of global trade in goods. The industry leader is China State Shipbuilding Corporation (CSSC), which alone holds a 21.5 per cent share of the global shipbuilding market.[14] The sprawling SOE was formed in 2019 after the merger of China's two largest shipbuilders, and today it directly controls over 100 subsidiaries. CSSC is a lynchpin in Beijing's MCF strategy and is more than just a commercial shipbuilding giant. It also produces warships for the Chinese navy. Under the MCF, the construction of maritime information infrastructure has also been expedited and comprises an all-weather, all-day, multi-method, three-dimensional, high-precision maritime battlefield situational awareness network, a military-civilian compatible communication network, a maritime target joint surveillance and management system, along with a national joint marine environment investigation and monitoring system.

In Xi Jinping's 19th Party Congress Report in October 2017, space and cyberspace domains were officially elevated for assuming 'great power' status. The significance of these domains was also evident in the 2019 Defense White Paper. In recent years, Chinese defence experts and analysts see space and cyber as offering the greatest asymmetric returns in both military and economic contexts. An interesting thing to note is that Xi's Cyber Great Power strategy goes beyond harnessing civilian technological innovation and infrastructure to include shaping public opinion at home and abroad. The cyber domain is a perfect embodiment of Xi Jinping's holistic national security concept, which sees 'political security' as the 'cardinal element'. In December 2016, the PLA Army signed an MCF strategic agreement with China Mobile that enables cooperation in seven areas, including joint construction of information infrastructure, emergency communications support, command and dispatch, 'smart' military camps, information system and resource development and utilisation, information security and informatisation talent training.

MCF-driven semiconductor investment has played a key role in countering the US-led technological containment by increasing state autonomy through subsidies, allowing for the replacement of outdated foreign made chips with 'new' domestic processors, especially in Chinese supercomputers, and permitting military-focused research to proceed without the threat of foreign sanctions. Shanghai-based Semiconductor Manufacturing International Corporation (SMIC) shocked the technology industry in August 2023 with the mass production of Huawei's Kirin 9000S processor. China's foundries do not currently have the capacity required to achieve full domestic production, but SMIC could quickly reach production levels required for military autonomy. China's mature-process capacity encompassing chips that are 28nm and above is expected to grow from 29 to 33 per cent by 2027, according to TrendForce, a Taiwan-based market research firm. We also see military capacities shifting to the civilian sector in case of semiconductors. Originally a military-focused graphical processing unit (GPU) design company, Jingjia Micro used its early support from the government to develop several generations of GPUs for deployment in radars and satellites. In 2019, Jingjia Micro leveraged its acquired knowhow to enter the civilian market for GPUs.[15]

Challenges in MCF Strategy

Under Xi, there has been a systematic trend to co-opt private sector and SOEs together to pursue strategic objectives with the Party-State giving guidance. This contrasts with his predecessors, who welcomed the private sector for larger economic growth and not security goals. In some cases, the private sector has willingly championed strategic sectors and even achieved success such as in the case of BYD and Huawei. In other cases, such as Alibaba and Tencent, they have had to bear the brunt of the Party's punishment to fall in line. This has created an environment of business uncertainty and suspicion, for both China's own private sector and international corporations. Further, centralised state guidance can be less than efficient in many outcomes. This can be seen in case of the China Integrated Circuit Industry Investment Fund, also known as the Big Fund, that was set up in 2014 to help China achieve semiconductor self-sufficiency. Big Fund II saw the second infusion of capital in 2019, of nearly $29 billion, but would witness more than ten of the high-profile sponsored semiconductor projects going bust. This prompted a strong probe of anti-corruption investigations in July 2022.

Since 2021, China's stock market has seen a nearly $6 trillion rout and strict US dollar withdrawals remain in place.[16] Though numerous policies were declared to bolster the private sector including announcement of a private economy development bureau under the NDRC in July 2023, there are real questions of whether private sector contribution to GDP would be allowed to increase beyond a certain threshold. As Xi has doubled down on MCF, he appears to have essentially abandoned efforts to reform large SOEs. The dominance of SOEs in the defence sectors thus remains predominant. Also, MCF has provoked a backlash from the West as the CPC weaponising its political dominance in a one-party state to provide the PRC with undue advantages. The US government has implemented export controls on emerging technologies to restrict China's ability to obtain advanced computing chips, develop and maintain supercomputers and manufacture advanced semiconductors. This has, in essence, removed the differential between civil and military use for equipment and technologies being exported to China. The US has also roped in its allies such as Japan and Netherlands to tighten restrictions in case of semiconductors.

Conclusion: Implications for India

Since elevating MCF to a national strategy, China has successfully created a national consensus and framework for its implementation that permeates the entire party, state and military structure of the PRC from Beijing to the provinces. However, implementation of the MCF strategy is still in its early stages and like many other PRC strategies or initiatives, such as the BRI, it has no clear date of completion. But, ironically, China's political system presents significant obstacles to the success of its own MCF strategy. MCF represents an attempt to allow for free flow of information and a dynamic market system with vibrant private sector participation, while at the same time retaining centralised control of the economy and society. Yet the successes of MCF in increasing China's dominance in numerous economic and technological sectors along with rapid military upgradation remains undeniable. Some key projects and initiatives pursued under MCF include the BeiDou Navigation Satellite System, DJI drones, Baidu, quantum computing, big data, semiconductors, 5G telecommunications, aerospace and AI.

In contrast, India's efforts at civil-military integration have a long way to go to harness civilian capabilities and synergise defence and civilian domains. There are strong silos between the civilian and military institutions. However, the setting up of the offices of the Chief of Defense Staff and Department for Military Affairs have been pathbreaking. But increasing jointness between the different armed services through theaterisation needs to precede efforts towards larger MCI or MCF. Despite the increasing number of defence startups, involvement of private sector in Indian defence industry also remains nascent. Further, in articulating our China policy, China's whole-of-nation approach will have to be factored in our defence planning. For instance, civilian infrastructure being created in Tibet, such as the rail links and Xiaokang villages, greatly enhance PLA's force induction and maintenance capabilities. The blurring of the divide between civilian and defence sectors also requires us to develop derisking strategy vis-a-vis China, including in the technology space. Some initial steps such as banning of digital apps such as TikTok have been useful endeavours in that regard to prevent China from gaining a pre-eminent position in India's information space. Above all, we need to be more systematic and intentional in evolving our own model of civil-military integration as China and the US have done.

Notes

1. Xia Yining and Han Wei, 'China's Debt-to-GDP Ratio Climbs to Record 287.8% in 2023', Nikkei Asia, 30 January 2024, https://asia.nikkei.com/Spotlight/Caixin/China-s-debt-to-GDP-ratio-climbs-to-record-287.8-in-2023.
2. 'Military and Security Developments Involving the People's Republic of China 2020', Annual Report to Congress, Office of the Secretary of Defense, https://media.defense.gov/2020/Sep/01/2002488689/-1/-1/1/2020-DOD-CHINA-MILITARY-POWER-REPORT-FINAL.PDF.
3. Alex Stone and Peter Wood for the China Aerospace Studies Institute, *China's Military-Civil Fusion Strategy: A View from Chinese Strategists*, 2020, https://www.airuniversity.af.edu/Portals/10/CASI/documents/Research/Other-Topics/2020-06-15%20CASI_China_Military_Civil_Fusion_Strategy.pdf.
4. Ibid., op cit 2.
5. Lt Col Saurabh Dixit, 'Military–Civil Fusion in China and Lessons for India', Synergy 2, no. 1(February 2023): 88–105, https://cenjows.in/wp-content/uploads/2023/03/5.-Military-Civil-Fusion-in-China-and-Lessons-for-India-By-Lt-Col-Saurabh-Dixit.pdf.
6. Ibid.
7. Ibid.

8. 'China Mulls New Law to Secure National Defense Transport', chinadaily.com.cn, 25 April 2016, https://www.chinadaily.com.cn/china/2016-04/25/content_24827399.htm.
9. Manoj Rawat, 'China's Emerging Strategy for Power Projection in the Indian Ocean', The Geopolitics, 1 August 2021, https://thegeopolitics.com/chinas-emerging-strategy-for-power-projection-in-the-indian-ocean/.
10. Matt Haldane, 'Explainer: What China's New Data Laws Are And Their Impact On Big Tech, *South China Morning Post*, 1 September 2021, https://www.scmp.com/tech/policy/article/3147040/what-chinas-new-data-laws-are-and-their-impact-big-tech.
11. US Department of Defense, 'Military and Security Developments Involving the People's Republic of China 2023', A Report to Congress, https://media.defense.gov/2023/Oct/19/2003323409/-1/-1/1/2023-MILITARY-AND-SECURITY-DEVELOPMENTS-INVOLVING-THE-PEOPLES-REPUBLIC-OF-CHINA.PDF.
12. Ibid.
13. Mia Nulimaimaiti, 'China's Maritime Ambitions Boosted, Claims Largest Shipping Fleet Title from Greece', *South China Morning Post*, 14 August 2023, https://www.scmp.com/economy/china-economy/article/3231041/chinas-maritime-ambitions-boosted-claims-largest-shipping-fleet-title-greece.
14. Matthew P. Funaiole, Brian Hart, Joseph S. Bermudez Jr, 'In the Shadow of Warships, How Foreign Companies Help Modernize China's Navy', Center for Strategic and International Studies (CSIS), https://features.csis.org/china-shadow-warships/.
15. Braddford Waldie, 'How Military-Civil Fusion Steps up China's Semiconductor Industry', DigiChina: Stanford University, 1 April 2022, https://digichina.stanford.edu/work/how-military-civil-fusion-helps-chinas-semiconductor-industry-step-up/.
16. 'China's $6 Trillion Stock Wipeout Exposes Deeper Problems for Xi', Bloomberg, 25 January 2024, https://www.bloomberg.com/news/features/2024-01-25/can-xi-jinping-reverse-china-s-6-trillion-stock-market-crisis.

Index

Abdalla, Hassan, 207
Abraham Accords, 204
Academy for Military Sciences (AMS), 351, 398
Act East Policy, 198
ADMM Plus, 152
Afghanistan, 100, 151, 184, 192, 204, 341
Africa, 23, 197, 201, 222, 231, 234, 235, 238
Agniveer scheme, 59
Agreement on Confidence Building Measures in the Military Field Along the LAC, 55
Air defence system S-400, 110
Aksai Chin, 370, 373
Alibaba, 279
Al-Jadaan, Mohammed, 207
Amarsaikhan, S., 342
America First Trade Policy, 28, 33
Ant Group, 42
Anti-corruption campaigns, 46, 47, 53, 78, 90, 245
Anti-Foreign Sanctions Law, 2021, 402
Arabian Sea, 189
Arab–Islamic Summit, 197
Arctic Council, 107
Ardagh–Johnson Line of 1897, 368
Arms exporter, 103
Artificial intelligence (AI), 42, 278–279
Arunachal Pradesh, 15, 56, 62, 336, 343, 373
ASEAN-centric security institutions, 152
ASEAN Defense Ministers' Meeting (ADMM), 152
ASEAN Outlook on the Indo-Pacific (AOIP), 157
ASEAN Regional Forum (ARF), 24, 152
Asian Development Bank, 190, 332, 343
Asian geopolitics, 150–151,
Asian Infrastructure Bank, 25
Asian Infrastructure Investment Bank (AIIB), 87
Asia Pacific Economic Cooperation (APEC), 86
Association of Southeast Asian Nations (ASEAN), 62, 89, 121, 122, 156–157, 162, 222, 234, 292
Asymmetric deterrence, 57–59
AUKUS, 88, 99, 104, 124, 158, 296

Austin, Lloyd J., 124
Australia, 20, 26, 38, 60, 64, 88, 89, 105, 124, 142, 153, 162, 296
Australia Strategic Policy Institute (ASPI), 49
Authoritarian state, 47, 90
Azhar, Masood, 185

Bahrain, 200
Ballistic missile early warning system (BMEWS), 386
Balloon incident, 127
Balochistan, 185
Baltic Sea, 103
Bangladesh, 13, 19, 168, 176–177, 219
Bangladesh, China, India, Myanmar (BCIM) corridor, 171
Bangladesh–China relationship, 169
  bilateral trade gap, 173
  BNS Sheikh Hasina, 170
  BRI initiative, 171
  debt to China, 171–172
  defence cooperation, 170
  economic crises, 175
  FM-90 missile maintenance centre, 170
  infrastructural support, 168–169
Beckley, Michael, 48
Belt and Road Initiative (BRI), 18, 27, 31, 46, 51–52, 77, 87, 91, 108, 135–137, 144, 151, 156, 197, 216–238, 297, 400
  advantage to China, 234–236
  agreements signed by China, 222
  agricultural development, 227
  background, 216
  bad debt, perceptions of, 236
  China–Europe rail, 220–221
  Chinese contracts under, 217–218
  decade of, 216
  energy security, 226–227
  engagement across globe, 218–220
  financial integration, 230–231
  geographical footprint, 222–223
  headwinds, 232
  health sector, investment in, 228

implications for India, 236–238
investments under, 217–219
maritime logistic chains, 228–229
military maritime advantage, 229–230
new sectors of engagement, 227–228
One Belt One Road, 216
other allied initiatives, 232–234
partner countries, agreements with, 217
political alignment, 223
quantum of engagement, 227
rail connectivity, 220–221
regional investment, 224–225
resource security, 226
sectoral investment, 225
setting standards, 232
smart city development initiatives, 231
synergy with regional development initiatives, 223–224
technology proliferation, 231
Belt and Road Initiative Tax Administration Cooperation Mechanism (BRITACOM), 230
Bessent, Scott, 61
Bhatta, Lekh Raj, 177
Bhutan, 15, 40, 168, 179, 341, 367
Biden, Joe, 28, 32, 35, 37, 88, 90, 108, 113, 115, 121–129, 153–154, 163, 204, 206, 295, 296, 385
Big Fund, 406
Blinken, Antony, 122, 125, 127, 197
Blockchain technology, 282
Bloomberg report, 61
Blue Pacific, 122
Blue water navy, 151
Bolt, Paul J., 108
Border infrastructure, improvement in, 58
Border management, 54–56. *See also* India–China border
Border Peace and Tranquillity Agreement of 1993, 16
Boundary settlement, 56
Brands, Hal, 48
Brazil, 44, 105, 203, 382
Bretton Woods institutions, 52
BRICS (Brazil, Russia, India, China and South Africa), 63, 86, 102, 105, 109, 142, 203, 382
BRICS Summit, Kazan, 3–4
Britain, 100, 367
Buddhism, 337–340,
Buffer zones, 54
'Build Back Better for the World' plan, 153–154

Bureau for the Development of the Private Economy, 257
Burns, Nick, 127

Cai Qi, 245
Cambodia, 153, 161
Canada, 8, 61, 105
Carney, Richard W., 200
Center for Global Development study, 28
Central Asia, 223
Central Commission for Military–Civilian Fusion Development (CCMCFD), 397
Central Economic Work Conference (CEWC), 253. *See also* Economic trajectory, of China, 2022 CEWC, 254, 290
 2023 CEWC, 253, 263–266
 food security concerns, 289
 2023 meeting, 253
Central Foreign Affairs Work Conference, 2014, 25
Central Military Commission (CMC), 75, 80, 349, 396
 control over military, 80–82
 PAP under, 80
Central Science and Technology Commission, 277
Centre for Disease Control (CDC), 305
Century of humiliation, 22, 29
Chen Quanguo, 314, 316–321, 339
Chile, 226, 230
China Aerospace and Science Industry Corporation (CASIC), 381
China Aerospace Science and Technology Corporation (CASC), 381
China–Africa Cooperation (FOCAC), 208
China–Arab relations, 212–213. *See also* Middle East (West Asia), China and China–Arab States Cooperation Forum (CASCF), 212
China–Arab States Cooperation Ministerial Forum (CACMF), 199
China–Arab Summit, Saudi Arabia, 199
China, as great power, 51–53
China Coast Guard (CCG), 39, 40
China–Europe rail, 220–221
China–Gulf Cooperation Council (C-GCC), 204,
China Index 2022, 187
China Institute of Contemporary International Relations (CICIR), 143, 335
China–Maldives Friendship Bridge, 168
China–Myanmar Economic Corridor (CMEC), 160, 172, 223

Index

China National Petroleum Corporation (CNPC), 105
China–Pakistan cross-border optical fibre cable (OFC), 230
China–Pakistan Economic Corridor (CPEC), 18–19, 171, 184, 188–190, 202, 223, 227, 236–237, 334
China's Civilisational Project, 84
China shock 2.0, 37
China Standards 2035, 276
China State Shipbuilding Corporation (CSSC), 404
China Study Group (CSG roads), 58
China virus, 32
Chinese Academy of Sciences, 278
Chinese civilisation, 84
Chinese Communist Party (CCP). *See also* Communist Party of China (CPC); People's Liberation Army (PLA); Xi Jinping
control of, 79
foreign policy of China, 135–145
goals and strategies, 79–80
18th Party Congress, 75, 76, 86, 135
19th Party Congress, 86, 135, 257, 259, 398, 405
20th Party Congress, 75, 78–80, 86, 135
Xi Jinping supremacy in, 75–76, 79, 135
Chinese currency, internationalisation of, 230
Chinese Dream, 363, 364
Chinese economy, 29. *See also* Economic trajectory, of China; Economy/economic growth,
Chinese Overseas Port Holdings Company (COPHC), 190
Chinese 'technology sphere', 227, 235
Chinh, Pham Minh, 253
CHIPS and Science Act, 2022, 126
Choices: Inside the Making of India (Shivshankar Menon), 369
Chumar, 12, 15, 372
Civil– Military Integration (CMI), 381–382, 396
Climate change, 10, 26, 88, 122, 128, 144, 162, 233, 290
Clinton, Hillary, 24
Cold War era, 203–204
Collective Security Treaty Organization (CSTO), 106
Colombo Port City, 171
Communist Party of China (CPC), 26, 41, 53, 100, 216, 243, 253, 288–289, 303, 395.
See also Communist Party of China (CPC)

China's civilisation and culture, 84–85
China's economy and challenges, 248–251
co-prosperity promotion, 83
legitimacy of, 45
Military–Civil Fusion (MCF) strategy, 395–407
Politburo Standing Committee (PBSC), 244–245
response to COVID-19, 304–311
on rise of China, 29–30
technology, importance on, 85
20th National Congress, 244
Xi's third term and challenges, 243–251
Zero-COVID policy, protest against, 245–247, 290
Communist Party of Soviet Union (CPSU), 76
Community of Common Destiny, 24
Comprehensive and Progressive Agreement for Trans-Pacific Partnership (CPTPP), 163
Comprehensive National Security doctrine, 296
Conference on Interaction and Conference Building (CICA), 153
Confidence building measures (CBMs), 369, 371
Confucianism, 30
Core interests, 21, 25, 51, 60, 86, 99, 137, 143, 144, 145, 177
Corruption, in Chinese military, 47
Counterespionage Law, 2021, 402–403
Counterterrorism Law, 2015, 401
Country Garden, 294
COVID-19 pandemic, 46, 55, 77, 145, 155, 161–162, 173, 228, 303–311, 319
Chinese state behaviour, 155
CPC response to, 304–311
deaths from infections, 41, 310
early stages of, 304–306
economic impact, 28, 46, 77, 284
foreign investments, 83
implications for China, 310–311
initial response of US to, 161
supply chain resilience, 163
US–China relations after, 32
vaccines for COVID-19, 307
Zero-COVID policy, 41, 46–47, 77, 245–247, 254, 307–310
Crimea, 108
Cross-border terrorism, 151
Cross, Sharyl N., 108
Cultural Revolution, 244, 275
Cyber Security Law, 2017, 402

Dai Bingguo, 370
Dalai Lama, 62, 337, 340
  selection of, 62–63
Data Security Law, 2021, 402
DeepSeek AI, 49
De-escalation of troops, 3, 6, 7, 12, 54–56
Defence budget, 80
  China, 14
  India, 58
Defence export destinations of China, 19
Demchok, 6, 15, 20, 54
Democratic People's Republic of Korea (DPRK), 151
Deng Xiaoping, 16, 21–24, 40, 41, 55, 101, 136, 316, 332, 348, 378, 396
Dependence cluster, 191
Depsang, 6, 15, 20, 54
Diaoyu Islands. *See* Senkaku Islands
Diego Garcia, 170
Digital economy, 85
Digital Silk Road (DSR), 230, 235, 238
Ding Xuexiang, 245, 295
Discord Leaks, 192
Disengagement from friction points, 5–7, 54–55
Dolam (Doklam), 15, 372
Domestic consumption, 49, 254–255, 291
Doshi, Rush, 23
Doval, Ajit, 4
Dual circulation strategy, 44, 49
Dual containment policy of the West, 106
Dwivedi, Upendra, 6

East Asian Summit (EAS), 152, 157, 158
East China Sea, 24, 26, 40, 76, 155, 156
Eastern Ladakh, 3, 5, 9, 15, 18, 54, 56, 59, 367, 370, 371, 372–373
Economic globalisation, 99
Economic reforms, in China, 45–46
  step-by-step approach, 45–46
  15th Five Year Plan, 83–84
  top design approach, 46, 49
Economic slowdown, 42–44, 48, 83, 249
Economic trajectory, of China, 253, 267
  agenda 2024, 263–266
  2022 CEWC, 254, 256, 257, 261
  domestic demand, expansion of, 254–255
  foreign investment, boosting of, 261–263
  high-quality growth, concept of, 258
  key risks, addressing of, 258–261
  local government debt, 260
  modern industrial system, building of, 255–257
  private sector, approach to, 257–258
  real estate sector, 258–260
  state-owned enterprise reform, 257
  twists and turns, 253–254
Economy/economic growth, 21, 39–43, 47–49, 75, 80–82, 88, 242. *See also* Economic trajectory, of China
Egypt, 200, 203, 207, 211
Electric vehicles, 49, 256
  duty on, 45
Elkhereiji, Waleed, 206
Enlai Zhou, 379
Eskelund, Jens, 44
Eurasia, 222
Europe, 8, 31, 37, 50, 77, 89, 103, 106, 218, 223
European Union, 20, 37, 44, 109, 292
Evergrande (real estate company), 83, 293–294
Export dominance, of China, 50
External balancing, policy of, 60

Fang Fang, 306
Fatemi, Syed Tariq, 191
Fenfa Youwei, 25
Find, Test, Trace, Isolate and Support (FTTIS) strategy, 288, 291
Fiscal stimulation package, 43
5G technology, 281–282
Foreign companies in China, challenges faced by, 44
Foreign Direct Investment (FDI), 83, 261
Foreign policy, 23–26, 40, 85–91
  BRI projects, 137
  China Dream, 139–140
  China Rejuvenation, 140
  community of common destiny, 140
  diplomatic concepts, 139–143
  foreign affairs work conferences, 138–139
  Global Civilisation Initiative, 142
  Global Development Initiative, 140–141
  Global Security Initiative, 141–142
  Group of Friends in UN, 141
  national security, emphasis on, 138
  party perspectives, 137–139
  problems/losses faced, 144–145
  role in global and regional orders, 144
  18th CCP Congress, 137
  19th CCP Congress, 137–138
  20th CCP Congress, 138
  transformation in diplomatic practice, 143–144
  wolf warrior diplomacy, 142
  under Xi Jinping, 135–145

Index

Xi Jinping Thought on Diplomacy, 139
Forum on China–Africa Cooperation (FOCAC), 51, 224
France, 37, 85, 88, 100, 143, 262, 379
Friction points, 5
Fulton, Jonathan, 209
Fuqiang, 22
Future of China, 48–54, 77
    after Xi Jinping, 53–54
    domestic consumption/dual circulation, 49
    economic resilience, 49
    export dominance, 50
    innovation power, 48–49
    military strength, 50
    notion of China peaking, 48–51
    traits of China as great power, 51–53
Fuxing/rejuvenation, 22, 30
Fu Ying, 113

Gagarin, Yuri, 378
Galwan Valley, 3, 10, 13, 54, 297, 327, 336, 371
Gandhi, Rajiv, 9, 55, 334
García-Herrero, Alicia, 44, 50
Gazprom (Russian gas major), 105
GDPs of China and India, 12, 50
Georgia, 108
Germany, 37, 50, 105, 109, 220, 262, 296
G695 in Aksai Chin, 18
Global Civilisation Initiative (GCI), 51, 52, 86, 136, 142, 198, 233–23
Global Development Initiative (GDI), 51, 52, 86, 87, 136, 140–141, 198, 233
Global economy, 86
    contribution to, 21
Global Financial Crisis, 23, 24, 150
Global governance, 25
Global image of China, 91
Global Initiative on Data Security (GIDS), 238
Globalisation, 21, 26, 48, 145, 157, 288
'Global Maritime Fulcrum', 159
Global Security Initiative (GSI), 51, 52, 86, 88, 136, 141–142, 198
Global South, Chinese engagement with, 37–38
Global supply chains, 38, 44, 290–292, 295, 297, 308
Global war on terrorism (GWT), 313
Gokhale, Vijay, 62
The Golden Road: How Ancient India Transformed the World (William Dalrymple), 31
Gou, Terry, 290

Green energy, 37, 44, 79
Grey zone operations, 26, 38–40, 57
Grid Style Social Governance Management system, 339
G20 Summit, 4, 20, 63, 109
Guo Boxiang, 47
Gwadar port, 177, 188–191, 202, 229, 232
Gyaltsen Norbu, 337, 338

Hambantota port, 19, 28, 171, 189, 232, 236
Han Zheng, 32
Han Zhifeng, 257
Haq Do Tehreek (Gwadar Rights Movement), 190
Hasina, Sheikh, 170, 172, 177
Hathongla–Lungrola–Sulula ridgeline, 55
Health Silk Road (HSR), 228
He Lifeng, 295
High fence, small yard approach, 32
High-tech manufacturing, 42
Himalayan states, 341–342
Hometown diplomacy gesture, 11
Hong Kong, 44, 50, 199
Hoodbhoy, Pervez, 189
Hua Chunying, 142
Huang Hua, 169
Huawei Marine Technology (HMT), 230
Huawei Technologies, 125, 235, 279
Hu Jintao, 23–25, 193, 244, 396, 404
Humanitarian assistance and disaster relief (HADR), 152
Hungary, 230
Hu Shisheng, 334–335
Hydropower project in Tibet, 13

IEA (International Energy Agency), 209
Independent Power Producers (IPP), 189, 191
India, 13, 38, 51, 61, 88, 121, 153, 162, 163, 176, 201, 203, 296
    ASEAN countries and, 163–164
    Belt and Road Initiative, 236–238
    border issue with China, 15–16, 368–371
    China not supportive of rise of, 13–14
    China's engagement in South Asia, 178–180
    China's trade with, 16–17
    civil-military integrated (CMI) approach, 389–390
    defence budget, 14, 58–59
    economic engagement with China, 17–18
    fear and apprehension about China's intentions, 176

GDPs of China and India, 14
human rights violations in Xinjiang, 326–327
hydropower project in Tibet, impact of, 13
import dependency on China, 16–17
'Neighbourhood first' policy, 177
nuclear doctrine, 59–60
perspective within Quad, 154
PLAN in Indian Ocean, 19–20
Russia–China relationship, 115
Russia defence cooperation with, 104
space vision, 389–390
threat perception from terrorist groups, 151
India–ASEAN Dialogue Partnership, 164
India–China border, 136, 328, 359–369. *See also* Line of Actual Control (LAC)
1993 agreement, 369
1996 agreement, 369
2013 agreement, 369–370
Border Personnel Meetings (BPMs), 370
future of, 373–375
historical perspective, 368–371
Joint Working Group (JWG), 370
Karakoram Pass, 368
Ladakh–Tibet border demarcation, 368
premeditated expansionism by PLA, 371–373
Special Representative (SR) mechanism, 378
thrust for India on border issue, 375–376
un-demarcated border, 368–371
unilaterally defined 1959 LAC by Zhou, 369
India–China relations, 3, 54, 64, 374
asymmetric deterrence, 57–59
bilateral relations, development of, 10
border areas, 3, 5–7, 9–10, 15–16, 374
border management, 54–56
boundary settlement, 56
COVID-19 crisis, 155
disengagement from friction points, 5–7
economic relations, 60–62
external balancing vis-à-vis China, 60
management of, suggestions on, 54–64
Modi Years and, 11–14
new paradigm, 63–64
nuclear matters, discussion on, 59–60
2014–19 period, 11
sensitive issues, 62–63
stabilisation/normalisation of, 3–6, 9
state of borders and, 10

strategic dialogue for, 56–57
structural problems/challenges in, 11–20
Track 1.5/Track-2 interactions, 4, 7, 54, 57
trans-border rivers issue, 13
Trumpian approach and, 8–9, 56
working together in minilateral platforms, 63
Zero-COVID period, 297–298
Indian Ocean, 168, 229
Indian Ocean Region (IOR), 19, 170
Indonesia, 154, 157, 158, 159–160, 223, 234, 235
Indo-Pacific, 89, 157, 197
China challenge in, 120–123
Indo-Pacific Economic Framework (IPEF), 121, 122, 163
Indo-Pacific initiatives, 104
Indo-Pacific strategy, 120–123
Industrial policies, 42, 49
Innovation
growth and, 42
as key driver of sustainable development, 141
and MCF, 403–404
and total factor productivity, 42
Innovation and Competition Act, US, 125
Innovation power, 48–49
Intelligence Law, 2017, 402
International Court of Arbitration, Hague, 30, 39
International environment, worsening of, 91
International Lunar Research Station (ILRS), 386
International Monetary Fund (IMF), 173, 174, 190, 265
International North–South Transport Corridor (INSTC), 238
International Space Station (ISS), 379
'Invest in China' campaign, 262
Iqbal, Ahsan, 188
Iran, 89, 201, 203, 206, 229, 230, 234
Iran–Saudi rapprochement, 238, 296
Iraq, 203, 205, 207
ISEAS Yusof-Ishak think tank survey, 27
Israel, 201, 204
Israel–Hamas war, 197, 198, 200
Ivan Chen, 332

Jack Ma, 42
Jaishankar, S., 6
Jamaat-ud-Dawa (JuD), 185, 193
Jamaat-ul-Ahrar, 193

Index

Jammu and Kashmir, 368
Japan, 20, 31, 38, 39, 40, 44, 48, 60, 64, 77, 88, 89, 108, 123, 125, 151, 153, 154, 162, 288, 96, 406
Jianan La (Daban), 373
Jiang Zemin, 244
Jian-Wei Pan, 281
Jingjia Micro, 405
Johnson–Ardagh Line, 368
Johnson, Boris, 296
Johnson, Ian, 46
Johnson Line of 1865, 368
Johnson, William, 368
Joint Comprehensive Plan of Action (JCPOA), 206

Kailash–Mansarovar Yatra, 4
Kamal, Mustafa, 175
Kani, Ali Bagheri, 206
Karakoram Highway, 101
Karakoram Pass, 368
Kazakhstan, 222, 231
Kerry, John, 128
Khan, Imran, 185
Khar, Hina Rabbani, 192
King Gan, 79
Kishida, Fumio, 123
Kissinger, Henry, 185, 379
Korea, 108, 122, 151
Kumar, R. Hari, 19
Kupchan, Charles, 114
Kuwait, 200
Kyrgyzstan, 231

Ladakh, 337. *See also* Eastern Ladakh
Ladakh–Tibet border, border demarcation of, 368
Laden, Osama bin, 185
Lai Ching-te, 40
Lakhvi, Zakiur-Rehman, 185
Lalwani, Sameer, 186–187
Laos, 153, 161
Latin America, 23, 89, 143, 217, 233
Law on Guarding State Secrets, 263
Leading nation, China as, 22
Lebanon, 200
Lee Hsein Loong, 162
Lee, John, 156
Lee Shangfu, 79
Letpadaung copper mine, Myanmar, 232
Li Jiming, 176

Li Keqiang, 244, 254, 289
Line of Actual Control (LAC), 54–56, 369–370. *See also* India–China border
 1993 agreement, 369
 1996 agreement, 369
 2013 agreement, 369–370
 bilateral agreements of 1993 and 1996, 16
 China's encroachments across, 40
 differences on, 16
 2024 India–China patrolling agreement over, 178
 military presence on, 18
 perceptions of, 375–376
 unilaterally defined 1959 LAC by Zhou, 369
Li Qiang, 245, 256, 261–262, 290, 295, 324
Li Shangfu, 47
Li Shien-Nien, 169
Lithium-ion batteries, 256
Liu Bocheng, 332
Liu He, 42, 259
Liu Jianchao, 5
Liu Liehong, 263
Liu Shao-chi, 184
Liu Xiaoming, 142
Living Buddhas of Tibet, 62–63
Li Wenliang, 305
Lo, Bobo, 107
Long Dingbin, 192
Lu Shaoye, 142
Lu Shaye, 143

Macartney–MacDonald Line of 1899, 368
Made in China 2025, 46, 49, 275, 399–400
Major power diplomacy, 51
Makin, Mohamed, 213
Malabar Exercise, 162
Malacca Straits, 168, 189
Malaysia, 152, 158, 161, 234
Maldives, 168, 176
 BRI initiative, 171
 China support to, 169, 170
 debt to China, 175
 infrastructural support/grants, 172
Mao Ning, 373
Mao Tse-tung, 396
Mao Zedong, 21, 22, 30, 41, 53, 100, 136, 244, 253, 378, 379
Marcos, Ferdinand, 154, 159
Maritime power, 19–20
Maritime Silk Road, 19, 20

Ma Xingrui, 322
McMahon, Henry, 57
McMahon Line, 57, 333–334
Mearsheimer, John J., 164
Mega-Engineering Programmes (MEPs), 276, 277
Mekong River, 13
Mercator Institute for China Studies (MERICS), 42, 61
Mexico, 8, 33, 44, 61, 226
Miao Hua, 47
Micius (quantum satellite), 281
Middle East (West Asia), China and, 197, 213, 218–219, 223
  anti-piracy operations, 201
  Arab Policy Paper, 209
  BRICS and SCO, 203
  BRI investments and projects, 210–211
  challenge for India, 213
  conflict management and peace talks, 202, 203
  connectivity relationships, 204
  COVID-19 pandemic, 204
  defense relationships, 205
  economic engagements, 211–212
  energy and economic cooperation, 196, 226–227
  financial architecture, 207–208
  geo-economic calculations, 209–210
  geo-strategic and geopolitical context, 199–200
  Gulf Cooperation Council (GCC) countries, 197, 198, 204
  institutional interactive frameworks, 208
  investments in infrastructure/sunrise sectors, 200–201
  Israel–Hamas war, 197, 198, 200, 202
  MENAT corridor, 210
  oil export and energy supplies to China, 209–210
  One Belt One Road (OBOR) initiative, 200
  partnership agreement with Iran, 201
  politically value-neutral approach, 198
  Russia–Ukraine war, 203
  securitisation of West Asian policy, 209
  security and development models, 198
  security, technology and defence partnership, 203–209
  soft power projection, 212–213
  strategic autonomy oriented foreign policy, 207
  strategic partnerships, 201
  trade with Middle East, 210
  weapon exports to Arab world, 205
  Xi Jinping visit to Riyadh, 207, 208
  Xi Jinping visit to Saudi Arabia, 198
  yuanisation, 207
Military–Civil Fusion Research Center, 398
Military–Civil Fusion (MCF) strategy, 80, 81, 280, 350, 395–407
  challenges in, 405–406
  China's national rejuvenation goals and, 395
  focus priorities of, 404–405
  implications for India, 406–407
  innovation and, 403–404
  institutionalising of, 396–398
  interrelated efforts, 396
  lawfare under, 401–403
  logistics under, 400–401
  private sector and, 399–400
  semiconductor investment, 405
  talent cultivation under, 403
Military, modernisation of, 80–81
Military strength, of China, 50, 80–81
Misri, Vikram, 3–5
Mitter, Rana, 30
Modi, Narendra, 3, 11, 54, 110, 213
Mongolia, 108
Morrison, Scott, 143
Muizzu, Mohamed, 176
Multi-Domain Precision Warfare (MDPW), 354
Multilateralism, genuine, 102
Multipolar world, 51, 99, 102
Myanmar, 19, 160–161, 163, 221, 232, 333
Myanmar–China relationship, 175–176
  BRI initiative, 171, 172
  defence cooperation, 170
  infrastructural projects, 172–173
Myitsone Dam, Myanmar, 232

National Committee of Chinese People's Political Consultative Conference (NCCPPCC), 78
National Defense Transportation Law, 2016, 401
National Defense University (NDU), 351, 398
National Medium- and Long-Term Plan for the Development of Science and Technology MLP), 276, 277, 279
National Natural Science Foundation of China (NSFC), 277
National People Congress (NPC), 78
National Science & Technology Programmes (NSTPs), 277

Index

National Security Adviser (NSA), 4
National Security Law, 2015, 401
National Security Strategy (NSS) (US), 153
National Strategy for Development Driven by Innovation, 276
National University of Defence Technology (NUDT), 351
2022 NATO Strategic Concept, 124
Nehru, Jawaharlal, 333, 368
Neijuan (involution), 47
Nepal, 168, 177, 230, 340
    bilateral ties with China, 169
    BRI initiative, 171
    debt to China, 174, 175
    infrastructural support/grants, 172
    military cooperation, 170
    Pokhara international airport, 172, 174
    trade gap with China, 173
    Trans-Himalayan Economic Corridor, 172
Netherlands, 125, 406
New Cultural Mission, 84
'Nine Dash Line', 159
Nithiyanandam, Y., 13
Nixon, Richard, 8
Nong Rong, 191
North Atlantic Treaty Organization (NATO), 89
North Korea, 163
Nuclear deterrence, 59
Nuclear Suppliers Group (NSG), 12, 187
Nuland, Victoria, 128
Nyingchi, Yadong and Gyrong, in Tibet, 18

Obama, B., 155
Offensive realism, theory of, 164
Okinawa Island, Japan, 123
Okinawa Marine Littoral Regiment (MLR), 123
2008 Olympics, 24
One Belt One Road, 25
One-China policy, 100, 199
On Xi Jinping: How Xi's Marxist Nationalism Is Shaping China and the World (Kevin Rudd), 21
Opium Wars, 29
Organisation of Islamic Cooperation (OIC), 185, 212
Organisation of Petroleum Exporting Countries (OPEC+), 207

Pacific islands, 222
Pacific Islands Summit, 2022, 122
Pakistan, 19, 60, 101, 151, 219, 234, 237, 341

Pakistan and East Africa Connecting Europe (PEACE) cable, 235
Pakistan–China relations, 151, 169, 184–194. *See also* China–Pakistan Economic Corridor (CPEC)
    background, 185
    bilateral relations, 185
    BRI initiative, 167, 188
    Chinese influence in Pakistan, 191–192
    commonality of interests, 184, 186
    CPEC, 188–190
    debt to China, 173
    defence cooperation, 169–170, 186–187
    diplomatic support to Pakistan, 185
    economic relations, 187–188
    free trade agreement, 188
    funds from China, 171
    Gwadar Port, 190–191
    joint military exercises, 186
    kill and dump policy, 185
    nuclear cooperation, 187
    problems in relationship, 192–193
    role in Pak domestic politics, 192
    weapons systems from China, 186, 187
Palestine, 204
Panchen Lama, 337, 338
Patel, Vallabhbhai, 368
Peace and tranquillity, in border areas, 10
Peaceful development (Heping Fazhan), 23
Peking University, 278
Pelosi, Nancy, 40, 89, 127
Peng Liyuan, 253
People Armed Police (PAP), 80, 94
People's Liberation Army (PLA), 75, 81, 336, 347, 362–364, 403, 405
    apex-level reforms, 2016–22, 351–353
    CCP's mandate to, 347
    concepts and policies, 348–349
    joint services exercises, 354
    Military–Civil Fusion (MCF) policy, 350
    modernisation and restructuring, 350–351
    Multi-Domain Precision Warfare (MDPW), 354
    new era force restructure, 350
    operational objectives, 361–362
    pivotal role, 347–348
    PLA Air Force (PLAAF), 350, 359–361
    PLA Army (PLAA), 350, 355–357, 405
    PLA Army Navy (PLAN), 350, 357–359
    process of modernisation, 348–349
    service-specific and force structuring, 355–361

strategising and war preparedness, 353–354
support services, 361
Western Theatre Command, 334, 336
People's Republic of China (PRC), 21–23, 100, 216, 217, 333, 347
Peripheral Diplomacy, 24, 26
Peru, 226
Pew survey, 143
Philippines, 30, 39, 124, 154, 159
PLA Air Force (PLAAF), 350, 359–361
PLA Joint Logistic Support Force (PLAJLSF), 94
PLA Navy (PLAN), 15, 19, 20, 52, 93n15, 229, 357–359
and Indian Navy, 15
PLA Rocket Forces (PLARF), 350, 352, 361
PLA Strategic Support Force (PLASSF), 350, 352, 361
Political security, 250
Portland Soft Power Index, 143
Port projects, 52
Post-9/11 global politics, 313
Private entrepreneurs, 257, 258
Private sector, support to, 257
Productivity-Linked Incentive (PLI) scheme, 297
Property developers, 259
Putin, Vladimir, 8, 36, 99, 101, 104, 105, 107–109, 113, 289

Qatar, 200
Qian Xuesen, 378
Qin Gang, 127, 136
Quad (Quadrilateral Security Dialogue), 13–14, 88, 104, 152, 153, 157, 162–163, 176, 295
Quantum communications, 281

Rahman, Mujibur, 169
Rail, high-speed, 49
Raimondo, Gina, 128
Raisi, Ebrahim, 206
Rajagopalan, Rajeshwari Pillai, 388
Rao, Narasimha, 334
Real estate sector, 83, 255, 258–260, 293–294
Regional Comprehensive Economic Partnership (RCEP), 17, 152
Regional disparities, 83, 90
Regional trouble-spots, handling of, 26
Rempang Eco-City, Indonesia, 232
Research and development (R&D), 275
investments in, 277–278
tax incentives, 276

Reverse Nixon, 8, 36
Rhodium Group report, 61, 236
Rise of China, 20–21, 29, 77, 85, 151, 164–165
Chinese narratives, 29–31
military importance in, 80–82
new power balance, 77
strategic challenge posed by, 155–157
RMB, 87, 230
Rosneft (Russian oil company), 105
Rubio, Marco, 33
Rudd, Kevin, 52
Rulemaking cluster, 191
Rules-based order, 102
Russia, 8, 32, 36, 37, 50, 64, 89, 102, 113, 200, 201, 203, 206–207, 222, 230, 296
influence in Africa, 109
international isolation of, 109
Russia–China relationship, 36, 99, 110–112
analytical pitfalls, 107–110
bilateral strategic ties, 99, 102–104
defence cooperation, 103
implications for India, 115
joint military exercises, 103
joint statement, 99
limiting western influence in Central Asia, 102
Putin–Xi tango, 102–104
Treaty of Good Neighbourliness, Friendship and Cooperation, 101, 111
Ukraine effect, 104–107
unequal treaties and cross-border interference, 100, 111
US's approach, 112–115
Russia–India–China dialogue, 102
Russia–Ukraine war, 88, 89, 173, 197, 203

Salami slicing, 39, 54
Saudi Arabia, 89, 109, 200, 201, 203, 204–206, 210, 223, 234
Scholz, Olaf, 105, 109
Science and technology innovation (S&TI), 275, 285–286
artificial intelligence, 280–281
blockchain, 282, 285
challenges to system, 283–284
China Standards 2035, 276, 284
education and training system, 278–279
exporting of technologies, 285
5G, 281–282
future trajectory, 284–285
industry structure, 279–280

Index

integration of technologies, 285
Long-Term Goals for 2035, 276
Made in China 2025, 275
militarisation of technologies, 284
MLP, 276
National Strategy for Development, 276
quantum, 281, 285
R&D tax incentives, 276
reorganising infrastructure, 277–278
semiconductors, 282–283, 285
6G, 282
state support, 275–277
S&TI 2030 Mega-Programmes, 276
strengths of system, 283
Scientific and technological (S&T) institutions, 91
Semiconductor Manufacturing International Corporation (SMIC), 405
Semiconductors, 125, 282–283, 40
Senkaku Islands, 39–40, 140
Seshadri, V.S., 61
Severe acute respiratory syndrome (SARS), 304
Shambaugh, David, 38
Shanghai Cooperation Organization (SCO), 63, 86, 101, 104, 105, 109, 141, 153, 203
Sharif, Shehbaz, 192
Shenzhen, 46
Shepard, Alan, 378
Shi Yan 6, 171
Shyok River Valley, 367
Silk Road, 31, 87
Silk Road Economic Belt (SREB), 222
Simla Convention, 334
Singapore, 158, 161, 162, 235
Singh, Maharaja Gulab, 368
Sinocentric international system, 114
Sino-European relations, 37
Sino-Russian relations, 36
Sino-Thai ethnic minority, 161
Sino-US relations, 164
Sino-Vietnamese relations, 158
6G technology, 282
Skinner, Kiron, 142
Small, Andrew, 187, 193
Socialism with Chinese characteristics, 30
Solar cells, 256
Solar panels, 49, 61, 91
Sonadia deep sea project, 175
South Asia, 231, 234, 237
South Asia, China's engagement in, 18–19, 168–180, 219

advantages in South Asia, 178
background/overview, 168–169
bilateral engagements, 169
bilateral trade gap and debt issues, 173–176
BRI initiative, 168, 171
continued engagement, 176–177
defence cooperation, 169–170
economic packages for neighbours, 168
future trends, 178–180
implications for India, 178–180
infrastructural support, 168, 171–173
political, economic, developmental partnerships, 168
related concerns, 177–178
South Asia policy, 91
South China Sea, 24, 26, 30–31, 39, 60, 76, 77, 103, 104, 140, 152–153, 154, 155, 156, 159, 162, 234
Southeast Asia, 27, 234, 237
Southeast Asia and Indo-Pacific, strategic competition in, 150–165
South Korea, 20, 26, 89, 123
South Sudan, 26
Soviet Union, 378, 379
Space programme, China's, 378–391
Chang'e-1 lunar orbital spacecraft, 379
Chinese Yaogan satellites, 388
commercial space sector, 380–381
concerns on, 386–387
Congressionally-mandated Pentagon Report, 387
consequences on India's national security, 388
construction of Tiangong space station, 379
contested heavens, 384–388
cooperation with Russia, 386
Document 60, 380
Gaofen satellites, 388
India approach to space, 388–390
journey to Tiantang, 378–381
man into space, 379
militarisation of space, 378, 387
peaceful approach to space, 382
race for space, 378
space aspirations of China, 378
strategic vision, 381–383
telecommunications satellite manufacturer, 379
threat US perceives from China, 383–384
US as competitor and threat, 383

US as dominant player, 378
white papers on space, 381
Special Economic Zones (SEZs), 46, 83
Special Representatives (SRs), 4, 5, 54, 56
Sputnik satellite, 378
Sri Lanka, 19, 28, 168, 189, 219, 230, 341
Sri Lanka–China relationship, 169, 177
    BRI initiative, 171
    debt to China, 173–174
    defence cooperation, 170
    economic crisis, 174, 175
    funds from China, 171
    infrastructural support, 171
    Sirimavo Bandaranaike's visit to China, 169
Srinivasan, Krishna, 43
State Administration for Science, Technology and Industry for National Defense (SASTIND), 387, 398, 399, 404
State-owned enterprises (SOEs), 82, 257, 275, 279, 291, 398–399, 406
Statist tilt, in economy, 41–42
Status quoist power, 52
S&TI 2030 Mega-Programmes, 276
Stockholm International Peace Research Institute (SIPRI), 14, 15, 19
Strait of Hormuz, 209, 229
Strategic Competition Act, US, 125
Subansiri Valley, Arunachal Pradesh, 7
Sullivan, Jake, 32, 123, 127, 128
Sumdorong Chu and Namkha Chu valleys, Chinese intrusions in, 54–55
Summit-level meetings, 64
Sun Weidong, 5
Supply-side Structural Reform (SSSR), 395
Supreme leader syndrome, 41
Surveillance state, 47
SWIFT payment system, 207, 208
Syria, 203

Tai, Katherine, 128
Taiwan, 26, 79, 123, 127, 176, 199, 283
Taiwan Straits, 40, 60, 76, 89
Technology, self-reliance in, 85
Technosphere, Chinese-dependent, 235
Teesta River Comprehensive Management Project, 176
Tehran, 199, 204
Tel Aviv, 199, 204
Telecom companies, Chinese, 231
Tencent, 279
Territorial claims, 38–40
    Bhutan, 40
    East China Sea, 39–40
    grey zone warfare, 39
    India–China borders, 40
    South China Sea, 39
    Taiwan, 40
THAAD missile defence system, 26
Thailand, 161
Theatre commands (TCs), 80, 81
Thousand Talents Programme (TTP), 279
Three Gorges Dam, 13
Tiananmen Square, 101
Tianxia, concept of, 29
Tibet, 26, 62–63, 332, 367
    China's occupation of, 332–333
    contested narrative on, 333
    importance for India and China, 332
    Sinicisation of Tibetan Buddhism, 337–343
    as 'Water Tower' of Asia, 332
    Zhou Enlai's visit to India, 333–337
Tibetan Buddhism, 337–340
Tibet Autonomous Region (TAR), 336–337, 339, 341
Tokyo Quad summit, 121
Tongyu Tao, Dr, 329–330
Total factor productivity (TFP), 42
Totalitarian state, 47
Township and village enterprises (TVEs), 46
Trade gap with China, 173
Trans-Pacific Partnership (TPP), 159, 163
Trans-Regional Himalayan Corridor (THRC), 341
Treaty of Aigun, 1858, 100
Treaty of Nerchinsk, 1689, 100
Treaty of Peking, 1860, 100
Trump, Donald, 8, 28, 31–35, 37, 64, 88, 113, 295
Tsinghua University, 278
Turkey, 201, 203, 210, 212
'Two bombs, one satellite' project, 396
Two Guides (Liangge Yindao) policy, 26
Two-ocean strategy, 19

UAE, 200, 201, 203, 206, 207
Ukraine, 26, 28, 32, 36, 37, 50, 103
Ukraine war, 6. *See also* Russia–Ukraine war
    Russia–China relationship, 104–107
UN, 52
Unemployment, 249–250, 289
United States (US), 8, 13, 24, 27, 49, 50, 60, 64, 77, 88–90, 105, 106, 109, 162, 192, 204, 249, 292
    Chinese assessment of, 50

Indonesia and, 160
Indo-Pacific Strategy, 153
Israel–Hamas war, 197, 200
leader in space technologies, 383
technology-denial by, 48
trade sanctions on China, 153
Trump administration and China, 8
Vietnam and, 159
United States Institute of Peace (USIP), 186
UN Security Council (UNSC), 12, 14, 185
Urumqi incident, 309
US–China relations, 31, 35–38, 77, 90, 100–101, 127, 128, 153, 384
  Biden administration, 32
  China as strategic adversary, 32–33
  Chinese companies, 43
  COVID-19 pandemic, 32, 155
  de-risking strategy, 32
  tariff threats and trade tensions, 33–35, 45
  termination of, 101
  territorial claims and, 39–40
  Trump administration, 31–34
US–China rivalry, 27–28, 35–36, 78, 88, 115, 156–157, 295, 384–385, 388
US–China trade war, 151, 288, 291
US Department of Defense Space Strategy of 2020, 385
US National Security Strategy, 107
US response to China challenge, 119
  aligning efforts with allies and partners, 120–123
  Biden administration, 119–129
  competing with China, 125–126
  cooperation, 126–129
  Indo-Pacific Strategy, 120–123
  Interim National Security Strategy, 119
  National Security Strategy (NSS), 119
  Obama administration, 120
  perception and defining of challenge, 119–120
  security partnerships, 123–124
  Trump administration, 119–120
US–Russia relations, 36, 389
US–Soviet competition, 203
US tariffs and export controls, 151
US–Vietnam relationship, 118–119,
Uyghur Forced Labor Prevention Act, 2021, 126
Uyghurs, 84, 100, 184, 185, 193, 199. *See also* Xinjiang
Uzbekistan, 231

Vajpayee, Atal Bihari, 62

Vanguard, 170
Vietnam, 20, 44, 109, 122, 154, 159, 162, 163, 234, 253, 297
Von Richthofen, Baron, 31

Waltz, Michael, 33
Wang Huning, 245
Wang Jingazi, 213
Wang Junzheng, 341
Wang Wenbin, 142
Wang Wentao, 128
Wang Yang, 244
Wang Yi, 4, 5, 11, 63, 128, 176, 199, 206, 342, 373
Wang Zhigang, 278
Washington Institute survey, 200
Wei Fenghe, 47
Weinberger, Casper, 55
Wen Jiabao, 185
West Asia, 237
Western liberal democracy, 30
Western Pacific, 19, 58
Widodo, Joko, 123, 154, 157, 160
Winter Olympics, 289
Wolf Amendment, 384
Wolf warrior diplomacy, 77, 91, 142
Working Mechanism for Coordination and Consultation (WMCC) talks, 372, 373
World Bank, 14, 174, 175, 190, 332, 342
World Health Organization (WHO), 228, 304
World Trade Organisation (WTO), 77, 86
Worldview and grand strategy, of China, 21–29

Xie Feng, 128
Xie Zhenhua, 128
Xi Jinping, 3, 8, 11, 21, 29, 31, 32, 36, 40, 51, 53, 54, 59, 63, 75–77, 86, 90, 91–92, 99, 105, 108, 128, 191, 198, 206, 253, 282, 288, 308, 316, 324, 401
  anti-corruption campaign, 46, 47
  BRI initiative, 27–28, 31, 87
  China after, 53–54
  on China's rise today, 29–30
  Chinese dream, 21–23, 25, 30, 31, 41, 139
  Community with a Shared Future for Mankind, concept of, 233
  control over military, 80–82
  culture, emphasis on, 84–85
  Cyber Great Power strategy, 405
  foreign policy, 25, 26–27, 86–87, 135–145
  innovation and technology led development model, 49

on military-civil fusion, 81, 397
national core interests, 25
party, control over, 79–80
personalised polity, 41
politics in command, 45
rejuvenation and new era for China, 25–26
statist tilt in economy, 41–42
supremacy, 79
territorial integrity and sovereignty, 38–39
third term and challenges, 243–251
19th Party Congress report, 25–26, 28
20th Party Congress report, 26, 45
top design approach, 46, 49
vision for private sector, 42–43, 82–83
Zero-COVID policy, 41, 245–247, 254, 288
Xinjiang, 192, 313, 325
COVID restrictions, 318–322
detention of Uyghur and other Muslims, 318
discrimination towards major minority group, 313–314
governance of, style of, 316–318
human rights violation, 325
laws/amendments to take drastic steps, 317
lockdown, 322–323
measures to fight terrorism, 315
overview of conflict, 314–316
protests against Zero-COVID policies, 322, 324
signs of extremist tendency, 318
surveillance measures by Chen, 317–318
three evil forces, 313, 315
tourism in Xinjiang during COVID, 321
Urumqi incident, 324
Uyghur Muslim community, policies against, 315
violence and interethnic tensions, 315–316
Zero-COVID policies and protests, 321–324

Xinjiang Uyghur Autonomous Region (XUAR). *See* Xinjiang
Xu Caihou, 47
Xu Jianwei, 44

Yameen, Abdulla, 176
Yang Jiechi, 24
Yang Liwei, 379
Yangtse, 7
Yan Xuetong, 25
Yao Wen, 171
Yarlung Tsangpo, 13, 342
Yellen, Janet, 126
Yeltsin, 101
Yunus, Uzair, 190

Zangnan, 62
Zelenskyy, Volodymyr, 7, 105
Zero-COVID policy, 41, 46–47, 77, 245–247, 307–310, 322
abandonment of, 288, 290
domestic politics, 288–291
economic management, 291–295
emergency measures, 288
external environment, 295–297
foreign trade, 291–293
impact of, 288–298
implications for India, 297–298
protest against, 245–247, 290, 309
real estate sector, 293–294
technology sector, 294–295
Zhang Chunxian, 315
Zhang Kejian, 399
Zhang Qingli, 338
Zhang Yijiong, 338–339
Zhao Leji, 245
Zhao Lijian, 142–143
Zhou Enlai, 16, 333–334, 368

About the Editor

Ashok K. Kantha is a Distinguished Fellow at the Vivekananda International Foundation (VIF). He is also an Honorary Fellow and former Director of the Institute of Chinese Studies and a Distinguished Fellow at the Council for Strategic and Defence Research. A former career diplomat, he served as Secretary (East) at the Ministry of External Affairs (MEA) and as Ambassador/High Commissioner of India to China, Sri Lanka and Malaysia. In his diplomatic career, Kantha specialised in India's neighbourhood and extended neighbourhood with particular focus on China and South Asia. Apart from three diplomatic assignments in China, he handled relations with China in policy positions at the MEA for eight years. He also serves as the chair of the Core Group on China at the Confederation of Indian Industry, New Delhi.

About the Contributors

Lieutenant General Gautam Banerjee, PVSM, AVSM, YSM, was a former Chief of Staff, Central Command, former Commandant of the Officers' Training Academy, Chennai. He is now Senior Fellow at the VIF.

Debasish Chaudhuri, Visiting Fellow at the Institute of Chinese Studies, Delhi, is an independent researcher. He holds a PhD in Chinese Studies from the University of Delhi. Chaudhuri is the author of *Xinjiang and the Chinese State: Violence in the Reform Era*.

Air Marshal Diptendu Choudhury, PVSM, AVSM, VM, VSM, is a former Commandant of the National Defence College, New Delhi. An experienced pilot with over 5000 sorties on fighters, he has commanded a fighter squadron, the IAF's prestigious Tactics Air Combat Development Establishment and two frontline fighter wings. He has extensive experience in the development and execution of air operations at Command, Air Force and Joint Operations levels.

Sreeradha Datta is a professor at Jindal University and Senior Fellow at ISAS, National University of Singapore. She is the author of *Act East Policy and Northeast India*, editor of *BIMSTEC: The Journey and Way Ahead* and co-editor of *Bangladesh at 50: Development and Challenges*.

Tilak Devasher is the author of three widely acclaimed books on Pakistan: *Pakistan: Courting the Abyss*, *Pakistan: At the Helm* and *Pakistan: The Balochistan Conundrum*. Tilak retired as Special Secretary, Cabinet Secretariat, Government of India in October 2014. He is currently a member of the National Security Advisory Board (NSAB) and a consultant with the Vivekananda International Foundation.

Prerna Gandhi is Associate Fellow at the VIF. She has an MPhil in Japanese Studies and an MA in East Asian Studies from the Department of East Asian Studies, University of Delhi. With close to a decade of working in international relations research, Prerna writes and speaks on the interplay of developments in China, Japan, the Korean Peninsula, Indo-Pacific, ASEAN, and the USA.

About the Contributors

Arvind Gupta is the Director of the Vivekananda International Foundation, New Delhi. He was the Deputy National Security Adviser and Secretary, National Security Council, Government of India 2014–2017. His most recent book, *Opportunity for India in a Changing World*, was published in 2021.

Manoj Kewalramani is the Chairperson of the Indo-Pacific Studies Programme and a China Studies fellow at the Takshashila Institution, a leading Indian public policy education centre. Manoj is the author of *Smokeless War: China's Quest for Geopolitical Dominance*, which discusses China's political, diplomatic, economic and narrative responses to the COVID-19 pandemic.

Srikanth Kondapalli is the former Dean of School of International Studies and Professor of China Studies at Jawaharlal Nehru University, New Delhi, India. Kondapalli is a frequent writer and commentator in the national and international media.

Ananth Krishnan is the China correspondent for *The Hindu* and has lived in China since 2008. In 2019, he was a Visiting Fellow at Brookings India. He was previously the Beijing-based Associate Editor at the India Today Group.

Biren Nanda served in the Indian Foreign Service from 1978 to 2015 and is a distinguished former career diplomat with extensive experience of working in East Asia. He has been India's High Commissioner to Australia (2012–2015); Ambassador to Indonesia, Timor-Leste and the ASEAN (2008–2012); India's Deputy Chief of Mission in Tokyo (2000–2004); and Consul General in Shanghai (1996–2000). Ambassador Nanda has also served in Indian Missions in Beijing, Washington DC and Singapore.

Madhurima Nundy is a Fellow in Health and Human Development at the Centre for Social and Economic Progress, New Delhi. She holds a PhD in Public Health from the Centre of Social Medicine and Community Health, Jawaharlal Nehru University, New Delhi.

Santosh Pai has been offering legal services to clients in the India–China corridor since 2010. His areas of interest include Chinese investments in India, India–China comparative law and policy, cross-cultural negotiations and board governance. He holds a BA, LLB degree from NLSIU, Bangalore, an LLM (Chinese law) from Tsinghua University, Beijing, and an MBA from Vlerick University, Belgium (Peking University campus). His manuscript 'Practical Guide on Investing in India for Chinese Investors' has been translated into Chinese and published by China Law Press.

P.S. Raghavan is the chairman of National Security Advisory Board (NSAB), which advises India's National Security Council on strategic and security issues. From 1979 to 2016, he held diplomatic positions in the USSR, the UK, Poland, South Africa and Vietnam, and was India's Ambassador to the Czech Republic, Ireland and Russia.

Jayadeva Ranade is a former member of the National Security Advisory Board (NSAB) and the President of the Centre for China Analysis and Strategy. A former Additional Secretary in the Cabinet Secretariat, Government of India, he is also a member of the Core Group on China of the Indian Council of World Affairs (ICWA) and Distinguished Fellow at the Institute for Peace and Conflict Studies (IPCS), New Delhi.

Group Captain Chandan Sharda is a recipient of the Vayu Sena Medal. He was formerly affiliated with the CCCS, the MEA's think tank on China.

Lieutenant General Rakesh Sharma was commissioned in Gorkha Rifles in 1977 and had a career spanning forty years in the Indian army culminating as the head of human resources of the Indian Army as the Adjutant General. He commanded the Fire and Fury Corps in Ladakh, facing both Pakistan and China. He has had extensive operational experience in Jammu and Kashmir, the North-East and the Western Borders. He currently holds the General Bipin Rawat Chair of Excellence at USI, New Delhi, and is Distinguished Fellow with the Vivekananda International Foundation (VIF) and the Centre for Land Warfare Studies (CLAWS).

Arun K. Singh was India's Ambassador to the United States (2015–2016), France (2013–2015) and Israel (2005–2008). Currently, he is a member of India's National Security Advisory Board; Visiting Professor at Ashoka University; and a Distinguished Non-Resident Senior Fellow in the Asia Program at the Washington DC-based German Marshall Fund of the USA.

Commodore Gopal Suri has held important command and staff appointments on shore and at sea in the Indian navy and is currently Senior Fellow at the VIF.

Anil Trigunayat is a member of the Indian Foreign Service. Prior to his superannuation in May 2016, he served as Ambassador of India to Jordan and Libya and High Commissioner to Malta (2012–2016).